# Essentials *of*
# SOCIOLOGY
## A Down-to-Earth Approach

*Edition*

8

# James M. Henslin
Southern Illinois University, Edwardsville

PEARSON

Boston    New York    San Francisco

Mexico City    Montreal    Toronto    London    Madrid    Munich    Paris

Hong Kong    Singapore    Tokyo    Cape Town    Sydney

*Senior Series Editor:* Jeff Lasser
*Development Editor:* Jennifer Albanese
*Series Editorial Assistant:* Lauren Macey
*Senior Marketing Manager:* Kelly May
*Editorial Production Service:* Nesbitt Graphics, Inc. and
    The Book Company
*Manufacturing Buyer:* Debbie Rossi
*Electronic Composition:* Nesbitt Graphics, Inc.
*Interior Design:* Gina Hagen
*Photo Research:* Katharine S. Cebik (new) & Myrna Engler Photo Research (reuse)
*Cover Administrator:* Kristina Mose-Libon

For related titles and support materials, visit our online catalog at www.ablongman.com.

Between the time website information is gathered and then published, it is not unusual for some sites to have closed. Also, the transcription of URLs can result in typographical errors. The publisher would appreciate notification where these errors occur so that they may be corrected in subsequent editions.

ISBN-13: 978-0-205-57870-2      ISBN-10: 0-205-57870-5

Library of Congress Cataloging-in-Publication Data
Henslin, James M.
  Essentials of sociology : a down-to-earth approach / James M. Henslin. -- 8th ed.
    p. cm.
  Includes bibliographical references and index.
  ISBN 0-205-57870-5 (pbk)
  1. Sociology.  I. Title.

  HM586.H43  2009
  301--dc22
                        2008032598

Printed in the United States of America

10 9 8 7 6 5 4 3 2  CKV 12 11 10 09

*To my fellow sociologists, who do such creative research on social life and who communicate the sociological imagination to generations of students.*

*With my sincere admiration and appreciation,*

Jim Henslin

# What's New?

Because sociology is about social life and we live in a changing global society, an introductory sociology text must reflect the national and global changes that engulf us, as well as new sociological research. This revision of *Essentials of Sociology: A Down-to-Earth Approach*, features a new photo essay of the author's recent research in Spain. It also has 15 new boxes, 35 new illustrations, over 90 new suggested readings, 180 new instructional photos (each tied into the text), and 250 new references. Here are some of the new topics, illustrations, tables, figures, and boxed features.

## CHAPTER 1

**Figure 1.1** Comparing African American and White Methods of Suicide

**Cultural Diversity in the United States box:** Studying Job Discrimination: A Surprising Example of Applied Sociology

## CHAPTER 2

**Topic:** Moral holiday places: Locations where norms are expected to be broken

**Cultural Diversity in the United States box:** Culture Shock: The Arrival of the Hmong

## CHAPTER 3

**Topic:** *Anime* as a medium of gender socialization

**By the Numbers:** Socialization

## CHAPTER 4

**Topics:**

The Amish reaction to a shooting

Eye contact: Invitation to intimacy?

Applied body language: Training of airport personnel and interrogators

Applied impression management: Helping female executives get promoted

## CHAPTER 5

**Topics:**

"Torture warrants"

The Peter Principle in bureaucracies

The "maximum security society"

The United States' involvement in Iraq as an example of groupthink

**Sociology and the New Technology box:** Cyberloafers and Cybersleuths: Surfing at Work

## CHAPTER 6

**Topics:**

Degradation ceremonies: An extreme form of shaming

Attention deficit disorder (ADD): An example of the medicalization of deviance

**Down-to-Earth Sociology box:** Shaming: Making a Comeback?

**Down-to-Earth Sociology box:** Gang Leader for a Day: Adventures of a Rogue Sociologist

**Cultural Diversity around the World box:** "What Kind of Prison Is This?"

**By the Numbers:** Deviance and Social Control

## CHAPTER 7

**Topics:** Controlling information: zFone, voice encryption for telephone calls; the Chinese government control of the Internet

## CHAPTER 8

**Figure 8.9** Births to Single Mothers by Education of the Mother

**By the Numbers:** Social Class in the United States

## CHAPTER 9

**Topics:**

The subprime crisis and discrimination

*Proposition 2* of the Michigan state constitution

**Down-to-Earth Sociology box:** The Man in the Zoo

**Cultural Diversity box:** The Illegal Travel Guide

**Figure 9.4** Race–Ethnicity of the U.S. Population

**Table 9.4** Race–Ethnicity and Income Extremes

**By the Numbers:** Race and Ethnicity

## CHAPTER 10

**Topic:** Gerotranscendence theory

**Down-to-Earth Sociology box:** Feisty to the End: Gender Roles Among the Elderly

**Table 10.2** Relationship of Rapists to Their Victims

**By the Numbers:** Inequalities of Gender and Age

## CHAPTER 11

**Topics:**

Frustrations to the unity of the European Union

Transcreation: The cultural adaptation of cartoons

**Down-to-Earth Sociology box:** How Can "Good" People Torture Others?

**Down-to-Earth Sociology box:** The Child Soldiers

**Cultural Diversity around the World box:** The Child Workers

**By the Numbers:** Politics and the Economy

## CHAPTER 12

**Topics:**

Today's parents are spending more time with their children

Finding brides for dead sons in China

Division of marital labor; Housework, child care, and paid labor (Bianchi et. al. research)

Lingering attachments: The "continuities" of ex-spouses

**Sociology and the New Technology box:** Finding a Mate: Not the Same as It Used to Be

**Figure 12.6** Married Women Who Never Give Birth

**Figure 12.13** The Marital History of U.S. Brides and Grooms

**By the Numbers:** Marriage and Family

## CHAPTER 13

**Topic:** Splintering of the Episcopal church upon the election of a gay bishop

**Through the Author's Lens:** Holy Week in Spain

**Mass Media in Social Life box:** School Shootings: Exploding a Myth

**Down-to-Earth Sociology box:** The New Face of Religion: Pentecostals and the Spanish-Speaking Immigrants

**Figure 13.3** Social Class, Ability, and College Attendance

**By the Numbers:** Education and Religion

## CHAPTER 14

**Figure 14.8** Country of origin of unauthorized immigrants

**By the Numbers:** Population and Urbanization

## CHAPTER 15

**Topics:**

Identity chips: Big Brother?

China's challenge to U.S. dominance by shooting down an orbiting satellite

Russia's threat to strike Poland with nuclear weapons

U.S. and Poland agreement to locate a missile defense in Poland

Report of the UN's Intergovernmental Panel on Climate Change

**Table 15.2** Ogburn's Processes of Social Change

# Brief Contents

# Contents

## PART I  The Sociological Perspective

# CHAPTER 4
## Social Structure and Social Interaction     84

## Through the Author's Lens

### When a Tornado Strikes
### Social Organization Following a Natural Disaster

As I was watching television on March 20, 2003, I heard a report that a tornado had hit Camilla, Georgia. "Like a big lawn mower," the report said, it had cut a path of destruction through this little town. In its fury, the tornado had left behind six dead and about 200 injured. (pages 110–111)

# PART II Social Groups and Social Control

# PART III  Social Inequality

## CHAPTER 7
## Global Stratification          170

## Through the Author's Lens

### The Dump People
### Working and Living and Playing in the City Dump of Phnom Penh, Cambodia

I went to Phnom Penh, the capital of Cambodia, to inspect orphanages, to see how well the children were being cared for. While there, I was told about people who live in the city dump. *Live* there? I could hardly believe my ears. I knew that people made their living by picking scraps from the city dump, but I didn't know they actually lived among the garbage. This I had to see for myself. (pages 188–189)

# CHAPTER 10
# Gender and Age     260

## Through the Author's Lens

### Work and Gender
**Women at work in India**

Traveling through India was both a pleasure and an eye-opening experience. The country is incredibly diverse, the people friendly, and the land culturally rich. For this photo essay, wherever I went—whether city, village, or countryside—I took photos of women at work. (pages 266–267)

# PART IV  Social Institutions

## Through the Author's Lens

### Small Town USA
### Stuggling to Survive

All across the nation, small towns are struggling to survive. Parents and town officials are concerned because so few young adults remain in their home town. There is little to keep them there, and when they graduate from high school, most move to the city. With young people leaving and old ones dying, the small towns are shriveling. I took most of these photos in the south. (pages 316–317)

# CHAPTER 12
## Marriage and Family    328

# CHAPTER 13
## Education and Religion    358

## Through the Author's Lens

### Holy Week in Spain

Taking these photos of Holy Week being observed in Spain—in Malaga, a capital city, and Almuñecar, a small town in Granada—was both enjoyable and a challenge. The rituals here, like those of religious groups everywhere, are designed to evoke memories, create awe, inspire reverence, and stimulate social solidarity. (pages 380–381)

# PART V  Social Change

## CHAPTER 14
### Population and Urbanization    392

## Through the Author's Lens
### A Walk Through El Tiro in Medellin, Colombia

One of the most significant changes in our time is the global rush of poor, rural people to the cities of the Least Industrialized Nations. Some of these settlements are dangerous. I was fortunate to be escorted by an insider through this section of Medellin, Colombia. (pages 408–409)

# Boxed Features

## Cultural Diversity in the United States

## MASS MEDIA in SOCIAL LIFE

Why Do Native Americans Like Westerns?

Although Western movies go through a cycle of popularity, their themes are a mainstay of Holly-wood. It is easy to see why Anglos might like

## SOCIOLOGY and the NEW TECHNOLOGY

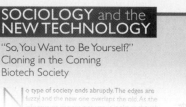

"So, You Want to Be Yourself?" Cloning in the Coming Biotech Society

No type of society ends abruptly. The edges are fuzzy, and the new one overlaps the old. As the

When genetic duplicates appear, the questio

## ThinkingCRITICALLY

# Guide to Social Maps

Social Maps illustrate the old Chinese saying, "A picture is worth ten thousand words." They allow you to see at a glance how social characteristics are distributed among the fifty United States or among the nations of the world. The U.S. Social Maps are a concise way of illustrating how our states compare on such factors as divorce, voting, poverty, or women in the work force. The global Social Maps show how the world's nations rank on such characteristics as income, the percentage of elderly, and the number of large cities.

These Social Maps are unique to this text. I have produced them for you from original data. At a glance, you can see how your state compares with your region and the other states—or you can see how the United States compares with other countries. I hope that you find these Social Maps informative. If you have suggestions for other Social Maps that you would like to see in the next edition, please share them with me.

*Jim Henslin*

# To the Student...
## from the Author

**W**ELCOME TO SOCIOLOGY! I've loved sociology since I was in my teens, and I hope you enjoy it, too. Sociology is fascinating because it is about human behavior, and many of us find that it holds the key to understanding social life.

If you like to watch people and try to figure out why they do what they do, you will like sociology. Sociology pries open the doors of society so you can see what goes on behind them. *Essentials of Sociology: A Down-to-Earth Approach* stresses how profoundly our society and the groups to which we belong influence us. Social class, for example, sets us on a particular path in life. For some, the path leads to more education, more interesting jobs, higher income, and better health, but for others it leads to dropping out of school, dead-end jobs, poverty, and even a higher risk of illness and disease. These paths are so significant that they affect our chances of making it to our first birthday, as well as of getting in trouble with the police. They even influence our satisfaction in marriage, the number of children we will have—and whether or not we will read this book in the first place.

When I took my first course in sociology, I was "hooked." Seeing how marvelously my life had been affected by these larger social influences opened my eyes to a new world, one that has been fascinating to explore. I hope that you will have this experience, too.

From how people become homeless to how they become presidents, from why people commit suicide to why women are discriminated against in every society around the world—all are part of sociology. This breadth, in fact, is what makes sociology so intriguing. We can place the sociological lens on broad features of society, such as social class, gender, and race–ethnicity, and then immediately turn our focus on the smaller, more intimate level. If we look at two people interacting—whether quarreling or kissing—we see how these broad features of society are being played out in their lives.

We aren't born with instincts. Nor do we come into this world with preconceived notions of what life should be like. At birth, we have no concepts of race–ethnicity, gender, age, or social class. We have no idea, for example, that people "ought" to act in certain ways because they are male or female. Yet we all learn such things as we grow up in our society. Uncovering the "hows" and the "whys" of this process is also part of what makes sociology so fascinating.

One of sociology's many pleasures is that as we study life in groups (which can be taken as a definition of sociology), whether those groups are in some far-off part of the world or in some nearby corner of our own society, we gain new insights into who we are and how we got that way. As we see how *their* customs affect *them,* the effects of our own society on us become more visible.

This book, then, can be part of an intellectual adventure, for it can lead you to a new way of looking at your social world—and, in the process, help you to better understand both society and yourself.

I wish you the very best in college—and in your career afterward. It is my sincere desire that *Essentials of Sociology: A Down-to-Earth Approach* will contribute to that success.

**James M. Henslin**
**Department of Sociology**
**Southern Illinois University, Edwardsville**

P.S. I enjoy communicating with students, so feel free to comment on your experiences with this text. Because I travel a lot, it is best to reach me by e-mail: henslin@aol.com

# To the Instructor...
## from the Author

**R**EMEMBER WHEN YOU FIRST GOT "HOOKED" on sociology, how the windows of perception opened as you began to see life-in-society through the sociological perspective? For most of us, this was an eye-opening experience. This text is designed to open those windows onto social life, so students can see clearly the vital effects of group membership on their lives. Although few students will get into what Peter Berger calls "the passion of sociology," we at least can provide them the opportunity.

To study sociology is to embark on a fascinating process of discovery. We can compare sociology to a huge jigsaw puzzle. Only gradually do we see how the intricate pieces fit together. As we begin to see these interconnections, our perspective changes as we shift our eyes from the many small, disjointed pieces to the whole that is being formed. Of all the endeavors we could have entered, we chose sociology because of the ways in which it joins together the "pieces" of society and the challenges it poses to "ordinary" thinking. To share with students this process of awareness and discovery called the sociological perspective is our privilege.

As instructors of sociology, we have set ambitious goals for ourselves: to teach both social structure and social interaction and to introduce students to the sociological literature—both the classic theorists and contemporary research. As we accomplish this, we would also like to enliven the classroom, encourage critical thinking, and stimulate our students' sociological imagination. Although formidable, these goals *are* attainable, and this book is designed to help you reach them. Based on many years of frontline (classroom) experience, its subtitle, *A Down-to-Earth Approach,* was not proposed lightly. My goal is to share the fascination of sociology with students and thereby make your teaching more rewarding.

Over the years, I have found the introductory course especially enjoyable. It is singularly satisfying to see students' faces light up as they begin to see how separate pieces of their world fit together. It is a pleasure to watch them gain insight into how their social experiences give shape to even their innermost desires. This is precisely what this text is designed to do—to stimulate your students' sociological imagination so they can better perceive how the "pieces" of society fit together—and what this means for their own lives.

Filled with examples from around the world as well as from our own society, this text helps to make today's multicultural, global society come alive for students. From learning how the international elite carve up global markets to studying the intimacy of friendship and marriage, students can see how sociology is the key to explaining contemporary life—and their own place in it.

In short, this text is designed to make your teaching easier. There simply is no justification for students to have to wade through cumbersome approaches to sociology. I am firmly convinced that the introduction to sociology should be enjoyable and that the introductory textbook can be an essential tool in sharing the discovery of sociology with students.

*xxvii*

# THE ORGANIZATION OF THIS TEXT

This text is laid out in five parts. Part I focuses on the sociological perspective, which is introduced in the first chapter. We then look at how culture influences us (Chapter 2), examine socialization (Chapter 3), and compare macrosociology and microsociology (Chapter 4).

Part II, which focuses on social groups and social control, adds to the students' understanding of how far-reaching society's influence is—how group membership penetrates even their thinking, attitudes, and orientations to life. We first examine the different types of groups that have such profound influences on us and then look at the fascinating area of group dynamics (Chapter 5). After this, we focus on how groups "keep us in line" and sanction those who violate their norms (Chapter 6).

In Part III, we turn our focus on social inequality, examining how it pervades society and its impact on our own lives. Because social stratification is so significant, I have written two chapters on this topic. The first (Chapter 7), with its global focus, presents an overview of the principles of stratification. The second (Chapter 8), with its emphasis on social class, focuses on stratification in U.S. society. After establishing this broader context of social stratification, we examine inequalities of race and ethnicity (Chapter 9) and then those of gender and age (Chapter 10).

Part IV helps students become more aware of how social institutions encompass their lives. We first look at politics and the economy, our overarching social institutions (Chapter 11). After examining the family (Chapter 12), we then turn our focus on education and religion (Chapter 13). One of the emphases in this part of the book is how our social institutions are changing and how their changes, in turn, influence our orientations and decisions.

With its focus on broad social change, Part V provides an appropriate conclusion for the book. Here we examine why our world is changing so rapidly, as well as catch a glimpse of what is yet to come. We first analyze trends in population and urbanization, those sweeping forces that affect our lives so significantly but that ordinarily remain below our level of awareness (Chapter 14). We conclude the book with an analysis of technology, social movements, and the environment (Chapter 15), which takes us to the cutting edge of the vital changes that engulf us all.

# THEMES AND FEATURES

Six central themes run throughout this text: down-to-earth sociology, globalization, cultural diversity, critical thinking, the new technology, and the influence of the mass media on our lives. For each of these themes, except globalization, which is incorporated in several of the others, I have written a series of boxes. These boxed features are one of my favorite components of the book. They are especially useful to introduce the controversial topics that make sociology such a lively activity.

Let's look at these six themes.

## Down-to-Earth Sociology

As many years of teaching have shown me, all too often textbooks are written to appeal to the adopters of texts rather than to the students who must learn from them. Therefore, a central concern in writing this book has been to present sociology in a way that not only facilitates understanding but also shares its excitement. During the course of writing other texts, I often have been told that my explanations and writing style are "down-to-earth," or accessible and inviting to students—so much so that I chose this phrase as the book's subtitle. The term is also featured in my introductory reader, *Down-to-Earth Sociology: Introductory Readings,* now in its 14th edition (New York: The Free Press, 2007).

This first theme is highlighted by a series of boxed features that explore sociological processes that underlie everyday life. The topics that we review in these **Down-to-Earth Sociology** boxes are highly diverse. Here are some of them:

- the experiences of Du Bois, an early sociologist, in studying U.S. race relations (Chapter 1)

- the relationship of heredity and the environment (Chapter 3)

- boot camp as a total institution (Chapter 3)

- how football can help us understand social structure (Chapter 4)

- social consequences of beauty (Chapter 4)

- the McDonaldization of society (Chapter 5)

- how a sociologist became a gang leader (for a day) (Chapter 6)

- serial killers (Chapter 6)

- what life is like after hitting it big in the lottery (Chapter 8)

- the taken-for-granted privileges attached to being white (Chapter 9)

- how a man became a live exhibit in a New York zoo (Chapter 9)

- the gender gap in math and science (Chapter 10)

- greedy surgeons and their women victims (Chapter 10)

- how "good" people can torture and mutilate (Chapter 11)

- child soldiers (Chapter 11)

- our chances of getting divorced (Chapter 12)

- how cohabitation means different things to people—and how this affects their chances of marriage (Chapter 12)

- terrorism in the name of God (Chapter 13)

- how the tsunami can help us to understand world population growth (Chapter 14)

- the gentrification of Harlem (Chapter 14)

- the coming Star Wars (Chapter 15)

- pollution and corporate welfare (Chapter 15)

This first theme is actually a hallmark of the text, as my goal is to make sociology "down to earth." To help students grasp the fascination of sociology, I continuously stress sociology's relevance to their lives. To reinforce this theme, I avoid unnecessary jargon and use concise explanations and clear and simple (but not reductive) language. I also use student-relevant examples to illustrate key concepts, and I base several of the chapters' opening vignettes on my own experiences in exploring social life. That this goal of sharing sociology's fascination is being reached is evident from the many comments I receive from instructors and students alike that the text helps make sociology "come alive."

## Globalization

In the second theme, *globalization,* we explore the impact of global issues on our lives and on the lives of people around the world. All of us are feeling the effects of an increasingly powerful and encompassing global economy, one that intertwines the fates of nations. The globalization of capitalism influences the kinds of skills and knowledge we need, the types of work available to us, the costs of the goods and services we consume, and even whether our country is at war or peace—or in some uncharted middle ground between the two. In addition to the strong emphasis on global issues that runs throughout this text, I have written a separate chapter on global stratification (Chapter 7). I have also featured global issues in the chapters on

social institutions and the final chapters on social change: population, urbanization, social movements, and the environment.

What occurs in Russia, Japan, Germany, and China, as well as in much smaller nations such as Afghanistan and Iraq, has far-reaching consequences on our own lives. Consequently, in addition to the global focus that runs throughout the text, the next theme, cultural diversity, also has a strong global emphasis.

## Cultural Diversity around the World and in the United States

The third theme, *cultural diversity,* has two primary emphases. The first is cultural diversity around the world. Gaining an understanding of how social life is "done" in other parts of the world often challenges our taken-for-granted assumptions about social life. At times, when we learn about other cultures, we gain an appreciation for the life of other peoples; at other times, we may be shocked or even disgusted at some aspect of another group's way of life (such as female circumcision) and come away with a renewed appreciation of our own customs.

To highlight this subtheme, I have written a series of boxes called ***Cultural Diversity around the World.*** In them, we review these topics

- food customs that shock people from different cultures (Chapter 2)

- how Easterners and Westerners perceive the world differently (Chapter 3)

- human sexuality in Mexico and Kenya (Chapter 6)

- a prison that lets its inmates work at outside-of-prison jobs—and have guns (Chapter 6)

- selling brides in China (Chapter 10)

- female circumcision (Chapter 10)

- doing business in the global village (Chapter 11)

- love and arranged marriage in India (Chapter 12)

- child workers around the world (Chapter 12)

- female infanticide in India and China (Chapter 14)

- the destruction of the rain forests and indigenous peoples of Brazil (Chapter 15)

In the second subtheme, ***Cultural Diversity in the United States,*** we examine groups that make up the fascinating array of people who form the U.S. population. The boxes I have written with this subtheme review such topics as

- how studying job discrimination turned into applied sociology (Chapter 1)

- the Hmong's culture shock when they moved to the United States (Chapter 2)

- the controversy over the use of Spanish or English (Chapter 2)

- the terms that people choose to refer to their own race–ethnicity (Chapter 2)

- education and culture in conflict (Chapter 3)

- how the Amish resist social change (Chapter 4)

- how our own social networks contribute to social inequality (Chapter 5)

- the upward social mobility of African Americans (Chapter 8)

- how Tiger Woods represents a significant change in racial–ethnic identity (Chapter 9)

- the author's travels with a Mexican who transports undocumented workers to the U.S. border (Chapter 9)

- Pentecostalism among Latino immigrants (Chapter 13)

Seeing that there are so many ways of "doing" social life can remove some of our cultural smugness, making us more aware of how arbitrary our own customs are—and how even our foundational, taken-for-granted ways of thinking are rooted in culture. The stimulating contexts of these contrasts can help students develop their sociological imagination. They encourage students to see connections among key sociological concepts such as culture, socialization, norms, race–ethnicity, gender, and social class. As your students' sociological imagination grows, they can attain a new perspective on their experiences in their own corners of life—and a better understanding of the social structure of U.S. society.

## Critical Thinking

In our fourth theme, *critical thinking,* we focus on controversial social issues, inviting students to examine various sides of those issues. In these sections, titled **Thinking Critically,** I present objective, fair portrayals of positions and do not take a side—although occasionally I do play the "devil's advocate" in the questions that close each of the topics. Like the boxed features, these sections can enliven your classroom with a vibrant exchange of ideas. Among the issues addressed are

- managing diversity in the workplace (Chapter 5)

- our tendency to conform to evil authority, as uncovered by the Milgram experiments (Chapter 5)

- culture clash of immigrants (Chapter 6)

- unintended consequences of three-strike laws (Chapter 6)

- bounties paid to kill homeless children in Brazil (Chapter 7)

- *maquiladoras* on the Mexican–U.S. border (Chapter 7)

- social class inequality in the treatment of mental and physical illness (Chapter 8)

- the weaponization of space (Chapter 15)

- ecosabotage (Chapter 15)

These *Thinking Critically* sections are based on controversial social issues that either affect the student's own life or focus on topics that have intrinsic interest for students. Because of their controversial nature, these sections stimulate both critical thinking and lively class discussions. These sections also make provocative topics for in-class debates and small discussion groups.

Small discussion groups are an effective way to enliven a class and present sociological ideas. Based on extensive experience, I describe the nuts and bolts of this teaching technique in the Instructor's Manual.

## Sociology and the New Technology

The fifth theme, *sociology and the new technology,* explores an aspect of social life that has come to be central in our lives. We welcome these new technological tools, for they help us to be more efficient at performing our daily tasks, from making a living to communicating with others—whether those people are nearby or on the other side of the globe. The significance of our new technology, however, extends far beyond the tools and the ease and efficiency they bring to our lives. The new technology is better envisioned as a social revolution that will leave few aspects of our lives untouched. Its effects are so profound that it even shapes our thinking and leads to changed ways of viewing life.

This theme is introduced in Chapter 2, where technology is defined and presented as an essential aspect of culture. The impact of technology is then discussed throughout the text. Examples include how technology is related to cultural change (Chapter 2), the control of workers (Chapter 5), and the maintenance of global stratification (Chapter 7). We also examine how technology led to social inequality in early human history and how it now may lead to world peace—and to Big Brother's net encompassing us all (Chapter 11). The final chapter (Chapter 15), "Social Change and the Environment," concludes the book with a focus on this theme.

To highlight this theme, I have written a series of boxes titled **Sociology and the New Technology.** In these boxes, we explore how technology affects our lives as it changes society. We examine, for example, the implications of cloning for future relationships (Chapter 4), the use of technology to avoid work ("cyberloafing") (Chapter 5), and how technology is changing the way people find mates (Chapter 12).

## The Mass Media and Social Life

In the sixth theme, we stress how the *mass media* affect our behavior and permeate our thinking. We consider how they penetrate our consciousness to such a degree that they even influence how we perceive our own bodies. As your students consider this theme, they may begin to grasp how the mass media shape their attitudes. If so, they will come to view the mass media in a different light, which should further stimulate their sociological imagination.

To make this theme more prominent for students, I have written a series of boxed features called **Mass Media in Social Life.** In these boxes, we consider why Native Americans like Western novels and movies even though Indians are usually portrayed as losers (Chapter 2), the influence of computer games on images of gender (Chapter 3), the worship of thinness—and how this affects our own body images (Chapter 4), the reemergence of slavery in today's world (Chapter 7), how the mass media shape our perceptions of the elderly (Chapter 10), and the myth of increasing school shootings (Chapter 13).

### New Topics

It is always a goal—and a challenge—to keep *Essentials of Sociology* current with cutting-edge sociological research and to incorporate into the analyses major national and global changes that affect our lives. For a chapter-by-chapter listing of some of this edition's numerous new topics, see "What's New?" on page viii.

As is discussed in the next section, some of the most interesting—and even fascinating—new topics are presented in a visual form.

## New and Expanded Features

### Visual Presentations of Sociology

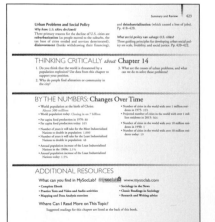

**Showing Changes Over Time**  In presenting social data, many of the figures and tables show how those data shift and change over time. This feature allows students to see trends in social life and to make predictions on how these trends might continue—and even affect their own lives. Examples include Figure 1.2, *U.S. Marriage, U.S. Divorce* (Chapter 1), Figure 10.16, *Trends in Poverty* (Chapter 10), and Figure 12.8, *Cohabitation in the United States.*

This hallmark feature of the text is now reinforced by a new feature, which appears at the end of most chapters: **By the Numbers.** By the Numbers pulls key data and statistics from the tables, figures, and text references in the chapter, and presents the data in paired comparisons. These comparisons represent some of the key changes occurring in our society and around the world.

**Through the Author's Lens**  Using this format, students are able to look over my shoulder as I experience other cultures or explore aspects of this one. These six photo essays should expand your students' sociological imagination and open their minds to other ways of doing social life, as well as stimulate thought-provoking class discussion.

*Holy Week in Spain*  New to this edition. I was fortunate to be able to photograph processions in two cities, Malaga, a provincial capital, and Almuñecar, a smaller city of Granada. Spain has a Roman Catholic heritage so deep that some of its city streets are named Conception, Piety, Humility, Calvary, Crucifxion, The Blessed Virgin, etc. In large and small towns throughout Spain, elaborate processions during Holy Week feature *tronos* that depict the biblical account of Jesus' suffering, death, and resurrection. As you will see in this photo essay, these events have a decidedly Spanish flavor.

I was also allowed to photograph the preparations for a procession, so this photo essay also includes some "behind-the-scenes" photos. During the processions in Malaga, the participants walk slowly for one or two minutes, then because of the weight of the *tronos,* they rest for one or two minutes. Except for Saturdays, this process repeats for about six hours each day during Holy Week, with different *tronos* featured and different bands and organizations participating. As you will see, some of the most interesting activities occur during the rest periods (Chapter 13).

*When a Tornado Strikes: Social Organization Following a Natural Disaster*  When a tornado hit a small town just hours from where I lived, I photographed the aftermath of the disaster. The police let me in to view the neighborhood where the tornado had struck, destroying homes and killing several people. I was impressed by how quickly people were putting their lives back together, the topic of this photo essay (Chapter 4).

*The Dump People: Working and Living and Playing in the City Dump of Phnom Penh, Cambodia*
Among the culture shocks I experienced in Cambodia was not to discover that people scavenge at Phnom Penh's huge city dump—this I knew about—but that they also live there. With the aid of an interpreter, I was able to interview these people, as well as photograph them as they went about their everyday lives. An entire community lives in the city dump, complete with restaurants amidst the smoke and piles of garbage. This photo essay reveals not just these people's activities but also their social organization (Chapter 7).

*Work and Gender: Women at Work in India*  As I traveled in India, I took photos of women at work in public places. The more I traveled in this country and the more photos I took, the more insight I gained into gender relations. Despite the general submissiveness of women to men in India, women's worlds are far from limited to family and home. Women are found at work throughout the society. What is even more remarkable is how vastly different "women's work" is in India than it is in the United States. This, too, is an intellectually provocative photo essay (Chapter 10).

*Small Town USA: Struggling to Survive*  To take the photos for this essay, I went off the beaten path. On a road trip from California to Florida, instead of following the interstates, I followed those "little black lines" on the map. They took me to out-of-the-way places that the national transportation system has bypassed. Many of these little towns are putting on a valiant face as they struggle to survive, but, as the photos show, the struggle is apparent, and, in some cases, so are the scars (Chapter 11).

*A Walk Through El Tiro in Medellín, Colombia:*  One of the most significant social changes in the world is taking place in the Least Industrialized Nations. There, in the search for a better life, people are abandoning rural areas. Fleeing poverty, they are flocking to the cities, only to find even more poverty. Some of these settlements of the new urban poor are dangerous. I was fortunate to be escorted by an insider through a section of Medellín, Colombia, that is controlled by gangs (Chapter 14).

**Other Photos by the Author**  Sprinkled throughout the text are photos that I took during travels to India and Cambodia. These photos illustrate sociological principles and topics better than photos available from commercial sources. As an example, while in the United States, I received a report about a feral child who had been discovered living with monkeys and who had been taken to an orphanage in Cambodia. The possibility of photographing and interviewing that child was one of the reasons that I went to Cambodia. That particular photo is on page 60. Another of my favorites is on page 142.

**Photo Essay on Subcultures**  To help students better understand subcultures, I have retained the photo essay on subcultures in Chapter 2. Because this photo essay consists of photos taken by others, it is not a part of the series, *Through the Author's Lens.* The variety of subcultures featured in this photo essay, however, should be instructive to your students.

**Photo Collages**  Because sociology lends itself so well to photographic illustrations, this text also includes photo collages. New to this edition is a photo collage that illustrates ethnic work (Chapter 9). As with the other photo collages that I have prepared, I found the process instructive, and I hope that your students also find it so. I have retained the photo collages in Chapters 2, 5, and 10. In Chapter 2 (page 41), students can catch a glimpse of the fascinating variety that goes into the cultural relativity of beauty. The collage in Chapter 5 (page 117) illustrates categories, aggregates, and primary and secondary groups, concepts that students sometimes wrestle to distinguish. The photo collage in Chapter 10 (page 263) lets students see how distinctively gender is portrayed in different cultures.

# Special Pedagogical Features

In addition to chapter summaries and reviews, key terms, and a comprehensive glossary, I have included several special features to aid students in learning sociology. **In Sum** sections help students review important points within the chapter before going on to new materials. I have also developed a series of **Social Maps,** which illustrate how social conditions vary by geography.

**Chapter-Opening Vignettes**  These accounts feature down-to-earth illustrations of a major aspect of each chapter's content. Some are based on my research with the homeless, the time I spent with them on the streets and slept in their shelters (Chapters 1 and 8). Others recount my travels in Africa (Chapters 2 and 10) and Mexico (Chapter 14). I also share my experiences when I spent a night with street people at Dupont Circle in Washington, D.C. (Chapter 4). For other vignettes, I use current and historical events (Chapters 9, 13, and 15), classic studies in the social sciences (Chapters 3 and 6), and even a scene from a novel (Chapter 11). Students have often told me that they find the vignettes compelling, that they stimulate interest in the chapter.

**Thinking Critically About the Chapters**  I close each chapter with three critical thinking questions. Each question focuses on a major feature of the chapter, asking students to consider some issue. Many of the questions ask the students to apply sociological findings and principles to their own lives.

**On Sources**  Sociological data are found in an amazingly wide variety of sources, and this text reflects that variety. Cited throughout this text are standard journals such as the *American Journal of Sociology, Social Problems, American Sociological Review,* and *Journal of Marriage and the Family,* as well as more esoteric journals such as the *Bulletin of the History of Medicine, Chronobiology International,* and *Western Journal of Black Studies.* I have also drawn heavily from standard news sources, especially the *New York Times* and the *Wall Street Journal,* as well as more unusual sources such as *El País.* In addition, I cite unpublished papers by sociologists.

# Acknowledgments

The gratifying response to earlier editions indicates that my efforts at making sociology down to earth have succeeded. The years that have gone into writing this text are a culmination of the many more years that preceded its writing—from graduate school to that equally demanding endeavor known as classroom teaching. No text, of course, comes solely from its author. Although I am responsible for the final words on the printed page, I have received excellent feedback from instructors who used the first seven editions. I am especially grateful to

## Reviewers

Sandra L. Albrecht, *University of Kansas*

David Allen, *Georgia Southern University*

Angelo A. Alonzo, *Ohio State University*

Kenneth Ambrose, *Marshall University*

Alberto Arroyo, *Baldwin-Wallace College*

Karren Baird-Olsen, *Kansas State University*

Linda Barbera-Stein, *University of Illinois*

Richard J. Biesanz, *Corning Community College*

Charles A. Brawner III, *Heartland Community College*

Shelly Breitenstein, *Western Wisconsin Technical College*

Richard D. Bucher, *Baltimore City Community College*

Richard D. Clark, *John Carroll University*

John K. Cochran, *University of Oklahoma*

Matthew Crist, *Moberly Area Community College*

Russell L. Curtis, *University of Houston*

William Danaher, *College of Charleston*

John Darling, *University of Pittsburgh–Johnstown*

Ray Darville, *Stephen F. Austin State University*

Nanette J. Davis, *Portland State University*

Tom DeDen, *Foothill College*

Paul Devereux, *University of Nevada*

Lynda Dodgen, *North Harris Community College*

James W. Dorsey, *College of Lake County*

Helen R. Ebaugh, *University of Houston*

Obi N. Ebbe, *State University of New York–Brockport*

Margaret C. Figgins-Hill, *University of Massachusetts–Lowell*

Robin Franck, *Southwestern College*

David O. Friedrichs, *University of Scranton*

Richard A. Garnett, *Marshall University*

George W. Glann, Jr., *Fayetteville Technical Community College*

Norman Goodman, *State University of New York–Stony Brook*

Anne S. Graham, *Salt Lake Community College*

Donald W. Hastings, *The University of Tennessee–Knoxville*

Penelope E. Herideen, *Holyoke Community College*

Michael Hoover, *Missouri Western State College*

Hua-Lun Huang, *University of Louisiana*

Charles E. Hurst, *The College of Wooster*

Dick Jobst, *Pacific Lutheran University*

Mark Kassop, *Bergen Community College*

Alice Abel Kemp, *University of New Orleans*

Dianna Kendall, *Austin Community College*

Gary Kiger, *Utah State University*

Ross Koppel, *University of Pennsylvania*

Jenifer Kunz, *West Texas A&M University*

David Kyle, *University of California–Davis*

Patricia A. Larson, *Cleveland State University*

Abraham Levine, *El Camino Community College*

Mike Lindner, *Gloucester County College*

Fr. Jeremiah Lowney, *Carroll College*

Cecile Lycan, *Spokane Community College*

John J. Malarky, *Wilmington College*

Patricia Masters, *George Mason University*

Bonita Sessing Matcha, *Hudson Valley Community College*

Ron Matson, *Wichita State University*

Armaund L. Mauss, *Washington State University*

Roger McVannan, *Broome Community College*

Evelyn Mercer, *Southwest Baptist University*

Robert Meyer, *Arkansas State University*

Richard B. Miller, *Missouri Southern State College*

Beth Mintz, *University of Vermont–Burlington*

Meryl G. Nason, *University of Texas, Dallas*

Craig J. Nauman, *Madison Area Technical College*

W. Lawrence Neuman, *University of Wisconsin–Whitewater*

Charles Norman, *Indiana State University*

Laura O'Toole, *University of Delaware*

Mike Pate, *Western Oklahoma State College*

William Patterson, *Clemson University*

Phil Piket, *Joliet Junior College*

Annette Prosterman, *Our Lady of the Lake University*

Adrian Rapp, *North Harris Community College*

Nancy Reeves, *Gloucester County College*

Donald D. Ricker, *Mott Community College*

Howard Robboy, *Trenton State College*

Terina Roberson, *Central Piedmont Community College*

Alden E. Roberts, *Texas Tech University*

Sybil Rosado, *Benedict College*

Kent Sandstrom, *University of Northern Iowa*

Don Shamblin, *Ohio University*

Walt Shirley, *Sinclair Community College*

Laura Siebuhr, *Centralia College*

Marc Silver, *Hofstra University*

Michael C. Smith, *Milwaukee Area Technical College*

Roberto E. Socas, *Essex County College*

Sherry Sperman, *Kansas State University*

Susan Sprecher, *Illinois State University*

Randolph G. Ston, *Oakland Community College*

Kathleen Tiemann, *University of North Dakota*

Tracy Tolbert, *California State University*

Suzanne Tuthill, *Delaware Technical Community College*

Lisa Waldner, *University of Houston–Downtown*

Larry Weiss, *University of Alaska*

Douglas White, *Henry Ford Community College*

Stephen R. Wilson, *Temple University*

Stuart Wright, *Lamar University*

Meifang Zhang, *Midlands Technical College*

I couldn't ask for a more outstanding team than the one that I have the pleasure to work with at Allyn and Bacon. I want to thank Jeff Lasser, whose counsel continues to be excellent; Dusty Friedman, who has overseen both the routine and the urgent while managing to maintain an exemplary attitude and encouraging me to excel; Judy Fiske, for wholeheartedly supporting my many suggestions and tolerating my many last-minute changes; Joan Pendleton, for the attention to detail that she has given in copy editing my manuscript, and even for a couple of surprising suggestions; Jenn Albanese, whose pursuit of countless research leads has been an ongoing help in this formidable task of keeping abreast of sociological changes; Kate Cebik, whose eye for photo composition and willingness to "keep on looking" for the "exact" photo have enhanced the visual appeal of this edition; and Gary Kliewer, for coordinating the many separate tasks that must be integrated into a whole.

I do so appreciate this team. It is difficult to heap too much praise on such fine, capable, and creative people. Often going "beyond the call of duty" as we faced nonstop deadlines, their untiring efforts coalesced with mine to produce this text. Students, whom we constantly kept in mind as we prepared this edition, are the beneficiaries of this intricate teamwork.

I would also like to thank those who prepared the many supplements that go with *Essentials of Sociology*. Their efforts, so often unacknowledged, are important in our goal of introducing students to sociology. The instructors who prepared supplements for this edition of *Essentials of Sociology* are Jessica Herrmeyer, Hawkeye Community College; Christopher Mele, SUNY Buffalo; Ralph Peters, Georgia Highlands College; Nancy Reeves, Goucester County College; and Anthony W. Zumpetta, West Chester University.

Since this text is based on the contributions of many, I would count it a privilege if you would share with me your teaching experiences with this book, including any suggestions for improving the text. Both positive and negative comments are welcome. It is in this way that I continue to learn.

I wish you the very best in your teaching. It is my sincere desire that *Essentials of Sociology: A Down-to-Earth Approach* contributes to your classroom success.

**James M. Henslin,**
**Professor Emeritus**
**Department of Sociology**
**Southern Illinois University, Edwardsville**

I welcome your correspondence. E-mail is the best way to reach me: henslin@aol.com

# A Note from the Publisher
## on the Supplements

## INSTRUCTOR'S SUPPLEMENTS

### Instructor's Manual *Jessica Herrmeyer, Hawkeye Community College*

For each chapter in the text, the Instructor's Manual provides At-a-Glance grids that link main concepts to key terms and theorists as well as to other supplements. Each chapter in the Instructor's Manual includes a list of key changes to the new edition, chapter summaries and outlines, learning objectives, key terms and people, classroom activities, discussion topics, recommended films, Web sites, and additional references. The Instructor's Manual also includes a section by James M. Henslin on using small in-class discussion groups. Adopters can request a print copy or download the electronic file by logging in to our Instructor Resource Center.

### Test Bank *Anthony W. Zumpetta, West Chester University*

The test bank contains approximately 150 questions per chapter in multiple choice, true/false, short answer, essay, and open-book formats. There is also a set of questions based on the text's figures, tables, and maps. All questions are labeled and scaled according to Bloom's Taxonomy. Adopters can request a print copy or download the electronic file by logging in to our Instructor Resource Center.

### Computerized Test Bank

The printed Test Bank is also available through Allyn and Bacon's computerized testing system, MyTest. This fully networkable test generator is delivered within Pegasus, Allyn and Bacon's course management system (and hosted nationally on our server). The user-friendly interface allows you to view, edit, and add questions, transfer questions to tests, and print tests in a variety of fonts. Search and sort features allow you to locate questions quickly and to arrange them in whatever order you prefer. Adopters can download the electronic file by logging in to our Instructor Resource Center.

### PowerPoint™ Presentation with Clicker Questions

*Nancy Reeves, Gloucester County College*

These PowerPoint slides feature lecture outlines for every chapter and corresponding artwork from the text. PowerPoint software is not required, as a PowerPoint viewer is included. Available on request at no additional cost to adopters. Available online from our Instructor Resource Center, and also on the Instructor's Resource CD-ROM.

### Instructor's Resource CD with PowerPoint Presentation

This CD contains electronic versions of all of our Instructor Supplements in two formats: as PDF files, and word processing files (which can be edited). Includes the Instructor's Manual, Test Bank, Study Guide, Study Guide Plus, and Telecourse Faculty Guide. The CD also includes the PowerPoint Presentation for this edition, and all the tables, graphs, and figures from the text in an easily accessible electronic format.

## Allyn and Bacon Transparencies for Henslin's Introductory Sociology

This package includes over 100 color acetates featuring illustrations from the Henslin texts. Available on request to adopters.

## ABC News Sociology Videos and DVDs

If you like to use news footage and documentary-style programs to illustrate sociological themes and stimulate classroom discussion, this series of videos contains material from popular ABC programs such as *Nightline, World News Tonight,* and *20/20.* Each video has an accompanying User's Guide. Individual videocassettes are available for the following topics: *Poverty and Stratification, Race and Ethnicity, Gender, Deviance,* and *Aging.* We also offer two DVDs that include a range of ABC programs for all topics typically covered in introductory sociology.

## The Video Professor: Applying Lessons in Sociology to Classic and Modern Films *Anthony W. Zumpetta, West Chester University*

This manual describes hundreds of commercially available videos that represent nineteen of the most important topics in introductory sociology textbooks. Each topic lists a number of movies, along with specific assignments and suggestions for class use. Adopters can request a print copy or download the electronic file by logging in to our Instructor Resource Center.

## Exploring Society Telecourse Faculty Guide

Allyn and Bacon provides special assistance for instructors who use the video series from Dallas TeleLearning, *Exploring Society.* This manual coordinates reading and video assignments, contains the entire content of the Telecourse Study Guide (see Student Supplements), and correlates all test questions in our Test Bank with twenty-two half-hour video programs. Adopters can download the electronic file by logging in to our Instructor Resource Center. For information about the *Exploring Society* Telecourse, contact Dallas TeleLearning directly (972-669-6650, http:/telelearning.deced.edu).

## InterWrite PRS (Personal Response System)

*Nancy Reeves, Gloucester County College*

Assess your students' progress with the Personal Response System—an easy-to-use wireless polling system that enables you to pose questions, record results, and display those results instantly in your classroom. Designed by teachers, for teachers, PRS is easy to integrate into your lectures:

- Each student uses a cell-phone-sized transmitter which they bring to class.
- You ask multiple-choice, numerical-answer, or matching questions during class; students simply click their answer into their transmitter.
- A classroom receiver (portable or mounted) connected to your computer tabulates all answers and displays them graphically in class.
- Results can be recorded for grading, attendance, or simply used as a discussion point.

Our partnership with PRS allows us to offer student rebate cards bundled with any Allyn and Bacon/Longman text. The rebate card is a direct value of $20.00 and can be redeemed with the purchase of a new PRS student transmitter. In addition, institutions that order 40 or more new textbook + rebate card bundles will receive the classroom receiver—a $250 value—software and support at no additional cost. Contact your Allyn and Bacon/Longman representative or visit **http://www.ablongman.com/prs** for more information.

# STUDENT SUPPLEMENTS

## Study Guide *Ralph Peters, Georgia Highlands College*

The Study Guide Plus includes successful study strategies, a glossary of words to know, chapter summaries, learning objectives, key terms and people, lecture outlines that correspond to the PowerPoint presentation for this text, and student projects. Practice tests with 80 questions per chapter in multiple-choice, true-false, short answer, matching, and essay formats help students prepare for quizzes and exams. An answer key is provided for all questions.

## Study Card for Introduction to Sociology

Compact, efficient, and laminated for durability, the Allyn and Bacon Study Card for Introductory Sociology condenses course information down to the basics, helping students quickly master fundamental facts and concepts and prepare for an exam.

## Exploring Social Life: Readings to Accompany *Essentials of Sociology: A Down-to-Earth Approach* *James M. Henslin*

This brief reader, revised for the Eighth Edition, contains one reading for each chapter of the text, chosen and introduced by James M. Henslin. The reader can be purchased separately at full price or packaged with this text for an additional $5 net to the bookstore. An Instructor's Manual for the reader is available electronically from our Instructor Resource Center.

# ONLINE COURSE MANAGEMENT

## MySocLab

MySocLab is a state-of-the-art interactive and instructive solution for introductory sociology, delivered within Pegasus, Allyn and Bacon's course management system (and hosted nationally on our server). MySocLab is designed to be used as a supplement to a traditional lecture course, or to completely administer an online course. Customize your course or use the materials as presented. Built around a complete e-book version of the text, MySocLab enables students to explore important sociological concepts, by watching television news stories, listening to interviews with prominent researchers and social scientists, reading current newspaper articles, analyzing data from graphs and maps in the text, and performing other hands-on activities. Customize your course or use the materials as presented. Available at no additional cost to students when the text is packaged with a MySocLab Pegasus Student Access Code Card.

MySocLab also incorporates the Exploring Society Telecourse Study Guide  The Telecourse Study Guide is designed to correlate *Essentials of Sociology* with the twenty-two video programs in the *Exploring Society* series from Dallas TeleLearning. Each section coordinates reading and video assignments and includes summaries, learning objectives, outlines, key terms and people, and student application projects. There is also a self-test section containing multiple-choice, true-false, fill-in-the-blank, matching, and essay questions.

## MySocLab—Website Version with GradeTracker

Provides virtually the same online content and interactivity as the CourseCompass MySocLab, without any of the course management features or requirements. Available at no additional cost to students when the text is packaged with a MySocLab Website Student Access Code.

## WebCT and Blackboard Test Banks

For colleges and universities with **WebCT™** and **Blackboard™** licenses, we have converted the complete Test Bank into these popular course management platforms. Adopters can request a copy on CD or download the electronic file by logging in to our Instructor Resource Center.

# ADDITIONAL SUPPLEMENTS

## Building Bridges: The Allyn and Bacon Guide to Service Learning *Doris Hamner*

This manual offers practical advice for students who must complete a service-learning project as part of their required course work. Packaged on request at no additional cost with this text.

## Careers in Sociology, Third Edition *W. Richard Stephens, Eastern Nazarene College*

This supplement explains how sociology can help students prepare for careers in such fields as law, gerontology, social work, business, and computers. It also examines how students of sociology enter the field. Packaged on request at no additional cost with this text.

## College and Society: An Introduction to the Sociological Imagination *Stephen Sweet, Ithaca College*

This supplemental text uses examples from familiar surroundings—the patterns of interaction, social structures, and expectations of conduct on a typical college campus—to help students see the ways in which large society also operates. Available for purchase separately or packaged with this text at a special discount.

## New! The Allyn and Bacon Social Atlas of the United States

*William H. Frey, University of Michigan, with Amy Beth Anspach and John Paul DeWitt*

This brief and accessible atlas uses colorful maps, graphs, and some of the best social science data available to survey the leading social, economic, and political indicators of American society. Available for purchase separately, or packaged with this text at a significant discount.

## Sociological Classics: A Prentice Hall Pocket Reader

*David Kauzlarich*

This reader features 14 classical readings by prominent names in sociology, including C. Wright Mills, W.E.B. DuBois, Jane Addams, and George Herbert Mead, with readings by female sociologists. Available for purchase separately, or packaged with this text at no charge.

# About the Author

The author at work—sometimes getting a little too close to "the action" (preparing the new "Through the Author's Lens" photo essay on pages 380–381).

JIM HENSLIN, who was born in Minnesota, graduated from high school and junior college in California and from college in Indiana. Awarded scholarships, he earned his master's and doctorate degrees in sociology at Washington University in St. Louis, Missouri. After this, he won a postdoctoral fellowship from the National Institute of Mental Health and spent a year studying how people adjust to the suicide of a family member. His primary interests in sociology are the sociology of everyday life, deviance, and international relations. Among his many books is *Down-to-Earth Sociology: Introductory Readings* (Free Press), now in its fourteenth edition, and *Social Problems* (Allyn and Bacon), now in its 9th edition. He has also published widely in sociology journals, including *Social Problems* and *American Journal of Sociology*.

While a graduate student, Jim taught at the University of Missouri at St. Louis. After completing his doctorate, he joined the faculty at Southern Illinois University, Edwardsville, where he is Professor Emeritus of Sociology. He says, "I've always found the introductory course enjoyable to teach. I love to see students' faces light up when they first glimpse the sociological perspective and begin to see how society has become an essential part of how they view the world."

Jim enjoys reading and fishing, and he also does a bit of kayaking. His two favorite activities are writing and traveling. He especially enjoys visiting and living in other cultures, for this brings him face to face with behaviors and ways of thinking that challenge his perspectives and "make sociological principles come alive." A special pleasure has been the preparation of the photo essays that appear in this text.

Jim moved to Latvia, an Eastern European country formerly dominated by the Soviet Union, where he observed firsthand how people struggle to adjust to capitalism. While there, he happened to be present at an historical event. See the two photos on page 429. He also interviewed aged political prisoners from Latvia who had survived the Soviet gulag. To better round out his cultural experiences, Jim is making extended stays in eastern and western Europe, South America, and Asia. He is developing more photo essays to reflect these fascinating cultures. He is grateful to be able to live in such exciting social, technological, and geopolitical times—and to have access to portable broadband Internet while he pursues his sociological imagination.

Chapter

1

The Sociological
Perspective

E ven from the glow of the faded red-and-white exit sign, its faint light barely illuminating the upper bunk, I could see that the sheet was filthy. Resigned to another night of fitful sleep, I reluctantly crawled into bed.

The next morning, I joined the long line of disheveled men leaning against the chain-link fence. Their faces were as downcast as their clothes were dirty. Not a glimmer of hope among them.

**I was determined. "I will experience what they experience," I kept telling myself.**

No one spoke as the line slowly inched forward.

When my turn came, I was handed a cup of coffee, a white plastic spoon, and a bowl of semiliquid that I couldn't identify. It didn't look like any food I had seen before. Nor did it taste like anything I had ever eaten.

My stomach fought the foul taste, every spoonful a battle. But I was determined. "I will experience what they experience," I kept telling myself. My stomach reluctantly gave in and accepted its morning nourishment.

The room was strangely silent. Hundreds of men were eating, each one immersed in his own private hell, his head awash with disappointment, remorse, bitterness.

As I stared at the Styrofoam cup that held my coffee, grateful for at least this small pleasure, I noticed what looked like teeth marks. I shrugged off the thought, telling myself that my long weeks as a sociological observer of the homeless were finally getting to me. "This must be some sort of crease from handling," I concluded.

I joined the silent ranks of men turning in their bowls and cups. When I saw the man behind the counter swishing out Styrofoam cups in a washtub of murky water, I began to feel sick to my stomach. I knew then that the jagged marks on my cup really had come from another person's mouth.

How much longer did this research have to last? I felt a deep longing to return to my family—to a welcome world of clean sheets, healthy food, and "normal" conversations.

*3*

# The Sociological Perspective

Why were these men so silent? Why did they receive such despicable treatment? What was I doing in that homeless shelter? After all, I hold a respectable, professional position, and I have a home and family.

Sociology offers a perspective, a view of the world. The *sociological perspective* (or imagination) opens a window onto unfamiliar worlds—and offers a fresh look at familiar worlds. In this text, you will find yourself in the midst of Nazis in Germany and warriors in South America, as well as the people I visited who live in a city dump in Cambodia. But you will also find yourself looking at your own world in a different light. As you view other worlds—or your own—the sociological perspective enables you to gain a new perception of social life. In fact, this is what many find appealing about sociology.

The sociological perspective has been a motivating force in my own life. Ever since I took my introductory course in sociology, I have been enchanted by the perspective that sociology offers. I have thoroughly enjoyed both observing other groups and questioning my own assumptions about life. I sincerely hope the same happens to you.

## Seeing the Broader Social Context

The **sociological perspective** stresses the social contexts in which people live. It examines how these contexts influence people's lives. At the center of the sociological perspective is the question of how groups influence people, especially how people are influenced by their **society**—a group of people who share a culture and a territory.

To find out why people do what they do, sociologists look at **social location,** the corners in life that people occupy because of where they are located in a society. Sociologists look at how jobs, income, education, gender, age, and race–ethnicity affect people's ideas and behavior. Consider, for example, how being identified with a group called *females* or with a group called *males* when we

are growing up shapes our ideas of who we are and what we should attain in life. Growing up as a female or a male influences not only our aspirations but also how we feel about ourselves. It also affects the way we relate to others in dating and marriage and at work.

Sociologist C. Wright Mills (1959) put it this way: "The sociological imagination [perspective] enables us to grasp the connection between history and biography." By *history,* Mills meant that each society is located in a broad stream of events. Because of this, each society has specific characteristics—such as its ideas about the proper roles of men and women. By *biography,* Mills referred to each individual's specific experiences. In short, people don't do what they do because of inherited internal mechanisms, such as instincts. Rather, *external* influences—our experiences—become part of our thinking and motivations. In short, the society in which we grow up, and our particular location in that society, lie at the center of what we do and how we think.

Consider a newborn baby. If we were to take the baby away from its U.S. parents and place it with the Yanomamö Indians in the jungles of South America, when the child begins to speak, his or her words will not be in English. You also know that the child will not think like an American. He or she will not grow up wanting credit cards, for example, or designer clothes, a car, a cell phone, an iPod, and the latest video game. Equally, the child will unquestioningly take his or her place in Yanomamö society—perhaps as a food gatherer, a hunter, or a warrior—and he or she will not even know about the world left behind at birth. And, whether male or female, the child will grow up assuming that it is natural to want many children, not debating whether to have one, two, or three children.

This brings us to *you*—to how *your* social groups have shaped *your* ideas and desires. Over and over in this text, you will see that

Examining the broad social context in which people live is essential to the *sociological perspective,* for this context shapes our beliefs and attitudes and sets guidelines for what we do. From this photo, you can see how distinctive those guidelines are for the Yanomamö Indians who live on the border of Brazil and Venezuela. How has this Yanomamö man been influenced by his group? How have groups influenced your views and behavior?

the way you look at the world is the result of your exposure to specific human groups. I think you will enjoy the process of self-discovery that sociology offers.

# Origins of Sociology

## Tradition Versus Science

Just how did sociology begin? In some ways, it is difficult to answer this question. Even ancient peoples tried to figure out how social life works. They, too, asked questions about why war exists, why some people become more powerful than others, and why some are rich but others are poor. However, they often based their answers on superstition, myth, or even the positions of the stars, and they did not *test* their assumptions.

*Science, in contrast, requires theories that can be tested by research.* Measured by this standard, sociology emerged about the middle of the 1800s, when social observers began to use scientific methods to test their ideas.

Sociology grew out of social upheaval. The Industrial Revolution had just begun. By the middle of the nineteenth century, Europe's economy was changing from agriculture to factory production. Masses of people were moving to cities in search of work. Their ties to the land were broken, distancing them from a culture that had provided ready answers to the difficult questions of life. The city greeted them with horrible working conditions: miserable pay; long hours; dangerous, exhausting work. For families to survive, even children had to work in these conditions; some children were even chained to factory machines to make certain they would not run away. With their world turned upside down, people could no longer count on tradition to provide the answers to questions about social life.

The success of the American and French revolutions also encouraged people to rethink social life. As new ideas emerged, they uprooted traditional social arrangements even further. Especially powerful was the new idea that individuals possess inalienable rights. As this idea caught fire, many traditional Western monarchies gave way to more democratic forms of government. Increasingly, people found the answers provided by tradition inadequate.

About this same time, **the scientific method**—using objective, systematic observations to test theories—was being tried out in chemistry and physics. This revealed many secrets that had been concealed in nature. With traditional answers failing, the logical step was to apply the scientific method to questions about social life. The result was the birth of sociology.

## Auguste Comte and Positivism

This idea of applying the scientific method to the social world, known as **positivism,** apparently was first proposed by Auguste Comte (1798–1857). With the social upheaval of the French Revolution still fresh in his mind, Comte left the small town in which he had grown up and moved to Paris. The changes he experienced in this move, combined with those France underwent in the revolution, led Comte to become interested in what holds society together. What creates social order, he wondered, instead of anarchy or chaos? And then, once society does become set on a particular course, what causes it to change?

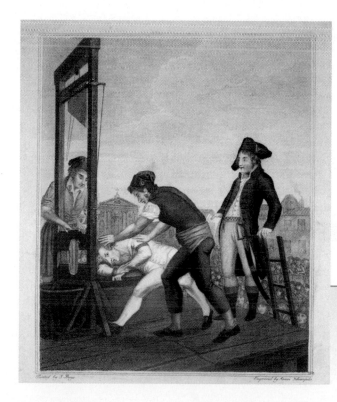

The French Revolution of 1789 not only overthrew the aristocracy but also upset the entire social order. This extensive change removed the past as a sure guide to the present. The events of this period stimulated Auguste Comte to analyze how societies change. His writings are often taken as the origin of sociology. This engraving depicts the 1794 execution of Maximilien Robespierre, a leader of the Revolution.

**Auguste Comte** (1798–1857), who is considered the founder of sociology, began to analyze the bases of the social order. Although he stressed that the scientific method should be applied to the study of society, he did not apply it himself.

**Herbert Spencer** (1820–1903), sometimes called the second founder of sociology, coined the term "survival of the fittest." Spencer thought that helping the poor was wrong, that this merely helped the "less fit" survive.

As Comte considered these questions, he concluded that the right way to answer them was to apply the scientific method to social life. Just as this method had revealed the law of gravity, so, too, it would uncover the laws that underlie society. Comte called this new science **sociology**—"the study of society" (from the Greek *logos,* "study of," and the Latin *socius,* "companion," or "being with others"). Comte stressed that this new science not only would discover social principles but also would apply them to social reform. Sociologists would reform the entire society, making it a better place to live.

To Comte, however, applying the scientific method to social life meant practicing what we might call "armchair philosophy"—drawing conclusions from informal observations of social life. He did not do what today's sociologists would call research, and his conclusions have been abandoned. Nevertheless, Comte's insistence that we must observe and classify human activities to uncover society's fundamental laws is well taken. Because he developed this idea and coined the term *sociology,* Comte often is credited with being the founder of sociology.

## Herbert Spencer and Social Darwinism

Herbert Spencer (1820–1903), who grew up in England, is sometimes called the second founder of sociology. Spencer disagreed profoundly with Comte that sociology should guide social reform. Spencer thought that societies evolve from lower ("barbarian") to higher ("civilized") forms. As generations pass, the most capable and intelligent ("the fittest") members of a society survive, while the less capable die out. Thus, over time, societies improve. To help the lower classes is to interfere with this natural process. The fittest members will produce a more advanced society—unless misguided do-gooders get in the way and help the less fit survive.

Spencer called this principle "the survival of the fittest." Although Spencer coined this phrase, it usually is attributed to his contemporary, Charles Darwin, who proposed that organisms evolve over time as they adapt to their environment. Because they are so similar to Darwin's ideas about the evolution of organisms, Spencer's views of the evolution of societies became known as *social Darwinism.*

Spencer did not conduct scientific studies. Like Comte, he simply developed ideas about society. Spencer gained a wide following in England and the United States, where he was sought after as a speaker, but eventually social Darwinism was discredited.

## Karl Marx and Class Conflict

Karl Marx (1818–1883) not only influenced sociology but also left his mark on world history. Marx's influence has been so great that even the *Wall Street Journal,* that staunch advocate of capitalism, has called him one of the three greatest modern thinkers (the other two being Sigmund Freud and Albert Einstein).

Marx, who came to England after being exiled from his native Germany for proposing revolution, believed that the engine of human history is **class conflict.** He said that the *bourgeoisie* (boo-shwa-ZEE) (the *capitalists,* those who own the means to produce wealth—capital, land, factories, and machines) are locked in conflict with the *proletariat* (the exploited workers, who do not own the means of production). This bitter struggle can end only when members of the working class unite and violently break their chains of bondage. This revolution will usher in a classless society, one free of exploitation. People will work according to their abilities and receive goods and services according to their needs (Marx and Engels 1848/1967).

**Karl Marx** (1818–1883) believed that the roots of human misery lay in class conflict, the exploitation of workers by those who own the means of production. Social change, in the form of the overthrow of the capitalists by the workers (proletariat), was inevitable from Marx's perspective. Although Marx did not consider himself a sociologist, his ideas have influenced many sociologists, particularly conflict theorists.

The French sociologist **Emile Durkheim** (1858–1917) contributed many important concepts to sociology. His comparison of the suicide rates of several countries revealed an underlying social factor: People are more likely to commit suicide if their ties to others in their communities are weak. Durkheim's identification of the key role of *social integration* in social life remains central to sociology today.

Marxism is not the same as communism. Although Marx proposed revolution as the only way that the workers could gain control of society, he did not develop the political system called *communism*. This is a later application of his ideas. Indeed, Marx himself felt disgusted when he heard debates about his insights into social life. After listening to some of the positions attributed to him, he shook his head and said, "I am not a Marxist" (Dobriner 1969b:222; Gitlin 1997:89).

## Emile Durkheim and Social Integration

The primary professional goal of Emile Durkheim (1858–1917) was to get sociology recognized as a separate academic discipline (Coser 1977). Up to this time, sociology had been viewed as part of history and economics. Durkheim, who grew up in eastern France and was educated in both Germany and France, achieved his goal in 1887. That year, at the University of Bordeaux, he became the world's first professor of sociology.

Durkheim also had another goal: to show how social forces affect people's behavior. To accomplish this, he conducted rigorous research. Comparing the suicide rates of several European countries, Durkheim (1897/1966) found that each country has a different suicide rate—and that these rates remain about the same year after year. He also found that different groups within a country have different suicide rates and that these, too, remain stable from year to year. His data showed that Protestants, males, and the unmarried kill themselves at a higher rate than do Catholics or Jews, females, and the married. From these observations, Durkheim concluded that suicide is not what it appears—simply a matter of individuals here and there deciding to take their lives for personal reasons. Instead,

*social factors underlie suicide,* which is why a group's rate remains fairly constant year after year.

But what are those social factors? Durkheim concluded that the main one is **social integration,** the degree to which people are tied to their social group. If people have weaker social ties, they are more likely to commit suicide. How does this apply to Protestants, males, and the unmarried, those who have the higher rates? Protestantism, said Durkheim, encourages greater freedom of thought and action; males are more independent than females; and the unmarried lack the ties and responsibilities that come with marriage. In other words, members of these groups have fewer of the social bonds that keep people from committing suicide. In Durkheim's terms, they have less social integration.

Despite the many years that have passed since Durkheim did his research, the principle he uncovered still applies: People who are less socially integrated have higher rates of suicide. Even today, those same groups that Durkheim identified—Protestants, males, and the unmarried—are more likely to kill themselves.

Here is the principle that was central in Durkheim's research: *Human behavior cannot be understood only in terms of the individual; we must always examine the social forces that affect people's lives.* Suicide, for example, appears to be such an intensely individual act that psychologists should study it, not sociologists. As Durkheim stressed, however, if we look at human behavior only in reference to the individual, we miss its *social* basis. For another glimpse of what Durkheim meant, look at Figure 1.1, on the next page, which shows the methods by which African Americans and whites commit suicide. I'm sure you'll be struck by how similar those methods are. Since these patterns remain year after year, they indicate something that goes beyond individuals. They reflect conditions in society, such as the popularity and accessibility of guns.

**FIGURE 1.1**   How Americans Commit Suicide

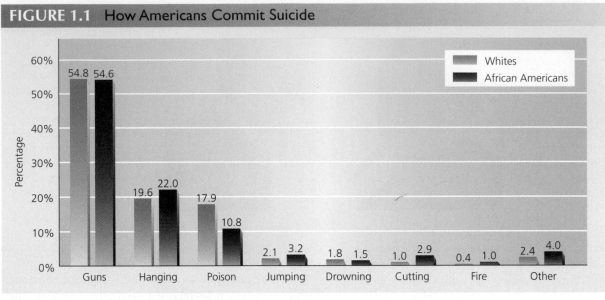

*Source:* By the author. Based on Centers for Disease Control 2006.

## Max Weber and the Protestant Ethic

Max Weber (Mahx VAY-ber) (1864–1920), a German sociologist and a contemporary of Durkheim's, also became a professor in the new academic discipline of sociology. Like Durkheim and Marx, Weber is one of the most influential of all sociologists, and you will come across his writings and theories in later chapters. Let's consider an issue Weber raised that remains controversial today.

**Religion and the Origin of Capitalism**   Weber disagreed with Marx's claim that economics is the central force in social change. That role, he said, belongs to religion. He came to this conclusion when he (1904/1958) contrasted the Roman Catholic and Protestant belief systems. Roman Catholics, he said, were taught that because they were members of the only true church, they were on the road to heaven. This made them comfortable with traditional ways of life. The Protestant belief system, in contrast, undermined the spiritual security of its followers, motivating them to embrace change. Protestants of the Calvinist tradition were told that they wouldn't know if they were saved until Judgment Day. Acutely uncomfortable with this uncertainty, they began to look for "signs" that they were in God's favor. Concluding that financial success was a divine blessing and that God did not want them to waste this blessing, they began to live frugal lives. Saving their money, they began to invest it to make even more. This fundamental change in the way money was viewed, said

Weber, produced the capital that brought about the birth of capitalism.

Weber called this self-denying approach to life the *Protestant ethic.* He termed the readiness to invest capital in order to make more money the *spirit of capitalism.* To test his theory, Weber compared the extent of capitalism in Roman Catholic and Protestant countries. In line with his theory, he found that capitalism was more likely to flourish in Protestant countries. Weber's conclusion that religion was the key factor in the rise of capitalism was controversial when he made it, and it continues to be debated today (Wade 2007). We'll explore these ideas in more detail in Chapter 13.

**Max Weber** (1864–1920) was another early sociologist who left a profound impression on sociology. He used cross-cultural and historical materials to trace the causes of social change and to determine how social groups affect people's orientations to life.

# Sexism in Early Sociology

## Attitudes of the Time

As you may have noticed, all the sociologists we have discussed are men. In the 1800s, sex roles were rigid, with women assigned the roles of wife and mother. In the classic German phrase, women were expected to devote themselves to the four K's: *Kirche, Küchen, Kinder, und Kleider* (church, cooking, children, and clothes). Trying to break out of this mold meant risking severe disapproval.

Few people, male or female, received any education beyond basic reading and writing and a little math. Higher education, for the rare few who received it, was reserved for men. A handful of women from wealthy families, however, did pursue higher education. A few even studied sociology, although the sexism so deeply entrenched in the universities stopped them from obtaining advanced degrees or becoming professors. In line with the times, the writings of women were almost entirely ignored. Jane Frohock, Lucretia Mott, and Elizabeth Cady Stanton, for example, were little known beyond a small circle. Frances Perkins, a sociologist and the first woman to hold a cabinet position (as Secretary of Labor under President Franklin Roosevelt), is no longer remembered.

## Harriet Martineau and Early Social Research

A classic example is Harriet Martineau (1802–1876), who was born into a wealthy family in England. When Martineau first began to analyze social life, she would hide her writing beneath her sewing when visitors arrived, for writing was "masculine" and sewing "feminine" (Gilman 1911:88). Martineau persisted in her interests, however, and eventually she studied social life in both Great Britain and the United States. In 1837, two or three decades before Durkheim and Weber were born, Martineau published *Society in America*. When I read this book, I was impressed with her analyses of this new nation's customs— family, race, gender, politics, and religion—an insightful examination of U.S. life that is still worth reading today. Martineau's research, however, met the same fate as the work of other early women sociologists and was ignored. Instead, she became known primarily for translating Comte's ideas into English.

Interested in social reform, **Harriet Martineau** (1802–1876) turned to sociology, where she discovered the writings of Comte. She became an advocate for the abolition of slavery, traveled widely, and wrote extensive analyses of social life.

# Sociology in North America

## Early History: The Tension Between Social Reform and Sociological Analysis

Transplanted to U.S. soil in the late nineteenth century, sociology first took root at the University of Kansas in 1890, at the University of Chicago in 1892, and at Atlanta University (then an all-black school) in 1897. From there, academic specialties in sociology spread throughout North America. The growth was gradual, however. It was not until 1922 that McGill University gave Canada its first department of sociology. Harvard University did not open its department of sociology until 1930, and the University of California at Berkeley did not follow until the 1950s.

Initially, the department at the University of Chicago, founded by Albion Small (1854–1926), dominated sociology. (Small also launched the *American Journal of Sociology*, serving as its editor from 1895 to 1925.) Members of this early sociology department whose ideas continue to influence today's sociologists include Robert E. Park (1864–1944), Ernest Burgess (1886–1966), and George Herbert Mead (1863–1931). Mead developed the symbolic interactionist perspective, which we will examine later.

The situation of women in North America was similar to that of European women, and their contributions to sociology met a similar fate. Among the early women sociologists were Jane Addams, Emily Greene Balch, Isabel

Eaton, Charlotte Perkins Gilman, Florence Kelley, Elsie Clews Parsons, and Alice Paul. Denied faculty appointments in sociology, many turned to social activism (Young 1995).

## Jane Addams and Social Reform

Although many North American sociologists combined the role of sociologist with that of social reformer, none was as successful as Jane Addams (1860–1935). Like Harriet Martineau, Addams came from a background of wealth and privilege. She attended the Women's Medical College of Philadelphia, but dropped out because of illness (Addams 1910/1981). On one of her trips to Europe, Addams was impressed with work being done to help London's poor. From then on, she worked tirelessly for social justice.

In 1889, Addams co-founded Hull-House, located in Chicago's notorious slums. Hull-House was open to people who needed refuge—to immigrants, the sick, the aged, the poor. Sociologists from the nearby University of Chicago were frequent visitors at Hull-House. With her piercing insights into the social classes, especially the ways in which workers were exploited and peasant immigrants adjust to city life, Addams strived to bridge the gap between the powerful and the powerless. She co-founded the American Civil Liberties Union and campaigned for the eight-hour work day and for laws against child labor. Her efforts at social reform were so outstanding that in 1931, she was a co-winner of the Nobel Prize for Peace, the first sociologist to win this coveted award.

## W. E. B. Du Bois and Race Relations

With the racism of this period, African American professionals also found life difficult. The most notable example is W. E. B. Du Bois (1868–1963), who, after earning a bachelor's degree from Fisk University, became the first African American to earn a doctorate at Harvard. After completing his education at the University of Berlin, where he attended lectures by Max Weber, Du Bois taught Greek and Latin at Wilberforce University. Hired by Atlanta University in 1897, he remained there for most of his career (Du Bois 1935/1992).

It is difficult to grasp how racist society was at this time. Du Bois once saw the fingers of a lynching victim displayed in a Georgia butcher shop (Aptheker 1990). Although Du Bois was invited to present a paper at the 1909 meetings of the American Sociological Society, he was too poor to attend, despite his education, faculty position, and accomplishments. When he could afford to attend meetings, discrimination was so prevalent that restaurants and hotels would not allow him to eat or room with the white sociologists. Later in life, when Du Bois had the money to travel, the U.S. State Department feared that he would criticize the United States and refused to issue him a passport (Du Bois 1968).

Each year between 1896 and 1914, Du Bois published a book on relations between African Americans and whites. Of his almost 2,000 writings, *The Philadelphia Negro* (1899/1967) stands out. In this analysis of how African Americans in Philadelphia coped with racism, Du Bois noted that some of the successful African Americans were breaking their ties with other African Americans in order to win acceptance by whites. This, he stressed, was weakening the African American community by depriving it of their influence. *The Souls of Black Folk* (1903), one of Du Bois' most elegantly written books, preserves a picture of race relations immediately after the Civil War. The Down-to-Earth Sociology box on the next page is taken from this book.

**Jane Addams** (1860–1935), a recipient of the Nobel Prize for Peace, worked on behalf of poor immigrants. With Ellen G. Starr, she founded Hull-House, a center to help immigrants in Chicago. She was also a leader in women's rights (women's suffrage), as well as the peace movement of World War I.

**W**(illiam) **E**(dward) **B**(urghardt) **Du Bois** (1868–1963) spent his lifetime studying relations between African Americans and whites. Like many early North American sociologists, Du Bois combined the role of academic sociologist with that of social reformer. He was also the editor of *Crisis*, an influential journal of the time.

# *Down-to-Earth Sociology*

## Early Sociology in North America: Du Bois and Race Relations

*In the 1800s, poverty was widespread in the United States. Most people were so poor that they expended their life energies on just getting enough food, fuel, and clothing to survive. Formal education beyond the first several grades was a luxury. This photo depicts the conditions of the people Du Bois worked with.*

W. E. B. Du Bois wrote more like an accomplished novelist than a sociologist. The following excerpts are from pages 66–68 of *The Souls of Black Folk* (1903). In this book, Du Bois analyzes changes that occurred in the social and economic conditions of African Americans during the thirty years following the Civil War.

For two summers, while he was a student at Fisk, Du Bois taught in a segregated school housed in a log hut "way back in the hills" of rural Tennessee. The following excerpts help us understand conditions at that time.

It was a hot morning late in July when the school opened. I trembled when I heard the patter of little feet down the dusty road, and saw the growing row of dark solemn faces and bright eager eyes facing me. . . . There they sat, nearly thirty of them, on the rough benches, their faces shading from a pale cream to deep brown, the little feet bare and swinging, the eyes full of expectation, with here and there a twinkle of mischief, and the hands grasping Webster's blue-black spelling-book. I loved my school, and the fine faith the children had in the wisdom of their teacher was truly marvelous. We read and spelled together, wrote a little, picked flowers, sang, and listened to stories of the world beyond the hill. . . .

On Friday nights I often went home with some of the children,—sometimes to Doc Burke's farm. He was a great, loud, thin Black, ever working, and trying to buy these seventy-five acres of hill and dale where he lived; but people said that he would surely fail and the "white folks would get it all." His wife was a magnificent Amazon, with saffron face and shiny hair, uncorseted and barefooted, and the children were strong and barefooted. They lived in a one-and-a-half-room cabin in the hollow of the farm near the spring. . . .

Often, to keep the peace, I must go where life was less lovely; for instance, 'Tildy's mother was incorrigibly dirty, Reuben's larder was limited seriously, and herds of untamed insects wandered over the Eddingses' beds. Best of all I loved to go to Josie's, and sit on the porch, eating peaches, while the mother bustled and talked: how Josie had bought the sewing-machine; how Josie worked at service in winter, but that four dollars a month was

"mighty little" wages; how Josie longed to go away to school, but that it "looked liked" they never could get far enough ahead to let her; how the crops failed and the well was yet unfinished; and, finally, how mean some of the white folks were.

For two summers I lived in this little world. . . . I have called my tiny community a world, and so its isolation made it; and yet there was among us but a half-awakened common consciousness, sprung from common joy and grief, at burial, birth, or wedding; from common hardship in poverty, poor land, and low wages, and, above all, from the sight of the Veil* that hung between us and Opportunity. All this caused us to think some thoughts together; but these, when ripe for speech, were spoken in various languages. Those whose eyes twenty-five and more years had seen "the glory of the coming of the Lord," saw in every present hindrance or help a dark fatalism bound to bring all things right in His own good time. The mass of those to whom slavery was a dim recollection of childhood found the world a puzzling thing: it asked little of them, and they answered with little, and yet it ridiculed their offering. Such a paradox they could not understand, and therefore sank into listless indifference, or shiftlessness, or reckless bravado.

*"The Veil" is shorthand for the Veil of Race, referring to how race colors all human relations. Du Bois' hope, as he put it, was that "sometime, somewhere, men will judge men by their souls and not by their skins" (p. 261).

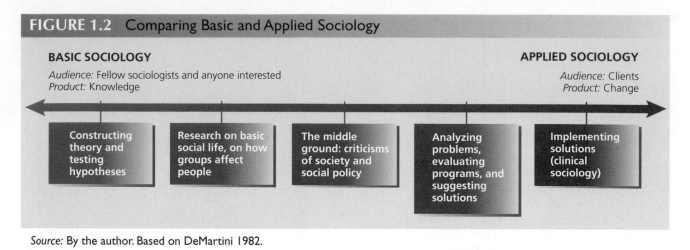

**FIGURE 1.2**   Comparing Basic and Applied Sociology

**BASIC SOCIOLOGY**
*Audience:* Fellow sociologists and anyone interested
*Product:* Knowledge

**APPLIED SOCIOLOGY**
*Audience:* Clients
*Product:* Change

- Constructing theory and testing hypotheses
- Research on basic social life, on how groups affect people
- The middle ground: criticisms of society and social policy
- Analyzing problems, evaluating programs, and suggesting solutions
- Implementing solutions (clinical sociology)

*Source:* By the author. Based on DeMartini 1982.

At first, Du Bois was content to collect and interpret objective data. Later, frustrated that racism continued, he turned to social action. Along with Jane Addams and others from Hull-House, Du Bois founded the National Association for the Advancement of Colored People (NAACP) (Deegan 1988). Continuing to battle racism both as a sociologist and as a journalist, Du Bois eventually embraced revolutionary Marxism. At age 93, dismayed that so little improvement had been made in race relations, he moved to Ghana, where he is buried (Stark 1989).

## Talcott Parsons and C. Wright Mills: Theory Versus Reform

During the 1940s, the emphasis shifted from social reform to social theory. Talcott Parsons (1902–1979), an influential sociologist of this period, developed abstract models of society that influenced a generation of sociologists. Parsons' models of how the parts of society work together harmoniously did nothing to stimulate social activism.

Deploring the theoretical abstractions of this period, C. Wright Mills (1916–1962) urged sociologists to get back to social reform. He warned that the nation faced an imminent threat to freedom—the coalescing of interests of a group he called the *power elite,* the top leaders of business, politics, and the military. Shortly after Mills' death came the turbulent 1960s and 1970s. This precedent-shaking era sparked interest in social activism, making Mills' ideas popular among a new generation of sociologists.

## The Continuing Tension and the Rise of Applied Sociology

The apparent contradiction of these two aims—analyzing society versus working toward its reform—created a tension in sociology that is still with us today. Some sociologists consider that their proper role is to analyze some aspect of society and to publish their findings in sociology journals. This is called *basic* (or *pure*) *sociology.* Others say that basic sociology is not enough, that sociologists have an obligation to help bring justice to the poor and to try to make society a better place in which to live.

Somewhere between these extremes lies **applied sociology,** using sociology to solve problems. (See Figure 1.2, which contrasts basic and applied sociology.) The founding of the National Association for the Advancement of Colored People by W. E. B. Du Bois, Jane Addams, and others was one of the first attempts at applied sociology—and one of the most successful. As illustrated in the Down-to-Earth Sociology box on the next page, applied sociologists work in a variety of settings. Some work for business firms to solve problems in the workplace. Others investigate social problems such as pornography, rape, environmental pollution, or the spread of AIDS. A new application of sociology is determining ways to disrupt

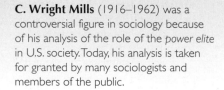

**C. Wright Mills** (1916–1962) was a controversial figure in sociology because of his analysis of the role of the *power elite* in U.S. society. Today, his analysis is taken for granted by many sociologists and members of the public.

terrorist groups (Ebner 2005). As illustrated by the Cultural Diversity box on the next page, studying job discrimination is also part of applied sociology.

Today's applied sociology has created a new tension, with criticism coming from two directions. The first is from those who want sociologists to focus on social reform. They say that although sociology is applied in some specific setting, there is no goal of rebuilding society, as early sociologists envisioned. The second criticism comes from sociologists who want the emphasis to remain on discovering knowledge. Their position is that when sociology is applied, it is no longer sociology. For example, if sociologists use sociological principles to help teenagers escape from pimps, what makes it sociology and not social work?

At this point, let's consider how theory fits into sociology.

## Down-to-Earth Sociology
### Careers in Sociology: What Applied Sociologists Do

Most sociologists teach in colleges and universities, sharing sociological knowledge with college students, as your instructor is doing with you in this course. Applied sociologists, in contrast, work in a wide variety of areas—from counseling children to studying how diseases are transmitted. Some even make software more "user-friendly." (They study how people use software and give feedback to the programmers who design those products [Guice 1999].) To give you an idea of this variety, let's look over the shoulders of four applied sociologists.

Leslie Green, who does marketing research at Vanderveer Group in Philadelphia, Pennsylvania, earned her bachelor's degree in sociology at Shippensburg University. She helps to develop strategies to get doctors to prescribe particular drugs. She sets up the meetings, locates moderators for the discussion groups, and arranges payments to the physicians who participate in the research. "My training in sociology," she says, "helps me in 'people skills.' It helps me to understand the needs of different groups, and to interact with them."

Stanley Capela, whose master's degree is from Fordham University, works as an applied sociologist at HeartShare Human Services in New York City. He evaluates how children's programs—such as ones that focus on housing, AIDS, group homes, and preschool education—actually work, compared with how they are supposed to work. He spots problems and suggests solutions. One of his assignments was to find out why it was taking so long to get children adopted, even though there was a long list of eager adoptive parents. Capela pinpointed how the paperwork got bogged down as it was routed through the system and suggested ways to improve the flow of paperwork.

Laurie Banks, who received her master's degree in sociology from Fordham University, analyzes statistics for the New York City Health Department. As she examined death certificates, she noticed that a Polish neighborhood had a high rate of stomach cancer. She alerted the Centers for Disease Control, which conducted interviews in the neighborhood. They traced the cause to eating large amounts of sausage. In another case, Banks compared birth records with school records. She found that problems at birth—low birth weight, lack of prenatal care, and birth complications—were linked to low reading skills and behavior problems in school.

Daniel Knapp, who earned a doctorate from the University of Oregon, decided to apply sociology by going to the city dump. Moved by the idea that urban wastes could be recycled and reused, he first tested this idea in a small way—by scavenging at the city dump at Berkeley, California. After starting a company called Urban Ore, Knapp (2005) did studies on how to recycle urban wastes and worked to change waste disposal laws. As a founder of the recycling movement in the United States, Knapp's application of sociology continues to influence us all.

From just these few examples, you can catch a glimpse of the variety of work that applied sociologists do. Some work for corporations, some are employed by government and private agencies, and others run their own businesses. You can also see that you don't need a doctorate in order to work as an applied sociologist.

## Cultural Diversity in the United States

### Studying Job Discrimination: A Surprising Example of Applied Sociology

Sometimes sociologists do basic sociology—research aimed at learning more about some behavior—and then someone else applies it.

Devah Pager was a graduate student at the University of Wisconsin in Madison. When she was doing volunteer work, homeless men told her how hard it was to find work if they had been in prison.

Pager decided to find out just what difference a prison record made in getting a job. She sent pairs of college men to apply for 350 entry-level jobs in Milwaukee. One team was African American, and one was white. Pager prepared identical résumés for the teams, but with one difference: On each team, one of the men said he had served 18 months in prison for possession of cocaine.

Figure 1.3 shows the difference that the prison record made. Men without a prison record were two or three times as likely to be called back.

But Pager came up with another significant finding. Look at the difference that race–ethnicity made. White men with a prison record were more likely to be offered a job than African American men who had a clean record!

The application of this research? Pager didn't apply anything, but others did. After President Bush was told of these results, he announced in his State of the Union

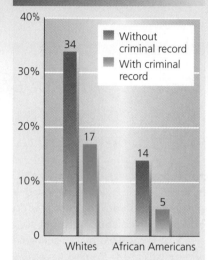

**FIGURE 1.3   Call-Back Rates by Race–Ethnicity and Criminal Record**

*Source:* Courtesy of Devah Pager.

speech that he wanted Congress to fund a $300 million program to provide mentoring and other support to help former prisoners get jobs (Kroeger 2004).

As you can see, sometimes only a thin line separates basic and applied sociology.

### For Your Consideration

What findings would you expect if women had been included in this study?

## Theoretical Perspectives in Sociology

Facts never interpret themselves. To make sense out of life, we use our common sense. That is, to understand our experiences (our "facts"), we place them into a framework of more-or-less related ideas. Sociologists do this, too, but

they place their observations into a conceptual framework called a theory. A **theory** is a general statement about how some parts of the world fit together and how they work. It is an explanation of how two or more "facts" are related to one another.

Sociologists use three major theories: symbolic interactionism, functional analysis, and conflict theory. Let's first examine the main elements of these theories. Then let's apply each theory to the U.S. divorce rate, to see why it is so high. As we do this, you will see how each theory, or perspective, provides a distinct interpretation of social life.

## Symbolic Interactionism

We can trace the origins of **symbolic interactionism** to the Scottish moral philosophers of the eighteenth century, who noted that individuals evaluate their own conduct by comparing themselves with others (Stryker 1990). This perspective was brought to sociology by Charles Horton Cooley (1864–1929), William I. Thomas (1863–1947), and George Herbert Mead (1863–1931). Let's look at the main elements of this theory.

**Symbols in Everyday Life**    Symbolic interactionists study how people use *symbols*—the things to which we attach meaning—to develop their views of the world and to communicate with one another. Without symbols, our social life would be no more sophisticated than that of animals. For example, without symbols we would have no aunts or uncles, employers or teachers—or even brothers and sisters. I know that this sounds strange, but it is symbols that define our relationships. There would still be reproduction, of course, but no symbols to tell us how we are related to whom. We would not know to whom we owe respect and obligations, or from whom we can expect privileges—the essence of human relationships.

Look at it like this: If you think of someone as your aunt or uncle, you behave in certain ways, but if you think of that person as a boyfriend or girlfriend, you behave quite differently. It is the symbol that tells you how you are related to others—and how you should act toward them.

To make this clearer:

Suppose that you have fallen head-over-heels in love and are going to marry. The night before your wedding, your mother confides that she had a child before she married your father, a child that she gave up for adoption. She then adds that she has just discovered that the person you are going to marry is this child.

You can see how the symbol will change overnight!— and your behavior, too!

Symbols allow not only relationships to exist, but also society. Without symbols, we could not coordinate our actions with those of others. We could not make plans for a future day, time, and place. Unable to specify times, materials, sizes, or goals, we could not build bridges and highways. Without symbols, there would be no movies or

musical instruments. We would have no hospitals, no government, no religion. The class you are taking could not exist—nor could this book. On the positive side, there would be no war.

In short, symbolic interactionists analyze how our behaviors depend on the ways we define ourselves and others. They study face-to-face interaction, examining how people make sense out of life and their place in it. Symbolic interactionists point out that even the *self* is a symbol, for it consists of the ideas we have about who we are. And the self is a changing symbol: As we interact with others, we adjust our views of who we are based on how we interpret the reactions of others to us. We'll get more into this later.

**Applying Symbolic Interactionism**    To better understand symbolic interactionism, let's see how changes in symbols (meanings) help to explain the high U.S. divorce rate shown in Figure 1.4 on the next page. For background, you should understand that marriage used to be a lifelong commitment. Getting divorced was viewed as an immoral act, a flagrant disregard for public opinion, and the abandonment of adult responsibilities.

Slowly, the meaning of marriage began to change. In 1933, sociologist William Ogburn observed that personality was becoming more important in mate selection. In 1945, sociologists Ernest Burgess and Harvey Locke noted the growing importance of mutual affection, understanding, and compatibility in marriage. Gradually, people's views changed. No longer did they see marriage as a lifelong commitment based on duty and obligation. Instead, they began to view marriage as an arrangement, often temporary, that was based on feelings of intimacy. The meaning of divorce also changed. Formerly a symbol of failure, it became an indicator of freedom and new beginnings. Removing the stigma from divorce shattered a strong barrier that had prevented husbands and wives from breaking up.

Symbolic interactionists note that related symbols also changed—and that none of these changes strengthen marriage. For example, tradition's guidelines were firm, letting newlyweds know what to expect from each other. In contrast, today's guidelines are vague, and couples must figure out how to divide up responsibilities for work, home, and children. As they struggle to do so, many flounder. Although couples find it a relief not to have to conform to what they consider to be burdensome notions, those traditional expectations (or symbols) did provide a structure that made marriages last. When these symbols changed, the structure they had created was

**FIGURE 1.4**    U.S. Marriage, U.S. Divorce

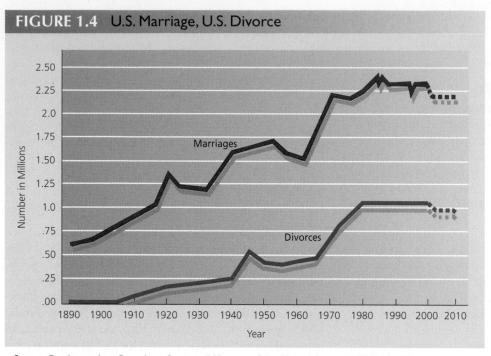

*Source:* By the author. Based on *Statistical Abstract of the United States* 1998:Table 92 and 2007:Table 119; earlier editions for earlier years. The broken lines indicate the author's estimates.

weakened, making marriage more fragile and divorce more common.

Similarly, ideas of parenthood and childhood used to be quite different. Parents had little responsibility for their children beyond providing food, clothing, shelter, and moral guidance. And this was for only a short time, because children began to contribute to the support of the family early in life. Among many people, parenthood is still like this. In Colombia, for example, children of the poor often are expected to support themselves by the age of 8 or 10. In advanced industrial societies, however, we assume that children are vulnerable beings who must depend on their parents for financial and emotional support for many years—often until they are well into their 20s. That this is not the case in many cultures often comes as a surprise to Americans, who assume that their own situation is some sort of worldwide, natural arrangement. The greater responsibilities that we assign to parenthood place heavy burdens on today's couples and, with them, more strain on marriage.

**In Sum:** Symbolic interactionists look at how changing ideas (or symbols) put pressure on married couples. No single change is *the* cause of our divorce rate, but, taken together, these changes provide a strong push toward divorce.

## Functional Analysis

The central idea of **functional analysis** is that society is a whole unit, made up of interrelated parts that work together. Functional analysis, also known as *functionalism* and *structural functionalism,* is rooted in the origins of sociology. Auguste Comte and Herbert Spencer viewed society as a kind of living organism. Just as a person or animal has organs that function together, they wrote, so does society. And like an organism, if society is to function smoothly, its parts must work together in harmony.

Emile Durkheim also viewed society as being composed of many parts, each with its own function. When all the parts of society fulfill their functions, society is in a "normal" state. If they do not fulfill their functions, society is in an "abnormal" or "pathological" state. To understand society, then, functionalists say that we need to look at both *structure* (how the parts of a society fit together to make the whole) and *function* (what each part does, how it contributes to society).

**Robert Merton and Functionalism**    Robert Merton (1910–2003) dismissed the organic analogy, but he did maintain the essence of functionalism—the image of society as a whole composed of parts that work together.

Merton used the term *functions* to refer to the beneficial consequences of people's actions: Functions help keep a group (society, social system) in balance. In contrast, *dysfunctions* are consequences that harm a society: They undermine a system's equilibrium.

Functions can be either manifest or latent. If an action is *intended* to help some part of a system, it is a *manifest function*. For example, suppose that government officials become concerned about our low rate of childbirth. Congress offers a $10,000 bonus for every child born to a married couple. The intention, or manifest function, of the bonus is to increase childbearing within the family unit. Merton pointed out that people's actions can also have *latent functions;* that is, they can have *unintended* consequences that help a system adjust. Let's suppose that the bonus works. As the birth rate jumps, so does the sale of diapers and baby furniture. Because the benefits to these businesses were not the intended consequences, they are latent functions of the bonus.

Of course, human actions can also hurt a system. Because such consequences usually are unintended, Merton called them *latent dysfunctions.* Let's assume that the government has failed to specify a "stopping point" with regard to its bonus system. To collect more bonuses, some people keep on having children. The more children they have, however, the more they need the next bonus to survive. Large families become common, and

poverty increases. Welfare is reinstated, taxes jump, and the nation erupts in protest. Because these results were not intended and because they harmed the social system, they would represent latent dysfunctions of the bonus program.

**Applying Functional Analysis** Now let's apply functional analysis to the U.S. divorce rate. Functionalists stress that industrialization and urbanization undermined the traditional functions of the family. For example, before industrialization, the family formed an economic team. On the farm, where most people lived, each family member had jobs or "chores" to do. The wife was in charge not only of household tasks but also of raising small animals, such as chickens. Milking cows, collecting eggs, and churning butter were also her responsibility—as were cooking, baking, canning, sewing, darning, washing, and cleaning. The daughters helped her. The husband was responsible for caring for large animals, such as horses and cattle, for planting and harvesting, and for maintaining buildings and tools. The sons helped him. Together, they formed an economic unit in which each depended on the others for survival.

Other functions also bound family members to one another: educating the children, teaching them religion, providing home-based recreation, and caring for the sick and elderly. To see how sharply family functions have changed, look at this example from the 1800s:

When Phil became sick, he was nursed by Ann, his wife. She cooked for him, fed him, changed the bed linens, bathed him, read to him from the Bible, and gave him his medicine. (She did this in addition to doing the housework and taking care of their six children.) Phil was also surrounded by the children, who shouldered some of his chores while he was sick.

When Phil died, the male neighbors and relatives made the casket while Ann, her mother, and female friends washed and dressed the body. Phil was then "laid out" in the front parlor (the formal living room), where friends,

Sociologists who use the *functionalist perspective* stress how industrialization and urbanization undermined the traditional *functions* of the family. Before industrialization, members of the family worked together as an economic unit, as in this 1860 photo of a farm family in France. Note that everyone has a job to do. As production moved away from the home, it took with it first the father and, more recently, the mother. One consequence of industrialization, then, is the weakening of family ties.

neighbors, and relatives paid their last respects. From there, friends moved his body to the church for the final message and then to the grave they themselves had dug.

**In Sum:** The family has lost many of its traditional functions, and others are presently under assault. Especially significant are changes in economic production. No longer is this a cooperative, home-based effort, with husbands and wives depending on one another for their interlocking contributions to a mutual endeavor. Husbands and wives today earn individual paychecks and increasingly function as separate components in an impersonal, multinational, and even global system. When outside agencies take over family functions, the family becomes more fragile and an increase in divorce is inevitable. The fewer functions that family members share, the fewer are their "ties that bind"—and these ties are what help husbands and wives get through the problems they inevitably experience.

## Conflict Theory

Conflict theory provides a third perspective on social life. Unlike the functionalists, who view society as a harmonious whole, with its parts working together, conflict theorists stress that society is composed of groups that are competing with one another for scarce resources. Although the surface may show alliances or cooperation, scratch that surface and you will find a struggle for power.

**Karl Marx and Conflict Theory**   Karl Marx, the founder of conflict theory, witnessed the Industrial Revolution that transformed Europe. He saw that peasants who had left the land to seek work in cities had to work for wages that barely provided enough to eat. Things were so bad that the average worker died at age 30, the average wealthy person at age 50 (Edgerton 1992:87). Shocked by this suffering and exploitation, Marx began to analyze society and history. As he did so, he developed **conflict theory.** He concluded that the key to human history is *class conflict.* In each society, some small group controls the means of production and exploits those who are not in control. In industrialized societies, the struggle is between the *bourgeoisie,* the small group of capitalists who own the means to produce wealth, and the *proletariat,* the mass of workers who are exploited by the bourgeoisie. The capitalists also control the legal and political system: If the workers rebel, the capitalists call on the power of the state to subdue them.

When Marx made his observations, capitalism was in its infancy, and workers were at the mercy of their employers. Workers had none of what we take for granted

today—minimum wages, eight-hour days, coffee breaks, five-day workweeks, paid vacations and holidays, medical benefits, sick leave, unemployment compensation, Social Security, and, for union workers, the right to strike. Marx's analysis reminds us that these benefits came not from generous hearts, but by workers forcing concessions from their employers.

**Conflict Theory Today**   Many sociologists extend conflict theory beyond the relationship of capitalists and workers. They examine how opposing interests permeate every layer of society—whether that be a small group, an organization, a community, or the entire society. For example, when police, teachers, and parents try to enforce conformity, which they must do, this creates resentment and resistance. It is the same when a teenager tries to "change the rules" to gain more independence. There is, then, a constant struggle throughout society to determine who has authority or influence and how far that dominance goes (Turner 1978; Bartos and Wehr 2002).

Sociologist Lewis Coser (1913–2003) pointed out that conflict is most likely to develop among people who are in close relationships. These people have worked out ways to distribute power and privilege, responsibilities and rewards. Any change in this arrangement can lead to hurt feelings, resentment, and conflict. Even in intimate relationships, then, people are in a constant balancing act, with conflict lying uneasily just beneath the surface.

**Feminists and Conflict Theory**   Just as Marx examined conflict between capitalists and workers, many feminists analyze conflict between men and women. A primary focus is the historical, contemporary, and global inequalities of men and women—and how the traditional dominance by men can be overcome to bring about equality of the sexes. Feminists are not united by the conflict perspective, however. They tackle a variety of topics and use whatever theory applies. (Feminism is discussed in Chapter 10.)

**Applying Conflict Theory**   To explain why the U.S. divorce rate is high, conflict theorists focus on how men's and women's relationships have changed. For millennia, men dominated women. Women had few alternatives other than to accept their exploitation. Then industrialization ushered in a new world, one in which women can meet their basic survival needs outside of marriage. Industrialization also fostered a culture in which females participate in social worlds beyond the home. With this new ability to refuse to bear burdens that earlier generations accepted as inevitable, today's women are likely to dissolve a marriage that becomes intolerable—or even unsatisfactory.

**In Sum:** The dominance of men over women was once considered natural and right. As women gained education and earnings, however, they first questioned and then rejected this assumption. As wives strove for more power and grew less inclined to put up with relationships that they defined as unfair, the divorce rate increased. From the conflict perspective, then, the significance of our high divorce rate is not that marriage has weakened, but, rather, that women are making headway in their historical struggle with men.

## Levels of Analysis: Macro and Micro

A major difference between these three theoretical perspectives is their level of analysis. Functionalists and conflict theorists focus on the **macro level;** that is, they examine large-scale patterns of society. In contrast, symbolic interactionists usually focus on the **micro level,** on **social interaction**—what people do when they are in one another's presence. These levels are summarized in Table 1.1 below.

To make this distinction between micro and macro levels clearer, let's return to the example of the homeless, with which we opened this chapter. To study homeless people, symbolic interactionists would focus on the micro level. They would analyze what homeless people do when they are in shelters and on the streets. They would also

analyze their communications, both their talk and their **nonverbal interaction** (gestures, silence, use of space, and so on). The observations I made at the beginning of this chapter about the silence in the homeless shelter, for example, would be of interest to symbolic interactionists.

This micro level, however, would not interest functionalists and conflict theorists. They would focus instead on the macro level. Functionalists would examine how changes in the parts of society have increased homelessness. They might look at how changes in the family (fewer children, more divorce) and economic conditions (inflation, fewer unskilled jobs, loss of jobs to workers overseas) cause homelessness among people who are unable to find jobs and who have no family to fall back on. For their part, conflict theorists would stress the struggle between social classes. They would be especially interested in how decisions by international elites on global production and trade affect the local job market and, along with it, unemployment and homelessness.

**Putting the Theoretical Perspectives Together** Which theoretical perspective should we use to study human behavior? Which level of analysis is the correct one? As you have seen, these three perspectives produce contrasting pictures of social life. In the case of divorce, these interpretations are quite different from the commonsense understanding that

**TABLE 1.1  Major Theoretical Perspectives in Sociology**

| Perspective | Usual Level of Analysis | Focus of Analysis | Key Terms | Applying the Perspective to the U.S. Divorce Rate |
|---|---|---|---|---|
| **Symbolic Interactionism** | Microsociological: examines small-scale patterns of social interaction | Face-to-face interaction, how people use symbols to create social life | Symbols Interaction Meanings Definitions | Industrialization and urbanization changed marital roles and led to a redefinition of love, marriage, children, and divorce. |
| **Functional Analysis (also called functionalism and structural functionalism)** | Macrosociological: examines large-scale patterns of society | Relationships among the parts of society; how these parts are functional (have beneficial consequences) or dysfunctional (have negative consequences) | Structure Functions (manifest and latent) Dysfunctions Equilibrium | As social change erodes the traditional functions of the family, family ties weaken, and the divorce rate increases. |
| **Conflict Theory** | Macrosociological: examines large-scale patterns of society | The struggle for scarce resources by groups in a society; how the elites use their power to control the weaker groups | Inequality Power Conflict Competition Exploitation | When men control economic life, the divorce rate is low because women find few alternatives to a bad marriage. The high divorce rate reflects a shift in the balance of power between men and women. |

two people are simply "incompatible." *Because each theory focuses on different features of social life, each provides a distinct interpretation. Consequently, we need to use all three theoretical lenses to analyze human behavior. By combining the contributions of each, we gain a more comprehensive picture of social life.*

## How Theory and Research Work Together

Theory cannot stand alone. As sociologist C. Wright Mills (1959) argued so forcefully, if theory isn't connected to research, it will be abstract and empty. It won't represent the way life really is. It is the same for research. Without theory, Mills said, research is also of little value; it is simply a collection of meaningless "facts."

Theory and research, then, go together like a hand and glove. Every theory must be tested, which requires research. And as sociologists do research, they often come up with surprising findings. Those findings must be explained, and for that, we need theory. As sociologists study social life, then, they combine research and theory.

# Doing Sociological Research

Around the globe, people make assumptions about the way the world "is." Common sense, the things that "everyone knows are true," may or may not be true, however. It takes research to find out. To move beyond guesswork and common sense, sociologists do research on just about every aspect of social life. Before we look at how they do their research, you can test your own "common sense" by taking the "fun quiz" on the next page.

## A Research Model

As shown in Figure 1.5, scientific research follows eight basic steps. This is an ideal model, however, and in the real world of research, some of these steps may run together. Some may even be omitted.

1. *Selecting a Topic.* What do you want to know more about? Let's use spouse abuse as our example.
2. *Defining the Problem.* The next step is to narrow the topic. Spouse abuse is too broad; you need to focus on a specific area. For example, you may want to know why men are more likely than women to be the abusers. Or perhaps you want to know what can be done to reduce spouse abuse.

3. *Reviewing the Literature.* You must read what has been published on your topic. You don't want to waste your time rediscovering what is already known.
4. *Formulating a Hypothesis.* The fourth step is to formulate a **hypothesis,** a statement of what you expect to find according to predictions from a theory. A hypothesis predicts a relationship between or among **variables,** factors that change, or vary, from one person or situation to another. For example, the statement "Men who are more socially isolated are more likely to abuse their wives than are men who are more socially integrated" is a hypothesis.

    Your hypothesis will need **operational definitions**—that is, precise ways to measure the variables. In this example, you would need operational definitions for three variables: social isolation, social integration, and spouse abuse.
5. *Choosing a Research Method.* The means by which you collect your data is called a **research method** (or *research design*). Sociologists use six basic research methods, which are outlined in the next section. You will want to choose the method that will best answer your particular questions.

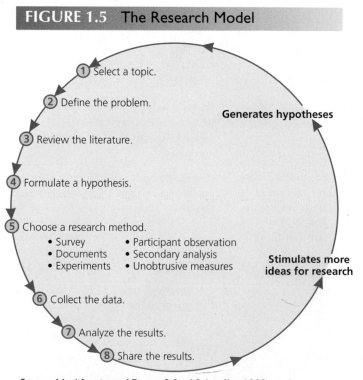

**FIGURE 1.5   The Research Model**

① Select a topic.
② Define the problem.
③ Review the literature.
④ Formulate a hypothesis.
⑤ Choose a research method.
- Survey
- Documents
- Experiments
- Participant observation
- Secondary analysis
- Unobtrusive measures
⑥ Collect the data.
⑦ Analyze the results.
⑧ Share the results.

**Generates hypotheses**

**Stimulates more ideas for research**

*Source:* Modification of Figure 2.2 of Schaeffer 1989.

## *Down-to-Earth Sociology*
## Enjoying a Sociology Quiz—Sociological Findings Versus Common Sense

Some findings of sociology support commonsense understandings of social life, but others contradict them. Can you tell the difference? To enjoy this quiz, complete *all* the questions before turning the page to check your answers.

1. **True/False**   More U.S. students are killed in school shootings now than ten or fifteen years ago.
2. **True/False**   The earnings of U.S. women have just about caught up with those of U.S. men.
3. **True/False**   It is more dangerous to walk near topless bars than fast-food restaurants.
4. **True/False**   Most rapists are mentally ill.
5. **True/False**   Most people on welfare are lazy and looking for a handout. They could work if they wanted to.
6. **True/False**   Compared with women, men make more eye contact in face-to-face conversations.
7. **True/False**   Couples who live together before marriage are usually more satisfied with their marriages than couples who do not live together before marriage.
8. **True/False**   Most husbands of employed wives who themselves get laid off from work take up the slack and increase the amount of housework they do.
9. **True/False**   Because bicyclists are more likely to wear helmets now than just a few years ago, their rate of head injuries has dropped.
10. **True/False**   Students in Japan are under such intense pressure to do well in school that their suicide rate is about double that of U.S. students.

---

6. *Collecting the Data.* When you gather your data, you have to take care to assure their **validity;** that is, your operational definitions must measure what they are intended to measure. In this case, you must be certain that you really are measuring social isolation, social integration, and spouse abuse—and not something else. Spouse abuse, for example, seems to be obvious. Yet what some people consider to be abuse is not regarded as abuse by others. Which will you choose? In other words, you must define your operational definitions so precisely that no one has any question about what you are measuring.

You must also be sure that your data are reliable. **Reliability** means that if other researchers use your operational definitions, their findings will be consistent with yours. If your operational definitions are sloppy, husbands who have committed the same act of violence might be included in some research but excluded from other studies. You would end up with erratic results. If you show a 10 percent rate

Because sociologists find all human behavior to be valid research topics, their research runs from the unusual to the routines of everyday life. Their studies range from broad scale social change, such as the globalization of capitalism, to smaller scale social interaction, such as people having fun.

## Down-to-Earth Sociology
### Sociological Findings Versus Common Sense—Answers to the Sociology Quiz

1. **False.** More students were shot to death at U.S. schools in the early 1990s than now (National School Safety Center 2007).
2. **False.** Over the years, the wage gap has narrowed, but only slightly. On average, full-time working women earn less than 70 percent of what full-time working men earn. This low figure is actually an improvement over earlier years. See Figures 10.5 and 10.6 on pages 277–278.
3. **False.** The crime rate outside fast-food restaurants is considerably higher. The likely reason for this is that topless bars hire private security and parking lot attendants (Linz et al. 2004).
4. **False.** Sociologists compared the psychological profiles of prisoners convicted of rape and prisoners convicted of other crimes. Their profiles were similar. Like robbery, rape is a learned behavior (Scully and Marolla 1984/2007).
5. **False.** Most people on welfare are children, the old, the sick, the mentally and physically handicapped, or young mothers with few skills. Less than 2 percent fit the stereotype of an able-bodied man. See page 216.
6. **False.** Women make considerably more eye contact (Henley et al. 1985).
7. **False.** The opposite is true. The likely reason is that many couples who cohabit before marriage are less committed to marriage in the first place—and a key to marital success is a strong commitment to one another (Larson 1988; Dush et al. 2003).
8. **False.** Most husbands who have employed wives and who themselves get laid off from work *reduce* the amount of housework they do (Hochschild 1989; Brines 1994).
9. **False.** Bicyclists today are more likely to wear helmets, but their rate of head injuries is higher. Apparently, they take more risks because the helmets make them feel safer (Barnes 2001).
10. **False.** The suicide rate of U.S. students is about double that of Japanese students (Lester 2003).

of spouse abuse, for example, but another researcher determines it to be 30 percent, the research is unreliable.

7. *Analyzing the Results.* You can choose from a variety of techniques to analyze the data you gather. If a hypothesis has been part of your research, it is during this step that you will test it. (Some research, especially that done by participant observation, has no hypothesis. You may know so little about the setting you are going to research that you cannot even specify the variables in advance.)

With today's software, in just seconds you can run tests on your data that used to take days or even weeks to perform. Two basic programs that sociologists and many undergraduates use are Microcase and the Statistical Package for the Social Sciences (SPSS). Some software, such as the Methodologist's Toolchest, provides advice about collecting data and even about ethical issues.

8. *Sharing the Results.* To wrap up your research, you will write a report to share your findings with the scientific community. You will review how you did your research, including your operational definitions. You will also show how your findings fit in with what has already been published on the topic and how they support or disagree with the theories that apply to your topic. As Table 1.2 illustrates, sociologists often summarize their findings in tables.

Let's look in greater detail at the fifth step to see what research methods sociologists use.

## TABLE 1.2 How to Read a Table

Tables summarize information. Because sociological findings are often presented in tables, it is important to understand how to read them. Tables contain six elements: title, headnote, headings, columns, rows, and source. When you understand how these elements fit together, you know how to read a table.

1. The **title** states the topic. It is located at the top of the table. What is the title of this table? Please determine your answer before looking at the correct answer at the bottom of the page.

2. The **headnote** is not always included in a table. When it is, it is located just below the title. Its purpose is to give more detailed information about how the data were collected or how data are presented in the table. What are the first eight words of the headnote of this table?

3. The **headings** tell what kind of information is contained in the table. There are three headings in this table. What are they? In the second heading, what does *n* = 25 mean?

4. The **columns** present information arranged vertically. What is the fourth number in the second column and the second number in the third column?

5. The **rows** present information arranged horizontally. In the fourth row, which husbands are more likely to have less education than their wives?

6. The **source** of a table, usually listed at the bottom, provides information on where the data in the table originated. Often, as in this instance, the information is specific enough for you to consult the original source. What is the source for this table?

### Comparing Violent and Nonviolent Husbands

*Based on interviews with 150 husbands and wives in a Midwestern city who were getting a divorce.*

| Husband's Achievement and Job Satisfaction | Violent Husbands *n* = 25 | Nonviolent Husbands *n* = 125 |
|---|---|---|
| He started but failed to complete high school or college. | 44% | 27% |
| He is very dissatisfied with his job. | 44% | 18% |
| His income is a source of constant conflict. | 84% | 24% |
| He has less education than his wife. | 56% | 14% |
| His job has less prestige than his father-in-law's. | 37% | 20% |

*Source: Modification of Table 1 in O'Brien 1975.*

Some tables are much more complicated than this one, but all follow the same basic pattern. To apply these concepts to a table with more information, see page 247.

ANSWERS

1. Comparing Violent and Nonviolent Husbands
2. Based on interviews with 150 husbands and wives
3. Husband's Achievement and Job Satisfaction, Violent Husbands, Nonviolent Husbands. The *n* is an abbreviation for number, and *n* = 25 means that 25 violent husbands were in the sample.
4. 56%, 18%
5. Violent Husbands
6. A 1975 article by O'Brien (listed in the References section of this text).

ods

methods (or *research designs*)
will continue our example of
see, the method you choose will
s you want to answer. So that you
ca........... for comparison, you will want to
know wh............. is in your study. Table 1.3 below discusses ways to ..... ure average.

## Surveys

Let's suppose that you want to know how many wives are
abused each year. Some husbands also are abused, of

course, but let's assume that you are going to focus on
wives. An appropriate method for this purpose would be
the **survey,** in which you would ask individuals a series of
questions. Before you begin your research, however, you
must deal with practical matters that face all researchers.
Let's look at these issues.

**Selecting a Sample**   Ideally, you might want to learn
about all wives in the world. Obviously, your resources
will not permit such research, and you will have to narrow
your **population,** the target group that you are going to
study.

Let's assume that your resources (money, assistants,
time) allow you to investigate spouse abuse only on your
campus. Let's also assume that your college enrollment is

---

| TABLE 1.3 | Three Ways to Measure "Average" | |
|---|---|---|
| **The Mean** | **The Median** | **The Mode** |
| The term *average* seems clear enough. As you learned in grade school, to find the average you add a group of numbers and then divide the total by the number of cases that you added. Assume that the following numbers represent men convicted of battering their wives: | To compute the second average, the *median*, first arrange the cases in order—either from the highest to the lowest or the lowest to the highest. That arrangement will produce the following distribution. | The third measure of average, the *mode*, is simply the cases that occur the most often. In this instance the mode is 57, which is way off the mark. |

EXAMPLE

| | |
|---|---|
| 321 | |
| 229 | |
| 57 | |
| 289 | |
| 136 | |
| 57 | |
| 1,795 | |

EXAMPLE

| | or | |
|---|---|---|
| 57 | | 1,795 |
| 57 | | 321 |
| 136 | | 289 |
| 229 | **or** | 229 |
| 289 | | 136 |
| 321 | | 57 |
| 1,795 | | 57 |

EXAMPLE

| |
|---|
| 57 |
| 57 |
| 136 |
| 229 |
| 289 |
| 321 |
| 1,795 |

| **The Mean** | **The Median** | **The Mode** |
|---|---|---|
| The total is 2,884. Divided by 7 (the number of cases), the average is 412. Sociologists call this form of average the *mean*.<br><br>The mean can be deceptive because it is strongly influenced by extreme scores, either low or high. Note that six of the seven cases are less than the mean.<br><br>Two other ways to compute averages are the median and the mode. | Then look for the middle case, the one that falls halfway between the top and the bottom. That number is 229, for three numbers are lower and three numbers are higher. When there is an even number of cases, the median is the halfway mark between the two middle cases. | Because the mode is often deceptive, and only by chance comes close to either of the other two averages, sociologists seldom use it. In addition, not every distribution of cases has a mode. And if two or more numbers appear with the same frequency, you can have more than one mode. |

large, so you won't be able to survey all the married women. Now you must select a **sample,** individuals from among your target population. How you choose a sample is crucial, for your choice will affect the results of your research. For example, married women enrolled in introductory sociology and engineering courses might have quite different experiences. If so, surveying just one or the other would produce skewed results.

Because you want to generalize your findings to your entire campus, you need a sample that accurately represents the campus. How can you get a representative sample?

The best way is to use a **random sample.** This does *not* mean that you stand on some campus corner and ask questions of any woman who happens to walk by. *In a random sample, everyone in your population (the target group) has the same chance of being included in the study.* In this case, because your population is every married woman enrolled in your college, all married women— whether first-year or graduate students, full- or part-time—must have the same chance of being included in your sample.

How can you get a random sample? First, you need a list of all the married women enrolled in your college. Then you assign a number to each name on the list. Using a table of random numbers, you then determine which of these women become part of your sample. (Tables of random numbers are available in statistics books and online, or they can be generated by a computer.)

A random sample will represent your study's population fairly—in this case, married women enrolled at your college. This means that you can generalize your findings to *all* the married women students on your campus, even if they were not included in your sample.

What if you want to know only about certain subgroups, such as freshmen and seniors? You could use a **stratified random sample.** You would need a list of the freshmen and senior married women. Then, using random numbers, you would select a sample from each group. This would allow you to generalize to all the freshmen and senior married women at your college, but you would not be able to draw any conclusions about the sophomores or juniors.

**Asking Neutral Questions**    After you have decided on your population and sample, your next task is to make certain that your questions are neutral. Your questions must allow **respondents,** the people who answer your questions, to express their own opinions. Otherwise, you will end up with biased answers—which are worthless. For example, if you were to ask, "Don't you think that men who beat their wives should go to prison?" you would be tilting the answer toward agreement with a prison sentence. The *Doonesbury* cartoon below illustrates a more blatant example of biased questions. For examples of flawed research, see the Down-to-Earth Sociology box on the next page.

**Types of Questions**    You must also decide whether to use closed- or open-ended questions. **Closed-ended questions** are followed by a list of possible answers. This format would work for recording someone's age (possible ages would be listed), but it wouldn't work for many other items. For example, how could you list all the opinions that people hold about what should be done to spouse abusers? The answers provided for closed-ended questions can miss the respondent's opinions.

As Table 1.4 on page 27 illustrates, the alternative is **open-ended questions,** which allow people to answer in their own words. Open-ended questions allow you to tap the full range of people's opinions, but they make it difficult

**Doonesbury**    BY GARRY TRUDEAU

Improperly worded questions can steer respondents toward answers that are not their own, thus producing invalid results.

# Down-to-Earth Sociology
## Loading the Dice: How *Not* to Do Research

The methods of science lend themselves to distortion, misrepresentation, and downright fraud. Consider these findings from surveys:

*Americans overwhelmingly prefer Toyotas to Chryslers.*
*Americans overwhelmingly prefer Chryslers to Toyotas.*

Obviously, these opposite conclusions cannot both be true. In fact, both are misrepresentations, even though the responses came from surveys conducted by so-called independent researchers. These researchers, however, are biased, not independent and objective.

It turns out that some consumer researchers load the dice. Hired by firms that have a vested interest in the outcome of the research, they deliver the results their clients are looking for (Armstrong 2007). Here are six ways to load the dice.

1. **Choose a biased sample.** If you want to "prove" that Americans prefer Chryslers over Toyotas, interview unemployed union workers who trace their job loss to Japanese imports. The answer is predictable. You'll get what you're looking for.

2. **Ask biased questions.** Even if you choose an unbiased sample, as in the *Doonesbury* cartoon on page 25, you can phrase questions in such a way that you direct people to the answer you're looking for. Suppose that you ask this question: "We are losing milllions of jobs to workers overseas who work for just a few dollars a day. After losing their jobs, some Americans are even homeless and hungry. Do you prefer a car that gives jobs to Americans, or one that forces our workers to lose their homes?" Questions like this—usually more subtle— are designed to channel people's thinking toward a predetermined answer—quite contrary to the standards of scientific research.

3. **List biased choices.** Another way to load the dice is to use closed-ended questions that push people into the answers you want. Consider this finding:

    U.S. college students overwhelmingly prefer Levis 501 to the jeans of any competitor.

Sound good? Before you rush out to buy Levis, note what these researchers did: In asking students which jeans would be the most popular in the coming year, their list of choices included no other jeans but Levis 501!

4. **Discard undesirable results.** Researchers can keep silent about results they find embarrassing, or they can continue to survey samples until they find one that matches what they are looking for.

As stressed in this chapter, research must be objective if it is to be scientific. Obviously, none of the preceding results qualifies. The underlying problem with the research cited here—and with so many surveys bandied about in the media as fact—is that survey research has become big business. Simply put, the money offered by corporations has corrupted some researchers.

The beginning of the corruption is subtle. Paul Light, dean at the University of Minnesota, put it this way: "A funder will never come to an academic and say, 'I want you to produce finding X, and here's a million dollars to do it.' Rather, the subtext is that if the researchers produce the right finding, more work—and funding—will come their way."

The first four sources of bias are inexcusable, intentional fraud. The next two sources of bias reflect sloppiness, which is also inexcusable in science.

5. **Misunderstand the subjects' world.** This route can lead to errors every bit as great as those just cited. Even researchers who use an adequate sample and word their questions properly can end up with skewed results. They may, for example, fail to anticipate that people may be embarrassed to express an opinion that isn't "politically correct." For example, surveys show that 80 percent of Americans are environmentalists. Most Americans, however, are probably embarrassed to tell a stranger otherwise. Today, that would be like going against the flag, motherhood, and apple pie.

6. **Analyze the data incorrectly.** Even when researchers strive for objectivity, the sample is good, the wording is neutral, and the respondents answer the questions honestly, the results can still be skewed. The researchers may make a mistake in their calculations, such as entering incorrect data into a computer program. This, too, of course, is inexcusable in science.

*Sources:* Based on Crossen 1991; Goleman 1993; Barnes 1995; Resnik 2000; Hotz 2007.

to compare answers. For example, how would you compare these answers to the question "What do you think causes men to abuse their wives?"

"They're sick."

"I think they must have had problems with their mother."

"We ought to string them up!"

**Establishing Rapport**   Will women who have been abused really give honest answers to strangers? The answer is yes, but first you have to establish **rapport** (ruh-POUR), a feeling of trust, with your respondents. We know from studies of rape that once rapport is gained (often by first asking nonsensitive questions), victims will talk about personal, sensitive issues.

To go beyond police statistics, each year researchers interview a random sample of 100,000 Americans. They ask them whether they have been victims of burglary, robbery, and other crimes. After establishing rapport, the researchers ask about rape. They find that rape victims will talk about their experiences. The national crime victimization survey shows that the actual incidence of rape is three times higher than the official statistics (*Statistical Abstract* 2007: page 188).

A new technique to gather data on sensitive areas, Computer-Assisted Self-Interviewing, overcomes lingering problems of distrust. In this technique, the interviewer gives a laptop computer to the respondent, then moves aside, while the individual enters his or her own answers into the computer. In one version of this method, the respondent listens to the questions on a headphone and answers them on the computer screen. When the respondent clicks the "Submit" button, the interviewer has no idea how the respondent answered any questions (Mosher et al. 2005).

## Participant Observation (Fieldwork)

In **participant observation** (or **fieldwork**), the researcher *participates* in a research setting while *observing* what is happening in that setting. Obviously, this method does not mean that you would sit around and watch someone being abused. But let's suppose that you are interested in learning how the abuse has changed the victims' hopes and goals, their attitudes toward men, or their self-concept. For such questions, you could use participant observation.

For example, if your campus has a crisis intervention center, you might be able to observe victims of spouse abuse from the time they report the attack through their participation in counseling. With good rapport, you might even be able to spend time with them in other settings, observing further aspects of their lives. What they

| TABLE 1.4 | Closed and Open-Ended Questions |
| --- | --- |
| **A. Closed-Ended Question** | **B. Open-Ended Question** |
| Which of the following best fits your idea of what should be done to someone who has been convicted of spouse abuse?<br>1. probation<br>2. jail time<br>3. community service<br>4. counseling<br>5. divorce<br>6. nothing—it's a family matter | What do you think should be done to someone who has been convicted of spouse abuse? |

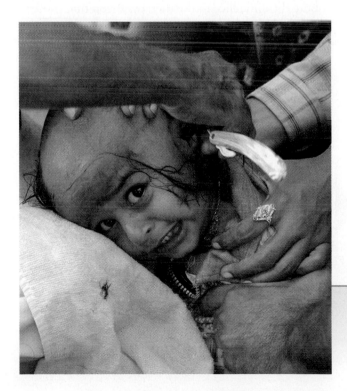

*Participant observation*, participating and observing in a research setting, is usually supplemented by interviewing, asking questions to better understand why people do what they do. In this instance, the sociologist would want to know what this hair removal ceremony in Gujarat, India, means to the child's family and to the community.

say and how they interact with others might help you to understand how the abuse has affected them. This, in turn, could give you insight into how to improve college counseling services.

## Secondary Analysis

In **secondary analysis,** researchers analyze data that others have collected. For example, if you were to analyze the original interviews from a study of women who had been abused by their husbands, you would be doing secondary analysis.

## Documents

**Documents,** recorded sources, include books, newspapers, diaries, bank records, police reports, video and audio recordings, and so on. To study spouse abuse, you might examine police reports and court records. These could reveal the percentage of complaints that result in arrest and the percentage of the arrested men who are charged, convicted, or put on probation. But if you want to learn about the victims' social and emotional adjustment, those records would tell you little. Other documents, though, might provide answers. For example, diaries kept by victims could yield insight into how their attitudes and relationships change. Perhaps the director of a crisis intervention center might ask clients to keep diaries for you—or get the victims' permission for you to examine records of their counseling sessions.

## Experiments

Is there a way to change a wife abuser into a loving husband? No one has made this claim, but a lot of people say

that abusers need therapy. Yet no one knows whether therapy really works. Because **experiments** are useful for determining cause and effect, let's suppose that you propose an experiment to a judge and she gives you access to men who have been arrested for spouse abuse. As in Figure 1.6 below, you would randomly divide the men into two groups. This helps to ensure that their individual characteristics (attitudes, number of arrests, severity of crimes, education, race–ethnicity, age, and so on) are distributed evenly between the groups. You then would arrange for the men in the **experimental group** to receive some form of therapy. The men in the **control group** would not get therapy.

Your **independent variable,** something that causes a change in another variable, would be therapy. Your **dependent variable,** the variable that might change, would be the men's behavior: whether they abuse women after they get out of jail. Unfortunately, your operational definition of the men's behavior will be sloppy: either reports from the wives or records indicating which men were rearrested for abuse. This is sloppy because some of the women will not report the abuse, and some of the men who abuse their wives will not be arrested. Yet it may be the best you can do.

Let's assume that you choose rearrest as your operational definition. If you find that the men who received therapy are *less* likely to be rearrested for abuse, you can attribute the difference to the therapy. If you find *no difference* in rearrest rates, you can conclude that the therapy was ineffective. If you find that the men who received the therapy have a *higher* rearrest rate, you can conclude that the therapy backfired.

## FIGURE 1.6    The Experiment

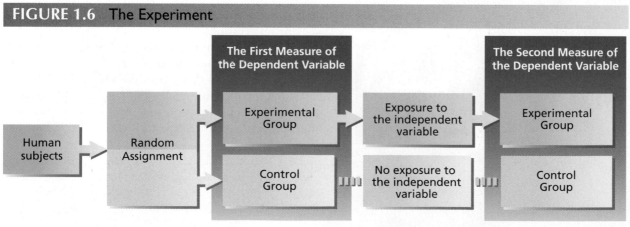

Human subjects → Random Assignment → The First Measure of the Dependent Variable [Experimental Group / Control Group] → Exposure to the independent variable / No exposure to the independent variable → The Second Measure of the Dependent Variable [Experimental Group / Control Group]

*Source:* By the author.

## Unobtrusive Measures

Researchers sometimes use **unobtrusive measures,** observing the behavior of people who are not aware that they are being studied. For example, researchers studied the level of whisky consumption in a town that was legally "dry" by counting empty bottles in trashcans (Lee 2000). Casino operators use chips that transmit radio frequencies, allowing them to track how much their high rollers are betting at every hand of poker or blackjack (Sanders 2005). Billboards can read information embedded on a chip in your car key. As you drive by, the billboard displays *your* name with a personal message (Feder 2007). The same device can *collect* information as you drive by.

It would be considered unethical to use most unobtrusive measures to research spouse abuse. You could, however, analyze 911 calls. Also, if there were a public forum held by abused or abusing spouses on the Internet, you could record and analyze the online conversations. Ethics are still a matter of dispute: To secretly record the behavior of people in public settings, such as a crowd, is generally considered acceptable, but to do so in private settings is not.

## Ethics in Sociological Research

In addition to choosing an appropriate research method, we must also follow the ethics of sociology (American Sociological Association 1999). Research ethics require honesty, truth, and openness (sharing findings with the scientific community). Ethics clearly forbid the falsification of results. They also condemn plagiarism—that is, stealing someone else's work. Another ethical guideline states that research subjects should generally be informed that they are being studied and never be harmed by the research. Ethics also require that sociologists protect the anonymity of those who provide information. Sometimes people reveal things that are intimate, potentially embarrassing, or otherwise harmful to themselves. Finally, although not all sociologists agree, it generally is considered unethical for researchers to misrepresent themselves.

Sociologists take their ethical standards seriously. To illustrate the extent to which they will go to protect their respondents, consider the research conducted by Mario Brajuha.

## Protecting the Subjects: The Brajuha Research

Mario Brajuha, a graduate student at the State University of New York at Stony Brook, was doing participant observation of restaurant workers. He lost his job as a waiter when the restaurant where he was working burned down—a fire of "suspicious origin," as the police said. When detectives learned that Brajuha had taken field notes (Brajuha and Hallowell 1986), they

A major concern of sociologists and other social scientists is that their research methods do not influence their findings. Respondents often change their behavior when they know they are being studied.

THE FAR SIDE® BY GARY LARSON

"Anthropologists! Anthropologists!"

asked to see them. Because he had promised to keep the information confidential, Brajuha refused to hand them over. When the district attorney subpoenaed the notes, Brajuha still refused. The district attorney then threatened to put Brajuha in jail. By this time, Brajuha's notes had become rather famous, and unsavory characters—perhaps those who had set the fire—also wanted to know what was in them. They, too, demanded to see them, accompanying their demands with threats of a different nature. Brajuha found himself between a rock and a hard place.

For two years, Brajuha refused to hand over his notes, even though he grew anxious and had to appear at several court hearings. Finally, the district attorney dropped the subpoena. When the two men under investigation for setting the fire died, the threats to Brajuha, his wife, and their children ended.

## Misleading the Subjects: The Humphreys Research

Sociologists agree on the necessity to protect respondents, and they applaud the professional manner in which Brajuha handled himself. Although it is considered acceptable for sociologists to do covert participant observation (studying some situation without announcing that they are doing research), to deliberately misrepresent oneself is considered unethical. Sociologists who violate this norm can become embroiled in ethical controversy. Let's look at the case of Laud Humphreys, whose research forced sociologists to rethink and refine their ethical stance.

Laud Humphreys, a classmate of mine at Washington University in St. Louis, was an Episcopal priest who decided to become a sociologist. For his Ph.D. dissertation, Humphreys (1970, 1971, 1975) studied social interaction in "tearooms," public restrooms where some men go for quick, anonymous oral sex with other men.

Humphreys found that some restrooms in Forest Park, just across from our campus, were tearooms. He began a participant observation study by hanging around these restrooms. He found that in addition to the two men having sex, a third man—called a "watch queen"—served as a lookout for police and other unwelcome strangers. Humphreys took on the role of watch queen, not only watching for strangers but also observing what the men did. He wrote field notes after the encounters.

Humphreys decided that he wanted to learn about the regular lives of these men. For example, what was the significance of the wedding rings that many of the men wore? He came up with an ingenious technique: Many of the men parked their cars near the tearooms, and Humphreys recorded their license plate numbers. A friend in the St. Louis police department gave Humphreys each man's address. About a year later, Humphreys arranged for these men to be included in a medical survey conducted by some of the sociologists on our faculty.

Disguising himself with a different hairstyle and clothing, Humphreys visited the men's homes. He interviewed the men, supposedly for the medical study. He found that they led conventional lives. They voted, mowed their lawns, and took their kids to Little League games. Many reported that their wives were not aroused sexually or were afraid of getting pregnant because their religion did not allow them to use birth control. Humphreys concluded that heterosexual men were also using the tearooms for a form of quick sex.

This study stirred controversy among sociologists and nonsociologists alike. Many sociologists criticized Humphreys, and a national columnist even wrote a scathing denunciation of "sociological snoopers" (Von Hoffman 1970). One of our professors even tried to get Humphreys' Ph.D. revoked. As the controversy heated up and a court case loomed, Humphreys feared that his list of respondents might be subpoenaed. He gave me the list to take from Missouri to Illinois, where I had begun teaching. When he called and asked me to destroy it, I burned the list in my backyard.

Was this research ethical? This question is not decided easily. Although many sociologists sided with Humphreys—and his book reporting the research won a highly acclaimed award—the criticisms continued. At first, Humphreys defended his position vigorously, but five years later, in a second edition of his book (1975), he stated that he should have identified himself as a researcher.

# Values in Sociological Research

Max Weber raised an issue that remains controversial among sociologists. He said that sociology should be **value free.** By this, he meant that a sociologist's values—beliefs about what is good or desirable in life and the way the world ought to be—should not affect research. Weber wanted **objectivity,** total neutrality, for he said that if values influence research, sociological findings will be biased.

That bias has no place in research is not a matter of debate. All sociologists agree that no one should distort data to make them fit preconceived ideas or personal values. It is equally clear, however, that because sociologists—like everyone else—are members of a particular society at a given point in history, they, too, are infused with values of all sorts. These values inevitably play a role in the topics we choose to research. For example, values are part of the reason that one sociologist chooses to do research on the Mafia, while another turns a sociological eye on kindergarten students.

Because values can lead to unintended distortions in how we interpret our findings, sociologists stress the need for **replication,** repeating a study in order to compare the new results with the original findings. If an individual's values have distorted research findings, replication by other sociologists should uncover the bias and correct it.

Despite this consensus, however, values remain hotly debated in sociology (Holmwood 2007). As summarized in Figure 1.7, the disagreement centers on the proper purposes and uses of sociology. Some sociologists say that the purpose of sociology is to advance understanding of social life. Sociologists should do research on whatever interests them and then use the best theory available to interpret their findings. Others are convinced that the purpose of research should be to help improve society, to do research that helps alleviate poverty, racism, sexism, and other forms of human exploitation.

**FIGURE 1.7    The Debate over Values in Sociological Research**

**The Purposes of Social Research**

To understand human behavior  *versus*  To investigate harmful social arrangements

**The Uses of Social Research**

Can be used by anyone for any purpose  *versus*  Should be used to reform society

This debate illustrates again the tension in sociology that we discussed earlier, the goal of analyzing social life versus the goal of social reform.

In the midst of this controversy, sociologists study the major issues facing our society. From racism and sexism to the globalization of capitalism—these are all topics that sociologists study and that we will explore in this book. Sociologists also examine face-to-face interaction—talking, touching, and gestures. These, too, will be the subject of our discussions in the upcoming chapters. This beautiful variety in sociology—and the contrast of going from the larger picture to the smaller one and back again—is part of the reason that sociology holds such fascination for me. I hope that you also find this variety appealing as you read the rest of this book.

# SUMMARY *and* REVIEW

## The Sociological Perspective

*What is the sociological perspective?*

The **sociological perspective** stresses that people's social experiences—the groups to which they belong and their experiences within these groups—underlie their behavior. C. Wright Mills referred to this as the intersection of biography (the individual) and history (social factors that influence the individual). Pp. 4–5.

## Origins of Sociology

*When did sociology first appear as a separate discipline?*

Sociology emerged as a separate discipline in the mid-1800s in western Europe, during the onset of the Industrial

Revolution. Industrialization affected all aspects of human existence—where people lived, the nature of their work, their relationships, and how they viewed life. Early sociologists who focused on these social changes include Auguste Comte, Herbert Spencer, Karl Marx, Emile Durkheim, Max Weber, Harriet Martineau, and W. E. B. Du Bois. Pp. 5–8.

## Sexism in Early Sociology

*What was the position of women in early sociology?*
Sociology developed during a historical period when deep sexism was common. Consequently, the few women who received the education necessary to become sociologists, such as Harriet Martineau, were ignored. P. 9.

## Sociology in North America

*When were the first academic departments of sociology established in the United States?*
The earliest departments of sociology were established in the late 1800s at the universities of Kansas, Chicago, and Atlanta. During the 1940s, the University of Chicago dominated sociology. Today, no single university or theoretical perspective dominates. In sociology's early years, the contributions of women and minorities were largely ignored. Pp. 9–12.

*What is the difference between basic (or pure) and applied sociology?*
*Basic* (or *pure*) *sociology* is sociological research whose purpose is to make discoveries. In contrast, **applied sociology** is the use of sociology to solve problems. Pp. 12–14.

## Theoretical Perspectives in Sociology

*What is a theory?*
A **theory** is a general statement about how facts are related to one another. A theory provides a conceptual framework for interpreting facts. P. 14.

*What are sociology's major theoretical perspectives?*
Sociologists use three primary theoretical frameworks to interpret social life. **Symbolic interactionists** examine how people use symbols to develop and share their views of the world. Symbolic interactionists usually focus on the **micro level**—on small-scale, face-to-face interaction. **Functionalists,** in contrast, focus on the **macro level**—on large-scale patterns of society. They stress that a social system is made up of interrelated parts. When working properly, each part fulfills a function that contributes to the system's stability. **Conflict theorists** also focus on

large-scale patterns of society. They stress that society is composed of competing groups that struggle for scarce resources.

With each perspective focusing on select features of social life and each providing a unique interpretation, no single theory is adequate. The combined insights of all three perspectives yield a more comprehensive picture of social life. Pp. 14–20.

*What is the relationship between theory and research?*
Theory and research depend on one another. Sociologists use theory to interpret the data they gather. Theory also generates questions that need to be answered by research. Research, in turn, helps to generate theory: Findings that don't match what is expected can indicate a need to modify theory. P. 20.

## Doing Sociological Research

*Why do we need sociological research when we have common sense?*
Common sense doesn't provide reliable information. When subjected to scientific research, commonsense ideas often are found to be limited or false. Pp. 20–22.

*What are the eight basic steps of sociological research?*
1. Selecting a topic, 2. Defining the problem, 3. Reviewing the literature, 4. Formulating a **hypothesis,** 5. Choosing a research method, 6. Collecting the data, 7. Analyzing the results, and 8. Sharing the results. These steps are explained in detail on pp. 20–23.

## Research Methods

*How do sociologists gather data?*
To collect data, sociologists use six **research methods** (or research designs): **surveys, participant observation** (fieldwork), **secondary analysis, documents, experiments,** and **unobtrusive measures.** Pp. 24–29.

## Ethics in Sociological Research

*How important are ethics in sociological research?*
Ethics are of fundamental concern to sociologists, who are committed to openness, honesty, truth, and protecting their subjects from harm. The Brajuha research on restaurant workers and the Humphreys research on "tearooms" were cited to illustrate ethical issues that concern sociologists. Pp. 29–30.

## Values in Sociological Research

*What value dilemmas do sociologists face?*

Max Weber stressed that social research should be **value free:** The researcher's personal beliefs must be set aside to permit objective findings. Like everyone else, however, sociologists are members of a particular society at a given point in history and are infused with **values** of all sorts. To overcome the distortions that values can cause, sociologists stress **replication,** the repetition of a study by other researchers in order to compare results. Values present a second dilemma for researchers: whether to do research solely to analyze human behavior (basic or pure sociology) or to reform harmful social arrangements. Pp. 30–31.

# THINKING CRITICALLY *about* Chapter 1

1. Do you think that sociologists should try to reform society or to study it dispassionately?

2. Of the three theoretical perspectives, which one would you like to use if you were a sociologist? Why?

3. Considering the macro- and micro-level approaches in sociology, which one do you think better explains social life? Why?

# ADDITIONAL RESOURCES

## What can you find in MySocLab? mysoclab  www.mysoclab.com

- **Complete Ebook**
- **Practice Tests and Video and Audio activities**
- **Mapping and Data Analysis exercises**

- **Sociology in the News**
- **Classic Readings in Sociology**
- **Research and Writing advice**

## Where Can I Read More on This Topic?

Suggested readings for this chapter are listed at the back of this book.

chapter

2

Culture

I had never felt heat like this before. This was *northern* Africa, and I wondered what it must be like closer to the equator. Sweat poured off me as the temperature climbed past 110 degrees Fahrenheit.

As we were herded into the building—which had no air conditioning—hundreds of people lunged toward the counter at the rear of the structure. With body crushed against body, we waited as the uniformed officials behind the windows leisurely examined each passport. At times like this, I wondered what I was doing in Africa.

> Everyone stared. No matter where I went, they stared.

When I first arrived in Morocco, I found the sights that greeted me exotic—not far from the scenes in *Casablanca, Raiders of the Lost Ark,* and other movies. The men, women, and even the children really did wear those white robes that reached down to their feet. What was especially striking was that the women were almost totally covered. Despite the heat, they wore not only full-length gowns but also head coverings that reached down over their foreheads and veils that covered their faces from the nose down. All you could see were their eyes—and every eye seemed the same shade of brown.

And how short everyone was! The Arab women looked to be, on average, 5 feet, and the men only about 3 or 4 inches taller. As the only blue-eyed, blonde, 6-foot-plus person around, and the only one who was wearing jeans and a pullover shirt, in a world of white-robed short people I stood out like a creature from another planet. Everyone stared. No matter where I went, they stared. Wherever I looked, I found brown eyes watching me intently. Even staring back at those many dark brown eyes had no effect. It was so different from home, where, if you caught someone staring at you, that person would look embarrassed and immediately glance away.

And lines? The concept apparently didn't even exist. Buying a ticket for a bus or train meant pushing and shoving toward the ticket man (always a man—no women were visible in any public position), who took the money from whichever outstretched hand he decided on.

And germs? That notion didn't seem to exist here either. Flies swarmed over the food in the restaurants and the unwrapped loaves of bread in the stores. Shopkeepers would considerately shoo off the flies before handing me a loaf. They also offered home delivery.

I watched a bread vendor deliver a loaf to a woman who was standing on a second-floor balcony. She first threw her money to the bread vendor, and he then threw the unwrapped bread up to her. Only, his throw was off. The bread bounced off the wrought-iron balcony railing and landed in the street, which was filled with people, wandering dogs, and the ever-present, urinating and defecating donkeys. The vendor simply picked up the unwrapped loaf and threw it again. This certainly wasn't his day, for he missed again. But he made it on his third attempt. The woman smiled as she turned back into her apartment, apparently to prepare the noon meal for her family.

As I left Morocco, I entered a crowded passport-check building on the Algerian border. With no air conditioning, the oppressive summer heat—about 115° Fahrenheit—was made all the worse as body crushed against body. As people pushed to get to the front, tempers began to flare. When a fight broke out, a little man in uniform appeared, shouting and knocking people aside as he forced his way to a little wooden box nailed to the floor. Climbing onto this makeshift platform, he shouted at the crowd, his arms flailing about him. The people fell silent. But just as soon as the man left, the shouting and shoving began again.

The situation had become unbearable. His body pressed against mine, the man behind me decided that this was a good time to take a nap. Determining that I made a good support, he placed his arm against my back and leaned his head against his arm. Sweat streamed down my back at the point where his arm and head touched me.

Finally, I realized that I had to abandon U.S. customs. So I pushed my way forward, forcing my frame into every square inch of vacant space that I could create. At the counter, I shouted in English. The official looked up at the sound of this strange tongue, and I thrust my long arms over the heads of three people, shoving my passport into his hand.

# What Is Culture?

What is culture? The concept is sometimes easier to grasp by description than by definition. For example, suppose you meet a young woman from India who has just arrived in the United States. That her culture is different from yours is immediately evident. You first see it in her clothing, jewelry, makeup, and hairstyle. Next you hear it in her speech. It then becomes apparent by her gestures. Later, you might hear her express unfamiliar beliefs about relationships or what is valuable in life. All of these characteristics are indicative of **culture**—the language, beliefs, values, norms, behaviors, and even material objects that are passed from one generation to the next.

In northern Africa, I was surrounded by a culture quite alien to my own. It was evident in everything I saw and heard. The **material culture**—such things as jewelry, art, buildings, weapons, machines, and even eating utensils, hairstyles, and clothing—provided a sharp contrast to what I was used to seeing. There is nothing inherently "natural" about material culture. That is, it is no more natural (or unnatural) to wear gowns on the street than it is to wear jeans.

I also found myself immersed in an unfamiliar **nonmaterial culture,** that is, a group's ways of thinking (its beliefs, values, and other assumptions about the world) and doing (its common patterns of behavior, including language, gestures, and other forms of interaction). North African assumptions that it is acceptable to stare at others in public and to push people aside to buy tickets are examples of nonmaterial culture. So are U.S. assumptions that it is wrong to do either of these things. Like material culture, neither custom is "right." People simply become comfortable with the customs they learn during childhood, and—as in the case of my visit to northern Africa—uncomfortable when their basic assumptions about life are challenged.

## Culture and Taken-for-Granted Orientations to Life

To develop a sociological imagination, it is essential to understand how culture affects people's lives. If we meet someone from a different culture, the encounter may make us aware of culture's pervasive influence on all aspects of a person's life. Attaining the same level of awareness regarding our own culture, however, is quite another matter. *Our* speech, *our* gestures, *our* beliefs, and *our* customs are usually taken for granted. We assume that they are "normal" or "natural," and we almost always follow them without question. As anthropologist Ralph Linton (1936) said, "The last thing a fish would ever notice would be water." So also with people: Except in unusual circumstances, most characteristics of our own culture remain imperceptible to us.

Yet culture's significance is profound; it touches almost every aspect of who and what we are. We came into this life without a language; without values and morality; with no ideas about religion, war, money, love, use of space, and so on. We possessed none of these fundamental orientations that are so essential in determining the type of people we become. Yet by this point in our lives, we all have acquired them—and take them for granted. Sociologists call this *culture within us.* These learned and shared ways of believing and of doing (another definition of culture) penetrate our beings at an early age and quickly become part of our taken-for-granted assumptions about what normal behavior is. *Culture becomes the lens through which we perceive and evaluate what is going on around us.* Seldom do we question these assumptions, for, like water to a fish, the lens through which we view life remains largely beyond our perception.

The rare instances in which these assumptions are challenged, however, can be upsetting. Although as a sociologist I should be able to look at my own culture "from the outside," my trip to Africa quickly revealed how fully I had internalized my culture. My upbringing in Western culture had given me assumptions about aspects of social life that had become rooted deeply in my being—appropriate eye contact, proper hygiene, and the use of space. But in this part of Africa these assumptions were useless in helping me navigate everyday life. No longer could I count on people to stare only surreptitiously, to take precautions against invisible microbes, or to stand in line in an orderly fashion, one behind the other.

As you can tell from the opening vignette, I found these unfamiliar behaviors upsetting, for they violated my basic expectations of "the way people *ought* to be"—and I did not even realize how firmly I held these expectations until they were challenged so abruptly. When my nonmaterial culture failed me—when it no longer enabled me to make sense out of the world—I experienced a disorientation known as **culture shock.** In the case of buying tickets, the fact that I was several inches taller than most Moroccans and thus able to outreach others helped me to adjust partially to their different ways of doing things. But I never did get used to the idea that pushing ahead of others was "right," and I always felt guilty when I used my size to receive preferential treatment.

We are talking about a two-way street, of course. You can imagine what a cultural shock people from a tribal society would experience if they were thrust into the United States. It would be severe, as the Cultural Diversity box on the next page describes.

An important consequence of culture within us is **ethnocentrism,** a tendency to use our own group's ways of doing things as a yardstick for judging others. All of us learn that the ways of our own group are good, right, and even superior to other ways of life. As sociologist William Sumner (1906), who developed this concept, said, "One's own group is the center of everything, and all others are scaled and rated with reference to it." Ethnocentrism has both positive and negative consequences. On the positive side, it creates in-group loyalties. On the negative side, ethnocentrism can lead to discrimination against people whose ways differ from ours.

The many ways in which culture affects our lives fascinate sociologists. In this chapter, we'll examine how profoundly culture influences everything we are and do. This will serve as a basis from which you can start to analyze your own assumptions of reality. I should give you a warning at this point: You might develop a changed perspective on social life and your role in it. If so, life will never look the same.

**In Sum:** To avoid losing track of the ideas under discussion, let's pause for a moment to summarize and, in some instances, clarify the principles we have covered.

1. There is nothing "natural" about material culture. Arabs wear gowns on the street and feel that it is natural to do so. Americans do the same with jeans.
2. There is nothing "natural" about nonmaterial culture. It is just as arbitrary to stand in line as to push and shove.
3. Culture penetrates deeply into our thinking, becoming a taken-for-granted lens through which we see the world and obtain our perception of reality.
4. Culture provides implicit instructions that tell us what we ought to do and how we ought to think. It provides a fundamental basis for our decision making.
5. Culture also provides a "moral imperative"; that is, the culture that we internalize becomes the "right" way of doing things. (I, for example, believed deeply that it was wrong to push and shove to get ahead of others.)
6. Coming into contact with a radically different culture challenges our basic assumptions of life. (I experienced culture shock when I discovered that my deeply ingrained cultural ideas about hygiene and the use of personal space no longer applied.)
7. Although the particulars of culture differ from one group of people to another, culture itself is universal. That is, all people have culture, for a society cannot exist without developing shared, learned ways of dealing with the challenges of life.
8. All people are ethnocentric, which has both positive and negative consequences.

# Cultural Diversity in the United States

## Culture Shock: The Arrival of the Hmong

Imagine that you were a member of a small tribal group in the mountains of Laos. Village life and the clan were all you knew. There were no schools, and you learned everything you needed to know from your relatives. U.S. agents recruited the men of your village to fight communists, and they gained a reputation as fierce fighters. When the U.S. forces were defeated in Vietnam, your people were moved to the United States so that they wouldn't be killed in reprisal.

Here is what happened. Keep in mind that you had never seen a television or a newspaper and that you had never gone to school. Your entire world had been the village.

They put you in a big house with wings. It flew.

They gave you strange food on a tray. The Sani-Wipes were hard to chew.

After the trip, you were placed in a house. This was an adventure. You had never seen locks before, as no one locked up anything in the village. Most of the village homes didn't even have doors, much less locks.

You found the bathroom perplexing. At first, you tried to wash rice in the bowl of water, which seemed to be provided for this purpose. But when you pressed the handle, the water and rice disappeared. After you learned what the toilet was for, you found it difficult not to slip off the little white round thing when you stood on it. In the village, you didn't need a white thing when you squatted to defecate.

When you threw water on the electric stove to put out the burner, it sparked and smoked. You became afraid to use the stove because it might explode.

And no one liked it when you tried to plant a vegetable garden in the park.

*Children make the fastest adjustment to a new culture, although they remain caught between the old and new ones.*

Your new world was so different that, to help you adjust, the settlement agency told you (Fadiman 1997):

1. To send mail, you must use stamps.
2. The door of the refrigerator must be shut.
3. Do not stand or squat on the toilet since it may break.
4. Always ask before picking your neighbor's flowers, fruit, or vegetables.
5. In colder areas you must wear shoes, socks, and appropriate outerwear. Otherwise, you may become ill.
6. Always use a handkerchief or a tissue to blow your nose in public places or inside a public building.
7. Picking your nose or ears in public is frowned upon in the United States.
8. Never urinate in the street. This creates a smell that is offensive to Americans. They also believe that it causes disease.

To help the Hmong assimilate, U.S. officials dispersed them across the nation. This, they felt, would help them to adjust to the dominant culture and prevent a Hmong subculture from developing. The dispersal brought feelings of isolation to the clan- and village-based Hmong. As soon as they had a chance, the Hmong moved from these towns scattered across the country to the same areas, the major one being in California's Central Valley. Here they united, renewing village relationships and helping one another adjust to the society they had never desired to join.

## For Your Consideration

Do you think you would have reacted differently if you had been a displaced Hmong? Why did the Hmong need one another more than their U.S. neighbors to adjust to their new life? What cultural shock do you think a U.S.-born 19-year-old Hmong would experience if his or her parents decided to return to Laos?

## Practicing Cultural Relativism

To counter our tendency to use our own culture as the standard by which we judge other cultures, we can practice **cultural relativism;** that is, we can try to understand a culture on its own terms. This means looking at how the elements of a culture fit together, without judging those elements as superior or inferior to our own way of life.

With our own culture embedded so deeply within us, however, practicing cultural relativism can challenge our orientations to life. For example, most U.S. citizens appear to have strong feelings against raising bulls for the purpose of stabbing them to death in front of crowds that shout "Olé!" According to cultural relativism, however, bullfighting must be viewed from the perspective of the culture in which it takes place—*its* history, *its* folklore, *its* ideas of bravery, and *its* ideas of sex roles.

You may still regard bullfighting as wrong, of course, if your culture, which is deeply ingrained in you, has no history of bullfighting. We all possess culturally specific ideas about cruelty to animals, ideas that have evolved slowly and match other elements of our culture. In the United States, for example, practices that once were common in some areas—cock fighting, dog fighting, bear–dog fighting, and so on—have been gradually eliminated.

None of us can be entirely successful at practicing cultural relativism. Look at the Cultural Diversity box on the next page. My best guess is that you will evaluate these "strange" foods through the lens of your own culture. Applying cultural relativism, however, is an attempt to refocus that lens so we can appreciate other ways of life rather than simply asserting, "Our way

is right." As you view the photos on page 41, try to appreciate the cultural differences in standards of beauty.

Although cultural relativism helps us to avoid cultural smugness, this view has come under attack. In a provocative book, *Sick Societies* (1992), anthropologist Robert Edgerton suggests that we develop a scale for evaluating cultures on their "quality of life," much as we do for U.S. cities. He also asks why we should consider cultures that practice female circumcision, gang rape, or wife beating or cultures that sell little girls into prostitution as morally equivalent to those that do not. Cultural values that result in exploitation, he says, are inferior to those that enhance people's lives.

Edgerton's sharp questions and incisive examples bring us to a topic that comes up repeatedly in this text: the disagreements that arise among scholars as they confront contrasting views of reality. It is such questioning of assumptions that keeps sociology interesting.

# Components of Symbolic Culture

Sociologists sometimes refer to nonmaterial culture as **symbolic culture,** because its central component is the symbols that people use. A **symbol** is something to which people attach meaning and that they then use to communicate with one another. Symbols include gestures, language, values, norms, sanctions, folkways, and mores. Let's look at each of these components of symbolic culture.

Many Americans perceive bullfighting, which is illegal in the United States, as a cruel activity that should be abolished everywhere. For many Spaniards, in contrast, bullfighting is a beautiful sport, a form of artistry in which matador and bull blend into a unifying image of power, courage, and glory. *Cultural relativism* requires that we suspend our own perspectives in order to grasp the perspectives of others, something that is much easier described than attained.

# Cultural Diversity around the World

## You Are What You Eat? An Exploration in Cultural Relativity

Here is a chance to test your ethnocentrism and ability to practice cultural relativity. You probably know that the French like to eat snails and that in some Asian cultures, chubby dogs and cats are considered a delicacy ("Ah, lightly browned with a little doggy sauce!"). But did you know that cod sperm is a delicacy in Japan (Raisfeld and Patronite 2006)?

Marston Bates (1967), a zoologist, noted this ethnocentric reaction to food:

> I remember once, in the llanos of Colombia, sharing a dish of toasted ants at a remote farmhouse. . . . My host and I fell into conversation about the general question of what people eat or do not eat, and I remarked that in my country people eat the legs of frogs.
>
> The very thought of this filled my ant-eating friends with horror; it was as though I had mentioned some re-pulsive sex habit.

Then there is the experience of the production co-ordinator of this text, Dusty Friedman, who told me:

> When traveling in Sudan, I ate some interesting things that I wouldn't likely eat now that I'm back in our society. Raw baby camel's liver with chopped herbs was a delicacy. So was camel's milk cheese patties that had been cured in dry camel's dung.

You might be able to see yourself eating frog legs, toasted ants, perhaps cod sperm and raw camel liver,

*What some consider food, even delicacies, can turn the stomachs of others. These little critters were for sale in a market in Laos.*

maybe even dogs and cats, but here's another test of your ethnocentrism and cultural relativity. Maxine Kingston (1975), an English professor whose parents grew up in China, wrote:

> "Do you know what people in [the Nantou region of] China eat when they have the money?" my mother began. "They buy into a monkey feast. The eaters sit around a thick wood table with a hole in the middle. Boys bring in the monkey at the end of a pole. Its neck is in a collar at the end of the pole, and it is screaming. Its hands are tied behind it. They clamp the monkey into the table; the whole table fits like another collar around its neck. Using a surgeon's saw, the cooks cut a clean line in a circle at the top of its head. To loosen the bone, they tap with a tiny hammer and wedge here and there with a silver pick. Then an old woman reaches out her hand to the monkey's face and up to its scalp, where she tufts some hairs and lifts off the lid of the skull. The eaters spoon out the brains."

### For Your Consideration

1. What is your opinion about eating toasted ants? About eating fried frog legs? About eating cod sperm? About eating puppies and kittens? About eating brains scooped out of a living monkey?
2. If you were reared in U.S. society, more than likely you think that eating frog legs is okay; eating ants is disgusting; and eating cod sperm, dogs, cats, and monkey brains is downright repugnant. How would you apply the concepts of ethnocentrism and cultural relativism to your perceptions of these customs?

## Gestures

**Gestures,** movements of the body to communicate with others, are shorthand ways to convey messages without using words. Although people in every culture of the world use gestures, a gesture's meaning may change com-pletely from one culture to another. North Americans, for example, communicate a succinct message by raising the middle finger in a short, upward stabbing motion. I wish to stress "North Americans," for this gesture does not con-vey the same message in most parts of the world.

Peru

New Guinea

Thailand

China

Cameroon

Tibet

Kenya

United States

## Standards of Beauty

Standards of beauty vary so greatly from one culture to another that what one group finds attractive, another may not. Yet, in its *ethnocentrism*, each group thinks that its standards are the best—that the appearance reflects what beauty "really" is.

As indicated by these photos, around the world men and women aspire to their group's norms of physical attractiveness. To make themselves appealing to others, they try to make their appearance reflect those standards.

I was surprised to find that this particular gesture was not universal, having internalized it to such an extent that I thought everyone knew what it meant. When I was comparing gestures with friends in Mexico, however, this gesture drew a blank look from them. After I explained its intended meaning, they laughed and showed me their rudest gesture—placing the hand under the armpit and moving the upper arm up and down. To me, they simply looked as if they were imitating monkeys, but to them the gesture meant "Your mother is a whore"— the worst possible insult in that culture.

With the current political, military, and cultural dominance of the United States, "giving the finger" is becoming well known in other cultures. Following the September 11, 2001, terrorist attack, the United States began to photograph and fingerprint foreign visitors. Feeling insulted, Brazil retaliated by doing the same to U.S. visitors. Angry at this, a U.S. pilot raised his middle finger while being photographed. Having become aware of the meaning of this gesture, Brazilian police arrested him. To gain his release, the pilot had to pay a fine of $13,000 ("Brazil Arrests" . . . 2004).

Gestures not only facilitate communication but also, because they differ around the world, can lead to misunderstanding, embarrassment, or worse. One time in Mexico, for example, I raised my hand to a certain height to indicate how tall a child was. My hosts began to laugh. It turned out that Mexicans use three hand gestures to indicate height: one for people, a second for animals, and yet another for plants. They were amused because I had ignorantly used the plant gesture to indicate the child's height. (See Figure 2.1.)

To get along in another culture, then, it is important to learn the gestures of that culture. If you don't, you will fail to achieve the simplicity of communication that gestures allow, and you may overlook or misunderstand much of what is happening, run the risk of appearing foolish, and possibly offend people. In some cultures, for example, you would provoke deep offense if you were to offer food or a gift with your left hand, because the left hand is reserved for dirty tasks, such as wiping after going to the toilet. Left-handed Americans visiting Arabs, please note!

Suppose for a moment that you are visiting southern Italy. After eating one of the best meals in your life, you are so pleased that when you catch the waiter's eye, you smile broadly and use the standard U.S. "A-OK" gesture of putting your thumb and forefinger together and making a large "**O**." The waiter looks horrified, and you are struck speechless when the manager asks you to leave. What have you done? Nothing on purpose, of course, but in that culture this gesture refers to a certain lower part of the human body that is not mentioned in polite company (Ekman et al. 1984).

Some gestures are so closely associated with emotional messages that the gestures themselves summon up emotions. For example, my introduction to Mexican gestures took place at a dinner table. It was evident that my husband-and-wife hosts were trying to hide their embarrassment at using their culture's obscene gesture at their

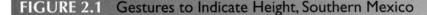

**FIGURE 2.1** Gestures to Indicate Height, Southern Mexico

dinner table. And I felt the same way—not about *their* gesture, of course, which meant nothing to me—but about the one I was teaching them.

## Language

The primary way in which people communicate with one another is through **language**—symbols that can be combined in an infinite number of ways for the purpose of communicating abstract thought. Each word is actually a symbol, a sound to which we have attached some particular meaning. Although all human groups have language, there is nothing universal about the meanings given to particular sounds. Like gestures, in different cultures the same sound may mean something entirely different—or may have no meaning at all. In German, for example, *gift* means poison, so if you give a box of chocolate to a non-English speaking German and say, "Gift, eat," . . .

Because *language allows culture to exist,* its significance for human life is difficult to overstate. Consider the following effects of language.

### Language Allows Human Experience to Be Cumulative

By means of language, we pass ideas, knowledge, and even attitudes on to the next generation. This allows others to build on experiences in which they may never directly participate. As a result, humans are able to modify their behavior in light of what earlier generations have learned. Hence the central sociological significance of language: *Language allows culture to develop by freeing people to move beyond their immediate experiences.*

Without language, human culture would be little more advanced than that of the lower primates. If we communicated by grunts and gestures, we would be limited to a short time span—to events now taking place, those that have just taken place, or those that will take place immediately—a sort of slightly extended present. You can grunt and gesture, for example, that you want a drink of water, but in the absence of language how could you share ideas concerning past or future events? There would be little or no way to communicate to others what event you had in mind, much less the greater complexities that humans communicate—ideas and feelings about events.

### Language Provides a Social or Shared Past
Without language, our memories would be extremely limited, for we associate experiences with words and then use words to recall the experience. Such memories as would exist in the absence of language would be highly individualized, for only rarely and incompletely could we communicate them to others, much less discuss them and agree on something. By attaching words to an event, however, and then using those words to recall it, we are able to discuss the event. As we talk about past events, we develop shared understandings about what those events mean. In short, through talk, people develop a shared past.

### Language Provides a Social or Shared Future
Language also extends our time horizons forward. Because language enables us to agree on times, dates, and places, it allows us to plan activities with one another. Think about it for a moment. Without language, how could you ever plan

Although most *gestures* are learned, and therefore vary from culture to culture, some gestures that represent fundamental emotions such as sadness, anger, and fear appear to be inborn. This crying child whom I photographed in India differs little from a crying child in China—or the United States or anywhere else on the globe. In a few years, however, this child will demonstrate a variety of gestures highly specific to his Hindu culture.

future events? How could you possibly communicate goals, times, and plans? Whatever planning could exist would be limited to rudimentary communications, perhaps to an agreement to meet at a certain place when the sun is in a certain position. But think of the difficulty, perhaps the impossibility, of conveying just a slight change in this simple arrangement, such as "I can't make it tomorrow, but my neighbor can take my place, if that's all right with you."

**Language Allows Shared Perspectives**  Our ability to speak, then, provides us a social (or shared) past and future. This is vital for humanity. It is a watershed that distinguishes us from animals. But speech does much more. When we talk with one another, we are exchanging ideas about events; that is, we are sharing perspectives. Our words are the embodiment of our experiences, distilled into a readily exchangeable form, one that is mutually understandable to people who have learned that language. *Talking about events allows us to arrive at the shared understandings that form the basis of social life.* Not sharing a language while living alongside one another, however, invites miscommunication and suspicion. This risk, which comes with a diverse society, is discussed in the Cultural Diversity box on the next page.

**Language Allows Shared, Goal-Directed Behavior**  Common understandings enable us to establish a *purpose* for getting together. Let's suppose you want to go on a picnic. You use speech not only to plan the picnic but also to decide on reasons for having the picnic—which may be anything from "because it's a nice day and it shouldn't be wasted studying" to "because it's my birthday." Language permits you to blend individual activities into an integrated sequence. In other words, through discussion you decide where you will go; who will drive; who will bring the hamburgers, the potato chips, the soda; where you will meet; and so on. Only because of language can you participate in such a common yet complex event as a picnic—or build roads and bridges or attend college classes.

**In Sum:**  The sociological significance of language is that it takes us beyond the world of apes and allows culture to develop. Language frees us from the present, actually giving us a social past and a social future. That is, language gives us the capacity to share understandings about the past and to develop shared perceptions about the future. Language also allows us to establish underlying purposes for our activities. In short, *language is the basis of culture.*

## Language and Perception: The Sapir-Whorf Hypothesis

In the 1930s, two anthropologists, Edward Sapir and Benjamin Whorf, became intrigued when they noted that the Hopi Indians of the southwestern United States had no words to distinguish among the past, the present, and the future. English, in contrast—as well as French, Spanish, Swahili, and other languages—distinguishes carefully among these three time frames. From this observation, Sapir and Whorf began to think that words might be more than labels that people attach to things. *Eventually, they concluded that language has embedded within it ways of looking at the world.* In other words, language not only expresses our thoughts and perceptions but also shapes the way we think and perceive. When we learn a language, we learn not only words but also ways of thinking and perceiving (Sapir 1949; Whorf 1956).

The **Sapir-Whorf hypothesis** reverses common sense: It indicates that rather than objects and events forcing themselves onto our consciousness, it is our language that determines our consciousness and, hence, our perception of objects and events. Sociologist Eviatar Zerubavel (1991) gives a good example. Hebrew, his native language, does not have separate words for jam and jelly. Both go by the same term, and only when Zerubavel learned English could he "see" this difference, which is "obvious" to native English speakers. Similarly, if you learn to classify students as Jocks, Goths, Stoners, Skaters, and Preps, you will perceive students in an entirely different way from someone who does not know these classifications.

Although Sapir and Whorf's observation that the Hopi do not have tenses was inaccurate (Edgerton 1992:27), they did stumble onto a major truth about social life. Learning a language means not only learning words but also acquiring the perceptions embedded in that language. In other words, language both reflects and shapes our cultural experiences (Drivonikou et al. 2007). The racial–ethnic terms that our culture provides, for example, influence how we see both ourselves and others, a point that is discussed in the Cultural Diversity box on page 46.

## Values, Norms, and Sanctions

To learn a culture is to learn people's **values,** their ideas of what is desirable in life. When we uncover people's values, we learn a great deal about them, for values are the standards by which people define what is good and

Florida

# Cultural Diversity in the United States

## Miami—The Controversy over Language

Immigration from Cuba and other Spanish-speaking countries has been so vast that most residents of Miami are Latinos. Half of Miami's 385,000 residents have trouble speaking English. Only *one-fourth* of Miamians speak English at home. As is well-known, the English-speakers want the Spanish-speakers to learn English, but many Spanish-speakers think that learning language should be a two-way street. Pedro Falcon, an immigrant from Nicaragua who is studying English, wonders why more people don't try to learn his language. "Miami is the capital of Latin America," he says. "The population speaks Spanish."

*Mural from Miami.*

As the English-speakers see it, this pinpoints the problem: Miami is in the United States, not in Latin America.

Controversy over immigrants and language isn't new. The millions of Germans who moved to the United States in the 1800s brought their language with them. They not only held their religious services in German, but they also opened private schools in which the instruction was in German, published German-language newspapers, and spoke German at home and in the taverns.

Some of their English-speaking neighbors didn't like this a bit. "Why don't those Germans assimilate?" they wondered. "Just whose side would they fight on if we had a war?"

This question was answered, of course, with the participation of German Americans in two world wars. It was even a general of German descent (Eisenhower) who led the armed forces that defeated Hitler.

But what happened to all this German language? The first generation of immigrants spoke German almost exclusively. The second generation assimilated, speaking English at home, but also speaking German when they visited their parents. For the most part, the third generation knew German only as "that language" that their grandparents spoke.

The same thing is happening with Spanish speakers. Spanish, however, is being kept alive longer because Mexico borders the United States, and there is constant traffic between the countries. In addition, the continuing migration from Mexico and other Spanish-speaking countries feeds the language.

If Germany bordered the United States, there would still be a lot of German spoken here.

In the midst of our current controversy over language, Miami officials have declared English to be the official language of Miami. In one small way, at least, they have succeeded. When we tried to get a photograph of *"Bienvenidos a Miami"* for this box, we were told that such a sign would be illegal!

*Sources:* Based on Sharp 1992; Usdansky 1992; Kent and Lalasz 2007.

---

bad, beautiful and ugly. Values underlie our preferences, guide our choices, and indicate what we hold worthwhile in life.

Every group develops expectations concerning the right way to reflect its values. Sociologists use the term **norms** to describe those expectations (or rules of behavior) that develop out of a group's values. The term **sanctions** refers to the reactions people receive for following or breaking norms. A **positive sanction** expresses approval for following a norm, and a **negative sanction** reflects disapproval for breaking a norm. Positive sanctions can be material, such as a prize, a trophy, or money, but in everyday life they usually consist of hugs, smiles, a pat on the back, or even handshakes and "high fives." Negative sanctions can also be material—being fined in court is one example—but negative sanctions, too, are more likely to be symbolic: harsh words, or gestures such as frowns, stares, clenched jaws, or raised fists. Getting a

# Cultural Diversity in the United States

## Race and Language: Searching for Self-Labels

The groups that dominate society often determine the names that are used to refer to racial–ethnic groups. If those names become associated with oppression, they take on negative meanings. For example, the terms *Negro* and *colored people* came to be associated with submissiveness and low status. To overcome these meanings, those referred to by these terms began to identify themselves as *black* or *African American*. They infused these new terms with respect—a basic source of self-esteem that they felt the old terms denied them.

In a twist, African Americans—and to a lesser extent Latinos, Asian Americans, and Native Americans—have changed the rejected term *colored people* to *people of color*. Those who embrace this modified term are imbuing it with meanings that offer an identity of respect. The term also has political meanings. It indicates bonds that cross racial–ethnic lines, mutual ties, and a sense of identity rooted in historical oppression.

*The ethnic terms we choose—or which are given to us—are major self-identifiers. They indicate both membership in some group and a separation from other groups.*

There is *always* disagreement about racial–ethnic terms, and this one is no exception. Although most rejected the term *colored people,* some found in it a sense of respect and claimed it for themselves. The acronym NAACP, for example, stands for the National Association for the Advancement of Colored People. The new term, *people of color,* arouses similar feelings. Some individuals whom this term would include claim that it is inappropriate. They point out that this new label still makes color the primary identifier of people. They stress that humans transcend race–ethnicity, that what we have in common as human beings goes much deeper than what you see on the surface. They stress that we should avoid terms that focus on differences in the pigmentation of our skin.

The language of self-reference in a society that is so conscious of skin color is an ongoing issue. As long as our society continues to emphasize such superficial differences, the search for adequate terms is not likely to ever be "finished." In this quest for terms that strike the right chord, the term *people of color* may become a historical footnote. If it does, it will be replaced by another term that indicates a changing self-identification in a changing historical context.

---

raise at work is a positive sanction, indicating that you have followed the norms clustering around work values. Getting fired, however, is a negative sanction, indicating that you have violated these norms. The North American finger gesture discussed earlier is, of course, a negative sanction.

Because people can find norms stifling, some cultures relieve the pressure through *moral holidays,* specified times when people are allowed to break norms. Moral holidays such as Mardi Gras often center on getting rowdy. Some activities for which people would otherwise be arrested are permitted—and expected—including public drunkenness and some nudity. The norms are never completely dropped, however—just loosened a bit. Go too far, and the police step in.

Some societies have *moral holiday places,* locations where norms are expected to be broken. One of the more interesting examples is "Party Cove" at Lake of the Ozarks in Missouri, a fairly straightlaced area of the country. During the summer, hundreds of boaters—from those operating cabin cruisers to jet skis—moor their vessels together in a highly publicized cove, where many get drunk, take off their clothes, and dance on the boats. In one of the more humorous incidents, boaters complained that a nude woman was riding a jet ski outside of the cove. The water patrol investigated but refused to arrest the woman because she was within the law—she had sprayed shaving cream on certain parts of her body.

## Folkways and Mores

Norms that are not strictly enforced are called **folkways.** We expect people to comply with folkways, but we are likely to shrug our shoulders and not make a big deal about it if they don't. If someone insists on passing you on the right side of the sidewalk, for example, you are unlikely to take corrective action, although if the sidewalk is crowded and you must move out of the way, you might give the person a dirty look.

Other norms, however, are taken much more seriously. We think of them as essential to our core values, and we insist on conformity. These are called **mores** (MORE-rays). A person who steals, rapes, or kills has violated some of society's most important mores. As sociologist Ian Robertson (1987:62) put it,

**A man who walks down a street wearing nothing on the upper half of his body is violating a folkway; a man who walks down the street wearing nothing on the lower half of his body is violating one of our most important mores, the requirement that people cover their genitals and buttocks in public.**

It should also be noted that one group's folkways may be another group's mores. Although a man walking down the street with the upper half of his body uncovered is deviating from a folkway, a woman doing the same thing is violating the mores. In addition, the folkways and mores of a subculture (discussed in the next section) may be the opposite of mainstream culture. For example, to walk down the sidewalk in a nudist camp with the entire body uncovered would conform to that subculture's folkways.

A **taboo** refers to a norm so strongly ingrained that even the thought of its violation is greeted with revulsion. Eating human flesh and parents having sex with their children are examples of such behaviors. When someone breaks a taboo, the individual is usually judged unfit to live in the same society as others. The sanctions are severe and may include prison, banishment, or death.

The violation of *mores* is a serious matter. In this case, it is serious enough that the police at this rugby match in Dublin, Ireland, have swung into action to protect the public from seeing a "disgraceful" sight, at least one so designated by this group.

# Many Cultural Worlds

## Subcultures

Groups of people who focus on some activity or who occupy some small corner in life tend to develop specialized ways to communicate with one another. To outsiders, their talk, even if it is in English, can seem like a foreign language. Here is one of my favorite quotes by a politician:

> There are things we know that we know. There are known unknowns; that is to say, there are things that we now know we don't know. But there are also unknown unknowns; there are things we do not know we don't know. (Dickey and Barry 2006:38)

Whatever Donald Rumsfeld, the former secretary of defense under George W. Bush, meant by his statement probably will remain a known unknown. (Or would it be an unknown known?)

People who specialize in some occupation—from cabbies to politicians—tend to develop a **subculture,** *a world within the larger world of the dominant culture.* Subcultures are not limited to occupations, for they include any corner in life in which people's experiences lead them to have distinctive ways of looking at life or some aspect of it. Even if we cannot understand the preceding quote, it makes us aware that politicians don't view life in quite the same way most of us do.

U.S. society contains *thousands* of subcultures. Some are as broad as the way of life we associate with teenagers, others as narrow as those we associate with bodybuilders—or with politicians. Some U.S. ethnic groups also form subcultures: Their values, norms, and foods set them apart. So might their religion, music, language, and clothing. Even sociologists form a subculture. As you are learning, they also use a unique language in their efforts to understand the world.

For a visual depiction of subcultures, see the photo essay on pages 50–51.

## Countercultures

Consider this quote from another subculture:

> If everyone applying for welfare had to supply a doctor's certificate of sterilization, if everyone who had committed a felony were sterilized, if anyone who had mental illness to any degree were sterilized—then our economy could easily take care of these people for the rest of their lives, giving them a decent living standard—but getting them out of the way. That way there would be no children abused, no surplus population, and, after a while, no pollution. . . .
>
> Now let's talk about stupidity. The level of intellect in this country is going down, generation after generation. The average IQ is always 100 because that is the accepted average. However, the kid with a 100 IQ today would have tested out at 70 when I was a lad. You get the concept . . . the marching morons. . . .
>
> When the . . . present world system collapses, it'll be good people like you who will be shooting people in the streets to feed their families. (Zellner 1995:58, 65)

Welcome to the world of the survivalists, where the message is much clearer than that of politicians—and much more disturbing.

The values and norms of most subcultures blend in with mainstream society. In some cases, however, as with these survivalists, some of the group's values and norms place it at odds with the dominant culture. Sociologists use the term **counterculture** to refer to such groups. To better see this distinction, consider motorcycle enthusiasts and motorcycle gangs. Motorcycle enthusiasts—who emphasize personal freedom and speed *and* affirm cultural values of success through work or education—are members of a subculture. In contrast, the Hells Angels, Pagans, and Bandidos not only stress freedom and speed but also value dirtiness and contempt toward women, work, and education. This makes them a counterculture.

An assault on core values is always met with resistance. To affirm their own values, members of the mainstream culture may ridicule, isolate, or even attack members of the counterculture. The Mormons, for example, were driven out of several states before they finally settled in Utah, which was then a wilderness. Even there, the federal government would not let them practice *polygyny* (one man having more than one wife), and Utah's statehood was made conditional on its acceptance of monogamy (Anderson 1942/1966).

# Values in U.S. Society

## An Overview of U.S. Values

As you know, the United States is a **pluralistic society,** made up of many different groups. The United States has numerous religious and racial–ethnic groups, as well as countless interest groups that focus on activities as divergent as collecting Barbie dolls and hunting deer. This state of affairs makes the job of specifying U.S. values difficult. Nonetheless, sociologists have tried to identify the underlying core values that are shared by most of the groups that make up U.S. society. Sociologist Robin Williams (1965) identified the following:

1. *Achievement and success.* Americans place a high value on personal achievement, especially outdoing others. This value includes getting ahead at work and school and attaining wealth, power, and prestige.

2. *Individualism.* Americans cherish the ideal that an individual can rise from the bottom of society to its very top. If someone fails to "get ahead," Americans generally find fault with that individual rather than with the social system for placing roadblocks in his or her path.

3. *Activity and work.* Americans expect people to work hard and to be busy doing some activity even when not at work. This value is becoming less important.

4. *Efficiency and practicality.* Americans award high marks for getting things done efficiently. Even in everyday life, Americans consider it important to do things fast, and they seek ways to increase efficiency.

5. *Science and technology.* Americans have a passion for applied science, for using science to control nature—to tame rivers and harness winds—and to develop new technology, from iPods to Segways.

6. *Progress.* Americans expect rapid technological change. They believe that they should constantly build "more and better" gadgets that will help them move toward some vague goal called "progress."

7. *Material comfort.* Americans expect a high level of material comfort. This comfort includes not only good nutrition, medical care, and housing but also late-model cars and recreational playthings—from Land Rovers to iPhones.

8. *Humanitarianism.* Americans emphasize personal kindness, aid in mass disasters, and organized philanthropy.

9. *Freedom.* This core value pervades U.S. life. It underscored the American Revolution, and Americans pride themselves on their personal freedom. The Mass Media in Social Life box on page 52 highlights an interesting study on how this core value applies to Native Americans.

10. *Democracy.* By this term, Americans refer to majority rule, to the right of everyone to express an opinion, and to representative government.

11. *Equality.* It is impossible to understand Americans without being aware of the central role that the value of equality plays in their lives. Equality of opportunity (part of the ideal culture discussed later) has significantly influenced U.S. history and continues to mark relations among the groups that make up U.S. society.

12. *Racism and group superiority.* Although it contradicts the values of freedom, democracy, and equality, Americans regard some groups more highly than others and have done so throughout their history. The slaughter of Native Americans and the enslavement of Africans are the most notorious examples.

In an earlier publication, I updated Williams' analysis by adding these three values:

13. *Education.* Americans are expected to go as far in school as their abilities and finances allow. Over the years, the definition of an "adequate" education has changed, and today a college education is considered an appropriate goal for most Americans. Those who have an opportunity for higher education and do not take it are sometimes viewed as doing something "wrong"—not merely as making a bad choice, but as somehow being involved in an immoral act.

14. *Religiosity.* There is a feeling that "every true American ought to be religious." This does not mean that everyone is expected to join a church, synagogue, or mosque, but that everyone ought to acknowledge a belief in a Supreme Being and follow some set of matching precepts. This value is so pervasive that Americans stamp "In God We Trust" on their money and declare in their national pledge of allegiance that they are "one nation under God."

15. *Romantic love.* Americans feel that the only proper basis for marriage is romantic love. Songs, literature, mass media, and "folk beliefs" all stress this value. They especially love the theme that "love conquers all."

## Value Clusters

As you can see, values are not independent units; some cluster together to form a larger whole. In the **value**

# Looking at **Subcultures**

**S**ubcultures can form around any interest or activity. Each subculture has its own values and norms that its members share, giving them a common identity. Each also has special terms that pinpoint the group's corner of life and that its members use to communicate with one another. Some of us belong to several subcultures simultaneously.

As you can see from these photos, most subcultures are compatible with the values of the dominant or mainstream culture. They represent specialized interests around which its members have chosen to build tiny worlds. Some subcultures, however, conflict with the mainstream culture. Sociologists give the name counterculture to subcultures whose values (such as those of outlaw motorcyclists) or activities and goals (such as those of terrorists) are opposed to the mainstream culture. Countercultures, however, are exceptional, and few of us belong to them.

Membership in this subculture is not easily awarded. High-steel ironworkers must prove not only that they are able to work at great heights but also that they fit into the group socially. Newcomers are tested by members of the group, and they must demonstrate that they can take joking without offense.

Values and interests are perhaps the two main characteristics of subcultures. What values and interests distinguish the modeling subculture?

The cabbies' subculture, centering on their occupational activities and interest, is also broken into smaller subcultures that reflect their experiences of race–ethnicity.

Participants in the rodeo subculture "advertise" their membership by wearing special clothing. The clothing symbolizes a set of values that unites its members. Among those values is the awarding of hyper-masculine status through the conquest of animals—or in this instance, the attempted conquest.

The subculture that centers on tattooing previously existed on the fringes of society, with seamen and circus folk its main participants. It now has entered the mainstream of society.

This subculture, with its fierce traditions, used to consist of white men. The subculture's painful adjustment to changed times is evident in its name being changed from firemen to fire-fighters.

Each subculture provides its members with values and distinctive ways of viewing the world. What values and perceptions do you think are common among body builders?

People who raise champion rams belong to a small subculture, in which the norms are explicit and high conformity is expected.

Why would people decorate themselves like this? Among the many reasons, one is to show their solidarity with the basket-ball subculture.

# MASS MEDIA in SOCIAL LIFE

## Why Do Native Americans Like Westerns?

Although Western movies go through a cycle of popularity, their themes are a mainstay of Hollywood. It is easy to see why Anglos might like Westerns. In their standard form, it is they who tame the wilderness while they defend themselves from the attacks of cruel, savage Indians who are intent on their destruction. But why would Indians like Westerns?

Sociologist JoEllen Shively, a Chippewa who grew up on Indian reservations in Montana and North Dakota, observed that Westerns are so popular that Native Americans bring bags of paperbacks into taverns to trade with one another. They even call each other "cowboy."

Intrigued, Shively decided to investigate the matter by showing a Western to adult Native Americans and Anglos in a reservation town. She matched the groups in education, age, income, and percentage of unemployment. To select the movie, Shively (1991, 1992) previewed more than seventy Westerns. She chose a John Wayne movie, *The Searchers,* because it not only focuses on conflict between Indians and cowboys but also shows the cowboys defeating the Indians. After the movie, the viewers filled out questionnaires, and Shively interviewed them.

She found something surprising: *All* Native Americans and Anglos identified with the cowboys; *none* identified with the Indians. Anglos and Native Americans, however, identified with the cowboys in different ways. Each projected a different fantasy onto the story. While Anglos

*Although John Wayne often portrayed an Anglo who kills Indians, Wayne is popular among Indian men. These men tend to identify with the cowboys, who reflect their values of bravery, autonomy, and toughness.*

saw the movie as an accurate portrayal of the Old West and a justification of their own status in society, Native Americans, in contrast, saw it as embodying a free, natural way of life. In fact, Native Americans said that they were the "real cowboys." They said, "Westerns relate to the way I wish I could live"; "He's not tied down to an eight-to-five job, day after day"; "He's his own man."

Shively adds,

> What appears to make Westerns meaningful to Indians is the fantasy of being free and independent like the cowboy. . . . Indians . . . find a fantasy in the cowboy story in which the important parts of their ways of life triumph and are morally good, validating their own cultural group in the context of a dramatically satisfying story.
>
> To express their real identity—a combination of marginality on the one hand, with a set of values which are about the land, autonomy, and being free—they [use] a cultural vehicle written for Anglos about Anglos, but it is one in which Indians invest a distinctive set of meanings that speak to their own experience, which they can read in a manner that affirms a way of life they value, or a fantasy they hold to.

In other words, values, not ethnicity, are the central issue. If a Native American film industry were to portray Native Americans with the same values that the Anglo movie industry projects onto cowboys, then Native Americans would identify with their own group. Thus, says Shively, Native Americans make cowboys "honorary Indians," for the cowboys express their values of bravery, autonomy, and toughness.

---

**cluster** that surrounds success, for example, we find hard work, education, efficiency, material comfort, and individualism bound up together. Americans are expected to go far in school, to work hard afterward, to be efficient, and then to attain a high level of material comfort, which, in turn, demonstrates success. Success is attributed to the individual's efforts; lack of success is blamed on his or her faults.

## Value Contradictions

Not all values fall into neat, integrated packages. Some even contradict one another. The value of group superiority contradicts freedom, democracy, and equality, producing a **value contradiction.** There simply cannot be full expression of freedom, democracy, and equality along with racism and sexism. Something has to give. One way in which Americans sidestepped this contradiction in the past was to say that freedom, democracy, and equality applied only to some groups. The contradiction was bound to surface over time, however, and so it did with the Civil War and the women's liberation movement. *It is precisely at the point of value contradictions, then, that one can see a major force for social change in a society.*

## Emerging Values

A value cluster of four interrelated core values—leisure, self-fulfillment, physical fitness, and youthfulness—is emerging in the United States. So is a fifth core value—concern for the environment.

1. *Leisure.* The emergence of leisure as a value is reflected in a huge recreation industry—from computer games, boats, vacation homes, and spa retreats to sports arenas, home theaters, extreme vacations, and luxury cruises.
2. *Self-fulfillment.* This value is reflected in the "human potential" movement, which emphasizes becoming "all one can be," and in magazine articles, books, and talk shows that focus on "self-help," "relating," and "personal development."
3. *Physical fitness.* Physical fitness is not a new U.S. value, but its increased emphasis is moving it into this emerging cluster. This trend is evident in the stress on nutrition and organic foods; obsessive attention to weight and diet; the growing number of joggers, cyclists, and backpackers; and the countless health clubs and physical fitness centers.
4. *Youthfulness.* Although valuing youth and disparaging old age are not new, some note a new sense of urgency. They attribute this to the huge number of aging baby boomers, who, aghast at the physical changes that accompany their advancing years, attempt to deny or at least postpone their biological fate. An extreme view is represented by a physician who claims that "aging is not a normal life event, but a disease" (Cowley 1996). It is not surprising, then, that techniques for maintaining and enhancing a youthful appearance—from cosmetic surgery to exotic creams and Botox injections—have become popular.

This emerging value cluster is a response to fundamental changes in U.S. society. Earlier generations of Americans were focused on forging a nation and fighting for economic survival. Today, millions of Americans are freed from long hours of work, and millions more are able to retire from work at an age when they anticipate decades of life ahead of them. This value cluster centers on helping people to maintain their health and vigor during their younger years and enabling them to enjoy their years of retirement.

5. *Concern for the environment.* During most of U.S. history, the environment was viewed as something to be exploited—a wilderness to be settled, forests to be cleared for farm land and lumber, rivers and lakes to be fished, and animals to be hunted. One result was the near extinction of the bison and the extinction in

The many groups that comprise the United States contribute to its culture. With their growing numbers, Latinos are making a greater impact on U.S. art, entertainment, music, and literature. This is also true of other areas of everyday life, such as customized vehicles. These "tricked out" cars at a show at Sturgeon Bay, Wisconsin, feature bumping hydraulics and ornate paint jobs.

*Values*, both those held by individuals and those that represent a nation or people, can undergo deep shifts. It is difficult for many of us to grasp the pride with which earlier Americans destroyed trees that took thousands of years to grow, that are located on only one tiny speck of the globe, and that we today consider part of the nation's and world's heritage. But this is a value statement, representing current views. The pride expressed on these woodcutters' faces represents another set of values entirely.

1915 of the passenger pigeon, a species of bird previously so numerous that its annual migration would darken the skies for days. Today, Americans have developed a genuine and apparently long-term concern for the environment.

This emerging value of environmental concern is related to the current stage of U.S. economic development: People act on environmental concerns only after they have met their basic needs. At this point in their development, for example, the world's poor nations have a difficult time "affording" this value.

## Culture Wars: When Values Clash

Challenges in core values are met with strong resistance by the people who hold them dear. They see changes as a threat to their way of life, an undermining of both their present and their future. Efforts to change gender roles, for example, arouse intense controversy, as does support for the marriage of homosexuals. Alarmed at such onslaughts against their values, traditionalists fiercely defend historical family relationships and the gender roles they grew up with. Today's clash in values is so severe that the term *culture wars* has been coined to refer to it. Compared with the violence directed against the Mormons, however, today's reactions to such controversies are mild.

## Values as Blinders

Just as values and their supporting beliefs paint a unique picture of reality, so they also form a view of what life *ought* to be like. Americans value individualism so highly, for example, that they tend to see almost everyone as free to pursue the goal of success. This value blinds them to circumstances that keep people from reaching this goal. The dire consequences of family poverty, parents' low education, and dead-end jobs tend to drop from sight. Instead, Americans cling to the notion that everyone can make it—if they put forth enough effort. And they "know" they are right, for every day, dangling before their eyes are enticing stories of individuals who have succeeded despite huge handicaps.

## "Ideal" Versus "Real" Culture

Many of the norms that surround cultural values are followed only partially. Differences always exist between a group's ideals and what its members actually do. Consequently, sociologists use the term **ideal culture** to refer to the values, norms, and goals that a group considers ideal, worth aspiring to. Success, for example, is part of ideal culture. Americans glorify academic progress, hard work, and the display of material goods as signs of individual achievement. What people actually do, however, usually falls short of the cultural ideal. Compared with their abilities, for example, most people don't work as hard as they could or go as far as they could in school. Sociologists call the norms and values that people actually follow **real culture.**

# Technology in the Global Village

## The New Technology

The gestures, language, values, folkways, and mores that we have discussed—all are part of symbolic or nonmaterial culture. Culture, as you recall, also has a material aspect: a group's *things*, from its houses to its toys. Central to a group's material culture is its technology. In its simplest sense, **technology** can be equated with tools. In a broader sense, technology also includes the skills or procedures necessary to make and use those tools.

We can use the term **new technology** to refer to an emerging technology that has a significant impact on social life. People develop minor technologies all the time. Most are slight modifications of existing technologies. Occasionally, however, they develop a technology that makes a major impact on human life. It is primarily to these innovations that the term *new technology* refers. For people 500 or 600 years ago, the new technology was the printing press. For us, the new technology consists of computers, satellites, and the Internet.

The sociological significance of technology goes far beyond the tool itself. *Technology sets the framework for a group's nonmaterial culture.* If a group's technology changes, so do people's ways of thinking and how they relate to one another. An example is gender relations. Through the centuries and throughout the world, it has been the custom (the nonmaterial culture of a group) for men to dominate women. Today's global communications (the material culture) make this custom more difficult to maintain. For example, when Arab

The adoption of new forms of communication by people who not long ago were cut off from events in the rest of the world is bound to change their *nonmaterial culture.* How do you think the views of the world of this man in Varanasi, India, are changing?

women watch Western television, they observe much freer gender relations. As these women talk to other women by e-mail and telephone, their communications both convey and create discontent, as well as feelings of sisterhood. These communications motivate some of them to agitate for social change.

In today's world, the long-accepted idea that it is proper to withhold rights on the basis of someone's sex can no longer be sustained. What is usually beyond our awareness in this revolutionary change is the role of the new technology, which joins the world's nations into a global communications network.

## Cultural Lag and Cultural Change

About three generations ago, sociologist William Ogburn (1922/1938), a functional analyst, coined the term **cultural lag.** By this, Ogburn meant that not all parts of a culture change at the same pace. When one part of a culture changes, other parts lag behind.

Ogburn pointed out that *a group's material culture usually changes first, with the nonmaterial culture lagging behind,* playing a game of catch-up. For example, when we get sick, we can type our symptoms into a computer and get an immediate diagnosis and a recommended course of treatment. In some tests, computers outperform physicians. Yet our customs have not caught up with our technology, and we continue to visit the doctor's office.

Sometimes nonmaterial culture never catches up. Instead, we rigorously hold onto some outmoded form—one that once was needed, but that long ago was bypassed by technology. A striking example is our nine-month school year. Have you ever wondered why it is nine months long, and why we take summers off? For most of us, this is "just the way it's always been," and we have never questioned it. But there is more to this custom than meets the eye, for it is an example of cultural lag.

In the late 1800s, when universal schooling came about, the school year matched the technology of the time, which was labor-intensive. Most parents were farmers, and for survival, they needed their children's help at the crucial times of planting and harvesting. Today, generations later, when few people farm and there is no need for the school year to be so short, we still live with this cultural lag.

## Technology and Cultural Leveling

For most of human history, communication was limited and travel slow. Consequently, in their relative isolation, human groups developed highly distinctive ways of life as they responded to the particular situations they faced. The unique characteristics they developed that distinguished one culture from another tended to change little over time. The Tasmanians, who lived on a remote island off the coast of Australia, provide an extreme example. For thousands of years, they had no contact with other people. They were so isolated that they did not even know how to make clothing or fire (Edgerton 1992).

Except in such rare instances, humans have always had *some* contact with other groups. During these contacts, people learned from one another, adopting things they found desirable. In this process, called **cultural diffusion,** groups are most open to changes in their technology or material culture. They usually are eager, for example, to adopt superior weapons and tools. In remote jungles in South America one can find metal cooking pots, steel axes, and even bits of clothing spun in mills in South Carolina. Although the direction of cultural diffusion today is primarily from the West to other parts of the world, cultural diffusion is not a one-way street—as bagels, woks, hammocks, and sushi in the United States attest.

With today's travel and communications, cultural diffusion is occurring rapidly. Air travel has made it possible to journey around the globe in a matter of hours. In the not-so-distant past, a trip from the United States to Africa was so unusual that only a few adventurous people made it, and newspapers would herald their feat. Today, hundreds of thousands make the trip each year.

The changes in communication are no less vast. Communication used to be limited to face-to-face speech, written messages that were passed from hand to hand, and visual signals such as smoke or light that was reflected from mirrors. Despite newspapers, people in some parts of the United States did not hear that the Civil War had ended until weeks and even months after it was over. Today's electronic communications transmit messages across the globe in a matter of seconds, and we learn almost instantaneously what is happening on the other side of the world. During Gulf War II, reporters traveled with U.S. soldiers, and for the first time in history, the public was able to view live video reports of battles and deaths as they occurred.

Travel and communication unite us to such an extent that there is almost no "other side of the world" anymore. One result is **cultural leveling,** a process in which cultures become similar to one another. The globalization of capitalism brings with it both technology and Western culture. Japan, for example, has adopted not only capitalism but also Western forms of dress and music. These changes have transformed Japan into a blend of Western and Eastern cultures.

Cultural leveling is occurring rapidly around the world, as is apparent to any traveler. The Golden Arches of McDonald's welcome today's visitors to Tokyo, Paris, London, Madrid, Moscow, Hong Kong, and Beijing. When I visited a jungle village in India—no electricity, no running water, and so remote that the only entrance was by a footpath—I saw a young man sporting a cap with the Nike emblem.

Although the bridging of geography and culture by electronic signals and the exportation of Western icons do not in and of themselves mark the end of traditional cultures, the inevitable result is some degree of *cultural leveling,* some blander, less distinctive way of life—U.S. culture with French, Japanese, and Brazilian accents, so to speak. Although the "cultural accent" remains, something vital is lost forever.

# SUMMARY *and* REVIEW

## What Is Culture?

All human groups possess **culture**—language, beliefs, values, norms, and material objects that are passed from one generation to the next. **Material culture** consists of objects (art, buildings, clothing, weapons, tools). **Nonmaterial** (or **symbolic**) **culture** is a group's ways of thinking and its patterns of behavior. **Ideal culture** is a group's ideal values, norms, and goals. **Real culture** is the group's actual behavior, which often falls short of its cultural ideals. Pp. 36–38.

*What are cultural relativism and ethnocentrism?*

People are naturally **ethnocentric;** that is, they use their own culture as a yardstick for judging the ways of others. In contrast, those who embrace **cultural relativism** try to understand other cultures on those cultures' own terms. P. 39.

## Components of Symbolic Culture

*What are the components of nonmaterial culture?*

The central component is **symbols,** anything to which people attach meaning and that they use to communicate with others. Universally, the symbols of nonmaterial culture are **gestures, language, values, norms, sanctions, folkways,** and **mores.** Pp. 39–43.

*Why is language so significant to culture?*

**Language** allows human experience to be goal-directed, cooperative, and cumulative. It also lets humans move beyond the present and share a past, future, and other common perspectives. According to the **Sapir-Whorf hypothesis,** language even shapes our thoughts and perceptions. Pp. 43–44.

*How do values, norms, sanctions, folkways, and mores reflect culture?*

All groups have **values,** standards by which they define what is desirable or undesirable, and **norms,** rules or expectations about behavior. Groups use **positive sanctions** to show approval of those who follow their norms and **negative sanctions** to show disapproval of those who do not. Norms that are not strictly enforced are called **folkways,** while **mores** are norms to which groups demand conformity because they reflect core values. Pp. 44–47.

## Many Cultural Worlds

*How do subcultures and countercultures differ?*

A **subculture** is a group whose values and related behaviors distinguish its members from the general culture. A **counterculture** holds some values that stand in opposition to those of the dominant culture. P. 48.

## Values in U.S. Society

*What are the core U.S. values?*

Although the United States is a **pluralistic society,** made up of many groups, each with its own set of values, certain values dominate: achievement and success, individualism, activity and work, efficiency and practicality, science and technology, progress, material comfort, equality, freedom, democracy, humanitarianism, racism and group superiority, education, religiosity, and romantic love. Some values cluster together (**value clusters**) to form a larger whole. **Value contradictions** (such as equality and racism) indicate areas of tension, which are likely points of social change. Leisure, self-fulfillment, physical fitness, youthfulness, and concern for the environment are emerging core values. Core values do not change without opposition. Pp. 48–55.

## Technology in the Global Village

*How is technology changing culture?*

William Ogburn coined the term **cultural lag** to describe how a group's nonmaterial culture lags behind its changing technology. With today's technological advances in travel and communications, **cultural diffusion** is occurring rapidly. This leads to **cultural leveling,** groups adopting Western culture in place of their own customs. Much of the richness of the world's diverse cultures is being lost in the process. Pp. 55–56.

# THINKING CRITICALLY *about* Chapter 2

1. Do you favor ethnocentrism or cultural relativism? Explain your position.

2. Do you think that the language change in Miami, Florida (discussed on page 45) is an indicator of the future of the United States? Why or why not?

3. Are you a member of any subcultures? Which one(s)? Why do you think that your group is a subculture? What is your group's relationship to the mainstream culture?

# ADDITIONAL RESOURCES

## What can you find in MySocLab? mysoclab www.mysoclab.com

- **Complete Ebook**
- **Practice Tests and Video and Audio activities**
- **Mapping and Data Analysis exercises**

- **Sociology in the News**
- **Classic Readings in Sociology**
- **Research and Writing advice**

## Where Can I Read More on This Topic?

Suggested readings for this chapter are listed at the back of this book.

# Socialization

The old man was horrified when he found out. Life never had been good since his daughter lost her hearing when she was just 2 years old. She couldn't even talk—just fluttered her hands around trying to tell him things.

Over the years, he had gotten used to that. But now . . . he shuddered at the thought of her being pregnant. No one would be willing to marry her; he knew that. And the neighbors, their tongues would never stop wagging. Everywhere he went, he could hear people talking behind his back.

> Her behavior toward strangers, especially men, was almost that of a wild animal, manifesting much fear and hostility.

If only his wife were still alive, maybe she could come up with something. What should he do? He couldn't just kick his daughter out into the street.

After the baby was born, the old man tried to shake his feelings, but they wouldn't let loose. Isabelle was a pretty name, but every time he looked at the baby he felt sick to his stomach.

He hated doing it, but there was no way out. His daughter and her baby would have to live in the attic.

Unfortunately, this is a true story. Isabelle was discovered in Ohio in 1938 when she was about 6½ years old, living in a dark room with her deaf-mute mother. Isabelle couldn't talk, but she did use gestures to communicate with her mother. An inadequate diet and lack of sunshine had given Isabelle a disease called rickets:

> [Her legs]were so bowed that as she stood erect the soles of her shoes came nearly flat together, and she got about with a skittering gait. Her behavior toward strangers, especially men, was almost that of a wild animal, manifesting much fear and hostility. In lieu of speech she made only a strong croaking sound. (Davis 1940/2007:156–157)

When the newspapers reported this case, sociologist Kingsley Davis decided to find out what had happened to Isabelle after her discovery. We'll come back to that later, but first let's use the case of Isabelle to gain insight into human nature.

# What Is Human Nature?

For centuries, people have been intrigued with the question of what is human about human nature. How much of a person's characteristics comes from "nature" (heredity) and how much from "nurture" (the **social environment,** contact with others)? One way to answer this question is to study identical twins who were separated at birth and reared in different environments, such as those discussed in the Down-to-Earth Sociology box on the next page. Another way is to examine children who have had little human contact. Let's consider such children.

## Feral Children

Over the centuries, people have occasionally found children living in the forests. Supposedly, these children could not speak; they bit, scratched, growled, and walked on all fours. They drank by lapping water, ate grass, tore ravenously at raw meat, and showed an insensitivity to pain and cold. These stories of what are called **feral children** sound like exaggerations, and it is easy to dismiss them as folk myth.

Because of what happened in 1798, however, we can't be so sure. In that year, a child who walked on all fours and could not speak was found in the forests of Aveyron, France. "The wild boy of Aveyron," as this child became known, would have been simply another of those legends, except that French scientists took the child to a laboratory and studied him. Like the children in the earlier informal reports, this child, too, gave no indication of feeling the cold. Most startling, though, the boy would growl when he saw a small animal, pounce on it, and devour it uncooked. Even today, the scientists' detailed reports make fascinating reading (Itard 1962).

Ever since I read Itard's account of this boy, I've been fascinated by the seemingly fantastic possibility that animals could rear human children. In 2002, I received a report from a contact in Cambodia that a feral child had been found in the jungles. When I had the opportunity the following year to visit the child and interview his caregivers, I grabbed it. The boy's photo is to the right.

If we were untouched by society, would we be like feral children? By nature, would our behavior be like that of wild animals? That is the sociolog-

ical question. Unable to study feral children, sociologists have studied isolated children, like Isabelle in our opening vignette.

## Isolated Children

Reports of isolated children are well documented. What can they tell us about human nature? We can first conclude that humans have no natural language, for Isabelle and others like her are unable to speak.

But maybe Isabelle was mentally impaired, and she simply was not able to progress through the usual stages of development. When Isabelle was given her first intelligence test, she scored practically zero. But after a few months of intensive language training, she was able to speak in short sentences. In about a year, she could write a few words, do simple addition, and retell stories after hearing them. Seven months later, she had a vocabulary of almost 2,000 words. In just two years, Isabelle reached the intellectual level that is normal for her age. She then went on to school, where she was "bright, cheerful, energetic . . . and participated in all school activities as normally as other children" (Davis 1940/2007:157–158).

As discussed in the previous chapter, language is the key to human development. Without language, people have no mechanism for developing and communicating thought. Unlike animals, humans have no instincts that take the place of language. If an individual lacks language, he or she lives in an isolated world—a world of internal silence, without shared ideas, lacking connections to others.

*Without language, there can be no culture—no shared way of life—and culture is the key to what people become.* Each of us possesses a biological heritage, but this heritage does not

One of the reasons I went to Cambodia was to interview a feral child—the boy shown here—who supposedly had been raised by monkeys. When I arrived at the remote location where the boy was living, I was disappointed to find that the story was only partially true. During its reign of terror, the Khmer Rouge had shot and killed the boy's parents, leaving him, at about the age of two, abandoned on an island. Some months later, villagers found him in the care of monkeys. They shot the female monkey who was carrying the boy. Not quite a feral child—but the closest I'll ever come to one.

## *Down-to-Earth Sociology*
## Heredity or Environment? The Case of Jack and Oskar, Identical Twins

Identical twins share exactly the same genetic heredity. One fertilized egg divides to produce two embryos. If heredity determines personality—or attitudes, temperament, skills, and intelligence—then identical twins should be identical not only in their looks but also in these characteristics.

The fascinating case of Jack and Oskar helps us unravel this mystery. From their experience, we can see the far-reaching effects of the environment—how social experiences take precedence over biology.

Jack Yufe and Oskar Stohr are identical twins born in 1932 to a Jewish father and a Catholic mother. They were separated as babies after their parents divorced. Jack was reared in Trinidad by his father. There, he learned loyalty to Jews and hatred of Hitler and the Nazis. After the war, Jack and his father moved to Israel. When he was 17, Jack joined a kibbutz and later served in the Israeli army.

Oskar's upbringing was a mirror image of Jack's. Oskar was reared in Czechoslovakia by his mother's mother, who was a strict Catholic. When Oskar was a toddler, Hitler annexed this area of Czechoslovakia, and Oskar learned to love Hitler and to hate Jews. He joined the Hitler Youth (a sort of Boy Scout organization, except that this one was designed to instill the "virtues" of patriotism, loyalty, obedience—and hatred).

In 1954, the two brothers met. It was a short meeting, and Jack had been warned not to tell Oskar that they were Jews. Twenty-five years later, in 1979, when they were 47 years old, social scientists at the University of Minnesota brought them together again. These researchers figured that because Jack and Oskar had the same genes, any differences they showed would have to be the result of their environment—their different social experiences.

Not only did Jack and Oskar hold different attitudes toward the war, Hitler, and Jews but their basic orientations to life were also different. In their politics, Jack was liberal, while Oskar was more conservative. Jack was a workaholic, while Oskar enjoyed leisure. And, as you can predict, Jack was very proud of being a Jew. Oskar, who by this time knew that he was a Jew, wouldn't even mention it.

*The question of the relative influence of heredity and the environment in human behavior has fascinated and plagued researchers. To try to answer this question, researchers have studied identical twins. Some human behaviors, such as beliefs, political and otherwise, are clearly due to the environment, but uncertainty remains about the origin of other behaviors.*

That would seem to settle the matter. But there was another side. The researchers also found that Jack and Oskar had both excelled at sports as children, but had difficulty with math. They also had the same rate of speech, and both liked sweet liqueur and spicy foods. Strangely, both flushed the toilet both before and after using it and enjoyed startling people by sneezing in crowded elevators.

### For Your Consideration

Heredity or environment? How much influence does each one have? The question is not yet settled, but at this point it seems fair to conclude that the *limits* of certain physical and mental abilities are established by heredity (such as ability at sports and aptitude for mathematics), while attitudes are the result of the environment. Basic temperament, though, seems to be inherited. Although the answer is still fuzzy, we can put it this way: For some parts of life, the blueprint is drawn by heredity; but even here the environment can redraw those lines. For other parts, the individual is a blank slate, and it is up to the environment to determine what is written on that slate.

*Sources:* Based on Begley 1979; Chen 1979; Wright 1995; Segal and Hershberger 2005.

determine specific behaviors, attitudes, or values. It is our culture that superimposes the specifics of what we become onto our biological heritage.

## Institutionalized Children

Other than language, what else is required for a child to develop into what we consider a healthy, balanced, intelligent human being? We find part of the answer in an intriguing experiment from the 1930s. Back then, parents died a lot younger, and orphanages were common throughout the United States. Children reared in orphanages often had difficulty establishing close bonds with others—and they tended to have low IQs. "Common sense" (which we noted in Chapter 1 is unreliable) told everyone that the cause of mental retardation is biological ("They're just born that way"). But then two psychologists, H. M. Skeels and H. B. Dye (1939), began to suspect a social cause.

For background on their experiment, Skeels (1966) provides this account of a "good" orphanage in Iowa during the 1930s, where he and Dye were consultants:

> Until about six months, they were cared for in the infant nursery. The babies were kept in standard hospital cribs that often had protective sheeting on the sides, thus effectively limiting visual stimulation; no toys or other objects were hung in the infants' line of vision. Human interactions were limited to busy nurses who, with the speed born of practice and necessity, changed diapers or bedding, bathed and medicated the infants, and fed them efficiently with propped bottles.

Perhaps, thought Skeels and Dye, the absence of stimulating social interaction was the problem, not some biological incapacity on the part of the children. To test their controversial idea, they selected thirteen infants whose mental retardation was so obvious that no one wanted to adopt them. They placed them in an institution for the mentally retarded. Each infant, then about 19 months old, was assigned to a separate ward of women ranging in mental age from 5 to 12 and in chronological age from 18 to 50. The women were pleased with this arrangement. Not only did they take care of the infants' physical needs—diapering, feeding, and so on—but also they loved to play with the children. They cuddled them and showered them with attention. They even competed to see which ward would have "its baby" walking or talking first. Each child also had one woman who became "particularly attached" and figuratively adopted him or her.

As a consequence, an intense one-to-one adult-child relationship developed, which was supplemented by the less intense but frequent interactions with the other adults in the environment. Each child had some one person with whom he [or she] was identified and who was particularly interested in him [or her] and his [or her] achievements. (Skeels 1966)

The researchers left a control group of twelve infants at the orphanage. These infants were also thought to have low IQs, but they were considered higher in intelligence than the other thirteen. They received the usual care. Two and a half years later, Skeels and Dye tested all the children's intelligence. Their findings were startling: Those assigned to the care of women in the institution had gained an average of 28 IQ points while those who remained in the orphanage had lost 30 points.

What happened after these children were grown? Did these initial differences matter? Twenty-one years later, Skeels and Dye did a follow-up study. Those in the control group who had remained in the orphanage had, on average, less than a third-grade education. Four still lived in state institutions, while the others held low-level jobs. Only two had married. In contrast, the average level of education for the thirteen individuals in the experimental group was twelve grades (about normal for that period). Five had completed one or more years of college. One had even gone to graduate school. Eleven had married. All thirteen were self-supporting or were homemakers (Skeels 1966). Apparently, then, one characteristic that we take for granted as being a basic "human" trait—high intelligence—depends on early, close relations with other humans.

A recent experiment in India confirms the Skeels and Dye research. Many of India's orphanages are similar to the ones that Skeels and Dye studied, dismal places where unattended children lie in bed all day. When experimenters added stimulating play and interaction to the children's activities, the children's motor skills improved and their IQs increased (Taneja et al. 2002). The longer that children lack stimulating interaction, though, the more difficulty they have intellectually (Meese 2005).

Let's consider one other case, the story of Genie:

> In 1970, California authorities found Genie, a 13-year-old girl who had been locked in a small room and tied to a chair since she was 20 months old. Apparently her father (70 years old when Genie was discovered) hated children, and probably had caused the death of two of Genie's siblings. Her 50-year-old mother was partially blind and frightened of her husband. Genie could not speak, did not know how to chew, was unable to stand upright, and could

not straighten her hands and legs. On intelligence tests, she scored at the level of a 1-year-old. After intensive training, Genie learned to walk and use simple sentences (although they were garbled). As she grew up, her language remained primitive, she took anyone's property if it appealed to her, and she went to the bathroom wherever she wanted. At the age of 21, Genie went to live in a home for adults who cannot live alone. (Pines 1981)

**In Sum:** From Genie's pathetic story and from reports of institutionalized children, we can conclude that the basic human traits of intelligence and the ability to establish close bonds with others depend on early interaction with other humans. In addition, apparently there is a period prior to age 13 in which children must experience language and human bonding if they are to develop high intelligence and the ability to be sociable and follow social norms.

## Deprived Animals

Finally, let's consider animals that have been deprived of normal interaction. In a series of experiments with rhesus monkeys, psychologists Harry and Margaret Harlow demonstrated the importance of early learning. The Harlows (1962) raised baby monkeys in isolation. They gave each monkey two artificial mothers. One "mother" was only a wire frame with a wooden head, but it did have a nipple from which the baby could nurse. The frame of the other "mother," which had no bottle, was covered with soft terrycloth. To obtain food, the baby monkeys nursed at the wire frame.

When the Harlows (1965) frightened the baby monkeys with a mechanical bear or dog, the babies did not run to the wire frame "mother." Instead, as shown by this photo, they would cling pathetically to their terrycloth "mother." The Harlows concluded that infant–mother bonding is not the result of feeding but, rather, of what they termed "intimate physical contact." To most of us, this phrase means cuddling.

In one of their many experiments, the Harlows isolated baby monkeys for different lengths of time. They found that when monkeys were isolated for shorter periods (about three months), they were able to overcome the effects of their isolation. Those isolated for six months or more, however, were unable to adjust to normal monkey life. They could not play or engage in pretend fights, and the other monkeys rejected them. In other words, the longer the period of isolation, the more difficult its effects are to overcome. In addition, a critical learning stage may exist: If that stage is missed, it may be impossible to compensate for what has been lost. This may have been the case with Genie.

Because humans are not monkeys, we must be careful about extrapolating from animal studies to human behavior. The Harlow experiments, however, support what we know about children who are reared in isolation.

**In Sum: Society Makes Us Human** Apparently, babies do not develop "naturally" into human adults. If children are reared in isolation, their bodies grow, but they become little more than big animals. Without the concepts that language provides, they can't experience or even grasp relationships between people (the "connections" we call brother, sister, parent, friend, teacher, and so on). And without warm, friendly interactions, they don't become "friendly" in the accepted sense of the term, nor do they cooperate with others. In short, it is through human contact that people learn to be members of the human community. This process by which we learn the ways of society (or of particular groups), called **socialization,** is what sociologists have in mind when they say "Society makes us human."

# Socialization into the Self and Mind

At birth, babies have no idea that they are separate beings. They don't even know that they are a he or she. How do we humans develop a **self,** our image of who we are? How do we develop our ability to reason? Let's see how this occurs.

Like humans, monkeys need interaction to thrive. Those raised in isolation are unable to interact satisfactorily with other monkeys. In this photograph, we see one of the monkeys described in the text. Purposefully frightened by the experimenter, the monkey has taken refuge in the soft terrycloth draped over its artificial "mother."

## Cooley and the Looking-Glass Self

About a hundred years ago, Charles Horton Cooley (1864–1929), a symbolic interactionist who taught at the University of Michigan, concluded that this unique aspect of "humanness" called the self is socially created. He said that *our sense of self develops from interaction with others.* Cooley (1902) coined the term **looking-glass self** to describe the process by which our sense of self develops. He summarized this idea in the following couplet:

**Each to each a looking-glass**
**Reflects the other that doth pass.**

The looking-glass self contains three elements:

1. *We imagine how we appear to those around us.* For example, we may think that others perceive us as witty or dull.
2. *We interpret others' reactions.* We come to conclusions about how others evaluate us. Do they like us for being witty? Do they dislike us for being dull?
3. *We develop a self-concept.* How we interpret others' reactions to us frames our feelings and ideas about ourselves. A favorable reflection in this *social mirror* leads to a positive self-concept; a negative reflection leads to a negative self-concept.

Note that the development of the self does *not* depend on accurate evaluations. Even if we grossly misinterpret how others think about us, those misjudgments become part of our self-concept. Note also that *although the self-concept begins in childhood, its development is an ongoing, lifelong process.* The three steps of the looking-glass self are a part of our everyday lives: As we monitor how others react to us, we continually modify the self. The self, then, is never a finished product—it is always in process, even into old age.

## Mead and Role Taking

Another symbolic interactionist, George Herbert Mead (1863–1931), who taught at the University of Chicago,

added that play is crucial to the development of a self. In play, children learn to **take the role of the other,** that is, to put themselves in someone else's shoes—to understand how someone else feels and thinks and to anticipate how that person will act.

Only gradually do children attain this ability (Mead 1934; Denzin 2007). Psychologist John Flavel (1968) asked 8- and 14-year-olds to explain a board game to some children who were blindfolded and to others who were not. The 14-year-olds gave more detailed instructions to those who were blindfolded, but the 8-year-olds gave the same instructions to everyone. The younger children could not yet take the role of the other, while the older children could.

As they develop this ability, at first children are able to take only the role of **significant others,** individuals who significantly influence their lives, such as parents or siblings. By assuming their roles during play, such as dressing up in their parents' clothing, children cultivate the ability to put themselves in the place of significant others.

As the self gradually develops, children internalize the expectations of more and more people. Their ability to take the roles of others eventually extends to being able

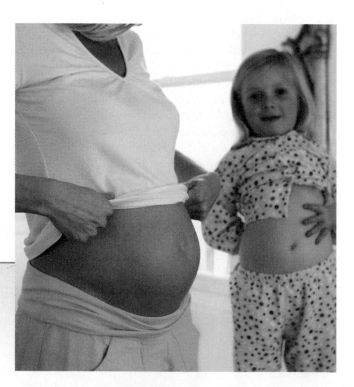

Mead analyzed *taking the role of the other* as an essential part of learning to be a full-fledged member of society. At first, we are able to take the role only of *significant others,* as this child is doing. Later we develop the capacity to take the role of *the generalized other,* which is essential not only for extended cooperation but also for the control of antisocial desires.

to take the role of "the group as a whole." Mead used the term **generalized other** to refer to our perception of how people in general think of us.

Taking the role of others is essential if we are to become cooperative members of human groups—whether they be our family, friends, or co-workers. This ability allows us to modify our behavior by anticipating how others will react—something Genie never learned.

As Figure 3.1 illustrates, we go through three stages as we learn to take the role of the other:

1. *Imitation.* Children under age 3 can only mimic others. They do not yet have a sense of self separate from others, and they can only imitate people's gestures and words. (This stage is actually not role taking, but it prepares the child for it.)
2. *Play.* During the second stage, from the ages of about 3 to 6, children pretend to take the roles of specific people. They might pretend that they are a firefighter, a wrestler, a nurse, Supergirl, Spiderman, a princess, and so on. They also like costumes at this stage and enjoy dressing up in their parents' clothing or tying a towel around their neck to "become" Spiderman or Wonder Woman.
3. *Team Games.* This third stage, organized play, or team games, begins roughly with the early school years. The significance for the self is that to play these games the individual must be able to take multiple roles. One of Mead's favorite examples was that of a baseball game, in which each player must be able to take the role of all the other players. To play baseball, the child not only must

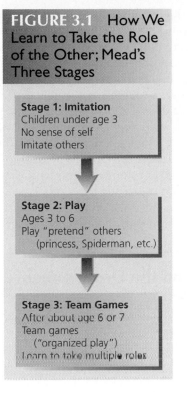

**FIGURE 3.1    How We Learn to Take the Role of the Other; Mead's Three Stages**

**Stage 1: Imitation**
Children under age 3
No sense of self
Imitate others

↓

**Stage 2: Play**
Ages 3 to 6
Play "pretend" others
(princess, Spiderman, etc.)

↓

**Stage 3: Team Games**
After about age 6 or 7
Team games
("organized play")
Learn to take multiple roles

know his or her own role but also must be able to anticipate who will do what when the ball is hit or thrown.

Mead also said there were two parts of the self, the "I" and the "me." The "*I*" is *the self as subject*, the active, spontaneous, creative part of the self. In contrast, the "*me*" is *the self as object*. It is made up of attitudes we internalize from our interactions with others. Mead chose these pronouns because in English "I" is the active agent, as in "I shoved him," while "me" is the object of action, as in "He shoved me." Mead stressed that we are not

To help his students understand the term *generalized other*, Mead used baseball as an illustration. Why are team sports and organized games such excellent examples to use in explaining this concept?

passive in the socialization process. We are not like robots, passively absorbing the responses of others. Rather, our "I" is active. It evaluates the reactions of others and organizes them into a unified whole. Mead added that the "I" even monitors the "me," fine-tuning our actions to help us better match what others expect of us.

Mead also drew a conclusion that some find startling: *Both the self and the human mind are social products.* Mead stressed that we cannot think without symbols. But where do these symbols come from? Only from society, which gives us our symbols by giving us language. If society did not provide the symbols, we would not be able to think and thus would not possess what we call the mind. The mind, then, like language, is a product of society.

## Piaget and the Development of Reasoning

An essential part of being human is the ability to reason. How do we learn this skill?

This question intrigued Jean Piaget (1896–1980), a Swiss psychologist who noticed that young children give similar wrong answers when they take intelligence tests. He thought that young children might be using some consistent, but incorrect, reasoning to figure out their answers. Perhaps children go through a natural process as they learn how to reason.

To find out, Piaget set up a laboratory where he could give children of different ages various problems to solve (Piaget 1950, 1954; Flavel et al. 2002). After years of testing, Piaget concluded that children go through four stages as they develop their ability to reason. (If you mentally substitute "reasoning skills" for the term *operational* in the following explanations, Piaget's findings will be easier to understand.)

1. **The sensorimotor stage** (from birth to about age 2) During this stage, understanding is limited to direct contact with the environment—sucking, touching, listening, looking. Infants do not "think" in any sense that we understand. During the first part of this stage, they do not even know that their bodies are separate from the environment. Indeed, they have yet to discover that they have toes. Neither can infants recognize cause and effect. That is, they do not know that their actions cause something to happen.

2. **The preoperational stage** (from about age 2 to age 7) During this stage, children *develop the ability to use symbols.* However, they do not yet understand common concepts such as size, speed, or causation. Although they can count, they do not really understand what numbers mean. Nor do they yet have the ability to take the role of the other. Piaget asked preoperational children to describe a clay model of a mountain range. They did just fine. But when he asked them to describe how the mountain range looked from where another child was sitting, they couldn't do it. They could only repeat what they saw from their view.

3. **The concrete operational stage** (from the age of about 7 to 12) Although reasoning abilities are more developed, they remain *concrete*. Children can now understand numbers, causation, and speed, and they are able to take the role of the other and to participate in team games. Without concrete examples, however, they are unable to talk about concepts such as truth, honesty, or justice. They can explain why Jane's answer was a lie, but they cannot describe what truth itself is.

4. **The formal operational stage** (after the age of about 12) Children are now capable of abstract thinking. They can talk about concepts, come to conclusions based on general principles, and use rules to solve abstract problems. During this stage, children are likely to become young philosophers (Kagan 1984). If shown a photo of a slave, for example, a child at the concrete operational stage might have said, "That's wrong!" However, a child at the formal operational stage is likely to add, "If our county was founded on equality, how could people have owned slaves?"

## Global Aspects of the Self and Reasoning

Cooley's conclusions about the looking-glass self appear to be true for everyone around the world. So do Mead's conclusions about role taking and the mind as a social product, although researchers are finding that the self may develop earlier than Mead indicated. The stages of reasoning that Piaget identified probably also occur worldwide, although researchers have found that the stages are not as distinct as Piaget concluded and the ages at which individuals enter the stages differ from one person to another (Flavel et al. 2002). Even during the sensorimotor stage, for example, children show early signs of reasoning, which may indicate an innate ability that is wired into the brain.

Although Piaget's theory is being refined, his contribution remains: *A basic structure underlies the way we develop our ability to reason, and children all over the world begin with the concrete and move to the abstract.*

Interestingly, some people seem to get stuck in the concreteness of the third stage and never reach the fourth stage of abstract thinking (Kohlberg and Gilligan 1971; Suizzo 2000). College, for example, nurtures the fourth stage, and most people without this experience apparently have less ability for abstract thought. Social experiences, then, can modify these stages. Also, there is much that we don't yet know about how culture influences the way we think, a topic explored in the Cultural Diversity box below.

# Cultural Diversity around the World

## Do You See What I See? Eastern and Western Ways of Perceiving and Thinking

**W**hich two of these items go together: a panda, a monkey, and a banana? Please answer before you read further. You probably said the panda and the monkey. Both are animals, while the banana is a fruit. This is logical.

At least this is the logic of Westerners. Someone from Japan, however, is more likely to reply that the monkey and the banana go together. Westerners typically see categories (animals and fruit), but Asians typically see relationships (monkeys eat bananas). This distinction illustrates how culture sets the stage for our perception.

In one study, Japanese and U.S. students were shown a picture of an aquarium that contained one big, fast-moving fish and several smaller fish, along with plants, a rock, and bubbles. Later, when the students were asked what they had seen, the Japanese students were 60 percent more likely to remember background elements. They also referred more to relationships, such as the "the little pink fish was in front of the blue rock."

The students were also shown ninety-six objects and asked which of them had been in the picture.

*What do you see when you look at this aquarium? Perception depends not only on biology but also on culture.*

The Japanese students did much better at remembering when the object was shown in its original surroundings. The U.S. students, in contrast, had not noticed the background.

Westerners pay more attention to the focal object—in this case, the fish—while Asians are more attuned to the overall surroundings. The implications of this difference run deep: Easterners attribute less causation to actors and more to context, while Westerners minimize the context and place greater emphasis on individual actors.

Differences in how Westerners and Easterners perceive the world and think about it are just being uncovered. We know practically nothing about how these differences originate. *Because these initial findings indicate deep, culturally based, fundamental differences in perception and thinking, this should prove to be a fascinating area of research.*

### For Your Consideration

In our global village, differences in perception and thinking can have potentially devastating effects. Consider a crisis between the United States and North Korea. How might Easterners and Westerners see the matter differently? How might they attribute cause differently and, without knowing it, "talk past one another"?

*Sources:* Based on Nisbett 2003; Davies 2007.

# Learning Personality, Morality, and Emotions

Our personality, morality, and emotions are vital aspects of who we are. Let's look at how we learn these essential aspects of our being.

## Freud and the Development of Personality

Along with the development of our mind and the self comes the development of our personality. Sigmund Freud (1856–1939) developed a theory of the origin of personality that has had a major impact on Western thought. Freud, a physician in Vienna in the early 1900s, founded *psychoanalysis,* a technique for treating emotional problems through long-term, intensive exploration of the subconscious mind. Let's look at his theory.

Freud believed that personality consists of three elements. Each child is born with the first element, an **id,** Freud's term for inborn drives that cause us to seek self-gratification. The id of the newborn is evident in its cries of hunger or pain. The pleasure-seeking id operates throughout life. It demands the immediate fulfillment of basic needs: food, safety, attention, sex, and so on.

The id's drive for immediate gratification, however, runs into a roadblock: primarily the needs of other people, especially those of the parents. To adapt to these constraints, a second component of the personality emerges, which Freud called the ego. The **ego** is the balancing force between the id and the demands of society that suppress it. The ego also serves to balance the id and the **superego,** the third component of the personality, more commonly called the *conscience.*

The superego represents *culture within us,* the norms and values we have internalized from our social groups. As the *moral* component of the personality, the superego provokes feelings of guilt or shame when we break social rules or pride and self-satisfaction when we follow them.

The id and the superego are always in conflict. When the id gets out of hand, pleasure rules. We break society's norms, and get in trouble. When the superego gets out of hand, we go in the other direction. Becoming overly rigid in following society's norms, we end up wearing a strait-jacket of rules that inhibit our lives. In the emotionally healthy individual, the ego succeeds in balancing these conflicting demands. In the maladjusted individual, however, the ego fails to control this conflict between the id and the superego. Either the id or the superego dominates this person, leading to internal confusion and problem behaviors.

**Sociological Evaluation**    Sociologists appreciate Freud's emphasis on socialization—his assertion that the social group into which we are born transmits norms and values that restrain our biological drives. Sociologists, however, object to the view that inborn and subconscious motivations are the primary reasons for human behavior. *This denies the central principle of sociology:* that factors such as social class (income, education, and occupation) and people's roles in groups underlie their behavior (Epstein 1988; Bush and Simmons 1990).

Feminist sociologists have been especially critical of Freud. Although what we just summarized applies to both females and males, Freud assumed that what is "male" is "normal." He even said that females are inferior, castrated males (Chodorow 1990; Gerhard 2000). It is obvious that sociologists need to continue to research how we develop personality.

## Socialization into Emotions

Emotions, too, are an essential aspect of who we become. Sociologists who research this area of our "humanness" find that emotions also are not simply the results of biology. Like the mind, emotions depend on socialization (Hochschild 1975, 1983; Wang and Roberts 2006). This may sound strange. Don't all people get angry? Doesn't everyone cry? Don't we all feel guilt, shame, sadness, happiness, fear? What has socialization to do with emotions?

Sports are a powerful agent of socialization. That sumo wrestling teaches a form of masculinity should be apparent from this photo. What else do you think these boys are learning?

What emotions are these people expressing? Are these emotions global? Is their way of expressing them universal?

**Global Emotions**    At first, it may look as though socialization is not relevant, that we simply express universal feelings. Paul Ekman (1980), an anthropologist who studied emotions in several countries, concluded that everyone experiences six basic emotions: anger, disgust, fear, happiness, sadness, and surprise. He also observed that we all show the same facial expressions when we feel these emotions. A person from Zimbabwe, for example, could tell from just the look on an American's face that she is angry, disgusted, or fearful, and we could tell from the Zimbabwean's face that he is happy, sad, or surprised. Because we all show the same facial expressions when we experience these six emotions, Ekman concluded that they are built into our biology, "a product of our genes."

**Expressing Emotions**    The existence of universal facial expressions for these basic emotions does *not* mean that socialization has no effect on how we express them. Facial expressions are only one way in which we show emotions. Other ways vary with gender. For example, U.S. women are allowed to express their emotions more freely, while U.S. men are expected to be more reserved. To express delighted surprise, for example, women are allowed to make "squeals of glee" in public places, even to jump a bit as they hug one another. Men are not. Such an expression would be a fundamental violation of their gender role.

Then there are culture, social class, and relationships. Consider culture. Two close Japanese friends who meet after a long separation don't shake hands or hug—they bow. Two Arab men will kiss. Social class is also significant, for it cuts across many other lines, even gender. Upon seeing a friend after a long absence, upper-class women and men are likely to be more reserved in expressing their delight than are lower-class women and men. Relationships also make a big difference. We express our emotions more openly if we are with close friends, more guardedly if we are at a staff meeting with the corporate CEO. A good part of childhood socialization centers on learning these "norms of emotion"—how to express our emotions in a variety of settings.

**What We Feel**    The matter goes deeper than this. Socialization not only leads to different ways of expressing emotions but even affects *what* we feel (Clark 1997; Shields 2002). People in one culture may even learn to experience feelings that are unknown in another culture. For example, the Ifaluk, who live on the Caroline Islands of Micronesia, use the word *fago* to refer to the feelings they have when they see someone suffer. This comes close to what we call sympathy or compassion. But the Ifaluk also use this term to refer to what they feel when they are with someone who has high status, someone they highly respect or admire (Kagan 1984). To us, these are two distinct emotions, and they require separate words to express them.

**Research Needed**    Although Ekman identified only six emotions that are universal in feeling and facial expression, I suspect that other emotions are common to people around the world—and that everyone shows similar facial expressions when they experience them. I suggest that feelings of helplessness, despair, confusion, and shock are among these universal emotions. We need cross-cultural research to find out whether this is so. We also need research into how culture guides children to feel and express emotions.

## Society Within Us: The Self and Emotions as Social Control

Much of our socialization is intended to turn us into conforming members of society. Socialization into the self and emotions is an essential part of this process, for both the self and our emotions mold our behavior. Although we like to think that we are "free," consider for a moment just some of the factors that influence how we act: the expectations of friends and parents, of neighbors and teachers; classroom norms and college rules; city, state, and federal laws. For example, if in a moment of intense frustration, or out of a devilish desire to shock people, you wanted to tear off your clothes and run naked down the street, what would stop you?

The answer is your socialization—*society within you.* Your experiences in society have resulted in a self that thinks along certain lines and feels particular emotions. This helps to keep you in line. Thoughts such as "Would I get kicked out of school?" and "What would my friends (parents) think if they found out?" represent an awareness of the self in relationship to others. So does the desire to avoid feelings of shame and embarrassment. Our *social mirror,* then—the result of being socialized into a self and emotions—sets up effective controls over our behavior. In fact, socialization into self and emotions is so effective that some people feel embarrassed just thinking about running nude in public!

**In Sum:** Socialization is essential for our development as human beings. From interaction with others, we learn how to think, reason, and feel. The net result is the shaping of our behavior—including our thinking and emotions—according to cultural standards. This is what sociologists mean when they refer to "*society within us.*"

# Socialization into Gender

## Learning the Gender Map

For a child, society is unchartered territory. A major signpost on society's map is **socialization into gender.** As we learn what is expected of us *because* we are a male or a female, we are nudged into different lanes in life, into contrasting attitudes and behaviors. We take direction so well that, as adults, most of us act, think, and even feel according to this gender map, our culture's guidelines of what is appropriate for our sex.

The significance of gender is emphasized throughout this book, and we focus specifically on gender in Chapter 10. For now, though, let's briefly consider some of the "gender messages" that we get from our family and the mass media.

## Gender Messages in the Family

Our parents are the first significant others who show us how to follow the gender map. Their own gender orientations have become embedded so firmly that they do most of this teaching without being aware of what they are doing. This is illustrated in a classic study by psychologists Susan

Goldberg and Michael Lewis (1969), whose results have been confirmed by other researchers (Fagot et al. 1985; Connors 1996).

> Goldberg and Lewis asked mothers to bring their 6-month-old infants into their laboratory, supposedly to observe the infants' development. Covertly, however, they also observed the mothers. They found that the mothers kept their daughters closer to them. They also touched their daughters more and spoke to them more frequently than they did to their sons.
>
> By the time the children were 13 months old, the girls stayed closer to their mothers during play, and they returned to their mothers sooner and more often than the boys did. When Goldberg and Lewis set up a barrier to separate the children from their mothers, who were holding toys, the girls were more likely to cry and motion for help; the boys, to try to climb over the barrier.

Goldberg and Lewis concluded that mothers subconsciously reward daughters for being passive and dependent, and sons for being active and independent.

These lessons continue throughout childhood. On the basis of their sex, children are given different kinds of toys. Boys are more likely to get guns and "action figures" that destroy enemies. Girls are more likely to get dolls and jewelry. Parents also subtly encourage the boys to participate in more rough-and-tumble play. They expect their sons to get dirtier and to be more defiant, their daughters to be daintier and more compliant (Gilman 1911/1971; Henslin 2007). In large part, they get what they expect. Such experiences in socialization lie at the heart of the sociological explanation of male–female differences.

We should note, however, that some sociologists would consider biology to be the cause, proposing that Goldberg and Lewis were simply observing innate differences in the children. In short, were the mothers creating those behaviors (the boys wanting to get down and play more, and the girls wanting to be hugged more), or were they responding to natural differences in their children? It is similarly the case with toys. In an intriguing experiment with monkeys, researchers discovered that male monkeys prefer cars and balls more than do female monkeys, who are more likely to prefer dolls and pots (Alexander and Hines 2002). We shall return to this controversial issue of nature versus nurture in Chapter 10.

## Gender Messages from Peers

Sociologists stress how this sorting process that begins in the family is reinforced as the child is exposed to other aspects of society. Of those other influences, one of the

**Frank and Ernest**

SOON WE'LL GIVE UP DOLLS AND HOPSCOTCH---BUT THEY'LL BE INTO FOOTBALL FOREVER.

12-10 THAVES

www.cartoonistgroup.com

The *gender roles* that we learn during childhood become part of our basic orientations to life. Although we refine these roles as we grow older, they remain built round the framework established during childhood.

most powerful is the **peer group,** individuals of roughly the same age who are linked by common interests. Examples of peer groups are friends, classmates, and "the kids in the neighborhood."

As you grew up, you regularly saw girls and boys teach one another what it means to be a female or a male. You might not have recognized what was happening, however, so let's eavesdrop on a conversation between two eighth-grade girls studied by sociologist Donna Eder (2007). You can see how these girls are reinforcing images of appearance and behavior that they think are appropriate for females.

CINDY:  The only thing that makes her look anything is all the makeup . . .
PENNY:  She had a picture, and she's standing like this. (Poses with one hand on her hip and one by her head)
CINDY:  Her face is probably this skinny, but it looks that big 'cause of all the makeup she has on it.
PENNY:  She's ugly, ugly, ugly.

Boys, of course, also reinforce cultural expectations of gender (Pascoe 2003). When sociologist Melissa Milkie (1994) studied junior high school boys, she found that much of their talk centered on movies and TV programs. Of the many images they saw, the boys would single out sex and violence. They would amuse one another by repeating lines, acting out parts, and joking and laughing at what they had seen.

If you know boys in their early teens, you've probably seen behavior like this. You may have been amused or even have shaken your head in disapproval. As a sociologist, however, Milkie peered beneath the surface. She concluded that the boys were using media images to develop their identity as males. They had gotten the message: "Real" males are obsessed with sex and violence. Not to joke and laugh about murder and promiscuous sex would have marked a boy as a "weenie," a label to be avoided at all costs.

## Gender Messages in the Mass Media

Also guiding us in learning our gender map are the **mass media,** forms of communication that are directed to large audiences. Let's look at how their images reinforce **gender roles,** the behaviors and attitudes considered appropriate for our sex.

**Television**  Television reinforces stereotypes of the sexes. On prime-time television, male characters outnumber female characters. Male characters are also more likely to be portrayed in higher-status positions (Glascock 2001). Sports news also maintains traditional stereotypes. Sociologists who studied the content of televised sports news in Los Angeles found that female athletes receive little coverage (Messner et al. 2003). When they do, they are sometimes trivialized by male newscasters who focus on humorous events in women's sports or turn the female athlete into a sexual object. Newscasters even manage to emphasize breasts and bras and to engage in locker-room humor.

Stereotype-breaking characters, in contrast, are a sign of changing times. In comedies, women are more verbally aggressive than men (Glascock 2001). The powers of the teenager *Buffy, The Vampire Slayer,* were remarkable. On *Alias,* Sydney Bristow exhibited extraordinary strength. In cartoons, Kim Possible divides her time between cheerleading practice and saving the world from evil, while, also with tongue in cheek, the Powerpuff Girls are touted as "the most elite kindergarten crime-fighting force ever assembled." This new gender portrayal continues in a variety of programs, such as *Totally Spies.*

The gender messages on these programs are mixed. Girls are powerful, but they have to be skinny and gorgeous and wear the latest fashions, too. Such messages present a dilemma for girls, as this is almost impossible to replicate in real life.

**Video Games**   One of the hallmarks of today's society is video games. Even preschoolers are involved: One-fourth of 4- to 6-year-olds play them for an average of an hour a day (Rideout and Vandewater 2003). You've probably noticed that college students, especially men, relieve stress by escaping into video games. The first members of the "Nintendo Generation," now in their thirties, are still playing video games—with babies on their laps.

Sociologists have begun to study how the sexes are portrayed in video games, but their influence on the players' ideas of gender is still unknown (Dietz 2000; Berger 2002). Because these games are on the cutting edge of society, they sometimes also reflect cutting-edge changes in sex roles, the topic of the Mass Media in Social Life box on the next page.

**Anime**   *Anime* is a Japanese cartoon form targeted at children. Because anime crosses boundaries of video games, television, movies, and books (comic), we shall consider it as a separate category. As shown below, perhaps the most recognizable feature of anime is the big-eyed little girls and the fighting little boys. Japanese parents are concerned about anime's antisocial heroes and its depiction of violence, but to keep peace they reluctantly buy anime for their children (Khattak 2007). In the United States, the mass media aimed at children often depict violence—so, with its cute characters, anime is unlikely to bother U.S. parents. Anime's depiction of active, dominant little boys and submissive little girls leads to the question, of course, of what gender lessons it is giving children.

**In Sum:** "Male" and "female" are such powerful symbols that learning them forces us to interpret the world in terms of gender. As children learn their society's symbols of gender, they learn that different behaviors and attitudes are expected of boys and girls. First transmitted by the family, these gender messages are reinforced by other social institutions. As they become integrated into our views of the world, gender messages form a picture of "how" males and females "are." Because gender serves as a primary basis for **social inequality**—giving privileges and obligations to one group of people while denying them to another—gender images are especially important to understand.

# Agents of Socialization

People and groups that influence our orientations to life—our self-concept, emotions, attitudes, and behavior—are called **agents of socialization.** We have already considered how three of these agents—the family, our peers, and the mass media—influence our ideas of gender. Now we'll look more closely at how agents of socialization prepare us to take our place in society. We shall first consider the family, then the neighborhood, religion, day care, school and peers, and the workplace.

## The Family

Around the world, the first group to have a major impact on us is our family. Sociologists have found that middle-class and working-class families socialize their children differently,

*Anime* is increasing in popularity—cartoons and comics aimed at children and pornography targeted to adults. Its gender messages, especially those directed to children, are yet to be explored.

## MASS MEDIA in SOCIAL LIFE

### Lara Croft, Tomb Raider: Changing Images of Women in the Mass Media

*The mass media not only reflect gender stereotypes but they also play a role in changing them. Sometimes they do both simultaneously. The images of Lara Croft not only reflect women's changing role in society, but also, by exaggerating the change, they mold new stereotypes.*

The mass media reflect traditional and changing roles of women. Amidst the portrayals of women as passive, as subordinate, or as mere background objects, a new image has broken through. This new image, as exaggerated as it is, illustrates a fundamental change in gender relations. Lara Croft is an outstanding example of this change.

Like books and magazines, video games are made available to a mass audience. And with digital advances, they have crossed the line from what are traditionally thought of as games to something that more closely resembles interactive movies. Costing an average of $10 million to produce and another $10 million to market, video games have intricate subplots and use celebrity voices for the characters (Nussenbaum 2004).

Sociologically, what is significant is that the *content* of video games socializes their users. As they play, gamers are exposed not only to action but also to ideas and images. The gender images of video games communicate powerful messages, just as they do in other forms of the mass media.

Lara Croft, an adventure-seeking archaeologist and star of *Tomb Raider* and its many sequels, is the essence of the new gender image. Lara is smart, strong, and able to utterly vanquish foes. With both guns blazing, she is the cowboy of the twenty-first century, the term *cowboy* being purposefully chosen, as Lara breaks stereotypical gender roles and dominates what previously was the domain of men. She was the first female protagonist in a field of muscle-rippling, gun-toting macho caricatures (Taylor 1999).

Yet the old remains powerfully encapsulated in the new. As the photo on this page makes evident, Lara is a fantasy girl for young men of the digital generation. No matter her foe, no matter her predicament, Lara oozes sex. Her form-fitting outfits, which flatter her volup-

tuous physique, reflect the mental images of the men who fashioned this digital character.

Lara has caught young men's fancy to such an extent that they have bombarded corporate headquarters with questions about her personal life. Lara is the star of two movies and a comic book. There is even a Lara Croft candy bar.

### For Your Consideration

A sociologist who reviewed this text said, "It seems that for women to be defined as equal, we have to become symbolic males—warriors with breasts." Why is gender change mostly one-way—females adopting traditional male characteristics? To see why men get to keep their gender roles, these two questions should help: Who is moving into the traditional territory of the other? Do people prefer to imitate power or weakness?

Finally, consider just how far stereotypes have actually been left behind. For completing certain tasks, the reward is to see Lara in a swimsuit or lingerie.

a process with lifelong consequences for children. Sociologist Melvin Kohn (1959, 1963, 1976, 1977; Kohn et al. 1986) found that working-class parents are mainly concerned that their children stay out of trouble. They also tend to use physical punishment. Middle-class parents, in contrast, focus more on developing their children's curiosity, self-expression, and self-control. They are more likely to reason with their children than to use physical punishment.

These findings were a sociological puzzle. Just why would working-class and middle-class parents rear their children so differently? Kohn knew that life experiences of some sort held the key, and he found that key in the world of work. Bosses usually tell blue-collar workers exactly what to do. Since blue-collar parents expect their children's lives to be like theirs, they stress obedience. At their work, in contrast, middle-class parents take more initiative. Expecting their children to work at similar jobs, middle-class parents socialize them into the qualities they have found valuable.

Kohn was still puzzled, for some working-class parents act more like middle-class parents, and vice versa. As Kohn probed this puzzle, the pieces fell into place. The key was the parents' type of job. Middle-class office workers, for example, are closely supervised, and Kohn found that they follow the working-class pattern of child rearing, emphasizing conformity. And some blue-collar workers, such as those who do home repairs, have a good deal of freedom. These workers follow the middle-class model in rearing their children (Pearlin and Kohn 1966; Kohn and Schooler 1969).

## The Neighborhood

As all parents know, some neighborhoods are better than others for their children. Parents try to move to those neighborhoods—if they can afford them. Their common-sense evaluations are borne out by sociological research. Children from poor neighborhoods are more likely to get in trouble with the law, to become pregnant, to drop out of school, and even to have worse mental health in later life (Brooks-Gunn et al. 1997; Sampson et al. 2001; Wheaton and Clarke 2003; Yonas et al. 2006).

Sociologists have also found that the residents of more affluent neighborhoods watch out for the children more than do the residents of poor neighborhoods (Sampson et al. 1999). This isn't because the adults in poor neighborhoods care less about children. Rather, the more affluent neighborhoods have fewer families in transition, so the adults are more likely to know the local children and their parents. This better equips them to help keep the children safe and out of trouble.

## Religion

How important is religion in your life? You could be among the two-thirds of Americans who belong to a local congregation, but what if you are among the other third? Why would religion be significant for you? To see the influence of religion, we can't look only at people who are religious. Even in the extreme—people who wouldn't be caught dead near a church, synagogue, or mosque—religion plays a powerful role. Perhaps this is the most significant aspect of religion: Religious ideas so pervade U.S. society that they provide the foundation of morality for both the religious and the nonreligious. For many Americans, the influence of religion is more direct. This is especially true for the two of every five Americans who report that during a typical week they attend a religious service (Gallup Poll 2007; *Statistical Abstract* 2007:Tables 73, 75). Through their participation in congregational life, they learn doctrine, values, and morality, but the effects on their lives are not limited to these obvious factors. For example, people who participate in religious services learn not only beliefs about the hereafter but also ideas about what kinds of clothing, speech, and manners are appropriate for formal occasions. Life in congregations also provides a sense of identity for its participants, giving them a feeling of belonging. It also helps to integrate immigrants into their new society, offers an avenue of social mobility for the poor, provides social contacts for jobs, and in the case of African American churches, has been a powerful influence in social change.

## Day Care

It is rare for social science research to make national news, but occasionally it does. This is what happened when researchers published their findings on 1,200 kindergarten children they had studied since they were a month old. They observed the children multiple times both at home and at day care. They also videotaped and made detailed notes on the children's interaction with their mothers (National Institute of Child Health and Human Development 1999; Guensburg 2001). What caught the media's attention? Children who spend more time in day care have weaker bonds with their mothers and are less affectionate to them. They are also less cooperative with others and more likely to fight and to be "mean." By the time they get to kindergarten, they are more likely to talk back to teachers and to disrupt the classroom. This holds true regardless of the quality of the day care, the family's social class, or whether the child is a girl or a boy (Belsky 2006). On the positive side, the children also scored higher on language tests.

Are we producing a generation of "smart but mean" children? This is not an unreasonable question, since the study was designed well, and an even larger study of children in England has come up with similar findings (Belsky 2006). Some point out that the differences between children who spend a lot of time in day care and those who spend less time are slight. Others stress that with several million children in day care (*Statistical Abstract* 2007:Table 564), slight differences can be significant for society. The researchers are following these children as they continue in school. The most recent report on the children, when they were in the 6th grade, indicates that these patterns are continuing (Belsky et al. 2007).

## The School and Peer Groups

As a child's experiences with agents of socialization broaden, the influence of the family decreases. Entry into school marks only one of many steps in this transfer of allegiance and learning of new values. The Cultural Diversity box on the next page explores how these new values and ways of looking at the world sometimes even replace those the child learns at home.

When sociologists Patricia and Peter Adler (1998) observed children at two elementary schools in Colorado, they saw how children separate themselves by sex and develop their own worlds with unique norms. The norms that made boys popular were athletic ability, coolness, and toughness. For girls, popularity was based on family background, physical appearance (clothing and use of makeup), and the ability to attract popular boys. In this children's subculture, academic achievement pulled in opposite directions: For boys, high grades lowered their popularity, but for girls, good grades increased their standing among peers.

You know from your own experience how compelling peer groups are. It is almost impossible to go against a peer group, whose cardinal rule seems to be "conformity or rejection." Anyone who doesn't do what the others want becomes an "outsider," a "nonmember," an "outcast." For preteens and teens just learning their way around in the world, it is not surprising that the peer group rules.

As a result, the standards of our peer groups tend to dominate our lives. If your peers, for example, listen to rap, Nortec, death metal, rock and roll, country, or gospel, it is almost inevitable that you also prefer that kind of music. It is the same for clothing styles and dating standards. Peer influences also extend to behaviors that violate social norms. If your peers are college-bound and upwardly striving, that is most likely what you will be; but if they use drugs, cheat, and steal, you are likely to do so, too.

## The Workplace

Another agent of socialization that comes into play somewhat later in life is the workplace. Those initial jobs that we take in high school and college are much more than just a way to earn a few dollars. From the people we rub shoulders with at work, we learn not only a set of skills but also perspectives on the world.

Most of us eventually become committed to some particular line of work, often after trying out many jobs. This may involve **anticipatory socialization,** learning to play a role before entering it. Anticipatory socialization is a sort of mental rehearsal for some future activity. We may talk to people who work in a particular career, read novels about that type of work, or take a summer internship in that field. Such activities allow us to gradually identify with the role, to become aware of what would be expected of us. Sometimes this helps people avoid committing themselves to an unrewarding career, as with some of my students who tried student teaching, found that they couldn't stand it, and then moved on to other fields more to their liking.

An intriguing aspect of work as a socializing agent is that the more you participate in a line of work, the more the work becomes a part of your self-concept. Eventually you come to think of yourself so much in terms of the job that if someone asks you to describe yourself, you are likely to include the job in your self-description. You might say, "I'm a teacher," "I'm a nurse," or "I'm a sociologist."

## Resocialization

What does a woman who has just become a nun have in common with a man who has just divorced? The answer is that they both are undergoing **resocialization;** that is, they are learning new norms, values, attitudes, and behaviors to match their new situation in life. In its most common form, resocialization occurs each time we learn something contrary to our previous experiences. A new boss who insists on a different way of doing things is resocializing you. Most resocialization is mild—only a slight modification of things we have already learned.

Resocialization can also be intense. People who join Alcoholics Anonymous (AA), for example, are surrounded by reformed drinkers who affirm the destructive effects of excessive drinking. Some students experience an intense period of resocialization when they leave high school and start college—especially during those initially scary days before they find companions, start to fit in, and feel comfortable. To join a cult or to begin psychotherapy is even more profound, for this immerses people in views that conflict with

# Cultural Diversity in the United States

## Caught Between Two Worlds

It is a struggle to learn a new culture, for its behaviors and ways of thinking may be at odds with ones already learned. This can lead to inner turmoil. One way to handle the conflict is to cut ties with your first culture. Doing so, however, can create a sense of loss, perhaps one that is recognized only later in life.

Richard Rodriguez, a literature professor and essayist, was born to working-class Mexican immigrants. Wanting their son to be successful in their adopted land, his parents named him Richard instead of Ricardo. While his English-Spanish hybrid name indicates the parents' aspirations for their son, it was also an omen of the conflict that Richard would experience.

Like other children of Mexican immigrants, Richard first spoke Spanish—a rich mother tongue that introduced him to the world. Until the age of 5, when he began school, Richard knew only fifty words in English. He describes what happened when he began school:

> The change came gradually but early. When I was beginning grade school, I noted to myself the fact that the classroom environment was so different in its styles and assumptions from my own family environment that survival would essentially entail a choice between both worlds. When I became a student, I was literally "re-made"; neither I nor my teachers considered anything I had known before as relevant. I had to forget most of what my culture had provided, because to remember it was a disadvantage. The past and its cultural values became detachable, like a piece of clothing grown heavy on a warm day and finally put away.

As happened to millions of immigrants before him, whose parents spoke German, Polish, Italian, and so on, learning English eroded family and class ties and ate away at his ethnic roots. For Rodriguez, language and education were not simply devices that eased the transition to the dominant culture. Instead, they slashed at the roots that had given him life.

To face conflicting cultures is to confront a fork in the road. Some turn one way and withdraw from the new culture—a clue that helps to explain why so many Latinos drop out of U.S. schools. Others go in the opposite direction. Cutting ties with their family and cultural roots, they wholeheartedly adopt the new culture.

Rodriguez took the second road. He excelled in his new language—so well, in fact, that he graduated from Stanford University and then became a graduate student in English at the University of California at Berkeley. He was even awarded a Fulbright fellowship to study English Renaissance literature at the University of London.

But the past shadowed Rodriguez. Prospective employers were impressed with his knowledge of Renaissance literature. At job interviews, however, they would skip over the Renaissance training and ask him if he would teach the Mexican novel and be an adviser to Latino students. Rodriguez was also haunted by the image of his grandmother, the warmth of the culture he had left behind, and the language and thought to which he had become a stranger.

Richard Rodriguez represents millions of immigrants—not just those of Latino origin but those from other cultures, too—who want to be a part of life in the United States without betraying their past. They fear that to integrate into U.S. culture is to lose their roots. They are caught between two cultures, each beckoning, each offering rich rewards.

## For Your Consideration

I saw this conflict firsthand with my father, who did not learn English until after the seventh grade (his last in school). German was left behind, but broken English and awkward expressions remained for a lifetime. Then, too, there were the lingering emotional connections to old ways, as well as the suspicions, haughtiness, and slights of more assimilated Americans. His longing for security by grasping the past was combined with his wanting to succeed in the everyday reality of the new culture. Have you seen anything similar?

*Sources:* Based on Richard Rodriguez 1975, 1982, 1990, 1991, 1995.

their earlier socialization. If these ideas take, not only does the individual's behavior change but he or she also learns a fundamentally different way of looking at life.

## Total Institutions

Relatively few of us experience the powerful agent of socialization that sociologist Erving Goffman (1961) called the **total institution.** He coined this term to refer to a place in which people are cut off from the rest of society and where they come under almost total control of the officials who are in charge. Boot camp, prisons, concentration camps, convents, some religious cults, and some military schools, such as West Point, are total institutions.

A person entering a total institution is greeted with a **degradation ceremony** (Garfinkel 1956), an attempt to remake the self by stripping away the individual's current identity and stamping a new one in its place. This unwelcome greeting may involve fingerprinting, photographing, shaving the head, and banning the individual's *personal identity kit* (items such as jewelry, hairstyles, clothing, and other body decorations used to express individuality). Newcomers may be ordered to strip, undergo an examination (often in a humiliating, semipublic setting), and then put on a uniform that designates their new status. (For prisoners, the public reading of the verdict and being led away in handcuffs by armed police are also part of the degradation ceremony.)

Total institutions are isolated from the public. The walls, bars, gates, and guards not only keep the inmates in but also keep outsiders out. Staff members closely supervise the day-to-day lives of the residents. Eating, sleeping, showering, recreation—all are standardized. Inmates learn that their previous statuses—student, worker, spouse, parent—mean nothing. The only thing that counts is their current status.

No one leaves a total institution unscathed, for the experience brands an indelible mark on the individual's self and colors the way he or she sees the world. Boot camp, as described in the Down-to-Earth Sociology box on the next page, is brutal but swift. Prison, in contrast, is brutal and prolonged. Neither recruit nor prisoner, however, has difficulty in pinpointing how the institution affected the self.

# Socialization Through the Life Course

You are at a particular stage in your life now, and college is a good part of it. You know that you have more stages ahead of you as you go through life. These stages, from birth to death, are called the **life course** (Elder 1975; 1999). The sociological significance of the life course is twofold. First, as you pass through a stage, it affects your behavior and orientations. You simply don't think about life in the same way when you are 30, are married, and have a baby and a mortgage, as you do when you are 18 or 20, single, and in college. (Actually, you don't even see life the same as a freshman and as a senior.) Second, your life course differs by social location. Your social class, race–ethnicity, and gender, for example, map out distinctive worlds of experience.

This means that the typical life course differs for males and females, the rich and the poor, and so on. To emphasize this major sociological point, in the sketch that follows I will stress the *historical* setting of people's lives. Because of your particular social location, your own life course may differ from this sketch, which is a composite of stages that others have suggested (Levinson 1978; Carr et al. 1995; Quadagno 2007).

## Childhood (from birth to about age 12)

Consider how different your childhood would have been if you had grown up in another historical era. Historian Philippe Ariès (1965) noticed that in European paintings from about 1000 to 1800 A.D., children were always dressed in adult clothing. If they were not depicted stiffly posed, as in a family portrait, they were shown doing adult activities.

From this, Ariès drew a conclusion that sparked a debate among historians: He believed that during this era in Europe, childhood was not regarded as a special time of life. He said that adults viewed children as miniature adults and put them to work at very early ages. At the age of 7, for example, a boy might leave home for good to learn to be a jeweler or a stonecutter. A girl, in contrast, stayed home until she married, but by the age of 7 she was expected to assume her share of the household tasks. Historians do not deny that these were the customs of that time, but some say that Ariès' conclusion is ridiculous. They say that other evidence of that period indicates that childhood was viewed as a special time of life (Orme 2002).

Having children work like adults did not disappear with the Middle Ages. It is still common in the Least Industrialized Nations, where children still work in many occupations—from blacksmiths to waiters. They are most visible as street peddlers, hawking everything from shoelaces to chewing gum and candy. The photo on the upper left of page 189 not only illustrates different activities, but it also reflects a view of children remarkably different from the one common in the Most Industrialized Nations.

# Down-to-Earth Sociology
## Boot Camp as a Total Institution

The bus arrives at Parris Island, South Carolina, at 3 A.M. The early hour is no accident. The recruits are groggy, confused. Up to a few hours ago, the young men were ordinary civilians. Now, as a sergeant sneeringly calls them "maggots," their heads are buzzed (25 seconds per recruit), and they are quickly thrust into the harsh world of Marine boot camp.

Buzzing the boys' hair is just the first step in stripping away their identity so that the Marines can stamp a new one in its place. The uniform serves the same purpose. There is a ban on using the first person "I." Even a simple request must be made in precise Marine style or it will not be acknowledged. ("Sir, Recruit Jones requests permission to make a head call, Sir.")

Every intense moment of the next eleven weeks reminds the recruits, men and women, at Parris Island that they are joining a subculture of self-discipline. Here pleasure is suspect and sacrifice is good. As they learn the Marine way of talking, walking, and thinking, they are denied the diversions they once took for granted: television, cigarettes, cars, candy, soft drinks, video games, music, alcohol, drugs, and sex.

Lessons are bestowed with fierce intensity. When Sgt. Carey checks brass belt buckles, Recruit Robert Shelton nervously blurts, "I don't have one." Sgt. Carey's face grows red as his neck cords bulge. "I?" he says, his face just inches from the recruit. With spittle flying from his mouth, he screams, "'I' is gone!"

"Nobody's an individual" is the lesson that is driven home again and again. "You are a team, a Marine. Not a civilian. Not black or white, not Hispanic or Indian or some hyphenated American—but a Marine. You will live like a Marine, fight like a Marine, and, if necessary, die like a Marine."

Each day begins before dawn with close-order formations. The rest of the day is filled with training in hand-to-hand combat, marching, running, calisthenics, Marine history, and—always—following orders.

"An M-16 can blow someone's head off at 500 meters," Sgt. Norman says. "That's beautiful, isn't it?"

"Yes, sir!" shout the platoon's fifty-nine voices.

"Pick your nose!" Simultaneously fifty nine index fingers shoot into nostrils.

*Resocialization is often a gentle process. Usually we are gradually exposed to different ways of thinking and doing. Sometimes, however, resocialization can be swift and brutal, as it is during boot camp in the Marines. This private at Parris Island is learning a world vastly unlike the civilian world he left behind.*

The pressure to conform is intense. Those who are sent packing for insubordination or suicidal tendencies are mocked in cadence during drills. ("Hope you like the sights you see/Parris Island casualty.") As lights go out at 9 P.M., the exhausted recruits perform the day's last task: The entire platoon, in unison, chants the virtues of the Marines.

Recruits are constantly scrutinized. Subperformance is not accepted, whether it be a dirty rifle or a loose thread on a uniform. The subperformer is shouted at, derided, humiliated. The group suffers for the individual. If a recruit is slow, the entire platoon is punished.

The system works.

One of the new Marines (until graduation, they are recruits, not Marines) says, "I feel like I've joined a new society or religion."

He has.

## For Your Consideration

Of what significance is the recruits' degradation ceremony? Why are recruits not allowed video games, cigarettes, or calls home? Why are the Marines so unfair as to punish an entire platoon for the failure of an individual? Use concepts in this chapter to explain why the system works.

*Sources:* Based on Garfinkel 1956; Goffman 1961; Ricks 1995; Dyer 2007.

In contemporary Western societies such as the United States, children are viewed as innocent and in need of protection from adult responsibilities such as work and self-support. Ideas of childhood vary historically and cross-culturally. From paintings, such as this 1642 British portrait by the Le Nain brothers, *A Woman and Five Children,* some historians conclude that Europeans once viewed children as miniature adults who assumed adult roles at the earliest opportunity.

Child rearing, too, was remarkably different. In earlier centuries, parents and teachers considered it their moral duty to terrorize children to keep them in line. They would lock children in dark closets, frighten them with bedtime stories of death and hellfire, and force them to witness gruesome events. Consider this:

A common moral lesson involved taking children to visit the gibbet [an upraised post on which executed bodies were left hanging from chains], where they were forced to inspect rotting corpses hanging there as an example of what happens to bad children when they grow up. Whole classes were taken out of school to witness hangings, and parents would often whip their children afterwards to make them remember what they had seen. (DeMause 1975)

Industrialization transformed the way we perceive children. With children having the leisure to go to school, they came to be thought of as tender and innocent, as needing more adult care, comfort, and protection. Over time, such attitudes of dependency grew, and today we view children as needing gentle guidance if they are to develop emotionally, intellectually, morally, even physically. We take our view for granted—after all, it is only "common sense." Yet, as you can see, our view is not "natural." It is, instead, rooted in geography and history.

**In Sum:** Childhood is more than biology. Everyone's childhood occurs at some point in history and is embedded in particular social locations, especially social class and gender. *These social factors are as vital as our biology, for they determine what childhood will be like for us.* Although a child's *biological* characteristics (such as being small and dependent) are universal, the child's *social* experiences (the kind of life the child lives) are not. Because of this, sociologists say that childhood varies from culture to culture.

## Adolescence (ages 13–17)

Adolescence is not a "natural" age division. It is a social invention. In earlier centuries, people simply moved from childhood into young adulthood, with no stopover in between. The Industrial Revolution brought such an abundance of material surpluses, however, that for the first time in history, millions of people in their teens were able to remain outside the labor force. At the same time, education became a more important factor in achieving success. The convergence of these two forces in industrialized societies created a gap between childhood and adulthood. In the early 1900s, the term *adolescence* was coined to indicate this new stage in life (Hall 1904), one that has become renowned for inner turmoil.

To ground the self-identity of children and mark their passage into adulthood, tribal societies hold *initiation rites.* In the industrialized world, however, adolescents must "find" themselves on their own. As they attempt to carve out an identity that is distinct from both the "younger" world being left behind and the "older" world that is still out of range, adolescents develop their own subcultures, with distinctive clothing, hairstyles, language, gestures, and music. We usually fail to realize that contemporary society, not biology, created this period of inner turmoil that we call *adolescence.*

## Transitional Adulthood (ages 18–29)

If society invented adolescence, can it also invent other periods of life? As Figure 3.2 illustrates, this is actually happening now. Postindustrial societies are adding a period of extended youth to the life course, which sociologists call **transitional adulthood** (also known as *adultolescence*). After high school, millions of young adults go to college, where they postpone adult responsibilities. They are mostly freed from the control of their parents, yet they don't have to support themselves. Even after college, many return home, so they can live cheaply while they establish themselves in a career—and, of course, continue to "find themselves." During this time, people are "neither psychological adolescents nor sociological adults" (Keniston 1971). At some point during this period of extended youth, young adults gradually ease into adult responsibilities. They take a full-time job, become serious about a career, engage in courtship rituals, get married—and go into debt.

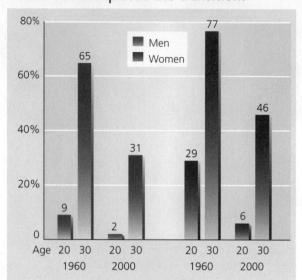

### FIGURE 3.2 Transitional Adulthood: A New Stage in the Life Course

**Who has completed the transition?**

The data show the percentage who have completed the transition to adulthood, as measured by leaving home, finishing school, getting married, having a child, and being financially independent.
*Source:* Furstenberg et al. 2004.

## The Middle Years (ages 30–65)

**The Early Middle Years (ages 30–49)**   During their early middle years, most people are more sure of themselves and of their goals in life. As with any point in the life course, however, the self can receive severe jolts. Common in this period are divorce and losing jobs. It may take years for the self to stabilize after such ruptures.

The early middle years pose a special challenge for many U.S. women, who have been given the message, especially by the media, that they can "have it all." They can be superworkers, superwives, and supermoms—all rolled into one. The reality, however, usually consists of

In many societies, manhood is not bestowed upon males simply because they reach a certain age. Manhood, rather, signifies a standing in the community that must be achieved. Shown here are 10- to 12-year old Aboriginal boys in Australia, prepared for their initiation circumcision ceremony. Except for their loin cloths, their "clothing" has been painted on their bodies.

conflicting pressures—too little time, too many demands, even too little sleep. Something has to give, and attempts to resolve this dilemma are anything but easy.

**The Later Middle Years (ages 50–65)** During the later middle years, health issues and mortality begin to loom large as people feel their bodies change, especially if they watch their parents become frail, fall ill, and die. The consequence is a fundamental reorientation in thinking—*from time since birth to time left to live* (Neugarten 1976). With this changed orientation, people attempt to evaluate the past and come to terms with what lies ahead. They compare what they have accomplished with what they had hoped to achieve. Many people also find themselves caring not only for their own children but also for their aging parents. Because of this set of burdens, which is often crushing, people in the later middle years sometimes are called the "sandwich generation."

Life during this stage isn't stressful for everyone. Many find late middle age to be the most comfortable period of their lives. They enjoy job security and a standard of living higher than ever before; they have a bigger house (one that may even be paid for), drive newer cars, and take longer and more exotic vacations. The children are grown, the self is firmly planted, and fewer upheavals are likely to occur.

As they anticipate the next stage of life, however, most people do not like what they see.

## The Older Years (about age 65 on)

In industrialized societies, the older years begin around the mid-60s. This, too, is recent, for in agricultural societies, when most people died early, old age was thought to begin at around age 40. Industrialization brought about improved nutrition and public health, which prolonged life. Today, people in good health who are over the age of 65 often experience this period not as old age, but as an extension of the middle years. People who continue to work or to do things they enjoy are less likely to perceive themselves as old (Neugarten 1977). Although frequency of sex declines, most men and women in their 60s and 70s are sexually active (Denney and Quadagno 1992).

Because we have a self and can reason abstractly, we can contemplate death. Initially, we regard death as a vague notion, a remote possibility. But as people see their parents and friends die and observe their own bodies no longer functioning as before, the thought of death becomes less abstract. Increasingly during this stage in the life course, people feel that "time is closing in" on them.

# Are We Prisoners of Socialization?

From our discussion of socialization, you might conclude that sociologists think of people as robots: The socialization goes in, and the behavior comes out. People cannot help what they do, think, or feel, for everything is simply a result of their exposure to socializing agents.

Sociologists do *not* think of people in this way. Although socialization is powerful and affects us all profoundly, we have a self. Established in childhood and continually modified by later experience, the self is dynamic. Our self is not a sponge that passively absorbs influences from the environment, but, rather, a vigorous, essential part of our being that allows us to act on our environment.

Indeed, it is precisely because individuals are not robots that their behavior is so hard to predict. The countless reactions of other people merge in each of us. As the self develops, each person internalizes or "puts together" these innumerable reactions, producing a unique whole called the *individual*. Each individual uses his or her own mind to reason and to make choices in life.

In this way, *each of us is actively involved in the construction of the self*. For example, although our experiences in the family lay down the basic elements of our personality, including fundamental orientations to life, we are not doomed to keep those orientations if we do not like them. We can purposely expose ourselves to groups and ideas that we prefer. Those experiences, in turn, will have their own effects on our self. In short, although socialization is powerful, we can change even the self within the limitations of the framework laid down by our social locations. And that self—along with the options available within society—is the key to our behavior.

# SUMMARY *and* REVIEW

## What Is Human Nature?

*How much of our human characteristics come from "nature" (heredity) and how much from "nurture" (the social environment)?*

Observations of isolated, institutionalized, and **feral children** help to answer this question, as do experiments with monkeys that were raised in isolation. Language and intimate social interaction—aspects of "nurture"—are essential to the development of what we consider to be human characteristics. Pp. 60–63.

## Socialization into the Self, Mind, and Emotions

*How do we acquire a self and reasoning skills?*

Humans are born with the *capacity* to develop a **self,** but the self must be socially constructed; that is, its contents depend on social interaction. According to Charles Horton Cooley's concept of the **looking-glass self,** our self develops as we internalize others' reactions to us. George Herbert Mead identified the ability to **take the role of the other** as essential to the development of the self. Mead concluded that even the mind is a social product. Jean Piaget identified four stages that children go through as they develop the ability to reason. Pp. 63–67.

## Learning Personality, Morality, and Emotions

*How do sociologists evaluate Freud's psychoanalytic theory of personality development?*

Freud viewed personality development as the result of our **id** (inborn, self-centered desires) clashing with the demands of society. The **ego** develops to balance the id and the **superego,** the conscience. Sociologists, in contrast, do not examine inborn or subconscious motivations, but, instead, study how *social* factors—social class, gender, religion, education, and so forth—underlie personality development. P. 68.

*How does socialization influence emotions?*

**Socialization** influences not only *how we express our emotions* but also *what emotions we feel.* Socialization into emotions is one of the means by which society produces conformity. Pp. 68–70.

## Socialization into Gender

*How does gender socialization affect our sense of self?*

**Gender socialization**—sorting males and females into different roles—is a primary means of controlling human behavior. Children receive messages about gender even in infancy. A society's ideals of sex-linked behaviors are reinforced by its social institutions. Pp. 70–72.

## Agents of Socialization

*What are the main agents of socialization?*

The **agents of socialization** include the family, neighborhood, religion, day care, school, **peer groups,** the **mass media,** and the workplace. Each has its particular influences in socializing us into becoming full-fledged members of society. Pp. 72–75.

## Resocialization

*What is resocialization?*

**Resocialization** is the process of learning new norms, values, attitudes, and behavior. Most resocialization is voluntary, but some, as with residents of **total institutions,** is involuntary. Pp. 75–77.

## Socialization Through the Life Course

*Does socialization end when we enter adulthood?*

Socialization occurs throughout the life course. In industrialized societies, the **life course** can be divided into childhood, adolescence, young adulthood, the middle years, and the older years. The West is adding a new stage, transitional adulthood. Life course patterns vary by social location such as history, gender, race–ethnicity, and social class, as well as by individual experiences such as health and age at marriage. Pp. 77–81.

## Are We Prisoners of Socialization?

Although socialization is powerful, we are not merely the sum of our socialization experiences. Just as socialization influences human behavior, so humans act on their environment and influence even their self-concept. P. 81.

# THINKING CRITICALLY *about* Chapter 3

1. What two agents of socialization have influenced you the most? Can you pinpoint their influence on your attitudes, beliefs, values, or other orientations to life?

2. Summarize your views of the "proper" relationships of women and men. What in your socialization has led you to have these views?

3. What is your location in the life course? How does the text's summary of that location match your experiences? Explain the similarities and differences.

# BY THE NUMBERS: Changes Over Time

- Percentage of Americans belonging to a local church or synagogue in 1970s (see Ch. 13): 71%
- Percentage of Americans belonging to a local church or synagogue today: 65%

- Percentage of men completing the transition to adulthood by age 30 in the 1960s: 65%
- Percentage of men completing the transition to adulthood by age 30 today: 31%

- Percentage of women completing the transition to adulthood by age 30 in the 1960s: 77%
- Percentage of women completing the transition to adulthood by age 30 today: 46%

- The age marking the beginning of old age in pre-industrialized times: 40
- The age marking the beginning of old age today: 65

# ADDITIONAL RESOURCES

## What can you find in MySocLab? mysoclab  www.mysoclab.com

- **Complete Ebook**
- **Practice Tests and Video and Audio activities**
- **Mapping and Data Analysis exercises**

- **Sociology in the News**
- **Classic Readings in Sociology**
- **Research and Writing advice**

## Where Can I Read More on This Topic?

Suggested readings for this chapter are listed at the back of this book.

# Social Structure and Social Interaction

My curiosity had gotten the better of me. When the sociology convention finished, I climbed aboard the first city bus that came along. I didn't know where the bus was going, and I didn't know where I would spend the night.

"Maybe I overdid it this time," I thought, as the bus began winding down streets I had never seen before. Actually, this was my first visit to Washington, D.C., so everything was unfamiliar to me. I had no destination, no plans, not even a map. I carried no billfold, just a driver's license shoved into my jeans for emergency identification, some pocket change, and a $10 bill tucked into my sock. My goal was simple: If I saw something interesting, I would get off the bus and check it out.

**Suddenly one of the men jumped up, smashed the empty bottle against the sidewalk, and . . .**

"Nothing but the usual things," I mused, as we passed row after row of apartment buildings and stores. I could see myself riding buses the entire night. Then something caught my eye. Nothing spectacular—just groups of people clustered around a large circular area where several streets intersected.

I climbed off the bus and made my way to what turned out to be Dupont Circle. I took a seat on a sidewalk bench and began to observe what was going on around me. As the scene came into focus, I noticed several streetcorner men drinking and joking with one another. One of the men broke from his companions and sat down next to me. As we talked, I mostly listened.

As night fell, the men said that they wanted to get another bottle of wine. I contributed. They counted their money and asked if I wanted to go with them.

Although I felt my stomach churning—a combination of hesitation and fear—I heard a confident "Sure!" come out of my mouth. As we left the circle, the three men began to cut through an alley. "Oh, no," I thought. "This isn't what I had in mind."

I had but a split second to make a decision. I found myself continuing to walk with the men, but holding back half a step so that none of the three was behind me. As we walked, they passed around the remnants of their bottle. When my turn came, I didn't know what to do. I shuddered to think about the diseases lurking within that bottle. I made another quick decision. In the semidarkness I faked it, letting only my thumb and forefinger touch my lips and nothing enter my mouth.

When we returned to Dupont Circle, we sat on the benches, and the men passed around their new bottle of Thunderbird. I couldn't fake it in the light, so I passed, pointing at my stomach to indicate that I was having digestive problems.

Suddenly one of the men jumped up, smashed the emptied bottle against the sidewalk, and thrust the jagged neck outward in a menacing gesture. He glared straight ahead at another bench, where he had spotted someone with whom he had some sort of unfinished business. As the other men told him to cool it, I moved slightly to one side of the group—ready to flee, just in case.

# Levels of Sociological Analysis

On this sociological adventure, I almost got in over my head. Fortunately, it turned out all right. The man's "enemy" didn't look our way, the man put the broken bottle next to the bench "just in case he needed it," and my intriguing introduction to a life that up until then I had only read about continued until dawn.

Sociologists Elliot Liebow (1967/1999), Mitchell Duneier (1999), and Elijah Anderson (1978, 1990, 2006) have written fascinating accounts about men like my companions from that evening. Although streetcorner men may appear to be disorganized—simply coming and going as they please and doing whatever feels good at the moment—sociologists have analyzed how, like us, these men are influenced by the norms and beliefs of our society. This will become more apparent as we examine the two levels of analysis that sociologists use.

## Macrosociology and Microsociology

The first level, **macrosociology,** focuses on broad features of society. Conflict theorists and functionalists use this approach to analyze such things as social class and how groups are related to one another. If they were to analyze streetcorner men, for example, they would stress that these men are located at the bottom of the U.S. social class system. Their low status means that many opportunities are closed to them: The men have few job skills, little education, hardly anything to offer an employer. As "able-bodied" men, however, they are not eligible for welfare—even for a two-year limit—so they hustle to survive. As a consequence, they spend their lives on the streets.

In the second level, **microsociology,** the focus is on **social interaction,** what people do when they come together. Sociologists who use this approach are likely to analyze the men's rules or "codes" for getting along; their survival strategies ("hustles"); how they divide up money, wine, or whatever other resources they have; their relationships with girlfriends, family, and friends; where they spend their time and what they do there; their language; their pecking order; and so on. Microsociology is the primary focus of symbolic interactionists.

Because each approach has a different focus, macrosociology and microsociology yield distinctive perspectives, and both are needed to gain a fuller understanding of social life. We cannot adequately understand streetcorner men, for example, without using *macrosociology.* It is essential that we place the men within the broad context of how groups in U.S. society are related to one another—for, as is true for ourselves, the social class of these men helps to shape their attitudes and behavior. Nor can we adequately understand these men without *microsociology,* for their everyday situations also form a significant part of their lives—as they do for all of us.

Let's look in more detail at how these two approaches in sociology work together to help us understand social life.

# The Macrosociological Perspective: Social Structure

Why did the street people in our opening vignette act as they did, staying up all night drinking wine, prepared to use a lethal weapon? Why don't *we* act like this? Social structure helps us answer such questions.

## The Sociological Significance of Social Structure

To better understand human behavior, we need to understand *social structure,* the framework of society that was already laid out before you were born. **Social structure** refers to the typical patterns of a group, such as its usual relationships between men and women or students and teachers. *The sociological significance of social structure is that it guides our behavior.*

Because this term may seem vague, let's consider how you experience social structure in your own life. As I write this, I do not know your race–ethnicity. I do not know your religion. I do not know whether you are young or old,

Sociologists use both macro and micro levels of analysis to study social life. Those who use *macrosociology* to analyze the homeless—or any human behavior—focus on broad aspects of society, such as the economy and social classes. Sociologists who use the *microsociological approach* analyze how people interact with one another. This photo illustrates social structure—the disparities between power and powerlessness.

tall or short, male or female. I do not know whether you were reared on a farm, in the suburbs, or in the inner city. I do not know whether you went to a public high school or to an exclusive prep school. But I do know that you are in college. And this, alone, tells me a great deal about you.

From this one piece of information, I can assume that the social structure of your college is now shaping what you do. For example, let's suppose that today you felt euphoric over some great news. I can be fairly certain (not absolutely, mind you, but relatively confident) that when you entered the classroom, social structure overrode your mood. That is, instead of shouting at the top of your lungs and joyously throwing this book into the air, you entered the classroom in a fairly subdued manner and took your seat.

The same social structure influences your instructor, even if he or she, on the one hand, is facing a divorce or has a child dying of cancer or, on the other, has just been awarded a promotion or a million-dollar grant. Your instructor may

feel like either retreating into seclusion or celebrating wildly, but most likely he or she will conduct class in the usual manner. In short, social structure tends to override personal feelings and desires.

Just as social structure influences you and your instructor, so it also establishes limits for street people. They, too, find themselves in a specific location in the U.S. social structure—although it is quite different from yours or your instructor's. Consequently, they are affected in different ways. Nothing about their social location leads them to take notes or to lecture. Their behaviors, however, are as logical an outcome of where they find themselves in the social structure as are your own. In their position in the social structure, it is just as "natural" to drink wine all night as it is for you to stay up studying all night for a crucial examination. It is just as "natural" for you to nod and say, "Excuse me," when you enter a crowded classroom late and have to claim a desk on which someone has already placed books as it is for them to break off the neck of a wine bottle and glare at an enemy. To better understand social structure, read the Down-to-Earth Sociology box on football on the next page.

In short, people learn their behaviors and attitudes because of their location in the social structure (whether they be privileged, deprived, or in between), and they act accordingly. This is as true of street people as it is of us. *The differences in behavior and attitudes are due not to biology (race, sex, or any other supposed genetic factors), but to people's location in the social structure.* Switch places with street people and watch your behaviors and attitudes change!

Because social structure so crucially affects who we are and what we are like, let's look more closely at its major components: culture, social class, social status, roles, groups, social institutions, and societies.

## Culture

In Chapter 2, we considered culture's far-reaching effects on our lives. At this point, let's simply summarize its main impact. Sociologists use the term *culture* to refer to a group's

# *Down-to-Earth Sociology*
## College Football as Social Structure

To gain a better idea of what *social structure* is, think of college football (see Dobriner 1969a). You probably know the various positions on the team: center, guards, tackles, ends, quarterback, running backs, and the like. Each is a *status*; that is, each is a social position. For each of the statuses shown on Figure 4.1, there is a *role*; that is, each of these positions has certain expectations attached to it. The center is expected to snap the ball, the quarterback to pass it, the guards to block, the tackles to tackle or block, the ends to receive passes, and so on. Those role expectations guide each player's actions; that is, the players try to do what their particular role requires.

Let's suppose that football is your favorite sport and you never miss a home game at your college. Let's also suppose that you graduate, get a great job, and move across the country. Five years later, you return to your campus for a nostalgic visit. The climax of your visit is the biggest football game of the season. When you get to the game, you might be surprised to see a different coach, but you are not surprised that each playing position is occupied by people you don't know, for all the players you knew have graduated, and their places have been filled by others.

This scenario mirrors *social structure,* the framework around which a group exists. In football, that framework consists of the coaching staff and the eleven playing positions. The game does not depend on any particular individual but, rather, on *social statuses,* the positions that the individuals occupy. When someone leaves a position, the game can go on because someone else takes over

**FIGURE 4.1**   Team Positions (Statuses) in Football

that position or status and plays the role. The game will continue even though not a single individual remains from one period of time to the next. Notre Dame's football team endures today even though Knute Rockne, the Gipper, and his teammates are long dead.

Even though you may not play football, you do live your life within a clearly established social structure. The statuses that you occupy and the roles you play were already in place before you were born. You take your particular positions in life, others do the same, and society goes about its business. Although the specifics change with time, the game—whether of life or of football—goes on.

language, beliefs, values, behaviors, and even gestures. Culture also includes the material objects that a group uses. Culture is the broadest framework that determines what kind of people we become. If we are reared in Chinese, Arab, or U.S. culture, we will grow up to be like most Chinese, Arabs, or Americans. On the outside, we will look and act like them; and on the inside, we will think and feel like them.

## Social Class

To understand people, we must examine the social locations that they hold in life. Especially significant is *social class,* which is based on income, education, and occupational prestige. Large numbers of people who have similar amounts of income and education and who work at jobs that are roughly comparable in prestige make up a

*Social class* is one of the most significant factors in social life. Fundamental to what we become, social class lays down our orientations to life. Can you see how this photo illustrates this point?

The status may also be looked down on, as in the case of a streetcorner man, an ex-convict, or a thief.

All of us occupy several positions at the same time. You may simultaneously be a son or daughter, a worker, a date, and a student. Sociologists use the term **status set** to refer to all the statuses or positions that you occupy. Obviously your status set changes as your particular statuses change. For example, if you graduate from college and take a full-time job, get married, buy a home, have children, and so on, your status set changes to include the positions of worker, spouse, homeowner, and parent.

Like other aspects of social structure, statuses are part of our basic framework of living in society. The example I gave of students and teachers who come to class and do what others expect of them despite their particular circumstances and moods illustrates how statuses affect our actions—and those of the people around us. Our statuses—whether daughter or son, worker or date—serve as guides for our behavior.

**Ascribed and Achieved Statuses**    An **ascribed status** is involuntary. You do not ask for it, nor can you choose it. At birth, you inherit ascribed statuses such as your race–ethnicity, sex, and the social class of your parents, as well as your statuses as female or male, daughter or son, niece or nephew. Others, such as teenager and senior citizen, are related to the life course discussed in Chapter 3 and are given to you later in life.

**Achieved statuses,** in contrast, are voluntary. These you earn or accomplish. As a result of your efforts you become a student, a friend, a spouse, a lawyer, or a member of the clergy. Or, for lack of effort (or for efforts that others fail to appreciate), you become a school dropout, a former friend, an ex-spouse, a debarred lawyer, or a defrocked member of the clergy. In other words, achieved statuses can be either positive or negative; both college president and bank robber are achieved statuses.

*Each status provides guidelines for how we are to act and feel.* Like other aspects of social structure, statuses set limits on what we can and cannot do. Because social statuses are an essential part of the social structure, they are found in all human groups.

**Status Symbols**    People who are pleased with their social status often want others to recognize their particular position. To elicit this recognition, they use **status symbols,**

**social class.** It is hard to overemphasize this aspect of social structure, for our social class influences not only our behaviors but even our ideas and attitudes. We have this in common, then, with the street people described in the opening vignette: We both are influenced by our location in the social class structure. Theirs may be a considerably less privileged position, but it has no less influence on their lives. Social class is so significant that we shall spend an entire chapter (Chapter 8) on this topic.

## Social Status

When you hear the word *status,* you are likely to think of prestige. These two words are welded together in people's minds. As you saw in the box on football, however, sociologists use **status** in a different way—to refer to the *position* that someone occupies. That position may carry a great deal of prestige, as in the case of a judge or an astronaut, or it may bring little prestige, as in the case of a convenience store clerk or a waitress at the local truck stop.

signs that identify a status. For example, people wear wedding rings to announce their marital status; uniforms, guns, and badges to proclaim that they are police officers (and not so subtly to let you know that their status gives them authority over you); and "backward" collars to declare that they are Lutheran ministers or Roman Catholic or Episcopal priests.

Some social statuses are negative and so, therefore, are their status symbols. The scarlet letter in Nathaniel Hawthorne's book by the same title is one example. Another is the CONVICTED DUI (Driving Under the Influence) bumper sticker that some U.S. courts require convicted drunk drivers to display if they wish to avoid a jail sentence.

Status symbols are part of our lives. *All* of us use them to announce our statuses to others and to help smooth our interactions in everyday life. Can you identify your own status symbols and what they communicate? For example, how does your clothing announce your statuses of sex, age, and college student?

**Master Statuses**   A **master status** cuts across your other statuses. Some master statuses are ascribed. An example is your sex. Whatever you do, people perceive you as a male or as a female. If you are working your way through college by flipping burgers, people see you not only as a burger flipper and a student but also as a *male* or *female* burger flipper and a *male* or *female* college student. Other master statuses are race and age.

Some master statuses are achieved. If you become very, very wealthy (and it doesn't matter whether your wealth comes from a successful invention or from winning the lottery—it is still *achieved* as far as sociologists are concerned), your wealth is likely to become a master status. For example, people might say, "She is a very rich burger flipper"—or, more likely, "She's very rich, and she used to flip burgers!"

Similarly, people who become disfigured find, to their dismay, that their condition becomes a master status. For example, a person whose face is scarred from severe burns will be viewed through this unwelcome master status regardless of occupation or accomplishments. In the same way, people who are confined to wheelchairs can attest to how their handicap overrides all their other statuses and influences others' perceptions of everything they do.

Although our statuses usually fit together fairly well, some people have a contradiction or mismatch between their statuses. This is known as **status inconsistency** (or discrepancy). A 14-year-old college student is an example. So is a 40-year-old married woman who is dating a 19-year-old college sophomore.

These examples reveal an essential aspect of social statuses: Like other components of social structure, they come with built-in *norms* (that is, expectations) that guide our behavior. When statuses mesh well, as they usually do, we know what to expect of people. This helps social interaction to unfold smoothly. Status inconsistency, however,

*Master statuses* are those that overshadow our other statuses. Shown here is Stephen Hawking, who is severely disabled by Lou Gehrig's disease. For many, his *master status* is that of a person with disabilities. Because Hawking is one of the greatest physicists who has ever lived, however, his outstanding achievements have given him another *master status,* that of world-class physicist in the ranking of Einstein.

upsets our expectations. In the preceding examples, how are you supposed to act? Are you supposed to treat the 14-year-old as you would a young teenager or as you would your college classmate? Do you react to the married woman as you would to the mother of your friend or as you would to a classmate's date?

## Roles

> All the world's a stage
> And all the men and women merely players.
> They have their exits and their entrances;
> And one man in his time plays many parts . . .
> (William Shakespeare, *As You Like It,* Act II, Scene 7)

Like Shakespeare, sociologists see roles as essential to social life. When you were born, **roles**—the behaviors, obligations, and privileges attached to a status—were already set up for you. Society was waiting with outstretched arms to teach you how it expected you to act as a boy or a girl. And whether you were born poor, rich, or somewhere in between, that, too, attached certain behaviors, obligations, and privileges to your statuses.

The difference between role and status is that you *occupy* a status, but you *play* a role (Linton 1936). For example, being a son or daughter is your status, but your expectations of receiving food and shelter from your parents—as well as their expectations that you show respect to them—are part of your role. Or, again, your status is student, but your role is to attend class, take notes, do homework, and take tests.

Roles are like a fence. They allow us a certain amount of freedom, but for most of us that freedom doesn't go very far. Suppose that a woman decides that she is not going to wear dresses—or a man that he will not wear suits and ties—regardless of what anyone says. In most situations, they'll stick to their decision. When a formal occasion comes along, however, such as a family wedding or a funeral, they are likely to cave in to norms that they find overwhelming. Almost all of us follow the guidelines for what is "appropriate" for our roles. Few of us are bothered by such constraints, for our socialization is so thorough that we usually *want* to do what our roles indicate is appropriate.

*The sociological significance of roles is that they lay out what is expected of people.* As individuals throughout society perform their roles, those roles mesh together to form this thing called *society*. As Shakespeare put it, people's roles provide "their exits and their entrances" on the stage of life. In short, roles are remarkably effective at keeping people in line—telling them when they should "enter" and when they should "exit," as well as what to do in between.

## Groups

A **group** consists of people who regularly interact with one another. Ordinarily, the members of a group share similar values, norms, and expectations. Just as social class, statuses, and roles influence our actions, so, too, the groups to which we belong are powerful forces in our lives. In fact, *to belong to a group is to yield to others the right to make certain decisions about our behavior.* If we belong to a group, we assume an obligation to act according to the expectations of other members of that group.

In the next chapter, we will examine groups in detail, but for now let's look at the next component of social structure, social institutions.

## Social Institutions

At first glance, the term *social institution* may seem cold and abstract—with little relevance to your life. In fact, however, **social institutions**—the ways that each society develops to meet its basic needs—vitally affect your life. By weaving the fabric of society, social institutions shape our behavior. They even color our thoughts. How can this be? Look at what social institutions are: the family, religion, education, economics, medicine, politics, law, science, the military, and the mass media.

In industrialized societies, social institutions tend to be more formal; in tribal societies, they are more informal. Education in industrialized societies, for example, is highly structured, while in tribal societies it usually consists of children informally learning what adults do. Figure 4.2 on the next page summarizes the basic social institutions. Note that each institution has its own groups, statuses, values, and norms. Social institutions are so significant that Part IV of this book focuses on them.

## Societies—and Their Transformation

How did our society develop? You know that it didn't spring full-blown on the human scene. To better understand this framework that surrounds us, that sets the stage for our experiences in life, let's trace the evolution of societies. Look at Figure 4.3 on page 93, which illustrates how changes in technology brought changes to **society**—people who share a culture and a territory. As we review these sweeping changes, picture yourself as a member of each society. Consider how your life—even your thoughts and values—would be different in each society.

## FIGURE 4.2    Social Institutions in Industrial and Postindustrial Societies

| Social Institution | Basic Needs | Some Groups or Organizations | Some Statuses | Some Values | Some Norms |
|---|---|---|---|---|---|
| Family | Regulate reproduction, socialize and protect children | Relatives, kinship groups | Daughter, son, father, mother, brother, sister, aunt, uncle, grandparent | Sexual fidelity, providing for your family, keeping a clean house, respect for parents | Have only as many children as you can afford, be faithful to your spouse |
| Religion | Concerns about life after death, the meaning of suffering and loss; desire to connect with the Creator | Congregation, synagogue, mosque, denomination, charity; clergy associations | Priest, minister, rabbi, imam, worshipper, teacher, disciple, missionary, prophet, convert | Reading and adhering to holy texts such as the Bible, the Torah, and the Koran; honoring God | Attend worship services, contribute money, follow the teachings |
| Education | Transmit knowledge and skills across generations | School, college, student senate, sports team, PTA, teachers' union | Teacher, student, dean, principal, football player, cheerleader | Academic honesty, good grades, being "cool" | Do homework, prepare lectures, don't snitch on classmates |
| Economy | Produce and distribute goods and services | Credit unions, banks, credit card companies, buying clubs | Worker, boss, buyer, seller, creditor, debtor, advertiser | Making money, paying bills on time, producing efficiently | Maximize profits, "the customer is always right," work hard |
| Medicine | Heal the sick and injured, care for the dying | AMA, hospitals, pharmacies, insurance companies, HMOs | Doctor, nurse, patient, pharmacist, medical insurer | Hippocratic oath, staying in good health, following doctor's orders | Don't exploit patients, give best medical care available |
| Politics | Allocate power, determine authority, prevent chaos | Political party, congress, parliament, monarchy | President, senator, lobbyist, voter, candidate, spin doctor | Majority rule, the right to vote as a privilege and a sacred trust | One vote per person, be informed about candidates |
| Law | Maintain social order | Police, courts, prisons | Judge, police officer, lawyer, defendant, prison guard | Trial by one's peers, innocence until proven guilty | Give true testimony, follow the rules of evidence |
| Science | Master the environment | Local, state, regional, national, and international associations | Scientist, researcher, technician, administrator, journal editor | Unbiased research, open dissemination of research findings, originality | Follow scientific method, be objective, disclose findings, don't plagiarize |
| Military | Protection from enemies, support of national interests | Army, navy, air force, marines, coast guard, national guard | Soldier, recruit, enlisted person, officer, veteran, prisoner, spy | To die for one's country is an honor, obedience unto death | Follow orders, be ready to go to war, sacrifice for your buddies |
| Mass Media (an emerging institution) | Disseminate information, mold public opinion, report events | TV networks, radio stations, publishers, association of bloggers | Journalist, newscaster, author, editor, publisher, blogger | Timeliness, accuracy, large audiences, freedom of the press | Be accurate, fair, timely, and profitable |

## FIGURE 4.3   The Social Transformations of Society

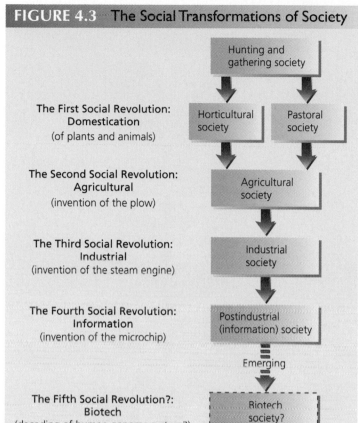

Hunting and gathering society

The First Social Revolution:
**Domestication**
(of plants and animals)

Horticultural society    Pastoral society

The Second Social Revolution:
**Agricultural**
(invention of the plow)

Agricultural society

The Third Social Revolution:
**Industrial**
(invention of the steam engine)

Industrial society

The Fourth Social Revolution:
**Information**
(invention of the microchip)

Postindustrial (information) society

Emerging

The Fifth Social Revolution?:
**Biotech**
(decoding of human genome system?)

Biotech society?

*Source:* By the author.

### Hunting and Gathering Societies

The members of **hunting and gathering societies** have few social divisions and little inequality. As the name implies, these groups depend on hunting animals and gathering plants for their survival. In some groups, the men do the hunting, and the women the gathering. In others, both men and women (and children) gather plants, the men hunt large animals, and both men and women hunt small animals. Although these groups give greater prestige to the men hunters, who supply the major source of meat, the women gatherers contribute more food to the group, perhaps even four-fifths of their total food supply (Bernard 1992).

Because a region cannot support a large number of people who hunt animals and gather plants (group members do not plant—they only gather what is already there), hunting and gathering societies are small. They usually consist of only twenty-five to forty people. These groups are nomadic. As their food supply dwindles in one area, they move to another location. Because of disease, drought, and pestilence, children have only about a fifty-fifty chance of surviving to adulthood (Lenski and Lenski 1987).

Of all societies, hunters and gatherers are the most egalitarian. Because what they hunt and gather is perishable, the people accumulate few personal possessions. Consequently, no one becomes wealthier than anyone else. There are no rulers, and most decisions are arrived at through discussion.

### Pastoral and Horticultural Societies

About ten thousand years ago, some groups found that they could tame and breed some of the animals they hunted—primarily goats, sheep, cattle, and camels. Others discovered that they could cultivate plants. As a result, hunting and gathering societies branched into two directions, each with different means of acquiring food.

The key to understanding the first branching is the word *pasture;* **pastoral** (or herding) **societies** are based on the *pasturing of animals*. Pastoral societies developed in regions where low rainfall made it impractical to build life around growing crops. Groups that took this turn remained nomadic, for they

The simplest forms of societies are called *hunting and gathering societies*. Members of these societies have adapted well to their environments, and they have more leisure than the members of other societies. Shown here are Inuits in the tundra of Greenland.

followed their animals to fresh pasture. The key to understanding the second branching is the word *horticulture*, or plant cultivation. **Horticultural** (or gardening) **societies** are based on the *cultivation of plants by the use of hand tools.* Because they no longer had to abandon an area as the food supply gave out, these groups developed permanent settlements.

As shown in Figure 4.4, the domestication of animals and plants transformed society, ushering in the *first social revolution.* Groups grew larger because the more dependable food supply supported more people. Because it was no longer necessary for everyone to work to provide food, a *division of labor* emerged. Some people began to make jewelry, others tools, others weapons, and so on. This led to a surplus of objects, which, in turn, stimulated trade. With trading, groups began to accumulate objects they prized, such as gold, jewelry, and utensils.

These changes set the stage for *social inequality.* Some families (or clans) acquired more goods than others. With the possession of animals, pastures, croplands, jewelry, and other material goods, groups began to fight. War, in turn, opened the door to slavery, for people found it convenient to let captives do their drudge work. As individuals passed their possessions on to their descendants, wealth grew more concentrated. So did power, and for the first time, some individuals became chiefs.

**Agricultural Societies** When the plow was invented about five or six thousand years ago, social life once again changed forever. Compared with hoes and digging sticks, the use of animals to pull plows was immensely efficient. The larger food surplus allowed even more people to engage in activities other than farming. In this new **agricultural society,** people developed cities and what is popularly known as "culture," such as philosophy, art, music, literature, and architecture. Accompanied by the inventions of the wheel, writing, and numbers, the changes were so profound that this period is sometimes referred to as "the dawn of civilization."

The social inequality of pastoral and horticultural societies was only a forerunner of what was to come. When some people managed to gain control of the growing surplus of resources, *inequality became a fundamental feature of life in society.* To protect their expanding privileges and power, this elite surrounded itself with armed men. This small group even levied taxes on others, who now had become their "subjects." As conflict theorists point out, this concentration of resources and power—along with the oppression of people not in power—was the forerunner of the state.

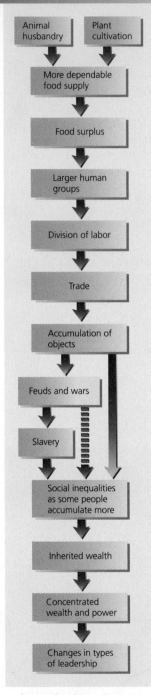

**FIGURE 4.4** Consequences of Animal Domestication and Plant Cultivation

*Source:* By the author.

**Industrial Societies**    The *third* social invention also turned society upside down. The **Industrial Revolution** began in Great Britain in 1765 when the steam engine was first used to run machinery. Before this, a few machines (such as windmills and water wheels) had been used to harness nature, but most machines depended on human and animal power. The new form of production in the **industrial society** brought even greater surplus—and with it another leap in social inequality. Some early industrialists accumulated such wealth that their riches outran the imagination of royalty. The masses, in contrast, were thrown off the land as feudal society came to an end. Homeless, they moved to the cities, where they faced the choice of stealing, starving, or working for wages barely sufficient to sustain life (the equivalent of a loaf of bread for a day's work).

Through a bitter struggle too detailed for us to review here, workers won their fight for better working conditions, reversing the earlier pattern of growing inequality. Home ownership became common, as did the ownership of automobiles and an incredible variety of consumer goods. Today's typical worker in industrial society enjoys a high standard of living in terms of health care, longevity, material possessions, and access to libraries and education. On an even broader scale, with industrializa-tion came the abolition of slavery, the shift from monarchies to more representative political systems, and the rights to a jury trial, to vote, and to travel. A recent extension of these equalities is the right to set up your own Internet blog, where you can bemoan life in your school or criticize the president.

**Postindustrial (Information) Societies**    If you were to choose one word that characterizes our society, what would it be? Of the many candidates, the word *change* would have to rank high among them. The primary source of the sweeping changes that are transforming our lives is the technology centering on the microchip. The change is so vast that sociologists say that a new type of society has emerged. They call it the **postindustrial** (or **information**) **society.**

Unlike the industrial society, the hallmark of this new type of society is not raw materials and manufacturing. Rather, its basic component is *information*. Teachers pass on knowledge to students, while lawyers, physicians, bankers, pilots, and interior decorators sell their specialized knowledge of law, the body, money, aerodynamics, and color schemes to clients. Unlike the factory workers of an industrial society, these individuals don't *produce* anything. Rather, they transmit or use information to provide services that others are willing to pay for.

Some social changes come without a whimper, others only violently. In this 1934 photo, a striking dock worker flees San Francisco police officers. The right to strike came with struggle—and loss of life.

The United States was in the forefront of this *fourth social revolution.* It was the first country to have more than 50 percent of its workforce in service industries such as education, health, research, government, counseling, banking, investments, insurance, sales, law, and mass media. Australia, New Zealand, western Europe, and Japan soon followed. This trend away from manufacturing and toward selling information and services shows no sign of letting up.

## Biotech Societies: Is a New Type of Society Emerging?

- Tobacco that fights cancer. ("Yes, smoke your way to health!")
- Corn that fights herpes and is a contraceptive. ("Corn flakes in the morning—and safe sex all day!")
- Goats whose milk contains spider silk (to make fishing lines and body armor) ("Got milk? The best bulletproofing.")
- Animals that are part human so they produce medicines for humans. ("Ah, those liver secretions. Good for what ails you.")
- No-Sneeze kitties—hypoallergenic cats at $4,000 each. (You can write your own jingle for this one.)

I know that such products sound like science fiction, but we *already* have the goats that make spider silk, and human genes have been inserted into animals so that they produce medicine (Elias 2001; Kristoff 2002; Osborne 2002). The no-sneeze cats are for sale—and there is a waiting list (Rosenthal 2006). Some suggest that the changes in which we are immersed are so extensive that we are entering another new type of society. In this new **biotech society,** the economy will center on applying and altering genetic structures—both plant and animal—to produce food, medicine, and materials.

If there is a new society, when did it begin? There are no firm edges to new societies, for each new one overlaps the one it is replacing. The opening to the biotech society could have been 1953, when Francis Crick and James Watson identified the double-helix structure of DNA. Or perhaps historians will trace the date to the decoding of the human genome in 2001.

Whether the changes that are swirling around us are part of a new type of society is not the main point. The larger group called society always profoundly affects people's thinking and behavior. *The sociological significance of these changes, then, is that as society is transformed, we will be swept along with it. The transformation will change even the ways we think about the self and life.*

Projecting a new type of society so soon after the arrival of the information society is risky. The wedding of genetics and economics could turn out to be simply another aspect of our information society—or we really may have just stepped into a new type of society. With cloning and bioengineering, we could even see changes in the human species. The Sociology and the New Technology box on the next page examines implications of cloning.

**In Sum:** Our society sets boundaries around our lives. By laying out a framework of statuses, roles, groups, and social institutions, society establishes the values and beliefs that prevail. It also determines the type and extent of social inequality. These factors, in turn, set the stage for relationships between men and women, racial–ethnic groups, the young and the elderly, the rich and the poor, and so on.

It is difficult to overstate the sociological principle that the type of society in which we live is the fundamental reason why we become who we are—why we feel about things the way we do and even why we think our particular thoughts. On the obvious level, if you lived in a hunting and gathering society, you would not be listening to your favorite music, watching TV programs, or playing video games. On a deeper level, you would not feel the same about life, have the same beliefs, or hold your particular aspirations for the future.

## What Holds Society Together?

With its many, often conflicting, groups and its extensive social change, how does society manage to hold together? Let's examine two answers that sociologists have proposed.

**Mechanical and Organic Solidarity**    Sociologist Emile Durkheim (1893/1933) found the key to **social integration**—the degree to which members of a society are united by shared values and other social bonds—in what he called **mechanical solidarity.** By this term, Durkheim meant that people who perform similar tasks develop a shared consciousness. Think of a farming community in which everyone is involved in planting, cultivating, and harvesting. Members of this group have so much in common that they know how almost everyone else in the community feels about life. Societies with mechanical solidarity tolerate little diversity in thinking and attitudes, for their unity depends on similar thinking.

# SOCIOLOGY and the NEW TECHNOLOGY

## "So, You Want to Be Yourself?" Cloning in the Coming Biotech Society

No type of society ends abruptly. The edges are fuzzy, and the new one overlaps the old. As the information society matures, it looks as though it is being overtaken by a biotech society. Let's try to peer over the edge of our current society to glimpse the one that may be arriving. What will life be like? There are many issues we could examine, but since space is limited, let's consider just one: cloning.

Consider this scenario:

Your four-year-old daughter has drowned, and you can't get over your sorrow. You go to the regional cloning clinic, where you have stored DNA from all members of your family. You pay the standard fee, and the director hires a surrogate mother to bring your daughter back as a newborn.

Will cloning humans become a reality? Since human embryos already have been cloned, it seems inevitable that some group somewhere will complete the process. If cloning humans becomes routine—well, consider these scenarios:

Suppose that a couple can't have children. Testing shows that the husband is sterile. The couple talk about their dilemma, and the wife agrees to have her husband's genetic material implanted into one of her eggs. Would this woman, in effect, be rearing her husband as a little boy?

Or suppose that you love your mother dearly, and she is dying. With her permission, you decide to clone her. Who is the clone? Would you be rearing your own mother?

What if a woman gave birth to her own clone? Would the clone be her daughter or her sister?

When genetic duplicates appear, the questions of what humans are, what their relationship to their "parents" is, and indeed what "parents" and children" are, will be brought up at every kitchen table.

## For Your Consideration

As these scenarios show, the issue of cloning provokes profound questions. Perhaps the most weighty concerns the future of society. Let's suppose that mass cloning becomes possible.

Many people object that cloning is immoral, but some will argue the opposite. They will ask why we should leave human reproduction to people who have inferior traits—genetic diseases, low IQs, perhaps even the propensity for crime and violence. They will suggest that we select people with the finer characteristics—high creative ability, high intelligence, compassion, and a propensity for peace.

Let's assume that geneticists have traced the characteristics just mentioned to specific genes—along with the ability to appreciate and create beautiful poetry, music, and architecture; to excel in mathematics, science, and other intellectual pursuits; and to be successful in love. Do you think that it should be our moral obligation to populate society with people like this? To try to build a society that is better for all—one without terrorism, war, violence, and greed? Could this perhaps even be our evolutionary destiny?

*Source:* Based on Kaebnick 2000; McGee 2000; Bjerklie et al. 2001; Davis 2001; Weiss 2004; Regalado 2005.

---

As societies get larger, their **division of labor** (how they divide up work) becomes more specialized. Some people mine gold, others sell it, while still others turn it into jewelry. This division of labor makes people depend on one another—for the work of each person contributes to the well-being of the whole group.

Durkheim called this new form of solidarity based on interdependence **organic solidarity.** To see why he used this

The warm, more intimate relationships of *Gemeinschaft* society are apparent in the photo taken during *Oktoberfest* in Munich, Germany. The more impersonal relationships of *Gesellschaft* society are evident in the Internet cafe, where customers are ignoring one another.

term, think about how you depend on your teacher to guide you through this introductory course in sociology. At the same time, your teacher needs you and other students in order to have a job. You and your teacher are *like organs in the same body.* (The "body" in this case is the college or university.) Although each of you performs different tasks, you depend on one another. This creates a form of unity.

**Gemeinschaft and Gesellschaft**   Ferdinand Tönnies (1887/1988) also analyzed this fundamental shift in relationships. He used the term **Gemeinschaft** (Guh-MINE-shoft), or "intimate community," to describe village life, the type of society in which everyone knows everyone else. He noted that in the society that was emerging, the personal ties, kinship connections, and lifelong friendships that marked village life were being crowded out by short-term relationships, individual accomplishments, and self-interest. Tönnies called this new type of society **Gesellschaft** (Guh-ZELL-shoft), or "impersonal association." He did not mean that we no longer have intimate ties to family and friends, but, rather, that our lives no longer center on them. Few of us take jobs in a family business, for example, and contracts replace handshakes. Much of our time is spent with strangers and short-term acquaintances.

**In Sum:** Whether the terms are *Gemeinschaft* and *Gesellschaft* or *mechanical solidarity* and *organic solidarity*, they indicate that as societies change, so do people's orientations to life. *The sociological point is that social structure sets the context for what we do, feel, and think and ultimately, then, for the kind of people we become.* As you read the Cultural Diversity box on the next page, which describes one of the few remaining Gemeinschaft societies in the United States, think of how fundamentally different you would be had you been reared in an Amish family.

# The Microsociological Perspective: Social Interaction in Everyday Life

Where macrosociology stresses the broad features of society, microsociology focuses on a narrower slice of social life. Microsociologists examine *face-to-face interaction*—what people do when they are in one another's presence. This is the primary focus of symbolic interactionists, who are especially interested in the symbols that people use. They want to know how people look at things and how this, in turn, affects their behavior and orientations to life. Of the many areas of social life they study, let's look at stereotypes, personal space, eye contact, and body language.

# Cultural Diversity in the United States

## The Amish: *Gemeinschaft* Community in a *Gesellschaft* Society

Ferdinand Tönnies' term, *Gesellschaft,* certainly applies to the United States. Impersonal associations pervade our everyday life. Local, state, and federal governments regulate many of our activities. Corporations hire and fire people not on the basis of personal relationships, but on the basis of the bottom line. And, perhaps even more significantly, millions of Americans do not even know their neighbors.

Within the United States, a handful of small communities exhibits characteristics distinct from those of the mainstream society. One such community is the Old Order Amish, followers of a sect that broke away from the Swiss-German Mennonite church in the 1600s and settled in Pennsylvania around 1727. Today, about 150,000 Old Order Amish live in the United States. About 75 percent live in just three states: Pennsylvania, Ohio, and Indiana. The largest concentration, about 22,000, resides in Lancaster County, Pennsylvania. The Amish, who believe that birth control is wrong, have doubled in population in just the past two decades.

Because Amish farmers use horses instead of tractors, most of their farms are one hundred acres or less. To the 5 million tourists who pass through Lancaster County each year, the rolling green pastures, white farmhouses, simple barns, horse-drawn buggies, and clotheslines hung with somber-colored garments convey a sense of peace and innocence reminiscent of another era. Although just sixty-five miles from Philadelphia, "Amish country" is a world away.

Amish life is based on separation from the world—an idea taken from Christ's Sermon on the Mount—and obedience to the church's teachings and leaders. This rejection of worldly concerns, writes sociologist Donald Kraybill in *The Riddle of Amish Culture* (2002), "provides the foundation of such Amish values as humility, faithfulness, thrift, tradition, communal goals, joy of work, a slow-paced life, and trust in divine providence."

The *Gemeinschaft* of village life that has been largely lost to industrialization remains a vibrant part of Amish life. The Amish make their decisions in weekly meetings, where, by consensus, they follow a set of rules, or *Ordnung,* to guide their behavior. Religion and discipline are the glue that holds the Amish together. Brotherly love and the welfare of the community are paramount values. In times of birth, sickness, and death, neighbors pitch in with the chores. In these ways, they maintain the bonds of intimate community.

The Amish are bound by other ties, including language (a dialect of German known as Pennsylvania Dutch), plain clothing—often black, whose style has remained unchanged for almost 300 years—and church-sponsored schools. Nearly all Amish marry, and divorce is forbidden. The family is a vital ingredient in Amish life; all major events take place in the home, including weddings, births, funerals, and church services. Amish children attend church schools, but only until the age of 13. (In 1972, the Supreme Court ruled that Amish parents had the right to take their children out of school after the eighth grade.) To go to school beyond the eighth grade would expose them to values and "worldly concerns" that would drive a wedge between the children and their community. The Amish believe that violence is bad, even personal self-defense, and they register as conscientious objectors during times of war. They pay no Social Security, and they receive no government benefits.

The Amish cannot resist all change, of course. Instead, they try to adapt to change in ways that will least disrupt their core values. Because urban sprawl has driven up the price of farmland, about half of Amish men work at jobs other than farming, most in farm-related businesses or in woodcrafts. They go to great lengths to avoid leaving the home. The Amish believe that when a husband works away from home, all aspects of life change, from the marital relationship to the care of the children—certainly an astute sociological insight. They also believe that if a man receives a paycheck, he will think that his work is of more value than his wife's. For the Amish, intimate, or *Gemeinschaft,* society is essential for maintaining their way of life.

Perhaps this is the most poignant illustration of how the Amish approach to life differs from that of the dominant culture: When in 2006 a non-Amish man shot several Amish girls at a one-room school, the Amish community established charitable funds not only for the families of the dead children but also for the family of the killer.

*Sources:* Hostetler 1980; Aeppel 1996; Kephart and Zellner 2001; Kraybill 2002; Dawley 2003; Johnson-Weiner 2007.

## Stereotypes in Everyday Life

You are familiar with how strong first impressions are and the way they set the tone for interaction. When you first meet someone, you cannot help but notice certain features, especially the person's sex, race–ethnicity, age, and clothing. Despite your best intentions, your assumptions about these characteristics shape your first impressions. They also affect how you act toward that person—and, in turn, how that person acts toward you. These fascinating aspects of our social interaction are discussed in the Down-to-Earth Sociology box on the next page.

## Personal Space

We all surround ourselves with a "personal bubble" that we go to great lengths to protect. We open the bubble to intimates—to our friends, children, parents, and so on—but we're careful to keep most people out of this space. In a crowded hallway between classes, we might walk with our books clasped in front of us (a strategy often chosen by females). When we stand in line, we make certain there is enough space so that we don't touch the person in front of us and aren't touched by the person behind us.

The amount of space that people prefer varies from one culture to another. South Americans, for example, like to be closer when they speak to others than do people reared in the United States. Anthropologist Edward Hall (1959; Hall and Hall 2007) recounts a conversation with a man from South America who had attended one of his lectures.

He came to the front of the class at the end of the lecture. . . . We started out facing each other, and as he talked I became dimly aware that he was standing a little too close and that I was beginning to back up. Fortunately I was able to suppress my first impulse and remain stationary because there was nothing to communicate aggression in his behavior except the conversational distance. . . .

By experimenting I was able to observe that as I moved away slightly, there was an associated shift in the pattern of interaction. He had more trouble expressing himself. If I shifted to where I felt comfortable (about twenty-one inches), he looked somewhat puzzled and hurt, almost as though he were saying, "Why is he acting that way? Here I am doing everything I can to talk to him in a friendly manner and he suddenly withdraws. Have I done anything wrong? Said something I shouldn't?" Having ascertained that distance had a direct effect on his conversation, I stood my ground, letting him set the distance.

After Hall (1969; Hall and Hall 2007) analyzed situations like this, he observed that North Americans use four different "distance zones."

1. *Intimate distance.* This is the zone that the South American unwittingly invaded. It extends to about 18 inches from our bodies. We reserve this space for comforting, protecting, hugging, intimate touching, and lovemaking.
2. *Personal distance.* This zone extends from 18 inches to 4 feet. We reserve it for friends and acquaintances and ordinary conversations. This is the zone in which Hall would have preferred speaking with the South American.

Social space is one of the many aspects of social life studied by sociologists who have a microsociological focus. What do you see in common in these two photos?

# Down-to-Earth Sociology
## Beauty May Be Only Skin Deep, But Its Effects Go on Forever

Mark Snyder, a psychologist, wondered whether **stereotypes**—our assumptions of what people are like—might be self-fulfilling. He came up with an ingenious way to test this idea. He (1993) gave college men a Polaroid snapshot of a woman (supposedly taken just moments before) and told them that he would introduce them to her after they talked with her on the telephone. Actually, the photographs—showing either a pretty or a homely woman—had been prepared before the experiment began. The photo was not of the woman the men would talk to.

Stereotypes came into play immediately. As Snyder gave each man the photograph, he asked him what he thought the woman would be like. The men who saw the photograph of the attractive woman said that they expected to meet a poised, humorous, outgoing woman. The men who had been given a photo of the unattractive woman described her as awkward, serious, and unsociable.

The men's stereotypes influenced the way they spoke to the women on the telephone, who did *not* know about the photographs. The men who had seen the photograph of a pretty woman were warm, friendly, and humorous. This, in turn, affected the women they spoke to, for they responded in a warm, friendly, outgoing manner. And the men who had seen the photograph of a homely woman? On the phone, they were cold, reserved, and humorless, and the women they spoke to became cool, reserved, and humorless. Keep in mind that the women did not know that their looks had been evaluated—and that the photographs were not even of them. In short, stereotypes tend to produce behaviors that match the stereotype. This principle is illustrated in Figure 4.5.

Although beauty might be only skin deep, its consequences permeate our lives (Katz 2007). Not only does beauty bestow an advantage in everyday interaction, but people who are physically attractive are also likely to make more money. Researchers in both Holland and the United States found that advertising firms with better-looking executives have higher revenues (Bosman et al. 1997; Pfann et al. 2000). The reason? The researchers suggest that people are more willing to associate with individuals whom they perceive as good-looking.

## For Your Consideration
Stereotypes have no single, inevitable effect, but they do affect how we react to one another.

Instead of beauty, consider gender and race–ethnicity. How do they affect those who do the stereotyping and those who are stereotyped?

 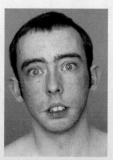

*Based on the experiment summarized here, how do you think women would modify their interactions if they were to meet the two men?*

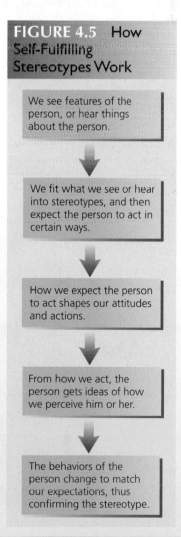

**FIGURE 4.5    How Self-Fulfilling Stereotypes Work**

We see features of the person, or hear things about the person.

↓

We fit what we see or hear into stereotypes, and then expect the person to act in certain ways.

↓

How we expect the person to act shapes our attitudes and actions.

↓

From how we act, the person gets ideas of how we perceive him or her.

↓

The behaviors of the person change to match our expectations, thus confirming the stereotype.

3. *Social distance.* This zone, extending out from us about 4 to 12 feet, marks impersonal or formal relationships. We use this zone for such things as job interviews.

4. *Public distance.* This zone, extending beyond 12 feet, marks even more formal relationships. It is used to separate dignitaries and public speakers from the general public.

## Eye Contact

One way that we protect our personal bubble is by controlling eye contact. Letting someone gaze into our eyes—unless the person is our eye doctor—can be taken as a sign that we are attracted to that person and can even be taken as an invitation to intimacy. Wanting to become "the friendliest store in town," a chain of supermarkets in Illinois ordered its checkout clerks to make direct eye contact with each customer. Female clerks complained that male customers were taking their eye contact the wrong way, as an invitation to intimacy. Management said they were exaggerating. The clerks' reply was, "We know the kind of looks we're getting back from men," and they refused to make direct eye contact with them.

## Applied Body Language

While we are still little children, we learn to interpret **body language,** the ways people use their bodies to give messages to others. This skill in correctly interpreting facial expressions, posture, and gestures is essential for getting us through everyday life. Without it—as is the case for people who have Asperger's syndrome—we wouldn't know how to react to other people. It would even be difficult to know whether someone were serious or joking. This common and essential skill for traversing everyday life is now becoming one of the government's tools in its fight against terrorism. Because many of our body messages lie beneath our consciousness, airport personnel and interrogators are being trained to look for telltale facial signs—from a quick downturn of the mouth to rapid blinking—that might indicate nervousness or lying (Davis et al. 2002).

This is an interesting twist for an area of sociology that had been entirely theoretical. Let's now turn to dramaturgy, a special area of symbolic interactionism.

## Dramaturgy: The Presentation of Self in Everyday Life

It was their big day, two years in the making. Jennifer Mackey wore a white wedding gown adorned with an 11-foot train and 24,000 seed pearls that she and her mother had sewn onto the dress. Next to her at the altar in Lexington, Kentucky, stood her intended, Jeffrey Degler, in black tie. They said their vows, then turned to gaze for a moment at the four hundred guests.

In *dramaturgy*, a specialty within sociology, social life is viewed as similar to the theater. In our everyday lives, we all are actors like those in this cast of *Grey's Anatomy.* We, too, perform roles, use props, and deliver lines to fellow actors—who, in turn, do the same.

That's when groomsman Daniel Mackey collapsed. As the shocked organist struggled to play Mendelssohn's "Wedding March," Mr. Mackey's unconscious body was dragged away, his feet striking—loudly—every step of the altar stairs.

"I couldn't believe he would die at my wedding," the bride said. (Hughes 1990)

Sociologist Erving Goffman (1922–1982) added a new twist to microsociology when he recast the artistic term **dramaturgy** (or dramaturgical analysis) into a sociological term. By this term, Goffman meant that social life is like a drama or a stage play: Birth ushers us onto the stage of everyday life, and our socialization consists of learning to perform on that stage. The self that we studied in the previous chapter lies at the center of our performances. We have ideas of how we want others to think of us, and we use our roles in everyday life to communicate those ideas. Goffman called these efforts to manage the impressions that others receive of us **impression management.**

**Stages**    Everyday life, said Goffman, involves playing our assigned roles. We have *front stages* on which to perform them, as did Jennifer and Jeffrey. (By the way, Daniel Mackey didn't really die—he had just fainted.) But we don't have to look at weddings to find front stages. Every-

day life is filled with them. Where your teacher lectures is a front stage. And if you make an announcement at a meal, you are using a front stage. In fact, you spend most of your time on front stages, for a front stage is wherever you deliver your lines. We also have *back stages,* places where we can retreat and let our hair down. When you close the bathroom or bedroom door for privacy, for example, you are entering a back stage.

**Role Performance, Conflict, and Strain**    Everyday life brings with it many roles. As discussed earlier, the same person may be a student, a teenager, a shopper, a worker, and a date, as well as a daughter or a son. Although a role lays down the basic outline for a performance, it also allows a great deal of flexibility. The particular emphasis or interpretation that we give a role, our "style," is known as **role performance.** Consider your role as son or daughter. You may play the role of ideal daughter or son—being respectful, coming home at the hours your parents set, and so forth. Or this description may not even come close to your particular role performance.

Ordinarily, our statuses are sufficiently separated that we find minimal conflict between them. Occasionally, however, what is expected of us in one status (our role) is incompatible with what is expected of us in another status. This problem, known as **role conflict,** is illustrated in Figure 4.6, in

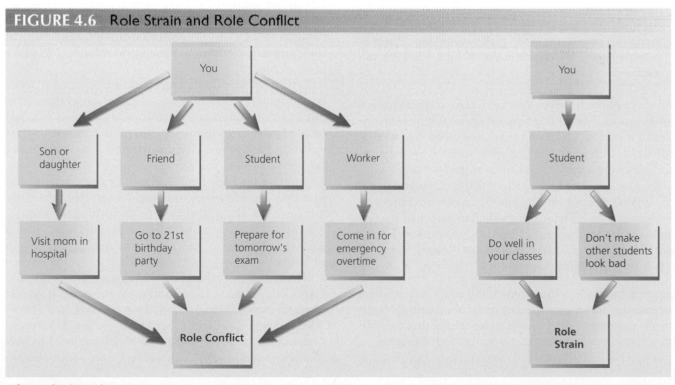

## FIGURE 4.6    Role Strain and Role Conflict

*Source:* By the author.

which family, friendship, student, and work roles come crashing together. Usually, however, we manage to avoid role conflict by segregating our statuses, although doing so can require an intense juggling act.

Sometimes the *same* status contains incompatible roles, a conflict known as **role strain.** Suppose that you are exceptionally well prepared for a particular class assignment. Although the instructor asks an unusually difficult question, you find yourself knowing the answer when no one else does. If you want to raise your hand, yet don't want to make your fellow students look bad, you will experience role strain. As illustrated in Figure 4.6, the difference between role conflict and role strain is that role conflict is conflict *between roles,* while role strain is conflict *within* a role.

**Teamwork**    Being a good role player brings positive recognition from others, something we all covet. To accomplish this, we often use **teamwork**—two or more people working together to make certain that a performance goes off as planned. When a performance doesn't come off quite right, however, it may require **face-saving behavior.** We may, for example, ignore flaws in someone's performance, which Goffman defines as *tact.*

> Suppose your teacher is about to make an important point. Suppose also that her lecturing has been outstanding and the class is hanging on every word. Just as she pauses for emphasis, her stomach lets out a loud growl. She might then use a *face-saving technique* by remarking, "I was so busy preparing for class that I didn't get breakfast this morning."

It is more likely, however, that both class and teacher will simply ignore the sound, giving the impression that no one heard a thing—a face-saving technique called *studied non-observance.* This allows the teacher to make the point or, as Goffman would say, it allows the performance to go on.

Because our own body is identified so closely with the self, a good part of impression management centers on "body messages." The messages that are attached to various body shapes change over time, but, as explored in the Mass Media in Social Life box on pages 106 and 107, thinness currently screams "desirability."

**Applying Impression Management**    I can just hear someone saying, "Impression management is interesting, but is it really important?" In fact, it is so significant that the right impression management can make a vital difference in your career. To be promoted, you must be perceived as

someone who *should* be promoted. You must appear dominant. You certainly cannot go unnoticed. But how you manage this impression is crucial. If a female executive tries to appear dominant by wearing loud clothing, using garish makeup, and cursing, this will get her noticed—but it will not put her on the path to promotion. How, then, can she exhibit dominance in the right way? To help women walk this fine line between femininity and dominance, career counselors advise women on fine details of impression management. Here are two things they recommend—that women place their hands on the table during executive sessions, not in their lap, and that they carry a purse that looks more like a briefcase (Needham 2006).

Male or female, in your own life you will have to walk this thin line, finding the best way to manage impressions in order to further your career. Much success in the work world depends not on what you actually know but, instead, on your ability to give the impression that you know what you should know.

## Ethnomethodology: Uncovering Background Assumptions

Certainly one of the strangest words in sociology is *ethnomethodology.* To better understand this term, consider the word's three basic components. *Ethno* means "folk" or "people"; *method* means how people do something; *ology* means "the study of." Putting them together, then, *ethno-method-ology* means "the study of how people do things." Specifically, **ethnomethodology** is the study of how people use commonsense understandings to make sense of life.

Let's suppose that during a routine office visit, your doctor remarks that your hair is rather long, then takes out a pair of scissors and starts to give you a haircut. You would feel strange about this, for your doctor would be violating **background assumptions**—your ideas about the way life is and the way things ought to work. These assumptions, which lie at the root of everyday life, are so deeply embedded in our consciousness that we are seldom aware of them, and most of us fulfill them unquestioningly. Thus, your doctor does not offer you a haircut, even if he or she is good at cutting hair and you need one!

The founder of ethnomethodology, sociologist Harold Garfinkel, conducted some interesting exercises designed to reveal our background assumptions. Garfinkel (1967, 2002) asked his students to act as though they did not understand the basic rules of social life. Some tried to bargain with supermarket clerks; others would inch close to people and stare directly at them. They were met with surprise, bewilderment, even anger. In one exercise Garfinkel asked students to take words literally. One conversation went like this:

ACQUAINTANCE:   How are you?
STUDENT:   How am I in regard to what?
My health, my finances, my schoolwork, my peace of mind, my . . .?
ACQUAINTANCE:   (red in the face): Look! I was just trying to be polite. Frankly, I don't give a damn how you are.

Students who are asked to break background assumptions can be highly creative. The young children of one of my students were surprised one morning when they came down for breakfast to find a sheet spread across the living room floor. On it were dishes, silverware, lit candles—and bowls of ice cream. They, too, wondered what was going on, but they dug eagerly into the ice cream before their mother could change her mind.

This is a risky assignment to give students, however, for breaking some background assumptions can make people suspicious. When a colleague of mine gave this assignment, a couple of his students began to wash dollar bills at a laundromat. By the time they put the bills in the dryer, the police had arrived.

**In Sum:** Ethnomethodologists explore *background assumptions,* the taken-for-granted ideas about the world that underlie our behavior. Most of these assumptions, or basic rules of social life, are unstated. We learn them as we learn our culture, and we violate them only with risk. Deeply embedded in our minds, they give us basic directions for living everyday life.

## The Social Construction of Reality

Symbolic interactionists stress how our ideas help determine our reality. In what has become known as *the definition of the situation,* or the **Thomas theorem,** sociologists W. I. and Dorothy S. Thomas said, "If people define situations as real, they are real in their consequences." Consider the following incident:

On a visit to Morocco, in northern Africa, I decided to buy a watermelon. When I indicated to the street vendor that the knife he was going to use to cut the watermelon was dirty (encrusted with filth would be more apt), he was very obliging. He immediately bent down and began to swish the knife in a puddle on the street. I shuddered as I looked

All of us have *background assumptions,* deeply ingrained assumptions of how the world operates. How do you think the background assumptions of this Londoner differ from those of this Ecuadoran shaman, who is performing a healing ceremony to rid London of its evil spirits?

at the passing burros that were urinating and defecating as they went by. Quickly, I indicated by gesture that I preferred my melon uncut after all.

For that vendor, germs did not exist. For me, they did. And each of us acted according to our definition of the

# MASS MEDIA in SOCIAL LIFE

## You Can't Be Thin Enough: Body Images and the Mass Media

An ad for Kellogg's Special K cereal shows an 18-month-old girl wearing nothing but a diaper. She has a worried look on her face. A bubble caption over her head has her asking, "Do I look fat?" (Krane et al. 2001)

When you stand before a mirror, do you like what you see? To make your body more attractive, do you watch your weight or work out? You have ideas about what you should look like. Where did you get them?

TV and magazine ads keep pounding home the message that our bodies aren't good enough, that we've got to improve them. The way to improve them, of course, is to buy the advertised products: hair extensions for women, hairpieces for men, hair transplants, padded bras, diet programs, anti-aging products, and exercise equipment. Muscular hulks show off machines that magically produce "six-pack abs" and incredible biceps—in just a few minutes a day. Female movie stars effortlessly go through their own tough workouts without even breaking into a sweat. Women and men get the feeling that attractive members of the opposite sex will flock to them if they purchase that wonder-working workout machine.

Although we try to shrug off such messages, knowing that they are designed to sell products, the messages still get our attention. They penetrate our thinking and feelings, helping to shape ideal images of how we "ought" to look. Those models so attractively clothed and coiffed as they walk down the runway, could they be any thinner? For women, the message is clear: You can't be thin enough. The men's message is also clear: You can't be muscular enough.

Woman or man, your body isn't good enough. It sags where it should be firm. It bulges where it should be smooth. It sticks out where it shouldn't, and it doesn't stick out enough where it should.

And—no matter what you weigh—it's too much. You've got to be thinner.

Exercise takes time, and getting in shape is painful. Once you do get in shape, let yourself slack off for just a few days, and your body seems to sag into its previous slothful, drab appearance. You can't let up, you can't exercise enough, and you can't diet enough.

*All of us contrast the reality we see when we look in the mirror with our culture's ideal body types. The thinness craze, discussed in this box, encourages some people to extremes, as with Keira Knightley. It also makes it difficult for larger people to have positive self-images. Overcoming this difficulty, Jennifer Hudson is in the forefront of promoting an alternative image.*

But who can continue at such a torrid pace, striving for what are unrealistic cultural ideals? A few people, of course, but not many. So liposuction is appealing. Just lie there, put up with a little discomfort, and the doctor will vacuum the fat right out of your body. Surgeons can transform flat breasts into super breasts overnight. They can lower receding hairlines and smooth furrowed brows. They can remove lumps with their magical tummy tucks and can take off a decade with their rejuvenating skin peels, face lifts, and Botox injections.

With impossibly shaped models at *Victoria's Secret* and skinny models showing off the latest fashions in *Vogue* and *Seventeen*, half of U.S. adolescent girls feel fat and count calories (Hill 2006). Some teens even call the plastic surgeon. Anxious lest their child violate peer ideals and trail behind in her race for popularity, parents foot the bill. Some parents pay $25,000 just to give their daughters a flatter tummy (Gross 1998).

With peer pressure to alter the body already intense, surgeons keep stoking the fire. A sample ad: "No Ifs, Ands or Butts. You Can Change Your Bottom Line in Hours!" Some surgeons even offer gift certificates—so you can give your loved ones liposuction or Botox injections along with their greeting card (Dowd 2002).

The thinness craze has moved to the East, where glossy magazines feature skinny models. In China and India, a little extra padding was once valued as a sign of good health. Today, the obsession is thinness, and not-so-subtle ads scream that fat is bad (Prystay and Fowler 2003; Jung and Forbes 2007). In China, some teas come with a package of diet pills. Weight-loss machines, with electrodes attached to acupuncture pressure points, not only reduce fat but also build breasts—or so the advertisers claim.

Not limited by our rules, advertisers in Japan and China push a soap that supposedly "sucks up fat through the skin's pores" (Marshall 1995). What a dream product! After all, even though our TV models smile as they go through their paces, those exercise machines do look like a lot of hard work.

Then there is the other bottom line: Attractiveness does pay off. U.S. economists studied physical attractiveness and earnings. The result? "Good-looking" men and women earn the most, "average-looking" men and women earn more than "plain" people, and the "ugly" earn the least (Hamermesh and Biddle 1994). In Europe, too, the more attractive workers earn more (Brunello and D'Hombres 2007). Then there is that potent cash advantage that "attractive" women have: They attract and marry higher-earning men (Kanazawa and Kovar 2004).

More popularity *and* more money? Maybe you can't be thin enough after all. Maybe those exercise machines are a good investment. If only we could catch up with the Japanese and develop a soap that would suck the fat right out of our pores. You can practically hear the jingle now.

## For Your Consideration

What image do you have of your body? How do cultural expectations of "ideal" bodies underlie your image? Can you recall any advertisement or television program that has affected your body image?

What is considered ideal body size differs with historical periods and from one ethnic group to another. The women who posed for sixteenth-century European sculptors and painters, for example, were much "thicker" than the so-called "ideal" young women of today. (As I was looking at a painting in the Vatican, I heard a woman remark, "Look at those rolls of fat!") Why do you think that this difference exists?

Most advertising and television programs that focus on weight are directed at women. Women are more concerned than men about weight, more likely to have eating disorders, and more likely to be dissatisfied with their bodies (Honeycutt 1995; Hill 2006). Do you think that the targeting of women in advertising creates these attitudes and behaviors? Or do you think that these attitudes and behaviors would exist even if there were no such ads? Why?

situation. My perception and behavior did not come from the fact that germs are real, but, rather, from *my having grown up in a society that teaches they are real.* Microbes, of course, *objectively* exist, and whether or not germs are part of our thought world makes no difference as to whether we are infected by them. Our behavior, however, does not depend on the *objective* existence of something but, rather, on our *subjective interpretation,* on what sociologists call our *definition of reality.* In other words, it is not the reality of microbes that impresses itself on us, but society that impresses the reality of microbes on us.

This is the **social construction of reality.** Our society, or the social groups to which we belong, holds particular views of life. From our groups (the *social* part of this process), we learn ways of looking at life—whether that be our view of Hitler or Osama bin Laden (they're good, they're evil), germs (they exist, they don't exist), or *anything else in life.* In short, through our interaction with others, we *construct reality;* that is, we learn ways of interpreting our experiences in life.

**Gynecological Examinations**　To better understand the social construction of reality, let's consider an extended example.

To do research on vaginal examinations, I interviewed a gynecological nurse who had been present at about 14,000 examinations. I focused on how doctors construct social reality in order to define this examination as nonsexual (Henslin and Biggs 1971/2007). It became apparent that the pelvic examination unfolds much as a stage play does. I will use "he" to refer to the physician because only male physicians were part of this study. Perhaps the results would be different with women gynecologists.

**Scene 1 (the patient as person)**　In this scene, the doctor maintains eye contact with his patient, calls her by name, and discusses her problems in a professional manner. If he decides that a vaginal examination is necessary, he tells a nurse, "Pelvic in room 1." By this statement, he is announcing that a major change will occur in the next scene.

**Scene 2 (from person to pelvic)**　This scene is the depersonalizing stage. In line with the doctor's announcement, the patient begins the transition from a "person" to a "pelvic." The doctor leaves the room, and a female nurse enters to help the patient make the transition. The nurse prepares the "props" for the coming examination and answers any questions the woman might have.

What occurs at this point is essential for the social construction of reality, for *the doctor's absence removes even the suggestion of sexuality.* To undress in front of him could suggest either a striptease or intimacy, thus undermining the reality so carefully being defined: that of nonsexuality.

The patient also wants to remove any hint of sexuality, and during this scene she may express concern about what to do with her panties. Some mutter to the nurse, "I don't want him to see these." Most women solve the problem by either slipping their panties under their other clothes or placing them in their purse.

**Scene 3 (the person as pelvic)**　This scene opens when the doctor enters the room. Before him is a woman lying on a table, her feet in stirrups, her knees tightly together, and her body covered by a drape sheet. The doctor seats himself on a low stool before the woman and says, "Let your knees fall apart" (rather than the sexually loaded "Spread your legs"), and begins the examination.

The drape sheet is crucial in this process of desexualization, for it *dissociates the pelvic area from the person:* Leaning forward and with the drape sheet above his head, the physician can see only the vagina, not the patient's face. Thus dissociated from the individual, the vagina is dramaturgically transformed into an object of analysis. If the doctor examines the patient's breasts, he also dissociates them from her person by examining them one at a time, with a towel covering the unexamined breast. Like the vagina, each breast becomes an isolated item dissociated from the person.

In this third scene, the patient cooperates in being an object, becoming, for all practical purposes, a pelvis to be examined. She withdraws eye contact from the doctor and usually from the nurse, is likely to stare at the wall or at the ceiling, and avoids initiating conversation.

**Scene 4 (from pelvic to person)**　In this scene, the patient becomes "repersonalized." The doctor has left the examining room; the patient dresses and fixes her hair and makeup. Her reemergence as a person is indicated by such statements to the nurse as, "My dress isn't too wrinkled, is it?" indicating a need for reassurance that the metamorphosis from "pelvic" back to "person" has been completed satisfactorily.

**Scene 5 (the patient as person)**　In this final scene, the patient is once again treated as a person rather than as an object. The doctor makes eye contact with her and addresses her by name. She, too, makes eye contact with the doctor, and the usual middle-class interaction patterns are followed. She has been fully restored.

**In Sum:** To an outsider to our culture, the custom of women going to a male stranger for a vaginal examination might seem bizarre. But not to us. We learn that pelvic examinations are nonsexual. To sustain this definition requires teamwork—patients, doctors, and nurses working together to *socially construct reality.*

It is not just pelvic examinations or our views of microbes that make up our definitions of reality. Rather, *our behavior depends on how we define reality.* Our definitions (or constructions) provide the basis for what we do and how we feel about life. To understand human behavior, then, we must know how people define reality.

# The Need for Both Macrosociology and Microsociology

As was noted earlier, both microsociology and macrosociology make vital contributions to our understanding of human behavior. Our understanding of social life would be vastly incomplete without one or the other. The photo essay on the next two pages should help to make clear why we need *both* perspectives.

To illustrate this point, let's consider two groups of high school boys studied by sociologist William Chambliss (1973/2007). Both groups attended Hannibal High School. In one group were eight middle-class boys who came from "good" families and were perceived by the community as "going somewhere." Chambliss calls this group the "Saints." The other group consisted of six lower-class boys who were seen as headed down a dead-end road. Chambliss calls this group the "Roughnecks."

Boys in both groups skipped school, got drunk, and did a lot of fighting and vandalism. The Saints were actually somewhat more delinquent, for they were truant more often and engaged in more vandalism. Yet the Saints had a good reputation, while the Roughnecks were seen by teachers, the police, and the general community as no good and headed for trouble.

The boys' reputations set them on distinct paths. Seven of the eight Saints went on to graduate from college. Three studied for advanced degrees: One finished law school and became active in state politics, one finished medical school, and one went on to earn a Ph.D. The four other college graduates entered managerial or executive training programs with large firms. After his parents divorced, one Saint failed to graduate from high school on time and had to repeat his senior year. Although this boy tried to go to college by attending night school, he never finished. He was unemployed the last time Chambliss saw him.

In contrast, only four of the Roughnecks finished high school. Two of these boys did exceptionally well in sports and were awarded athletic scholarships to college. They both graduated from college and became high school coaches. Of the two others who graduated from high school, one became a small-time gambler and the other disappeared "up north," where he was last reported to be driving a truck. The two who did not complete high school were convicted of separate murders and sent to prison.

To understand what happened to the Saints and the Roughnecks, we need to grasp *both* social structure and social interaction. Using *macrosociology,* we can place these boys within the larger framework of the U.S. social class system. This reveals how opportunities open or close to people depending on their social class and how people learn different goals as they grow up in different groups. We can then use *microsociology* to follow their everyday lives. We can see how the Saints manipulated their "good" reputations to skip classes and how their access to automobiles allowed them to protect those reputations by spreading their troublemaking around different communities. In contrast, the Roughnecks, who did not have cars, were highly visible. Their lawbreaking, which was limited to a small area, readily came to the attention of the community. Microsociology also reveals how their respective reputations opened doors of opportunity to the first group of boys while closing them to the other.

It is clear that we need both kinds of sociology, and both are stressed in the following chapters.

# When a **Tornado Strikes**

## Social Organization Following a Natural Disaster

**a**s I was watching television on March 20, **2003, I heard** a report that a tornado had hit Camilla, Georgia. "Like a big lawn mower," the report said, it had cut a path of destruction through this little town. In its fury, the tornado had left behind six dead and about 200 injured.

From sociological studies of natural disasters, I knew that immediately after the initial shock the survivors of natural disasters work together to try to restore order to their disrupted lives. I wanted to see this restructuring process firsthand. The next morning, I took off for Georgia.

These photos, taken the day after the tornado struck, tell the story of people in the midst of trying to put their lives back together. I was impressed at how little time people spent commiserating about their misfortune and how quickly they took practical steps to restore their lives.

As you look at these photos, try to determine why you need both microsociology and macrosociology to understand what occurs after a natural disaster.

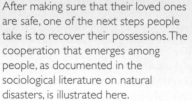

After making sure that their loved ones are safe, one of the next steps people take is to recover their possessions. The cooperation that emerges among people, as documented in the sociological literature on natural disasters, is illustrated here.

◀ The owners of this house invited me inside to see what the tornado had done to their home. In what had been her dining room, this woman is trying to salvage whatever she can from the rubble. She and her family survived by taking refuge in the bathroom. They had been there only five seconds, she said, when the tornado struck.

▲ In addition to the inquiring sociologist, television teams also were interviewing survivors and photographing the damage. This was the second time in just three years that a tornado had hit this neighborhood.

▲ No building or social institution escapes a tornado as it follows its path of destruction. Just the night before, members of this church had held evening worship service. After the tornado someone mounted a U.S. flag on top of the cross, symbolic of the church members' patriotism and religiosity—and of their enduring hope.

▲ Personal relationships are essential in putting lives together. Consequently, reminders of these relationships are one of the main possessions that people attempt to salvage. This young man, having just recovered the family photo album, is eagerly reviewing the photos.

▲ For children, family photos are not as important as toys. This girl has managed to salvage a favorite toy, which will help anchor her to her previous life.

▲ Formal organizations also help the survivors of natural disasters recover. In this neighborhood, I saw representatives of insurance companies, the police, the fire department, and an electrical co-op. The Salvation Army brought meals to the neighborhood.

▲ A sign of the times. Like electricity and gas, cable television also has to be restored as soon as possible.

# SUMMARY *and* REVIEW

## Levels of Sociological Analysis

### What two levels of analysis do sociologists use?

Sociologists use macrosociological and microsociological levels of analysis. In **macrosociology,** the focus is placed on large-scale features of social life, while in **microsociology,** the focus is on **social interaction.** Functionalists and conflict theorists tend to use a macrosociological approach, while symbolic interactionists are more likely to use a microsociological approach. P. 86.

## The Macrosociological Perspective: Social Structure

### How does social structure influence our behavior?

The term **social structure** refers to the social envelope that surrounds us and establishes limits on our behavior. Social structure consists of culture, social class, social statuses, roles, groups, and social institutions. Our location in the social structure underlies our perceptions, attitudes, and behaviors.

Culture lays the broadest framework, while **social class** divides people according to income, education, and occupational prestige. Each of us receives **ascribed statuses** at birth; later we add **achieved statuses.** Our behaviors and orientations are further influenced by the **roles** we play, the **groups** to which we belong, and our experiences with social institutions. These components of society work together to help maintain social order. Pp. 86–91.

### What are social institutions?

**Social institutions** are the standard ways that a society develops to meet its basic needs. As summarized in Figure 4.2 (page 92), industrial and postindustrial societies have ten social institutions—the family, religion, education, economics, medicine, politics, law, science, the military, and the mass media. Pp. 91–92.

### What social revolutions have transformed society?

The discovery that animals and plants could be domesticated marked the *first* social revolution. This transformed **hunting and gathering societies** into **pastoral** and **horticultural societies.** The invention of the plow brought about the *second* social revolution, as societies became **agricultural.** The invention of the steam engine, which led to **industrial societies,** marked the *third* social revolution.

The *fourth* social revolution was ushered in by the invention of the microchip, leading to the **postindustrial** or **information society.** Another new type of society, the **biotech society,** may be emerging. As in the previous social revolutions, little will remain the same. Our attitudes, ideas, expectations, behaviors, relationships—all will be transformed. Pp. 91–96.

### What holds society together?

According to Emile Durkheim, in agricultural societies people are united by **mechanical solidarity** (having similar views and feelings). With industrialization comes **organic solidarity** (people depend on one another to do their more specialized jobs). Ferdinand Tönnies pointed out that the informal means of control in *Gemeinschaft* (small, intimate) societies are replaced by formal mechanisms in *Gesellschaft* (larger, more impersonal) societies. Pp. 96–98.

## The Microsociological Perspective: Social Interaction in Everyday Life

### What is the focus of symbolic interactionism?

In contrast to functionalists and conflict theorists, who, as macrosociologists, focus on the "big picture," symbolic interactionists tend to be microsociologists, who focus on face-to-face social interaction. Symbolic interactionists analyze how people define their worlds and how their definitions, in turn, influence their behavior. Pp. 98–99.

### How do stereotypes affect social interaction?

**Stereotypes** are assumptions of what people are like. When we first meet people, we classify them according to our perceptions of their visible characteristics. Our ideas about those characteristics guide our behavior toward them. Our behavior, in turn, may influence them to behave in ways that reinforce our stereotypes. Pp. 100–101.

### Do all human groups share a similar sense of personal space?

In examining how people use physical space, symbolic interactionists stress that we surround ourselves with a "personal bubble" that we carefully protect. People from different cultures use "personal bubbles" of varying sizes, so the answer to the question is no. Americans typically use four different "distance zones": intimate, personal, social, and public. Pp. 100, 102.

### What is dramaturgy?

Erving Goffman developed **dramaturgy** (or dramaturgical analysis), in which everyday life is analyzed in terms of the stage. At the core of this analysis is **impression management,** our attempts to control the impressions we make on others. Our performances often call for **teamwork** and **face-saving behavior.** Pp. 102–105.

### What is the social construction of reality?

The phrase **the social construction of reality** refers to how we construct our views of the world, which, in turn, underlie our actions. **Ethnomethodology** is the study of how people make sense of everyday life. Ethnomethodologists try to uncover **background assumptions,** our basic ideas about the way life is. Pp. 105–109.

## The Need for Both Macrosociology and Microsociology

### Why are both levels of analysis necessary?

Because each focuses on different aspects of the human experience, both microsociology and macrosociology are necessary for us to understand social life. P. 109.

## THINKING CRITICALLY *about* Chapter 4

1. The major components of social structure are culture, social class, social status, roles, groups, and social institutions. Use social structure to explain why Native Americans have such a low rate of college graduation. (See Table 9.3 on page 248.)

2. Dramaturgy is a form of microsociology. Use dramaturgy to analyze a situation with which you are intimately familiar (such as interaction with your family or friends, or in one of your college classes).

3. To illustrate why we need both macrosociology and microsociology to understand social life, analyze the situation of a student getting kicked out of college as an example.

## ADDITIONAL RESOURCES

### What can you find in MySocLab? mysoclab  www.mysoclab.com

- **Complete Ebook**
- **Practice Tests and Video and Audio activities**
- **Mapping and Data Analysis exercises**

- **Sociology in the News**
- **Classic Readings in Sociology**
- **Research and Writing advice**

### Where Can I Read More on This Topic?

Suggested readings for this chapter are listed at the back of this book.

## chapter 5

# Social Groups and Formal Organizations

**W**hen Kody Scott joined the L.A. Crips, his initiation had two parts. Here's the first:

"How old is you now anyway?"

"Eleven, but I'll be twelve in November."

I never saw the blow to my head come from Huck. Bam! And I was on all fours. . . . Kicked in the stomach, I was on my back counting stars in the blackness. Grabbed by the collar, I was made to stand again. A solid blow to my chest exploded pain on the blank screen that had now become my mind. Bam! Another, then another. Blows rained on me from every direction. . . .

> Kody, you got eight shots, you don't come back to the car unless they all are gone.

Up until this point not a word had been spoken. . . . Then I just started swinging, with no style or finesse, just anger and the instinct to survive. . . . (This) reflected my ability to represent the set [gang] in hand-to-hand combat. The blows stopped abruptly. . . . My ear was bleeding, and my neck and face were deep red. . . .

Scott's beating was followed immediately by the second part of his initiation. For this, he received the name *Monster*, which he carried proudly:

"Give Kody the pump." [12-gauge pump action shotgun] . . . Tray Ball spoke with the calm of a football coach. "Tonight we gonna rock they world." . . . Hand slaps were passed around the room. . . . "Kody, you got eight shots, you don't come back to the car unless they all are gone."

"Righteous," I said, eager to show my worth. . . .

Hanging close to buildings, houses, and bushes, we made our way, one after the other, to within spitting distance of the Bloods. . . . Huck and Fly stepped from the shadows simultaneously and were never noticed until it was too late. Boom! Boom! Heavy bodies hitting the ground, confusion, yells of dismay, running. . . . By my sixth shot I had advanced past the first fallen bodies and into the street in pursuit of those who had sought refuge behind cars and trees. . . .

Back in the shack we smoked more pot and drank more beer. I was the center of attention for my acts of aggression. . . .

Tray Ball said. "You got potential, 'cause you eager to learn. Bangin' [being a gang member] ain't no part-time thang, it's full-time, it's a career. It's bein' down when ain't nobody else down with you. It's gettin' caught and not tellin'. Killin' and not caring, and dyin' without fear. It's love for your set and hate for the enemy. You hear what I'm sayin'?"

Kody adds this insightful remark:

> **Though never verbally stated, death was looked upon as a sort of reward, a badge of honor, especially if one died in some heroic capacity for the hood. . . . The supreme sacrifice was to "take a bullet for a homie" [fellow gang member]. The set functioned as a religion. Nothing held a light to the power of the set. If you died on the trigger you surely were smiled upon by the Crip God.**

Excerpts from Scott 1994:8–13, 103.

# Groups Within Society

Could you shoot strangers in cold blood—just because others tell you to pull the trigger? Although none of us want to think that we could be like Kody, don't bet on it. You are going to read some surprising things about groups in this chapter.

**Groups,** people who think of themselves as belonging together and who interact with one another, are the essence of life in society. Groups are vital for our well-being. They provide intimate relationships and a sense of belonging, something that we all need. This chapter, then, is highly significant for your life.

Before we analyze groups, we should clarify the concept. Two terms sometimes confused with group are *aggregate* and *category*. An **aggregate** consists of people who temporarily share the same physical space but who do not see themselves as belonging together. Shoppers standing in a checkout line or drivers waiting at a red light are an aggregate. A **category** is simply a statistic. It consists of people who share similar characteristics, such as all college women who wear glasses or all men over 6 feet tall. Unlike group members, the individuals who make up a category don't think of themselves as belonging together and they don't interact with one another. These concepts are illustrated in the photos on the next page.

Groups are so influential that they determine who we are. If you think that this is an exaggeration, recall what you read in Chapter 3, that even our minds are a product of society—or, more specifically phrased, of the groups to which we belong. To better understand the influence of groups on your own life, let's begin by looking at the types of groups that make up our society.

As society—the largest and most complex type of group—changes, so, too, do the groups, activities, and, ultimately, the type of people who form that society. This photo of Russian and Austrian wrestlers in the Olympics at Greece captures some of the changes occurring in Western societies. What social changes can you identify from this photo?

# Categories, Aggregates, Primary and Secondary Groups

Groups have a deep impact on our views, orientations, even what we feel and think about life. Yet, as illustrated by these photos, not everything that appears to be a group is actually a group in the sociological sense.

▲ **Aggregates** are simply people who happen to be in the same place at the same time.

▲ The outstanding trait that these three people have in common does not make them a group, but a **category.**

◀ **Secondary groups** are larger and more anonymous, formal, and impersonal than primary groups. Why are the participants of a dog show an example of a secondary group?

▶ **Primary groups** such as the family play a key role in the development of the self. As a small group, the family also serves as a buffer from the often-threatening larger group known as society. The family has been of primary significance in forming the basic orientations of this couple, as it will be for their son.

## Primary Groups

Our first group, the family, gives us our basic orientations to life. Later, among friends, we find more intimacy and an expanded sense of belonging. These groups are what sociologist Charles Cooley called **primary groups.** By providing intimate, face-to-face interaction, they give us an identity, a feeling of who we are. As Cooley (1909) put it,

> By primary groups I mean those characterized by intimate face-to-face association and cooperation. They are primary in several senses, but chiefly in that they are fundamental in forming the social nature and ideals of the individual.

**Producing a Mirror Within**    Cooley called primary groups the "springs of life." By this, he meant that primary groups, such as family and friends, are essential to our emotional well-being. As humans, we have an intense need for face-to-face interaction that generates feelings of self-esteem. By offering a sense of belonging and a feeling of being appreciated—and sometimes even loved—primary groups are uniquely equipped to meet this basic need. From our opening vignette, you can see that gangs are also primary groups.

Primary groups are also significant because their values and attitudes become fused into our identity. We internalize their views, which then become the lenses through which we view life. Even when we are adults—no matter how far we move away from our childhood roots—early primary groups remain "inside" us. There, they continue to form part of the perspective from which we look out onto the world. Ultimately, then, it is difficult, if not impossible, for us to separate the self from our primary groups, for the self and our groups merge into a "we."

## Secondary Groups

Compared with primary groups, **secondary groups** are larger, more anonymous, more formal, and more impersonal. Secondary groups are based on some common interest or activity, and their members are likely to interact on the basis of specific statuses, such as president, manager, worker, or student. Examples are a college class, the American Sociological Association, and the Democratic Party. Contemporary society could not function without secondary groups. They are part of the way we get our education, make our living, spend our money, and use our leisure time.

As necessary as secondary groups are for contemporary life, they often fail to satisfy our deep needs for intimate association. Consequently, *secondary groups tend to break down into primary groups.* At school and work, we form friendships. Our interaction with our friends is so important that we sometimes feel that if it weren't for them, school or work "would drive us crazy." The primary groups that we form within secondary groups, then, serve as a buffer between ourselves and the demands that secondary groups place on us.

**Voluntary Associations**    A special type of secondary group is a **voluntary association,** a group made up of volunteers who organize on the basis of some mutual interest. Some groups are local, consisting of only a few volunteers; others are national, with a paid professional staff.

Americans love voluntary associations and use them to express a wide variety of interests. A visitor entering one of the thousands of small towns that dot the U.S. landscape is often greeted by a highway sign proclaiming the town's voluntary associations: Girl Scouts, Boy Scouts, Kiwanis, Lions, Elks, Eagles, Knights of Columbus, Chamber of Commerce, American Legion, Veterans of Foreign Wars, and perhaps a host of others. One type of voluntary association is so prevalent that a separate sign sometimes indicates which varieties are present in the town: Roman Catholic, Baptist, Lutheran, Methodist, Episcopalian, and so on. Not listed on these signs are many other voluntary associations, such as political parties, unions, health clubs, the National Right to Life, the National Organization for Women, Alcoholics Anonymous, Gamblers Anonymous, Association of Pinto Racers, and Citizens United For or Against This and That.

**The Inner Circle and the Iron Law of Oligarchy**    A significant aspect of a voluntary association is that its key members, its inner circle, often grow distant from the regular members. They become convinced that only they can be trusted to make the group's important decisions. To see this principle at work, let's look at the Veterans of Foreign Wars (VFW).

Sociologists Elaine Fox and George Arquitt (1985) studied three local posts of the VFW, a national organization of former U.S. soldiers who have served in foreign wars. They found that although the leaders conceal their attitudes from the other members, the inner circle views the rank and file as a bunch of ignorant boozers. Because the leaders can't stand the thought that such people might represent them in the community and at national meetings, a curious situation arises. Although the VFW constitution makes rank-and-file members eligible for top leadership positions, they never become leaders. In fact, the inner circle is so effective in controlling these top positions that even before an election they can tell you who is going to win. "You need to meet Jim," the sociologists were told. "He's the next post commander after Sam does his time."

At first, the researchers found this puzzling. The election hadn't been held yet. As they investigated further, they found that leadership is actually determined behind the scenes. The current leaders appoint their favored people to chair the key committees. This spotlights their names and accomplishments, propelling the members to elect them. By appointing its own members to highly visible positions, then, the inner circle maintains control over the entire organization.

Like the VFW, most organizations are run by only a few of their members. Building on the term *oligarchy*, a system in which many are ruled by a few, sociologist Robert Michels (1876–1936) coined the term **the iron law of oligarchy** to refer to how organizations come to be dominated by a small, self-perpetuating elite (Michels 1911/1949). Most members of voluntary associations are passive, and an elite inner circle keeps itself in power by passing the leadership positions among its members.

What many find disturbing about the iron law of oligarchy is that people are excluded from leadership because they don't represent the inner circle's values—or, in some instances, their background. This is true even of organizations that are committed to democratic principles. For example, U.S. political parties—supposedly the backbone of the nation's representative government—are run by an inner circle that passes leadership positions from one elite member to another. This principle also shows up in the U.S. Senate. With their statewide control of political machinery and access to free mailing, about 90 percent of U.S. senators who choose to run are reelected (*Statistical Abstract* 2006:Table 394).

## In-Groups and Out-Groups

Groups toward which we feel loyalty are called **in-groups;** those toward which we feel antagonism are called **out-groups.** For Monster Kody in our opening vignette, the Crips were an in-group, while the Bloods were an out-group. That the Crips—and we—make such a fundamental division of the world has far-reaching consequences for our lives.

**Implications for a Socially Diverse Society: Shaping Perception and Morality**   The sense of belonging that membership in a group brings often leads to positive consequences. A common example is our tendency to excuse the faults of people we love and to encourage them to do better. Unfortunately, dividing the world into a "we" and "them" also leads to discrimination, hatred, and, as we saw in our opening vignette, even murder.

At the center of it all is how in-group membership shapes our perception of the world. Let's look at two examples. The first you see regularly, prejudice and discrimination on the basis of sex. As sociologist Robert Merton (1968) said, our favoritism creates a fascinating double standard. We tend to view the traits of our in-group as virtues, while we perceive those *same* traits as vices in out-groups. Men may perceive an aggressive man as assertive but an aggressive woman as pushy. They may think that a male employee who doesn't speak up "knows when to keep his mouth shut," while they

"So long, Bill. This is my club. You can't come in."

How our participation in social groups shapes our self-concept is a focus of symbolic interactionists. In this process, knowing who we are *not* is as significant as knowing who we are.

consider a quiet woman as too timid to make it in the business world.

The "we" and "they" division of the world can lead to such twisted perception that harming others comes to be viewed as right. The Nazis provide one of the most startling examples. For them, the Jews were an out-group who symbolized an evil that should be eliminated. Many ordinary, "good" Germans shared this view and defended the Holocaust as "dirty work" that someone had to do (Hughes 1962/2005).

An example from way back then, you might say—and the world has moved on since then. But our inclination to divide the world into in-groups and out-groups has not moved on—nor has the twisting of perception that follows. After the terrorist attacks of September 11, 2001, top U.S. officials came to view Arabs as sinister, bloodthirsty villains. They even said that it was OK for interrogators to be "cruel, inhuman, and degrading" to prisoners—as long as they didn't call it torture (Gonzales 2002). Alan Dershowitz, a professor at Harvard Law School, who usually takes very liberal views, went even further. He said that we should make torture legal, but, he added, judges should determine if torture is necessary and, if so, issue "torture warrants" (Schulz 2002). After 9/11, cruel interrogation and torture—justified for the sake of the in-group—became "dirty work" that someone had to do. Can you see the principle at work—and understand that in-group/out-group thinking can be so severe that even "good people" can torture and kill? And with a good conscience.

Economic downturns are especially perilous in this regard. The Nazis took power during a depression so severe that it was wiping out the middle classes. If such a depression were to occur in the United States, immigrants would be transformed from "nice people who for low wages will do jobs that Americans think are beneath them" to "sneaky people who steal jobs from friends and family." A national anti-immigration policy would follow, accompanied by a resurgence of hate groups such as the neo-Nazis, the Ku Klux Klan, and skinheads.

In short, to divide the world into in-groups and out-groups is a natural part of social life. But in addition to bringing functional consequences, it also brings dysfunctional ones.

## Reference Groups

Suppose you have just been offered a good job. It pays double what you hope to make even after you graduate from college. You have only two days to make up your mind. If you accept it, you will have to drop out of college. As you consider the matter, thoughts like this may go through your mind: "My friends will say I'm a fool if I don't take the job . . . but Dad and Mom will practically go crazy. They've made sacrifices for me, and they'll be crushed if I don't finish college. They've always said I've got to get my education first, that good jobs will always be there. . . . But, then, I'd like to see the look on the faces of those neighbors who said I'd never amount to much!"

**Evaluating Ourselves**    This is an example of how people use **reference groups,** the groups we refer to when we eval-

All of us have *reference groups*—the groups whose standards we use to evaluate ourselves. How do you think the reference groups of these members of the KKK who are demonstrating in Jaspar, Texas, differ from those of the police officer who is protecting their right of free speech? Although the KKK and this police officer use different groups to evaluate their attitudes and behaviors, the process is the same.

uate ourselves. Your reference groups may include your family, neighbors, teachers, classmates, co-workers, and the Scouts or the members of a church, synagogue, or mosque. If you were like Monster Kody in our opening vignette, the "set" would be your main reference group. Even a group you don't belong to can be a reference group. For example, if you are thinking about going to graduate school, graduate students or members of the profession you want to join may form a reference group. You would consider their standards as you evaluate your grades or writing skills.

Reference groups exert tremendous influence over our lives. For example, if you want to become a corporate executive, you might start to dress more formally, try to improve your vocabulary, read the *Wall Street Journal,* and change your major to business or law. In contrast, if you want to become a rock musician, you might wear jewelry in several places where you have pierced your body, get elaborate tattoos, dress in ways your parents and many of your peers consider extreme, read *Rolling Stone,* drop out of college, and hang around clubs and rock groups.

**Exposure to Contradictory Standards in a Socially Diverse Society**   From these examples, you can see how we use reference groups to evaluate our behavior. When we see ourselves as measuring up to a reference group's stan-

dards, we feel no conflict. If our behavior—or even aspirations—does not match the group's standards, however, the mismatch can lead to inner turmoil. For example, wanting to become a corporate executive would create no inner turmoil for most of us. It would, however, for someone who had grown up in an Amish home. The Amish strongly disapprove of such aspirations for their children. They ban high school and college education, suits and ties, and corporate employment. Similarly, if you want to join the military and your parents are dedicated pacifists, you likely would feel deep conflict, as your parents would have quite different aspirations for you.

Two chief characteristics of our society are social diversity and social mobility. This exposes most of us to standards and orientations that are inconsistent with those we learned during childhood. The "internal recordings" that play contradictory messages from different reference groups, then, are one price we pay for our social mobility.

## Social Networks

Although we live in a huge and diverse society, we don't experience social life as a sea of nameless, strange faces. Instead, we interact within social networks. The term **social network** refers to people who are linked to one another. Your social network includes your family, friends, acquaintances, people at work and school, and even "friends of friends." Think of your social network as lines that extend outward from yourself, gradually encompassing more and more people.

If you are a member of a large group, you probably associate regularly with a few people within that group. In a sociology class I was teaching at a commuter campus, six women who didn't know one another ended up working together on a project. They got along well, and they began to sit together. Eventually they planned a Christmas party at one of their homes. This type of social network, the clusters within a group, or its internal factions, is called a **clique** (cleek).

"Network analysis" has moved from theory and laboratory study to the practical world. One of the most striking examples is how U.S. forces located Saddam Hussein. Social scientists analyzed people's relationship to Hussein. They then drew up a "people map," placing names and

*Social networks* start with the people we associate with and expand outward from there. How do you think the social networks and *reference groups* of these two people differ from your own? How do you think they are similar?

photos of these people closer and farther from a central photo of Hussein. This let them see who was close enough to Hussein to know where he might be but distant enough to perhaps be willing to cooperate. It worked.

**The Small World Phenomenon**   Social scientists have wondered just how extensive the connections are between social networks. If you list everyone you know, each of those individuals lists everyone he or she knows, and you keep doing this, would almost everyone in the United States eventually be included on those lists?

It would be too cumbersome to test this hypothesis by drawing up such lists, but psychologist Stanley Milgram (1933–1984) came up with an interesting idea. In a classic study known as "the small world phenomenon," Milgram (1967) addressed a letter to "targets": the wife of a divinity student in Cambridge and a stockbroker in Boston. He sent the letter to "starters," who did not know these people. He asked them to send the letter to someone they knew on a first-name basis, someone they thought might know the "target." The recipients, in turn, were asked to mail the letter to someone they knew who might know the "target," and so on. The question was: Would the letters ever reach the "target"? If so, how long would the chain be?

Think of yourself as part of this study. What would you do if you were a "starter," but the "target" lived in a state in which you knew no one? You would send the letter to someone you know who might know someone in that state. This, Milgram reported, is just what happened. Although none of the senders knew the targets, the letters reached the designated individual in an average of just six jumps.

Milgram's study caught the public's fancy, leading to the phrase "six degrees of separation." This expression means that, on average, everyone in the United States is separated by just six individuals. Milgram's conclusions have become so popular that a game, "Six Degrees of Kevin Bacon," was built around it.

**Is the Small World Phenomenon an Academic Myth?**   Unfortunately, things are not this simple. There is a problem with Milgram's research, as psychologist Judith Kleinfeld (2002a, 2002b) discovered when she decided to replicate Milgram's study. When she went to the archives at Yale University Library to get more details, she found that Milgram had stacked the deck in favor of finding a small world. The "starters" came from mailing lists of people who were likely to have higher incomes and therefore were not representative of average people. In addition, one of the "targets" was a stockbroker, and that person's "starters" were investors in blue-chip stocks. Kleinfeld also

found another discrepancy: On average, only 30 percent of the letters reached their "target." In one of Milgram's studies, the success rate was just 5 percent.

Since most letters did *not* reach their targets, even with the deck stacked in favor of success, we can draw the *opposite* conclusion from the one that Milgram reported: People who don't know one another are dramatically separated by social barriers. How great the barriers are is illustrated by another attempt to replicate Milgram's study, this one using e-mail. Only 384 of 24,000 chains reached their targets (Dodds et al. 2003).

As Kleinfeld says, "Rather than living in a small world, we may live in a world that looks a lot like a bowl of lumpy oatmeal, with many small worlds loosely connected and perhaps some small worlds not connected at all." Somehow, I don't think that the phrase "lumpy oatmeal phenomenon" will become standard, but the criticism of Milgram's research is valid.

**Implications for a Socially Diverse Society**   Besides geography, the barriers that separate us into many small worlds are primarily those of social class, gender, and race–ethnicity. Overcoming these social barriers is difficult because even our own social networks contribute to social inequality, a topic that we explore in the Cultural Diversity box on the next page.

**Implications for Science**   Kleinfeld's revelations of the flaws in Milgram's research reinforce the need for replication, a topic discussed in Chapter 1. For our knowledge of social life, we cannot depend on single studies—there may be problems of generalizability on the one hand, or those of negligence or even fraud on the other. Replication by objective researchers is essential to build and advance solid social knowledge.

## A New Group: Electronic Communities

In the 1990s, a new type of human group, the **electronic community,** made its appearance. People "meet" online in chat rooms to talk about almost any conceivable topic, from donkey racing and bird watching to sociology and quantum physics. Some online encounters meet our definition of *group,* people who interact with one another and who think of themselves as belonging together. They pride themselves on the distinctive nature of their interests and knowledge—factors that give them a common identity and bind them together. Although sociologists have begun to study these groups, the results are preliminary and tentative.

# Cultural Diversity in the United States

## How Our Own Social Networks Perpetuate Social Inequality

Consider some of the principles we have reviewed. People tend to form in-groups with which they identify; they use reference groups to evaluate their attitudes and behavior; and they interact in social networks. Our in-groups, reference groups, and social networks are likely to consist of people whose backgrounds are similar to our own. For most of us, this means that just as social inequality is built into society, so it is built into our own relationships. One consequence is that we tend to perpetuate social inequality.

To see why, suppose that an outstanding job—great pay, interesting work, opportunity for advancement—has just opened up where you work. Whom are you going to tell? Most likely it will be someone you know, a friend or at least someone to whom you owe a favor. And most likely your social network is made up of people who look much like you do—especially in terms of their age, social class, race–ethnicity, and probably also gender. This tends to keep good jobs moving in the direction of people whose characteristics are similar to those of the people already in an organization. You can see how our social networks both reflect the inequality that characterizes our society and help to perpetuate it.

Consider a network of white men who are established in an organization. As they learn of opportunities (jobs, investments, real estate, and so on), they share this information with their networks. Opportunities and good jobs flow to people who have characteristics similar to their own. Those who benefit from

Social networks, *which open and close doors of opportunity, are important for careers. Despite the official program of business and professional conventions, much of the "real" business centers around renewing and extending social networks.*

this information, in turn, reciprocate with similar information when they learn of it. This bypasses people who have different characteristics—in this example, women and minorities—while it perpetuates the "good old boy" network. No intentional discrimination need be involved.

To overcome this barrier, women and minorities do **networking.** They try to meet people who can help advance their careers. Like the "good old boys," they go to parties and join clubs, churches, synagogues, mosques, and political parties. African American leaders, for example, cultivate a network of African American leaders. As a result, the network of African American leaders is so tight that one-fifth of the people composing the entire national African American leadership are personal acquaintances. Add some "friends of a friend," and *three-fourths* of the entire leadership belong to the same network (Taylor 1992).

Similarly, women cultivate a network of women. As a result, some women who reach top positions end up in a circle so tight that the term "new girl" network is being used, especially in the field of law. Remembering those who helped them and sympathetic to those who are trying to get ahead, these women tend to steer business to other women. Like the "good old boys" who preceded them, the new insiders have a ready set of reasons to justify their exclusionary practice (Jacobs 1997).

## For Your Consideration

The perpetuation of social inequality does not require intentional discrimination. Just as social inequality is built into society, so is it built into our personal relationships. How do you think your own social network helps to perpetuate social inequality? How do you think we can break this cycle? (The key must lie in creating diversity in social networks.)

# Bureaucracies

About 100 years ago, sociologist Max Weber analyzed the *bureaucracy,* a group that has since become dominant in social life. To achieve more efficient results, this form of social organization shifts the emphasis from traditional relationships based on personal loyalties to the "bottom line." As we look at the characteristics of bureaucracies, we will also consider their implications for our lives.

## The Characteristics of Bureaucracies

What do the Russian army and the U.S. postal service have in common? Or the government of Mexico and your col-

lege? The sociological answer is that all are *bureaucracies.* As Weber (1913/1947) pointed out, **bureaucracies** have

1. *Clear levels, with assignments flowing downward and accountability flowing upward.* Each level assigns responsibilities to the level beneath it, while each lower level is accountable to the level above it for fulfilling those assignments. Figure 5.1 below shows the bureaucratic structure of a typical university.
2. *A division of labor.* Each worker has a specific task to fulfill, and all the tasks are coordinated to accomplish the purpose of the organization. In a college, for example, a teacher does not fix the heating system, the president does not approve class schedules, and a secretary does not evaluate textbooks. These tasks are distributed among people who have been trained to do them.

**FIGURE 5.1**   **The Typical Bureaucratic Structure of a Medium-Sized University**

This is a scaled-down version of a university's bureaucratic structure. The actual lines of a university are likely to be much more complicated than those depicted here. A large university may have a chancellor and several presidents under the chancellor, each president being responsible for a particular campus. Although in this figure extensions of authority are shown only for the Vice President for Administration and the College of Social Sciences, each of the other vice presidents and colleges has similar positions. If the figure were to be extended, departmental secretaries would be shown and, eventually, somewhere, even students.

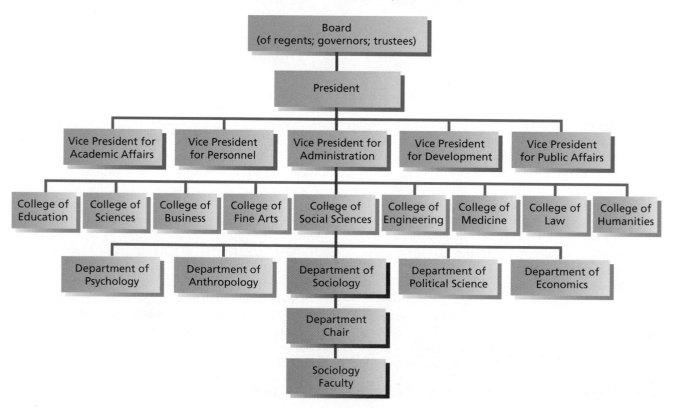

3. *Written rules.* In their attempt to become efficient, bureaucracies stress written procedures. In general, the longer a bureaucracy exists and the larger it grows, the more written rules it has.

4. *Written communications and records.* Records are kept of much of what occurs in a bureaucracy ("Be sure to CC all immediate supervisors."). In some organizations, workers spend a fair amount of time sending memos and e-mail back and forth.

5. *Impersonality and replaceability.* It is the office that is important, not the individual who holds the office. You work for the organization, not for the replaceable person who heads some post in the organization.

Weber viewed bureaucracies as such a powerful form of social organization that he predicted they would come to dominate social life. He called this process **the rationalization of society,** meaning that bureaucracies, with their rules and emphasis on results, would increasingly dominate our lives. Weber was right. These five characteristics have made bureaucracies so successful that, as illustrated by the Down-to-Earth Sociology box on the next page, they have even begun to take over cooking, one of the most traditional areas of life.

## The Perpetuation of Bureaucracies

Bureaucracies have become a standard feature of our lives because they are a powerful form of social organization. They harness people's energies to reach specific goals. Once in existence, however, bureaucracies tend to take on a life of their own. In a process called **goal displacement,** even after the organization achieves its goal and no longer has a reason to continue, continue it does.

A classic example is the March of Dimes, organized in the 1930s with the goal of fighting polio (Sills 1957). At that time, the origin of polio was a mystery. The public was alarmed and fearful, for overnight a healthy child could be stricken with this crippling disease. To raise money to find a cure, the March of Dimes placed posters of children on crutches near cash registers in almost every store in the United States. (See the photo below.) The organization raised money beyond its wildest dreams. When Dr. Jonas Salk developed a vaccine for polio in the 1950s, the threat was wiped out almost overnight.

Did the staff that ran the March of Dimes quietly fold up their tents and slip away? Of course not. They had jobs to protect, so they targeted a new enemy—birth defects. But then in 2001, researchers finished mapping the human genome system. Perceiving that this information could help to eliminate birth defects—and their jobs—officials of the March of Dimes came up with a new slogan, "Breakthroughs for Babies." This latest goal should ensure the organization's existence forever: It is so vague that we are not likely to ever run out of the need for "breakthroughs."

The March of Dimes was founded by President Franklin Roosevelt in the 1930s to fight polio. When a vaccine for polio was discovered in the 1950s, the organization did not declare victory and disband. Instead, its leaders kept the organization intact by creating new goals—fighting birth defects. Sociologists use the term *goal displacement* to refer to this process of adopting new goals.

## Down-to-Earth Sociology

## The McDonaldization of Society

*McDonalds in Tokyo, Japan*

The McDonald's restaurants that seem to be all over the United States—and, increasingly, the world—have a significance that goes far beyond the convenience of quick hamburgers and milk shakes. As sociologist George Ritzer (1993, 1998, 2001) says, our everyday lives are being "McDonaldized." Let's see what he means by this.

**The McDonaldization of society** does not refer just to the robotlike assembly of food. This term refers to the standardization of everyday life, a process that is transforming our lives. Want to do some shopping? Shopping malls offer one-stop shopping in controlled environments. Planning a trip? Travel agencies offer "package" tours. They will transport middle-class Americans to ten European capitals in fourteen days. All visitors experience the same hotels, restaurants, and other scheduled sites—and no one need fear meeting a "real" native. Want to keep up with events? *USA Today* spews out McNews—short, bland, non-analytical pieces that can be digested between gulps of the McShake or the McBurger.

Efficiency brings dependability. You can expect your burger and fries to taste the same whether you buy them in Los Angeles or Beijing. Although efficiency also lowers prices, it does come at a cost. Predictability washes away spontaneity, changing the quality of our lives. It produces a sameness, a bland version of what used to be unique experiences. In my own travels, for example, had I taken packaged tours, I never would have had the eye-opening experiences that have added so much to my appreciation of human diversity. (Bus trips with chickens in Mexico, hitchhiking in Europe and

Africa, sleeping on a granite table in a nunnery in Italy and in a cornfield in Algeria are just not part of tour agendas.)

For good or bad, our lives are being McDonaldized, and the predictability of packaged settings seems to be our social destiny. When education is rationalized, no longer will our children have to put up with real professors, who insist on discussing ideas endlessly, who never come to decisive answers, and who come saddled with idiosyncrasies. At some point, such an approach to education is going to be a bit of quaint history.

Our programmed education will eliminate the need for discussion of social issues—we will have packaged solutions to social problems, definitive answers that satisfy our need for closure. Computerized courses will teach the same answers to everyone—the approved, "politically correct" ways to think about social issues. Mass testing will ensure that students regurgitate the programmed responses.

Our coming prepackaged society will be efficient, of course. But it also means that we will be trapped in the "iron cage" of bureaucracy—just as Weber warned would happen.

---

Then there is NATO (North Atlantic Treaty Organization), founded during the Cold War to prevent Russia from invading Western Europe. When the Cold War ended, removing the organization's purpose, the Western powers tried to find a reason to continue their organization. I mean, why waste a perfectly good bureaucracy? They appear to have found one: to create "rapid response forces" to combat terrorism and "rogue nations" (Tyler

2002). To keep this bureaucracy going, they even allowed Russia to become a junior partner.

## Dysfunctions of Bureaucracies

Although in the long run no other form of social organization is more efficient, as Weber recognized, bureaucracies also have a dark side. Let's look at some of their dysfunctions.

This is the way that some people view bureaucracies: stilted, slow-moving, and destructive to the individual. Bureaucracies can be like this, but not all bureaucracies are alike. Some are innovative and unleash creative energy.

**Red Tape: A Rule Is a Rule**    Bureaucracies can be so bound by red tape that when officials apply their rules, the results can defy all logic. I came across an example so ridiculous that it can make your head swim—if you don't burst from laughing first.

> In Spain, the Civil Registry of Barcelona recorded the death of a woman named Maria Antonieta Calvo in 1992. Apparently, Maria's evil brother had reported her dead so he could collect the family inheritance.
>
> When Maria learned that she was supposedly dead, she told the Registry that she was very much alive. The bureaucrats at this agency looked at their records, shook their heads, and insisted that she was dead. Maria then asked lawyers to represent her in court. They all refused—because no dead person can bring a case before a judge.
>
> When Maria's boyfriend asked her to marry him, the couple ran into a serious obstacle: No living man in Spain (or elsewhere, I presume) can marry a dead woman—so these bureaucrats said, "So sorry, but no license."
>
> After years of continuing to insist that she was alive, Maria finally got a hearing in court. When the judges looked at Maria, they believed that she really was a living person, and they ordered the Civil Registry to declare her alive.

The ending of this story gets even happier, for now that Maria was alive, she was able to marry her boyfriend. I don't know if the two lived happily ever after, but, after overcoming the bureaucrats, they at least had that chance ("Mujer 'resucita'. . ." 2006).

**Bureaucratic Alienation**    Perceived in terms of roles, rules, and functions rather than as individuals, many workers begin to feel more like objects than people. Marx termed these reactions **alienation**, a result, he said, of workers being cut off from the finished product of their labor. He pointed out that before industrialization, workers used their own tools to produce an entire product, such as a chair or table. Now the capitalists own the tools (machinery, desks, computers) and assign each worker only a single step or two in the entire production process. Relegated to performing repetitive tasks that seem remote from the final product, workers no longer identify with what they produce. They come to feel estranged not only from the results of their labor but also from their work environment.

**Resisting Alienation**    Because workers need to feel valued and want to have a sense of control over their work, they resist alienation. Forming primary groups at work is a major form of that resistance. Workers band together in informal settings—at lunch, around desks, or for a drink after work. There, they give one another approval for jobs well done and express sympathy for the shared need to put up with cantankerous bosses, meaningless routines, and endless rules. In these contexts, they relate to one another not just as workers, but as people who value one another. They flirt, laugh and tell jokes, and talk about their families and goals. Adding this multidimensionality to their work relationships maintains their sense of being individuals rather than mere cogs in a machine.

Workers develop many ways to avoid becoming a depersonalized unit in a bureaucratic-economic machine. In this photo, which I took at a major publisher, you can see how Rebecca, by personalizing her work setting, is claiming an identity that transcends that of worker. What "personalized messages" do you see in this photo?

As in the photo above, workers often decorate their work areas with personal items. The sociological implication is that of workers who are striving to resist alienation. By staking a claim to individuality, the workers are rejecting an identity as machines that exist simply to perform functions.

**Bureaucratic Incompetence**    In a tongue-in-cheek analysis of bureaucracies, Laurence Peter proposed what has become known as the **Peter principle:** Each employee of a bureaucracy is promoted to his or her *level of incompetence* (Peter and Hull 1969). People who perform well in a bureaucracy come to the attention of those higher up the chain of command and are promoted. If they continue to perform well, they are promoted again. This process continues *until* they are promoted to a level at which they can no longer handle the responsibilities well—their level of incompetence. There they hide behind the work of others, taking credit for the accomplishments of employees under their direction.

Although the Peter principle contains a grain of truth, if it were generally true, bureaucracies would be staffed by incompetents, and these organizations would fail. In reality, bureaucracies are remarkably successful. Sociologists Peter Evans and James Rauch (1999) examined the government bureaucracies of thirty-five developing countries. They found that prosperity comes to the countries with central bureaucracies that hire workers on the basis of merit and offer them rewarding careers.

# Working for the Corporation

Since you are likely to end up working in a bureaucracy, let's look at how its characteristics might affect your career.

## Self-Fulfilling Stereotypes in the "Hidden" Corporate Culture

As you might recall from Chapter 4, stereotypes can be self-fulfilling. That is, stereotypes can produce the very characteristics that they are built around. The example used in Chapter 4 concerned stereotypes of appearance and personality. You might want to review the Down-to-Earth Sociology box on page 101.

Stereotypes also operate in corporate life—and are so powerful that they can affect *your* career. Here's how they work.

**Self-Fulfilling Stereotypes and Promotions**    Corporate and department heads have ideas of "what it takes" to get ahead. Not surprisingly, since they themselves got ahead, they look for people who have characteristics similar to their own. They feed better information to workers with these characteristics, bring them into stronger networks, and put them in "fast track" positions. With such advantages, these workers perform better and become more committed to the company. This, of course, confirms the boss's initial expectation, or stereotype. But for workers who don't look or act like the corporate leaders, the opposite happens. Thinking of them as less capable, the bosses give them fewer opportunities and challenges. When these workers see others get ahead and realize that they are working beneath their own abilities, they lose morale, become less committed to the company, and don't perform as well. This, of course, confirms the stereotypes the bosses had of them.

In her studies of U.S. corporations, sociologist Rosabeth Moss Kanter (1977, 1983) found such self-fulfilling stereotypes to be part of a "hidden" **corporate culture.** That is, these stereotypes and their powerful effects on workers remain hidden to everyone, even the bosses. What bosses and workers see is the surface: The workers getting promoted are those who have superior performance and greater commitment to the company. To everyone, this seems to be just the way it should be. Hidden below this surface, however, as Kanter found, are these higher and lower expectations and the open and closed opportunities that produce the attitudes and accomplishments—or the lack of them.

As corporations grapple with growing diversity, the stereotypes in the hidden corporate culture are likely to give way, although slowly and grudgingly. In the following Thinking Critically section, we'll consider other aspects of diversity in the workplace.

# ThinkingCRITICALLY
## Managing Diversity in the Workplace

Times have changed. The San Jose, California, electronic phone book lists *ten* times more *Nguyens* than *Joneses* (Albanese 2007). More than half of U.S. workers are minorities, immigrants, and women. Diversity in the workplace is much more than skin color. Diversity includes age, ethnicity, gender, religion, sexual orientation, and social class.

In our growing global context of life, diversity is increasing. In the past, the idea was for people to join the "melting pot," to give up their distinctive traits and become like the dominant group. Today, with the successes of the civil rights and women's movements, people are more likely to prize their distinctive traits. Realizing that assimilation (being absorbed into the dominant culture) is probably not the wave of the future, most large companies have "diversity training" (Johnson 2004; Hymowitz 2007). They hold lectures and workshops so that employees can learn to work with colleagues of diverse cultures and racial–ethnic backgrounds.

Coors Brewery is a prime example of this change. Coors went into a financial tailspin after one of the Coors brothers gave a racially charged speech in the 1980s. Today, Coors offers diversity workshops, has sponsored a gay dance, and has paid for a corporate-wide mammography program. In 2004, Coors opposed an amendment to the Colorado constitution that would ban the marriage of homosexuals. The company has even had rabbis certify its suds as kosher. Its proud new slogan: "Coors cares" (Cloud 1998). Now, that's quite a change.

What Coors cares about, of course, is the bottom line. It's the same with other corporations. Blatant racism and sexism once made no difference to profitability. Today, they do. To promote profitability, companies must promote diversity—or at least pretend to. The sincerity of corporate leaders is not what's important; diversity in the workplace is.

Diversity training has the potential to build bridges, but it can backfire. Managers who are chosen to participate can resent it, thinking that it is punishment for some unmentioned insensitivity on their part (Sanchez and Medkik 2004). Some directors of these programs are so incompetent that they create antagonisms and reinforce stereotypes. For example, the leaders of a diversity training session at the U.S. Department of Transportation had women grope men as the men ran by. They encouraged blacks and whites to insult one another and to call each other names (Reibstein 1996). The intention may have been good (understanding the other through role reversal and getting hostilities "out in the open"), but the approach was moronic. Instead of healing, such behaviors wound and leave scars.

Pepsi provides a positive example of diversity training. Managers at Pepsi are given the assignment of sponsoring a group of employees who are unlike themselves. Men sponsor women, African Americans sponsor whites, and so on. The executives are expected to try to understand work from the perspective of the people they sponsor, to identify key talent, and to personally mentor at least three people in their group. Accountability is built in—the sponsors have to give updates to executives even higher up (Terhune 2005).

### For Your Consideration

Do you think that corporations and government agencies should offer diversity training? If so, how can we develop diversity training that fosters mutual respect? Can you suggest practical ways to develop workplaces that are not divided by gender and race–ethnicity?

# Technology and the Control of Workers

As mentioned in the last chapter, the microchip has revolutionized society. Among the changes it has ushered in is the greater ease of keeping tabs on people. Computers make it easier for governments to operate a police state by monitoring our every move (Bradsher 2007b). The Big Brother in Orwell's classic novel *1984* may turn out to be a master computer to which we all become servants.

We'll know shortly. Already, many workers are closely monitored by computers. In some workplaces, cameras even transmit workers' facial expressions for computer analysis (Neil 2008). These cameras, called "little brothers" (as compared with Orwell's "Big Brother"), are making their appearance in shopping malls, on streetcorners, and in our homes. As some analysts suggest, we seem to be moving to a *maximum-security society* (Marx 1995).

Maximum-security society seems an apt term. As with the workers in the Sociology and the New Technology box on the next page, few of us realize how extensively our actions are being monitored.

# Group Dynamics

As you know from personal experience, the lively interaction *within* groups—who does what with whom—has profound consequences for how you adjust to life. Sociologists use the term **group dynamics** to refer to how groups influence us and how we affect groups. Let's consider how the size of a group makes a difference and then examine leadership, conformity, and decision making.

Before doing so, we should see how sociologists define the term *small group.* In a **small group,** there are few enough members that each one can interact directly with all the other members. Small groups can be either primary or secondary. A wife, husband, and children make up a primary small group, as do workers who take their breaks together, while bidders at an auction and students in an introductory sociology class are secondary small groups.

## Effects of Group Size on Stability and Intimacy

Writing in the early 1900s, sociologist Georg Simmel (1858–1918) noted the significance of group size. He used the term **dyad** for the smallest possible group, which consists of two people. Dyads, which include marriages, love affairs, and close friendships, show two distinct qualities. First, they are the most intense or intimate of human groups. Because only two people are involved, the interaction is focused on them. Second, because dyads require that both members participate and be committed, it takes just one member to lose interest for the dyad to collapse. In larger groups, by contrast, even if one member withdraws, the group can continue, for its existence does not depend on any single member (Simmel 1950).

A **triad** is a group of three people. As Simmel noted, the addition of a third person fundamentally changes the group. With three people, interaction between the first two decreases. This can create strain. For example, with the birth of a child, hardly any aspect of a couple's relationship goes untouched. Attention focuses on the baby, and interaction between the husband and wife diminishes. Despite this, the marriage usually becomes stronger. Although the intensity of interaction is less in triads, they are inherently stronger and give greater stability to a relationship.

Yet, as Simmel noted, triads, too, are inherently unstable. They tend to form **coalitions**—some group members aligning themselves against others. In a triad, it is not uncommon for two members to feel a stronger bond and to prefer one another. This leaves the third person feeling hurt and excluded. Another characteristic of triads is that they often produce an arbitrator or mediator, someone who tries to settle disagreements between the other two. In one-child families, you can often observe both of these characteristics of triads—coalitions and arbitration.

The general principle is this: *As a small group grows larger, it becomes more stable, but its intensity, or intimacy, decreases.* To see why, look at Figure 5.2 on page 132. As each new person comes into a group, the connections among people multiply. In a dyad, there is only 1 relationship; in a triad, there are 3; in a group of four, 6; in a group of five, 10. If we expand the group to six, we have 15 relationships, while a group of seven yields 21 relationships. If we continue adding members, we soon are unable to follow the connections: A group of eight has 28 possible relationships; a group of nine, 36 relationships; a group of ten, 45; and so on.

It is not only the number of relationships that makes larger groups more stable. As groups grow, they also tend to develop a more formal structure to accomplish their goals. For example, leaders emerge and more specialized roles come into play. This often results in such familiar offices as president, secretary, and treasurer. This structure provides a framework that helps the group survive over time.

# SOCIOLOGY and the NEW TECHNOLOGY

## Cyberloafers and Cybersleuths: Surfing at Work

Few people work constantly at their jobs. Most of us take breaks and, at least once in a while, goof off. We meet fellow workers at the coffee machine, and we talk in the hallway. Much of this interaction is good for the company, for it bonds us to fellow workers and ties us to our jobs.

Our personal lives may even cross over into our workday. Some of us make personal calls from the office. Bosses know that we need to check in with our child's preschool or make arrangements for a babysitter. They expect such calls. Some even wink as we make a date or nod as we arrange to have our car worked on. And most bosses make personal calls of their own from time to time. It's the abuse that bothers bosses, and it's not surprising that they fire anyone who talks on the phone all day for personal reasons.

Using computers at work for personal purposes is called *cyberslacking*. Many workers fritter away some of their workday online. They trade stocks, download music, gamble, and play games. They read books, shop, exchange jokes, send personal e-mail, post messages in chat rooms, and visit online red-light districts. Some cyberslackers even operate their own businesses online—when they're not battling virtual enemies during "work."

To take a day off without the boss knowing it, some use remote devices to make their computer switch screens and their printer spew out documents (Spencer 2003). It looks as though they just stepped away from their desk. Some equip their cell phones with audio recordings: Although they may be sitting on the beach when they call the office, their boss hears background sounds of a dentist's drill or of honking horns (Richtel 2004).

Some workers defend their cyberloafing. They argue, reasonably enough, that since their work invades their homes—forcing them to work evenings and weekends—employers should accommodate their personal lives. Some Web sites protect cyberloafers: They feature a panic button in case the boss pokes her head in your office. Click the button and a phony spreadsheet pops onto your screen while typing sounds emerge from your speakers.

Cyberslacking has given birth to the *cybersleuth*. With specialized software, cybersleuths can recover every note employees have written and every Web site they have visited (Nusbaum 2003). They can bring up every file that employees have deleted, even every word they've erased. What some workers don't know (and what some of us forget) is that "delete" does not mean erase. Hitting the delete button simply pushes the text into the background of our hard drive. With a few clicks, the cybersleuth, like magic ink, exposes our "deleted" information, opening our hidden diary for anyone to read.

## For Your Consideration

Do you think that cybersleuthing is an abuse of power? An invasion of privacy? Or do employers have a right to check on what their employees are doing with company computers on company time? Can you think of a less invasive solution to cyberloafing?

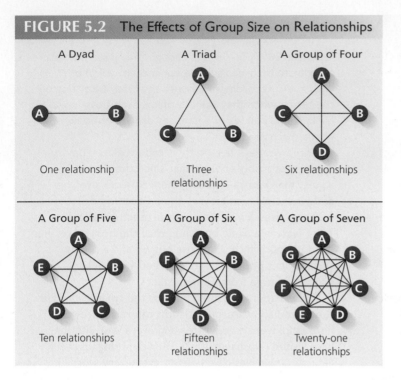

**FIGURE 5.2**   The Effects of Group Size on Relationships

A Dyad — One relationship

A Triad — Three relationships

A Group of Four — Six relationships

A Group of Five — Ten relationships

A Group of Six — Fifteen relationships

A Group of Seven — Twenty-one relationships

## Effects of Group Size on Attitudes and Behavior

Imagine that your social psychology professors have asked you to join a few students to discuss your adjustment to college life. When you arrive, they tell you that to make the discussion anonymous they want you to sit unseen in a booth. You will participate in the discussion over an intercom, talking when your microphone comes on. The professors say that they will not listen to the conversation, and they leave.

You find the format somewhat strange, to say the least, but you go along with it. You have not seen the other students in their booths, but when they talk about their experiences, you find yourself becoming wrapped up in the problems that they begin to share. One student even mentions how frightening he has found college because of his history of epileptic seizures. Later, you hear this individual breathe heavily into the microphone. Then he stammers and cries for help. A crashing noise follows, and you imagine him lying helpless on the floor.

Nothing but an eerie silence follows. What do you do?

Your professors, John Darley and Bibb Latané (1968), staged the whole thing, but you don't know this. No one had a seizure. In fact, no one was even in the other booths. Everything, except your comments, was on tape.

Some participants were told that they would be discussing the topic with just one other student, others with two, others with three, four, and five. Darley and Latané found that all students who thought they were part of a dyad rushed out to help. If they thought they were part of a triad, only 80 percent went to help—and they were slower in leaving the booth. In six-person groups, only 60 percent went to see what was wrong—and they were even slower.

This experiment demonstrates how deeply group size influences our attitudes and behavior: It even affects our willingness to help one another. Students in the dyad knew that it was up to them to help the other student. The professor was gone, and if they didn't help there was no one else. In the larger groups, including the triad, students felt *a diffusion of responsibility:* Giving help was no more their responsibility than anyone else's.

You probably have observed the second consequence of group size firsthand. When a group is small, its members act informally, but as the group grows, the members lose their sense of intimacy and become more formal with one another. No longer can the members assume that the others are "insiders" in sympathy with what they say. Now they must take a "larger audience" into consideration, and instead of merely "talking," they begin to "address" the group. As their speech becomes more formal, their body language stiffens.

You probably have observed a third aspect of group dynamics, too. In the early stages of a party, when only a few people are present, almost everyone talks with everyone else. But as others arrive, the guests break into smaller groups. Some hosts, who want their guests to mix together, make a nuisance of themselves trying to achieve *their* idea of what a group should be like. The division into small groups is inevitable, however, for it follows the basic sociological principles that we have just reviewed. Because the addition of each person rapidly increases connections (in this case, "talk lines"), conversation becomes more difficult. The guests break into smaller groups in which they can look at each other directly and interact comfortably with one another.

## Leadership

All of us are influenced by leaders, so it is important to understand leadership. Let's look at how people become leaders, the types of leaders there are, and their different styles of leadership. Before we do this, though, it is important to clarify that leaders don't necessarily hold formal positions in a group. **Leaders** are simply people who influence the behaviors, opinions, or attitudes of others. Even a group of friends has leaders.

**Who Becomes a Leader?**    Are leaders born with characteristics that propel them to the forefront of a group? No sociologist would agree with such an idea. In general, people who become leaders are perceived by group members as strongly representing their values or as able to lead a group out of a crisis (Trice and Beyer 1991). Leaders also tend to be more talkative and to express determination and self-confidence.

These findings may not be surprising, as such traits appear to be related to leadership. Researchers, however, have also discovered traits that seem to have no bearing on the ability to lead. For example, taller people and those who are judged better looking are more likely to become leaders (Stodgill 1974; Judge and Cable 2004). The taller and more attractive are also likely to earn more, but that is another story (Deck 1968; Feldman 1972; Case and Paxson 2006).

Many other factors underlie people's choice of leaders, most of which are quite subtle. A simple experiment performed by social psychologists Lloyd Howells and Selwyn Becker (1962) uncovered one of these factors. They formed groups of five people who did not know one another, seating them at a rectangular table, three on one side and two on the other. After discussing a topic for a set period of time, each group chose a leader. The findings are startling: Although only 40 percent of the people sat on the two-person side, 70 percent of the leaders emerged from that side. The explanation is that we tend to direct more interactions to people facing us than to people to the side of us.

**Types of Leaders**    Groups have two types of leaders (Bales 1950, 1953; Cartwright and Zander 1968). The first is easy to recognize. This person, called an **instrumental leader** (or *task-oriented leader*), tries to keep the group moving toward its goals. These leaders try to keep group members from getting sidetracked, reminding them of what they are trying to accomplish. The **expressive leader** (or *socioemotional leader*), in contrast, usually is not recognized as a leader, but he or she certainly is one. This person is likely to crack jokes, to offer sympathy, or to do other things that help to lift the group's morale. Both types of leadership are essential: the one to keep the group on track, the other to increase harmony and minimize conflicts.

It is difficult for the same person to be both an instrumental and an expressive leader, for these roles contradict one another. Because instrumental leaders are task oriented, they sometimes create friction as they prod the group to get on with the job. Their actions often cost them popularity. Expressive leaders, in contrast, who stimulate personal bonds and reduce friction, are usually more popular (Olmsted and Hare 1978).

**Leadership Styles**    Let's suppose that the president of your college has asked you to head a task force to determine how the college can improve race relations on campus. Although this position requires you to be an instrumental leader, you can adopt a number of **leadership styles,** or ways of expressing yourself as a leader. The three basic styles are those of **authoritarian leader,** one who gives orders; **democratic leader,** one who tries to gain a consensus; and **laissez-faire leader,** one who is highly permissive. Which style should you choose?

Social psychologists Ronald Lippitt and Ralph White (1958) carried out a classic study of these leadership styles. Boys who were matched for IQ, popularity, physical energy, and leadership were assigned to "craft clubs" made up of five boys each. The experimenters trained adult men in the three leadership styles. As the researchers peered through peepholes, taking notes and making movies, each adult rotated among the clubs, playing all three styles to control possible influences of their individual personalities.

The *authoritarian* leaders assigned tasks to the boys and told them exactly what to do. They also praised or condemned the boys' work arbitrarily, giving no explanation for why they judged it good or bad. The *democratic* leaders discussed the project with the boys, outlining the steps that would help them reach their goals. They also suggested alternative approaches and let the boys work at their own pace. When they evaluated the project, they gave "facts" as the bases for their decisions. The *laissez-faire* leaders were passive. They gave the boys almost total freedom to do as they wished. They offered help when asked, but made few suggestions. They did not evaluate the boys' projects, either positively or negatively.

The results? The boys who had authoritarian leaders grew dependent on their leader and showed a high degree of internal solidarity. They also became either aggressive or apathetic, with the aggressive boys growing hostile toward their leader. In contrast, the boys who had democratic leaders were friendlier and looked to one another for mutual approval. They did less scapegoating, and when the leader left the room they continued to work at a steadier pace. The boys with laissez-faire leaders asked more questions, but they made fewer decisions. They were notable for their lack of achievement. The researchers concluded that the democratic style of leadership works best. Their conclusion, however, may have been biased, as the researchers favored a democratic style of leadership in the first place (Olmsted and Hare 1978). Apparently, this same bias in studies of leadership continues (Cassel 1999).

You may have noticed that only boys and men were involved in this experiment. It is interesting to speculate how the results might differ if we were to repeat the experiment with all-girl groups and with mixed groups of girls and boys—and if we used both men and women as leaders. Perhaps you will become the sociologist to study such variations of this classic experiment.

**Leadership Styles in Changing Situations** Different situations require different styles of leadership. Suppose, for example, that you are leading a dozen backpackers in the Sierra Madre mountains north of Los Angeles, and it is time to make dinner. A laissez-faire style would be appropriate if the backpackers had brought their own food, or perhaps a democratic style if everyone were supposed to pitch in. Authoritarian leadership—you telling the hikers how to prepare their meals—would create resentment. This, in turn, would likely interfere with meeting the primary goal of the group, which in this case is to have a good time while enjoying nature.

Now assume the same group but a different situation: One of your party is lost, and a blizzard is on its way. This situation calls for you to exercise authority. To simply shrug your shoulders and say "You figure it out" would invite disaster—and probably a lawsuit.

## The Power of Peer Pressure: The Asch Experiment

How influential are groups in our lives? To answer this, let's look first at *conformity* in the sense of going along with our peers. Our peers have no authority over us, only the influence that we allow.

Imagine that you are taking a course in social psychology with Dr. Solomon Asch and you have agreed to participate in an experiment. As you enter his laboratory, you see seven chairs, five of them already filled by other students. You are given the sixth. Soon the seventh person arrives. Dr. Asch stands at the front of the room next to a covered easel. He explains that he will first show a large

card with a vertical line on it, then another card with three vertical lines. Each of you is to tell him which of the three lines matches the line on the first card. (See Figure 5.3)

Dr. Asch then uncovers the first card with the single line and the comparison card with the three lines. The correct answer is easy, for two of the lines are obviously wrong, and one is exactly right. Each person, in order, states his or her answer aloud. You all answer correctly. The second trial is just as easy, and you begin to wonder why you are there.

Then on the third trial, something unexpected happens. Just as before, it is easy to tell which lines match. The first student, however, gives a wrong answer. The second gives the same incorrect answer. So do the third and

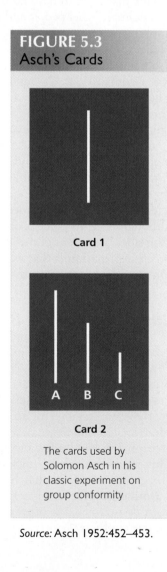

**FIGURE 5.3**
Asch's Cards

Card 1

Card 2

The cards used by Solomon Asch in his classic experiment on group conformity

*Source:* Asch 1952:452–453.

the fourth. By now, you are wondering what is wrong. How will the person next to you answer? You can hardly believe it when he, too, gives the same wrong answer. Then it is your turn, and you give what you know is the right answer. The seventh person also gives the same wrong answer.

On the next trial, the same thing happens. You know that the choice of the other six is wrong. They are giving what to you are obviously wrong answers. You don't know what to think. Why aren't they seeing things the same way you are? Sometimes they do, but in twelve trials they don't. Something is seriously wrong, and you are no longer sure what to do.

When the eighteenth trial is finished, you heave a sigh of relief. The experiment is finally over, and you are ready to bolt for the door. Dr. Asch walks over to you with a big smile on his face, and thanks you for participating in the experiment. He explains that you were the only real subject in the experiment! "The other six were stooges. I paid them to give those answers," he says. Now you feel real relief. Your eyes weren't playing tricks on you after all.

What were the results? Asch (1952) tested fifty people. One-third (33 percent) gave in to the group half the time, providing what they knew to be wrong answers. Another two out of five (40 percent) gave wrong answers, but not as often. One out of four (25 percent) stuck to their guns and always gave the right answer. I don't know how I would do on this test (if I knew nothing about it in advance), but I like to think that I would be part of the 25 percent. You probably feel the same way about yourself. But why should we feel that we wouldn't be like *most* people?

The results are disturbing, and researchers are still replicating Asch's experiment (Bond 2005). In our "land of individualism," the group is so powerful that most people are willing to say things that they know are not true. And this was a group of strangers! How much more conformity can we expect when our group consists of friends, people we value highly and depend on for getting along in life? Again, maybe you will become the sociologist to run that variation of Asch's experiment, perhaps using female subjects.

## The Power of Authority: The Milgram Experiment

Even more disturbing are the results of the experiment described in the following Thinking Critically section.

# ThinkingCRITICALLY
## If Hitler Asked You to Execute a Stranger, Would You?
## The Milgram Experiment

Imagine that you are taking a course with Dr. Stanley Milgram (1963, 1965), a former student of Dr. Asch's. Assume that you do not know about the Asch experiment and have no reason to be wary. You arrive at the laboratory to participate in a study on punishment and learning. You and a second student draw lots for the roles of "teacher" and "learner." You are to be the teacher. When you see that the learner's chair has protruding electrodes, you are glad that you are the teacher. Dr. Milgram shows you the machine you will run. You see that one side of the control panel is marked "Mild Shock, 15 volts," while the center says "Intense Shock, 350 Volts," and the far right side reads "DANGER: SEVERE SHOCK."

"As the teacher, you will read aloud a pair of words," explains Dr. Milgram. "Then you will repeat the first word, and the learner will reply with the second word. If the learner can't remember the word, you press this lever on the shock generator. The shock will serve as punishment, and we can then determine if punishment improves memory." You nod, now very relieved that you haven't been designated the learner.

"Every time the learner makes an error, increase the punishment by 15 volts," instructs Dr. Milgram. Then, seeing the look on your face, he adds, "The shocks can be extremely painful, but they won't cause any permanent tissue damage." He pauses, and then says, "I want you to see." You then follow him to the "electric chair," and Dr. Milgram gives you a shock of 45 volts. "There. That wasn't too bad, was it?" "No," you mumble.

The experiment begins. You hope for the learner's sake that he is bright, but unfortunately he turns out to be rather dull. He gets some answers right, but you have to keep turning up the dial. Each turn makes you more and more uncomfortable. You find yourself hoping that the learner won't miss another answer. But he does. When he received the first shocks, he let out some moans and groans, but now he is screaming in agony. He even protests that he suffers from a heart condition.

*How far do you turn that dial?*

By now, you probably have guessed that there was no electricity attached to the electrodes and that the

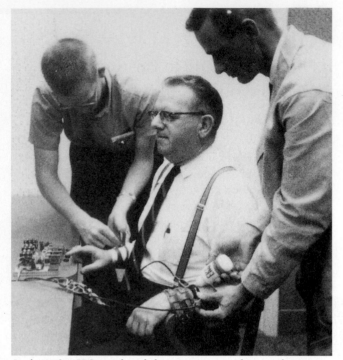

*In the 1960s, U.S. social psychologists ran a series of creative but controversial experiments. From this photo of the "learner" being prepared for one of Stanley Milgram's experiments, you can get an idea of how convincing the situation would be for the "teacher."*

"learner" was a stooge who only pretended to feel pain. The purpose of the experiment was to find out at what point people refuse to participate. Does anyone actually turn the lever all the way to "DANGER: SEVERE SHOCK"?

Milgram wanted the answer because millions of ordinary people did nothing to stop the Nazi slaughter of Jews, gypsies, Slavs, homosexuals, people with disabilities, and others whom the Nazis designated as "inferior." The cooperation of so many ordinary people in the face of all this killing seemed bizarre, and Milgram wanted to see how ordinary, intelligent Americans might react in an analogous situation.

Milgram was upset by what he found. Many "teachers" broke into a sweat and protested that the experiment was inhuman and should be stopped. But when the experimenter calmly replied that the experiment must go on, this assurance from an "authority" ("scientist, white coat, university laboratory") was enough for most "teachers" to continue, even though the "learner" screamed in agony. Even "teachers" who were "reduced to twitching, stuttering wrecks" continued to follow orders.

Milgram varied the experiments (Nestar and Gregory 2005). He used both men and women. In some experi-

ments, he put the "teachers" and "learners" in the same room, so the "teacher" could clearly see the suffering. In others, he put the "learners" in a separate room and had them pound and kick the wall during the first shocks and then go silent. The results varied. When there was no verbal feedback from the "learner," 65 percent of the "teachers" pushed the lever all the way to 450 volts. Of those who could see the "learner," 40 percent turned the lever all the way. When Milgram added a second "teacher," a stooge who refused to go along with the experiment, only 5 percent of the "teachers" turned the lever all the way, a result that bears out some of Asch's findings.

A stormy discussion about research ethics erupted. Not only were researchers surprised and disturbed by what Milgram found, but they were also alarmed at his methods. Universities began to require that subjects be informed of the nature and purpose of social research. Researchers agreed that to reduce subjects to "twitching, stuttering wrecks" was unethical, and almost all deception was banned.

## For Your Consideration

What connections do you see between Milgram's experiment and the actions of Monster Kody in our opening vignette? Taking into account how significant these findings are, do you think that the scientific community overreacted to Milgram's experiments? Should we allow such research? Consider both the Asch and Milgram experiments, and use symbolic interactionism, functionalism, and conflict theory to explain why groups have such influence over us.

## Global Consequences of Group Dynamics: Groupthink

Suppose you are a member of the president's inner circle. It is midnight, and the president has just called an emergency meeting to deal with a terrorist attack. At first, several options are presented. Eventually, these are narrowed to only a couple of choices, and at some point, everyone seems to agree on what now appears to be "the only possible course of action." To express doubts at that juncture will bring you into conflict with all the other important people in the room. To criticize will mark you as not being a "team player." So you keep your mouth shut, with the result that each step commits you—and them—more and more to the "only" course of action.

From the Milgram and Asch experiments, we can see the power of authority and the influence of peers. Under some circumstances, as in this example, these factors can lead to **groupthink.** Sociologist Irving Janis (1972, 1982) coined this term to refer to the collective tunnel vision that group members sometimes develop. As they begin to think alike, they become convinced that there is only one "right" viewpoint and a single course of action to follow. They take any suggestion of alternatives as a sign of disloyalty. With their perspective narrowed and fully convinced that they are right, they may even put aside moral judgments and disregard risk (Hart 1991; Flippen 1999).

Groupthink can bring serious consequences. Consider the *Columbia* space shuttle disaster of 2003.

**Foam broke loose during launch, and engineers were concerned that it might have damaged tiles on the nose cone. Because this would make reentry dangerous, they sent e-mails to NASA officials, warning them about the risk. One engineer even suggested that the crew do a "space walk" to examine the tiles (Vartabedian and Gold 2003). The team in charge of the Columbia shuttle, however, disregarded the warnings. Convinced that a piece of foam weighing less than two pounds could not seriously harm the shuttle, they refused to even consider the possibility (Wald and Schwartz 2003). The fiery results of their closed minds were transmitted around the globe.**

The consequences of groupthink can be even greater than this. In 1941, President Franklin D. Roosevelt and his chiefs of staff had evidence that the Japanese were preparing to attack Pearl Harbor. They simply refused to believe it and decided to continue naval operations as usual. The destruction of the U.S. naval fleet ushered the United States into World War II. In the war with Vietnam, U.S. officials had evidence of the strength and determination of the North Vietnamese military. They arrogantly threw such evidence aside, refusing to believe that "little, uneducated, barefoot people in pajamas" could defeat the U.S. military.

In each of these cases, options closed as officials committed themselves to a single course of action. Questioning the decisions would have indicated disloyalty and disregard for "team playing." Those in power plunged ahead, unable to see alternative perspectives. No longer did they try to objectively weigh evidence as it came in; instead, they interpreted everything as supporting their one "correct" decision.

Groupthink knows few bounds. Consider the aftermath of 9/11, when government officials defended torture as moral, "the lesser of two evils." Groupthink narrowed thought to the point that the U.S. Justice Department ruled that the United States was not bound by the Geneva Convention that prohibits torture. Facing protests, the Justice Department backed down (Lewis 2005).

The U.S. military involvement in Iraq appears to be a similar example. Top leaders, convinced that they made the right decision to go to war and that they were finding success in building a new Iraqi society, continuously interpreted even disconfirming evidence as favorable. Opinions and debate that contradicted their mind-set were written off as signs of ignorance and disloyalty. Despite mounting casualties, negative public sentiment, and even political opposition to the war, it was as though the president and his advisors had been blinded by groupthink.

**Preventing Groupthink** Groupthink is a danger for government leaders, who tend to surround themselves with an inner circle that closely reflects their own views. In "briefings," written summaries, and "talking points," this inner circle spoon-feeds the leaders the information it has selected. The result is that top leaders, such as the president, become cut off from information that does not support their own opinions.

Perhaps the key to preventing the mental captivity and intellectual paralysis known as groupthink is the widest possible circulation—especially among a nation's top government officials—of research that has been conducted by social scientists independent of the government and information that has been gathered freely by media reporters. If this conclusion comes across as an unabashed plug for sociological research and the free exchange of ideas, it is. Giving free rein to diverse opinions can curb groupthink, which—if not prevented—can lead to the destruction of a society and, in today's world of nuclear, chemical, and biological weapons, the obliteration of Earth's inhabitants.

# SUMMARY *and* REVIEW

## Groups Within Society

### What is a group?

Sociologists use many definitions of groups, but, in general, **groups** consist of people who think of themselves as belonging together and who interact with one another. P. 116.

### How do sociologists classify groups?

Sociologists divide groups into primary groups, secondary groups, in-groups, out-groups, reference groups, and networks. The cooperative, intimate, long-term, face-to-face relationships provided by **primary groups** are fundamental to our sense of self. **Secondary groups** are larger, relatively temporary, and more anonymous, formal, and impersonal than primary groups. **In-groups** provide members with a strong sense of identity and belonging. **Out-groups** also foster identity by showing in-group members what they are *not*. **Reference groups** are groups whose standards we refer to as we evaluate ourselves. **Social networks** consist of social ties that link people together. Developments in communications technology have given birth to a new type of group, the **electronic community**. Pp. 116–123.

### What is "the iron law of oligarchy"?

Sociologist Robert Michels noted that formal organizations have a tendency to become controlled by an inner circle that limits leadership to its own members. The dominance of a formal organization by an elite that keeps itself in power is called **the iron law of oligarchy**. Pp. 118–119.

## Bureaucracies

### What are bureaucracies?

**Bureaucracies** are social groups characterized by a hierarchy, division of labor, written rules and communications, and impersonality and replaceability of positions. These characteristics make bureaucracies efficient and enduring. Pp. 124–126.

### What dysfunctions are associated with bureaucracies?

The dysfunctions of bureaucracies include alienation, red tape, **goal displacement,** and incompetence (as seen in the **Peter principle**). The impersonality of bureaucracies tends to produce **alienation** among workers—the feeling that no one cares about them and that they do not really fit in. Pp. 126–128.

## Working for the Corporation

### How does the corporate culture affect workers?

The term **corporate culture** refers to an organization's traditions, values, and unwritten norms. Much of corporate culture, such as its hidden values and stereotypes, is not readily visible. Often, a **self-fulfilling stereotype** is at work: People who match a corporation's hidden values tend to be put on career tracks that enhance their chance of success, while those who do not match those values are set on a course that minimizes their performance. Pp. 128–129.

## Technology and the Control of Workers

### What is the maximum-security society?

It is the use of computers and surveillance devices to monitor people, especially in the workplace. This technology is being extended to monitoring our everyday lives. P. 130.

## Group Dynamics

### How does a group's size affect its dynamics?

The term **group dynamics** refers to how individuals affect groups and how groups influence individuals. In a **small group,** everyone can interact directly with everyone else. As a group grows larger, its intensity decreases but its stability increases. A **dyad,** consisting of two people, is the most unstable of human groups, but it provides the most intense of intimate relationships. The addition of a third person, forming a **triad,** fundamentally alters relationships. Triads are unstable, as **coalitions** (the alignment of some members of a group against others) tend to form. Pp. 130–132.

### What characterizes a leader?

A **leader** is someone who influences others. **Instrumental leaders** try to keep a group moving toward its goals, even though this causes friction and they lose popularity. **Expressive leaders** focus on creating harmony and raising group morale. Both types are essential to the functioning of groups. Pp. 132–133.

### What are the three main leadership styles?

**Authoritarian leaders** give orders, **democratic leaders** try to lead by consensus, and **laissez-faire leaders** are highly permissive. An authoritarian style appears to be more effective in emergency situations, a democratic style works best for most situations, and a laissez-faire style is usually ineffective. Pp. 133–134.

*How do groups encourage conformity?*
The Asch experiment was cited to illustrate the power of peer pressure, the Milgram experiment to illustrate the influence of authority. Both experiments demonstrate how easily we can succumb to **groupthink,** a kind of collective tunnel vision. Preventing groupthink requires the free circulation of diverse and opposing ideas. Pp. 134–137.

# THINKING CRITICALLY *about* Chapter 5

1. Identify your in-groups and your out-groups. How have your in-groups influenced the way you see the world? And what influence have your out-groups had on you?

2. You are likely to work for a bureaucracy. How do you think this will affect your orientation to life? How can you make the "hidden culture" work to your advantage?

3. Milgram's and Asch's experiments illustrate the power of peer pressure. How has peer pressure operated in your life? Think about something that you did not want to do but did anyway because of peer pressure.

# ADDITIONAL RESOURCES

## What can you find in MySocLab? mysoclab   www.mysoclab.com

- **Complete Ebook**
- **Practice Tests and Video and Audio activities**
- **Mapping and Data Analysis exercises**

- **Sociology in the News**
- **Classic Readings in Sociology**
- **Research and Writing advice**

## Where Can I Read More on This Topic?

Suggested readings for this chapter are listed at the back of this book.

# Deviance and Social Control

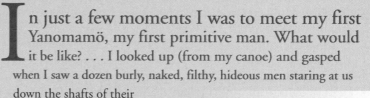

**I**n just a few moments I was to meet my first Yanomamö, my first primitive man. What would it be like? . . . I looked up (from my canoe) and gasped when I saw a dozen burly, naked, filthy, hideous men staring at us down the shafts of their drawn arrows. Immense wads of green tobacco were stuck between their lower teeth and lips, making them look even more hideous, and strands of dark-green slime dripped or hung from their noses. We arrived at the village while the men were blowing a hallucinogenic drug up their noses. One of the side effects of the drug is a runny nose. The mucus is always saturated with the green powder, and the Indians usually let it run freely from their nostrils. . . . I just sat there holding my notebook, helpless and pathetic. . . .

> **They would "clean" their hands by spitting slimy tobacco juice into them.**

The whole situation was depressing, and I wondered why I ever decided to switch from civil engineering to anthropology in the first place. . . . (Soon) I was covered with red pigment, the result of a dozen or so complete examinations. . . . These examinations capped an otherwise grim day. The Indians would blow their noses into their hands, flick as much of the mucus off that would separate in a snap of the wrist, wipe the residue into their hair, and then carefully examine my face, arms, legs, hair, and the contents of my pockers. I said (in their language), "Your hands are dirty"; my comments were met by the Indians in the following way: they would "clean" their hands by spitting a quantity of slimy tobacco juice into them, rub them together, and then proceed with the examination.

\* \* \* \* \*

This is how Napoleon Chagnon describes the culture shock he felt when he met the Yanomamö tribe of the rain forests of Brazil. His ensuing months of fieldwork continued to bring surprise after surprise, and often Chagnon (1977) could hardly believe his eyes— or his nose.

If you were to list the deviant behaviors of the Yanomamö, what would you include? The way they appear naked in public? Use hallucinogenic drugs? Let mucus hang from their noses? Or the way they rub hands filled with mucus, spittle, and tobacco juice over a frightened stranger who doesn't dare to protest? Perhaps. But it isn't this simple, for as we shall see, deviance is relative.

# What Is Deviance?

Sociologists use the term **deviance** to refer to any violation of norms, whether the infraction is as minor as driving over the speed limit, as serious as murder, or as humorous as Chagnon's encounter with the Yanomamö. This deceptively simple definition takes us to the heart of the sociological perspective on deviance, which sociologist Howard S. Becker (1966) described this way: *It is not the act itself, but the reactions to the act, that make something deviant.* What Chagnon saw disturbed him, but to the Yanomamö those same behaviors represented normal, everyday life. What was deviant to Chagnon was *conformist* to the Yanomamö. From their viewpoint, you *should* check out strangers the way they did, and nakedness is good, as are hallucinogenic drugs and letting mucus be "natural."

Chagnon's abrupt introduction to the Yanomamö allows us to see the *relativity of deviance,* a major point made by symbolic interactionists. Because different groups have different norms, *what is deviant to some is not deviant to others.* (See the photo on this page.) This principle holds both *within* a society as well as across cultures. Thus, acts that are acceptable in one culture—or in one group within a society—may be considered deviant in another culture or by another group within the same society. This idea is explored in the Cultural Diversity box on the next page.

This principle also applies to a specific form of deviance known as **crime,** the violation of rules that have been written into law. In the extreme, an act that is applauded by one group may be so despised by another group that it is punishable by death. Making a huge profit on business deals is one example. Americans who do this are admired. Like Donald Trump, Jack Welch, and Warren Buffet, they may even write books about their exploits. In China, however, until recently this same act was considered a crime called *profiteering.* Anyone who was found guilty was hanged in a public square as a lesson to all.

Unlike the general public, sociologists use the term *deviance* nonjudgmentally, to refer to any act to which people respond negatively. When sociologists use this term, it does not mean that they agree that an act is bad, just that people judge it negatively. To sociologists, then, *all* of us are deviants of one sort or another, for we all violate norms from time to time.

I took this photo on the outskirts of Hyderabad, India. Is this man deviant? If this were a U.S. street, he would be. But here? No houses have running water in his neighborhood, and the men, women, and children bathe at the neighborhood water pump. This man, then, would not be deviant in his culture. And yet, he is actually mugging for my camera, making the three bystanders laugh. Does this additional factor make this a scene of deviance?

To be considered deviant, a person does not even have to *do* anything. Sociologist Erving Goffman (1963) used the term **stigma** to refer to characteristics that discredit people. These include violations of norms of ability (blindness, deafness, mental handicaps) and norms of appearance (a facial birthmark, obesity). They also include involuntary memberships, such as being a victim of AIDS or the brother of a rapist. The stigma can become a person's master status, defining him or her as deviant. Recall from Chapter 4 that a master status cuts across all other statuses that a person occupies.

## How Norms Make Social Life Possible

No human group can exist without norms, for *norms make social life possible by making behavior predictable.* What would life be like if you could not predict what others would do? Imagine for a moment that you have gone to a store to purchase milk:

> **Suppose the clerk says, "I won't sell you any milk. We're overstocked with soda, and I'm not going to sell anyone milk until our soda inventory is reduced."**

# Cultural Diversity around the World

## Human Sexuality in Cross-Cultural Perspective

**H**uman sexuality illustrates how a group's *definition* of an act, not the act itself, determines whether it will be considered deviant. Let's look at some examples reported by anthropologist Robert Edgerton (1976).

Norms of sexual behavior vary so widely around the world that what is considered normal in one society may be considered deviant in another. In Kenya, a group called the Pokot place high emphasis on sexual pleasure, and they expect that both a husband and wife will reach orgasm. If a husband does not satisfy his wife, he is in trouble—especially if she thinks that his failure is because of adultery. If this is so, the wife and her female friends will sneak up on her husband when he is asleep. The women will tie him up, shout obscenities at him, beat him, and then urinate on him. As a final gesture of their contempt, before releasing him, they will slaughter and eat his favorite ox. The husband's hours of painful humiliation are intended to make him more dutiful concerning his wife's conjugal rights.

People can also become deviants for failing to understand that the group's ideal norms may not be its real

*Pokot married man, northern Kenya*

norms. As with many groups, the Zapotec Indians of Mexico profess that sexual relations should take place exclusively between husband and wife. Yet the only person in one Zapotec community who had not had any extramarital affairs was considered deviant. Evidently, these people have an unspoken understanding that married couples will engage in affairs, but be discreet about them.

When a wife learns that her husband is having an affair, she usually has one, too.

One Zapotec wife did not follow this covert norm. Instead, she would praise her own virtue to her husband—and then voice the familiar "headache" excuse. She also told other wives the names of the women their husbands were sleeping with. As a result, this virtuous woman was condemned by everyone in the village. Clearly, real norms can conflict with ideal norms—another illustration of the gap between ideal and real culture.

## For Your Consideration

How do the behaviors of the Pokot wife and husband look from the perspective of U.S. norms? Are there U.S. norms in the first place? How about the Zapotec woman? The rest of the Zapotec community? How does cultural relativity apply? (We discussed this concept in Chapter 2, pages 39–41.)

You don't like it, but you decide to buy a case of soda. At the checkout, the clerk says, "I hope you don't mind, but there's a $5 service charge on every fifteenth customer." You, of course, are the fifteenth.

Just as you start to leave, another clerk stops you and says, "We're not working any more. We decided to have a party." Suddenly a CD player begins to blast, and everyone in the store begins to dance. "Oh, good, you've brought the soda," says a different clerk, who takes your package and passes sodas all around.

Life is not like this, of course. You can depend on grocery clerks to sell you milk. You can also depend on paying the same price as everyone else and not being forced to attend a party in the store. Why can you depend on this? Because we are socialized to follow norms, to play the basic roles that society assigns to us.

Without norms, we would have social chaos. Norms lay out the basic guidelines for how we should play our roles and interact with others. In short, norms bring about **social order,** a group's customary social arrangements. Our lives are based on these arrangements, which is why deviance often is perceived as threatening: Deviance undermines predictability, the foundation of social life. Consequently, human groups develop a system of **social control**—formal and informal means of enforcing norms.

## Sanctions

As we discussed in Chapter 2, people do not enforce folkways strictly, but they become upset when people break mores (MORE-rays). Expressions of disapproval of deviance, called **negative sanctions,** range from frowns and gossip for breaking folkways to imprisonment and capital punishment for breaking mores. In general, the more seriously the group takes a norm, the harsher the penalty for violating it. In contrast, **positive sanctions**—from smiles to formal awards—are used to reward people for conforming to norms. Getting a raise is a positive sanction; being fired is a negative sanction. Getting an *A* in Intro to Sociology is a positive sanction; getting an *F* is a negative one.

Most negative sanctions are informal. You might stare if you observe someone dressed in what you consider to be inappropriate clothing, or you might gossip if a married person you know spends the night with someone other than his or her spouse. Whether you consider the breaking of a norm merely an amusing matter that warrants no severe sanction or a serious infraction that does, however, depends on your perspective. If a woman appears at your college graduation ceremonies in a bikini, you may stare and laugh, but if this is *your* mother, you are likely to feel that different sanctions are appropriate. Similarly, if it is *your* father

Much of our interaction is based on *background assumptions,* the unwritten, taken-for-granted "rules" that underlie our everyday lives. We don't have a "rule" that specifies "Adults, don't change clothes in a subway," yet anyone who is familiar with subways knows this rule exists. We also know it is a subset of the more general rule, "Don't change clothes in public."

who spends the night with an 18-year-old college freshman, you are likely to do more than gossip.

**In Sum:** In sociology, the term *deviance* refers to all violations of social rules, regardless of their seriousness. The term is not a judgment about the behavior. Deviance is relative, for what is deviant in one group may be conformist in another. Consequently, we must consider deviance from *within* a group's own framework, for it is the group's unwritten rules of social life that reflect how its members view right and wrong and what they expect of one another. The following Thinking Critically section focuses on this issue.

# Thinking CRITICALLY

## Is It Rape, or Is It Marriage?
## A Study in Culture Clash

Surrounded by cornfields, Lincoln, Nebraska, is about as provincial as a state capital gets. Most of its residents have little experience dealing with people who come from different ways of life. Their baptism into cultural diversity came as a shock.

Although the age of the brides was not typical, the wedding followed millennia-old Islamic practices (Annin and Hamilton 1996). A 39-year-old immigrant from Iraq had arranged for his two eldest daughters, ages 13 and 14, to marry two fellow Iraqi immigrants, ages 28 and 34. A Muslim cleric flew in from Ohio to perform the ceremony.

Nebraska went into shock. So did the immigrants. What is marriage in Iraq is rape in Nebraska. The husbands were charged with rape, the girls' father with child abuse, and their mother with contributing to the delinquency of minors.

The event made front page news in Saudi Arabia, where people shook their heads in amazement at Americans. Nebraskans shook their heads in amazement, too.

In Fresno, California, a Hmong immigrant took a group of friends to a local college campus. There, they picked up the Hmong girl whom he had selected to be his wife (Sherman 1988; Lacayo 1993). The men brought her to his house, where he had sex with her. The woman, however, was not in agreement with this plan.

The Hmong call this *zij poj niam*, "marriage by capture." For them, this is an acceptable form of mate selection, one that mirrors Hmong courtship ideals of strong men and virtuous, resistant women. The Fresno District Attorney, however, called it kidnapping and rape.

As migration intensifies, other countries are experiencing similar culture shock. Germans awoke one morning to the news that a 28-year-old Turkish man had taken his 11-year-old wife to the registry office in Düsseldorf to get her an ID card. The shocked officials detained the girl and shipped her back to Turkey (Stephens 2006).

In Bishkek, Kyrgyzstan, a former republic of the Soviet Union, one father said that he wouldn't mind if a man kidnapped his daughter to marry her. "After all," he said, "that's how I got my wife" (Smith 2005).

## For Your Consideration

To apply *symbolic interactionism* to these real-life dramas, ask how the perspectives of the people involved explain why they did what they did. To apply *functionalism*, ask how the U.S. laws that were violated are "functional" (that is, what are their benefits, and to whom?). To apply *conflict theory*, ask what groups are in conflict in these examples. (Do not focus on the individuals involved, but on the groups to which they belong.)

Understanding events in terms of different theoretical perspectives does not tell us which reaction is "right" when cultures clash. Science can analyze causes and consequences, but it cannot answer questions of what is "right" or moral. Any "ought" that you feel about these cases comes from your values, which brings us, once again, to the initial issue: the relativity of deviance.

*Because the marriage customs of one culture can violate the norms of another culture, as migration increases so does the possibility of culture clash. Shown here is a Kyrgyzstan family. The woman, now married for 16 years, was kidnapped after she rejected a marriage proposal.*

## Competing Explanations of Deviance: Sociology, Sociobiology, and Psychology

If social life is to exist, norms are essential. So why do people violate them? To better understand the reasons, it is useful to know how sociological explanations differ from biological and psychological ones.

*Sociobiologists* explain deviance by looking for answers *within* individuals. They assume that **genetic predispositions** lead people to such deviances as juvenile delinquency and crime (Lombroso 1911; Wilson and Herrnstein 1985; Goozen et al. 2007). Among their explanations are the following three theories: (1) intelligence—low intelligence leads to crime; (2) the "XYY" theory—an extra Y chromosome in males leads to crime; and (3) body type—people with "squarish, muscular" bodies are more likely to commit **street crime**—acts such as mugging, rape, and burglary.

How have these theories held up? We should first note that most people who have these supposedly "causal" characteristics do not become criminals. Regarding intelligence, you already know that some criminals are very intelligent and that most people of low intelligence do not commit crimes. Regarding the extra Y chromosome, most men who commit crimes have the normal XY chromosome combination, and most men with the XYY combination do not become criminals. No women have this combination of genes, so this explanation can't even be applied to female criminals. Regarding body type, criminals exhibit the full range of body types, and most people with "squarish, muscular" bodies do not become street criminals.

*Psychologists* also focus on abnormalities *within* the individual. They examine what are called **personality disorders.** Their supposition is that deviating individuals have deviating personalities (Barnes 2001; Mayer 2007) and that subconscious motives drive people to deviance. No specific childhood experience, however, is invariably linked with deviance. For example, children who had "bad toilet training," "suffocating mothers," or "emotionally aloof fathers" may become embezzling bookkeepers—or good accountants. Just as college students, teachers, and police officers represent a variety of bad—and good—childhood experiences, so do deviants. Similarly, people with "suppressed anger" can become freeway snipers or military heroes—or anything else. In short, there is no inevitable outcome of any childhood experience. Deviance is not associated with any particular personality.

In contrast with both sociobiologists and psychologists, *sociologists* search for factors *outside* the individual. They look for social influences that "recruit" people to break norms. To account for why people commit crimes, for example, sociologists examine such external influences as socialization, membership in subcultures, and social class. *Social class,* a concept that we will discuss in depth in Chapter 8, refers to people's relative standing in terms of education, occupation, and especially income and wealth.

The point stressed earlier, that deviance is relative, leads sociologists to ask a crucial question: Why should we expect to find something constant within people to account for a behavior that is conforming in one society and deviant in another?

To see how sociologists explain deviance, let's contrast the three sociological perspectives—symbolic interactionism, functionalism, and conflict theory.

# The Symbolic Interactionist Perspective

As we examine symbolic interactionism, it will become more evident why sociologists are not satisfied with explanations that are rooted in biology or personality. A basic principle of symbolic interactionism is this: We act according to our interpretations of situations, not according to blind predisposition. Let's consider how our membership in groups influences our views of life and thus affects our behavior.

## Differential Association Theory

**The Theory**    Contrary to theories built around biology and personality, sociologists stress that people *learn* deviance. Edwin Sutherland coined the term **differential association** to indicate that we learn to deviate from or conform to society's norms primarily from the *different* groups we *associate* with (Sutherland 1924, 1947; Sutherland et al. 1992). On the most obvious level, some boys and girls join street gangs, while others join the Scouts. As sociologists have repeatedly demonstrated, what we learn influences us toward or away from deviance (Deflem 2006; Chambliss 1973/2007).

Sutherland's theory is actually more complicated than this, but he basically said that deviance is learned. This goes directly against the view that deviance is due to biology or

To experience a sense of belonging is a basic human need. Membership in groups, especially peer groups, is a primary way that people meet this need. Regardless of the orientation of the group—whether to conformity or to deviance—the process is the same. These members of a street gang in Cali, Colombia, are showing off their home-made guns.

mean instant death. If the neighbors feel that a victim deserved to be killed, they refuse to testify because "he got what was coming to him" (Kubrin and Weitzer 2003).

Some neighborhoods even develop subcultures in which killing is considered an honorable act:

Sociologist Ruth Horowitz (1983, 2005), who did participant observation in a lower-class Chicano neighborhood in Chicago, discovered how associating with people who have a certain concept of "honor" propels young men to deviance. The formula is simple. "A real man has honor. An insult is a threat to one's honor. Therefore, not to stand up to someone is to be less than a real man."

Now suppose you are a young man growing up in this neighborhood. You likely would do a fair amount of fighting, for you would interpret many things as attacks on your honor. You might even carry a knife or a gun, for words and fists wouldn't always be sufficient. Along with members of your group, you would define fighting, knifing, and shooting quite differently from the way most people do.

personality. Sutherland stressed that the different groups with which we associate (our "*differential* association") give us messages about conformity and deviance. We may receive mixed messages, but we end up with more of one than the other (an "excess of definitions," as Sutherland put it). The end result is an imbalance—attitudes that tilt us more toward one direction than another. Consequently, either we conform or we deviate.

**Families**    You know how important your family has been in forming your orientations to life, especially how it has directed you toward or away from deviance. Research has confirmed this informal observation. One of the outstanding findings is that delinquents are more likely to come from families that get in trouble with the law. One study stands out: Of all jail inmates across the United States, almost *half* have a father, mother, brother, sister, or spouse who has served time in prison (*Sourcebook of Criminal Justice Statistics* 2003:Table 6.0011). In short, families who are involved in crime tend to set their children on a law-breaking path.

**Friends, Neighborhoods, and Subcultures**    Most people don't know the term *differential association*, but they do know how it works. Most parents want to move out of "bad" neighborhoods because they know that if their kids have delinquent friends, they are likely to become delinquent, too. Sociological research supports this common observation (Miller 1958; Chung and Steinberg 2006; Yonas et al. 2006). Some neighborhoods develop a subculture of violence. In these places, even a teasing remark can

Members of the Mafia also intertwine ideas of manliness with violence. For them, *to kill is a measure of their manhood.* Not all killings are accorded the same respect, however, for "the more awesome and potent the victim, the more worthy and meritorious the killer" (Arlacchi 1980). Some killings are done to enforce norms. A member of the Mafia who gives information to the police, for example, has violated *omertà* (the Mafia's vow of secrecy). This offense can never be tolerated, for it threatens the very existence of the group. Mafia killings further illustrate just how relative deviance is. Although killing is deviant to mainstream society, for members of the Mafia, *not* to kill after certain rules are broken—such as when someone "squeals" to the cops—is the deviant act.

**Prison or Freedom?**    As was mentioned in Chapter 3, an issue that comes up over and over again in sociology is whether we are prisoners of socialization. Symbolic interactionists stress that we are not mere pawns in the hands of others. We are not destined to think and act as our group memberships dictate. Rather, we *help to produce our own orientations to life*. By joining one group rather than another (differential association), for example, we help to shape the self. For instance, one college student may join a feminist group that is trying to change the treatment of women in college; another may associate with a group of women who shoplift on weekends. Their choice of groups points them in different directions. The one who associates with shoplifters may become even more oriented toward criminal activities, while the one who joins the feminist group may develop an even greater interest in producing social change.

## Control Theory

Inside most of us, it seems, are desires to do things that would get us in trouble—inner drives, temptations, urges, hostilities, and so on. Yet most of the time we stifle these desires. Why?

**The Theory**    Sociologist Walter Reckless (1973), who developed **control theory,** stresses that two control systems work against our motivations to deviate. Our *inner controls* include our internalized morality—conscience, religious principles, ideas of right and wrong. Inner controls also include fears of punishment, feelings of integrity, and the desire to be a "good" person (Hirschi 1969; Rogers 1977; McShane and Williams 2007). Our *outer controls* consist of people—such as family, friends, and the police—who influence us not to deviate.

The stronger our bonds are with society, the more effective our inner controls are (Hirschi 1969). Bonds are based on *attachments* (feeling affection and respect for people who conform to mainstream norms), *commitments* (having a stake in society that you don't want to risk, such as a respected place in your family, a good standing at college, a good job), *involvements* (putting time and energy into approved activities), and *beliefs* (believing that certain actions are morally wrong).

This theory can be summarized as *self*-control, says sociologist Travis Hirschi. The key to learning high self-control

is socialization, especially in childhood. Parents help their children to develop self-control by supervising them and punishing their deviant acts (Gottfredson and Hirschi 1990). Do you think that more use of shaming, discussed in the Down-to-Earth Sociology box on the next page, could help increase people's internal controls?

**Applying the Theory**

Suppose that some friends have invited you to a night club. When you get there, you notice that everyone seems unusually happy—almost giddy would be a better description. They seem to be euphoric in their animated conversations and dancing. Your friends tell you that almost everyone here has taken the drug Ecstasy, and they invite you to take some with them.

What do you do? Let's not explore the question of whether taking Ecstasy in this setting is a deviant or a conforming act. That is a separate issue. Instead, concentrate on the pushes and pulls you would feel. The pushes toward taking the drug: your friends, the setting, and your curiosity. Then there are the inner controls: the inner voices of your conscience and your parents, perhaps of

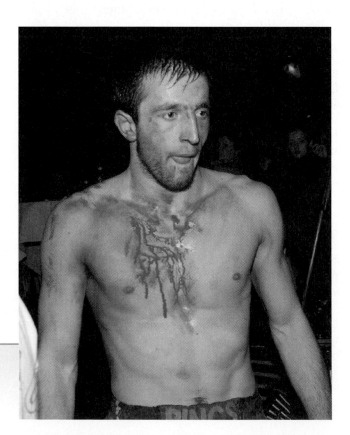

The social control of deviance takes many forms, some rather subtle. With its mayhem, "cage fighting" might look like the opposite of social control, but it is a way to channel aggressive impulses in a way that leaves no vendetta, feud, or "score to settle."

# Down-to-Earth Sociology
## Shaming: Making a Comeback?

Shaming can be effective, especially when members of a primary group use it. For this reason, parents sometimes use it to keep children in line. Shaming is also effective in small communities, where the individual's reputation is at stake. As our society grew large and urban, its sense of community diminished, and shaming lost its effectiveness. Shaming seems to be making a comeback. One Arizona sheriff makes the men in his jail wear pink underwear (Boxer 2001). Online shaming sites have also appeared. Captured on cell phone cameras are bad drivers, older men who leer at teenaged girls, and dog walkers who don't pick up their dog's poop (Saranow 2007). Some sites post photos of the offenders, as well as their addresses and phone numbers.

In small communities, shaming can be the centerpiece of the enforcement of norms, with the violator marked as a deviant and held up for all the world to see. In Nathaniel Hawthorne's *The Scarlet Letter*, town officials forced Hester Prynne to wear a scarlet A sewn on her dress. The A stood for *adulteress*. Wherever she went, Prynne had to wear this badge of shame, and the community expected her to wear it every day for the rest of her life.

Sociologist Harold Garfinkel (1956) gave the name **degradation ceremony** to an extreme form of shaming. The individual is called to account before the group, witnesses denounce him or her, the offender is pronounced guilty, and steps are taken to strip the individual of his or her identity as a group member. In some courts martial, officers who are found guilty stand at attention before their peers while the insignia of rank are ripped from their uniforms. This procedure screams that the individual is no longer a member of the group. Although Hester Prynne was not banished from the group physically, she was banished morally; her degradation ceremony proclaimed her a *moral* outcast from the community. The scarlet A marked her as "not one" of them.

Although we don't use scarlet A's today, informal degradation ceremonies still occur. Consider what happened to Joseph Gray (Chivers 2001):

*"If you drive and drink, you'll wear pink" is the slogan of a campaign to shame men who drive drunk in Phoenix, Arizona. Shown here are convicted drunk drivers who will pick up trash.*

Joseph Gray, a fifteen-year veteran of the New York City police force, was involved in a fatal accident. The *New York Times* and New York television stations reported that Gray had spent the afternoon drinking in a topless bar before plowing his car into a vehicle carrying a pregnant woman, her son, and her sister. All three died. Gray was accused of manslaughter and drunk driving. (He was later convicted on both counts.)

The news media kept hammering this story to the public. Three weeks later, as Gray left police headquarters after resigning from his job, an angry crowd gathered around him. Gray hung his head in public disgrace as Victor Manuel Herrera, whose wife and son were killed in the crash, followed him, shouting, "You're a murderer!"

## For Your Consideration

1. How do you think law enforcement officials might use shaming to reduce lawbreaking?
2. Do you think school officials could use shaming effectively? How?
3. Suppose that you were caught shoplifting at a store near where you live. Would you rather spend two nights in jail with no one but your family knowing it (and no permanent record) or a week walking in front of the store you stole from wearing a placard that says in bold red capital letters: I AM A THIEF! and in smaller letters: "I am sorry for stealing from this store and causing you to have to pay higher prices"? Why?

your teachers, as well as your fears of arrest and of the dangers of illegal drugs. There are also the outer controls—perhaps the uniformed security guard looking in your direction.

So, what *did* you decide? Which was stronger: your inner and outer controls or the pushes and pulls toward taking the drug? It is you who can best weigh these forces, for they differ with each of us.

## Labeling Theory

Symbolic interactionists have developed **labeling theory,** which focuses on the significance of the labels (names, reputations) that we are given. Labels tend to become a part of our self-concept and help to set us on paths that either propel us into or divert us from deviance. Let's look at how people react to society's labels—from "whore" and "pervert" to "cheat" and "slob."

### Rejecting Labels: How People Neutralize Deviance

Most people resist the negative labels that others try to pin on them. Some are so successful that even though they persist in deviance, they still consider themselves conformists. For example, even though they beat up people and vandalize property, some delinquents consider themselves to be conforming members of society. How do they do it?

Sociologists Gresham Sykes and David Matza (1957/1988) studied boys like this. They found that the boys used five **techniques of neutralization** to deflect society's norms.

*Denial of Responsibility* Some boys said, "I'm not responsible for what happened because . . ." and then they were quite creative about the "becauses." Some said that what happened was an "accident." Other boys saw themselves as "victims" of society. What else could you expect? They were like billiard balls shot around the pool table of life.

*Denial of Injury* Another favorite explanation of the boys was "What I did wasn't wrong because no one got hurt." They would define vandalism as "mischief," gang fights as a "private quarrel," and stealing cars as "borrowing." They might acknowledge that what they did was illegal, but claim that they were "just having a little fun."

*Denial of a Victim* Some boys thought of themselves as avengers. Vandalizing a teacher's car was done to get revenge for an unfair grade, while shoplifting was a way to even the score with "crooked" store owners. In short, even if the boys did accept responsibility and admit

that someone had gotten hurt, they protected their self-concept by claiming that the people "deserved what they got."

*Condemnation of the Condemners* Another technique the boys used was to deny that others had the right to judge them. They might accuse people who pointed their fingers at them of being "a bunch of hypocrites": The police were "on the take," teachers had "pets," and parents cheated on their taxes. In short, they said, "Who are *they* to accuse *me* of something?"

*Appeal to Higher Loyalties* A final technique the boys used to justify antisocial activities was to consider loyalty to the gang more important than following the norms of society. They might say, "I had to help my friends. That's why I got in the fight." Not incidentally, the boy may have shot two members of a rival group, as well as a bystander!

**In Sum:** These five techniques of neutralization have implications far beyond this group of boys, for it is not only delinquents who try to neutralize the norms of mainstream society. Look again at these five techniques—don't they sound familiar? (1) "I couldn't help myself"; (2) "Who really got hurt?"; (3) "Don't you think she deserved that, after what *she* did?"; (4) "Who are *you* to talk?"; and (5) "I had to help my friends—wouldn't you have done the same thing?" All of us attempt to neutralize the moral demands of society, for neutralization helps us to sleep at night.

### Embracing Labels: The Example of Outlaw Bikers

Although most of us resist attempts to label us as deviant, some people revel in a deviant identity. Some teenagers, for example, make certain by their clothing, choice of music, hairstyles, and "body art" that no one misses their rejection of adult norms. Their status among fellow members of a subculture—within which they are almost obsessive conformists—is vastly more important than any status outside it.

One of the best examples of a group that embraces deviance is motorcycle gangs. Sociologist Mark Watson (1980/2006) did participant observation with outlaw bikers. He rebuilt Harleys with them, hung around their bars and homes, and went on "runs" (trips) with them. He concluded that outlaw bikers see the world as "hostile, weak, and effeminate." They pride themselves on looking "dirty, mean, and generally undesirable" and take pleasure in provoking shocked reactions to their appearance and behavior. Holding the conventional world in contempt, they also pride themselves on getting into trouble, laughing at death, and treating women as lesser beings whose primary value is to provide them with services—especially sex. Outlaw bikers also regard themselves as losers, a factor that becomes woven into their unusual embrace of deviance.

**The Power of Labels: The Saints and the Roughnecks**
We can see how powerful labeling is by referring back to the study of the "Saints" and the "Roughnecks" that was cited in Chapter 4 (page 109). As you recall, both groups of high school boys were "constantly occupied with truancy, drinking, wild parties, petty theft, and vandalism." Yet their teachers looked on the Saints as "headed for success" and the Roughnecks as "headed for trouble." By the time they finished high school, not one Saint had been arrested, while the Roughnecks had been in constant trouble with the police.

Why did the members of the community perceive these boys so differently? Chambliss (1973/2007) concluded that this split vision was due to *social class.* As symbolic interactionists emphasize, social class vitally affects our perceptions and behavior. The Saints came from respectable, middle-class families, while the Roughnecks were from less respectable, working-class families. These backgrounds led teachers and the authorities to expect good behavior from the Saints but trouble from the Roughnecks. And, like the rest of us, teachers and police saw what they expected to see.

The boys' social class also affected their visibility. The Saints had automobiles, and they did their drinking and vandalism outside of town. Without cars, the Roughnecks hung around their own street corners, where their drinking and boisterous behavior drew the attention of police and confirmed the negative impressions that the community already had of them.

The boys' social class also equipped them with distinct *styles of interaction.* When police or teachers questioned them, the Saints were apologetic. Their show of respect for authority elicited a positive reaction from teachers and police, allowing the Saints to wiggle out of problems with the school and the law. The Roughnecks, said Chambliss, were "almost the polar opposite." When questioned, they were hostile. Even when they tried to assume a respectful attitude, everyone could see through it. Consequently, while teachers and police let the Saints off with warnings, they came down hard on the Roughnecks.

Although what happens in life is not determined by labels alone, the Saints and the Roughnecks did live up to the labels that the community gave them. As you may recall, all but one of the Saints went on to college. One earned a Ph.D., one became a lawyer, one a doctor, and

the others business managers. In contrast, only two of the Roughnecks went to college. They earned athletic scholarships and became coaches. The other Roughnecks did not fare so well. Two of them dropped out of high school, later became involved in separate killings, and were sent to prison. One became a local bookie, and no one knows the whereabouts of the other.

How do labels work? Although the matter is complex, because it involves the self-concept and reactions that vary from one individual to another, we can note that labels open and close doors of opportunity. Unlike its meaning in sociology, the term *deviant* in everyday usage is emotionally charged with a judgment of some sort. This label can lock people out of conforming groups and push them into almost exclusive contact with people who have been similarly labeled.

**In Sum:** Symbolic interactionists examine how people's definitions of the situation underlie whether they conform to or deviate from social norms. These theorists focus on group membership (differential association), how people balance pressures to conform and to deviate (control theory), and the significance of the labels that are placed on people (labeling theory).

# The Functionalist Perspective

When we think of deviance, its dysfunctions are likely to come to mind. Functionalists, in contrast, are as likely to stress the functions of deviance as they are to emphasize its dysfunctions.

## Can Deviance Really Be Functional for Society?

Most of us are upset by deviance, especially crime, and assume that society would be better off without it. The classic functionalist theorist Emile Durkheim (1893/1933, 1895/1964), however, came to a surprising conclusion. Deviance, he said—including crime—is functional for society, for it contributes to the social order. Durkheim saw three main functions of crime:

1. *Deviance clarifies moral boundaries and affirms norms.* A group's ideas about how people should think and act mark its *moral boundaries.* Deviant acts challenge those boundaries. To call a member into account is to say, in effect, "You broke an important rule, and we cannot tolerate that." Punishing deviants affirms

the group's norms and clarifies what it means to be a member of the group.

2. *Deviance promotes social unity.* To affirm the group's moral boundaries by punishing deviants fosters a "we" feeling among the group's members. In saying, "You can't get away with that," the group affirms the rightness of its own ways.

3. *Deviance promotes social change.* Groups do not always agree on what to do with people who push beyond their accepted ways of doing things. Some group members may even approve of the rule-breaking behavior. Boundary violations that gain enough support become new, acceptable behaviors. Thus, deviance may force a group to rethink and redefine its moral boundaries, helping groups—and whole societies—to change their customary ways.

## Strain Theory: How Social Values Produce Deviance

Functionalists argue that crime is a *natural* part of society, not an aberration or some alien element in our midst. Indeed, they say, some mainstream values actually generate crime. To understand what they mean, consider what sociologists Richard Cloward and Lloyd Ohlin (1960) identified as the crucial problem of the industrialized world: the need to locate and train the most talented people of every generation—whether they were born into wealth or into poverty—so that they can take over the key technical jobs of society. When children are born, no one knows which ones will have the ability to become dentists, nuclear physicists, or engineers. To get the most talented people to compete with one another, society tries to motivate *everyone* to strive for success. It does this by arousing discontent—making people feel dissatisfied with what they have so that they will try to "better" themselves.

Most people, then, end up with strong desires to reach **cultural goals** such as wealth or high status or to achieve whatever other objectives society holds out for them. However, not everyone has equal access to society's **institutionalized means,** the legitimate ways of achieving success. Some people find their path to education and good jobs blocked. These people experience *strain,* or frustration, which may motivate them to take a deviant path.

This perspective, known as **strain theory,** was developed by sociologist Robert Merton (1956, 1968). People who experience strain, he said, are likely to feel *anomie,* a sense of normlessness. Because mainstream norms (such as working hard or pursuing higher education) don't seem to be getting them anywhere, people who experience strain find it difficult to identify with these norms. They may even feel wronged by the system, and its rules may seem illegitimate.

Table 6.1 compares people's reactions to cultural goals and institutionalized means. The first reaction, which Merton said is the most common, is *conformity,* using socially acceptable means to try to reach cultural goals. In industrialized societies most people try to get good jobs, a good education, and so on. If well-paid jobs are unavailable, they take less desirable jobs. If they are denied access to Harvard or Stanford, they go to a state university. Others take night classes and go to vocational schools. In short, most people take the socially acceptable road.

**Four Deviant Paths** The remaining four responses, which are deviant, represent reactions to strain. Let's look at each. *Innovators* are people who accept the goals of society but use illegitimate means to try to reach them. Crack dealers, for instance, accept the goal of achieving wealth, but they reject the legitimate avenues for doing so. Other examples are embezzlers, robbers, and con artists.

The second deviant path is taken by people who become discouraged and give up on achieving cultural goals. Yet they still cling to conventional rules of conduct. Merton called this response *ritualism.* Although ritualists have given up on getting ahead at work, they survive by following the rules of their job. Teachers whose idealism is shattered (who are said to suffer from "burnout"), for example, remain in the classroom,

| TABLE 6.1 | How People Match Their Goals to Their Means | | |
|---|---|---|---|
| Do They Feel the Strain That Leads to Anomie? | Mode of Adaptation | Cultural Goals | Institutionalized Means |
| No | Conformity | Accept | Accept |
| | **Deviant Paths:** | | |
| | 1. Innovation | Accept | Reject |
| Yes | 2. Ritualism | Reject | Accept |
| | 3. Retreatism | Reject | Reject |
| | 4. Rebellion | Reject/Replace | Reject/Replace |

*Source:* Based on Merton 1968.

where they teach without enthusiasm. Their response is considered deviant because they cling to the job even though they have abandoned the goal, which may have been to stimulate young minds or to make the world a better place.

People who choose the third deviant path, *retreatism,* reject both the cultural goals and the institutionalized means of achieving them. Those who drop out of the pursuit of success by way of alcohol or drugs are retreatists. Women who enter a convent or men a monastery are also retreatists, although their path to withdrawal is certainly different.

The final type of deviant response is *rebellion.* Convinced that their society is corrupt, rebels, like retreatists, reject both society's goals and its institutionalized means. Unlike retreatists, however, rebels seek to give society new goals. Revolutionaries are the most committed type of rebels.

**In Sum:** Strain theory underscores the sociological principle that deviants are the product of society. Mainstream social values (cultural goals and institutionalized means to reach those goals) can produce strain (frustration, dissatisfaction). People who feel this strain are more likely than others to take the deviant (nonconforming) paths summarized in Table 6.1.

## Illegitimate Opportunity Structures: Social Class and Crime

One of the more interesting sociological findings in the study of deviance is that the social classes have distinct styles of crime. Let's see how unequal access to the institutionalized means to success helps to explain this.

**Street Crime** Functionalists point out that industrialized societies have no trouble socializing the poor into wanting to own things. Like others, the poor are bombarded with messages urging them to buy everything from Xboxes and iPods to designer jeans and new cars. Television and movies show images of middle-class people enjoying luxurious lives. These images reinforce the myth that all full-fledged Americans can afford society's many goods and services.

In contrast, the school system, the most common route to success, often fails the poor. The middle class runs it, and there the children of the poor confront a bewildering world, one that is at odds with their background. Their speech, with its nonstandard grammar, is often sprinkled with what the middle class considers obscenities. Their ideas of punctuality, as well as their poor preparation in paper-and-pencil skills, are also a mismatch with their new environment. Facing such barriers, the poor are more likely than their more privileged counterparts to drop out of school. Educational failure, in turn, closes the door on many legitimate avenues to financial success.

Not infrequently, however, different doors open to the poor, ones that Cloward and Ohlin (1960) called **illegitimate opportunity structures.** Woven into the texture of life in urban slums, for example, are robbery, burglary, drug dealing, prostitution, pimping, gambling, and other crimes, commonly called "hustles" (Sanchez-Jankowski 2003; Anderson 1978, 1990/2006). For many of the poor, the "hustler" is a role model—glamorous, in control, the image of "easy money," one of the few people in the area who comes close to attaining the cultural goal of success. For such reasons, then, these activities attract disproportionate numbers of the poor. As indicated in the Down-to-Earth Sociology box on the next page, studying people involved in these activities takes the researcher into a different world.

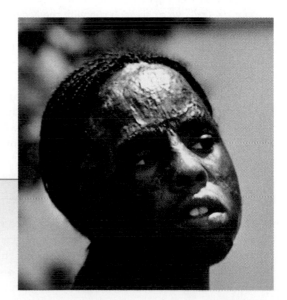

Most *white-collar crime* is a harmless nuisance, but some brings horrible costs. Shown here is Alisha Parker, who, with three siblings, was burned when the gas tank of a 1979 Chevrolet Malibu exploded after a rear-end collision. She also lost her right hand. Although General Motors executives knew about the problem with the Malibu gas tanks, they had ignored it. Outraged at the callousness of GM's conduct, the jury awarded these victims the staggering sum of $4.9 billion, which a judge later reduced to $1.2 billion.

# *Down-to-Earth Sociology*

## Gang Leader for a Day: Adventures of a Rogue Sociologist

Next to the University of Chicago is an area so dangerous that the professors warn students to avoid it. One of the graduate students in sociology, Sudhir Venkatesh, the son of immigrants from India, who was working on a research project with William Julius Wilson, decided to ignore the warning.

With clipboard in hand, Sudhir entered "the projects." Ignoring the glares of the young men standing around, he went into the lobby of a high-rise. Seeing a gaping hole where the elevator was supposed to be, he decided to climb the stairs, where he was almost overpowered by the smell of urine. After climbing five flights, Sudhir came upon some young men shooting craps in a dark hallway. One of them jumped up, grabbed Sudhir's clipboard, and demanded to know what he was doing there.

Sudhir blurted, "I'm a student at the university, doing a survey, and I'm looking for some families to interview."

One man took out a knife and began to twirl it. Another pulled out a gun, pointed it at Sudhir's head, and said, "I'll take him."

Then came a series of rapid-fire questions that Sudhir couldn't answer. He had no idea what they meant: "You flip right or left? Five or six? You run with the Kings, right?"

Grabbing Sudhir's bag, two of the men searched it. They could find only questionnaires, pen and paper, and a few sociology books. The man with the gun then told Sudhir to go ahead and ask him a question.

Sweating despite the cold, Sudhir read the first question on his survey, "How does it feel to be black and poor?" Then he read the multiple-choice answers: "Very bad, somewhat bad, neither bad nor good, somewhat good, very good."

As you might surmise, the man's answer was too obscenity laden to be printed here.

As the men deliberated Sudhir's fate ("If he's here and he don't get back, you know they're going to come looking for him"), a powerfully built man with glittery gold teeth and a sizable diamond earring appeared. The man, known as J. T., who, it turned out, directed the drug trade in the building, asked what was going on. When the

*Professor Sudhir Venkatesh at Columbia University, New York.*

younger men mentioned the questionnaire, J. T. said to ask *him* a question.

Amidst an eerie silence, Sudhir asked, "How does it feel to be black and poor?"

"I'm not black," came the reply.

"Well, then, how does it feel to be African American and poor?"

"I'm not African American either. I'm a nigger."

Sudhir was left speechless. Despite his naïveté, he knew better than to ask, "How does it feel to be a nigger and poor?"

As Sudhir stood with his mouth agape, J. T. added, "Niggers are the ones who live in this building. African Americans live in the suburbs. African Americans wear ties to work. Niggers can't find no work."

Not exactly the best start to a research project.

But this weird and frightening beginning turned into several years of fascinating research. Over time, J. T. guided Sudhir into a world that few outsiders ever see. Not only did Sudhir get to know drug dealers, crackheads, squatters, prostitutes, and pimps, but he also was present at beatings by drug crews, drive-by shootings done by rival gangs, and armed robberies by the police.

How Sudhir got out of his predicament in the stairwell, his immersion into a threatening underworld—the daily life for many people in "the projects"—and his moral dilemma at witnessing so many crimes are part of his fascinating experience in doing participant observation of the Black Kings.

Sudhir, who was reared in a middle-class suburb in California, even took over this Chicago gang for a day. This is one reason that he calls himself a rogue sociologist—the decisions he made that day were serious violations of law, felonies that could bring years in prison. There are other reasons, too: During the research, he kicked a man in the stomach, and he was present as the gang planned drive-by shootings.

Sudhir eventually completed his Ph.D., and he now teaches at Columbia University.

Based on Venkatesh 2008.

**White-Collar Crime**    The more privileged social classes are not crime free, of course, but for them different illegitimate opportunities beckon. They find *other forms* of crime to be functional. Physicians, for example, don't hold up cabbies, but many do cheat Medicare. You've heard about bookkeepers who embezzle from their employers and corporate officers who manipulate stock prices. In other words, rather than mugging, pimping, and committing burglary, the more privileged encounter "opportunities" for evading income tax, bribing public officials, embezzling, and so on. Sociologist Edwin Sutherland (1949) coined the term **white-collar crime** to refer to crimes that people of respectable and high social status commit in the course of their occupations.

A special form of white-collar crime is **corporate crime,** crimes committed by executives in order to benefit their corporation. For example, to increase corporate profits, Sears executives defrauded the poor of over $100 million by having debtors sign agreements that were illegal. Their victims were so poor that they had already filed for bankruptcy. To avoid a criminal trial, Sears pleaded guilty. This frightened the parent companies of Macy's and Bloomingdales, which had similar deceptive practices, and they settled with their debtors out of court (McCormick 1999b). Similarly, Citigroup had to pay $70 million for preying on the poor (O'Brien 2004). None of the corporate thieves at Sears, Macy's, Bloomingdales, or Citigroup spent a day in jail.

Seldom is corporate crime taken seriously, even when it results in death. One of the most notorious corporate crimes involved the decision by Firestone executives to allow faulty tires to remain on U.S. vehicles—even though they were recalling the tires in Saudi Arabia and Venezuela. These tires cost the lives of about 200 Americans (White et al. 2001). No Firestone executive went to jail.

Consider this: Under federal law, causing the death of a worker by willfully violating safety rules is a misdemeanor punishable by up to six months in prison. Yet harassing a wild burro on federal lands is punishable by a year in prison (Barstow and Bergman 2003).

At $400 billion a year (Reiman 2004), "crime in the suites" actually costs more than "crime in the streets." This refers only to dollar costs. No one has yet figured out a way to compare, for example, the suffering experienced by a rape victim with the pain felt by an elderly couple who have lost their life savings to white-collar fraud.

The greatest concern of Americans, however, is street crime. They fear the violent stranger who will change their life forever. As the Social Map below shows, the chances of such an encounter depend on where you live. From this map, you can see that entire regions are safer or more dangerous than others. In general, the northern states are the safest, and the southern states the most dangerous.

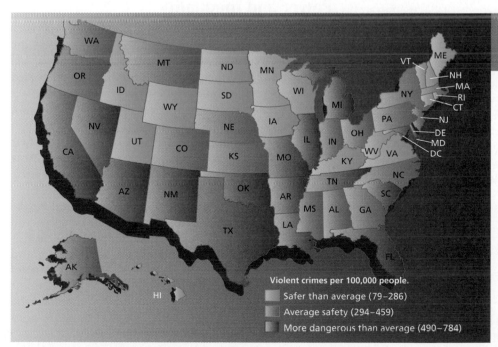

## FIGURE 6.1    Some States Are Safer: Violent Crime in the United States

Violent crimes are murder, rape, robbery, and aggravated assault. As this figure illustrates, violent crime varies widely among the states. The chances of becoming a victim of these crimes are ten times higher in South Carolina, the most dangerous state, than in North Dakota, the safest state. Washington, D.C., not a state, is in a class by itself. Its rate of 1,371 is three times the national average and over 17 times North Dakota's rate.

*Source:* By the author. Based on *Statistical Abstract of the United States* 2007:Table 297.

Violent crimes per 100,000 people.

- Safer than average (79–286)
- Average safety (294–459)
- More dangerous than average (490–784)

**Gender and Crime**   Like men, women are also enticed by illegitimate opportunities, and a major change in crime is the growing number of female offenders. As Table 6.2 below shows, women are committing a larger proportion of crime—from car theft to possession of illegal weapons. The basic reason for this increase is women's changed social location. As more women work in factories, corporations, and the professions, their opportunities for crime increase.

### TABLE 6.2   Women and Crime: What a Change

Of all those arrested, what percentage are women?

| Crime | 1992 | 2006[1] | Change |
|---|---|---|---|
| Car Theft | 10.8% | 17.7% | +64% |
| Burglary | 9.2% | 14.5% | +58% |
| Stolen Property[2] | 12.5% | 18.9% | +51% |
| Drunken Driving | 13.8% | 20.0% | +45% |
| Aggravated Assault | 14.8% | 20.7% | +40% |
| Robbery | 8.5% | 11.3% | +33% |
| Arson | 13.4% | 17.0% | +27% |
| Larceny/Theft | 32.1% | 37.7% | +17% |
| Illegal Drugs | 16.4% | 18.9% | +15% |
| Forgery and Counterfeiting | 34.7% | 39.1% | +13% |
| Illegal Weapons[3] | 7.5% | 8.0% | +7% |
| Fraud | 42.1% | 44.5% | +6% |

[1]Latest year available; national U.S. arrests.
[2]Buying, receiving, possessing.
[3]Carrying, possessing.

Source: By the author. Based on *Statistical Abstract of the United States* 1994: Table 317; *Crime in the United States* 2006: Table 42.

**In Sum:**   Functionalists conclude that much street crime is the consequence of socializing everyone into equating success with owning material possessions, while denying many in the lower social classes the legitimate means to attain that success. People from higher social classes encounter different opportunities to commit crimes. The growing crime rates of women illustrate how changing gender roles are giving more women access to illegitimate opportunities.

# The Conflict Perspective

## Class, Crime, and the Criminal Justice System

Sioux Manufacturing in North Dakota made helmets for the U.S. ground troops in Iraq and Afghanistan. Two former managers reported that the company had set its looms to use less Kevlar—a fabric that deflects some shrapnel and bullets—than they were supposed to. The government investigated. If the charge were true, then the company had endangered U.S. soldiers, perhaps causing some to die.

The charge turned out to be true. Employees had even doctored records to show that the company had used the correct amount of Kevlar. So how was Sioux Manufacturing punished? Were its executives put on trial and imprisoned?

Not at all. Sioux Manufacturing paid a fine—and the government gave it another contract to make more helmets. Of course, the company had to reset its looms (Lambert 2008).

Contrast the reaction to this corporate crime with the prison sentences given to poor people who have been caught stealing cars. How can a legal system that is supposed to provide "justice for all" be so inconsistent? According to conflict theorists, this question is central to the analysis of crime and the **criminal justice system**—the police, courts, and prisons that deal with people who are accused of having committed crimes. Let's see what conflict theorists have to say about this.

## Power and Inequality

Conflict theorists regard power and social inequality as the main characteristics of society. They stress that the power elite that runs society also controls the criminal justice system. This group makes certain that laws are passed that will protect its position in society.

Conflict theorists see the most fundamental division in capitalist society as that between the few who own the means of production and the many who sell their labor. Those who buy labor, and thereby control workers, make up the **capitalist class;** those who sell their labor form the **working class.** Toward the most depressed end of the working class is the **marginal working class:** people who have few skills, who are subject to layoffs, and whose jobs are low paying, part time, or seasonal. This class is marked by unemployment and poverty. From its ranks come most of the prison inmates in the United States. Desperate, these people commit street crimes; and because their crimes threaten the social order that keeps the elite in power, they are punished severely.

## The Law as an Instrument of Oppression

According to conflict theorists, the idea that the law operates impartially and administers a code that is shared by all is a cultural myth promoted by the capitalist class. These theorists see the law as an instrument of oppression, a tool designed by the powerful to maintain their privileged position (Spitzer 1975; Reiman 2004; Chambliss 2000, 2007). Because the working class has the potential to rebel and overthrow the current social order, when its members get out of line, the law comes down hard on them.

For this reason, the criminal justice system does not focus on the owners of corporations and the harm they do through manufacturing unsafe products, creating pollution, and manipulating prices—or the crimes of Sioux Manufacturing mentioned on the previous page. Instead, it directs its energies against violations by the working class. The violations of the capitalist class cannot be ignored totally, however, for if they become too outrageous or oppressive, the working class might rise up and revolt. To prevent this, a flagrant violation by a member of the capitalist class is occasionally prosecuted. The publicity given to the case helps to stabilize the social system by providing evidence of the "fairness" of the criminal justice system.

Usually, however, the powerful are able to bypass the courts altogether, appearing instead before an agency that has no power to imprison (such as the Federal Trade Commission). People from wealthy backgrounds who sympathize with the intricacies of the corporate world direct these agencies. It is they who oversee most cases of manipulating the price of stocks, insider trading, violating fiduciary duty, and so on. Is it surprising, then, that the typical sanction for corporate crime is a token fine?

When groups that have been denied access to power gain that access, we can expect to see changes in the legal system. This is precisely what is occurring now. Racial–ethnic minorities and homosexuals, for example, have more political power today than ever before. In line with conflict theory, a new category called *hate crime* has been formulated. We analyze this change in a different context on pages 164–165.

**In Sum:** From the perspective of conflict theory, the power elite use the legal system to keep themselves in power, to control workers, and to stabilize the social order. They make certain that small penalties are imposed for crimes committed by the powerful and that heavy penalties come down on those whose crimes could upset the social order. The poor always pose a threat, for they could rebel as a group and dislodge the elite from their place of power. As viewed from this perspective, law enforcement is a cultural device through which the capitalist class carries out self-protective and repressive policies.

## Reactions to Deviance

Whether it involves cheating on a sociology quiz or holding up a liquor store, any violation of norms invites reaction. Reactions, though, vary with culture. Before we examine reactions in the United States, let's take a little side trip to Greenland, an island nation three times the size of Texas located between Canada and Denmark. I think you'll enjoy this little excursion in cultural diversity.

"*If you want justice, it's two hundred dollars an hour. Obstruction of justice runs a bit more.*"

The cartoonist's hyperbole makes an excellent commentary on the social class disparity of our criminal justice system. Not only are the crimes of the wealthy not as likely to come to the attention of authorities as are the crimes of the poor, but when they do, the wealthy can afford legal expertise that the poor cannot.

# Cultural Diversity around the World

## "What Kind of Prison Is This?"

The prison in Nuuk, the capital of Greenland, has no wall around it. It has no fence. It doesn't even have bars.

The other day, Meeraq Lendenhann, a convicted rapist, walked out of prison. He didn't run or hide. He just walked out. Meeraq went to a store he likes to shop at, bought a CD of his favorite group, U2, and then walked back to the prison.

If Meeraq tires of listening to music, he can send e-mail and play games on a computer. Like other prisoners, he also has a personal TV with satellite hookup.

The prison holds 60 prisoners—the country's killers, rapists, and a few thieves. The prisoners leave the prison to work at regular jobs, where they average $28,000 or so a year. But they have to return to the prison after work. And they are locked into their rooms at 9:30.

The prisoners have to work, because the prison charges them $150 a week for room and board. The extra money goes into their savings accounts or to help support their families.

And, of course, the prisoners can have guns. At least during the summer. A major summer sport for Greenlanders is hunting reindeer and seals. Prisoners don't want to miss out on the fun, so if they ask, they are given shotguns.

But gun use isn't as easy as it sounds. Judges have set a severe requirement: The prisoners have to be accompanied by armed guards. If that isn't bad enough, the judges have added another requirement—that the prisoners not get drunk while they hunt.

One woman prisoner who said she was going to a beauty salon got sidetracked and went to a bar instead. When it got late and she was quite drunk, she called the prison and asked someone to come and get her.

If someone from another culture asks about the prisoners running away, the head of the prison says, "Where would they run? It's warm inside, and cold outside."

*This photo was taken inside a "cell" at Nuuk—private room, personal TV with satellite connection, VCR, adjustable reading lamp, radio-CD player, and window to the outside. The inmate's coffee maker is on the other side of the room.*

Then, of course, the prisoners probably wouldn't want to miss breakfast—a buffet of five kinds of imported cheese, various breads, marmalade, honey, coffee, and tea.

## For Your Consideration

Greenland's unique approach arose out of its history of hunting and fishing for a living. If men were locked up, they wouldn't be able to hunt or fish, and their families would suffer. From this history has come the main goal of Greenland's prison—to integrate offenders into society. This treatment helps prisoners slip back into village life after they have served their sentence. The incorrigibles, those who remain dangerous—about 20 men—are sent to a prison in Copenhagen, Denmark. Meeraq, the rapist, is given injections of Androcur, a testosterone-reducing drug that lowers his sex drive. Alcoholics are given Antabuse, a drug that triggers nasty reactions if someone drinks alcohol.

How do you think we could apply Greenland's approach to the United States?

Based on Naik 2004.

## Street Crime and Prisons

Let's turn back to the United States. Figure 6.2 illustrates the remarkable growth in the U.S. prison population. The number of prisoners is actually higher than the total shown in this figure. If we add jail inmates, the total comes to over 2 million people—one out of every 143 citizens. Not only does the United States have more prisoners than any other nation, but it also has a larger percentage of its population in prison. The number of prisoners has grown so fast that the states hire private companies to operate additional jails for them. About 110,000 prisoners are in these "private" jails (*Sourcebook of Criminal Justice Statistics* 2006:Table 6.32).

To better understand U.S. prisoners, let's compare them with the U.S. population. As you look at Table 6.3 on the next page, several things may strike you. Almost all prisoners (87 percent) are ages 18 to 44, and almost all of them are men. Then there is this remarkable statistic: Although African Americans make up just 12.8 percent of the U.S. population, close to half of all prisoners are African Americans. On any given day, about one in eight African American men ages 20 to 34 is in jail or prison (Butterfield 2003). Finally, note how marriage and education—two of the major techniques society has of "anchoring" us—provide protection from prison.

As I mentioned earlier, social class funnels some people into the criminal justice system and diverts others away from it. This table illuminates the power of education, a major component of social class. You can see how people who drop out of high school have a high chance of ending up in prison—and how unlikely it is for a college graduate to have this unwelcome destination in life.

For about the past 20 years or so, the United States has followed a "get tough" policy. One of the most significant changes was the "three strikes and you're out" laws. When someone is convicted of a third felony, judges are required to give a mandatory sentence, sometimes life imprisonment. While few of us would feel sympathy if a man convicted of a third brutal rape or a third murder were sent to prison for life, these laws have had unanticipated consequences, as you will see in the following Thinking Critically section.

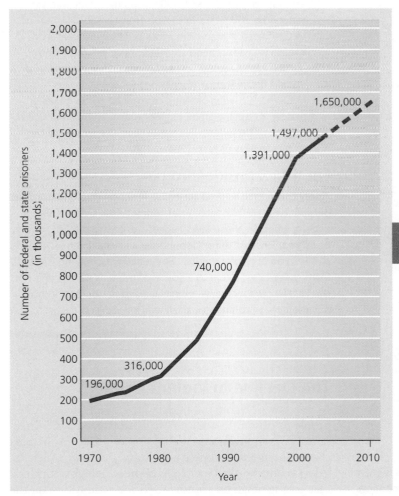

### FIGURE 6.2    How Much Is Enough? The Explosion in the Number of U.S. Prisoners

To better understand how remarkable this change is, compare the increase in U.S. prisoners with the increase in the U.S. population. Between 1970 and 2004, the U.S. population increased 43 percent, while the number of prisoners increased 764 percent, a rate that is *18 times greater*. If the number of prisoners had grown at the same rate as the U.S. population, there would be about 280,000 prisoners, only 13 percent of today's total. (Or, if the U.S. population had increased at the same rate as that of U.S. prisoners, the U.S. population would be 3,650,000,000—more than the population of China, India, Canada, Mexico, and all of Europe combined.)

*Sources:* By the author. Based on *Statistical Abstract of the United States* 1995:Table 349; 2007:Table 334. The broken line is the author's estimate.

## TABLE 6.3    Inmates in U.S. State Prisons

| Characteristics | Percentage of Prisoners with These Characteristics | Percentage of U.S. Population with These Characteristics |
|---|---|---|
| **Age** | | |
| 18–24 | 26.4% | 9.9% |
| 25–34 | 35.4% | 13.5% |
| 35–44 | 25.2% | 14.8% |
| 45–54 | 10.4% | 14.3% |
| 55 and older | 1.0% | 22.7% |
| **Race–Ethnicity** | | |
| African American | 47.3% | 12.8% |
| White | 36.9% | 66.9% |
| Latino | 14.2% | 14.4% |
| Asian Americans | 0.6% | 4.3% |
| Native Americans | 0.9% | 1.0% |
| **Sex** | | |
| Male | 93.4% | 49.3% |
| Female | 6.3% | 50.7% |
| **Marital Status** | | |
| Never Married | 59.8% | 28.2% |
| Divorced | 15.5% | 10.2% |
| Married | 17.3% | 58.6% |
| Widowed | 1.1% | 6.4% |
| **Education** | | |
| Less than high school | 39.7% | 14.8% |
| High school graduate | 49.0% | 32.2% |
| Some college | 9.0% | 25.4% |
| College graduate | 2.4% | 27.6% |

*Source:* By the author. Based on *Sourcebook of Criminal Justice Statistics* 2003: Tables 6.000b, 6.28; 2006: Tables 6.34, 6.45; *Statistical Abstract of the United States* 2007: Tables 12, 14, 23, 55, 216.

convicted of a third felony receives an automatic mandatory sentence. Judges are not allowed to consider the circumstances. Some mandatory sentences carry life imprisonment.

In their haste to appease the public, politicians did not limit the three-strikes laws to *violent* crimes. And they did not consider that some minor crimes are considered felonies. As the functionalists would say, this has led to unanticipated consequences.

Here are some actual cases:

- In Los Angeles, a 27-year-old man was sentenced to 25 years for stealing a pizza (Cloud 1998).
- In New York City, a man who was about to be sentenced for selling crack said to the judge, "I'm only 19. This is terrible." He then hurled himself out of a courtroom window, plunging to his death sixteen stories below (Cloud 1998).
- In Sacramento, a man who passed himself off as Tiger Woods to go on a $17,000 shopping spree was sentenced to 200 years in prison (Reuters 2001).
- In California, a man who stole nine videotapes from Kmart was sentenced to 50 years in prison without parole. He appealed to the U.S. Supreme Court, which upheld his sentence (Greenhouse 2003).
- In Utah, a 25-year-old was sentenced to 55 years in prison for selling small bags of marijuana to a police informant. The judge who sentenced the man said the sentence was unjust (Madigan 2004).

### For Your Consideration

Apply the symbolic interactionist, functionalist, and conflict perspectives to mandatory sentencing. For *symbolic interactionism*, what do these laws represent to the public? How does your answer differ depending on what part of "the public" you are referring to? For *functionalism*, who benefits from these laws? What are some of their dysfunctions? For the *conflict perspective*, what groups are in conflict? Who has the power to enforce their will on others?

# ThinkingCRITICALLY

## "Three Strikes and You're Out!" Unintended Consequences of Well-Intended Laws

In the 1980s, crimes of violence soared. As Americans grew fearful, they demanded that their lawmakers do something. Politicians heard the message, and some state legislatures responded by passing the "three-strikes" law. Anyone who is

## The Decline in Violent Crime

As you saw in Figure 6.2, judges have put more and more people in prison. In addition, legislators passed the three-strikes laws and reduced early releases of prisoners. As these changes occurred, the crime rate dropped sharply, which has led to a controversy in sociology. Some sociologists conclude that getting tough on criminals was the main reason for the drop in violent crime (Conklin 2003). Others point to higher employment, a drop in drug use, and even abortion

(Rosenfeld 2002; Reiman 2004; Blumstein and Wallman 2006). This matter is not yet settled, but both tough sentencing and the economy seem to be important factors.

## Recidivism

A major problem with prisons is that they fail to teach their clients to stay away from crime. Our **recidivism rate**—the percentage of former prisoners who are rearrested—is high. For those who are sentenced to prison for crimes of violence, within just three years of their release, two out of three (62 percent) are rearrested, and half (52 percent) are back in prison (*Sourcebook of Criminal Justice Statistics* 2003:Table 6.52). Figure 6.3 shows recidivism by type of crime. It is safe to conclude that if—and this is a big if—the purpose of prisons is to teach people that crime doesn't pay, they are colossal failures.

## The Death Penalty and Bias

**Capital punishment,** the death penalty, is the most extreme measure the state takes. The death penalty is mired in controversy, arousing impassioned opposition and support on both moral and philosophical grounds. Advances in DNA testing have given opponents of the death penalty a strong argument: Innocent people have been sent to death row, and some have been executed. Others are passionate about retaining the death penalty, pointing to such crimes as those of the serial killers discussed in the Down-to-Earth Sociology box on the next page.

Apart from anyone's personal position on the death penalty, it certainly is clear that the death penalty is not administered evenly. Consider geography: The Social Map on page 163 shows that where people commit murder greatly affects their chances of being put to death.

The death penalty also shows social class bias. As you know from news reports on murder and sentencing, it is rare for a rich person to be sentenced to death. Although the government does not collect statistics on social class and the death penalty, this common observation is borne out by the average education of the prisoners on death row. *Most* prisoners on death row (51 percent) have not finished high school (*Sourcebook of Criminal Justice Statistics* 2006:Table 6.81).

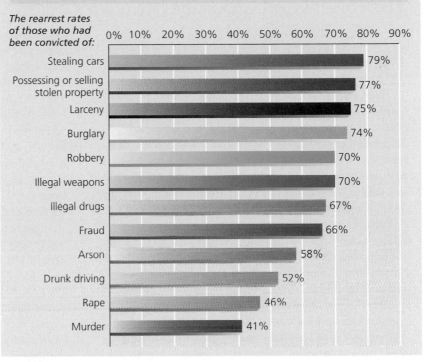

**FIGURE 6.3    Recidivism of U.S. Prisoners**

Of 272,000 prisoners released from U.S. prisons, what percentage were rearrested within three years?

The rearrest rates of those who had been convicted of:

|  |  |
|---|---|
| Stealing cars | 79% |
| Possessing or selling stolen property | 77% |
| Larceny | 75% |
| Burglary | 74% |
| Robbery | 70% |
| Illegal weapons | 70% |
| Illegal drugs | 67% |
| Fraud | 66% |
| Arson | 58% |
| Drunk driving | 52% |
| Rape | 46% |
| Murder | 41% |

*Note:* The individuals were not necessarily rearrested for the same crime for which they had originally been imprisoned.

*Source:* By the author. Based on *Sourcebook of Criminal Justice Statistics* 2003:Table 6.50.

Figure 6.5 on page 163 shows gender bias in the death penalty. It is almost unheard of for a woman to be sentenced to death. Although women commit 9.6 percent of the murders, they make up only 1.6 percent of death row inmates (*Sourcebook of Criminal Justice Statistics* 2006:Table 3.129). It is possible that this statistic reflects not only gender bias but also the relative brutality of the women's murders. We need research to determine this.

Bias used to be so flagrant that it once put a stop to the death penalty. Donald Partington (1965), a lawyer in Virginia, was shocked by the bias he saw in the courtroom, and he decided to document it. He found that 2,798 men had been convicted for rape and attempted rape in Virginia between 1908 and 1963—56 percent whites and 44 percent blacks. For attempted rape, 13 had been executed. For rape, 41 men had been executed. *All those executed were black.* Not one of the whites was executed.

# Down-to-Earth Sociology
## The Killer Next Door: Serial Murderers in Our Midst

I was stunned by the images. Television cameras showed the Houston police digging up dozens of bodies from under a boat storage shed. Fascinated, I waited impatiently for spring break. A few days later, I drove from Illinois to Houston, where 33-year-old Dean Corll had befriended Elmer Wayne Henley and David Brooks, two teenagers from broken homes. Together, they had killed 27 boys. Elmer and David would pick up young hitchhikers and deliver them to Corll to rape and kill. Sometimes they even brought him their high school classmates.

I talked to one of Elmer's neighbors, as he was painting his front porch. His 15-year-old son had gone to get a haircut one Saturday morning; it was the last time he had seen his son alive. The police insisted that the boy had run away, and they refused to investigate. On a city map, I plotted the locations of the homes of the local murder victims. Many clustered around the homes of the teenage killers.

I was going to spend my coming sabbatical writing a novel on this case, but, to be frank, I became frightened and didn't write the book. I didn't know if I could recover psychologically if I were to immerse myself in grisly details day after day for months on end. One of these details was a piece of plywood, with a hole in each of its four corners. Corll and the boys would spread-eagle their victims handcuffed to the plywood. There, they would torture the boys (no girl victims) for hours. Sometimes, they would even pause to order pizza.

My interviews confirmed what has since become common knowledge about serial killers: They lead double lives so successfully that their friends and family are unaware of their criminal activities. Henley's mother swore to me that her son was a good boy and couldn't possibly be guilty. Some of his high school friends told me the same thing. They stressed that Elmer couldn't be involved in homosexual rape and murder because he was interested only in girls. I conducted my interviews in Henley's bedroom, and for proof of what they told me, his friends pointed to a pair of girls' panties that were draped across a lamp shade.

**Serial murder** is the killing of several victims in three or more separate events. The murders may occur over several days, weeks, or years. The elapsed time between murders distinguishes serial killers from *mass murderers*, who do their killing all at once. Here are some infamous examples:

- During the 1960s and 1970s, Ted Bundy raped and killed dozens of women in four states.
- Between 1979 and 1981, Wayne Williams killed 28 boys and young men in Atlanta.
- In 2005, in Wichita, Kansas, Dennis Rader pleaded guilty to being the BTK (Bind, Torture, and Kill) strangler, a name he had proudly given himself. His 10 killings spanned 1974 to 1991.
- In the late 1980s and early 1990s, Aileen Wuornos, hitchhiking along Florida's freeways, killed 7 men after having sex with them.
- The serial killer with the most victims appears to be Harold Shipman of Manchester, England. From 1977 to 2000, this quiet, unassuming physician killed 230 to 275 of his elderly women patients. While making house calls, he gave the women lethal injections.

*One of the striking traits of most serial killers is how they blend in with the rest of society. Ted Bundy, shown here, was remarkable in this respect. Almost everyone who knew this law student liked him. Even the Florida judge who found him guilty said that he would have liked to have him practice law in his court, but, as he added, "You went the wrong way, partner." (Note the term partner—used even after Bundy was convicted of heinous crimes.)*

Is serial murder more common now than it used to be? Not likely. In the past, police departments had little communication with one another. When killings occurred in different jurisdictions, seldom did anyone connect them. Today's more efficient communications, investigative techniques, and DNA matching make it easier for the police to conclude that a serial killer is operating in an area. Part of the perception that there are more serial killers today is also due to ignorance of our history: In our frontier past, serial killers went from ranch to ranch. Some would say that mass murderers wiped out entire villages of Native Americans.

## For Your Consideration
Do you think that serial killers should be given the death penalty? Why or why not? How do your social locations influence your opinion?

## FIGURE 6.4    Executions in the United States

Executions since 1977, when the death penalty was reinstated.

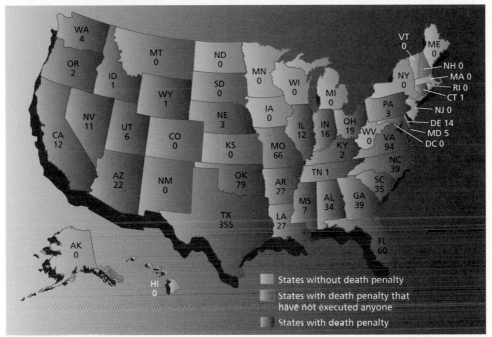

- States without death penalty
- States with death penalty that have not executed anyone
- States with death penalty

*Source:* By the author. Based on *Statistical Abstract of the United States* 2007:Table 341.

## FIGURE 6.5    Women and Men on Death Row

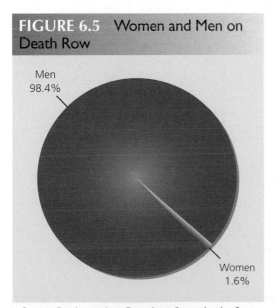

Men
98.4%

Women
1.6%

*Source:* By the author. Based on *Sourcebook of Criminal Justice Statistics* 2006:Table 6.81.

After listening to evidence like this, in 1972 the Supreme Court ruled in *Furman v. Georgia* that the death penalty, as applied, was unconstitutional. The execution of prisoners stopped—but not for long. The states wrote new laws, and in 1977 they again began to execute prisoners. Since then, 67 percent of those put to death have been white and 33 percent African American (*Statistical Abstract* 2007:Table 340). (Latinos are evidently counted as whites in this statistic.) Table 6.4 on the next page shows the race-ethnicity of the prisoners who are on death row.

## Legal Change

Did you know that it is a crime in Saudi Arabia for a woman to drive a car (Fattah 2007)? A crime in Florida to sell alcohol before 1 P.M. on Sundays? Or illegal in Wells, Maine, to advertise on tombstones? As has been stressed in this chapter, deviance, including the form called *crime,* is relative. It varies from one society to another, and from group to group within a society. Crime also varies from one time period to another, as opinions change or as different groups gain access to power.

Hate crimes are an example of legal change, the topic of the next Thinking Critically section.

**TABLE 6.4**    The Race–Ethnicity of the 3,486 Prisoners on Death Row

|  | Percentage | |
|---|---|---|
|  | on Death Row | in U.S. Population |
| Whites | 45% | 67% |
| African Americans | 42% | 13% |
| Latinos | 11% | 14% |
| Asian Americans | 1% | 4% |
| Native Americans | 1% | 1% |

*Source:* By the author. Based on *Sourcebook of Criminal Justice Statistics* 2007: Table 6.80 and Figure 9.4 of this text.

# ThinkingCRITICALLY
## Changing Views: Making Hate a Crime

Because crime consists of whatever acts authorities decide to assign that label, new crimes emerge from time to time. A prime example is juvenile delinquency, which Illinois lawmakers designated a separate type of crime in 1899. Juveniles committed crimes before this time, of course, but youths were not considered to be a separate type of lawbreaker. They were just young

Hate crimes, which range from murder and injury to defacing property with symbols of hatred, include arson, the suspected cause of the fire at this synagogue.

people who committed crimes, and they were treated the same as adults who committed the same crime. Sometimes new technology leads to new crimes. Motor vehicle theft, a separate crime in the United States, obviously did not exist before the automobile was invented.

In the 1980s, another new crime was born when state governments developed the classification **hate crime.** This is a crime that is motivated by *bias* (dislike, hatred) against someone's race–ethnicity, religion, sexual orientation, disability, or national origin. Before this, of course, people attacked others or destroyed their property out of these same motivations, but in those cases the motivation was not the issue. If someone injured or killed another person because of that person's race–ethnicity, religion, sexual orientation, national origin, or disability, he or she was charged with assault or murder. Today, motivation has become a central issue, and hate crimes carry more severe sentences than do the same acts that do not have hatred as their motive. Table 6.5 summarizes the victims of hate crimes.

**TABLE 6.5**    Hate Crimes

| Directed Against | Number of Victims | |
|---|---|---|
| **Race–Ethnicity** | | |
| African Americans | | 3,494 |
| Whites | | 1,027 |
| Latinos | | 646 |
| Asian Americans | | 272 |
| Native Americans | | 102 |
| **Religion** | | |
| Jews | | 1,086 |
| Muslims | | 202 |
| Catholics | | 68 |
| Protestants | | 48 |
| **Sexual Orientation** | | |
| Homosexual | | 1,429 |
|   Male homosexual | 902 | |
|   Female homosexual | 213 | |
|   General | 314 | |
| Heterosexual | | 32 |
| Bisexual | | 18 |
| **Disabilities** | | |
| Mental | | 49 |
| Physical | | 24 |

*Source: Statistical Abstract of the United States* 2007: Table 308.

We can be certain that the "evolution" of crime is not yet complete. As society changes and as different groups gain access to power, we can expect the definitions of crime to change accordingly.

## For Your Consideration

Why should we have a separate classification called hate crime? Why aren't the crimes of assault, robbery, and murder adequate? As one analyst (Sullivan 1999) said, "Was the brutal murder of gay college student Matthew Shepard [a hate crime] in Laramie, Wyoming, in 1998 worse than the abduction, rape, and murder of an eight-year-old Laramie girl [not a hate crime] by a pedophile that same year?"

How do you think your social location (race–ethnicity, gender, social class, sexual orientation, or physical ability) affects your opinion?

## The Medicalization of Deviance: Mental Illness

Another way in which society deals with deviance is to "medicalize" it. Let's look at what this entails.

**Neither Mental Nor Illness?**    To *medicalize* something is to make it a medical matter, to classify it as a form of illness that properly belongs in the care of physicians. For the past hundred years or so, especially since the time of Sigmund Freud (1856–1939), the Viennese physician who founded psychoanalysis, there has been a growing tendency toward the **medicalization of deviance.** In this view, deviance, including crime, is a sign of mental sickness. Rape, murder, stealing, cheating, and so on are external symptoms of internal disorders, consequences of a confused or tortured mind.

Thomas Szasz (1986, 1996, 1998), a renegade in his profession of psychiatry, argues that *mental illnesses are neither mental nor illnesses. They are simply problem behaviors.* Some forms of so-called mental illnesses have organic causes; that is, they are *physical* illnesses that result in unusual perceptions or behavior. Some depression, for example, is caused by a chemical imbalance in the brain, which can be treated by drugs. The depression, however, may appear in the forms of crying, long-term

sadness, and lack of interest in family, work, school, or one's appearance. When someone becomes deviant in ways that disturb others, *and* when these others cannot find a satisfying explanation for why the person is "like that," a "sickness in the head" is often taken as the cause of the unacceptable behavior.

Attention deficit disorder (ADD) is an excellent example. As Szasz says, "No one explains where this disease came from, why it didn't exist 50 years ago. No one is able to diagnose it with objective tests." It is diagnosed by a teacher or a parent complaining about a child misbehaving. Misbehaving children have been a problem throughout history, but now their problem behavior has become a sign of mental illness.

All of us have troubles. Some of us face a constant barrage of problems as we go through life. Most of us continue the struggle, perhaps encouraged by relatives and friends and motivated by job, family responsibilities, religious faith, and life goals. Even when the odds seem hopeless, we carry on, not perfectly, but as best we can.

Some people, however, fail to cope well with life's challenges. Overwhelmed, they become depressed, uncooperative, or hostile. Some strike out at others, while some, in Merton's terms, become retreatists and withdraw into their apartments or homes, refusing to come out. These are *behaviors, not mental illnesses,* stresses Szasz. They may be inappropriate coping devices, but they are coping devices nevertheless, not mental illnesses. Thus, Szasz concludes that "mental illness" is a myth foisted on a naive public by a medical profession that uses pseudoscientific jargon in order to expand its area of control and force nonconforming people to accept society's definitions of "normal."

Szasz's extreme claim forces us to look anew at the forms of deviance that we usually refer to as mental illness. To explain behavior that people find bizarre,

People whose behaviors violate norms often are called mentally ill. "Why else would they do such things?" is a common response to deviant behaviors that we don't understand. Mental illness is a label that contains the assumption that there is something wrong "within" people that "causes" their disapproved behavior. The surprise with this man, who changed his legal name to "Scary Guy," is that he speaks at schools across the country, where he promotes acceptance, awareness, love, and understanding.

he directs our attention not to causes hidden deep within the "subconscious," but, instead, to how people learn such behaviors. To ask, "What is the origin of someone's inappropriate or bizarre behavior?" then becomes similar to asking "Why do some women steal?" "Why do some men rape?" "Why do some teenagers cuss their parents and stalk out of the room, slamming the door?" *The answers depend on those people's particular experiences in life, not on an illness in their mind.* In short, some sociologists find Szasz's renegade analysis refreshing because it indicates that *social experiences,* not some illness of the mind, underlie bizarre behaviors—as well as deviance in general.

### The Homeless Mentally Ill

Jamie was sitting on a low wall surrounding the landscaped courtyard of an exclusive restaurant. She appeared unaware of the stares that were elicited by her layers of mismatched clothing, her matted hair and dirty face, and the shopping cart that overflowed with her meager possessions.

When I saw Jamie point to the street and concentrate, slowly moving her finger horizontally, I asked her what she was doing.

"I'm directing traffic," she replied. "I control where the cars go. Look, that one turned right there," she said, now withdrawing her finger.

"Really?" I said.

After a while she confided that her cart talked to her.

"Really?" I said again.

"Yes," she replied. "You can hear it, too." At that, she pushed the shopping cart a bit.

"Did you hear that?" she asked.

When I shook my head, she demonstrated again. Then it hit me. She was referring to the squeaking wheels!

I nodded.

When I left, Jamie was pointing to the sky, for, as she told me, she also controlled the flight of airplanes.

To most of us, Jamie's behavior and thinking are bizarre. They simply do not match any reality we know. Could you or I become like Jamie?

Suppose for a bitter moment that you are homeless and have to live on the streets. You have no money, no place to sleep, no bathroom. You do not know *if* you are going to eat, much less where. You have no friends or anyone you can trust, and you live in constant fear of rape and other violence. Do you think this might be enough to drive you over the edge?

Consider just the problems involved in not having a place to bathe. (Shelters are often so dangerous that many homeless people prefer to sleep in public settings.) At first, you try to wash in the restrooms of gas stations, bars, the bus station, or a shopping center. But you are dirty, and people stare when you enter and call the management when they see you wash your feet in the sink. You are thrown out and told in no uncertain terms never to come back. So you get dirtier and dirtier. Eventually, you come to think of being dirty as a fact of life. Soon, maybe, you don't even care. The stares no longer bother you—at least not as much.

No one will talk to you, and you withdraw more and more into yourself. You begin to build a fantasy life. You talk openly to yourself. People stare, but so what? They stare anyway. Besides, they are no longer important to you.

Jamie might be mentally ill. Some organic problem, such as a chemical imbalance in her brain, might underlie her behavior. But perhaps not. How long would it take you to exhibit bizarre behaviors if you were homeless—and hopeless? The point is that *just being on the streets can cause mental illness*—or whatever we want to label socially inappropriate behaviors that we find difficult to classify. *Homelessness and mental illness are reciprocal:* Just as "mental illness" can cause homelessness, so the trials of being homeless, of living on cold, hostile streets, can lead to unusual thinking and behaviors.

Mental illness is common among the homeless. This screaming man, who hangs out near Boston Commons in Boston, Massachusetts, has been homeless for 44 years. This gives you an idea of the depth of the problem of rehabilitation.

## The Need for a More Humane Approach

As Durkheim (1895/1964:68) pointed out, deviance is inevitable—even in a group of saints.

> Imagine a society of saints, a perfect cloister of exemplary individuals. Crimes, properly so called, will there be unknown; but faults which appear invisible to the layman will create there the same scandal that the ordinary offense does in ordinary society.

With deviance inevitable, one measure of a society is how it treats its deviants. Our prisons certainly don't say much good about U.S. society. Filled with the poor, they are warehouses of the unwanted. They reflect patterns of broad discrimination in our larger society. White-collar criminals continue to get by with a slap on the wrist while street criminals are punished severely. Some deviants, who fail to meet current standards of admission to either prison or mental hospital, take refuge in shelters, as well as in cardboard boxes tucked away in urban recesses. Although no one has *the* answer, it does not take much reflection to see that there are more humane approaches than these.

Because deviance is inevitable, we need to address the larger issues: finding ways to protect people from harmful deviance, tolerating those behaviors that are not harmful, and developing systems of fair treatment for deviants. In the absence of fundamental changes that would bring about a truly equitable social system, most efforts are, unfortunately, like putting a Band-Aid on a gunshot wound. What we need is a more humane social system, one that would prevent the social inequalities that are the focus of the next four chapters.

# SUMMARY *and* REVIEW

## What Is Deviance?

From a sociological perspective, **deviance** (the violation of norms) is relative. What people consider deviant varies from one culture to another and from group to group within the same society. As symbolic interactionists stress, it is not the act, but the reactions to the act, that make something deviant. All groups develop systems of **social control** to punish **deviants**—those who violate their norms. Pp. 142–145.

*How do sociological and individualistic explanations of deviance differ?*

To explain why people deviate, sociobiologists and psychologists look for reasons *within* the individual, such as **genetic predispositions** or **personality disorders.** Sociologists, in contrast, look for explanations *outside* the individual, in social experiences. P. 146.

## The Symbolic Interactionist Perspective

*How do symbolic interactionists explain deviance?*

Symbolic interactionists have developed several theories to explain deviance, such as **crime** (the violation of norms that are written into law). According to **differential association theory,** people learn to deviate by associating with others. According to **control theory,** each of us is propelled toward deviance, but most of us conform because of an effective system of inner and outer controls. People who have less effective controls deviate. Pp. 146–151.

**Labeling theory** focuses on how labels (names, reputations) help to funnel people into or divert them away from deviance. People who commit deviant acts often use **techniques of neutralization** to continue to think of themselves as conformists. Pp. 150–151.

## The Functionalist Perspective

*How do functionalists explain deviance?*

Functionalists point out that deviance, including criminal acts, is functional for society. Functions include affirming norms and promoting social unity and social change. According to **strain theory,** societies socialize their members into desiring **cultural goals.** Many people are unable to achieve these goals in socially acceptable ways—that is, by **institutionalized means.** *Deviants,* then, are people who either give up on the goals or use deviant means to attain them. Merton identified five types of responses to cultural goals and institutionalized means: conformity, innovation, ritualism, retreatism, and rebellion. **Illegitimate opportunity theory** stresses that some people have easier access to illegal means of achieving goals. Pp. 151–156.

## The Conflict Perspective

### How do conflict theorists explain deviance?

Conflict theorists take the position that the group in power (the **capitalist class**) imposes its definitions of deviance on other groups (the **working class** and the **marginal working class**). From the conflict perspective, the law is an instrument of oppression used to maintain the power and privilege of the few over the many. The marginal working class has little income, is desperate, and commits highly visible property crimes. The ruling class directs the **criminal justice system,** using it to punish the crimes of the poor while diverting its own criminal activities away from this punitive system. Pp. 156–157.

## Reactions to Deviance

### What are common reactions to deviance in the United States?

In following a "get-tough" policy, the United States has imprisoned millions of people. African Americans make up a disproportionate percentage of U.S. prisoners. The death penalty shows biases by geography, social class, race–ethnicity, and gender. In line with conflict theory, as groups gain political power, their views are reflected in the criminal code. **Hate crime** legislation was considered in this context. Pp. 157–165.

### What is the medicalization of deviance?

The medical profession has attempted to **medicalize** many forms of **deviance,** claiming that they represent mental illnesses. Thomas Szasz disagrees, asserting that they are problem behaviors, not mental illnesses. Research on homeless people illustrates how problems in living can lead to bizarre behavior and thinking. Pp. 165–166.

### What is a more humane approach?

Deviance is inevitable, so the larger issues are to find ways to protect people from deviance that harms themselves and others, to tolerate deviance that is not harmful, and to develop systems of fairer treatment for deviants. P. 167.

# THINKING CRITICALLY *about* Chapter 6

1. Select some deviance with which you are personally familiar. (It does not have to be your own—it can be something that someone you know did.) Choose one of the three theoretical perspectives to explain what happened.

2. As is explained in the text, deviance can be mild. Recall some instance in which you broke a social rule in dress, etiquette, or speech. What was the reaction? Why do you think people reacted like that? What was your response to their reactions?

3. What do you think should be done about the U.S. crime problem? What sociological theories support your view?

# BY THE NUMBERS: Changes Over Time

- Women made up this percentage of arrests for car theft in 1992: **10.8%**
- Women made up this percentage of arrests for car theft in 2006: **17.6%**

- Women made up this percentage of aggravated assault arrests in 1992: **14.8%**
- Women made up this percentage of aggravated assault arrests in 2006: **20.7%**

- Number of U.S. federal and state prisoners in 1970: **196,000**
- Number of U.S. federal and state prisoners today: **1,497,000**

# ADDITIONAL RESOURCES

## What can you find in MySocLab?  mysoclab  www.mysoclab.com

- **Complete Ebook**
- **Practice Tests and Video and Audio activities**
- **Mapping and Data Analysis exercises**

- **Sociology in the News**
- **Classic Readings in Sociology**
- **Research and Writing advice**

## Where Can I Read More on This Topic?

Suggested readings for this chapter are listed at the back of this book.

*Chapter* 7

# Global
# Stratification

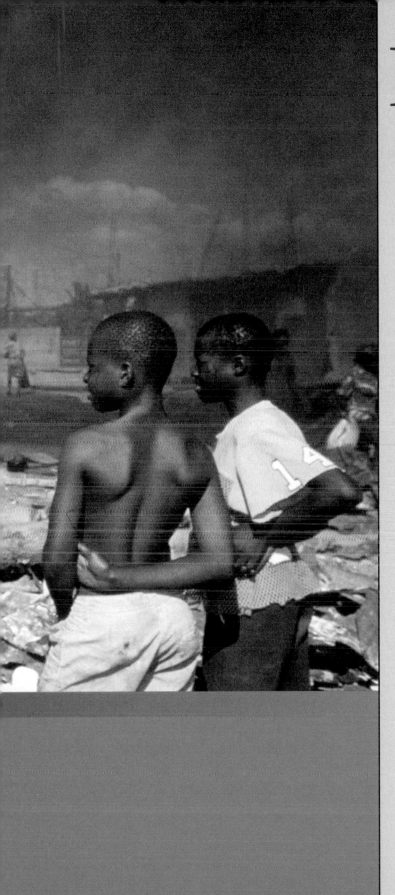

L et's contrast two "average" families in different parts of the world:

For Getu Mulleta, 33, and his wife, Zenebu, 28, of rural Ethiopia, life is a constant struggle to keep themselves and their seven children from starving.

They live in a 320-square-foot manure-plastered hut with no electricity, gas, or running water. They have a radio, but the battery is dead. The family farms teff, a grain, and survives on $130 a year.

**They live in a 320-square-foot manure-plastered hut with no electricity, gas, or running water.**

The Mulletas' poverty is not due to a lack of hard work. Getu works about eighty hours a week, while Zenebu puts in even more hours. "Housework" for Zenebu includes fetching water, cleaning animal stables, and making fuel pellets out of cow dung for the open fire over which she cooks the family's food. Like other Ethiopian women, she eats after the men.

In Ethiopia, the average male can expect to live to age 48, the average female to 50.

The Mulletas' most valuable possession is their oxen. Their wishes for the future: more animals, better seed, and a second set of clothing.

\* \* \* \* \*

Springfield, Illinois, is home to the Kellys—Rick, 36, Patti, 34, Julie, 10, and Michael, 7. The Kellys live in a four-bedroom, 2 1/2 bath, 2,434-square-foot, carpeted ranch-style house, with a fireplace, central heating and air conditioning, a basement, and a two-car garage. Their home is equipped with a refrigerator, washing machine, clothes dryer, dishwasher, garbage disposal, vacuum cleaner, food processor, microwave, and convection oven. They also own six telephones (three cellular), four color televisions (two high definition), two CD players, two digital cameras, digital camcorder, two DVD players, iPod, Xbox, a computer, and a printer-scanner-fax machine, not to mention two blow dryers, an answering machine, a juicer, and an espresso coffee maker. This count doesn't include such items as electric can openers, battery-powered tooth brushes, or the stereo-radio-CD/DVD players in their pickup truck and SUV.

Rick works forty hours a week as a cable splicer for a telephone company. Patti teaches school part time. Together they make $54,061, plus benefits. The Kellys can choose from among dozens of superstocked supermarkets. They spend $4,809 for food they eat at home, and another $3,362 eating out, a total of 15 percent of their annual income.

In the United States, the average life expectancy is 75 for males, 80 for females.

On the Kellys' wish list are a new hybrid car with satellite radio, a 160-gigabyte laptop with Bluetooth wi-fi, a 50-inch plasma TV with surround sound, a DVD camcorder, a boat, a motor home, an ATV, and, oh, yes, farther down the road, an in-ground heated swimming pool. They also have an eye on a cabin at a nearby lake.

*Sources:* Menzel 1994; *Statistical Abstract* 2007:Tables 99, 668, 676, 937.

# Systems of Social Stratification

Some of the world's nations are wealthy, others poor, and some in between. This division of nations, as well as the layering of groups of people within a nation, is called *social stratification*. Social stratification is one of the most significant topics we shall discuss in this book, for, as you saw in the opening vignette, it affects our life chances—from our access to material possessions to the age at which we die.

Social stratification also affects the way we think about life. If you had been born into the Ethiopian family in our opening vignette, for example, you would be illiterate and would assume that your children would be as well. You also would expect hunger to be a part of life and would not expect all of your children to survive. To be born into the U.S. family, however, would give you quite a different picture of the world. You would expect your children not only to survive, but to go to college as well. You can see that social stratification brings with it ideas of what we can expect out of life.

**Social stratification** is a system in which groups of people are divided into layers according to their relative property, power, and prestige. It is important to emphasize that social stratification does not refer to individuals. It is a way of ranking large groups of people into a hierarchy according to their relative privileges.

It is also important to note that *every society stratifies its members*. Some societies have greater inequality than others, but social stratification is universal. In addition, in every society of the world, *gender* is a basis for stratifying people. On the basis of their gender, people are either allowed or denied access to the good things offered by their society.

Let's consider three systems of social stratification: slavery, caste, and class.

## Slavery

**Slavery,** whose essential characteristic is that *some individuals own other people,* has been common throughout world history. The Old Testament even lays out rules for how owners should treat their slaves. So does the Koran. The Romans also had slaves, as did the Africans and Greeks. In classical Greece and Rome, slaves did the work, freeing citizens to engage in politics and the arts. Slavery was most widespread in agricultural societies and least common among nomads, especially hunters and gatherers (Landtman 1938/1968). As we examine the major causes and conditions of slavery, you will see how remarkably slavery has varied around the world.

**Causes of Slavery** Contrary to popular assumption, slavery was usually based not on racism but on one of three other factors. The first was *debt*. In some societies, creditors would enslave people who could not pay their debts. The second was *crime*. Instead of being killed, a murderer or thief might be enslaved by the victim's family as compensation for their loss. The third was *war*. When one group of people conquered another, they often enslaved some of the vanquished. Historian Gerda Lerner (1986) notes that women were the first people enslaved

Under slavery, humans are sold like a commodity. Wm. F. Talbott bought slaves in Kentucky for the market in New Orleans.

through warfare. When tribal men raided another group, they killed the men, raped the women, and then brought the women back as slaves. The women were valued for sexual purposes, for reproduction, and for their labor.

Roughly twenty-five hundred years ago, when Greece was but a collection of city-states, slavery was common. A city that became powerful and conquered another city would enslave some of the vanquished. Both slaves and slaveholders were Greek. Similarly, when Rome became the supreme power of the Mediterranean area about two thousand years ago, following the custom of the time, the Romans enslaved some of the Greeks they had conquered. More educated than their conquerors, some of these slaves served as tutors in Roman homes. Slavery, then, was a sign of debt, of crime, or of defeat in battle. It was not a sign that the slave was inherently inferior.

**Conditions of Slavery**   The conditions of slavery have varied widely around the world. *In some places, slavery was temporary.* Slaves of the Israelites were set free in the year of jubilee, which occurred every fifty years. Roman slaves ordinarily had the right to buy themselves out of slavery. They knew what their purchase price was, and some were able to meet this price by striking a bargain with their owner and selling their services to others. In most instances, however, slavery was a lifelong condition. Some criminals, for example, became slaves when they were given life sentences as oarsmen on Roman warships. There they served until death, which often came quickly to those in this exhausting service.

*Slavery was not necessarily inheritable.* In most places, the children of slaves were slaves themselves. But in some instances, the child of a slave who served a rich family might even be adopted by that family, becoming an heir who bore the family name along with the other sons or daughters of the household. In ancient Mexico, the children of slaves were always free (Landtman 1938/1968:271).

*Slaves were not necessarily powerless and poor.* In almost all instances, slaves owned no property and had no power. Among some groups, however, slaves could accumulate property and even rise to high positions in the community. Occasionally, a slave might even become wealthy, loan money to the master, and, while still a slave, own slaves himself or herself (Landtman 1938/1968). This, however, was rare.

**Slavery in the New World**   To meet their growing need for labor, some colonists tried to enslave Native Americans. This attempt failed miserably, in part because when Indians escaped, they knew how to survive in the wilderness and were able to make their way back to their tribe. The colonists then turned to Africans, who were being brought to North and South America by the Dutch, English, Portuguese, and Spanish.

Because slavery has a broad range of causes, some analysts conclude that racism didn't lead to slavery, but, rather, that slavery led to racism. Finding it profitable to make people slaves for life, U.S. slave owners developed an **ideology,** beliefs that justify social arrangements. Ideology leads to a perception of the world that makes current social arrangements seem necessary and fair. The colonists developed the view that their slaves were inferior. Some even said that they were not fully human. In short, the colonists wove elaborate justifications for slavery, built on the presumed superiority of their own group.

To make slavery even more profitable, slave states passed laws that made slavery *inheritable;* that is, the babies born to slaves became the property of the slave owners (Stampp 1956). These children could be sold, bartered, or traded. To strengthen their control, slave states passed laws making it illegal for slaves to hold meetings or to be away from the master's premises without carrying a pass (Lerner 1972). As sociologist W. E. B. Du Bois (1935/1992:12) noted, "gradually the entire white South became an armed camp to keep Negroes in slavery and to kill the black rebel."

The Civil War did not end legal discrimination. For example, until 1954 many states operated separate school systems for blacks and whites. Until the 1950s, in order to keep the races from "mixing," it was illegal in Mississippi for a white and an African American to sit together on the same seat of a car! There was no outright ban on blacks and whites being in the same car, however, because whites wanted to employ African American chauffeurs.

**Slavery Today**   Slavery has again reared its ugly head in several parts of the world. The Ivory Coast, Mauritania, Niger, and Sudan have a long history of slavery, and not until the 1980s was slavery made illegal in Mauritania and Sudan (Ayittey 1998). It took until 2004 for slavery to be banned in Niger (Andersson 2005). Although officially abolished, slavery in this region continues, the topic of the Mass Media box on the next page.

The enslavement of children for work and sex is a problem in Africa, Asia, and South America (LaFraniere 2006). A unique form of child slavery occurs in Kuwait, Qatar, and the United Arab Emirates. There, little boys are held in captivity because they are prized as jockeys in camel races (Brinkley 2005). It is thought that their screams make the camels run faster.

## Caste

The second system of social stratification is caste. In a **caste system,** status is determined by birth and is lifelong. Someone who is born into a low-status group will always

# MASS MEDIA in SOCIAL LIFE

## What Price Freedom? Slavery Today

Children of the Dinka tribe in rural Sudan don't go to school. They work. Their families depend on them to tend the cattle that are essential to their way of life.

On the morning of the raid, ten-year-old Adhieu had been watching the cattle. "We were very happy because we would soon leave the cattle camps and return home to our parents. But in the morning, there was shooting. There was yelling and crying everywhere. My uncle grabbed me by the hand, and we ran. We swam across the river. I saw some children drowning. We hid behind a rock."

By morning's end, 500 children were either dead or enslaved. Their attackers were their fellow countrymen—Arabs from northern Sudan. The children who were captured were forced to march hundreds of miles north. Some escaped on the way. Others tried to—and were shot (Akol 1998).

Journalists provided devastating accounts: In the United States, public television (PBS) ran film footage of captive children in chains. And escaped slaves recounted their ordeal in horrifying detail (Salopek 2003; Mende and Lewis 2005).

Although the United States bombed Kosovo (in Serbia) into submission for its crimes against humanity, in the face of this outrage it remained largely silent. A cynic might say that Kosovo was located at a politically strategic spot in Europe, but Sudan occupies an area of Africa in which the U.S. and European powers have had little interest. A cynic might add that these powers fear Arab retaliation, which might take the form of oil embargoes and terrorism. A cynic might also suggest that outrages against black Africans are not as significant to these powers as those against white Europeans. Finally, a cynic might add that this will change as Sudan's oil reserves become more strategic to Western interests.

When the world's most powerful governments didn't act on behalf of the slaves, private groups stepped in. One was Switzerland's Christian Solidarity International (CSI). CSI sent Arab "retrievers" to northern Sudan,

*In this photo, a representative of the Liaison Agency Network (on the left) is buying the freedom of the Sudanese slaves (in the background).*

where they either bought or abducted slaves. CSI paid the retrievers $50 per slave (Mabry 1999). Critics claimed that buying slaves, even to free them, encourages slavery. The money provides motivation to enslave people in order to turn around and sell them. Certainly $50 is a lot of money in Sudan, where people are lucky to make $50 a month (*Statistical Abstract* 2007: Table 1324).

CSI said that this was a bogus argument. What is intolerable, they said, is to leave women and children in slavery where they are deprived of their freedom and families and are beaten and raped by brutal masters.

## For Your Consideration

What do you think about buying the freedom of slaves? Can you suggest a workable alternative? Why do you think the U.S. government remained largely silent about this issue, when it invaded other countries such as Serbia and Haiti for human rights abuses? Do you think that, perhaps, political motivations outweigh human rights motivations? If not, why the silence in the face of slavery?

With the media coverage of this issue, some U.S. high schools—and even grade schools—raised money to participate in slave buyback programs. If you were a school principal, would you encourage this practice? Why or why not?

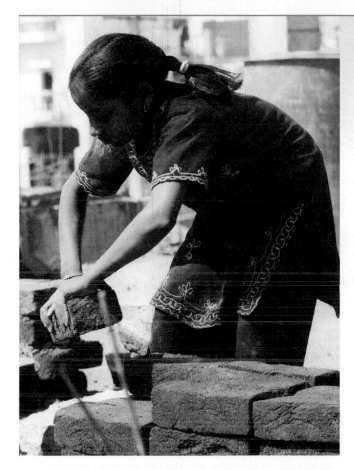

During my research in India, I interviewed this 8-year-old girl. Mahashury is a *bonded laborer* who was exchanged by her parents for a 2,000-rupee loan (about $14). To repay the loan, Mahashury must do construction work for one year. She will receive one meal a day and one set of clothing for the year. Because this centuries-old practice is now illegal, the master bribes Indian officials, who inform him when they are going to inspect the construction site. He then hides his bonded laborers. I was able to interview and photograph Mahashury because her master was absent the day I visited the construction site.

The lowest group listed in Table 7.1, the Dalit, make up India's "untouchables." If a Dalit touches someone of a higher caste, that person becomes unclean. Even the shadow of an untouchable can contaminate. Early morning and late afternoons are especially risky, for the long shadows of these periods pose a danger to everyone higher up the caste system. Consequently, Dalits are not allowed in some villages during these times. Anyone who becomes contaminated must follow *ablution,* or washing rituals, to restore purity.

Although the Indian government formally abolished the caste system in 1949, centuries-old practices cannot be eliminated so easily, and the caste system remains part of everyday life in India (Beckett 2007). The ceremonies people follow at births, marriages, and deaths, for example, are dictated by caste (Chandra 1993a). The upper castes dread the upward mobility of the untouchables, sometimes resisting it even with violence and ritual suicide (Crossette 1996; Jaffrelot 2006). From personal observations in India, I can add that in some villages Dalit children are not allowed in the government schools. If they try to enroll, they are beaten.

**A U.S. Racial Caste System**    Before leaving the subject of caste, we should note that when slavery ended in the United States, it was replaced by a *racial caste system.* From the moment of birth, everyone was marked for life (Berger 1963/2007). In this system, *all* whites, even if they were poor and uneducated, considered themselves to have a higher status than *all* African Americans. As in India and

have low status, no matter how much that person may accomplish in life. In sociological terms, a caste system is built on ascribed status (discussed on page 89). Achieved status cannot change an individual's place in this system.

Societies with this form of stratification try to make certain that the boundaries between castes remain firm. They practice **endogamy,** marriage within their own group, and prohibit intermarriage. To reduce contact between castes, they even develop elaborate rules about *ritual pollution,* teaching that contact with inferior castes contaminates the superior caste.

**India's Religious Castes**    India provides the best example of a caste system. Based not on race but on religion, India's caste system has existed for almost three thousand years (Chandra 1993a; Jaffrelot 2006). India's four main castes are depicted in Table 7.1. These four castes are subdivided into about three thousand subcastes, or *jati.* Each *jati* specializes in a particular occupation. For example, one subcaste washes clothes, another sharpens knives, and yet another repairs shoes.

| TABLE 7.1 | India's Caste System |
|---|---|
| Caste | Occupation |
| Brahman | Priests and teachers |
| Kshatriya | Rulers and soldiers |
| Vaishya | Merchants and traders |
| Shudra | Peasants and laborers |
| Dalit (untouchables) | The outcastes; degrading or polluting labor |

In a *caste system*, status is determined by birth and is lifelong. At birth, these women received not only membership in a lower caste but also, because of their gender, a predetermined position in that caste. When I photographed these women, they were carrying sand to the second floor of a house being constructed in Andhra Pradesh, India.

South Africa, the upper caste, fearing pollution from the lower caste, prohibited intermarriage and insisted on separate schools, hotels, restaurants, and even toilets and drinking fountains in public facilities. In the South, when any white met any African American on a sidewalk, the African American had to move aside—which the untouchables of India still must do when they meet someone of a higher caste (Deliege 2001).

## Class

As we have seen, stratification systems based on slavery and caste are rigid. The lines drawn between people are firm, and there is little or no movement from one group to another. A **class system,** in contrast, is much more open, for it is based primarily on money or material possessions, which can be acquired. This system, too, is in place at birth, when children are ascribed the status of their parents, but, unlike in the other systems, individuals can change their social class by what they achieve (or fail to achieve) in life. In addition, no laws specify people's occupations on the basis of birth or prohibit marriage between the classes.

A major characteristic of the class system, then, is its relatively fluid boundaries. A class system allows **social mobility,** movement up or down the class ladder. The potential for improving one's life—or for falling down the class ladder—is a major force that drives people to go far in school and to work hard. In the extreme, the family background that a child inherits at birth may present such obstacles that he or she has little chance of climbing very far—or it may provide such privileges that it makes it almost impossible to fall down the class ladder. Because

social class is so significant for our own lives, we will focus on class in the next chapter.

## Global Stratification and the Status of Females

In *every* society of the world, gender is a basis for social stratification. In no society is gender the sole basis for stratifying people, but gender cuts across *all* systems of social stratification—whether slavery, caste, or class (Huber 1990). In all these systems, on the basis of their gender, people are sorted into categories and given different access to the good things available in their society.

Apparently these distinctions always favor males. It is remarkable, for example, that in *every* society of the world men's earnings are higher than women's. Men's dominance is even more evident when we consider female circumcision (see the box on page 271). That most of the world's illiterate are females also drives home women's relative position in society. Of the several hundred million adults who cannot read, about two-thirds are women (UNESCO 2006). Because gender is such a significant factor in what happens to us in life, we shall focus on it more closely in Chapter 10.

## What Determines Social Class?

In the early days of sociology, a disagreement arose about the meaning of social class. Let's compare how Marx and Weber analyzed the issue.

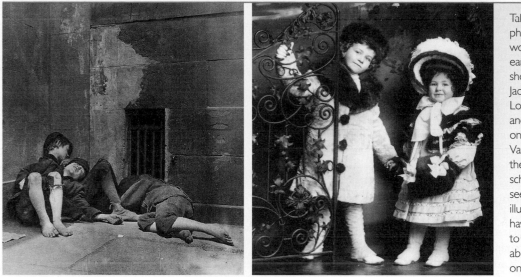

Taken at the end of the 1800s, these photos illustrate the contrasting worlds of *social classes* produced by early capitalism. The sleeping boys shown in this classic 1890 photo by Jacob Riis sold newspapers in London. They did not go to school, and they had no home. The children on the right, Cornelius and Gladys Vanderbilt, are shown in front of their parents' estate. They went to school and did not work. You can see how the social locations illustrated in these photos would have produced different orientations to life and, therefore, politics, ideas about marriage, values, and so on—the stuff of which life is made.

## Karl Marx: The Means of Production

As we discussed in Chapter 1, the breakup of the feudal system displaced masses of peasants from their traditional lands and occupations. Fleeing to cities, they competed for the few available jobs. Paid only a pittance for their labor, they wore rags, went hungry, and slept under bridges and in shacks. In contrast, the factory owners built mansions, hired servants, and lived in the lap of luxury. Seeing this great disparity between owners and workers, Karl Marx (1818–1883) concluded that social class depends on a single factor: people's relationship to the **means of production**—the tools, factories, land, and investment capital used to produce wealth (Marx 1844/1964; Marx and Engels 1848/1967).

Marx argued that the distinctions people often make among themselves—such as clothing, speech, education, paycheck, the neighborhood they live in, even the car they drive—are superficial matters. These things camouflage the only dividing line that counts. There are just two classes of people, said Marx: the **bourgeoisie** (*capitalists*), those who own the means of production, and the **proletariat** (*workers*), those who work for the owners. In short, people's relationship to the means of production determines their social class.

Marx did recognize other groups: farmers and peasants; a *lumpenproletariat* (people living on the margin of society, such as beggars, vagrants, and criminals); and a middle group of self-employed professionals. Marx did not consider these groups social classes, however, for they lack **class consciousness**—a shared identity based on their position in the means of production. In other words, they did not

perceive themselves as exploited workers whose plight could be solved by collective action. Consequently, Marx thought of these groups as insignificant in the future he foresaw—a workers' revolution that would overthrow capitalism.

The capitalists will grow even wealthier, Marx said, and the hostilities will increase. When workers come to realize that capitalists are the source of their oppression, they will unite and throw off the chains of their oppressors. In a bloody revolution, they will seize the means of production and usher in a classless society—and no longer will the few grow rich at the expense of the many. What holds back the workers' unity and their revolution is **false class consciousness,** workers mistakenly thinking of themselves as capitalists. For example, workers with a few dollars in the bank may forget that they are workers and instead see themselves as investors, or as capitalists who are about to launch a successful business.

The only distinction worth mentioning, then, is whether a person is an owner or a worker. This decides everything else, Marx stressed, for property determines people's lifestyles, establishes their relationships with one another, and even shapes their ideas.

## Max Weber: Property, Power, and Prestige

Max Weber (1864–1920) was an outspoken critic of Marx. Weber argued that property is only part of the picture. *Social class,* he said, has three components: property, power, and prestige (Gerth and Mills 1958; Weber 1922/1968). Some call these the three P's of social class. (Although Weber used the terms *class, power,* and *status,* some sociologists find *property, power,* and *prestige* to be clearer terms. To make them even clearer, you may wish to substitute *wealth* for *property.*)

*Property* (or wealth), said Weber, is certainly significant in determining a person's standing in society. On that point he agreed with Marx. But, added Weber, ownership is not the only significant aspect of property. For example, some powerful people, such as managers of corporations, *control* the means of production even though they do not *own* them. If managers can control property for their own benefit—awarding themselves huge bonuses and magnificent perks—it makes no practical difference that they do not own the property that they use so generously for their own benefit.

*Power,* the second element of social class, is the ability to control others, even over their objections. Weber agreed with Marx that property is a major source of power, but he added that it is not the only source. For example, prestige can be turned into power. Two well-known examples are actors Arnold Schwarzenegger, who became governor of California, and Ronald Reagan, who became governor of California and president of the United States. Figure 7.1 shows how property, power, and prestige are interrelated.

*Prestige,* the third element in Weber's analysis, is often derived from property and power, for people tend to admire the wealthy and powerful. Prestige, however, can be based on other factors. Olympic gold medalists, for example, might not own property or be powerful, yet they have high prestige. Some are even able to exchange their prestige for property—such as those who are paid a small fortune for endorsing a certain brand of sportswear or for claiming that they start their day with "the breakfast of champions." In other words, property and prestige are not one-way streets: Although property can bring prestige, prestige can also bring property.

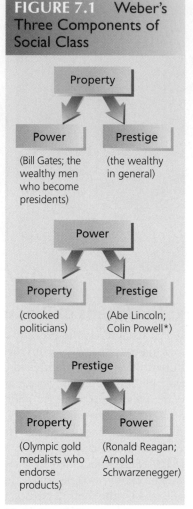

**FIGURE 7.1    Weber's Three Components of Social Class**

Property → Power (Bill Gates; the wealthy men who become presidents) / Prestige (the wealthy in general)

Power → Property (crooked politicians) / Prestige (Abe Lincoln; Colin Powell*)

Prestige → Property (Olympic gold medalists who endorse products) / Power (Ronald Reagan; Arnold Schwarzenegger)

*Colin Powell illustrates the circularity of these components. Powell's power as Chairman of the Joint Chiefs of Staff led to prestige. Powell's prestige, in turn, led to power when he was called from retirement to serve as Secretary of State in George W. Bush's first administration.

The text describes the many relationships among Weber's three components of social class: property, power, and prestige. Colin Powell is an example of power that was converted into prestige—which was then converted back into power. Power, of course, can be lost, as it was when Powell resigned after disagreeing with the Bush administration.

**In Sum:** For Marx, social class was based solely on a person's relationship to the means of production. One is a member of either the bourgeoisie or the proletariat. Weber argued that social class is a combination of property, power, and prestige.

# Why Is Social Stratification Universal?

What is it about social life that makes all societies stratified? We shall first consider the explanation proposed by functionalists, which has aroused controversy in sociology, and then explanations proposed by conflict theorists.

## The Functionalist View: Motivating Qualified People

Functionalists take the position that the patterns of behavior that characterize a society exist because they are functional for that society. Because social inequality is universal, inequality must help societies survive. But how?

**Davis and Moore's Explanation**     Two functionalists, Kingsley Davis and Wilbert Moore (1945, 1953), wrestled with this question. They concluded that stratification of society is inevitable because

1. Society must make certain that its positions are filled.
2. Some positions are more important than others.
3. The more important positions must be filled by the more qualified people.
4. To motivate the more qualified people to fill these positions, society must offer them greater rewards.

To flesh out this functionalist argument, consider college presidents and military generals. The position of college president is more important than that of student because the president's decisions affect a large number of people, including many students. College presidents are also accountable for their performance to boards of trustees. It is the same with generals. Their decisions affect many people and can determine life and death. Generals are accountable to superior generals and to the country's leader.

Why do people accept such high-pressure positions? Why don't they just take less demanding jobs? The answer, said Davis and Moore, is that society offers greater rewards—prestige, pay, and benefits—for its more demanding and accountable positions. To get highly qualified people to compete with one another, some positions offer a salary of $2 million a year, country club membership, a private jet and pilot, and a chauffeured limousine. For less demanding positions, a $30,000 salary without fringe benefits is enough to get hundreds of people to compete. If a job requires rigorous training, it, too, must offer more salary and benefits. If you can get the same pay with a high school diploma, why suffer through the many tests and term papers that college requires?

**Tumin's Critique of Davis and Moore**     Davis and Moore tried to explain *why* social stratification is universal, not to justify social inequality. Nevertheless, their view makes many sociologists uncomfortable, for they see it as coming close to justifying the inequalities in society. Its bottom line seems to be, The people who contribute more to society are paid more, while those who contribute less are paid less.

Melvin Tumin (1953) was the first sociologist to point out what he saw as major flaws in the functionalist position. Here are three of his arguments.

*First,* how do we know that the positions that offer the higher rewards are more important? A heart surgeon, for example, saves lives and earns much more than a garbage collector, but this doesn't mean that garbage collectors are less important to society. By helping to prevent contagious diseases, garbage collectors save more lives than heart surgeons do. We need independent methods of measuring importance, and we don't have them.

*Second,* if stratification worked as Davis and Moore described it, society would be a **meritocracy;** that is, positions would be awarded on the basis of merit. But is this what we have? The best predictor of who goes to college, for example, is not ability but income: The more a family earns, the more likely their children are to go to college (Carnevale and Rose 2003). This has nothing to do with merit. It is simply another form of the inequality that is built into society. In short, people's positions in society are based on many factors other than merit.

*Third,* if social stratification is so functional, it ought to benefit almost everyone. Yet social stratification is *dysfunctional* for many. Think of the people who could have made valuable contributions to society had they not been born in slums, dropped out of school, and taken menial jobs to help support their families. Then there are the many who, born female, are assigned "women's work," thus ensuring that they do not maximize their mental abilities.

**In Sum:** Functionalists argue that society works better if its most qualified people hold its most important positions. Therefore, those positions offer higher rewards. For example, to get highly talented people to become surgeons— to undergo years of rigorous training and then cope with life-and-death situations, as well as malpractice suits—society must provide a high payoff.

## The Conflict Perspective: Class Conflict and Scarce Resources

Conflict theorists don't just criticize details of the functionalist argument. Rather, they go for the throat and attack its basic premise. Conflict, not function, they stress, is the reason that we have social stratification. Let's look at the major arguments.

**Mosca's Argument** Italian sociologist Gaetano Mosca argued that every society will be stratified by power. This is inevitable, he said in an 1896 book titled *The Ruling Class,* because

1. No society can exist unless it is organized. This requires leadership of some sort in order to coordinate people's actions and get society's work done.
2. Leadership (or political organization) requires inequalities of power. By definition, some people take leadership positions, while others follow.
3. Human nature is self-centered. Therefore, people in power will use their positions to seize greater rewards for themselves.

There is no way around these facts of life, added Mosca. They make social stratification inevitable, and every society will stratify itself along lines of power.

**Marx's Argument** If he were alive to hear the functionalist argument, Karl Marx would be enraged. From his point of view, the people in power are not there because of superior traits, as the functionalists would have us believe. This view is simply an ideology that members of the elite use to justify their being at the top—and to seduce the oppressed into believing that their welfare depends on keeping society stable. Human history is the chronicle of class struggle, of those in power using society's resources to benefit themselves and to oppress those beneath them—and of oppressed groups trying to overcome domination.

Marx predicted that the workers would revolt. The day will come, he said, when class consciousness will overcome the ideology that now blinds workers. When they realize their common oppression, workers will rebel against the capitalists. The struggle to control the means of production may be covert at first, taking the form of work slowdowns or industrial sabotage. Ultimately, however, resistance will break out into the open. The revolution will not be easy, for the bourgeoisie control the police, the military, and even the educational system, where they implant false class consciousness in the minds of the workers' children.

**Current Applications of Conflict Theory** Just as Marx focused on overarching historic events—the accumulation of capital and power and the struggle between workers and capitalists—some of today's conflict sociologists are doing the same. Their focus is on the current capitalist triumph on a global level (Sklair 2001). They analyze both the use of armed forces to keep capitalist nations dominant and the exploitation of workers as capital is moved from the Most Industrialized Nations to the Least Industrialized Nations.

Some conflict sociologists, in contrast, examine conflict wherever it is found, not just as it relates to capitalists and workers. They examine how groups *within the same class* compete with one another for a larger slice of the pie (Schellenberg 1996; Collins 1988, 1999). Even within the same industry, for example, union will fight against union for higher salaries, shorter hours, and more power. A special focus has been conflict between racial–ethnic groups as they compete for education,

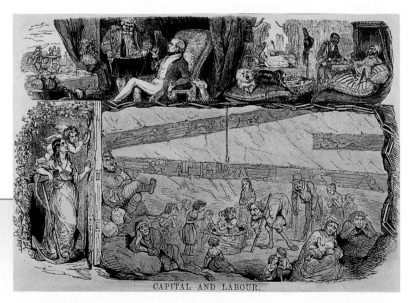

This cartoon of political protest appeared in London newspapers in 1843. It illustrates the severe exploitation of labor that occurred during early capitalism, which stimulated Marx to analyze relations between capitalists and workers.

CAPITAL AND LABOUR.

housing, and even prestige—whatever benefits society has to offer. Another focus has been relations between women and men, which conflict theorists say are best understood as a conflict over power—over who controls society's resources. Unlike functionalists, conflict theorists say that just beneath the surface of what may appear to be a tranquil society lies conflict that is barely held in check.

## Lenski's Synthesis

As you can see, functionalist and conflict theorists disagree sharply. Is it possible to reconcile their views? Sociologist Gerhard Lenski (1966) thought so. He suggested that surplus is the key. He said that the functionalists are right when it comes to groups that don't accumulate a surplus, such as hunting and gathering societies. These societies give a greater share of their resources to those who take on important tasks, such as warriors who risk their lives in battle. It is a different story, said Lenski, with societies that accumulate surpluses. In them, groups fight over the surplus, and the group that wins becomes an elite. This dominant group rules from the top, controlling the groups below it. In the resulting system of social stratification, where you are born in that society, not personal merit, becomes important.

**In Sum:** Conflict theorists stress that in every society groups struggle with one another to gain a larger share of their society's resources. Whenever a group gains power, it uses that power to extract what it can from the groups beneath it. This elite group also uses the social institutions to keep itself in power.

## How Do Elites Maintain Stratification?

Suppose that you are part of the ruling elite of your society. What can you do to make sure you don't lose your privileged position? The key lies in controlling people's ideas, the information they receive, and the threat and use of force.

## Ideology Versus Force

Medieval Europe provides a good example of the power of ideology. At that time, land was the primary source of wealth—and only the nobility and the church could own it. Almost everyone else was a peasant (or serf) who worked for these powerful landowners. The peasants farmed the land, took care of the livestock, and built the roads and bridges. Each year, they had to turn over a designated portion of their crops to their feudal lord. Year after year, for centuries, they did so. Why?

**Ideas Controlling the Masses**   Why didn't the peasants rebel and take over the land themselves? There were many reasons, not the least of which was that the nobility and church controlled the army. Coercion, however, goes only so far, for it breeds hostility and nourishes rebellion. How much more effective it is to get the masses to *want* to do what the ruling elite desires. This is where *ideology* (beliefs that justify the way things are) comes into play, and

The *divine right of kings* was an ideology that made the king God's direct representative on earth—to administer justice and punish evildoers. This theological-political concept was supported by the Roman Catholic Church, whose representatives crowned the king. Shown here is Pope Clement IV crowning Charles Anjou as king of Sicily in 1226.

the nobility and clergy used it to great effect. They developed an ideology known as the **divine right of kings**—the idea that the king's authority comes directly from God. The king delegates authority to nobles, who, as God's representatives, must be obeyed. To disobey is a sin against God; to rebel is to merit physical punishment on earth and eternal suffering in hell.

Controlling people's ideas can be remarkably more effective than using brute force. Although this particular ideology governs few peoples' minds today, the elite in *every* society develops ideologies to justify its position at the top. For example, around the world, schools teach that their country's form of government—*no matter what form of government that is*—is good. Religious leaders teach that we owe obedience to authority, that laws are to be obeyed. To the degree that their ideologies are accepted by the masses, the elite remains securely in power.

**Controlling Information and Using Technology**    To maintain their positions of power, elites try to control information. Fear is a favorite tactic of dictators. To muffle criticism, they imprison, torture, and kill reporters who dare to criticize their regime. (Under Saddam Hussein, the penalty for telling a joke about Hussein was having your tongue cut out [Nordland 2003].) Lacking such power, the ruling elites of democracies rely on more covert means. They manipulate the media by selectively releasing information—and by withholding information "in the interest of national security."

The new technology is another tool for the elite. Machines can read the entire contents of a computer in a second, without leaving evidence that they have done so. Security cameras—"Tiny Brothers"—have sprouted almost everywhere. Face-recognition systems can scan a crowd of thousands, instantly matching the scans with digitized files of individuals. With these devices, the elite can monitor citizens' activities without anyone knowing that they are being observed. Dictatorships have few checks on how they employ such technology, but in democracies, checks and balances, such as requiring court orders for search and seizure, at least partially curb their abuse. The threat of bypassing such restraints on power is always present, as with Homeland Security laws that allow officials to spy on citizens without their knowledge.

The new technology is a two-edged sword. Just as it gives the elite powerful tools for monitoring citizens, it also makes it more difficult for them to control information. Satellite communications, e-mail, and the Internet pay no respect to international borders. Information (both true and fabricated) flies around the globe in seconds. Internet users also have free access to PGP (Pretty Good Privacy), a code that

no government has been able to break. Then, too, there is zFone, a voice encryption for telephone calls that prevents wiretappers from understanding what people are saying.

Feeling threatened that their citizens will criticize them, Chinese leaders have put tight controls on Internet cafes and search engines (French 2005; Hutton 2007). U.S. officials, unable to wield the sword, have distributed fake news reports to be broadcast to the nation (Barstow and Stein 2005). We are still in the early stages of the new technology, so we will see how this cat and mouse game plays out.

**In Sum:** To maintain stratification within a society, the elite tries to dominate its society's institutions. In a dictatorship, the elite makes the laws. In a democracy, the elite influences the laws. In both, the elite controls the police and military and can give orders to crush a rebellion—or to run the post office or air traffic control if workers strike. Force has its limits, and a nation's elite prefers to maintain its stratification system by peaceful means, especially by influencing the thinking of its people.

# Comparative Social Stratification

Now that we have examined systems of social stratification, considered why stratification is universal, and looked at how elites keep themselves in power, let's compare social stratification in Great Britain and in the former Soviet Union. In the next chapter, we'll look at social stratification in the United States.

## Social Stratification in Great Britain

Great Britain is often called England by Americans, but England is only one of the countries that make up the island of Great Britain. The others are Scotland and Wales. In addition, Northern Ireland is part of the United Kingdom of Great Britain and Northern Ireland.

Like other industrialized countries, Great Britain has a class system that can be divided into a lower, a middle, and an upper class. Great Britain's population is about evenly divided between the middle class and the lower (or working) class. A tiny upper class, perhaps 1 percent of the population, is wealthy, powerful, and highly educated.

Compared with Americans, the British are very class conscious. Like Americans, they recognize class distinctions on the basis of the type of car a person drives or the stores someone patronizes. But the most striking characteristics of the British class system are language and education. Because these show up in accent, distinctive speech has a powerful impact on British life. As soon as someone speaks, the listener is aware of that person's social class—and treats him or her accordingly (Sullivan 1998).

Education is the primary way by which the British perpetuate their class system from one generation to the next. Almost all children go to neighborhood schools. Great Britain's richest 5 percent, however—who own *half* the nation's wealth—send their children to exclusive private boarding schools (which, strangely, they call "public" schools). There the children of the elite are trained in subjects that are considered "proper" for members of the ruling class. An astounding 50 percent of the students at Oxford and Cambridge, the country's most prestigious universities, come from this 5 percent of the population. To illustrate how powerfully this system of stratified education affects the national life of Great Britain, sociologist Ian Robertson (1987) said,

**Eighteen former pupils of the most exclusive of [England's high schools], Eton, have become prime minister. Imagine the chances of a single American high school producing eighteen presidents!**

## Social Stratification in the Former Soviet Union

Heeding Karl Marx's call for a classless society, Vladimir Ilyich Lenin (1870–1924) and Leon Trotsky (1879–1940) led a revolution in Russia in 1917. They, and the nations that followed their banner, never claimed to have achieved the ideal of communism, in which all contribute their labor to the common good and receive according to their needs. Instead, they used the term *socialism* to describe the intermediate step between capitalism and communism, in which social classes are abolished but some inequality remains.

To tweak the nose of Uncle Sam, the socialist countries would trumpet their equality and point a finger at glaring inequalities in the United States. These countries, however, also were marked by huge disparities in privilege. Their major basis of stratification was membership in the Communist party. Party members decided who would gain admission to the better schools or obtain the more desirable jobs and housing. The equally qualified son or daughter of a nonmember would be turned down, for such privileges came with demonstrated loyalty to the party.

The Communist party, too, was highly stratified. Most members occupied a low level, where they fulfilled such tasks as spying on fellow workers. For this, they might get easier jobs in the factory or occasional access to special stores to purchase hard-to-find goods. The middle level consisted of bureaucrats who were given better than average access to resources and privileges. At the top level was a small elite: Party members who enjoyed not only power but also limousines, imported delicacies, vacation homes, and even servants and hunting lodges. As with other stratification systems around the world, women held lower positions in the party. This was evident at each year's May Day, when the top members of the party reviewed the latest weapons paraded in Moscow's Red Square. Photos of these events showed only men.

The leaders of the USSR became frustrated as they saw the West thrive. They struggled with a bloated bureaucracy, the inefficiencies of central planning, workers who did the minimum because they could not be fired, and a military so costly that it spent one of every eight of the nation's rubles (*Statistical Abstract* 1993:1432, table dropped in later editions). Socialist ideology did not call for their citizens to be deprived, and in an attempt to turn things around, the Soviet leadership initiated reforms. They allowed elections to be held in which more than one candidate ran for an office. (Before this, voters had a choice of only one candidate per office.) They also sold huge chunks of state-owned businesses to the public. Overnight, making investments to try to turn a profit changed from a crime into a respectable goal.

Russia's transition to capitalism took a bizarre twist. As authority broke down, a powerful Mafia emerged (Varese 2005; Chazman 2006). These criminal groups are headed by gangsters, corrupt government officials (including members of the former KGB, now FSB), and crooked businessmen. In some towns, they buy the entire judicial system—the police force, prosecutors, and judges. They assassinate business leaders, reporters, and politicians who refuse to cooperate. They amass wealth, launder money through banks they control, and buy luxury properties in popular tourist areas around the world.

As Moscow reestablishes its authority, Mafia ties have brought wealth to some of the members of this central government. This group of organized criminals is taking its place as part of Russia's new capitalist class.

# Global Stratification: Three Worlds

As noted at the beginning of this chapter, just as the people within a nation are stratified by property, power, and prestige, so are the world's nations. Until recently, a simple model consisting of First, Second, and Third Worlds was used to depict global stratification. *First World* referred to the industrialized capitalist nations, *Second World* to the communist (or socialist) countries, and *Third World* to any nation that did not fit into the first two categories. The breakup of the Soviet Union in 1989 made these terms outdated. In addition, although *first, second,* and *third* did not mean "best," "better," and "worst," they implied it. An alternative classification that some now use—developed, developing, and undeveloped nations—has the same drawback. By calling ourselves "developed," it sounds as though we are mature and the "undeveloped" nations are somehow retarded.

To try to solve this problem, I use more neutral, descriptive terms: *Most Industrialized, Industrializing,* and *Least Industrialized* nations. We can measure industrialization with no judgment implied as to whether a nation's industrialization represents "development," ranks it "first," or is even desirable at all. The intention is to depict on a global level the three primary dimensions of social stratification: property, power, and prestige. The Most Industrialized Nations have much greater property (wealth), power (they usually get their way in international relations), and prestige (they are looked up to as world leaders). The two families sketched in the opening vignette illustrate the far-reaching effects of global stratification.

## The Most Industrialized Nations

The Most Industrialized Nations are the United States and Canada in North America; Great Britain, France, Germany, Switzerland, and the other industrialized countries of western Europe; Japan in Asia; and Australia and New Zealand in the area of the world known as Oceania. Although there are variations in their economic systems, these nations are capitalistic. As Table 7.2 shows, although these nations have only 16 percent of the world's people, they possess 31 percent of the earth's land. Their wealth is so enormous that even their poor live better and longer lives than do the average citizens of the Least Industrialized Nations. The Social Map on pages 186–187 shows the tremendous disparities in income among the world's nations.

## The Industrializing Nations

The Industrializing Nations include most of the nations of the former Soviet Union and its former satellites in eastern Europe. As Table 7.2 shows, these nations account for 20 percent of the earth's land and 16 percent of its people.

**TABLE 7.2**   Distribution of the World's Land and Population

|  | Land | Population |
|---|---|---|
| Most Industrialized Nations | 31% | 16% |
| Industrializing Nations | 20% | 16% |
| Least Industrialized Nations | 49% | 68% |

*Sources:* Computed from Kurian 1990, 1991, 1992.

The dividing points between the three "worlds" are soft, making it difficult to know how to classify some nations. This is especially the case with the Industrializing Nations. Exactly how much industrialization must a nation have to be in this category? Although soft, these categories do pinpoint essential differences among nations. Most people who live in the Industrializing Nations have much lower incomes and standards of living than do those who live in the Most Industrialized Nations. The majority, however, are better off than those who live in the Least Industrialized Nations. For example, on such measures as access to electricity, indoor plumbing, automobiles, telephones, and even food, most citizens of the Industrializing Nations rank lower than those in the Most Industrialized Nations, but higher than those in the Least Industrialized Nations. As you saw in the opening vignette, stratification affects even life expectancy.

The benefits of industrialization are uneven. Large numbers of people in the Industrializing Nations remain illiterate and desperately poor. Conditions can be gruesome, as we explore in the following Thinking Critically section.

# ThinkingCRITICALLY
## Open Season: Children as Prey

What is childhood like in the Industrializing Nations? The answer depends on who your parents are. If you are the son or daughter of rich parents, childhood can be pleasant—a world filled with luxuries and even servants. If you are born into poverty, but living in a rural area where there is plenty to eat, life can still be good—although there may be no books, television, and little education. If you live in a slum, however, life can be horrible—worse even than in the slums of the

Most Industrialized Nations. Let's take a glance at a notorious slum of Brazil.

Not enough food—this you can take for granted—along with wife abuse, broken homes, alcoholism and drug abuse, and a lot of crime. From your knowledge of slums in the Most Industrialized Nations, you would expect these things. What you may not expect, however, are the brutal conditions in which Brazilian slum (*favela*) children live.

Sociologist Martha Huggins (Huggins et al. 2002) reports that poverty is so deep that children and adults swarm through garbage dumps to try to find enough decaying food to keep them alive. You might also be surprised to discover that the owners of some of these dumps hire armed guards to keep the poor out—so that they can sell the garbage for pig food. And you might be shocked to learn that the Brazilian police and death squads murder some of these children. Although this is not typical, some shop owners have hired hit men. The pay for this dirty work is low, sometimes half a month's salary—figured at the low Brazilian minimum wage.

Life is cheap in the poor nations—but death squads for children? To understand this, we must first note that Brazil has a long history of violence. Brazil also has a high rate of poverty, has only a tiny middle class, and is controlled by a small group of families who, under a veneer of democracy, make the country's major decisions. Hordes of homeless children, with no schools or jobs, roam the streets. To survive, they wash windshields, shine shoes, beg, and steal (Huggins and Rodrigues 2004).

The "respectable" classes see these children as nothing but trouble. They hurt business, for customers feel intimidated when they see begging children—especially teenaged males—clustered in front of stores. Some shoplift; others dare to sell items that place them in competition with the stores. With no effective social institutions to care for these children, one solution is to kill them. As Huggins notes, murder sends a clear message—especially if it is accompanied by ritual torture: gouging out the eyes, ripping open the chest, cutting off the genitals, raping the girls, and burning the victim's body.

Not all life is bad in the Industrializing Nations, but this is about as bad as it gets.

## For Your Consideration

Do you think there is anything the Most Industrialized Nations can do about this situation? Or is it, though unfortunate, just an "internal" affair that is up to the Brazilians to handle as they wish?

Homeless people sleeping on the streets is a common sight in India's cities. I took this photo in Chennai (formerly Madras).

## The Least Industrialized Nations

In the Least Industrialized Nations, most people live on small farms or in villages, have large families, and barely survive. These nations account for 68 percent of the world's people but only 49 percent of the earth's land.

Poverty plagues these nations to such an extent that some families actually *live* in city dumps. This is hard to believe, but look at the photos on pages 188–189, which I took in Phnom Penh, the capital of Cambodia. Although wealthy nations have their pockets of poverty, *most* people in the Least Industrialized nations are poor. *Most* of them have no running water, indoor plumbing, or access to trained teachers or physicians. As we will discuss in Chapter 14, most of the world's population growth occurs in these nations, placing even greater burdens on their limited resources and causing them to fall farther behind each year.

**FIGURE 7.2   Global Stratification: Income[1] of the World's Nations**

### The Most Industrialized Nations

| | Nation | Income per Person |
|---|---|---|
| 1 | Luxembourg | $58,900 |
| 2 | United States | $39,820 |
| 3 | Norway | $38,680 |
| 4 | Switzerland | $35,660 |
| 5 | Ireland | $32,930 |
| 6 | Iceland | $31,900 |
| 7 | Austria | $31,800 |
| 8 | Denmark | $31,770 |
| 9 | Hong Kong (a part of China) | $31,560 |
| 10 | Belgium | $31,530 |
| 11 | United Kingdom | $31,430 |
| 12 | Netherlands | $31,360 |
| 13 | Canada | $30,760 |
| 14 | Sweden | $29,880 |
| 15 | Japan | $29,810 |
| 16 | Finland | $29,800 |
| 17 | France | $29,460 |
| 18 | Australia | $29,340 |
| 19 | Germany | $28,170 |
| 20 | Italy | $28,020 |
| 21 | Singapore | $27,370 |
| 22 | Taiwan | $25,300 |
| 23 | Israel | $23,770 |
| 24 | New Zealand | $22,260 |

### The Industrializing Nations

| | Nation | Income per Person |
|---|---|---|
| 25 | Spain | $24,750 |
| 26 | Greece | $22,230 |
| 27 | Slovenia | $20,830 |
| 28 | Korea, South | $20,530 |
| 29 | Portugal | $19,240 |
| 30 | Czech Republic | $18,420 |
| 31 | Hungary | $15,800 |
| 32 | Slovakia | $14,480 |
| 33 | Saudi Arabia | $13,810 |
| 34 | Estonia | $13,630 |
| 35 | Poland | $12,730 |
| 36 | Lithuania | $12,690 |
| 37 | Argentina | $12,530 |
| 38 | Croatia | $11,920 |
| 39 | Latvia | $11,820 |
| 40 | South Africa | $10,960 |
| 41 | Chile | $10,610 |
| 42 | Malaysia | $9,720 |
| 43 | Russia | $9,680 |
| 44 | Mexico | $9,640 |
| 45 | Costa Rica | $9,220 |
| 46 | Uruguay | $9,030 |
| 47 | Romania | $8,330 |
| 48 | Brazil | $7,940 |
| 49 | Bulgaria | $7,940 |
| 50 | Thailand | $7,930 |
| 51 | Bosnia | $7,230 |
| 52 | Colombia | $6,940 |
| 53 | Venezuela | $5,830 |

### The Least Industrialized Nations

| | Nation | Income per Person | | Nation | Income per Person |
|---|---|---|---|---|---|
| 54 | Botswana[3] | $9,580 | 70 | Lebanon | $5,550 |
| 55 | Turkey | $7,720 | 71 | Peru | $5,400 |
| 56 | Namibia | $7,520 | 72 | Albania | $5,070 |
| 57 | Tunisia | $7,430 | 73 | Philippines | $4,950 |
| 58 | Belarus | $6,970 | 74 | El Salvador | $4,890 |
| 59 | Kazakhstan | $6,930 | 75 | Paraguay | $4,820 |
| 60 | Dominican Republic | $6,860 | 76 | Jordan | $4,770 |
| 61 | Panama | $6,730 | 77 | Suriname | $4,300 |
| 62 | Macedonia | $6,560 | 78 | Guatemala | $4,260 |
| 63 | Belize | $6,500 | 79 | Morocco | $4,250 |
| 64 | Ukraine | $6,330 | 80 | Sri Lanka | $4,210 |
| 65 | Algeria | $6,320 | 81 | Egypt | $4,200 |
| 66 | China | $5,890 | 82 | Armenia | $4,160 |
| 67 | Gabon | $5,700 | 83 | Jamaica | $3,950 |
| 68 | Turkmenistan | $5,700 | 84 | Azerbaijan | $3,810 |
| 69 | Swaziland | $5,650 | 85 | Guyana | $3,800 |
| | | | 86 | Ecuador | $3,770 |

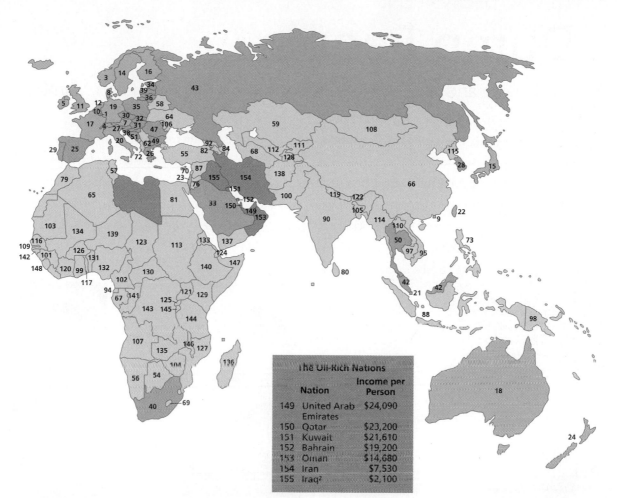

| The Oil-Rich Nations | | |
|---|---|---|
| | Nation | Income per Person |
| 149 | United Arab Emirates | $24,090 |
| 150 | Qatar | $23,200 |
| 151 | Kuwait | $21,610 |
| 152 | Bahrain | $19,200 |
| 153 | Oman | $14,680 |
| 154 | Iran | $7,530 |
| 155 | Iraq[2] | $2,100 |

### The Least Industrialized Nations

| | Nation | Income per Person | | Nation | Income per Person | | Nation | Income per Person | | Nation | Income per Person |
|---|---|---|---|---|---|---|---|---|---|---|---|
| 87 | Syria | $3,500 | 102 | Cameroon | $2,120 | 119 | Nepal | $1,480 | 135 | Zambia | $890 |
| 88 | Indonesia | $3,480 | 103 | Mauritania | $2,050 | 120 | Cote d'Ivoire | $1,470 | 136 | Madagascar | $840 |
| 89 | Nicaragua | $3,480 | 104 | Zimbabwe | $2,040 | 121 | Uganda | $1,450 | 137 | Yemen | $810 |
| 90 | India | $3,120 | 105 | Bangladesh | $1,970 | 122 | Bhutan | $1,400 | 138 | Afghanistan | $800 |
| 91 | Cuba | $3,000 | 106 | Moldova | $1,950 | 123 | Chad | $1,340 | 139 | Niger | $780 |
| 92 | Georgia | $2,900 | 107 | Angola | $1,930 | 124 | Djibouti | $1,300 | 140 | Ethiopia | $750 |
| 93 | Honduras | $2,760 | 108 | Mongolia | $1,900 | 125 | Rwanda | $1,240 | 141 | Congo | $740 |
| 94 | Equatorial Guinea | $2,700 | 109 | Gambia | $1,890 | 126 | Burkina Faso | $1,170 | 142 | Guinea-Bissau | $690 |
| 95 | Vietnam | $2,700 | 110 | Laos | $1,880 | 127 | Mozambique | $1,170 | 143 | Congo, Democratic Republic | $680 |
| 96 | Bolivia | $2,600 | 111 | Kyrgyzstan | $1,860 | 128 | Tajikistan | $1,160 | 144 | Tanzania | $670 |
| 97 | Cambodia | $2,310 | 112 | Uzbekistan | $1,860 | 129 | Kenya | $1,130 | 145 | Burundi | $660 |
| 98 | Papua-New Guinea | $2,280 | 113 | Sudan | $1,810 | 130 | Central African Republic | $1,100 | 146 | Malawi | $630 |
| 99 | Ghana | $2,220 | 114 | Burma | $1,700 | 131 | Benin | $1,090 | 147 | Somalia | $600 |
| 100 | Pakistan | $2,170 | 115 | Korea, North | $1,700 | 132 | Nigeria | $970 | 148 | Sierra Leone | $550 |
| 101 | Guinea | $2,160 | 116 | Senegal | $1,660 | 133 | Eritrea | $960 | | | |
| | | | 117 | Togo | $1,510 | 134 | Mali | $950 | | | |
| | | | 118 | Haiti | $1,500 | | | | | | |

[1]Income is a country's purchasing power parity based on its per capita gross domestic product measured in U.S. dollars. Since some totals vary widely from year to year, they must be taken as approximate. [2]Iraq's oil has been disrupted by war. [3]Botswana's relative wealth is based on its diamond mines.

*Sources:* By the author. Based on *Statistical Abstract of the United States* 2007: Table 1324, with a few missing countries taken from the CIA's latest *World Factbook*.

# The Dump People

Working and Living and Playing in the City Dump of Phnom Penh, Cambodia

**I** **went to Phnom Penh, the capital of Cambodia, to inspect** orphanages, to see how well the children were being cared for. While there, I was told about people who live in the city dump. *Live* there? I could hardly believe my ears. I knew that people made their living by picking scraps from the city dump, but I didn't know they actually lived among the garbage. This I had to see for myself.

I did. And there I found a highly developed social organization—an intricate support system. Because words are inadequate to depict the abject poverty of the Least Industrialized Nations, these photos can provide more insight into these people's lives than anything I could say.

This is a typical sight—family and friends working together. The trash, which is constantly burning, contains harmful chemicals. Why do people work under such conditions? Because they have few options. It is either this or starve.

The people live at the edge of the dump, in homemade huts (visible in the background). This woman, who was on her way home after a day's work, put down her sack of salvaged items to let me take her picture.

After the garbage arrives by truck, people stream around it, struggling to be the first to discover something of value. To sift through the trash the workers use metal picks, like the one the child is holding. Note that children work alongside the adults.

The children who live in the dump also play there. These children are riding bicycles on a "road," a packed, leveled area of garbage that leads to their huts. The huge stacks in the background are piled trash. Note the ubiquitous Nike.

One of my many surprises was to find food stands in the dump. Although this one primarily offers drinks and snacks, others serve more substantial food. One even has chairs for its customers.

I was surprised to learn that ice is delivered to the dump. This woman is using a hand grinder to crush ice for drinks for her customers. The customers, of course, are other people who also live in the dump.

At the day's end, the workers wash at the community pump. This hand pump serves all their water needs—drinking, washing, and cooking. There is no indoor plumbing. The weeds in the background serve that purpose.

Not too many visitors to Phnom Penh tell a cab driver to take them to the city dump. The cabbie looked a bit perplexed, but he did as I asked. Two cabs are shown here because my friends insisted on accompanying me.

I know they were curious themselves, but my friends had also discovered that the destinations I want to visit are usually not in the tourist guides, and they wanted to protect me.

# How Did the World's Nations Become Stratified?

How did the globe become stratified into such distinct worlds? The commonsense answer is that the poorer nations have fewer resources than the richer nations. As with many commonsense answers, however, this one, too, falls short. Many of the Industrializing and Least Industrialized Nations are rich in natural resources, while one Most Industrialized Nation, Japan, has few. Three theories explain how global stratification came about.

## Colonialism

The first theory, **colonialism,** stresses that the countries that industrialized first got the jump on the rest of the world. Beginning in Great Britain about 1750, industrialization spread throughout western Europe. Plowing some of their immense profits into powerful armaments and fast ships, these countries invaded weaker nations, making colonies out of them (Harrison 1993). After subduing these weaker nations, the more powerful countries left behind a controlling force in order to exploit the nations' labor and natural resources. At one point, there was even a free-for-all among the industrialized European countries as they rushed to divide up an entire continent. As they sliced Africa into pieces, even tiny Belgium got into the act and acquired the Congo, which was *seventy-five* times larger than itself.

The purpose of colonialism was to establish *economic colonies*—to exploit the nation's people and resources for the benefit of the "mother" country. The more powerful European countries would plant their national flags in a colony and send their representatives to run the government, but the United States usually chose to plant corporate flags in a colony and let these corporations dominate the territory's government. Central and South America are prime examples. There were exceptions, such as the conquest of the Philippines, which President McKinley said was motivated by the desire "to educate the Filipinos, and uplift and civilize and Christianize them" (Krugman 2002).

Colonialism, then, shaped many of the Least Industrialized Nations. In some instances, the Most Industrialized Nations were so powerful that when dividing their spoils, they drew lines across a map, creating new states without regard for tribal or cultural considerations (Kifner 1999). Britain and France did just this as they divided up North Africa and parts of the Middle East—which is why the national boundaries of Libya, Saudi Arabia, Kuwait, and other countries are so straight. This legacy of European conquests is a background factor in much of today's racial–ethnic and tribal violence: Groups with no history of national identity were incorporated arbitrarily into the same political boundaries.

## World System Theory

The second explanation of how global stratification came about was proposed by Immanuel Wallerstein (1974, 1979, 1990). According to **world system theory,** industrialization led to four groups of nations. The first group consists of the *core nations*, the countries that industrialized first (Britain, France, Holland, and later Germany), which grew rich and powerful. The second group is the *semiperiphery.* The economies of these nations, located around the Mediterranean, stagnated because they grew dependent on trade with the core nations. The economies of the third group, the *periphery,* or fringe nations, developed even less. These are the eastern European countries, which sold cash crops to the core nations. The fourth group of nations includes most of Africa and Asia. Called the *external area,* these nations were left out of the development of capitalism altogether. The current expansion of capitalism has changed the relationships among these groups. Most notably, Asia is no longer left out of capitalism.

The **globalization of capitalism**—the adoption of capitalism around the world—has created extensive ties among the world's nations. Production and trade are now so interconnected that events around the globe affect us all. Sometimes this is immediate, as happens when a civil war disrupts the flow of oil, or—perish the thought—as would be the case if terrorists managed to get their hands on nuclear or biological weapons. At other times, the effects are like a slow ripple, as when a government adopts some policy that gradually impedes its ability to compete in world markets. All of today's societies, then, no matter where they are located, are part of a *world system.*

The interconnections are most evident among nations that do extensive trading with one another. The following Thinking Critically section explores implications of Mexico's *maquiladoras.*

# Thinking CRITICALLY

## When Globalization Comes Home: *Maquiladoras* South of the Border

Two hundred thousand Mexicans rush to Juarez each year, fleeing the hopelessness of the rural areas in pursuit of a better life. They have no running water

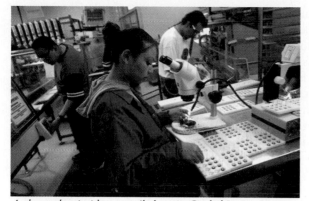

*A photo taken inside a* maquiladora *in Ciudad Juarez, Mexico.*

or plumbing, but they didn't have any in the country anyway, and here they have the possibility of a job, a weekly check to buy food for the kids.

The pay is $10 a day.

This may not sound like much, but it is more than twice the minimum daily wage in Mexico.

Assembly-for-export plants, known as *maquiladoras*, dot the Mexican border (Wise and Cypher 2007). The North American Free Trade Agreement (NAFTA) allows U.S. companies to import materials to Mexico without paying tax and to then export the finished products into the United States, again without tax. It's a sweet deal: few taxes and $10 a day for workers starved for jobs.

That these workers live in shacks, with no running water or sewage disposal, is not the employers' concern.

Nor is the pollution. The stinking air doesn't stay on the Mexican side of the border. Neither does the garbage. Heavy rains wash torrents of untreated sewage and industrial wastes into the Rio Grande (Lacey 2007).

There is also the loss of jobs for U.S. workers. Six of the fifteen poorest cities in the United States are located along the sewage-infested Rio Grande. NAFTA didn't bring poverty to these cities. They were poor before this treaty, but residents resent the jobs they've seen move across the border (Thompson 2001).

What if the *maquiladora* workers organize and demand better pay? Farther south, even cheaper labor beckons. Guatemala and Honduras will gladly take the *maquiladoras*. Mexico has already lost many of its *maquiladora* jobs to places where people even more desperate will work for even less (Luhnow 2004).

Many Mexican politicians would say that this presentation is one-sided. "Sure there are problems," they would say, "but that is always how it is when a country industrializes. Don't you realize that the *maquiladoras* bring jobs to people who have no work? They also bring roads, telephone

lines, and electricity to undeveloped areas." "In fact," said Vicente Fox, when he was the president of Mexico, "workers at the *maquiladoras* make more than the average salary in Mexico—and that's what we call fair wages" (Fraser 2001).

## For Your Consideration

Let's apply our three theoretical perspectives. Conflict theorists say that capitalists try to weaken the bargaining power of workers by exploiting divisions among them. In what is known as the *split labor market*, capitalists pit one group of workers against another to lower the cost of labor. How do you think that *maquiladoras* fit this conflict perspective?

When functionalists analyze a situation, they identify its functions and dysfunctions. What functions and dysfunctions of *maquiladoras* do you see?

Do *maquiladoras* represent exploitation or opportunity? As symbolic interactionists point out, reality is a perspective based on one's experience. What multiple realities do you see here?

*Where the workers live—no running water or sewage system.*

## Culture of Poverty

The third explanation of global stratification is quite unlike the other two. Economist John Kenneth Galbraith (1979) claimed that the cultures of the Least Industrialized Nations hold them back. Building on the ideas of anthropologist Oscar Lewis (1966a, 1966b), Galbraith argued that some nations are crippled by a **culture of poverty,** a way of life that perpetuates poverty from one generation to the next. He explained it this way: Most of the world's poor people are farmers who live on little plots of land. They barely produce enough food to survive. Living so close to the edge of starvation, they have little room for risk—so they stick closely to tried-and-true, traditional ways. To experiment with new farming techniques is to court disaster, for failure would lead to hunger and death.

Their religion also encourages them to accept their situation, for it teaches fatalism: the belief that an individual's position in life is God's will. For example, in India, the Dalits are taught that they must have done very bad things in a previous life to suffer so. They are supposed to submit to their situation—and in the next life maybe they'll come back in a more desirable state.

## Evaluating the Theories

Most sociologists prefer colonialism and world system theory. To them, an explanation based on a culture of poverty places blame on the victim—the poor nations themselves. It points to characteristics of the poor nations, rather than to international political arrangements that benefit the Most Industrialized Nations at the expense of the poor nations. But even taken together, these theories yield only part of the picture. None of these theories, for example, would have led anyone to expect that after World War II, Japan would become an economic powerhouse: Japan had a religion that stressed fatalism, two of its major cities had been destroyed by atomic bombs, and it had been stripped of its colonies.

Each theory, then, yields but a partial explanation, and the grand theorist who will put the many pieces of this puzzle together has yet to appear.

# Maintaining Global Stratification

Regardless of how the world's nations became stratified, why do the same countries remain rich year after year, while the rest stay poor? Let's look at two explanations of how global stratification is maintained.

## Neocolonialism

Sociologist Michael Harrington (1977) argued that when colonialism fell out of style it was replaced by **neocolonialism.** When World War II changed public sentiment about sending soldiers and colonists to exploit weaker countries, the Most Industrialized Nations turned to the international markets as a way of controlling the Least Industrialized Nations. By selling them goods on credit—especially weapons that their elite desire so they can keep themselves in power—the Most Industrialized Nations entrap the poor nations with a circle of debt.

As many of us learn the hard way, owing a large debt and falling behind on payments puts us at the mercy of our creditors. So it is with neocolonialism. The *policy* of selling weapons and other manufactured goods to the Least Industrialized Nations on credit turns those countries into eternal debtors. The capital they need to develop their own industries goes instead as payments toward the debt, which becomes bloated with mounting interest. Keeping these nations in debt forces them to submit to trading terms dictated by the neocolonialists (Carrington 1993; S. Smith 2001).

The oil-rich Middle Eastern nations provide an example of neocolonialism that has become highly significant for our own lives. Because of the two Gulf Wars and the terrorism that emanates from this region, it is worth focusing on Saudi Arabia (*Strategic Energy Policy* 2001; Mouawad 2007). Great Britain founded Saudi Arabia, drawing its boundaries and naming the country after the man (Ibn Saud) that Great Britain picked to lead it. The Most Industrialized Nations need low-priced oil to keep their factories running at a profit—and until recently the Saudis have been providing it. When other nations pumped less—no matter the cause, whether revolution or an attempt to raise prices—the Saudis made up the shortfall. For decades, this arrangement brought us low oil prices. In return, the United States overlooked the human rights violations of the Saudi royal family and propped them up by selling them the latest weapons. Oil shortages have short-circuited this arrangement, at least temporarily, and have brought higher gasoline prices at the pump.

## Multinational Corporations

**Multinational corporations,** companies that operate across many national boundaries, also help to maintain the global dominance of the Most Industrialized Nations. In some cases, multinational corporations exploit the Least Industrialized Nations directly. A prime example is the United Fruit Company, which used to control national and local politics in Central America. This U.S. corporation ran Central American nations as fiefdoms for the company's own profit while the U.S. Marines waited in the wings. An occasional invasion to put down dissidents reminded regional politicians of the military power that supported U.S. corporations.

Most commonly, however, it is simply by doing business that multinational corporations help to maintain international stratification. A single multinational corporation may manage mining operations in several countries, manufacture goods in others, and market its products around the globe. No matter where the profits are made, or where they are reinvested, the primary beneficiaries are the Most Industrialized Nations, especially the one in which the multinational corporation has its world headquarters.

In this game of profits, the elites of the Least Industrialized Nations are essential players (Sklair 2001; Wise and Cypher 2007). The multinational corporations funnel money to these elites, who, in return, create what is known as a "favorable business climate"—that is, low taxes and cheap labor. The money paid to the elites is politely called "subsidies" and "offsets," not bribes. Although most people in the Least Industrialized Nations live in remote villages where they eke out a meager living on small plots of land, the elites of these countries favor urban projects, such as building laboratories and computer centers in the capital city. The elites live a sophisticated upper-class life in the major cities of their home country, with many sending their children to prestigious Western universities, such as Oxford, the Sorbonne, and Harvard.

The money given to the elites (whether by direct payment or by sharing profits with companies the elites control) helps to maintain stratification. Not only do these payoffs allow the elites to maintain a genteel lifestyle but also they give them the ability to purchase high-tech weapons. This allows them to continue to oppress their people and to preserve their positions of dominance. The result is a political stability that keeps alive the diabolical partnership between the multinational corporations and the national elites.

This, however, is not the full story. Multinational corporations also play a role in changing international stratification. This is an unintentional by-product of their worldwide search for cheap resources and labor. When these corporations move manufacturing from the Most Industrialized Nations to the Least Industrialized Nations, not only do they exploit cheap labor but also they bring jobs and money to these nations. Although workers in the Least Industrialized Nations are paid a pittance, it is more than they can earn elsewhere. With new factories come opportunities to develop skills and a capital base.

This does not occur in all nations, but it did in the Pacific Rim nations, nicknamed the "Asian tigers" (Hong Kong, Singapore, South Korea, and Taiwan, with some "emerging tigers" now appearing in this region). In return for providing the "favorable business climate" just mentioned, the multinational corporations invested billions of dollars in this region. These nations now have such a strong capital base that they have begun to rival the older capitalist countries. Subject to capitalism's "boom and bust" cycles, many workers and investors in these nations, including those in the *maquiladoras* that you just read about, will have their dreams smashed as capitalism moves into its next downturn.

## Technology and Global Domination

The race between the Most and Least Industrialized Nations to develop and apply the new technologies is like a race between a marathon runner and someone with a broken leg. Can the outcome be in doubt? As the multinational corporations amass profits, they are able to invest huge sums in the latest technology. Gillette, for example, spent $100 million simply so that it could adjust its production "on an hourly basis" (Zachary 1995). These millions came from just one U.S. company. Many Least Industrialized Nations would love to have $100 million to invest in their entire economy, much less to use for fine-tuning the production of razor blades.

The race is not this simple, however. Although the Most Industrialized Nations have a seemingly insurmountable head start, some of the other nations are shortening the distance between themselves and the front runners. With cheap labor making their manufactured goods inexpensive, China and India are exporting goods on a massive scale. They are using the capital earned to extend their infrastructure (building dams, transportation, communication, and electrical systems), to develop their industry, and to adopt high technology. Although the maintenance of global domination is not in doubt at this point, it could be on the verge of a major shift from West to East.

**Unintended Public Relations**    Bono and other celebrities have used the media well in their campaign to pressure the world's wealthiest and most powerful nations to forgive the debts of some of the poorest nations. This has made a good story, which the mass media have promoted widely. With Bono at their side, the wealthy and powerful nations have basked in the spotlight. Amidst television reporters and global drum rolls, they have cancelled the debts of some poor nations. The image has been powerful—good-hearted capitalists having mercy on the poor. Behind the scenes was something vastly different: The wealthy nations had already written these debts off as uncollectible. But what a tool, for the publicity that accompanies their pronouncements helps to soften opposition to the global dominance of capitalism.

## A Concluding Note

The term *global stratification* is a remote-sounding term, so let's return to the two families featured in our opening vignette. These families represent distinct worlds of privilege and power—that is, unique locations in global stratification. By comparing these families, we can see how profoundly global stratification affects our life chances—from access to material possessions to our opportunity for education and even the likely age at which we will die. The division of the globe into interconnected units of nations with more or less wealth and more or less power and prestige, then, is much more than a matter of theoretical interest. In fact, it is *your* life we are talking about.

# SUMMARY *and* REVIEW

## Systems of Social Stratification

### What is social stratification?

**Social stratification** refers to a hierarchy of relative privilege based on property, power, and prestige. Every society stratifies its members, and in every society men as a group are placed above women as a group. P. 172.

### What are three major systems of social stratification?

Three major stratification systems are slavery, caste, and class. The essential characteristic of **slavery** is that some people own other people. Initially, slavery was based not on race but on debt, punishment, or defeat in battle. Slavery could be temporary or permanent and was not necessarily passed on to one's children. North American slaves had no legal rights, and the system was gradually buttressed by a racist **ideology.** In a **caste system,** status is determined by birth and is lifelong. A **class system** is much more open than these other systems, for it is based primarily on money or material possessions. Industrialization encourages the formation of class systems. Gender cuts across all forms of social stratification. Pp. 172–176.

## What Determines Social Class?

Karl Marx argued that a single factor determines social class: If you own the means of production, you belong to the **bourgeoisie;** if you do not, you are one of the **proletariat.** Max Weber argued that three elements determine social class: *property, power,* and *prestige.* Pp. 177–179.

## Why Is Social Stratification Universal?

To explain why stratification is universal, functionalists Kingsley Davis and Wilbert Moore argued that to attract the most capable people to fill its important positions, society must offer them greater rewards. Melvin Tumin said that if this view were correct, society would be a **meritocracy,** with all positions awarded on the basis of merit. Gaetano Mosca argued that stratification is inevitable because every society must have leadership, which by definition means inequality. Conflict theorists argue that stratification came about because resources are limited, and an elite emerges as groups struggle for them.

Gerhard Lenski suggested a synthesis between the functionalist and conflict perspectives. Pp. 179–181.

## How Do Elites Maintain Stratification?

To maintain social stratification within a nation, the ruling class adopts an ideology that justifies its current arrangements. It also controls information and uses technology. When all else fails, it turns to brute force. Pp. 181–182.

## Comparative Social Stratification

### What are key characteristics of stratification systems in other nations?

The most striking features of the British class system are speech and education. In Britain, accent reveals social class, and almost all of the elite attend "public" schools (the equivalent of U.S. private schools). In the former Soviet Union, communism was supposed to abolish class distinctions. Instead, it merely ushered in a different set of classes. Pp. 182–183.

## Global Stratification: Three Worlds

### How are the world's nations stratified?

The model presented here divides the world's nations into three groups: the Most Industrialized, the Industrializing, and the Least Industrialized. This layering represents relative property, power, and prestige. Pp. 183–189.

## How Did the World's Nations Become Stratified?

The main theories that seek to account for global stratification are **colonialism, world system theory,** and the **culture of poverty.** Pp. 190–192.

## Maintaining Global Stratification

### How do elites maintain global stratification?

There are two basic explanations for why the world's countries remain stratified. **Neocolonialism** is the ongoing dominance of the Least Industrialized Nations by the Most Industrialized Nations. The second explanation points to the influence of **multinational corporations.** The new technology gives further advantage to the Most Industrialized Nations. Pp. 192–194.

# THINKING CRITICALLY *about* **Chapter 7**

1. How do slavery, caste, and class systems of social stratification differ?

2. Why is social stratification universal?

3. Do you think that the low-wage factories of the multi-national corporations, located in such countries as Mexico, represent exploitation or opportunity? Why?

# ADDITIONAL RESOURCES

## What can you find in MySocLab?  mysoclab  www.mysoclab.com

- **Complete Ebook**
- **Practice Tests and Video and Audio activities**
- **Mapping and Data Analysis exercises**

- **Sociology in the News**
- **Classic Readings in Sociology**
- **Research and Writing advice**

## Where Can I Read More on This Topic?

Suggested readings for this chapter are listed at the back of this book.

## chapter 8

# Social Class in the United States

A h, New Orleans, that fabled city on the Mississippi Delta. Images from its rich past floated through my head—pirates, treasure, intrigue. Memories from a pleasant vacation stirred my thoughts—the exotic French Quarter with its enticing aroma of Creole food and sounds of earthy jazz drifting through the air.

> I was startled by a sight so out of step with the misery and despair that I had just experienced that I stopped and stared.

The shelter for the homeless, however, forced me back to an unwelcome reality. The shelter was just like those I had visited in the North, West, and East—only dirtier. The dirt, in fact, was the worst that I had encountered during my research, and this shelter was the only one to insist on payment in exchange for sleeping in one of its filthy beds.

The men looked the same—disheveled and haggard, wearing that unmistakable expression of despair—just like the homeless anywhere in the country. Except for the accent, you wouldn't know what region you were in. Poverty wears the same tired face wherever you are, I realized. The accent may differ, but the look remains the same.

I had grown used to the sights and smells of abject poverty. Those no longer surprised me. But after my fitful sleep with the homeless, I saw something that did. Just a block or so from the shelter, I was startled by a sight so out of step with the misery and despair I had just experienced that I stopped and stared.

Indignation swelled within me. Confronting me were life-size, full-color photos mounted on the transparent Plexiglas shelter of a bus stop. Staring back at me were images of finely dressed men and women proudly strutting about as they modeled elegant suits, dresses, diamonds, and furs.

A wave of disgust swept over me. "Something is cockeyed in this society," I thought, as my mind refused to stop juxtaposing these images of extravagance with the suffering I had just witnessed.

The disjunction that I felt in New Orleans was triggered by the ads, but it was not the first time that I had experienced this sensation. Whenever my research abruptly transported me from the world of the homeless to one of another social class, I experienced a sense of disjointed unreality. Each social class has its own way of being, and because these fundamental orientations to the world contrast so sharply, the classes do not mix well.

# What Is Social Class?

If you ask most Americans about their country's social class system, you are likely to get a blank look. If you press the matter, you are likely to get an answer like this: "There are the poor and the rich—and then there are you and I, neither poor nor rich." This is just about as far as most Americans' consciousness of social class goes. Let's try to flesh out this idea.

Our task is made somewhat difficult because sociologists have no clear-cut, agreed-on definition of social class. As was noted in the last chapter, conflict sociologists (of the Marxist orientation) see only two social classes: those who own the means of production and those who do not. The problem with this view, say most sociologists, is that it lumps too many people together. Teenage "order takers" at McDonald's who work for $15,000 a year are lumped together with that company's executives who make $500,000 a year—because they both are workers at McDonald's, not owners.

Most sociologists agree with Weber that there is more to social class than just a person's relationship to the means of production. Consequently, most sociologists use the components Weber identified and define **social class** as a large group of people who rank closely to one another in property, power, and prestige. These three elements separate people into different lifestyles, give them different chances in life, and provide them with distinct ways of looking at the self and the world.

Let's look at how sociologists measure these three components of social class.

## Property

**Property** comes in many forms, such as buildings, land, animals, machinery, cars, stocks, bonds, businesses, furniture, jewelry, and bank accounts. When you add up the value of someone's property and subtract that person's debts, you have what sociologists call **wealth.** This term can be misleading, as some of us have little wealth—especially most college students. Nevertheless, if your net total comes to $10, then that is your wealth. (Obviously, *wealth* as a sociological term does not mean *wealthy.*)

**Distinguishing Between Wealth and Income**    Wealth and income are sometimes confused, but they are not the same. Where *wealth* is a person's net worth, **income** is a flow of money. Income has many sources: The most common is a business or wages, but other sources are rent, interest, or royalties, even alimony, an allowance, or gambling. Some people have much wealth and little income. For example, a farmer may own much land (a form of wealth), but bad weather, combined with the high cost of fertilizers and machinery, can cause the income to dry up. Others have much income and little wealth. An executive with a $250,000 annual income may be debt-ridden. Below the surface prosperity—the exotic vacations, country club membership, private schools for the children, sports cars, and an elegant home—the credit cards may be maxed out, the sports cars in danger of being repossessed, and the mortgage payments "past due." Typically, however, wealth and income go together.

**Distribution of Property**    Who owns the property in the United States? One answer, of course, is "everyone." Although this statement has some merit, it overlooks how the nation's property is divided among "everyone."

Overall, Americans are worth a hefty sum, about $41 trillion (*Statistical Abstract* 2008:Table 701). This

A mere one-half of 1 percent of Americans owns over a quarter of the entire nation's wealth. Very few minorities are numbered among this 0.5 percent. An exception is Oprah Winfrey, who has had an ultra-successful career in entertainment and investing. Worth $1.3 billion, she is the 215th richest person in the United States. Winfrey, who has given millions of dollars to help minority children, is shown here as she talks with Tom Cruise.

includes all real estate, stocks, bonds, and business assets in the entire country. Figure 8.1 shows how highly concentrated this wealth is. Most wealth, 70 percent, is owned by only *10 percent* of the nation's families. As you can also see from this figure, 1 percent of Americans own one-third of all the U.S. assets.

**Distribution of Income**  How is income distributed in the United States? Economist Paul Samuelson (Samuelson and Nordhaus 2005) put it this way: "If we made an income pyramid out of a child's blocks, with each layer portraying $500 of income, the peak would be far higher than Mount Everest, but most people would be within a few feet of the ground."

Actually, if each block were 1½ inches tall, the typical American would be just 9 *feet off the ground,* for the average per capita income in the United States is about $36,000 per year. (This average income includes every American, even children.) The typical family climbs a little higher, for most families have more than one worker, and together they average about $56,000 a year. Compared with the few families who are on the mountain's peak, the average U.S. family would find itself only 14 feet off the ground (*Statistical Abstract* 2008:Tables 659, 674). Figure 8.2 portrays these differences.

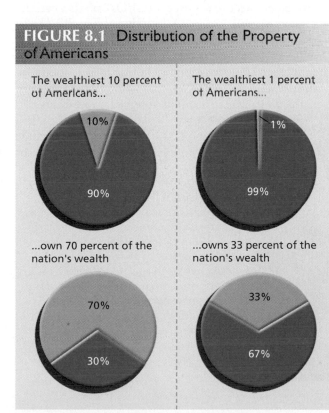

**FIGURE 8.1**  Distribution of the Property of Americans

The wealthiest 10 percent of Americans...

10%

90%

...own 70 percent of the nation's wealth

70%

30%

The wealthiest 1 percent of Americans...

1%

99%

...owns 33 percent of the nation's wealth

33%

67%

*Source:* By the author. Based on Beeghley 2008.

**FIGURE 8.2**  Distribution of the Income of Americans

Some U.S. families have incomes that exceed the height of Mt. Everest, 29,028 feet

**Average U.S. family income** $56,000 or 14 feet

**Average U.S. individual income** $36,000 or 9 feet

If a 1–1/2 inch child's block equals $500 of income, the average individual's annual income of $36,000 would represent a height of 9 feet, and the average family's annual income of $56,000 would represent a height of 14 feet. The income of some families, in contrast, would represent a height greater than that of Mt. Everest.

*Source:* By the author.

**FIGURE 8.3**    The More Things Change, the More They Stay the Same: The Percentage of the Nation's Income Received by Each Fifth of U.S. Families

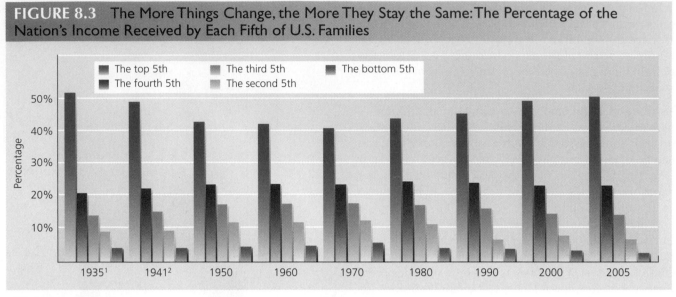

¹Earliest year available.
²No data for 1940.
*Source:* By the author. Based on *Statistical Abstract* 1960: Table 417; 1970: Table 489; 2008: Table 675.

The fact that some Americans enjoy the peaks of Mount Everest while most—despite their efforts—make it only 9 to 14 feet up the slope presents a striking image of income inequality in the United States. Another picture emerges if we divide the U.S. population into five equal groups and rank them from highest to lowest income. As Figure 8.3 shows, the top 20 percent of the population receive *half* (50.4 percent) of all income in the United States. In contrast, the bottom 20 percent of Americans receive only 3.4 percent of the nation's income.

Two features of Figure 8.3 are outstanding. First, notice how little change there has been in the distribution of income through the years. Second, look at how income inequality decreased from 1935 to 1970. *Since 1970, the richest 20 percent of U.S. families have grown richer, while the poorest 20 percent have grown poorer.* Despite numerous government antipoverty programs, the poorest 20 percent of Americans receive *less* of the nation's income today than they did decades ago. The richest 20 percent, in contrast, are receiving more, almost as much as they did in 1935.

The chief executive officers (CEOs) of the nation's largest corporations are especially affluent. The *Wall Street Journal* surveyed the 350 largest U.S. companies to find out what they paid their CEOs ("The Boss's Pay" 2007). Their median compensation (including salaries, bonuses, and stock options) came to $6,549,000 a year. (*Median* means that half received more than this amount, and half less.)

The CEOs' income—which does *not* include their income from interest, dividends, or rents, or

With a fortune of $48 billion, Bill Gates, a cofounder of Microsoft Corporation, is the wealthiest person in the world. His 40,000-square-foot home (sometimes called a "technopalace") in Seattle, Washington, was appraised at $110 million.

In addition to being the wealthiest person, Gates is also the most generous. He has given more money to the poor and minorities than any individual in history. His foundation is now focusing on fighting infectious diseases, developing vaccines, and improving schools.

| TABLE 8.1 | The Highest-Paid CEOs | |
|---|---|---|
| Executive | Company | Compensation |
| 1. John A. Thain | Merrill Lynch | $79 million |
| 2. Lloyd C. Blankfein | Goldman Sachs Group | $69 million |
| 3. Ray R. Irani | Occidental Petroleum | $61 million |
| 4. Kenneth I. Chenault | American Express | $46 million |
| 5. Richard S. Fuld Jr. | Lehman Brothers | $40 million |

Note: Compensation includes salary, bonuses, and stock options.
Source: "The Boss's Pay" 2008.

the value of company-paid limousines and chauffeurs, airplanes and pilots, and private boxes at the symphony and sporting events—is *166 times* higher than the average pay of U.S. workers (*Statistical Abstract* 2007:Table 629). To really see the disparity, consider this: The average U.S. worker would have to work *1,475 years* to earn the amount the highest-paid executive listed in Table 8.1 receives in *one year*.

Imagine how you could live with an income like this. And that is precisely the point. Beyond cold numbers lies a dynamic reality that profoundly affects people's lives. The difference in wealth between those at the top and those at the bottom of the U.S. class structure means that these individuals experience vastly different lifestyles. For example, a colleague of mine who was teaching at an exclusive Eastern university piqued his students' curiosity when he lectured on poverty in Latin America. That weekend, one of the students borrowed his parents' corporate jet and pilot, and in class on Monday, he and his friends related their personal observations on poverty in Latin America. Americans who are at the low end of the income ladder, in contrast, lack the funds to travel even to a neighboring town for the weekend. For young parents, choices may revolve around whether to spend the little they have at the laundromat or on milk for the baby. The elderly might have to choose between purchasing the medicines they need or buying food. In short, divisions of wealth represent not "mere" numbers, but choices that make vital differences in people's lives, a topic that we explore in the Down-to-Earth Sociology box on the next page.

## Power

Like many people, you may have said to yourself, "Sure, I can vote, but the big decisions are always made despite what I might think. Certainly *I* don't make the decision to send soldiers to Afghanistan or Iraq. *I* don't launch missiles against Kosovo or Baghdad. *I* don't decide to raise taxes or lower interest rates. It isn't *I* who decides to change Social Security or Medicare benefits."

And then another part of you may say, "But I do participate in these decisions through my representatives in Congress and by voting for president." True enough—as far as it goes. The trouble is, it just doesn't go far enough. Such views of being a participant in the nation's "big" decisions are a playback of the ideology we learn at an early age—an ideology that Marx said is promoted by the elites to both legitimate and perpetuate their power. Sociologists Daniel Hellinger and Dennis Judd (1991) call this the "democratic facade" that conceals the real source of power in the United States.

Back in the 1950s, sociologist C. Wright Mills (1956) was criticized for insisting that **power**—the ability to carry out your will despite resistance—was concentrated in the hands of a few, for his analysis contradicted the dominant ideology of equality. As was discussed in earlier chapters, Mills coined the term **power elite** to refer to those who make the big decisions in U.S. society.

Mills and others have stressed how wealth and power coalesce in a group of like-minded individuals who share ideologies, values, and world views. These individuals belong to the same private clubs, vacation at the same exclusive resorts, and even hire the same bands for their daughters' debutante balls. Their shared backgrounds and vested interests reinforce their view of both the world and their special place in it (Domhoff 1999a, 2006). This elite wields extraordinary power in U.S. society, so much so that *most* U.S. presidents have come from this group—millionaire white men from families with "old money" (Baltzell and Schneiderman 1988).

Continuing in the tradition of Mills, sociologist William Domhoff (1990, 2006) argues that this group is so powerful that the U.S. government makes no major decision without its approval. He analyzed how this group works behind the scenes with elected officials to determine both foreign and domestic policy—from setting Social Security taxes to imposing trade tariffs. Although Domhoff's conclusions are controversial—and alarming—they certainly follow logically from the principle that wealth brings power, and extreme wealth brings extreme power.

## Prestige

**Occupations and Prestige**    What are you thinking about doing after college? Chances are, you don't have the option of lolling under palm trees at the beach. Al-most all of us have to choose an occupation and go to work. Look at Table 8.2 to see how the career you are considering stacks up in terms of **prestige** (respect or regard). Because we are moving toward a global society, this table also shows how the rankings given by Ameri-

*Down-to-Earth Sociology*
## How the Super-Rich Live

It's good to see how other people live. It gives us a dif-ferent perspective on life. Let's take a glimpse at the life of John Castle (his real name). After earning a de-gree in physics at MIT and an MBA at Harvard, John went into banking and securities, where he made more than $100 million (Lublin 1999).

Wanting to be connected to someone famous, John bought President John F. Kennedy's "Winter White House," an oceanfront estate in Palm Beach, Florida. John spent $11 million to remodel the 13,000-square-foot house so that it would be more to his liking. Among those changes: adding bathrooms numbers 14 and 15. He likes to show off John F. Kennedy's bed and also the dresser that has the drawer labeled "black un-derwear," carefully hand-lettered by Rose Kennedy.

At his beachfront estate, John gives what he calls "re-fined feasts" to the glitterati ("On History . . ." 1999). If he gets tired of such activities—or weary of swimming in the Olympic-size pool where JFK swam the weekend before his assassination—he entertains himself by riding one of his thoroughbred horses at his nearby 10-acre ranch. If this fails to ease his boredom, he can relax aboard his custom-built 42-foot Hinckley yacht.

The yacht is a real source of diversion. John once boarded it for an around-the-world trip. He didn't stay on board, though—just joined the cruise from time to time. A captain and crew kept the vessel on course, and when-ever John felt like it he would fly in and stay a few days. Then he would fly back to the States to direct his busi-ness. He did this about a dozen times, flying perhaps 150,000 miles. An interesting way to go around the world.

How much does a custom-built Hinckley yacht cost? John can't tell you. As he says, "I don't want to know what anything costs. When you've got enough money, price doesn't make a difference. That's part of the free-dom of being rich."

*How do the super-rich live? This photo helps give you an idea of how different their lifestyles are from most of ours. Shown here is Wayne Huizenga, who is featured in this box, with one of his vintage automobiles.*

Right. And for John, being rich also means paying $1,000,000 to charter a private jet to fly Spot, his Appaloosa horse, back and forth to the vet. John didn't want Spot to have to endure a long trailer ride. Oh, and of course, there was the cost of Spot's medical treat-ment, another $500,000.

Other wealthy people put John to shame. Wayne Huizenga, the founder of Blockbuster, wanted more elbow room for his estate at Nantucket, so he added the house next door for $2.5 million (Fabrikant 2005). He also bought a 2,000-acre country club, complete with an 18-hole golf course, a 55,000-square-foot-clubhouse, and 68 slips for visiting vessels. The club is so exclusive that its only members are Wayne and his wife.

### For Your Consideration

What effects has social class had on your life? (Go be-yond possessions to values, orientations, and views on life.) How do you think you would see the world differ-ently if you were John Castle or Mrs. Wayne Huizenga?

cans compare with those of the residents of sixty other countries.

Why do people give more prestige to some jobs than to others? If you look at Table 8.2, you will notice that the jobs at the top share four features:

1. They pay more.
2. They require more education.
3. They entail more abstract thought.
4. They offer greater autonomy (independence, or self-direction).

If you look at the bottom of the list, you can see that people give less prestige to jobs with the opposite characteristics: These jobs are low-paying, require less preparation or education, involve more physical labor, and are closely supervised. In short, the professions and the white-collar jobs are at the top of the list, the blue-collar jobs at the bottom.

One of the more interesting aspects of these rankings is how consistent they are across countries and over time. For example, people in every country rank college professors higher than nurses, nurses higher than social workers, and social workers higher than janitors. Similarly, the occupations that were ranked high 25 years ago still rank high today—and likely will rank high in the years to come.

**Displaying Prestige**  People want others to acknowledge their prestige. In times past, in some countries only the emperor and his family could wear purple—for it was the royal color. In France, only the nobility could wear lace. In England, no one could sit while the king was on his throne. Some kings and queens required that subjects walk backward as they left the room—so that they would not "turn their back" on the "royal presence."

Concern with displaying prestige has not let up. For some, it is almost an obsession. Military manuals specify precisely who must salute whom. The U.S. president enters a room only after everyone else attending the function is present (to show that the president isn't the one waiting for others). Everyone must be standing when the president enters. In the courtroom, bailiffs, sometimes armed, make certain that everyone stands when the judge enters.

The display of prestige is not just something "out there." Think about your clothing. How much more are you willing to pay for clothing that bears some hot "designer" label? Purses, shoes, jeans, and shirts—many of us pay more if they have a little symbol than if they don't. As we wear them proudly, aren't we actually proclaiming, "See, I had the money to buy this particular

**TABLE 8.2  Occupational Prestige: How the United States Compares with 60 Countries**

| Occupation | United States | Average of 60 Countries |
|---|---|---|
| Physician | 86 | 78 |
| Supreme court Judge | 85 | 82 |
| College president | 81 | 86 |
| Astronaut | 80 | 80 |
| Lawyer | 75 | 73 |
| College professor | 74 | 78 |
| Architect | 73 | 72 |
| Biologist | 73 | 69 |
| Dentist | 72 | 70 |
| Civil engineer | 69 | 70 |
| Clergy | 69 | 60 |
| Psychologist | 69 | 66 |
| Pharmacist | 68 | 64 |
| High school teacher | 66 | 64 |
| Registered nurse | 66 | 54 |
| Professional athlete | 65 | 48 |
| Electrical engineer | 64 | 65 |
| Author | 63 | 62 |
| Banker | 63 | 67 |
| Police officer | 61 | 40 |
| Sociologist | 61 | 67 |
| Actor or actress | 58 | 52 |
| Chiropractor | 57 | 62 |
| Athletic coach | 53 | 50 |
| Social worker | 52 | 56 |
| Electrician | 51 | 44 |
| Undertaker | 49 | 34 |
| Real estate agent | 48 | 49 |
| Mail carrier | 47 | 33 |
| Secretary | 46 | 53 |
| Plumber | 45 | 34 |
| Carpenter | 43 | 37 |
| Barber | 36 | 30 |
| Store sales clerk | 36 | 34 |
| Truck driver | 30 | 33 |
| Cab driver | 28 | 28 |
| Garbage collector | 28 | 13 |
| Waiter or waitress | 28 | 23 |
| Bartender | 25 | 23 |
| Lives on public aid | 25 | 16 |
| Bill collector | 24 | 27 |
| Factory worker | 24 | 29 |
| Janitor | 22 | 21 |
| Shoe shiner | 17 | 12 |

*Note:* For four occupations not located in the 1994 source, the 1991 ratings were used: Supreme Court judge, astronaut, athletic coach, and lives on public aid.
*Sources:* Treiman 1977, Appendices A and D; Nakao and Treas 1991; 1994: Appendix D.

item!"? For many of us, prestige is a primary factor in deciding which college to attend. Everyone knows how the prestige of a generic sheepskin from Regional State College compares with a degree from Harvard, Princeton, Yale, or Stanford.

Status symbols vary with social class. Clearly, only the wealthy can afford certain items, such as yachts and huge estates. But beyond affordability lies a class-based preference in status symbols. For example, people who are striving to be upwardly mobile are quick to flaunt labels, Hummers, Land Rovers, and other symbols to show that they have "arrived," while the rich, more secure in their status, often downplay such images. The wealthy regard the designer labels of the "common" classes as cheap and showy. They, of course, flaunt their own status symbols, such as $50,000 Rolex watches and $20,000 diamond earrings. Like the other classes, they, too, try to outdo one another; they boast about who has the longest yacht or let others know that they have a helicopter fly them to their meetings or their golf games (Fabrikant 2005).

## Status Inconsistency

Ordinarily, a person has a similar rank on all three dimensions of social class—property, power, and prestige. The homeless men in the opening vignette are an example. Such people are **status consistent.** Sometimes that match is not there, however, and someone has a mixture of high and low ranks, a condition called **status inconsistency.**

Instant wealth, the topic of the Down-to-Earth Sociology box below, provides an interesting case of status inconsistency.

---

## *Down-to-Earth Sociology*
## The Big Win:
## Life After the Lottery

"If I just win the lottery, life will be good. These problems I've got, they'll be gone. I can just see myself now."

So goes the dream. And many Americans shell out megabucks every week, with the glimmering hope that "Maybe this week, I'll hit it big."

Most are lucky to get $20, or maybe just win another scratch-off ticket.

But there are the big hits. What happens to these winners? Are their lives all wine, roses, and chocolate afterward?

We don't have any systematic studies of the big winners, so I can't tell you what life is like for the average winner. But several themes are apparent from reporters' interviews.

The most common consequence of hitting it big is that life becomes topsy-turvy (Ross 2004). All of us are rooted somewhere. We have connections with others that provide the basis for our orientations to life and how we feel about the world. Sudden wealth can rip these moorings apart, and the resulting *status inconsistency* can lead to a condition sociologists call **anomie.**

First comes the shock. As Mary Sanderson, a telephone operator in Dover, New Hampshire, who won

Status inconsistency *is common for lottery winners, whose new wealth is vastly greater than the statuses that come with their education and occupation. Shown here are John and Sandy Jarrell of Chicago, after they learned that they were one of 13 families to share a $295 million jackpot. How do you think their $22 million will affect their lives?*

$66 million, said, "I was afraid to believe it was real, and afraid to believe it wasn't." Mary says that she never slept worse than her first night as a multimillionaire. "I spent the whole time crying—and throwing up" (Tresniowski 1999).

Reporters and TV camera operators appear on your doorstep. "What are you going to do with all that money?" they demand. You haven't the slightest idea, but in a daze you mumble something.

Sociologist Gerhard Lenski (1954, 1966) analyzed how people try to maximize their **status,** their position in a social group. Individuals who rank high on one dimension of social class but lower on others want people to judge them on the basis of their highest status. Others, however, who are trying to maximize their own position, may respond to status-inconsistent individuals according to their lowest ranking.

A classic study of status inconsistency was done by sociologist Ray Gold (1952). He found that after apartment-house janitors unionized, they made more money than some of the tenants whose garbage they carried out. Tenants became upset when they saw their janitors driving more expensive cars than they did. Some attempted to "put the janitor in his place" by making "snotty" remarks to him. For their part, the janitors took delight in knowing "dirty" secrets about the tenants, gleaned from their garbage.

Individuals with status inconsistency, then, are likely to confront one frustrating situation after another (Heames et al. 2006). They claim the higher status, but others acknowledge only the lower one. The significance of this condition, said Lenski (1954), is that such people tend to be more politically radical. An example is college professors. Their prestige is very high, as we saw in Table 8.2, but their incomes are relatively low. Hardly anyone in U.S. society is more educated, and yet college professors don't even come close to the top of the income pyramid. In line with Lenski's prediction, the politics of most college professors are left of center. This hypothesis may also hold true among academic departments; that is, the higher a department's average pay, the less radical are the members' politics. Teachers in departments of business and medicine, for example, are among the most highly paid in the university—and they also are the most politically conservative.

---

Then come the calls. Some are welcome. Your Mom and Dad call to congratulate you. But long-forgotten friends and distant relatives suddenly remember how close they really are to you—and strangely enough, they all have emergencies that your money can solve. You even get calls from strangers who have ailing mothers, terminally ill kids, sick dogs . . .

You have to unplug the phone and get an unlisted number.

You might be flooded with marriage proposals. You certainly didn't become more attractive or sexy overnight—or did you? Maybe money makes people sexy.

You can no longer trust people. You don't know what their real motives are. Before, no one could be after your money because you didn't have any. You may even fear kidnappers. Before, this wasn't a problem—unless some kidnapper wanted the ransom of a seven-year-old car.

The normal becomes abnormal. Even picking out a wedding gift is a problem. If you give the usual toaster, everyone will think you're stingy. But should you write a check for $25,000? If you do, you'll be invited to every wedding in town—and everyone will expect the same.

Here is what happened to some lottery winners:

As a tip, a customer gave a lottery ticket to Tonda Dickerson, a waitress at the Waffle House in Grand Bay, Alabama. She won $10 million. (Yes, just like the Nicholas Cage movie, *It Could Happen to You.*) Her co-workers sued her, saying that they had always agreed to split such winnings ("House Divided" 1999).

Then there is Michael Klinebiel of Rahway, New Jersey. When he won $2 million, his mother, Phyllis, said that half of it was hers, that she and her son had pooled $20 a month for years to play the lottery. He said they had done this—but he had bought the winning ticket on his own. Phyllis sued her son ("Sticky Ticket" 1998).

When Mack Metcalf, a forklift operator in Corbin, Kentucky, hit the jackpot for $34 million, he fulfilled a dream: He built and moved into a replica of George Washington's Mount Vernon home. Then his life fell apart—his former wife sued him, his current wife divorced him, and his new girlfriend got $500,000 while he was drunk. Within three years of his "good" fortune, Metcalf had drunk himself to death (Dao 2005).

Winners who avoid *anomie* seem to be people who don't make sudden changes in their lifestyle or their behavior. They hold on to their old friends and routines—the anchors in life that give them identity and a sense of belonging. Some even keep their old jobs—not for the money, of course, but because the job anchors them to an identity with which they are familiar and comfortable.

Sudden wealth, in other words, poses a threat that has to be guarded against.

And I can just hear you say, "I'll take the risk!"

### For Your Consideration
How do you think your life would change if you won a lottery jackpot of $10 million?

Display of prestige and social position varies over time and from one culture to another. Shown here is Elizabeth I, Queen of England and Ireland. Elizabeth became queen in 1558 at the age of 25 and ruled for 45 years, until 1603. This painting hangs in the National Portrait Gallery.

Compare these people with a man I know in Godfrey, Illinois, who used to fix cars in his backyard. As Frank gained a following, he quit his regular job, and in a few years he put up a building with five bays and an office. Frank is now a capitalist, for he employs five or six mechanics and owns the tools and the building (the "means of production"). But what does he have in common with a factory owner who controls the lives of one thousand workers? Not only is Frank's work different but so are his lifestyle and the way he looks at the world.

To resolve this problem, sociologist Erik Wright (1985) suggests that some people are members of more than one class at the same time. They occupy what he calls **contradictory class locations.** By this, Wright means that a person's position in the class structure can generate contradictory interests. For example, the automobile mechanic-turned-business owner may want his mechanics to have higher wages because he, too, has experienced their working conditions. At the same time, his current interests—making profits and remaining competitive with other repair shops—lead him to resist pressures to raise their wages.

Because of such contradictory class locations, Wright modified Marx's model. As summarized in Table 8.3, Wright identifies four classes: (1) *capitalists,* business owners who employ many workers; (2) *petty bourgeoisie,* small business owners; (3) *managers,* who sell their own labor but also exercise authority over other employees; and (4) *workers,* who simply sell their labor to others. As you can see, this model allows finer divisions than the one Marx proposed, yet it

## Sociological Models of Social Class

The question of how many social classes there are is a matter of debate. Sociologists have proposed several models, but no single model has gained universal support. There are two main models: one that builds on Marx, the other on Weber.

### Updating Marx

Marx argued that there are just two classes—capitalists and workers—with membership based solely on a person's relationship to the means of production (see Figure 8.4). Sociologists have criticized this view, saying that these categories are too broad. For example, because executives, managers, and supervisors don't own the means of production, they would be classified as workers. But what do these people have in common with assembly-line workers? The category of "capitalist" is also too broad. Some people, for example, employ a thousand workers, and their decisions directly affect a thousand families.

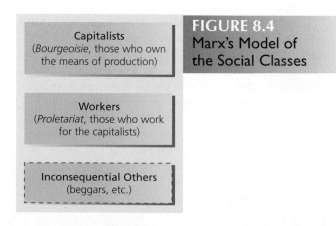

**FIGURE 8.4**
**Marx's Model of the Social Classes**

Capitalists
(*Bourgeoisie,* those who own the means of production)

Workers
(*Proletariat,* those who work for the capitalists)

Inconsequential Others
(beggars, etc.)

**TABLE 8.3**
Wright's Modification
of Marx's Model
of the Social Classes

1. Capitalists
2. Petty bourgeoisie
3. Managers
4. Workers

maitains the primary distinction between employer and employee.

## Updating Weber

Sociologists Joseph Kahl and Dennis Gilbert (Gilbert and Kahl 1998; Gilbert 2003) developed a six-tier model to portray the class structure of the United States and other capitalist countries. Think of this model, illustrated in Figure 8.5, as a ladder. Our discussion starts with the highest rung and moves downward. In line with Weber, on each lower rung you find less property (wealth), less power, and less prestige. Note that in this model education is also a primary measure of class.

**The Capitalist Class**    Sitting on the top rung of the class ladder is a powerful elite that consists of just 1 percent of the U.S. population. As you saw in Figure 8.1 on page 199, this capitalist class is so wealthy that it owns one-third of all U.S. assets. *This tiny 1 percent is worth more than the entire bottom 90 percent of the country* (Beeghley 2008).

Power and influence cling to this small elite. They have direct access to top politicians, and their decisions open or close job opportunities for millions of people. They even help to shape the consciousness of the nation: They own our major media and entertainment outlets—newspapers, magazines, radio and television stations, and sports franchises. They also control the boards of directors of our most influential colleges and universities. The super-rich perpetuate themselves in privilege by passing on their assets and social networks to their children.

**FIGURE 8.5    The U.S. Social Class Ladder**

| Social Class | Education | Occupation | Income | Percentage of Population |
|---|---|---|---|---|
| Capitalist | Prestigious university | Investors and heirs, a few top executives | $1,000,000+ | 1% |
| Upper Middle | College or university, often with postgraduate study | Professionals and upper managers | $125,000+ | 15% |
| Lower Middle | High school or college; often apprenticeship | Semiprofessionals and lower managers, craftspeople, foremen | About $60,000 | 34% |
| Working | High school | Factory workers, clerical workers, low-paid retail sales, and craftspeople | About $35,000 | 30% |
| Working Poor | Some high school | Laborers, service workers, low-paid salespeople | About $17,000 | 16% |
| Underclass | Some high school | Unemployed and part-time, on welfare | Under $10,000 | 4% |

*Source:* Based on Gilbert and Kahl 1998 and Gilbert 2003; income estimates are modified from Duff 1995.

The capitalist class can be divided into "old" and "new" money. The longer that wealth has been in a family, the more it adds to the family's prestige. The children of "old" money seldom mingle with "common" folk. Instead, they attend exclusive private schools where they learn views of life that support their privileged position. They don't work for wages; instead, many study business or enter the field of law so that they can manage the family fortune. These old-money capitalists (also called "blue bloods") wield vast power as they use their extensive political connections to protect their economic empires (Sklair 2001; Domhoff 1990, 1999b, 2006).

At the lower end of the capitalist class are the *nouveau riche,* those who have "new money." Although they have made fortunes in business, the stock market, inventions, entertainment, or sports, they are outsiders to the upper class. They have not attended the "right" schools, and they don't share the social networks that come with old money. Not blue bloods, they aren't trusted to have the right orientations to life. Even their "taste" in clothing and status symbols is suspect (Fabricant 2005). Donald Trump, whose money is "new," is not listed in the *Social Register,* the "White Pages" of the blue bloods that lists the most prestigious and wealthy one-tenth of 1 percent of the U.S. population. Trump says he "doesn't care," but he reveals his true feelings by adding that his heirs will be in it (Kaufman 1996). He is probably right, for the children of the new-moneyed can ascend into the top part of the capitalist class—if they go to the right schools *and* marry old money.

Many in the capitalist class are philanthropic. They establish foundations and give huge sums to "causes." Their motivations vary. Some feel guilty because they have so much while others have so little. Others seek prestige, acclaim, or fame. Still others feel a responsibility—even a sense of fate or purpose—to use their money for doing good. Bill Gates, who has given more money to the poor and to medical research than anyone else has, seems to fall into this latter category.

Sociologists use income, education, and occupational prestige to measure social class. For most people, this classification works well, but not for everyone. Entertainers sometimes are difficult to fit in. To what social class do Depp, Oh, Cruz, and James belong? Johnny Depp makes $10 million a year, Sandra Oh around $3 million, and Penelope Cruz $1 to 2 million. When Lebron James got out of high school, he signed more than $100 million in endorsement contracts, as well as a $4 million contract to play basketball for the Cleveland Cavaliers.

Johnny Depp

Sandra Oh

Penelope Cruz

LeBron James

**The Upper Middle Class**    Of all the classes, the upper middle class is the one most shaped by education. Almost all members of this class have at least a bachelor's degree, and many have postgraduate degrees in business, management, law, or medicine. These people manage the corporations owned by the capitalist class or else operate their own business or profession. As Gilbert and Kahl (1998) say,

> [These positions] may not grant prestige equivalent to a title of nobility in the Germany of Max Weber, but they certainly represent the sign of having "made it" in contemporary America. . . . Their income is sufficient to purchase houses and cars and travel that become public symbols for all to see and for advertisers to portray with words and pictures that connote success, glamour, and high style.

Consequently, parents and teachers push children to prepare for upper-middle-class jobs. About 15 percent of the population belong to this class.

**The Lower Middle Class**    About 34 percent of the population belong to the lower middle class. Members of this class have jobs that call for them to follow orders given by those who have upper-middle-class credentials. With their technical and lower-level management positions, they can afford a mainstream lifestyle, and many anticipate being able to move up the social class ladder. Feelings of insecurity are common, however, with the threat of inflation, recession, and job insecurity bringing a nagging sense that they might fall down the class ladder (Kefalas 2007).

The distinctions between the lower middle class and the working class on the next rung below are more blurred than those between other classes. In general, however, members of the lower middle class work at jobs that have slightly more prestige, and their incomes are generally higher.

**The Working Class**    About 30 percent of the U.S. population belong to this class of relatively unskilled blue-collar and white-collar workers. Compared with the lower middle class, they have less education and lower incomes. Their jobs are also less secure, more routine, and more closely supervised. One of their greatest fears is that of being laid off during a recession. With only a high school diploma, the average member of the working class has little hope of climbing up the class ladder. Job changes usually bring "more of the same," so most concentrate on getting ahead by achieving seniority on the job rather than by changing their type of work. They tend to think of themselves as having "real jobs" and regard the "suits" above them as paper pushers who have no practical experience (Morris and Grimes 2005).

**The Working Poor**    Members of this class, about 16 percent of the population, work at unskilled, low-paying, temporary and seasonal jobs, such as sharecropping, migrant farm work, housecleaning, and day labor. Most are high school dropouts. Many are functionally illiterate, finding it difficult to read even the want ads. They are not likely to vote (Gilbert and Kahl 1998; Beeghley 2008), for they believe that no matter what party is elected to office, their situation won't change.

Although they work full time, millions of the working poor depend on help such as food stamps and donations from local food pantries to survive on their meager incomes (O'Hare 1996b). It is easy to see how you can work full time and still be poor. Suppose that you are married and have a baby 3 months old and another child 3 years old. Your spouse stays home to care for them, so earning the income is up to you. But as a high-school dropout, all you can get is a minimum wage job. At $7.25 an hour, you earn $290 for 40 hours. In a year, this comes to $15,080—before deductions. Your nagging fear—and daily nightmare—is of ending up "on the streets."

**The Underclass**    On the lowest rung, and with next to no chance of climbing anywhere, is the **underclass.** Concentrated in the inner city, this group has little or no connection with the job market. Those who are employed—and some are—do menial, low-paying, temporary work. Welfare, if it is available, along with food stamps and food pantries, is their main support. Most members of other classes consider these people the "ne'er-do-wells" of society. Life is the toughest in this class, and it is filled with despair. About 4 percent of the population fall into this class.

The homeless men described in the opening vignette of this chapter, and the women and children like them, are part of the underclass. These are the people whom most Americans wish would just go away. Their presence on our city streets bothers passersby from the more privileged social classes—which includes just about everyone. "What are those obnoxious, dirty, foul-smelling people doing here, cluttering up my city?" appears to be a common response. Some people react with sympathy and a desire to do something. But what? Almost all of us just shrug our shoulders and look the other way, despairing of a solution and somewhat intimidated by their presence.

The homeless are the "fallout" of our postindustrial economy. In another era, they would have had plenty of work. They would have tended horses, worked on farms, dug ditches, shoveled coal, and run the factory looms. Some would have explored and settled the West. Others would have been lured to California, Alaska, and Australia by the

The homeless are classified by some sociologists as members of the *underclass*, by others as members of the lower-lower class. Whatever the name, members of this class receive the least of what society offers. Compare this photo with the one on page 202.

prospect of gold. Today, however, with no frontiers to settle, factory jobs scarce, and farms that are becoming technological marvels, we have little need for unskilled labor.

## Social Class in the Automobile Industry

Let's use the automobile industry to illustrate the social class ladder. The Fords, for example, own and control a manufacturing and financial empire whose net worth is truly staggering. Their power matches their wealth, for through their multinational corporation, their decisions affect production and employment in many countries. The family's vast fortune and its accrued power are now several generations old. Consequently, Ford children go to the "right" schools, know how to spend money in the "right" way, and can be trusted to make family and class interests paramount in life. They are without question at the top level of the *capitalist* class.

Next in line come top Ford executives. Although they may have an income of several hundred thousand dollars a year (and some, with stock options and bonuses, earn several million dollars annually), most are new to wealth

and power. Consequently, they would be classified at the lower end of the capitalist class.

A husband and wife who own a Ford dealership are members of the *upper middle class*. Their income clearly sets them apart from the majority of Americans, and their reputation in the community is enviable. More than likely, they also exert greater-than-average influence in their community, but their capacity to wield power is limited.

A Ford salesperson, as well as people who work in the dealership office, belongs to the *lower middle class*. Although there are some exceptional salespeople—even a few who make handsome incomes selling prestigious, expensive cars to the capitalist class—those at a run-of-the-mill Ford agency are lower middle class. Compared with the owners of the agency, their income is less, their education is likely to be less, and their work is less prestigious.

Mechanics who repair customers' cars are members of the *working class*. A mechanic who is promoted to supervise the repair shop joins the lower middle class. Those who "detail" used cars (making them appear newer by washing and polishing the car, painting the tires, spraying "new car scent" into the interior, and so on) belong to the *working poor*. Their income and education are low, and the prestige accorded to their work minimal. They are laid off when selling slows down.

Ordinarily, the *underclass* is not represented in the automobile industry. It is conceivable, however, that the dealership might hire a member of the underclass to do a specific job such as mowing the grass or cleaning up the used car lot. In general, however, personnel at the dealership do not trust members of the underclass and do not want to associate with them—even for a few hours. They prefer to hire someone from the working poor for such jobs.

# Consequences of Social Class

Each social class can be thought of as a broad subculture with distinct approaches to life. Social class affects people's health, family life, and education. It also influences their religion and politics and even their experiences with crime and the criminal justice system. Let's look at these consequences of social class.

## Physical Health

If you want to get a sense of how social class affects health, take a ride on Washington's Metro system. Start in the blighted Southeast section of downtown D.C. For every mile you travel to where the wealthy live in Montgomery County in Maryland, life expectancy rises about a year and a half. By the time you get off, you will find a twenty-year gap between the poor blacks where you started your trip and the rich whites where you ended it. (Cohen 2004).

*(The foldout at the front of the book illustrates these effects of social class.)*

The effects of social class on physical health are startling. The principle is simple: The lower a person's social class, the more likely that individual is to die before the expected age. This principle holds true at all ages. Infants born to the poor are more likely than other infants to die before their first birthday. In old age—whether 75 or 95—a larger proportion of the poor die each year than do the wealthy.

How can social class have such dramatic effects? While there is some controversy over the reasons, there seem to be three basic explanations. First, social class opens and closes doors to medical care. Consider this example:

Terry Takewell (his real name), a 21-year-old diabetic, lived in a trailer park in Somerville, Tennessee. When Zettie Mae Hill, Takewell's neighbor, found the unemployed carpenter drenched with sweat from a fever, she called an ambulance. Takewell was rushed to nearby Methodist Hospital, where, it turned out, he had an outstanding bill of $9,400. A notice posted in the emergency room told staff members to alert supervisors if Takewell ever returned.

When the hospital administrator was informed of the admission, Takewell was already in a hospital bed. The administrator went to Takewell's room, helped him to his feet, and escorted him to the parking lot. There, neighbors found him under a tree and took him home.

Takewell died about twelve hours later.

Zettie Mae Hill wonders whether Takewell would be alive today if she had directed his ambulance to a different hospital. She said, "I didn't think a hospital would just let a person die like that for lack of money." (Based on Ansberry 1988)

Why was Terry Takewell denied medical treatment and his life cut short? The fundamental reason is that health care in the United States is not a citizens' right but a commodity for sale. This gives us a two-tier system of medical care: superior care for those who can afford the cost and inferior care for those who cannot (Budrys 2003). Unlike the middle and upper classes, few poor people have a personal physician, and they often spend hours waiting in crowded public health clinics. After waiting most of a day, some don't even get to see a doctor. Instead, they are told to come back the next day. And when the poor are hospitalized, they are likely to find themselves in understaffed and underfunded public hospitals, treated by rotating interns who do not know them and cannot follow up on their progress.

A second reason is lifestyles, which are shaped by social class. People in the lower social classes are more likely to smoke, eat a lot of fats, be overweight, abuse drugs and alcohol, get little or no exercise, and practice unsafe sex (Chin et al. 2000; Navarro 2002; Liu 2007). This, to understate the matter, does not improve people's health.

There is a third reason, too. Life is hard on the poor. The persistent stresses they face cause their bodies to wear out faster (Spector 2007). The rich find life better. They have fewer problems and more resources to deal with the ones they have. This gives them a sense of control over their lives, a source of both physical and mental health.

## Mental Health

From the 1930s until now, sociologists have found that the mental health of the lower classes is worse than that of the higher classes (Faris and Dunham 1939; Srole et al. 1978; Pratt et al. 2007). Greater mental problems are part of the higher stress that accompanies poverty. Compared with middle- and upper-class Americans, the poor have less job security and lower wages. They are more likely to divorce, to be the victims of crime, and to have more physical illnesses. Couple these conditions with bill collectors and the threat of eviction, and you can see how they can deal severe blows to people's emotional well-being.

People higher up the social class ladder experience stress in daily life, of course, but their stress is generally less, and their coping resources are greater. Not only can they afford vacations, psychiatrists, and counselors but also *their class position gives them greater control over their lives, a key to good mental health.*

As is starkly evident from the following Thinking Critically section, social class is also important when it comes to the medical care people receive for their mental problems.

# ThinkingCRITICALLY

## Mental Illness and Inequality in Medical Care

Standing among the police, I watched as the elderly naked man, looking confused, struggled to put on his clothing. The man had ripped the wires out of the homeless shelter's main electrical box and then led the police on a merry chase as he ran from room to room.

I asked the officers where they were going to take the man, and they replied, "To Malcolm Bliss" (the state hospital). When I commented, "I guess he'll be in there for quite a while," they said, "Probably just a day or two. We picked him up last week—he was crawling under cars at a traffic light—and they let him out in two days."

The police explained that the man must be a danger to himself or to others to be admitted as a long-term patient. Visualizing this old man crawling under cars in traffic and thinking about the possibility of electrocution as he ripped out electrical wires with his bare hands, I marveled at the definition of "danger" that the hospital psychiatrists must be using.

Stripped of its veil, the two-tier system of medical care is readily visible. The poor—such as this confused naked man—find it difficult to get into mental hospitals. If they are admitted, they are sent to the dreaded state hospitals. In contrast, private hospitals serve the wealthy and those who have good insurance. The rich are likely to be treated with "talk therapy" (forms of psychotherapy), the poor with "drug therapy" (tranquilizers to make them docile, sometimes called "medicinal straitjackets").

## For Your Consideration

How can we improve the treatment of the mentally ill poor? Take into consideration that the public does not want higher taxes. What about the more fundamental issue—that of inequality in health care? Should medical care be a commodity that is sold to those who can afford it? Or do all citizens possess a fundamental right to high-quality health care?

## Family Life

Social class also plays a significant role in family life. It even affects our choice of spouse, our chances of getting divorced, and how we rear our children.

**Choice of Husband or Wife**    Members of the capitalist class place strong emphasis on family tradition. They stress the family's ancestors, history, and even a sense of purpose or destiny in life (Baltzell 1979; Aldrich 1989). Children of this class learn that their choice of husband or wife affects not just them but also the entire family, that their spouse will have an impact on the "family line." Because of these background expectations, the field of "eligible" marriage partners is much narrower than it is for the children of any other social class. As a result, parents in this class play a strong role in their children's mate selection.

**Divorce**    The more difficult life of the lower social classes, especially the many tensions that come from insecure jobs and inadequate incomes, leads to higher marital friction and a greater likelihood of divorce. Consequently, children of the poor are more likely to grow up in broken homes.

## Education

As we saw in Figure 8.5 on page 207, education increases as one goes up the social class ladder. It is not just the amount of education that changes, but also the type of education. Children of the capitalist class bypass public schools. They attend exclusive private schools where they are trained to take a commanding role in society. Prep schools such as Phillips Exeter Academy, Groton School, and Woodberry Forest School teach upper-class values and prepare their students for prestigious universities (Cookson and Persell 2005; Beeghley 2008).

Keenly aware that private schools can be a key to upward social mobility, some upper-middle-class parents do their best to get their children into the prestigious preschools that feed into these exclusive prep schools. Although some preschools cost $23,000 a year, they have a waiting list (Rohwedder 2007). Parents even get letters of recommendation for their 2- and 3-year-olds. Such parental expectations and resources are major reasons why children from the more privileged classes are more likely to go to college—and to graduate.

## Religion

One area of social life that we might think would not be affected by social class is religion. ("People are just religious, or they are not. What does social class have to do with it?") As we shall see in Chapter 13, however, the classes tend to cluster in different denominations. Episcopalians, for example, are more likely to attract the middle and upper classes, while Baptists draw heavily from the lower classes. Patterns of worship also follow class lines: The lower classes are attracted to more expressive worship services and louder music, while the middle and upper classes prefer more "subdued" worship.

## Politics

As I have stressed throughout this text, people perceive events from their own corner in life. Political views are no exception to this symbolic interactionist principle, and the rich and the poor walk different political paths. The higher that people are on the social class ladder, the more likely they are to vote for Republicans (Burris 2005). In contrast, most members of the working class believe that the government should intervene in the economy to provide jobs and to make citizens financially secure. They are more likely to vote for Democrats. Although the working class is more liberal on *economic* issues (policies that increase government spending), it is more conservative on *social* issues (such as opposing abortion and the Equal Rights Amendment) (Lipset 1959; Houtman 1995). People toward the bottom of the class structure are also less likely to be politically active—to campaign for candidates or even to vote (Soss 1999; Gilbert 2003; Beeghley 2008).

## Crime and Criminal Justice

If justice is supposed to be blind, it certainly is not when it comes to one's chances of being arrested (Henslin 2008). In Chapter 6 (pages 153–155), we discussed how the upper and lower social classes have different styles of crime. The white-collar crimes of the more privileged classes are more likely to be dealt with outside the criminal justice system, while the police and courts deal with the street crimes of the lower classes. One consequence of this class standard is that members of the lower classes are more likely to be in prison, on probation, or on parole. In addition, since people tend to commit crimes in or near their own neighborhoods, the lower classes are more likely to be robbed, burglarized, or murdered.

# Social Mobility

No aspect of life, then—from marriage to politics—goes untouched by social class. Because life is so much more satisfying in the more privileged classes, people strive to climb the social class ladder. What affects their chances?

## Three Types of Social Mobility

There are three basic types of social mobility: intergenerational, structural, and exchange. **Intergenerational mobility** refers to a change that occurs between generations—when grown-up children end up on a different rung of the social class ladder from the one occupied by their parents. If the child of someone who sells used cars graduates from college and buys a Saturn dealership, that person experiences **upward social mobility.** Conversely, if a child of the dealership's owner parties too much, drops out of college, and ends up selling cars, he or she experiences **downward social mobility.** As discussed in the Cultural Diversity box on the next page, social mobility comes at a cost.

We like to think that individual efforts are the reason people move up the class ladder—and their faults the reason they move down. In these examples, we can identify hard work, sacrifice, and ambition on the one hand versus indolence and substance abuse on the other. Although individual factors such as these do underlie social mobility, sociologists consider **structural mobility** to be the crucial factor. This second basic type of mobility refers to changes in society that cause large numbers of people to move up or down the class ladder.

To better understand structural mobility, think of how opportunities opened when computers were invented. New types of jobs appeared overnight. Huge numbers of

The term *structural mobility* refers to changes in society that push large numbers of people either up or down the social class ladder. A remarkable example was the stock market crash of 1929, when tens of thousands of people suddenly lost immense amounts of wealth. People who once "had it made" found themselves standing on street corners selling apples or, as depicted here, selling their possessions at fire-sale prices.

# *Cultural Diversity in the United States*

## Social Class and the Upward Social Mobility of African Americans

The overview of social class presented in this chapter doesn't apply equally to all the groups that make up U.S. society. Consider geography: What constitutes the upper class of a town of 5,000 people will be quite different from that of a city of a million. The extremes of wealth and the diversity and prestige of occupations will be less in the small town, where family background and local reputation play a significant role.

So, too, there are differences within racial–ethnic groups. While all racial–ethnic groups are marked by divisions of social class, what constitutes a particular social class can differ from one group to another—as well as from one historical period to another. Consider social class among African Americans (Cole and Omari 2003).

The earliest class divisions can be traced to slavery—to slaves who worked in the fields and those who worked in the "big house." Those who worked in the plantation home were exposed to more "genteel" manners and forms of speech. Their more privileged position—which brought with it better food and clothing, as well as lighter work—was often based on skin color. Mulattos, lighter-skinned slaves, were often chosen for this more desirable work. One result was the development of a "mulatto elite," a segment of the slave population that, proud of its distinctiveness, distanced itself from the other slaves. At this time, there also were free blacks. Not only were they able to own property but some of them even owned black slaves.

After the War Between the States (as the Civil War is known in the South), these two groups, the mulatto elite and the free blacks, became the basis of an upper class. Proud of their earlier status, they distanced them-selves from other blacks. From these groups came most of the black professionals.

After World War II, just as with whites, the expansion of the black middle class opened access to a wider range of occupations and residential neighborhoods. Beginning about 1960, the numbers of African Americans who were middle class surged. Today, more than half of all African American adults work at white-collar jobs, with 22 percent working at the professional or manage-rial level (Beeghley 2008). African Americans who move up the social class ladder experience a hidden cost: They feel an uncomfortable distancing from their roots, a separation from significant others—parents, siblings, and childhood friends (hooks 2000). The upwardly mobile individual has entered a world unknown to those left behind.

Trying to straddle two worlds makes anyone uncomfortable. The dominant culture is demanding: Anyone entering its domain must leave the old ways behind. Beyond such changes as those of appearance and speech, which in themselves are challenging, there is the much deeper threat to the self. Social mobility exposes the individual to a world of different values, aspirations, and ways of viewing the world. Social mobility often brings not just more contact with whites but also a sense of depriva-tion. As whites become a primary reference group, racism, mostly subtle, lurks beneath the surface, poison-ing what should be easy interaction among people who respect one another. Awareness that one is still per-ceived as different, as "the other," engenders frustration, dissatisfaction, and, ultimately, cynicism.

### For Your Consideration

If you review the box on upward social mobility on page 76, you will find that Latinos face a similar situation. Why do you think this is? What connections do you see among upward mobility, frustration, and strong racial–ethnic identity? How do you think that the up-ward mobility of whites is different? Why?

people attended workshops and took crash courses, switching from blue-collar to white-collar work. Although individual effort certainly was involved—for some seized the opportunity while others did not—the underlying cause was a change in the *structure* of work. Consider the opposite—how opportunities disappear during a depression, which forces millions of people downward on the class ladder. In this instance, too, their changed status is due less to individual behavior than to *structural* changes in society.

The third type of social mobility, **exchange mobility,** occurs when large numbers of people move up and down the social class ladder, but, on balance, the proportions of the social classes remain about the same. Suppose that a million or so working-class people are trained in some new technology, and they move up the class ladder. Suppose also that because of a surge in imports, about a million skilled workers have to take lower-status jobs. Although millions of people change their social class, there is, in effect, an *exchange* among them. The net result more or less balances out, and the class system remains basically untouched.

## Women in Studies of Social Mobility

In classic studies, sociologists concluded that about half of sons passed their fathers on the social class ladder, about one-third stayed at the same level, and about one-sixth moved down (Blau and Duncan 1967; Featherman and Hauser 1978; Featherman 1979).

Feminists objected that it wasn't good science to focus on sons and ignore daughters (Davis and Robinson 1988). They also pointed out that it was wrong to assume that women had no social class position of their own, that wives should not simply be assigned the class of their husbands. The defense made by male sociologists of the time was that too few women were in the labor force to make a difference.

With the huge numbers of women now working for pay, more recent studies include women (Gofen 2007; Beeghley 2008). Sociologists Elizabeth Higginbotham and Lynn Weber (1992), for example, studied 200 women from working-class backgrounds who became professionals, managers, and administrators in Memphis. They found that almost without exception, the women's parents had encouraged them while they were still little girls to postpone marriage and get an education. This study confirms how important the family is in the socialization process. It also supports the observation that the primary entry to the upper middle class is a college education. At the same time, if there had not been a *structural* change in society, the millions of new positions that women occupy would not exist.

# Poverty

Many Americans find that the "limitless possibilities" on which the American dream is based are quite elusive. As illustrated in Figure 8.5 on page 207, the working poor and underclass together form about one-fifth of the U.S. population. This translates into a huge number, about 60 million people. Who are these people?

## Drawing the Poverty Line

To determine who is poor, the U.S. government draws a **poverty line.** This measure was set in the 1960s, when poor people were thought to spend about one-third of their incomes on food. On the basis of this assumption, each year the government computes a low-cost food budget and multiplies it by 3. Families whose incomes are less than this amount are classified as poor; those whose incomes are higher—even by a dollar—are determined to be "not poor."

**WIZARD OF ID**

By permission of Johnny Hart and Creators Syndicate.

This cartoon pinpoints the arbitrary nature of the poverty line. This almost makes me think that the creators of the Wizard of Id have been studying sociology.

This official measure of poverty is grossly inadequate. Poor people actually spend only about 20 percent of their incomes on food, so to determine a poverty line, we ought to multiply their food budget by 5 instead of 3 (Uchitelle 2001). No political party in power wants to do this, as redrawing the line in this way would make it appear that poverty increased under their watch. Another problem with the poverty line is that some mothers work outside the home and have to pay for child care, but they are treated the same as mothers who don't have this expense. The poverty line is also the same for everyone across the nation, even though the cost of living is much higher in New York than in Alabama. In addition, the government does not count food stamps as income.

That a change in the poverty line would instantly make millions of people poor—or take away their poverty— would be a laughable matter, if it weren't so serious. (The absurdity has not been lost on Parker and Hart, as you can see from their sarcastic cartoon on page 215.) Although this line is arbitrary, it is the official measure of poverty, and the government uses it to decide who will receive help and who will not. On the basis of this line, let's see who in the United States is poor. Before we do this, though, com-

pare your ideas of the poor with the myths explored in the Down-to-Earth Sociology box below.

## Who Are the Poor?

**Geography**    As you can see from the Social Map on page 217, the poor are not distributed evenly among the states. Notice the clustering of poverty in the South, a pattern that has prevailed for more than 150 years.

A second aspect of geography is also significant. About 59 million Americans live in rural areas. Of these, 9 million are poor. At 16 percent, the rate of poverty of rural Americans is higher than the national average of 13 percent. The rural poor are less likely to be single parents and more likely to be married and to have jobs. Compared with urban Americans, the rural poor are less educated, and the jobs available to them pay less than similar jobs in urban areas (Lichter and Crowley 2002; Arsneault 2006).

Geography, however, is not the main factor in poverty. The greatest predictors of poverty are race–ethnicity, education, and the sex of the person who heads the family. Let's look at these factors.

## *Down-to-Earth Sociology*
## Exploring Myths About the Poor

**Myth 1  Most poor people are lazy. They are poor because they do not want to work.** Half of the poor are either too old or too young to work: About 40 percent are under age 18, and another 10 percent are age 65 or older. About 30 percent of the working-age poor work at least half the year.

**Myth 2  Poor people are trapped in a cycle of poverty that few escape.** Long-term poverty is rare. Most poverty lasts less than a year (Lichter and Crowley 2002). Only 12 percent remain in poverty for five or more consecutive years (O'Hare 1996a). Most children who are born in poverty are *not* poor as adults (Ruggles 1989; Corcoran 2001).

**Myth 3  Most of the poor are African Americans and Latinos.** As shown in Figure 8.7, the poverty rates of African Americans and Latinos are much higher than the poverty rate of whites. Because there

are so many more whites in the U.S. population, however, *most of the poor are white.* Of the U.S. poor, about 56 percent are white, 20 percent African American, 20 percent Latino, and 1 percent Native American (*Statistical Abstract* 2008: Tables 36, 691).

**Myth 4  Most of the poor are single mothers and their children.** Although about 38 percent of the poor match this stereotype, 34 percent of the poor live in married-couple families, 22 percent live alone or with nonrelatives, and 6 percent live in other settings.

**Myth 5  Most of the poor live in the inner city.** This one is close to fact, as about 42 percent do live in the inner city. But 36 percent live in the suburbs, and 22 percent live in small towns and rural areas.

**Myth 6  The poor live on welfare.** This stereotype is far from reality. Only about 25 percent of the income of poor adults comes from welfare. About half comes from wages and pensions, and about 22 percent from Social Security.

*Sources:* Primarily O'Hare 1996a, 1996b, with other sources as indicated.

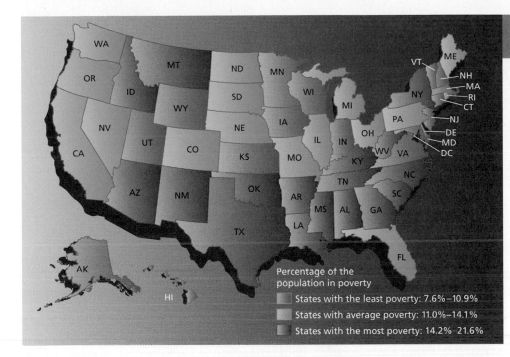

**FIGURE 8.6**
**Patterns of Poverty**

*Note:* Poverty varies tremendously from one state to another. In the extreme, poverty is about three times greater in Mississippi (21.6%) than in Connecticut and New Hampshire (7.6% each).
*Source:* By the author. Based on *Statistical Abstract of the United States* 2007:Table 690.

Percentage of the population in poverty

States with the least poverty: 7.6%–10.9%

States with average poverty: 11.0%–14.1%

States with the most poverty: 14.2%–21.6%

**Race–Ethnicity**    One of the strongest factors in poverty is race–ethnicity. As Figure 8.7 on the next page shows, only 11 percent of Asian Americans and whites are poor. In contrast, 22 percent of Latinos live in poverty, while the total jumps even higher, to 25 percent, for African Americans and Native Americans. The stereotype that most poor people are African Americans and Latinos is untrue. Because there are so many more whites in U.S. society, their much lower rate of poverty translates into larger numbers. As a result, most poor people are white.

**Education**    You are aware that education is a vital factor in poverty, but you may not know just how powerful it is. Figure 8.8 on the next page shows that 3 of 100 people who finish college end up in poverty, but 1 of every 4 people who drop out of high school is poor. As you can see, the chances that someone will be poor become less with each higher level of education. Although this principle applies regardless of race–ethnicity, this figure shows that at every level of education, race–ethnicity makes an impact.

**The Feminization of Poverty**    One of the best indicators of whether or not a family is poor is family structure. Families headed by both a mother and father are the least likely to be poor. Families headed by only a father or a mother are more likely to be poor, with poverty the most common among mother-headed families. The reason for this can be summed up in this one statistic: On average, women who head families earn only 70 percent of the income of men who head families (*Statistical Abstract* 2007:Table 679). With our high rate of divorce combined with our high

Beyond the awareness of most Americans are the rural poor, such as this family in Maine. This family is typical of the rural poor: white and headed by a woman. What do you think the future holds for these children?

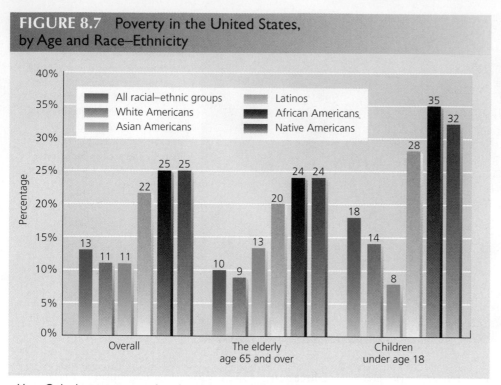

**FIGURE 8.7   Poverty in the United States, by Age and Race–Ethnicity**

*Note:* Only these groups are listed in the source. The poverty line on which this figure is based is $19,971 for a family of four.

*Source:* By the author. Based on *Statistical Abstract* 2005: Table 682; 2008: Tables 36, 658, 691.

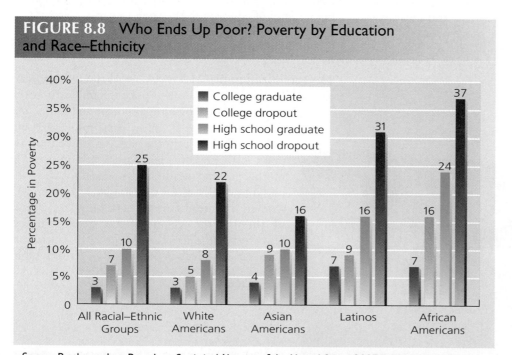

**FIGURE 8.8   Who Ends Up Poor? Poverty by Education and Race–Ethnicity**

*Source:* By the author. Based on *Statistical Abstract of the United States* 2007: Table 697.

number of births to single women, mother-headed families have become more common. This association of poverty with women has come to be known by sociologists as the **feminization of poverty.**

**Old Age**    As Figure 8.7 on page 218 shows, the elderly are *less* likely than the general population to be poor. This is quite a change. It used to be that growing old increased people's chances of being poor, but government policies to redistribute income—Social Security and subsidized housing, food, and medical care—slashed the rate of poverty among the elderly. This figure also shows how the prevailing racial–ethnic patterns carry over into old age. You can see how much more likely an elderly African American, Latino, or Native American is to be poor than an elderly white or Asian American.

## Children of Poverty

Children are more likely to live in poverty than are adults or the elderly. This holds true regardless of race–ethnicity, but from Figure 8.7 on page 218, you can see how much greater poverty is among Latino, African American, and Native American children. That millions of U.S. children are reared in poverty is shocking when one considers the wealth of this country and the supposed concern for the well-being of children. This tragic aspect of poverty is the topic of the following Thinking Critically section.

# ThinkingCRITICALLY

## The Nation's Shame:
## Children in Poverty

One of the most startling statistics in sociology is shown in Figure 8.7 on page 218. Look at the rate of childhood poverty: For Asian Americans, 1 of 12 children is poor; for whites, 1 of 7; for Latinos, 1 of 3 or 4; and for African Americans and Native Americans, an astounding 1 of 3. These percentages translate into incredible numbers—approximately *13 million* children live in poverty.

Why do so many U.S. children live in poverty? The main reason, said sociologist and former U.S. Senator Daniel Moynihan (1991), is an increase in births outside

marriage. In 1960, 1 of 20 U.S. children was born to a single woman. Today that total is about *seven times higher,* and single women now account for 1 of 3 (36 percent) of all U.S. births (*Statistical Abstract* 2007:Table 84). Sociologists Lee Rainwater and Timothy Smeeding (2003), who note that *the poverty rate of U.S. children is the highest in the industrialized world,* point to another cause: the lack of government support to children.

Births to single women follow patterns that are significant for their children's welfare. The less education a woman has, the more likely she is to bear children when she is not married. As you can see from Figure 8.9, births to single women drop with each gain in education. Because people with lower education earn less, this means that the single women who can least afford children are those most likely to give birth. Their children are likely to live in poverty and to face the suffering and obstacles to a satisfying life that poverty entails. They are more likely to die in infancy, to go hungry, to be malnourished, to develop more slowly, and to have more health problems. They also are more likely to drop out of school, to become involved in criminal activities, and to have children while still in their teens—thus perpetuating the cycle of poverty.

## For Your Consideration

With education so important to obtain jobs that pay better, in light of Figure 8.9, what programs would you suggest for helping women attain more education? Be specific and practical.

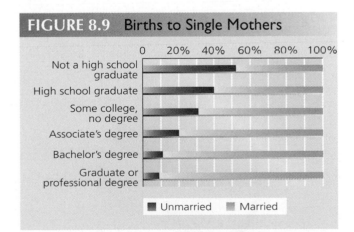

**FIGURE 8.9    Births to Single Mothers**

■ Unmarried  ■ Married

*Note:* Based on a national U.S. sample of all births in the preceding 12 months.

## The Dynamics of Poverty

Some have suggested that the poor tend to get trapped in a **culture of poverty** (Harrington 1962; Lewis 1966a). They assume that the values and behaviors of the poor "make them fundamentally different from other Americans, and that these factors are largely responsible for their continued long-term poverty" (Ruggles 1989:7).

Lurking behind this concept is the idea that the poor are lazy people who bring poverty on themselves. Certainly, some individuals and families match this stereotype—many of us have known them. But is a self-perpetuating culture—one that is transmitted across generations and that locks people in poverty—the basic reason for U.S. poverty?

Researchers who began following 5,000 U.S. families in 1968 uncovered some surprising findings. Contrary to common stereotypes, most poverty is short-lived, lasting only a year or less. The researchers found that most poverty comes about because of a dramatic life change such as divorce, the loss of a job, or even the birth of a child (O'Hare 1996a). As Figure 8.10 shows, only 12 percent of poverty lasts five years or longer. Contrary to the stereotype of lazy people content to live off the government, few poor people enjoy poverty—and they do what they can to avoid being poor.

Yet from one year to the next, the number of poor people remains about the same. This means that the people who move out of poverty are replaced by people who move *into* poverty. Most of these newly poor will also move out of poverty within a year. Some people even bounce back and forth, never quite making it securely out of poverty.

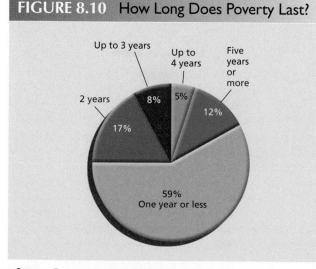

### FIGURE 8.10    How Long Does Poverty Last?

Up to 3 years
Up to 4 years
Five years or more
2 years
8%
5%
12%
17%
59%
One year or less

*Source:* Gottschalk et al. 1994:89.

Poverty, then, is dynamic, touching a lot more people than the official totals indicate. Although 13 percent of Americans may be poor at any one time, twice that number—about one-fourth of the U.S. population—is or has been poor for at least a year.

## Why Are People Poor?

Two explanations for poverty compete for our attention. The first, which sociologists prefer, focuses on *social structure.* Sociologists stress that *features of society* deny some people access to education or the learning of job skills. They emphasize racial–ethnic, age, and gender discrimination, as well as changes in the job market—the closing of plants, the elimination of unskilled jobs, and the increase in marginal jobs that pay poverty wages. In short, some people find their escape routes to a better life blocked.

A competing explanation focuses on the *characteristics of individuals* that are assumed to contribute to poverty. Sociologists reject individualistic explanations such as laziness and lack of intelligence, viewing these as worthless stereotypes. Individualistic explanations that sociologists reluctantly acknowledge include dropping out of school, bearing children in the teen years, and averaging more children than women in the other social classes. Most sociologists are reluctant to speak of such factors in this context, for they appear to blame the victim, something that sociologists bend over backward not to do.

## Welfare Reform

After decades of criticism, the U.S. welfare system was restructured in 1996. A federal law—the Personal Responsibility and Work Opportunity Reconciliation Act—requires states to place a lifetime cap on welfare assistance and compels welfare recipients to look for work and to take available jobs. The maximum length of time that someone can collect welfare is five years. In some states, it is less. Unmarried teen parents must attend school and live at home or in some other adult-supervised setting.

This law set off a storm of criticism. Some called it an attack on the poor. Defenders replied that the new rules would rescue people from poverty. They would transform welfare recipients into self-supporting and hard-working citizens—and reduce welfare costs. National welfare rolls plummeted, dropping by about 60 percent (Urban Institute 2006). Two out of five who left welfare also moved out of poverty (Hofferth 2002).

This is only the rosy part of the picture, however. Three of five are still in poverty or are back on welfare. A third of those who were forced off welfare have no jobs (Hage

A society's dominant ideologies are reinforced throughout the society, including its literature. Horatio Alger provided inspirational heroes for thousands of boys. The central theme of these many novels, immensely popular in their time, was rags to riches. Through rugged determination and self-sacrifice, a boy could overcome seemingly insurmountable obstacles to reach the pinnacle of success. (Girls did not strive for financial success, but were dependent on fathers and husbands.)

2004; Urban Institute 2006). Some can't work because they have health problems. Others lack transportation. Some are addicted to drugs and alcohol. Still others are trapped in economically depressed communities where there are no jobs. Then there are those who have jobs, but earn so little that they remain in poverty. Consider one of the "success stories":

> JoAnne Sims, 37, lives in Erie, New York, with her 7-year-old daughter Jamine. JoAnne left welfare, and now earns $7.25 an hour as a cook for Head Start. Her 37-hour week brings $268 before deductions. With the help of medical benefits and a mother who provides child care, JoAnne "gets by." She says, "From what I hear, a lot of us who went off welfare are still poor . . . let me tell you, it's not easy." (Peterson 2000; earnings updated)

Conflict theorists have an interesting interpretation of welfare. They say that the purpose of welfare is not to help people, but, rather, to maintain a *reserve labor force.* It is designed to keep the unemployed alive during economic downturns until they are needed during the next economic boom. The 1996 law that reduced the welfare rolls fits this model, as it was passed during the longest economic boom in U.S. history. Recessions are inevitable, however, and just as inevitable is surging unemployment. In line with conflict theory, we can predict that during the coming recession, welfare rules will be softened—in order to keep the reserve labor force ready for the next time they are needed.

## Where Is Horatio Alger? The Social Functions of a Myth

In the late 1800s, Horatio Alger was one of the country's most popular authors. The rags-to-riches exploits of his fictional boy heroes and their amazing successes in overcoming severe odds motivated thousands of boys of that period. Although Alger's characters have disappeared from U.S. literature, they remain alive and well in the psyche of Americans. From real-life examples of people of humble origin who climbed the social class ladder, Americans know that anyone who really tries can get ahead. In fact, they believe that most Americans, including minorities and the working poor, have an average or better-than-average chance of getting ahead—obviously a statistical impossibility (Kluegel and Smith 1986).

The accuracy of the **Horatio Alger myth** is less important than the belief that limitless possibilities exist for everyone. Functionalists would stress that this belief is functional for society. On the one hand, it encourages people to compete for higher positions or, as the song says, "to reach for the highest star." On the other hand, it places blame for failure squarely on the individual. If you don't make it—in the face of ample opportunities to get ahead—the fault must be your own. The Horatio Alger myth helps to stabilize society: Since the fault is viewed as the individual's, not society's, current social arrangements can be regarded as satisfactory. This reduces pressures to change the system.

As Marx and Weber pointed out, social class penetrates our consciousness, shaping our ideas of life and our "proper" place in society. When the rich look at the world around them, they sense superiority and anticipate control over their own destiny. When the poor look around them, they are more likely to sense defeat and to anticipate that unpredictable forces will batter their lives. Both rich and poor know the dominant ideology, that their particular niche in life is due to their own efforts, that the reasons for success—or failure—lie solely with the self. Like fish that don't notice the water, people tend not to perceive the effects of social class on their own lives.

# SUMMARY *and* REVIEW

## What Is Social Class?

### What is meant by the term social class?

Most sociologists have adopted Weber's definition of **social class:** a large group of people who rank closely to one another in terms of property (wealth), power, and prestige. **Wealth**—consisting of the value of property and income—is concentrated in the upper classes. From the 1930s to the 1970s, the trend in the distribution of wealth in the United States was toward greater equality. Since that time, it has been toward greater inequality. Pp. 198–201.

**Power** is the ability to get one's way even though others resist. C. Wright Mills coined the term **power elite** to refer to the small group that holds the reins of power in business, government, and the military. **Prestige** is linked to occupational status. People's rankings of occupational prestige have changed little over the decades and are similar from country to country. Globally, the occupations that bring greater prestige are those that pay more, require more education and abstract thought, and offer greater independence. Pp. 201–204.

### What is meant by the term status inconsistency?

**Status** is social position. Most people are **status consistent;** that is, they rank high or low on all three dimensions of social class. People who rank higher on some dimensions than on others are status inconsistent. The frustrations of **status inconsistency** tend to produce political radicalism. Pp. 204–205.

## Sociological Models of Social Class

### What models are used to portray the social classes?

Erik Wright developed a four-class model based on Marx: (1) capitalists (owners of large businesses), (2) petty bourgeoisie (small business owners), (3) managers, and (4) workers. Kahl and Gilbert developed a six-class model based on Weber. At the top is the capitalist class. In descending order are the upper middle class, the lower middle class, the working class, the working poor, and the **underclass.** Pp. 205–210.

## Consequences of Social Class

### How does social class affect people's lives?

Social class leaves no aspect of life untouched. It affects our chances of dying early, becoming ill, receiving good health care, and getting divorced. Social class membership also affects educational attainment, religious affiliation, political participation, the crimes people commit, and contact with the criminal justice system. Pp. 210–213.

## Social Mobility

### What are three types of social mobility?

The term **intergenerational mobility** refers to changes in social class from one generation to the next. **Structural mobility** refers to changes in society that lead large numbers of people to change their social class. **Exchange mobility** is the movement of large numbers of people from one class to another, with the net result that the relative proportions of the population in the classes remain about the same. Pp. 213–215.

## Poverty

### Who are the poor?

Poverty is unequally distributed in the United States. Racial–ethnic minorities (except Asian Americans), children, women-headed households, and rural Americans are more likely than others to be poor. The poverty rate of the elderly is less than that of the general population. Pp. 215–220.

### Why are people poor?

Some social analysts believe that characteristics of *individuals* cause poverty. Sociologists, in contrast, examine *structural* features of society, such as employment opportunities, to find the causes of poverty. Sociologists generally conclude that life orientations are a consequence, not the cause, of people's position in the social class structure. Pp. 220–221.

### How is the Horatio Alger myth functional for society?

The **Horatio Alger myth**—the belief that anyone can get ahead if only he or she tries hard enough—encourages people to strive to get ahead. It also deflects blame for failure from society to the individual. P. 221.

# THINKING CRITICALLY *about* Chapter 8

1. The belief that the United States is the land of opportunity draws millions of legal and illegal immigrants to the United States each year. How do the materials in this chapter support or undermine this belief?

2. How does social class affect people's lives?

3. What social mobility has your own family experienced? In what ways has this affected your life?

# BY THE NUMBERS: Changes Over Time

- Percentage of the nation's income received by the richest 20% of Americans in 1970: **41%**
- Percentage of the nation's income received by the richest 20% of Americans today: **50%**
- Percentage of the nation's income received by the poorest 20% of Americans in 1970: **6%**
- Percentage of the nation's income received by the poorest 20% of Americans today: **3%**
- Frequency of births outside of marriage in 1960: **1 in 20**
- Frequency of births outside of marriage today: **1 in 3**
- Amount that the national welfare rolls dropped from 1996 to today: **60%**

# ADDITIONAL RESOURCES

## What can you find in MySocLab? mysoclab www.mysoclab.com

- **Complete Ebook**
- **Practice Tests and Video and Audio activities**
- **Mapping and Data Analysis exercises**
- **Sociology in the News**
- **Classic Readings in Sociology**
- **Research and Writing advice**

## Where Can I Read More on This Topic?

Suggested readings for this chapter are listed at the back of this book.

# Race and Ethnicity

I magine that you are an African American man living in Macon County, Alabama, during the Great Depression of the 1930s. Your home is a little country shack with a dirt floor. You have no electricity or running water. You never finished grade school, and you make a living, such as it is, by doing odd jobs. You haven't been feeling too good lately, but you can't afford a doctor.

**You have just become part of one of the most callous experiments of all time.**

Then you hear the fantastic news. You rub your eyes in disbelief. It is just like winning the lottery! If you join *Miss Rivers' Lodge* (and it is free to join), you will get a lifetime of free physical examinations at Tuskegee University. You will even get free rides to and from the clinic, hot meals on examination days, and free treatment for minor ailments.

You eagerly join *Miss Rivers' Lodge*.

After your first physical examination, the doctor gives you the bad news. "You've got bad blood," he says. "That's why you've been feeling bad. Miss Rivers will give you some medicine and schedule you for your next exam. I've got to warn you, though. If you go to another doctor, there's no more free exams or medicine."

You can't afford another doctor anyway. You take your medicine and look forward to the next trip to the university.

What has really happened? You have just become part of what is surely slated to go down in history as one of the most callous experiments of all time, outside of the infamous World War II Nazi and Japanese experiments. With heartless disregard for human life, the U.S. Public Health Service told 399 African American men that they had joined a social club and burial society called "Miss Rivers' Lodge." What the men were *not* told was that they had syphilis. For forty years, the "Public Health Service" allowed these men to go without treatment for their syphilis—just "to see what would happen." There was even a control group of 201 men who were free of the disease (Jones 1993).

By the way, you do get one further benefit: a free autopsy to determine how syphilis ravaged your body.

# Laying the Sociological Foundation

As unlikely as it seems, this is a true story. It really did happen. Seldom do race and ethnic relations degenerate to this point, but reports of troubled race relations surprise none of us. Today's newspapers and TV news shows regularly report on racial problems. Sociology can contribute greatly to our understanding of this aspect of social life—and this chapter may be an eye-opener for you. To begin, let's consider to what extent race itself is a myth.

## Race: Myth and Reality

With its more than 6.5 billion people, the world offers a fascinating variety of human shapes and colors. People see one another as black, white, red, yellow, and brown. Eyes come in shades of blue, brown, and green. Lips are thick and thin. Hair is straight, curly, kinky, black, blonde, and red—and, of course, all shades of brown.

As humans spread throughout the world, their adaptations to diverse climates and other living conditions resulted in this profusion of complexions, hair textures and colors, eye hues, and other physical variations. Genetic mutations added distinct characteristics to the peoples of the globe. In this sense, the concept of **race**—a group of people with inherited physical characteristics that distinguish it from another group—is a reality. Humans do, indeed, come in a variety of colors and shapes.

In two senses, however, race is a myth, a fabrication of the human mind. The *first* myth is the idea that any race is superior to others. All races have their geniuses—and their idiots. As with language, no race is superior to another.

Ideas of racial superiority abound, however. They are not only false but also dangerous. Adolf Hitler, for example, believed that the Aryans were a superior race, responsible for the cultural achievements of Europe. The Aryans, he said, were destined to establish a superior culture and usher in a new world order. This destiny required them to avoid the "racial contamination" that would come from breeding with inferior races; therefore, it was necessary to isolate or destroy races that threatened Aryan purity and culture.

Put into practice, Hitler's views left an appalling legacy—the Nazi slaughter of those they deemed inferior: Jews, Slavs, gypsies, homosexuals, and people with mental and physical disabilities. Horrific images of gas ovens and emaciated bodies stacked like cordwood haunted the world's nations. At Nuremberg, the Allies, flush with victory, put the top Nazis on trial, exposing their heinous deeds to a shocked world. Their public executions, everyone assumed, marked the end of such grisly acts.

Obviously, they didn't. In the summer of 1994 in Rwanda, Hutus slaughtered about 800,000 Tutsis—mostly with machetes (Cowell 2006). A few years later, the Serbs in Bosnia massacred Muslims, giving us the new term "ethnic cleansing." As these events sadly attest, **genocide,** the attempt to destroy a group of people because of their presumed race or ethnicity, remains alive

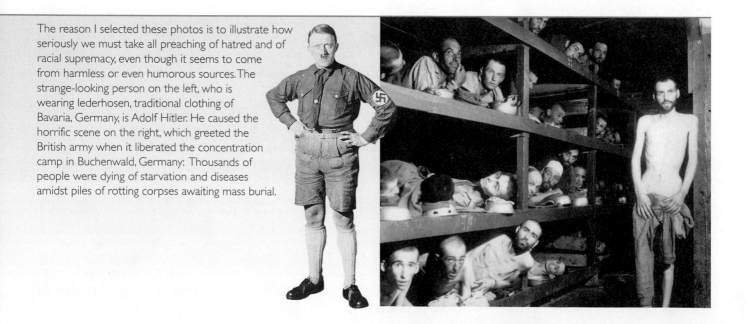

The reason I selected these photos is to illustrate how seriously we must take all preaching of hatred and of racial supremacy, even though it seems to come from harmless or even humorous sources. The strange-looking person on the left, who is wearing lederhosen, traditional clothing of Bavaria, Germany, is Adolf Hitler. He caused the horrific scene on the right, which greeted the British army when it liberated the concentration camp in Buchenwald, Germany: Thousands of people were dying of starvation and diseases amidst piles of rotting corpses awaiting mass burial.

and well. Although more recent killings are not accompanied by swastikas and gas ovens, the perpetrators' goal is the same.

The *second* myth is that "pure" races exist. Humans show such a mixture of physical characteristics—in skin color, hair texture, nose shape, head shape, eye color, and so on—that there are no "pure" races. Instead of falling into distinct types that are clearly separate from one another, human characteristics flow endlessly together. The mapping of the human genome system shows that humans are strikingly homogenous, that so-called racial groups differ from one another only once in a thousand subunits of the genome (Angler 2000). Humans, then, vary from one another in only very slight ways. As you can see from the example of Tiger Woods, discussed in the Cultural Diversity box on the next page, these minute gradations make any attempt to draw lines of race purely arbitrary.

Although large groupings of people can be classified by blood type and gene frequencies, these classifications do not uncover "race." Rather, race is so arbitrary that biologists and anthropologists cannot even agree on how many "races" there are. Ashley Montagu (1964, 1999), a physical anthropologist, pointed out that some scientists have classified humans into only two "races," while others have found as many as two thousand. Montagu (1960) himself classified humans into forty "racial" groups. As the Down-to-Earth Sociology box on page 230 illustrates, even a plane ride can change someone's race!

The *idea* of race, of course, is far from a myth. Firmly embedded in our culture, it is a powerful force in our everyday lives. That no race is superior and that even biologists cannot decide how people should be classified into races is not what counts. "I know what I see, and you can't tell me any different" seems to be the common attitude. As was noted in Chapter 4, sociologists W. I. and D. S. Thomas (1928) observed that "If people define situations as real, they are real in their consequences." In other words, people act on beliefs, not facts. As a result, we will always have people like Hitler and, as illustrated in our opening vignette, officials like those in the U.S. Public Health Service who

Humans show such remarkable diversity that, as the text explains, there are no pure races. Shown here are Verne Troyer, who weighs about 45 pounds and is 2 feet 8 inches short, and Yao Ming, who weighs 296 pounds and is 7 feet 5 inches tall.

thought that it was fine to experiment with people whom they deemed inferior. While few people hold such extreme views, most people appear to be ethnocentric enough to believe that their own race is—at least just a little—superior to others.

## Ethnic Groups

In contrast to *race,* which people use to refer to supposed biological characteristics that distinguish one group of people from another, **ethnicity** and **ethnic** refer to cultural characteristics. Derived from the word *ethnos* (a Greek word meaning "people" or "nation"), *ethnicity* and *ethnic* refer to people who identify with one another on the basis of common ancestry and cultural heritage. Their sense of belonging may center on their nation or region of origin, distinctive foods, clothing, language, music, religion, or family names and relationships.

People often confuse the terms *race* and *ethnic group.* For example, many people, including many Jews, consider Jews a race. Jews, however, are more properly considered an ethnic group, for it is their cultural characteristics, especially their religion, that bind them together. Wherever Jews have lived in the world, they have intermarried. Consequently, Jews in China may have Chinese features, while some Swedish Jews are blue-eyed blonds. The confusion of race and ethnicity is illustrated in the photo on page 229.

## Minority Groups and Dominant Groups

Sociologist Louis Wirth (1945) defined a **minority group** as people who are singled out for unequal treatment and who regard themselves as objects of collective discrimination. Worldwide, minorities share several conditions: Their physical or cultural traits are held in low esteem by the dominant group, which treats them unfairly, and they tend to marry within their own group (Wagley and Harris 1958). These conditions tend to create a sense of identity among minorities (a feeling of "we-ness"). In many instances, a sense of common destiny emerges (Chandra 1993b).

# Cultural Diversity in the United States

## Tiger Woods: Mapping the Changing Ethnic Terrain

Tiger Woods, perhaps the top golfer of all time, calls himself Cablinasian. Woods invented this term as a boy to try to explain to himself just who he was—a combination of Caucasian, Black, Indian, and Asian (Leland and Beals 1997; Hall 2001). Woods wants to embrace all sides of his family.

Like many of us, Tiger Woods' heritage is difficult to specify. Analysts who like to quantify ethnic heritage put Woods at one-quarter Thai, one-quarter Chinese, one-quarter white, an eighth Native American, and an eighth African American. From this chapter, you know how ridiculous such computations are, but the sociological question is why many people consider Tiger Woods an African American. The U.S. racial scene is indeed complex, but a good part of the reason is simply that this is the label the media placed on him. "Everyone has to fit somewhere" seems to be our attitude. If they don't, we grow uncomfortable. And for Tiger Woods, the media chose African American.

The United States once had a firm "color line"— barriers between racial–ethnic groups that you didn't dare cross, especially in dating or marriage. This invisible barrier has broken down, and today such marriages are common (*Statistical Abstract* 2007: Table 58). Several campuses have interracial student organizations. Harvard has two, one just for students who have one African American parent (Leland and Beals 1997).

As we march into unfamiliar ethnic terrain, our classifications are bursting at the seams. Consider how Kwame Anthony Appiah, of Harvard's Philosophy and Afro-American Studies Departments, described his situation:

"My mother is English; my father is Ghanaian. My sisters are married to a Nigerian and a Norwegian. I have nephews who range from blond-haired kids to very black kids. They are all first cousins. Now according to the American scheme of things, they're all black—even the guy with blond hair who skis in Oslo." (Wright 1994)

I marvel at what racial experts the U.S. census takers once were. When they took the census, which is done

*Tiger Woods as he answers questions at a news conference.*

every ten years, they looked at people and assigned them a race. At various points, the census contained these categories: mulatto, quadroon, octoroon, Negro, black, Mexican, white, Indian, Filipino, Japanese, Chinese, and Hindu. Quadroon (one-fourth black and three-fourths white) and octoroon (one-eighth black and seven-eighths white) proved too difficult to "measure," and these categories were used only in 1890. Mulatto appeared in the 1850 census, but disappeared in 1930. The Mexican government complained about Mexicans being treated as a race, and this category was used only in 1930. I don't know whose strange idea it was to make Hindu a race, but it lasted for three censuses, from 1920 to 1940 (Bean et al. 2004; Tafoya et al. 2005).

Continuing to reflect changing ideas about race—ethnicity, censuses have become flexible, and we now have a lot of choices. In the 2000 census, we were first asked to declare whether we were or were not "Spanish/Hispanic/ Latino." After this, we were asked to check "one or more races" that we "consider ourselves to be." We could choose from White; Black, African American, or Negro; American Indian or Alaska Native; Asian Indian, Chinese, Filipino, Japanese, Korean, Vietnamese, Native Hawaiian, Guamanian or Chamorro, Samoan, and other Pacific Islander. If these didn't do it, we could check a box called "Some Other Race" and then write whatever we wanted.

Perhaps the census should list Cablinasian, after all. There should also be ANGEL for African-Norwegian-German-English-Latino Americans, DEVIL for those of Danish-English-Vietnamese-Italian-Lebanese descent, and STUDY for Swedish-Turkish-Uruguayan-Djibouti-Yugoslavian Americans. As you read farther in this chapter, you will see why these terms make as much sense as the categories we currently use.

### For Your Consideration

Just why do we count people by "race" anyway? Why not eliminate race from the U.S. census? (Race became a factor in 1790 during the first census. To determine the number of representatives from each state, slaves were counted as three-fifths of whites!) Why is race so important to some people? Perhaps you can use the materials in this chapter to answer these questions.

Surprisingly, a minority group is not necessarily a *numerical* minority. For example, before India's independence in 1947, a handful of British colonial rulers dominated tens of millions of Indians. Similarly, when South Africa practiced apartheid, a smaller group of Dutch discriminated against a much larger number of blacks. And all over the world, females are a minority group. Accordingly, sociologists usually refer to those who do the discriminating not as the *majority,* but, rather, as the **dominant group,** for they have the greater power, privileges, and social status.

Possessing political power and unified by shared physical and cultural traits, the dominant group uses its position to discriminate against those with different—and supposedly inferior—traits. The dominant group considers its privileged position to be the result of its own innate superiority.

**Emergence of Minority Groups**    A group becomes a minority in one of two ways. The *first* is through the expansion of political boundaries. With the exception of females, tribal societies contain no minority groups. Everyone shares the same culture, including the same language, and belongs to the same group. When a group expands its political boundaries, however, it produces minority groups if it incorporates people with different customs, languages, values, and physical characteristics into the same political entity and discriminates against

them. For example, after defeating Mexico in war in 1848, the United States took over the Southwest. The Mexicans living there, who had been the dominant group prior to the war, were transformed into a minority group, a master status that has influenced their lives ever since. Referring to his ancestors, one Latino said, "We didn't move across the border—the border moved across us."

A *second* way in which a group becomes a minority is by migration. This can be voluntary, as with the millions of people who have chosen to move from Mexico to the United States, or involuntary, as with the millions of Africans who were brought in chains to the United States. (The way females became a minority group represents a third way, but, as discussed in the previous chapter, no one knows just how this occurred.)

## How People Construct Their Racial–Ethnic Identity

Some of us have a greater sense of ethnicity than others. Some of us feel firm boundaries between "us" and "them." Others have assimilated so extensively into the mainstream culture that they are only vaguely aware of their ethnic origins. With interethnic marrying common, some do not even know the countries from which their families originated—nor do they care. If asked to identify themselves ethnically, they respond

This photo illustrates the difficulty that assumptions about *race* and *ethnicity* posed for Israel. These Ethiopian Jews, shown here as they arrived in Israel, looked so different from other Jews that it took several years for Israeli authorities to acknowledge this group's "true Jewishness."

# Down-to-Earth Sociology
## Can a Plane Ride Change Your Race?

At the beginning of this text (pages 20–21), I mentioned that common sense and sociology often differ. This is especially so when it comes to race. According to common sense, our racial classifications represent biological differences between people. Sociologists, in contrast, stress that what we call races are *social* classifications, not biological categories.

Sociologists point out that *our "race" depends more on the society in which we live than on our biological characteristics.* For example, the racial categories common in the United States are merely one of *numerous* ways by which people around the world classify physical appearances. Although various groups use different categories, each group assumes that its categories are natural, merely a response to visible biology.

To better understand this essential sociological point—that race is more social than it is biological—consider this: In the United States, children born to the same parents are all of the same race. "What could be more natural?" Americans assume. But in Brazil, children born to the same parents may be of different races—if their appearances differ. "What could be more natural?" assume Brazilians.

Consider how Americans usually classify a child born to a "black" mother and a "white" father. Why do they usually say that the child is "black"? Wouldn't it be equally as logical to classify the child as "white"? Similarly, if a child has one grandmother who is "black," but all her other ancestors are "white," the child is often considered "black." Yet she has much more "white blood" than "black blood." Why, then, is she considered "black"? Certainly not because of biology. Rather, such thinking is a legacy of slavery. In an attempt to preserve the "purity" of their "race" in the face of numerous children whose fathers were white slave masters and whose mothers were black slaves, whites classified anyone with even a "drop of black blood" as black. This was actually known as the "one-drop" rule.

*What "race" are these two Brazillions? Is the child of a different "race" than the mother? The text explains why "race" is such an unreliable concept that it changes even with geography.*

*Even a plane trip can change a person's race.* In the city of Salvador in Brazil, people classify one another by color of skin and eyes, breadth of nose and lips, and color and curliness of hair. They use at least seven terms for what we call white and black. Consider again a U.S. child who has "white" and "black" parents. If she flies to Brazil, she is no longer "black"; she now belongs to one of their several "whiter" categories (Fish 1995).

If the girl makes such a flight, would her "race" actually change? Our common sense revolts at this, I know, but it actually would. We want to argue that because her biological characteristics remain unchanged, her race remains unchanged. This is because we think of race as biological, when *race is actually a label we use to describe perceived biological characteristics.* Simply put, the race we "are" depends on our social location—on who is doing the classifying.

"Racial" classifications are also fluid, not fixed. You can see change occurring even now in the classifications that are used in the United States. The category "multiracial," for example, indicates changing thought and perception.

## For Your Consideration

How would you explain to "Joe and Suzie Six-Pack" that race is more a social classification than a biological one? Can you come up with any arguments to refute this statement? How do you think our racial–ethnic categories will change in the future?

with something like "I'm Heinz 57—German and Irish, with a little Italian and French thrown in—and I think someone said something about being one-sixteenth Indian, too."

Why do some people feel an intense sense of ethnic identity, while others feel hardly any? Figure 9.1 portrays four factors, identified by sociologist Ashley Doane, that heighten or reduce our sense of ethnic identity. From this figure, you can see that the keys are relative size, power, appearance, and discrimination. If your group is relatively small, has little power, looks different from most people in society, and is an object of discrimination, you will have a heightened sense of ethnic identity. In contrast, if you belong to the dominant group that holds most of the power, look like most people in the society, and feel no discrimination, you are likely to experience a sense of "belonging"—and to wonder why ethnic identity is such a big deal.

We can use the term **ethnic work** to refer to the way people construct their ethnicity. For people who have a strong ethnic identity, this term refers to how they enhance and maintain their group's distinctions—from clothing, food, and language to religious practices and holidays. For people whose ethnic identity is not as firm, it refers to attempts to recover their ethnic heritage, such as trying to trace family lines or visiting the country or region of their family's origin. As illustrated by the photo essay on the next page, many Americans are engaged in ethnic work. This has confounded the experts who thought that the United States would be a **melting pot,** with most of its groups blending into a sort of ethnic stew. Because so many Americans have become fascinated with their "roots," some analysts have suggested that "tossed salad" is a more appropriate term than "melting pot."

# Prejudice and Discrimination

With prejudice and discrimination so significant in social life, let's consider the origin of prejudice and the extent of discrimination.

## Learning Prejudice

**Distinguishing Between Prejudice and Discrimination**
Prejudice and discrimination are common throughout the world. In Mexico, Hispanic Mexicans discriminate against Native American Mexicans; in Israel, Ashkenazi Jews, primarily of European descent, discriminate against Sephardi Jews from the Muslim world. In some places, the elderly discriminate against the young; in others, the young discriminate against the elderly. And all around the world, men discriminate against women.

**Discrimination** is an *action*—unfair treatment directed against someone. Discrimination can be based on many characteristics: age, sex, height, weight, skin color, clothing, income, education, marital status, sexual orientation, disease, disability, religion, and politics. When the basis of discrimination is someone's perception of race, it is known as **racism.** Discrimination is often the result of an *attitude* called **prejudice**—a prejudging of some sort, usually in a negative way. There is also *positive prejudice*, which exaggerates the virtues of a group, as when people think that some group (usually their own) is more capable than others. Most prejudice, however, is negative and involves prejudging a group as inferior.

**Learning from Association**   As with our other attitudes, we are not born with prejudice. Rather, we learn prejudice from the people around us. In a fascinating study, sociologist Kathleen Blee (2005) interviewed women who were members of the KKK and Aryan Nations. Her first finding is of the "ho hum" variety: Most women were recruited by someone who already belonged to the group. Blee's second finding, however, holds a surprise: Some women learned to be racists *after* they joined the group. They were attracted to the group not because it matched their racist beliefs but because someone they liked belonged to it. Blee found that their racism was not the *cause* of their joining but, rather, the *result* of their membership.

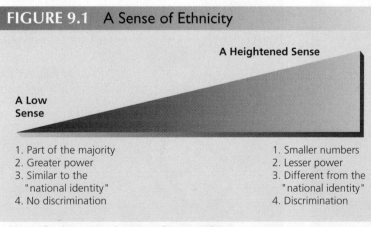

## FIGURE 9.1   A Sense of Ethnicity

A Heightened Sense

A Low Sense

| 1. Part of the majority | 1. Smaller numbers |
| 2. Greater power | 2. Lesser power |
| 3. Similar to the "national identity" | 3. Different from the "national identity" |
| 4. No discrimination | 4. Discrimination |

*Source:* By the author. Based on Doane 1997.

# Ethnic Work

## Explorations in Cultural Identity

**Ethnic work** refers to the ways that people establish, maintain, protect, and transmit their ethnic identity. As shown here, among the techniques people use to forge ties with their roots are dress, dance, and music.

Many African Americans are trying to get in closer contact with their roots. To do this, some use musical performances, as with this group in Philadelphia, Pennsylvania. Note the five-year old who is participating.

Having children participate in ethnic celebrations is a common way of passing on cultural heritage. Shown here is a Thai girl in Los Angeles getting final touches before she performs a temple dance.

Folk dancing (doing a traditional dance of one's cultural heritage) is often used to maintain ethnic identity. Shown here is a man in Arlington, Virginia, doing a Bolivian folk dance.

Many European Americans are also involved in ethnic work, attempting to maintain an identity more precise than "from Europe." These women of Czech ancestry are performing for a Czech community in a small town in Nebraska.

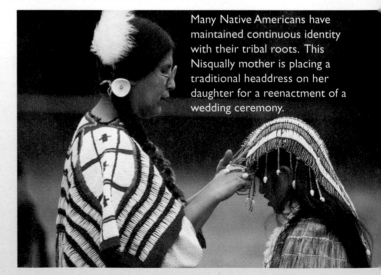

Many Native Americans have maintained continuous identity with their tribal roots. This Nisqually mother is placing a traditional headdress on her daughter for a reenactment of a wedding ceremony.

In the 1920s and 1930s, the Ku Klux Klan was a powerful political force in the United States. To get a sense of the prevailing mood at the time, consider the caption that accompanied this photo taken in Freeport, New York, when it appeared in the local newspaper: "Here's the Ladies in Their Natty Uniforms Marching in the Parade." Which theories would be most useful to explain this upsurge in racism among mainstream whites of the time?

**The Far-Reaching Nature of Prejudice**   It is amazing how much prejudice people can learn. In a classic article, psychologist Eugene Hartley (1946) asked people how they felt about several racial and ethnic groups. Besides Negroes, Jews, and so on, he included the Wallonians, Pireneans, and Danireans—names he had made up. Most people who expressed dislike for Jews and Negroes also expressed dislike for these three fictitious groups.

Hartley's study shows that prejudice does not depend on negative experiences with others. It also reveals that people who are prejudiced against one racial or ethnic group also tend to be prejudiced against other groups. People can be, and are, prejudiced against people they have never met—and even against groups that do not exist!

**Internalizing Dominant Norms**   People can even learn to be prejudiced against their *own* group. A national survey of black Americans conducted by black interviewers found that African Americans think that lighter-skinned African American women are more attractive than those with darker skin (Hill 2002). Sociologists call this *the internalization of the norms of the dominant group.*

To study the internalization of dominant norms, psychologists Mahzarin Banaji and Anthony Greenwald created the "Implicit Association Test." In one version of this test, good and bad words are flashed on a screen along with photos of African Americans and whites. Most subjects are quicker to associate positive words (such as *love, peace,* and *baby*) with whites and negative words (such as *cancer, bomb,* and *devil*) with blacks. Here's the clincher: This is true for *both* white and black subjects (Dasgupta et al. 2000; Greenwald and Krieger 2006). Apparently, we all learn the *ethnic maps* of our culture and, along with them, their route to biased perception.

In the early 1900s, the Ku Klux Klan was a powerful political force. By the 1950s, when this photo was taken in Montgomery, Alabama, the Klan possessed only a shadow of its former power. Today's Klan gets a headline here and there, but few are listening to its message. The group continues to have followers, however.

# Individual and Institutional Discrimination

Sociologists stress that we should move beyond thinking in terms of **individual discrimination,** the negative treatment of one person by another. Although such behavior creates problems, it is primarily an issue between individuals. With their focus on the broader picture, sociologists encourage us to examine **institutional discrimination,** that is, to see how discrimination is woven into the fabric of society. Let's look at two examples.

**Home Mortgages and Car Loans**    Bank lending provides an excellent illustration of institutional discrimination. As shown in Figure 9.2, race–ethnicity is a significant factor in getting a mortgage. When bankers looked at the statistics shown in this figure, they cried foul. It might *look* like discrimination, they said, but the truth is that whites have better credit histories. To see if this were true, researchers went over the data again, comparing the credit histories of the applicants. The lending gap did narrow a bit, but the bottom line was that even when applicants were identical in all these areas, African Americans and Latinos were *60 percent* more likely than whites to be rejected (Thomas 1992; Passell 1996).

Mortgage discrimination continues. Among the revelations of the subprime debacle that made national news and worried Congress was that, compared with whites, African Americans and Latinos had been hit the hardest. They had been charged higher interest rates and were more likely to lose their homes (Fernandez 2007; Fessenden 2007). They are also more likely to pay more for their car loans (Peters and Hakim 2005). In short, it is not a matter of a banker here or there discriminating according to personal prejudices; rather, discrimination is built into the country's financial institutions.

**Health Care**    Discrimination does not have to be deliberate. It can occur even though no one is aware of it: neither those being discriminated against *nor* those doing the discriminating. For example, white patients are more likely to receive knee replacements and coronary bypass surgery than are Latino and African American patients (Skinner et al. 2003; Smedley et al. 2003).

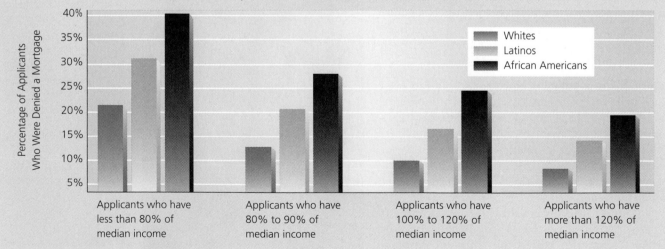

**FIGURE 9.2    Race-Ethnicity and Mortgages: An Example of Institutional Discrimination**

The Federal Reserve Board gathered data on the loans made by 9,300 financial institutions (Thomas 1991). As shown here, loan applicants who had the same income did not receive the same treatment. Note how much more likely banks were to turn down minorities.

This figure illustrates *institutional discrimination*. (Because the discrimination is part of the social *system*, it is also called *systemic discrimination*.) Being turned down for a mortgage is not due to discrimination by an individual banker here and there, but, rather, is a nationwide practice.

*Source:* By the author. Based on Thomas 1991.

Treatment after a heart attack follows a similar pattern: Whites are more likely than blacks to be given cardiac catheterization, a test to detect blockage of blood vessels. This study of 40,000 patients holds a surprise: Both black *and* white doctors are more likely to give this preventive care to whites (Stolberg 2001).

Researchers do not know why race–ethnicity is a factor in medical decisions. With both white and black doctors involved, we can be certain that physicians *do not intend* to discriminate. In ways we do not yet understand, discrimination is built into the medical delivery system. My guess (hypothesis) is that the implicit bias that apparently comes with the internalization of dominant norms becomes a subconscious motivation for giving or denying access to advanced medical procedures.

Institutional discrimination, then, is much more than a matter of inconvenience—it even translates into life and death. Table 9.1 also illustrates this point. Here you can see that an African American baby has more than *twice* the chance of dying in infancy that a white baby does and that an African mother is more than *three* times as likely to die in childbirth as a white mother. You can also see that African Americans die four to six years younger than whites. The reason for these differences is not biology, but social factors, in this case largely income—the key factor in determining who has access to better nutrition, housing, and medical care.

## Theories of Prejudice

Social scientists have developed several theories to explain prejudice. Let's first look at psychological explanations, then sociological ones.

## Psychological Perspectives

**Frustration and Scapegoats**    In 1939, psychologist John Dollard suggested that prejudice is the result of frustration. People who are unable to strike out at the real source of their frustration (such as unemployment) look for someone to blame. They unfairly attribute their troubles to a **scapegoat**—often a racial–ethnic or religious minority—and this person or group becomes a target on which they vent their frustrations. Gender and age also provide common bases for scapegoating.

Even mild frustration can increase prejudice. A team of psychologists led by Emory Cowen (1959) measured the prejudice of a sample of students. They then gave the students two puzzles to solve, making sure the students did not have enough time to solve them. After the students had worked furiously on the puzzles, the experimenters shook their heads in disgust and said that they couldn't believe the students hadn't finished such a simple task. They then retested the students and found that their scores on prejudice had increased. The students had directed their frustrations outward, transferring them to people who had nothing to do with the contempt the experimenters had directed toward them.

**The Authoritarian Personality**    Have you ever wondered whether personality is a cause of prejudice? Maybe some people are more inclined to be prejudiced, and others more fair-minded. For psychologist Theodor Adorno, who had fled from the Nazis, this was no idle speculation. With the horrors he had observed still fresh in his mind, Adorno wondered whether there might be a certain type of person who is more likely to fall for the racist spewings of people like Hitler, Mussolini, and those in the Ku Klux Klan.

To find out, Adorno (Adorno et al. 1950) tested about two thousand people, ranging from college professors to prison inmates. To measure their ethnocentrism, anti-Semitism (bias against Jews), and support for strong, authoritarian leaders, he gave them three tests. Adorno found that people who scored high on one test also scored high on the other two. For example, people who agreed with anti-Semitic statements also said that governments should be authoritarian and that foreign ways of life pose a threat to the "American" way.

Adorno concluded that highly prejudiced people are insecure conformists.

### TABLE 9.1   Race–Ethnicity and Health

|                   | Mother and Child Deaths | | Life Expectancy | |
|-------------------|------------|----------------|-------|---------|
|                   | Infant Deaths | Maternal Deaths | Males | Females |
| White Americans   | 5.7  | 8.7  | 75.7 | 80.8 |
| African Americans | 14.0 | 30.5 | 69.8 | 76.5 |

*Note:* The national database used for this table does not list these totals for other racial–ethnic groups. White refers to non-Hispanic whites. *Infant Deaths* refers to the number of deaths per year of infants under 1 year old per 1,000 live births. *Maternal Deaths* refers to the number of deaths per 100,000 women who give birth in a year.
*Source:* Statistical Abstract 2007: Tables 98, 106.

They have deep respect for authority and are submissive to superiors. He termed this the **authoritarian personality.** These people believe that things are either right or wrong. Ambiguity disturbs them, especially in matters of religion or sex. They become anxious when they confront norms and values that vary from their own. To view people who differ from themselves as inferior assures them that their own positions are right.

Adorno's research stirred the scientific community, stimulating more than a thousand research studies. In general, the researchers found that people who are older, less educated, less intelligent, and from a lower social class are more likely to be authoritarian. Critics say that this doesn't indicate a particular personality, just that the less educated are more prejudiced—which we already knew (Yinger 1965; Ray 1991). Nevertheless, researchers continue to study this concept (Stenner 2005).

## Sociological Perspectives

Sociologists find psychological explanations inadequate. They stress that the key to understanding prejudice cannot be found by looking *inside* people but, rather, by examining conditions *outside* them. For this reason, sociologists focus on how social environments influence prejudice. With this background, let's compare functionalist, conflict, and symbolic interactionist perspectives on prejudice.

**Functionalism**   In a telling scene from a television documentary, journalist Bill Moyers interviewed Fritz Hippler, a Nazi intellectual who at age 29 was put in charge of the entire German film industry. Hippler said that when Hitler came to power the Germans were no more anti-Semitic than the French, and probably less so. He was told to create anti-Semitism. Obediently, Hippler produced movies that contained vivid scenes comparing Jews to rats—with their breeding threatening to infest the population.

Why was Hippler told to create hatred? Prejudice and discrimination were functional for the Nazis. Germany was on its knees at this time. It had been defeated in World War I and was being devastated by fines levied by the victors. The middle class was being destroyed by runaway inflation. The Jews provided a scapegoat, a common enemy against which the Nazis could unite Germany. In addition, the Jews owned businesses, bank accounts, fine art, and other property that the Nazis could confiscate. Jews also held key positions (as university professors, reporters, judges, and so on) into which the Nazis could place their own flunkies. In the end, hatred also showed its

dysfunctional side, as the Nazi officials who were hanged at Nuremberg discovered.

Prejudice becomes practically irresistible when state machinery is harnessed to advance the cause of hatred. To produce prejudice, the Nazis exploited government agencies, the schools, police, courts, and mass media. The results were devastating. Recall the identical twins featured in the Down-to-Earth Sociology box on page 61. Jack and Oskar had been separated as babies. Jack was brought up as a Jew in Trinidad, while Oskar was reared as a Catholic in Czechoslovakia. Under the Nazi regime, Oskar learned to hate Jews, unaware that he himself was a Jew.

That prejudice is functional and is shaped by the social environment was demonstrated by psychologists Muzafer and Carolyn Sherif (1953). In a boys' summer camp, they assigned friends to different cabins and then had the cabin groups compete in sports. In just a few days, strong in-groups had formed. Even lifelong friends began to taunt one another, calling each other a "crybaby" and "sissy."

The Sherif study teaches us several important lessons about social life. Note how it is possible to arrange the social environment to generate either positive or negative feelings about people and how prejudice arises if we pit groups against one another in an "I win, you lose" situation. You can also see that prejudice is functional, how it creates in-group solidarity. And, of course, it is obvious how dysfunctional prejudice is, when you observe the way it destroys human relationships.

**Conflict Theory**   Conflict theorists also analyze how groups are pitted against one another, but they focus on how this arrangement benefits those with power. They begin by noting that workers want better food, health care, housing, and education. To attain these goals, workers need good jobs. If workers are united, they can demand higher wages and better working conditions, but if capitalists can keep workers divided, they can hold wages down. To do this, capitalists use two main tactics.

The first tactic is to keep workers insecure. Fear of unemployment works especially well. The unemployed serve as a **reserve labor force** for capitalists. The capitalists draw on the unemployed to expand production during economic booms; when the economy contracts, they release these workers to rejoin the ranks of the unemployed. The lesson is not lost on workers who have jobs. They fear eviction and worry about having their cars and furniture repossessed. Many know they are just one paycheck away from ending up "on the streets." This helps to keep workers docile.

The second tactic is encouraging and exploiting racial–ethnic divisions (Patterson 2007). Pitting worker against worker weakens labor's bargaining power. When white workers went on strike in California in the 1800s, owners of factories replaced them with Chinese workers. To break strikes by Japanese workers on plantations in Hawaii, owners used to hire Koreans (Xie and Goyette 2004). This division of workers along racial–ethnic and gender lines is known as a **split labor market** (Du Bois 1935/1992; Roediger 2002). Although today's exploitation is more subtle, fear and suspicion continue to split workers. Whites are aware that other groups are ready to take their jobs, African Americans often perceive Latinos as competitors (Cose 2006), and men know that women are eager to get promoted. All of this helps to make workers more docile.

The consequences are devastating, say conflict theorists. It is just like the boys in the Sherif experiment. African Americans, Latinos, whites, and others see themselves as able to make gains only at the expense of members of the other groups. This rivalry shows up along even finer racial–ethnic lines, such as that in Miami between Haitians and African Americans, who distrust each other as competitors. Divisions among workers deflect anger and hostility away from the power elite and direct these powerful emotions toward other racial and ethnic groups. Instead of recognizing their common class interests and working for their mutual welfare, workers learn to fear and distrust one another.

**Symbolic Interactionism**   While conflict theorists focus on the role of the capitalist class in exploiting racial and ethnic divisions, symbolic interactionists examine how labels affect perception and create prejudice.

**How Labels Create Prejudice**   Symbolic interactionists stress that *the labels we learn affect the way we perceive people.* Labels cause **selective perception;** that is, they lead us to see certain things while they blind us to others. If we apply a label to a group, we tend to perceive its members as all alike. We shake off evidence that doesn't fit (Simpson and Yinger 1972). Racial and ethnic labels are especially powerful. They are shorthand for emotionally charged stereotypes. The term *nigger,* for example, is not neutral. Nor are *honky, cracker, spic, mick, kike, limey, kraut, dago, guinea,* or any of the other scornful words people use to belittle ethnic groups. Such words overpower us with emotions, blocking out

rational thought about the people to whom they refer (Allport 1954).

**Labels and the Self-Fulfilling Stereotype**   Some stereotypes not only justify prejudice and discrimination but also produce the behaviors depicted in the stereotype. Let's consider Group X. Negative stereotypes characterize the members of Group X as lazy, so they don't deserve good jobs. ("They are lazy and undependable and wouldn't do the job well.") Denied the better jobs, most members of Group X are limited to doing "dirty work," the kind of employment thought appropriate for "that kind" of people. Since much "dirty work" is sporadic, members of Group X are often seen "on the streets." The sight of their idleness reinforces the original stereotype of laziness. The discrimination that created the "laziness" in the first place passes unnoticed.

To apply these three theoretical perspectives and catch a glimpse of how amazingly different things were in the past, read the Down-to-Earth Sociology box on the next page.

# Global Patterns of Intergroup Relations

Sociologists have studied racial–ethnic relations around the world. They have found six basic patterns that characterize the relationship of dominant groups and minorities. These patterns are shown in Figure 9.3 on page 239. Let's look at each.

## Genocide

Last century's two most notorious examples of genocide occurred in Europe and Africa. In Germany during the 1930s and 1940s, Hitler and the Nazis attempted to destroy all Jews. In the 1990s, in Rwanda, the Hutus tried to destroy all Tutsis. One of the horrifying aspects of these slaughters was that the killers did not crawl out from under a rock someplace. Rather, they were ordinary citizens whose participation was facilitated by labels that singled out the victims as enemies who deserved to die (Huttenbach 1991; Browning 1993; Gross 2001).

To better understand how ordinary people can participate in genocide, let's look at an example from the United States. To call the Native Americans "savages," as U.S. officials and white settlers did, was to label them as inferior, as somehow less than human. This identification made it easier to justify killing the Native Americans in order to take their resources.

# Down-to-Earth Sociology
## The Man in the Zoo

You are going to think I'm kidding, but listen to this:

> The Bronx Zoo in New York City used to keep a 22-year-old pygmy in the Monkey House. The man—and the orangutan he lived with—became the most popular exhibit at the zoo. Thousands of visitors would arrive daily and head straight for the Monkey House. Eyewitnesses to what they thought was a lower form of human in the long chain of evolution, the visitors were fascinated by the pygmy, especially by his sharpened teeth.
>
> To make the exhibit even more alluring, the zoo director had animal bones scattered in front of the man.

I know it sounds as though I must have made this up, but this is a true story. The World's Fair was going to be held in St. Louis in 1904, and the Department of Anthropology wanted to show villages from different cultures. They asked Samuel Verner, an explorer, if he could bring some pygmies to St. Louis to serve as live exhibits. Verner agreed, and on his next trip to Africa, in the Belgian Congo he came across Ota Benga (or Otabenga), a pygmy who had been enslaved by another tribe. Benga, then about age 20, said he was willing to go to St. Louis. After Verner bought Benga's freedom for a few yards of cloth, Benga recruited another half dozen pygmies to go with them.

*Ota Benga*

After the World's Fair, Verner took the pygmies back to Africa. When Benga found out that a hostile tribe had wiped out his village and killed his family, he asked Verner if he could return with him to the United States. Verner agreed.

When they returned to New York, Verner ran into financial trouble and cashed some bad checks. Unable to care for Benga, Verner dropped Benga off with friends at the American Museum of Natural History. After a few weeks, they grew tired of Benga's antics and turned him over to the Bronx Zoo. There, on exhibit in the Monkey House, living with an orangutan as a roommate, Benga became a sensation.

In their official bulletin, the New York Zoological Society described Benga as "an acquisition" of the Bronx Zoo. An article in the *New York Times* said it was fortunate that Benga couldn't think very deeply, or else he might be bothered by living with monkeys.

When the Colored Baptist Ministers' Conference protested that the zoo's exhibit was degrading, zoo officials replied that they were "taking excellent care of the little fellow." They added that "he has one of the best rooms at the primate house."

Not surprisingly, this didn't satisfy the ministers. As their protests grew more insistent, zoo officials decided to let Benga out of his cage. They put a white shirt on him and let him walk around the zoo. At night, Benga slept in the monkey house.

This limited freedom made life even more miserable for Benga. Zoo visitors would follow him, howling, jeering, laughing, and poking at him. Benga then made a little bow and some arrows and began shooting at the obnoxious visitors. At that point, all the fun was over for the zoo officials. They decided that Benga had to leave.

Benga ended up working as a laborer in a tobacco factory in Lynchburg, Virginia. Always treated as a freak, Benga was desperately lonely. In despair that he had no home or family to return to in Africa, in 1916, at the age of 26, Benga ended his misery by shooting himself in the heart.

Based on Bradford and Blume 1992; Crossen 2006; Richman 2006.

## For Your Consideration

1. See what different views emerge as you apply the three theoretical perspectives (functionalism, symbolic interactionism, and conflict theory) to exhibiting Benga at the Bronx Zoo.
2. How does the concept of ethnocentrism apply to this event?
3. Explain how the concepts of prejudice and discrimination apply to what happened to Benga.

## FIGURE 9.3    Global Patterns of Intergroup Relations: A Continuum

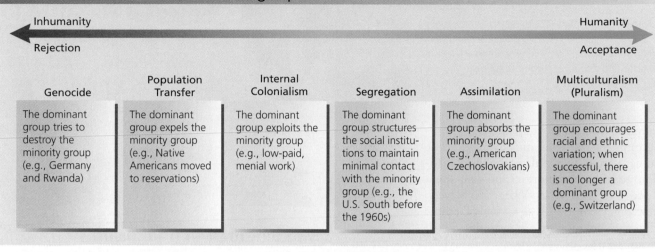

Inhumanity                                                                                    Humanity

Rejection                                                                                      Acceptance

| Genocide | Population Transfer | Internal Colonialism | Segregation | Assimilation | Multiculturalism (Pluralism) |
|---|---|---|---|---|---|
| The dominant group tries to destroy the minority group (e.g., Germany and Rwanda) | The dominant group expels the minority group (e.g., Native Americans moved to reservations) | The dominant group exploits the minority group (e.g., low-paid, menial work) | The dominant group structures the social institutions to maintain minimal contact with the minority group (e.g., the U.S. South before the 1960s) | The dominant group absorbs the minority group (e.g., American Czechoslovakians) | The dominant group encourages racial and ethnic variation; when successful, there is no longer a dominant group (e.g., Switzerland) |

When gold was discovered in northern California in 1849, the fabled "Forty-Niners" rushed in. With the region already inhabited by 150,000 Native Americans, the white government put a bounty on the heads of Native Americans. It even reimbursed the whites for their bullets. The result was the slaughter of 120,000 Native American men, women, and children. (Schaefer 2004)

Most Native Americans, however, died not from bullets but from diseases that the whites brought with them. The Native Americans had no immunity against diseases such as measles, smallpox, and the flu (Dobyns 1983; Schaefer 2004). The settlers also ruthlessly destroyed the Native Americans' food supply (buffalos, crops). As a result, about *95 percent* of Native Americans died (Thornton 1987; Churchill 1997).

The same thing was happening in other places. In South Africa, the Dutch settlers viewed the native Hottentots as jungle animals and totally wiped them out. In Tasmania, the British settlers stalked the local aboriginal population, hunting them for sport and sometimes even for dog food.

Labels are powerful. Those that dehumanize help people to **compartmentalize**—to separate their acts of cruelty from their sense of being good and moral people. To regard members of some group as inferior or even less than human means that it is okay to treat them inhumanely. Thus people can kill—and still retain a good self-concept (Bernard et al. 1971). In short, *labeling the targeted group as inferior or even less than fully human facilitates genocide.*

## Population Transfer

There are two types of **population transfer:** indirect and direct. *Indirect transfer* is achieved by making life so miserable for members of a minority that they leave "voluntarily." Under the bitter conditions of czarist Russia, for example, millions of Jews made this "choice." *Direct transfer* occurs when a dominant group expels a minority. Examples include the U.S. government relocating Native Americans to reservations and transferring Americans of Japanese descent to internment camps during World War II.

In the 1990s, a combination of genocide and population transfer occurred in Bosnia and Kosovo, parts of the former Yugoslavia. A hatred nurtured for centuries had been kept under wraps by Tito's iron-fisted rule from 1944 to 1980. After Tito's death, these suppressed, smoldering hostilities soared to the surface, and Yugoslavia split into warring factions. When the Serbs gained power, Muslims rebelled and began guerilla warfare. The Serbs vented their hatred by what they termed **ethnic cleansing:** They terrorized villages with killing and rape, forcing survivors to flee in fear.

## Internal Colonialism

In Chapter 7, the term *colonialism* was used to refer to one way that the Most Industrialized Nations exploit the Least Industrialized Nations (p. 190). Conflict theorists use the term **internal colonialism** to describe the way in which

Amid fears that Japanese Americans were "enemies within" who would sabotage industrial and military installations on the West Coast, in the early days of World War II Japanese Americans were transferred to "relocation camps." Many returned home after the war to find that their property had been confiscated or vandalized.

a country's dominant group exploits minority groups for its economic advantage. The dominant group manipulates the social institutions to suppress minorities and deny them full access to their society's benefits. Slavery, reviewed in Chapter 7, is an extreme example of internal colonialism, as was the South African system of *apartheid.* Although the dominant Afrikaners despised the minority, they found its presence necessary. As Simpson and Yinger (1972) put it, who else would do the hard work?

## Segregation

Internal colonialism is often accompanied by **segregation**— the separation of racial or ethnic groups. Segregation allows the dominant group to maintain social distance from the minority and yet to exploit their labor as cooks, cleaners, chauffeurs, nannies, factory workers, and so on. In the U.S. South until the 1960s, by law, African Americans and whites had to use separate public facilities such as hotels, schools, swimming pools, bathrooms, and even drinking fountains. In thirty-eight states, laws prohibited marriage between blacks and whites. Violators could be sent to prison (Mahoney and Kooistra 1995; Crossen 2004b). The last law of this type was repealed in 1967 (Spickard 1989). In the villages of India, an ethnic group, the Dalits (untouchables), is forbidden to use the village pump. Dalit women must walk long distances to streams or pumps outside of the village to fetch their water (author's notes).

## Assimilation

**Assimilation** is the process by which a minority group is absorbed into the mainstream culture. There are two types. In *forced assimilation,* the dominant group refuses to allow the minority to practice its religion, to speak its language, or to follow its customs. Before the fall of the Soviet Union, for example, the dominant group, the Russians, required that Armenian children attend schools where they were taught in Russian. Armenians could celebrate only Russian holidays, not Armenian ones. *Permissible assimilation,* in contrast, allows the minority to adopt the dominant group's patterns in its own way and at its own speed.

## Multiculturalism (Pluralism)

A policy of **multiculturalism,** also called **pluralism,** permits or even encourages racial–ethnic variation. The minority groups are able to maintain their separate identities, yet participate freely in the country's social institutions, from education to politics. Switzerland provides an outstanding example of multiculturalism. The Swiss population includes four ethnic groups: French, Italians, Germans, and Romansh. These groups have kept their own languages, and they live peacefully in political and economic unity. Multiculturalism has been so successful that none of these groups can properly be called a minority.

# Racial–Ethnic Relations in the United States

Writing about race–ethnicity is like stepping onto a minefield: One never knows where to expect the next explosion. Even basic terms are controversial. The term *African American,* for example, is rejected by those who ask why this term doesn't include white immigrants from South Africa. Some people classified as African Americans also reject this term because they identify themselves as blacks. Similarly, some Latinos prefer the term *Hispanic American,* but others reject it, saying that it ignores the Indian side of their heritage. Some would limit the term *Chicanos*—commonly used to refer to Americans from Mexico—to those who have a sense of ethnic oppression and unity; they say that it does not apply to those who have assimilated.

No term that I use here, then, will satisfy everyone. Racial–ethnic identity is fluid, constantly changing, and all terms carry a risk as they take on politically charged meanings. Nevertheless, as part of everyday life, we classify ourselves and one another as belonging to distinct racial–ethnic groups. As Figures 9.4 and 9.5 show, on the basis of these self-identities, whites make up 66 percent of the U.S. population, minorities (African Americans, Asian Americans, Latinos, and Native Americans) 32 percent. Between 1 and 2 percent claim membership in two or more racial–ethnic groups.

As you can see from the Social Map on the next page, the distribution of dominant and minority groups among the states seldom comes close to the national average. This is because minority groups tend to be clustered in regions.

**FIGURE 9.4   Race–Ethnicity of the U.S. Population**

- African Americans 13%
- Asian Americans 4%
- Native Americans 1%
- Claim two or more races 1.5%
- Latinos 14%
- Whites 66%

*Source:* By the author. See Figure 9.5.

## FIGURE 9.5   U.S. Racial–Ethnic Groups

**Americans of European Descent[a]**
198,700,000
66.3%

| Group | Number | Percentage |
|---|---|---|
| German | 48,208,000 | 16.0% |
| Irish[b] | 34,488,000 | 11.5% |
| English/British | 29,600,000 | 9.9% |
| Italian | 16,823,000 | 5.6% |
| French[c] | 11,730,000 | 3.9% |
| Scottish[d] | 11,075,000 | 3.7% |
| Polish | 9,385,000 | 3.1% |
| Dutch | 5,087,000 | 1.7% |
| Norwegian | 4,585,000 | 1.5% |
| Swedish | 4,326,000 | 1.4% |
| Russian | 3,017,000 | 1.0% |
| Welsh | 1,913,000 | 0.6% |
| Hungarian | 1,527,000 | 0.5% |
| Danish | 1,477,000 | 0.5% |
| Czech | 1,462,000 | 0.5% |
| Portuguese | 1,336,000 | 0.4% |
| Greek | 1,310,000 | 0.4% |
| Swiss | 1,033,000 | 0.3% |
| Others | 11,000,000 | 3.3% |

**Americans of African, Asian, and North, Central, and South American Descent**
96,146,000
32.1%

| Group | Number | Percentage |
|---|---|---|
| Latino[e] | 42,687,000 | 14.4% |
| African American | 37,909,000 | 12.8% |
| Asian American[f] | 12,687,000 | 4.3% |
| Native American[g] | 2,863,000 | 1.0% |

**Americans Who Claim Two or More Race-Ethnicities**
1.5%

4,579,000   1.5%

**Overall Total: 299,608,000**

Percentage of Americans (0   4%   8%   12%   16%)

*Notes:* [a]The totals in this figure should be taken as broadly accurate only. The totals for groups and even for the U.S. population vary from table to table in the source. Because the total of the individual white ethnic groups listed in the source is 10 percent above the total of whites, I arbitrarily reduced each white ethnic group by 10 percent.
[b]Interestingly, this total *is* six times higher than all the Irish who live in Ireland.
[c]Includes French Canadian.
[d]Includes "Scottish-Irish."
[e]Most Latinos trace at least part of their ancestry to Europe.
[f]In descending order, the largest groups of Asian Americans are from China, the Philippines, India, Korea, Vietnam, and Japan. See Figure 9.9 on page 251. Also includes those who identify themselves as Native Hawaiian or Pacific Islander.
[g]Includes Native American, Inuit, and Aleut.

*Source:* By the author. Based on *Statistical Abstract* 2007:Table 50.

USA—the land of diversity

The extreme distributions are represented by Maine and Vermont, each of which has only 4 percent minority, and by Hawaii, where minorities outnumber whites 77 percent to 23 percent. With this as background, let's review the major groups in the United States, going from the largest to the smallest.

## European Americans

Perhaps the event that best crystallizes the racial view of the nation's founders occurred during the first U.S. Congress. Its members passed the Naturalization Act of 1790, declaring that only white immigrants could apply for citizenship. The sense of superiority and privilege of **WASPs** (white Anglo-Saxon Protestants) was not limited to their views of race. They also viewed as inferior white Europeans from countries other than England. They greeted **white ethnics**—immigrants from Europe whose language and other customs differed from theirs—with disdain and negative stereotypes. They especially despised the Irish, viewing them as dirty, lazy drunkards, but they also painted Germans, Poles, Jews, Italians, and others with similarly broad disparaging brush strokes.

To get an idea of how intense these feelings were, consider this statement by Benjamin Franklin regarding immigrants from Germany:

> **Why should the Palatine boors be suffered to swarm into our settlements and by herding together establish their language and manners to the exclusion of ours? Why should Pennsylvania, founded by the English, become a colony of aliens, who will shortly be so numerous as to germanize us instead of our anglifying them? (In Alba and Nee 2003:17)**

The cultural and political dominance of the WASPs placed pressure on immigrants to assimilate into the mainstream culture. The children of most immigrants embraced the new way of life and quickly came to think of themselves as Americans rather than as Germans, French, Hungarians, and so on. They dropped their distinctive customs, especially their language, often viewing them as symbols of shame. This second generation of immigrants was sandwiched between two worlds: "the old country"

---

**FIGURE 9.6** **The Distribution of Dominant and Minority Groups**

This social map indicates how unevenly distributed U.S. minority groups are. The extremes are Hawaii with 77 percent minority and Maine and Vermont with 4 percent minority.

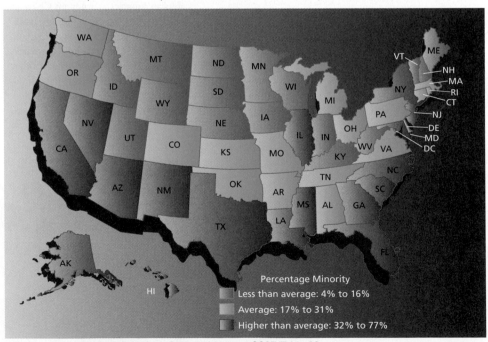

Percentage Minority
Less than average: 4% to 16%
Average: 17% to 31%
Higher than average: 32% to 77%

*Source:* By the author. Based on *Statistical Abstract* 2007:Table 23.

of their parents and their new home. Their children, the third generation, had an easier adjustment, for they had fewer customs to discard. As immigrants from other parts of Europe assimilated into this Anglo culture, the meaning of WASP expanded to include people of this descent.

**In Sum:** Because Protestant English immigrants settled the colonies, they established the culture—from the dominant language to the dominant religion. Highly ethnocentric, they regarded as inferior the customs of other groups. Because white Europeans took power, they determined the national agenda to which other ethnic groups had to react and conform. Their institutional and cultural dominance still sets the stage for current ethnic relations, a topic that is explored in the Down-to-Earth Sociology box below.

# Down-to-Earth Sociology
## Unpacking the Invisible Knapsack: Exploring Cultural Privilege

Overt racism in the United States has dropped sharply, but doors still open and close on the basis of the color of our skin. Whites have a difficult time grasping the idea that good things come their way because they are white. They usually fail to perceive how "whiteness" operates in their own lives.

Peggy McIntosh, of Irish descent, began to wonder why she was so seldom aware of her race–ethnicity, while her African American friends were so conscious of theirs. She realized that people are not highly aware of things that they take for granted—and that "whiteness" is a "taken-for-granted" background assumption of U.S. society. To explore this, she drew up a list of things that she can take for granted because of her "whiteness," what she calls her "invisible knapsack."

What is in this "knapsack"? That is, what taken-for-granted privileges can most white people in U.S. society assume? Because she is white, McIntosh (1988) says,

1. If I don't do well as a leader, I can be sure people won't say that it is because of my race.
2. When I go shopping, store detectives won't follow me.
3. When I watch television or look at the front page of the paper, I see people of my race presented positively.
4. When I study our national heritage, I see people of my color and am taught that they made our country great.
5. When I cash a check or use a credit card, my skin color does not make the clerk think that I may be financially irresponsible.
6. To protect my children, I do not have to teach them to be aware of racism.
7. I can talk with my mouth full and not have people put this down to my color.

*One of the cultural privileges of being white in the United States is less suspicion of wrongdoing.*

8. I can speak at a public meeting without putting my race on trial.
9. I can achieve something and not be "a credit to my race."
10. I am never asked to speak for all the people of my race.
11. If a traffic cop pulls me over, I can be sure that it isn't because I'm white.
12. I can be late to a meeting without people thinking I was late because "That's how *they* are."

### For Your Consideration
Can you think of other "background privileges" that come to whites because of their skin color? (McIntosh's list contains forty-six items.) Why are whites seldom aware that they carry this invisible knapsack?

## Latinos (Hispanics)

**A Note on Terms**   Before reviewing major characteristics of Latinos, it is important to stress that *Latino* and *Hispanic* refer not to a race but to ethnic groups. Latinos may identify themselves racially as black, white, or Native American. With changing self-identities, some Latinos who have an African heritage refer to themselves as Afro-Latinos (Navarro 2003).

**Numbers, Origins, and Location**   When birds still nested in the trees that would be used to build the *Mayflower*, Latinos had already established settlements in Florida and New Mexico (Bretos 1994). Today, Latinos are the largest minority group in the United States. As shown in Figure 9.7, about 28 million people trace their origin to Mexico, 3 to 4 million to Puerto Rico, 1 to 2 million to Cuba, and about 7 million to Central or South America.

Although Latinos are officially tallied at 42 million, another 7 million Latinos are living here illegally, 5 million from Mexico and 2 million from Central and South America (*Statistical Abstract* 2006:Table 7). Most Latinos are legal residents, but each year more than *1 million* Mexicans are apprehended at the border or at points inland and are returned to Mexico (*Statistical Abstract* 2007:Table 518). Several hundred thousand others manage to enter the United States each year. With this vast migration, there are millions more Latinos in the United States than there are Canadians in Canada (33 million). As Figure 9.8 shows, two-thirds live in just four states: California, Texas, Florida, and New York.

Public concern about the migration of Mexicans across the U.S. border has led to emotionally charged debates in the U.S. Congress. One response was to tighten the border, and, despite protests from the Mexican government,

**FIGURE 9.7   Geographical Origin of U.S. Latinos**

Cuba 1,540,000 3.7%
Other countries 2,170,000 5.2%
Puerto Rico 3,610,000 8.6%
Central and South America 6,910,000 16.5%
Mexico 27,620,000 66.0%

*Source:* By the author. Based on *Statistical Abstract* 2007:Table 44.

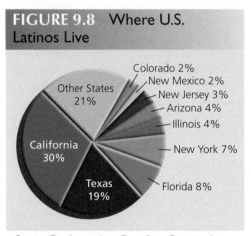

**FIGURE 9.8   Where U.S. Latinos Live**

Colorado 2%, New Mexico 2%, New Jersey 3%, Arizona 4%, Illinois 4%, New York 7%, Florida 8%, Texas 19%, California 30%, Other States 21%

*Source:* By the author. Based on *Statistical Abstract* 2007:Table 23.

The illegal migration of Mexicans into the United States has become a major social issue. For political reasons, including especially relations with Mexico, U.S. officials have hesitated to close the border. The appearance of citizen patrols proved an embarrassment to the official U.S. Border Patrol, as well as a threat to international relations.

U.S. officials built a wall at various points on the U.S. side of the border. Helping to shape the international debate was the arrival of volunteers, calling themselves Minutemen, organized through the Internet to patrol the border. Their arrival in Arizona spread fear among Mexicans and upset U.S. officials, who worried that there would be bloody clashes between the volunteers and the "coyotes" who were smuggling migrants (Peña 2005; Ramos 2005). The violence didn't happen, and the unwelcome unofficial patrolling of the border continued. So did the migration. Despite walls and patrols, as long as there is a need for unskilled labor and so many Mexicans live in poverty, this flow of undocumented workers will continue. To gain insight into why, see the Cultural Diversity box on the next page.

**Spanish Language**    The Spanish language distinguishes most Latinos from other U.S. ethnic groups. With 31 million people speaking Spanish at home, the United States has become one of the largest Spanish-speaking nations in the world (*Statistical Abstract* 2007:Table 51). Because about half of Latinos are unable to speak English, or can do so only with difficulty, many millions face a major obstacle to getting good jobs.

The growing use of Spanish has stoked controversy. Perceiving the prevalence of Spanish as a threat, Senator S. I. Hayakawa of California initiated an "English-only" movement in 1981. The constitutional amendment that he sponsored never got off the ground, but twenty-six states have passed laws that declare English their official language (Schaefer 2004).

**Diversity**    For Latinos, country of origin is highly significant. Those from Puerto Rico, for example, feel that they have little in common with people from Mexico, Venezuela, or El Salvador—just as earlier immigrants from Germany, Sweden, and England felt they had little in common with one another. A sign of these divisions is that many refer to themselves in terms of their country of origin, such as *puertorriqueños* or *cubanos,* rather than as Latino or Hispanic.

As with other ethnic groups, Latinos are separated by social class. The half-million Cubans who fled Castro's rise to power in 1959, for example, were mostly well-educated, well-to-do professionals or businesspeople. In contrast, the "boat people" who fled later were mostly lower-class refugees, people with whom the earlier arrivals would not have associated in Cuba. The earlier arrivals, who are firmly established in Florida and who control many businesses and financial institutions, distance themselves from the more recent immigrants.

These divisions of national origin and social class are a major obstacle to political unity. One consequence is a severe underrepresentation in politics. Because Latinos make up 14.4 percent of the U.S. population, we might expect fourteen or fifteen U.S. senators to be Latino. How many are there? *Two.* In addition, Latinos hold only 5 percent of the seats in the U.S. House of Representatives (*Statistical Abstract* 2007:Table 395).

The potential political power of Latinos is remarkable, and in coming years we will see more of this potential realized. As Latinos have become more visible in U.S. society and more vocal in their demands for equality, they have come face to face with African Americans who fear that Latino gains in employment and at the ballot box will come at their expense (Cose 2006). Together, Latinos and African Americans make up more than one-fourth of the U.S. population. If these two groups were to join together, their unity would produce an unstoppable political force.

For millions of people, the United States represents a land of opportunity and freedom from oppression. Shown here are Cubans who reached the United States by transforming their 1950s truck into a boat.

# Cultural Diversity in the United States

## The Illegal Travel Guide

Manuel was a drinking buddy of Jose, a man I had met in Colima, Mexico. At 45, Manuel was friendly, outgoing, and enterprising.

Manuel, who had lived in the United States for seven years, spoke fluent English. Preferring to live in his home town in Colima, where he palled around with his childhood friends, Manuel always seemed to have money and free time.

When Manuel invited me to go on a business trip with him, I accepted. I never could figure out what he did for a living or how he could afford a car, a luxury that none of his friends had. As we traveled from one remote village to another, Manuel would sell used clothing that he had heaped in the back of his older-model Ford station wagon.

At one stop, Manuel took me into a dirt-floored, thatched-roof hut. While chickens ran in and out, Manuel whispered to a slender man who was about 23 years old. The poverty was overwhelming. Juan, as his name turned out to be, had a partial grade school education. He also had a wife, four hungry children under the age of 5, and two pigs—his main food supply. Although eager to work, Juan had no job, for there was simply no work available in this remote village.

As we were drinking a Coke, which seems to be the national beverage of Mexico's poor, Manuel explained to me that he was not only selling clothing—he was also lining up migrants to the United States. For a fee, he would take a man to the border and introduce him to a "coyote," who would help him make a night crossing into the promised land.

*Mexicans crossing the Rio Grande. Photo taken from the Mexican side of the border, near Nuevo Laredo.*

When I saw the hope in Juan's face, I knew nothing would stop him. He was borrowing every cent he could from every friend and relative to scrape the money together. Although he risked losing everything if apprehended and he would be facing unknown risks, Juan would make the trip, for wealth beckoned on the other side. He knew people who had been to the United States and spoke glowingly of its opportunities. Manuel, of course, stoked the fires of hope.

Looking up from the children playing on the dirt floor with the chickens pecking about them, I saw a man who loved his family. In order to make the desperate bid for a better life, he would suffer an enforced absence, as well as the uncertainties of a foreign culture whose language he did not know.

Juan opened his billfold, took something out, and slowly handed it to me. I looked at it curiously. I felt tears as I saw the tenderness with which he handled this piece of paper. It was his passport to the land of opportunity: a Social Security card made out in his name, sent by a friend who had already made the trip and who was waiting for Juan on the other side of the border.

It was then that I realized that the thousands of Manuels scurrying about Mexico and the millions of Juans they were transporting could never be stopped, for only the United States could fulfill their dream of a better life.

## For Your Consideration

The vast stream of immigrants illegally crossing the Mexican–U.S. border has become a national issue. What do you think is the best way to deal with this issue? Why?

**Comparative Conditions**    To see how Latinos are doing on some major indicators of well-being, look at Table 9.2 below. As you can see, compared with white Americans and Asian Americans, Latinos have less income, higher unemployment, and more poverty. They are also less likely to own their homes. Now look at how closely Latinos rank with African Americans and Native Americans. From this table, you can also see how significant country of origin is. People from Cuba score higher on all these indicators of well-being, while those from Puerto Rico score lower.

The significance of country or region of origin is also underscored by Table 9.3 on the next page. You can see that people who trace their roots to Cuba attain considerably more education than do those who come from other areas. You can also see that Latinos are the most likely to drop out of high school and the least likely to graduate from college. In a postindustrial society that increasingly requires advanced skills, these totals indicate that huge numbers of Latinos will be left behind.

## African Americans

After slavery was abolished, the Southern states passed legislation (*Jim Crow* laws) to segregate blacks and whites. In 1896, the U.S. Supreme Court ruled in *Plessy v. Ferguson* that it was reasonable to use state power to require "separate but equal" accommodations for blacks. Whites used this ruling to strip blacks of the political power they had gained after the Civil War. One way they did this was to prohibit blacks from voting in "white" primaries. It was not until 1944 that the Supreme Court ruled that African Americans could vote in Southern primaries, and not until 1954 that they gained the legal right to attend the same public schools as whites (Schaefer 2004). Well into the 1960s, the South was still openly—and legally— practicing segregation.

### The Struggle for Civil Rights

It was 1955, in Montgomery, Alabama. As specified by law, whites took the front seats of the bus, and blacks went to

| TABLE 9.2 | Race–Ethnicity and Comparative Well-Being[1] | | | | | | | |
|---|---|---|---|---|---|---|---|---|
| | Income | | Unemployment | | Poverty | | Home Ownership | |
| Racial–Ethnic Group | Median Family Income | Compared to Whites | Percentage Unemployed | Compared to Whites | Percentage Below Poverty Line | Compared to Whites | Percentage Who Own Their Homes | Compared to Whites |
| Whites | $59,907 | — | 3.5% | — | 7.7% | — | 76.3% | — |
| Latinos | $36,820 | 39% lower | 4.8% | 37% higher | 21.9% | 184% higher | 49.4% | 35% lower |
| Country or Area of Origin | | | | | | | | |
| Cuba | NA[2] | NA | 2.0% | 57% lower | 14.5% | 88% higher | 61.3% | 20% lower |
| Central and South America | NA | NA | NA | NA | 17.8% | 131% higher | 39.2% | 49% lower |
| Mexico | NA | NA | 4.2% | 20% higher | 23.8% | 209% higher | 51.4% | 33% lower |
| Puerto Rico | NA | NA | 4.7% | 34% higher | 22.9% | 197% higher | 39.7% | 48% lower |
| African Americans | $34,851 | 42% lower | 7.5% | 114% higher | 24.5% | 218% higher | 49.5% | 35% lower |
| Asian Americans[3] | $65,132 | 9% higher | 3.5% | The same | 11.7% | 52% higher | 57.6% | 25% lower |
| Native Americans | $35,981 | 40% lower | NA | NA | 24.6% | 219% higher | 55.5% | 27% lower |

[1] Data are from 2004 and 2005.
[2] Not Available
[3] Includes Pacific Islanders
*Source:* By the author. Based on *Statistical Abstract* 2007: Tables 40, 41, 44, 613, 677.

**TABLE 9.3    Race–Ethnicity and Education**

| Racial–Ethnic Group | Education Completed | | | | Doctorates | | Percentage of U.S. Population |
| --- | --- | --- | --- | --- | --- | --- | --- |
| | Less than High School | High School | Some College | College (BA or Higher) | Number Awarded | Percentage of all U.S. Doctorates[1] | |
| Whites | 9.7% | 33.4% | 28.0% | 28.9% | 28,214 | 81.0% | 66.3% |
| Latinos | 41.1% | 27.3% | 19.6% | 12.1% | 1,662 | 4.7% | 14.4% |
| Country or Area of Origin | | | | | | | |
| Cuba | 26.5% | 30.4% | 18.4% | 24.7% | NA | NA | |
| Puerto Rico | 27.8% | 33.7% | 24.7% | 13.8% | NA | NA | |
| Central and South America | 37.6% | 25.6% | 18.3% | 18.5% | NA | NA | |
| Mexico | 47.7% | 26.6% | 17.4% | 8.3% | NA | NA | |
| African Americans | 19.4% | 36.0% | 27.0% | 17.6% | 2,900 | 8.1% | 12.8% |
| Asian Americans | 15.1% | 17.2% | 19.3% | 48.2% | 2,632 | 7.4% | 4.3% |
| Native Americans | 23.3% | 31.3% | 31.1% | 14.1% | 217 | 0.6% | 1.0% |

[1]Percentage after the doctorates awarded to nonresidents are deducted from the total.

*Source:* By the author. Based on *Statistical Abstract* 2007:Tables 41, 44, 289 and Figure 12.5 of this text.

the back. As the bus filled up, blacks had to give up their seats to whites.

When Rosa Parks, a 42-year-old African American woman and secretary of the Montgomery NAACP, was told that she would have to stand so that white folks could sit, she refused (Bray 1995). She stubbornly sat there while the bus driver raged and whites felt insulted. Her arrest touched off mass demonstrations, led 50,000 blacks to boycott the city's buses for a year, and thrust an otherwise unknown preacher into a historic role.

Reverend Martin Luther King, Jr., who had majored in sociology at Morehouse College in Atlanta, Georgia, took control. He organized car pools and preached nonviolence. Incensed at this radical organizer and at the stirrings in the normally compliant black community, segregationists also put their beliefs into practice—by bombing the homes of blacks and dynamiting their churches.

**Rising Expectations and Civil Strife**    The barriers came down, but they came down slowly. Not until 1964 did Congress pass the Civil Rights Act, making it illegal to discriminate on the basis of race. African Americans were finally allowed in "white" restaurants, hotels, theaters, and other public places. Then in 1965, Congress passed the Voting Rights Act, banning the fraudulent literacy tests that the Southern states had used to keep African Americans from voting.

Encouraged by these gains, African Americans experienced what sociologists call **rising expectations;** that is, they believed that better conditions would soon follow. The lives of the poor among them, however, changed little, if at all. Frustrations built, finally exploding in Watts in 1965, when people living in that African American ghetto of central Los Angeles took to the streets in the first of what were termed "urban revolts." When King was assassinated by a white supremacist on April 4, 1968, inner cities across the nation erupted in fiery violence. Under threat of the destruction of U.S. cities, Congress passed the sweeping Civil Rights Act of 1968.

**Continued Gains**    Since then, African Americans have made remarkable gains in politics, education, and jobs. At 10 percent, the number of African Americans in the U.S. House of Representatives is almost *three times* what it was a generation ago (*Statistical Abstract* 1989:Table 423; 2007:Table 395). As college enrollments increased, the middle class expanded, and today half of all African American families make more than $35,000 a year. One in three makes more than $50,000 a year, and one in six earns more than $75,000 (*Statistical Abstract* 2007:Table 675). Contrary to stereotypes, the average African American family is *not* poor.

The extent of African American political prominence was highlighted when Jesse Jackson (another sociology major) competed for the Democratic presidential nomination in 1984 and 1988. Political progress was further confirmed in 1989 when L. Douglas Wilder was elected governor of Virginia and again in 2006 when Deval Patrick became governor of Massachusetts. The most publicized African American politician is Barack Obama, who was elected to the U.S. Senate from Illinois in 2004 and then won the Democratic nomination for president in 2008.

**Current Losses**   Despite these gains, African Americans continue to lag behind in politics, economics, and education. Only *one* U.S. senator is African American, but on the basis of the percentage of African Americans in the U.S. population, we would expect about thirteen. As Tables 9.2 and 9.3 on pages 247 and 248 show, African Americans average only 58 percent of white income, have much more unemployment and poverty, and are less likely to own their home or to have a college education. That half of African American families have incomes over $35,000 is only part of the story. Table 9.4 shows the other part—that one of every five African American families makes less than $15,000 a year.

| TABLE 9.4 | Race–Ethnicity and Income Extremes | |
| --- | --- | --- |
| | Less than $15,000 | Over $75,000 |
| Asian Americans | 6.3% | 53.2% |
| Whites | 6.7% | 38.6% |
| African Americans | 21.1% | 17.7% |
| Latinos | 15.8% | 16.6% |

*Note:* These are family incomes. Only these groups are listed in the source.
*Source:* By the author: Based on *Statistical Abstract* 2007: Table 675.

The upper mobility of millions of African Americans into the middle class has created two worlds of African American experience—one educated and affluent, the other uneducated and poor. Concentrated among the poor are those with the least hope, the highest despair, and the violence that so often dominates the evening news. Although homicide rates have dropped to their lowest point in thirty years, African

Until the 1960s, the South's public facilities were segregated. Some were reserved for whites only, others for blacks only. This *apartheid* was broken by blacks and whites who worked together and risked their lives to bring about a fairer society. Shown here is a 1963 sit-in at a Woolworth's lunch counter in Jackson, Mississippi. Sugar, ketchup, and mustard are being poured over the heads of the demonstrators.

The political gains of African Americans have been stunning, but none greater than the accomplishments of Barack Obama. Since Obama's mother is a white American and his father is from Kenya, why is he referred to as African American? The explanation is in the text.

Americans are *six* times as likely to be murdered as are whites (*Statistical Abstract* 2007:Table 302). Compared with whites, African Americans are also *eleven* times more likely to die from AIDS (*Statistical Abstract* 2007:Table 117).

**Race or Social Class? A Sociological Debate**   This division of African Americans into "haves" and "have-nots" has fueled a sociological controversy. Sociologist William Julius Wilson (1978, 1987, 2000) argues that social class has become more important than race in determining the life chances of African Americans. Before civil rights legislation, he says, the African American experience was dominated by race. Throughout the United States, African Americans were excluded from avenues of economic advancement: good schools and good jobs. When civil rights legislation opened new opportunities, African Americans seized them. Just as legislation began to open doors to African Americans, however, manufacturing jobs dried up, and many blue-collar jobs were moved to the suburbs. As better-educated African Americans obtained middle-class, white-collar jobs and moved out of the inner city, they left behind the African Americans with poor education and few skills.

Wilson stresses the significance of these two worlds of African American experience. The group that is stuck in the inner city lives in poverty, attends poor schools, and faces dead-end jobs or welfare. This group is filled with hopelessness and despair, combined with apathy or hostility. In contrast, those who have moved up the social class ladder live in comfortable homes in secure neighborhoods. They work at jobs that provide decent incomes, and they send their children to good schools. Their middle-class experiences and lifestyle have changed their views on life, and their aspirations and values have little in common with those of African Americans who remain poor. According to Wilson, then, social class—not race—has become the most significant factor in the lives of African Americans.

Some sociologists reply that this analysis overlooks the discrimination that continues to underlie the African American experience. They note that even when African Americans do the same work as whites, they average less pay (Willie 1991; Herring 2002). This, they argue, points to racial discrimination, not to social class.

What is the answer to this debate? Wilson would reply that it is not an either-or question. My book is titled *The **Declining** Significance of Race,* he would say, not *The **Absence** of Race.* Certainly racism is still alive, he would add, but today social class is more central to the African American experience than is racial discrimination. He stresses that for the poor in the inner city, we need to provide jobs—for work provides an anchor to a responsible life (Wilson 1996, 2000).

**Racism as an Everyday Burden**   Today, racism is more subtle than it used to be, but it still walks among us (Perry 2006). To study discrimination in the job market, researchers sent out 5,000 résumés in response to help wanted ads in the Boston and Chicago Sunday papers (Bertrand and Mullainathan 2002). The résumés were identical, except for the names of the job applicants. Some applicants had white-sounding names, such as Emily and Brandon, while others had black-sounding names, such as Lakisha and Jamal. Although the qualifications of the supposed job applicants were identical, the white-sounding names elicited *50 percent* more callbacks than the black-sounding names.

African Americans who occupy higher statuses enjoy greater opportunities, and they also face less discrimination. The discrimination that they encounter, however, is no less painful. Unlike whites of the same social class, they feel discrimination constantly hovering over them. Here is how an African American professor described it:

> [One problem with] being black in America is that you have to spend so much time thinking about stuff that most white people just don't even have to think about. I worry when I get pulled over by a cop. . . . I worry what some white cop is going to think when he walks over to our car, because he's holding on to a gun. And I'm very aware of how many black folks accidentally get shot by cops. I worry when I walk into a store, that someone's going to think I'm in there shoplifting. . . . And I get resentful that I have to think about things that a lot of people, even my very close white friends whose politics are similar to mine, simply don't have to worry about. (Feagin 1999:398)

## Asian Americans

I have stressed in this chapter that our racial–ethnic categories are based more on social considerations than on biological ones. This point is again obvious when we examine the category Asian American. As Figure 9.9 shows, those who are called Asian Americans came to the United States from many nations. With no unifying culture or "race," why should they ever be clustered together in a single category—except that others perceive them as a unit? Think about it. What culture or race–ethnicity do Samoans and Vietnamese have in common? Or Laotians and Pakistanis? Or Native Hawaiians and Chinese? Or people from India and those from Guam? Yet all these groups—and more—are lumped together and called Asian Americans. Apparently, the U.S. government is not satisfied until it is able to pigeonhole everyone into a racial–ethnic category.

Since *Asian American* is a standard term, however, let's look at the characteristics of the 13 million people who are lumped together and assigned this label.

**A Background of Discrimination**    From their first arrival in the United States, Asian Americans confronted discrimination. Lured by gold strikes in the West and an urgent need for unskilled workers to build the railroads, 200,000 Chinese immigrated between 1850 and 1880. When the famous golden spike was driven at Promontory, Utah, in 1869 to mark the completion of the railroad to the West

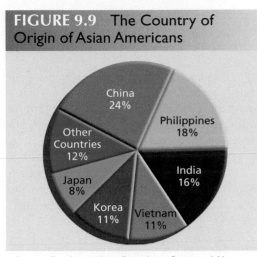

**FIGURE 9.9    The Country of Origin of Asian Americans**

*Source:* By the author. Based on *Statistical Abstract 2006:* Table 24.

Coast, white workers prevented Chinese workers from being in the photo—even though Chinese made up 90 percent of Central Pacific Railroad's labor force (Hsu 1971).

After the railroad was complete, the Chinese took other jobs. Feeling threatened by their cheap labor, Anglos formed vigilante groups to intimidate them. They also used the law. California's 1850 Foreign Miner's Act required Chinese (and Latinos) to pay a fee of $20 a month in order to work—when wages were a dollar a day. The California Supreme Court ruled that Chinese could not testify against whites (Carlson and Colburn 1972). In 1882, Congress passed the Chinese Exclusion Act, suspending all Chinese immigration for ten years. Four years later, the Statue of Liberty was dedicated. The tired, the poor, and the huddled masses it was intended to welcome were obviously not Chinese.

When immigrants from Japan arrived, they encountered *spillover bigotry,* a stereotype that lumped Asians together, depicting them as sneaky, lazy, and untrustworthy. After Japan attacked Pearl Harbor in 1941, conditions grew worse for the 110,000 Japanese Americans who called the United States their home. U.S. authorities feared that Japan would invade the United States and that the Japanese Americans would fight on Japan's side. They also feared that Japanese Americans would sabotage military installations on the West Coast. Although no Japanese American had been involved in even a single act of sabotage, on February 19, 1942, President Franklin D. Roosevelt ordered that everyone who was *one-eighth Japanese or more* be confined in detention centers (called "internment camps"). These people were charged with no crime, and they had no trials. Japanese ancestry was sufficient cause for being imprisoned.

**Diversity**　As you can see from Table 9.2 on page 247, the annual income of Asian Americans has outstripped that of whites. This has led to the stereotype that all Asian Americans are successful. Are they? Their poverty rate is actually 50 percent higher than that of whites, and between 1 and 2 million Asian Americans live in poverty. Like Latinos, country of origin is also significant: Poverty is unusual among Chinese and Japanese Americans, but it clusters among Americans from Southeast Asia.

**Reasons for Success**　The high average income of Asian Americans can be traced to three major factors: family life, educational achievement, and assimilation into mainstream culture.

Of all ethnic groups, including whites, Asian American children are the most likely to grow up with two parents and the least likely to be born to a single mother (*Statistical Abstract* 2007:Tables 53, 64). Most grow up in close-knit families that stress self-discipline, thrift, and hard work (Suzuki 1985; Bell 1991). This early socialization provides strong impetus for the other two factors.

The second factor is their high rate of college graduation. As Table 9.3 on page 248 shows, 48 percent of Asian Americans complete college. To realize how stunning this is, compare this with the other groups shown on this table. This educational achievement, in turn, opens doors to economic success.

The most striking indication of assimilation, the third factor, is a high rate of intermarriage. It is especially high among those who trace their descent from Japan and China—who are the most successful financially. In an unprecedented change, two of every three children born to a Japanese American have one parent who is not of Japanese descent (Schaefer 2004). The Chinese are close behind (Alba and Nee 2003).

Asian Americans are becoming more prominent in politics. With more than half of its citizens being Asian American, Hawaii has elected Asian American governors and sent several Asian American senators to Washington, including the two now serving there (Lee 1998, *Statistical Abstract* 2007:Table 395). The first Asian American governor outside of Hawaii was Gary Locke, who served as governor of Washington, a state in which Asian Americans make up less than 6 percent of the population, from 1997 to 2005.

## Native Americans

"I don't go so far as to think that the only good Indians are dead Indians, but I believe nine out of ten are—and I shouldn't inquire too closely in the case of the tenth. The most vicious cowboy has more moral principle than the average Indian."

—Teddy Roosevelt, 1886,
President of the United States, 1901–1909

**Diversity of Groups**　This quote from Teddy Roosevelt provides insight into the rampant racism of earlier generations. Yet, even today, thanks to countless grade B Westerns, some Americans view the original inhabitants of what became the United States as wild, uncivilized savages, a single group of people subdivided into separate tribes. The European immigrants to the colonies, however, encountered diverse groups of people with a variety of cultures—from nomadic hunters and gatherers to people who lived in wooden houses in settled agricultural communities. Altogether, they spoke over 700 languages (Schaefer 2004). Each group had its own norms and values—and the usual ethnocentric pride in its own culture. Consider what happened in 1744 when the colonists of Virginia offered college scholarships for "savage lads." The Iroquois replied:

"Several of our young people were formerly brought up at the colleges of Northern Provinces. They were instructed in all your sciences. But when they came back to us, they were bad runners, ignorant of every means of living in the woods, unable to bear either cold or hunger, knew neither how to build a cabin, take a deer, or kill an enemy. . . . They were totally good for nothing."

They added, "If the English gentlemen would send a dozen or two of their children to Onondaga, the great Council would take care of their education, bring them up in really what was the best manner and make men of them." (Nash 1974; in McLemore 1994)

Native Americans, who numbered about 10 million, had no immunity to the diseases the Europeans brought with them. With deaths due to disease—and warfare, a much lesser cause—their population plummeted. The low point came in 1890, when the census reported only 250,000 Native Americans. If the census and the estimate of the original population are accurate, Native Americans had been reduced to about *one-fortieth* their original size. The population has never recovered, but Native Americans now number almost 3 million (see

The Native Americans stood in the way of the U.S. government's westward expansion. To seize their lands, the government followed a policy of *genocide*, later replaced by *population transfer*. This depiction of Apache shepherds being attacked by the U.S. Cavalry is by Rufus Zogbaum, a popular U.S. illustrator of the 1880s.

Figure 9.5 on page 241). Native Americans, who today speak 150 different languages, do not think of themselves as a single people who fit neatly within a single label (McLemore 1994).

**From Treaties to Genocide and Population Transfer**    At first, the Native Americans tried to accommodate the strangers, since there was plenty of land for both the few newcomers and themselves. Soon, however, the settlers began to raid Indian villages and pillage their food supplies (Horn 2006). As wave after wave of settlers arrived, Pontiac, an Ottawa chief, saw the future—and didn't like it. He convinced several tribes to unite in an effort to push the Europeans into the sea. He almost succeeded, but failed when the English were reinforced by fresh troops (McLemore 1994).

A pattern of deception evolved. The U.S. government would make treaties to buy some of a tribe's land, with the promise to honor forever the tribe's right to what it had not sold. European immigrants, who continued to pour into the United States, would then disregard these boundaries. The tribes would resist, with death tolls on both sides. The U.S. government would then intervene—

not to enforce the treaty, but to force the tribe off its lands. In its relentless drive westward, the U.S. government embarked on a policy of genocide. It assigned the U.S. cavalry the task of "pacification," which translated into slaughtering Native Americans who "stood in the way" of this territorial expansion.

The acts of cruelty perpetrated by the Europeans against Native Americans appear endless, but two are especially notable. The first is the Trail of Tears. In the winter of 1838–1839, the U.S. Army rounded up 15,000 Cherokees and forced them to walk a thousand miles from the Carolinas and Georgia to Oklahoma. Coming from the South, many of the Cherokees wore only light clothing. Conditions were so inhumane that about 4,000 of those who were forced on this midwinter march died before they reached Oklahoma. About 50 years later came the symbolic end to Native American resistance to the European expansion. In 1890, at Wounded Knee, South Dakota, the U.S. cavalry gunned down 300 men, women, and children. After the massacre, the soldiers threw the bodies of the Dakota Sioux into a mass grave (Thornton 1987; Lind 1995; DiSilvestro 2006). These acts took place after the U.S. government had begun a policy called *Indian Removal,* forcefully confining Native Americans to specified areas called *reservations.*

**The Invisible Minority and Self-Determination**    Native Americans can truly be called the invisible minority. Because about half live in rural areas and one-third in just three states—Oklahoma, California, and Arizona—most other Americans are hardly aware of a Native American presence in the United States. The isolation of about half of Native Americans on reservations further reduces their visibility (Schaefer 2004).

The systematic attempts of European Americans to destroy the Native Americans' way of life and their forced resettlement onto reservations continue to have deleterious effects. The rate of suicide of Native Americans is the highest of any racial–ethnic group, and their life expectancy is lower than that of the nation as a whole (Murray et al. 2006; Centers for Disease Control 2007b). Table 9.3 on page 248 shows that their education also lags behind most groups: Only 14 percent graduate from college.

Native Americans are experiencing major changes. In the 1800s, U.S. courts ruled that Native Americans did not own the land on which they had been settled and determined that they had no right to develop its resources. Native Americans were made wards of the state and treated like children by the Bureau of Indian Affairs (Mohawk 1991; Schaefer 2004). Then, in the 1960s, Native Americans won a series of legal victories that gave them control over reservation lands. As a result, many Native American tribes have opened businesses—ranging from industrial parks serving metropolitan areas to fish canneries. The Skywalk, opened by the Hualapai, which offers breathtaking views of the Grand Canyon, gives an idea of the varieties of businesses to come.

It is the casinos, though, that have attracted the most attention. In 1988, the federal government passed a law that allowed Native Americans to operate gambling establishments on reservations. Now over 200 tribes operate casinos. *They bring in about $25 billion a year, twice as much as all the casinos in Las Vegas* (Werner 2007). The Oneida tribe of New York, which has only 1,000 members, runs a casino that nets $232,000 a year for each man, woman, and child (Peterson 2003). This huge amount, however, pales in comparison with that of the Pequot of Connecticut. With only 700 members, they bring in more than $2 million a day just from slot machines (Rivlin 2007). Incredibly, one tribe has only *one* member: She has her own casino (Barlett and Steele 2002).

One of the most significant changes is **pan-Indianism.** This emphasis on common elements that run through Native American cultures is an attempt to develop an identity that goes beyond the tribe. Pan-Indianism ("We are all Indians") is a remarkable example of the plasticity of ethnicity. The label "Indian"—originally imposed by whites—is embraced and substituted for individual tribal identities. As sociologist Irwin Deutscher (2002:61) puts it, "The peoples who have accepted the larger definition of who they are, have, in fact, little else in common with each other than the stereotypes of the dominant group which labels them."

A highly controversial issue is *separatism.* Because Native Americans were independent peoples when the Europeans arrived and they never willingly joined the United States, many tribes maintain the right to remain separate from the U.S. government and U.S. society. "Such decisions must be ours," say the Native Americans. "We are sovereign, and we will not take orders from the victors of past wars."

# Looking Toward the Future

Back in 1903, sociologist W. E. B. Du Bois said, "The problem of the twentieth century is the problem of the color line—the relation of the darker to the lighter races." Incredibly, over a hundred years later, the color line remains one of the most volatile topics facing the nation. From time to time, the color line takes on a different complexion, as with the war on terrorism and the corresponding discrimination directed against people of Middle Eastern descent.

In another hundred years, will yet another sociologist lament that the color of people's skin still affects human relationships? Given our past, it seems that although racial–ethnic walls will diminish, even crumble at some points, the color line is not likely to disappear. Let's close this chapter by looking at two issues we are currently grappling with, immigration and affirmative action.

The United States is the most racially–ethnically diverse society in the world. This can be our central strength, with our many groups working together to build a harmonious society, a stellar example for the world. Or it can be our Achilles heel, if we break into feuding groups, forming a Balkanized society that marks an ill-fitting end to a grand social experiment. Our reality will probably fall somewhere between these extremes.

## The Immigration Debate

Throughout its history, the United States has both welcomed immigration and feared its consequences. The gates opened wide (numerically, if not in attitude) for waves of immigrants in the 1800s and early 1900s. During the past twenty years, a new wave of immigration has brought close to a million new residents to the United States each year. Today, more immigrants (34 million) live in the United States than at any other time in the country's history (*Statistical Abstract* 2007:Tables 5, 45).

In contrast to earlier waves, in which immigrants came almost exclusively from western Europe, this current wave of immigrants is more diverse. In fact, it is changing the U.S. racial–ethnic mix. If current trends in immigration (and birth) persist, in about fifty years the "average" American will trace his or her ancestry to Africa, Asia, South America, the Pacific Islands, the Middle East—almost anywhere but white Europe. This change is discussed in the Cultural Diversity box on the next page.

In some states, the future is arriving much sooner than this. In California, racial–ethnic minorities have become the majority. California has 20 million minorities and 16 million whites (*Statistical Abstract* 2007:Table 23). Californians who request new telephone service from Pacific Bell can speak to customer service representatives in Spanish, Korean, Vietnamese, Mandarin, Cantonese— or in English.

As in the past, there is concern that "too many" immigrants will change the character of the United States. "Throughout the history of U.S. immigration," write sociologists Alejandro Portes and Rubén Rumbaut (1990), "a consistent thread has been the fear that the 'alien element' would somehow undermine the institutions of the country and would lead it down the path of disintegration and decay." A hundred years ago, the widespread fear was that the immigrants from southern Europe would bring communism with them. Today, some fear that Spanish-speaking immigrants threaten the primacy of the English language. In addition, the age-old fear that immigrants will take jobs away from native-born Americans remains strong. Finally, minority groups that struggled for political representation fear that newer groups will gain political power at their expense.

## Affirmative Action

The role of affirmative action in our multicultural society lies at the center of a national debate about racial–ethnic relations. In this policy, initiated by President Kennedy in 1961, goals based on race (and sex) are used in hiring, promotion, and college admission. Sociologist Barbara Reskin (1998) examined the results of affirmative action. She concluded that although it is difficult to separate the results of affirmative action from economic booms and busts and the greater numbers of women in the workforce, affirmative action has had a modest impact.

The results may have been modest, but the reactions to this program have been anything but modest. Affirmative action has been at the center of controversy for almost two generations. Liberals, both white and minority, say that this program is the most direct way to level the playing field of economic opportunity. If whites are passed over, this is an unfortunate cost that we must pay if we are to make up for past discrimination. In contrast, conservatives, both white and minority, agree that opportunity should be open to all, but claim that putting race (or sex) ahead of an individual's training and ability to perform a job is reverse discrimination. Because of their race (or sex), qualified people who had nothing to do with past inequity are discriminated against. They add that affirmative action stigmatizes the people who benefit from it, because it suggests that they hold their jobs because of race (or sex), rather than merit.

This national debate crystallized with a series of controversial rulings. One of the most significant was *Proposition 209*, a 1996 amendment to the California state constitution. This amendment made it illegal to give preference to minorities and women in hiring, promotion, and college admissions. Despite appeals by a coalition of civil rights groups, the U.S. Supreme Court upheld this California law.

A second significant ruling was made by the Supreme Court of Michigan in 2003. White students who had been denied admission to the University of Michigan claimed that they had been discriminated against because less qualified applicants had been admitted on the basis of their race. The Court ruled that universities can give minorities an edge in admissions, but there must be a meaningful review of individual applicants. Mechanical systems, such as giving extra points because of race, are unconstitutional. This murky message satisfied no one, as no one knew what it really meant.

To remove ambiguity, opponents of affirmative action in Michigan offered *Proposition 2*, an amendment to the state constitution that would make it illegal for public institutions to even consider race or sex in college admissions, in hiring, or in awarding contracts. Like the proposal in California, *Proposition 2* became law (Lewin 2007).

With opponents and proponents of affirmative action gearing up for similar battles in other states, the issue of

# Cultural Diversity in the United States

## Glimpsing the Future: The Shifting U.S. Racial–Ethnic Mix

During the next twenty-five years, the population of the United States is expected to grow by about 22 percent. To see what the U.S. population will look like at the end of that time, can we simply add 22 percent to our current racial–ethnic mix? The answer is a resounding no. As you can see from Figure 9.10, some groups will grow much more than others, giving us a different-looking United States. Some of the changes in the U.S. racial–ethnic mix will be dramatic. In twenty-five years, one of every nineteen Americans is expected to have an Asian background, and the most dramatic change—almost one of four is expected to be of Latino ancestry.

Two basic causes underlie this fundamental shift: immigration and birth rates. Immigration is by far the more important. The racial–ethnic groups have different rates of immigration and birth, and these will change their proportions of the U.S. population. From Figure 9.10, you can see how the proportion of non-Hispanic whites is expected to shrink, that of Native Americans to remain the same, that of African Americans to increase slightly, and that of Latinos to increase sharply.

## For Your Consideration

This shifting racial–ethnic mix is one of the most significant events occurring in the United States. To better understand its implications, apply the three theoretical perspectives.

Use the *conflict perspective* to identify the groups that are likely to be threatened by this change. Over what resources are struggles likely to develop? What impact do you think this changing mix might have on European Americans? On Latinos? On African Americans? On Asian Americans? On Native Americans? What changes in immigration laws (or their enforcement) can you anticipate?

To apply the *symbolic interactionist perspective,* consider how groups might perceive one another differently as their proportion of the population changes. How do you think that this changed perception will affect people's behavior?

To apply the *functionalist perspective,* try to determine how each racial–ethnic group will benefit from this changing mix. How will other parts of society (such as businesses) benefit? What functions and dysfunctions can you anticipate for politics, economics, education, or religion?

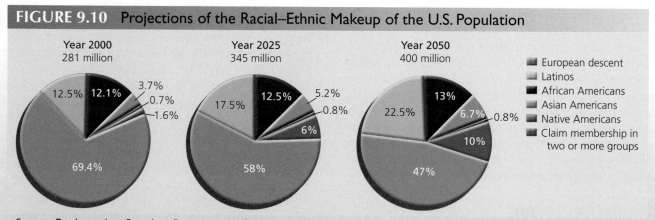

**FIGURE 9.10    Projections of the Racial–Ethnic Makeup of the U.S. Population**

Year 2000 — 281 million
12.5%  12.1%  3.7%  0.7%  1.6%  69.4%

Year 2025 — 345 million
17.5%  12.5%  5.2%  0.8%  6%  58%

Year 2050 — 400 million
22.5%  13%  6.7%  0.8%  10%  47%

- European descent
- Latinos
- African Americans
- Asian Americans
- Native Americans
- Claim membership in two or more groups

*Sources:* By the author. Based on Bernstein and Bergman 2003; *Statistical Abstract* 2004: Table 16; 2005: Table 16. I modified the projections based on the new census category of membership in two or more groups and trends in interethnic marriage.

affirmative action in a multicultural society is likely to remain center stage for quite some time.

## Toward a True Multicultural Society

The United States has the potential to become a society in which racial–ethnic groups not only coexist, but also respect one another—and thrive—as they work together for mutually beneficial goals. In a true multicultural society, the minority groups that make up the United States would participate fully in the nation's social institutions while maintaining their cultural integrity. Reaching this goal will require that we understand that "the biological differences that divide one race from another add up to a drop in the genetic ocean." For a long time, we have given racial categories an importance they never merited. Now we need to figure out how to reduce them to the irrelevance they deserve. In short, we need to make real the abstraction called equality that we profess to believe (Cose 2000).

# SUMMARY *and* REVIEW

## Laying the Sociological Foundation

### How is race both a reality and a myth?

In the sense that different groups inherit distinctive physical traits, race is a reality. There is no agreement regarding what constitutes a particular race, however, or even how many races there are. In the sense of one race being superior to another and of there being pure races, race is a myth. The *idea* of race is powerful, shaping basic relationships among people. Pp. 226–227.

### How do race and ethnicity differ?

**Race** refers to inherited biological characteristics; **ethnicity,** to cultural ones. Members of ethnic groups identify with one another on the basis of common ancestry and cultural heritage. P. 227.

### What are minority and dominant groups?

**Minority groups** are people who are singled out for unequal treatment by members of the **dominant group,** the group with more power, privilege, and social status. Minorities originate with migration or the expansion of political boundaries. Pp. 227–229.

### What heightens ethnic identity, and what is "ethnic work"?

A group's relative size, power, physical characteristics, and amount of discrimination heighten or reduce ethnic identity. **Ethnic work** is the process of constructing and maintaining an ethnic identity. For people without a firm ethnic identity, ethnic work is an attempt to recover their ethnic heritage. For those with strong ties to their culture of origin, ethnic work involves enhancing group distinctions. Pp. 229–231.

## Prejudice and Discrimination

### Why are people prejudiced?

**Prejudice** is an attitude, and **discrimination** is an action. Like other attitudes, **prejudice** is learned in association with others. Prejudice is so extensive that people can show prejudice against groups that don't even exist. Minorities also internalize the dominant norms, and some show prejudice against their own group. Pp. 231–233.

### How do individual and institutional discrimination differ?

**Individual discrimination** is the negative treatment of one person by another, while **institutional discrimination** is negative treatment that is built into social institutions. Institutional discrimination can occur without the awareness of either the perpetrator or the object of discrimination. Discrimination in health care is one example. Pp. 234–235.

## Theories of Prejudice

### How do psychologists explain prejudice?

Psychological theories of prejudice stress the **authoritarian personality** and frustration displaced toward **scapegoats.** Pp. 235–236.

### How do sociologists explain prejudice?

Sociological theories focus on how different social environments increase or decrease prejudice. *Functionalists* stress the benefits and costs that come from discrimination. *Conflict theorists* look at how the groups in power exploit racial–ethnic divisions in order to control workers and maintain power. *Symbolic interactionists* stress how labels create **selective perception** and self-fulfilling prophecies. Pp. 236–237.

## Global Patterns of Intergroup Relations

*What are the major patterns of minority and dominant group relations?*

Beginning with the least humane, they are **genocide, population transfer, internal colonialism, segregation, assimilation,** and **multiculturalism (pluralism).** Pp. 237–240.

## Racial–Ethnic Relations in the United States

*What are the major racial–ethnic groups in the United States?*

From largest to smallest, the major groups are European Americans, Latinos, African Americans, Asian Americans, and Native Americans. Pp. 240–243.

*What are some issues in racial–ethnic relations and characteristics of minority groups?*

Latinos are divided by social class and country of origin. African Americans are increasingly divided into middle and lower classes, with two sharply contrasting worlds of experience. On many measures, Asian Americans are better off than white Americans, but their well-being varies with their country of origin. For Native Americans, the primary issues are poverty, nationhood, and settling treaty obligations. The overarching issue for minorities is overcoming discrimination. Pp. 244–254.

## Looking Toward the Future

*What main issues dominate U.S. racial–ethnic relations?*

The main issues are immigration, affirmative action, and how to develop a true multicultural society. The answers affect our future. Pp. 254–257.

# THINKING CRITICALLY *about* Chapter 9

1. How many races do your friends think there are? Do they think that one race is superior to the others? What do you think their reaction would be to the sociological position that racial categories are primarily social?

2. A hundred years ago, sociologist W. E. B. Du Bois said, "The problem of the twentieth century is the problem of the color line—the relation of the darker to the lighter races." Why do you think that the color line remains one of the most volatile topics facing the nation?

3. If you were appointed head of the U.S. Civil Service Commission, what policies would you propose to reduce racial–ethnic strife in the United States? Be ready to explain the sociological principles that might give your proposals a higher chance of success.

# BY THE NUMBERS: Changes Over Time

- Number of possible racial–ethnic categories in the 1890 census: **8**
- Number of possible racial–ethnic categories in the 2000 census: **63**

- Percentage of U.S. Native Americans who were killed or died of disease by 1860: **95%**
- Percentage of Tutsis killed in Rwanda in 1994: **77%**

- Percentage of Americans of European descent in 2000: **69%**
- Projected percentage of Americans of European descent in 2050: **47%**

- Percentage of Americans of Latino descent in 2000: **12.5%**
- Projected percentage of Americans of Latino descent in 2050: **22.5%**

- Percentage of Americans of African descent in 2000: **12%**
- Projected percentage of Americans of African descent in 2050: **13%**

- Percentage of Americans who claim membership in two or more racial–ethnic groups in 2000: **1.6%**
- Projected percentage of Americans who will claim membership in two or more racial–ethnic groups in 2050: **10%**

# ADDITIONAL RESOURCES

## What can you find in MySocLab?    mysoclab    www.mysoclab.com

- **Complete Ebook**
- **Practice Tests and Video and Audio activities**
- **Mapping and Data Analysis exercises**
- **Sociology in the News**
- **Classic Readings in Sociology**
- **Research and Writing advice**

## Where Can I Read More on This Topic?

Suggested readings for this chapter are listed at the back of this book.

# Chapter 10

# Gender and Age

I n Tunis, the capital of Tunisia, on Africa's northern coast, I met some U.S. college students and spent a couple of days with them. They wanted to see the city's red light district, but I wondered whether it would be worth the trip. I already had seen other red light districts, including the unusual one in Amsterdam where the state licenses the women, requires that they have medical check-ups (certificates must be posted so that customers can check them), sets their prices, and pays them social security benefits upon retirement. The prostitutes sit behind lighted picture windows while customers stroll along the canal side streets and browse from the outside.

**In front of each open door stood a young woman. I could see . . . a well-worn bed.**

I decided to go with them. We ended up on a wharf that extended into the Mediterranean. Each side was lined with a row of one-room wooden shacks, crowded one against the next. In front of each open door stood a young woman. Peering from outside into the dark interiors, I could see that each door led to a tiny room with a well-worn bed.

The wharf was crowded with men who were eyeing the women. Many of the men wore sailor uniforms from countries that I couldn't identify.

As I looked more closely, I could see that some of the women had runny sores on their legs. Incredibly, with such visible evidence of their disease, customers still sought them out. Evidently, the $2 price was too low to resist.

With a sick feeling in my stomach and the desire to vomit, I kept a good distance between the beckoning women and myself. One tour of the two-block area was more than sufficient.

Somewhere nearby, out of sight, I knew that there were men whose wealth derived from exploiting these women, who were condemned to live short lives punctuated by fear and misery.

In the previous chapter, we considered how race–ethnicity affects people's well-being and their position in society. In this chapter, we examine **gender stratification**—males' and females' unequal access to property, power, and prestige. We also explore the prejudice and discrimination directed toward people because of their age.

Gender and age are especially significant because, like race–ethnicity, they are *master statuses;* that is, they cut across *all* aspects of social life. *We all are labeled male or female and are assigned an age category.* These labels are powerful, because they convey images and expectations about how we should act and serve as a basis of power and privilege.

# INEQUALITIES OF GENDER

Let's begin by considering the distinctions between sex and gender.

## Issues of Sex and Gender

When we consider how females and males differ, the first thing that usually comes to mind is **sex,** the *biological characteristics* that distinguish males and females. *Primary sex characteristics* consist of a vagina or a penis and other organs related to reproduction. *Secondary sex characteristics* are the physical distinctions between males and females that are not directly connected with reproduction. These characteristics become clearly evident at puberty when males develop more muscles and a lower voice and gain more body hair and height, while females develop breasts and form more fatty tissue and broader hips.

Gender, in contrast, is a *social,* not a biological characteristic. **Gender** consists of whatever behaviors and attitudes a group considers proper for its males and females. Consequently, gender varies from one society to another. *Sex* refers to male or female, but *gender* refers to masculinity or femininity. In short, you inherit your sex, but you learn your gender as you are socialized into the behaviors and attitudes your culture asserts are appropriate for your sex. As the photo montage on the next page illustrates, the expectations associated with gender differ around the world.

*The sociological significance of gender is that it is a device by which society controls its members.* Gender sorts us, on the basis of sex, into different life experiences. It opens and closes doors to property, power, and even prestige. Like social class, gender is a structural feature of society.

Before examining inequalities of gender, let's consider why the behaviors of men and women differ.

## Gender Differences in Behavior: Biology or Culture?

Why are most males more aggressive than most females? Why do women enter "nurturing" occupations such as teaching young children and nursing in far greater numbers than men? To answer such questions, many people respond with some variation of "They're just born that way."

Is this the correct answer? Certainly biology plays a significant role in our lives. Each of us begins as a fertilized egg. The egg, or ovum, is contributed by our mother, the sperm that fertilizes the egg by our father. At the very instant the egg is fertilized, our sex is determined. Each of us receives twenty-three pairs of chromosomes from the ovum and twenty-three pairs from the sperm. The egg has an X chromosome. If the sperm that fertilizes the egg also has an X chromosome, we become a girl (XX). If the sperm has a Y chromosome, we become a boy (XY).

That's the biology. Now, the sociological question is, Does this biological difference control our behavior? Does it, for example, make females more nurturing and submissive and males more aggressive and domineering? Almost all sociologists take the side of "nurture" in this "nature versus nurture" controversy, but a few do not. The dominant position in sociology is that social factors, not biology, are the reasons we behave the way we do. Our visible differences of sex do not come with meanings built into them. Rather, each human group makes its own interpretation of these physical differences and, on this basis, assigns males and females to separate groups. In these groups, people learn what is expected of them and are given different access to their society's privileges.

Most sociologists find compelling the argument that if biology were the principal factor in human behavior, all around the world we would find women behaving in one way and men in another. In fact, however, ideas of gender vary greatly from one culture to another—and, as a result, so do male–female behaviors.

## Opening the Door to Biology

The matter of "nature" versus "nurture" is not so easily settled, however, and some sociologists acknowledge that biological factors are involved in some human behavior other than reproduction and childbearing (Udry 2000). Alice Rossi, a feminist sociologist and former president of the American Sociological Association, has suggested that

Mexico

Jordan

Kenya

Ethiopia

Brazil

Chile

India

Tibet

## Standards of Gender

Each human group determines its ideas of "maleness" and "femaleness." As you can see from these photos of four women and four men, standards of gender are arbitrary and vary from one culture to another. Yet, in its ethnocentrism, each group thinks that its preferences reflect what gender "really" is. As indicated here, around the world men and women try to make themselves appealing by aspiring to their group's standards of gender.

women are better prepared biologically for "mothering" than are men. Rossi (1977, 1984) says that women are more sensitive to the infant's soft skin and to their nonverbal communications. She stresses that the issue is not either biology or society. Instead, nature provides biological predispositions, which are then overlaid with culture.

To see why the door to biology is opening just slightly in sociology, let's consider a medical accident and a study of Vietnam veterans.

**A Medical Accident**    The drama began in 1963, when 7-month-old identical twin boys were taken to a doctor for a routine circumcision (Money and Ehrhardt 1972). The inept physician, who was using a heated needle, turned the electric current too high and accidentally burned off the penis of one of the boys. You can imagine the parents' disbelief—and then their horror—as the truth sank in.

What can be done in a situation like this? The damage was irreversible. The parents were told that their boy could never have sexual relations. After months of soul-searching and tearful consultations with experts, the parents decided that their son should have a sex-change operation. When he was 22 months old, surgeons castrated the boy, using the skin to construct a vagina. The parents then gave the child a new name, Brenda, dressed him in frilly clothing, let his hair grow long, and began to treat him as a girl. Later, physicians gave Brenda female steroids to promote female pubertal growth (Colapinto 2001).

At first, the results were promising. When the twins were 4 years old, the mother said (remember that the children are biologically identical):

> One thing that really amazes me is that she is so feminine. I've never seen a little girl so neat and tidy. . . . She likes for me to wipe her face. She doesn't like to be dirty, and yet my son is quite different. I can't wash his face for anything. . . . She is very proud of herself, when she puts on a new dress, or I set her hair. . . . She seems to be daintier. (Money and Ehrhardt 1972)

About a year later, the mother described how their daughter imitated her while their son copied his father:

> I found that my son, he chose very masculine things like a fireman or a policeman. . . . He wanted to do what daddy does, work where daddy does, and carry a lunch kit. . . . [My daughter] didn't want any of those things. She wants to be a doctor or a teacher. . . . But none of the things that she ever wanted to be were like a policeman or a fireman, and that sort of thing never appealed to her. (Money and Ehrhardt 1972)

If the matter were this clear-cut, we could use this case to conclude that gender is entirely up to nurture. Seldom are things in life so simple, however, and a twist occurs in this story. Despite this promising start and her parents' coaching, Brenda did not adapt well to femininity. She preferred to mimic her father shaving, rather than her mother putting on makeup. She rejected dolls, favoring guns and her brother's toys, and liked rough-and-tumble games. She also insisted on standing up when she urinated. Classmates teased her and called her a "cavewoman" because she walked like a boy. At age 14, she was expelled from school for beating up a girl who teased her. Despite estrogen treatment, she was not attracted to boys, and at age 14, in despair over her inner turmoil, she was thinking of suicide. In a tearful confrontation, her father told her about the accident and her sex change.

"All of a sudden everything clicked. For the first time, things made sense, and I understood who and what I was," the twin said of this revelation. David (his new name) then had testosterone shots and, later, surgery to partially reconstruct a penis. At age 25, he married a woman and adopted her children (Diamond and Sigmundson 1997; Colapinto 2001). There is an unfortunate end to this story, however. In 2004, David committed suicide.

**The Vietnam Veterans Study**    Time after time, researchers have found that boys and men who have higher levels of testosterone tend to be more aggressive. In one study, researchers compared the testosterone levels of college men in a "rowdy" fraternity with those of men in a fraternity that had a reputation for academic achievement and social responsibility. Men in the "rowdy" fraternity had higher levels of testosterone (Dabbs et al. 1996). In another study, researchers found that prisoners who had committed sex crimes and acts of violence against people had higher levels of testosterone than those who had committed property crimes (Dabbs et al. 1995). The samples that the researchers used were small, however, leaving the nagging uncertainty that these findings might be due to chance.

Then in 1985, the U.S. government began a health study of Vietnam veterans. To be certain that the study was representative, the researchers chose a random sample of 4,462 men. Among the data they collected was a measurement of testosterone. This gave sociologists a large random sample to analyze, one that is still providing surprising clues about human behavior.

This sample supports earlier studies showing that men who have higher levels of testosterone tend to be more aggressive and to have more problems as a consequence. When the veterans with higher testosterone levels were boys, they were more likely to get in trouble with parents

Sociologists stress the social factors that underlie human behavior, the experiences that mold us, funneling us into different directions in life. The study of Vietnam veterans discussed in the text is one indication of how the sociological door is opening slowly to also consider biological factors in human behavior. This February 14, 1966, photo shows orderlies rushing a wounded soldier to an evacuation helicopter.

and teachers and to become delinquents. As adults, they were more likely to use hard drugs, to get into fights, to end up in lower-status jobs, and to have more sexual partners. Knowing this, you probably won't be surprised to learn that they also were less likely to marry—certainly their low-paying jobs and trouble with the police made them less appealing candidates for marriage. Those who did marry were more likely to have affairs, to hit their wives, and, it follows, to get divorced (Dabbs and Morris 1990; Booth and Dabbs 1993).

Fortunately, the Vietnam veterans study does not leave us sociologists with biology as the sole basis for behavior. Not all men with high testosterone get in trouble with the law, do poorly in school, or mistreat their wives. A chief difference, in fact, is social class. High-testosterone men from higher social classes are less likely to be involved in antisocial behaviors than are high-testosterone men from lower social classes (Dabbs and Morris 1990). *Social* factors such as socialization, life goals, and self-definitions, then, also play a part. The matter becomes even more complicated, for in some instances men with higher testosterone have better marriages (Booth et al. 2004). Discovering how social factors work in combination with testosterone level is of great interest to sociologists.

**In Sum:** The findings are preliminary, but significant and provocative. They indicate that human behavior is not a matter of either nature or nurture, but of the two working together. Some behavior that we sociologists usually assume to be due entirely to socialization is apparently influenced by biology. In the years to come, this should prove to be an exciting—and controversial—area of soci-

ological research. One level of research will be to determine whether any behaviors are due only to biology. The second level will be to discover the ways that social factors modify biology. The third level will be, in sociologist Janet Chafetz's (1990:30) phrase, to determine how "different" becomes translated into "unequal."

"Nature or nurture?" The matter continues to be controversial. In the Down-to-Earth Sociology box on page 268, we see that gender differences have even become the focus of national attention.

## How Females Became a Minority Group

Around the world, gender is *the* primary division between people. To catch a glimpse of how remarkably gender expectations differ with culture, look at the photo essay on pages 266–267.

Every society has barriers that, on the basis of sex, prevent equal access to property, power, and prestige. The barriers *always* favor men-as-a-group. After reviewing the historical record, historian and feminist Gerda Lerner (1986) concluded that "there is not a single society known where women-as-a-group have decision-making power over men (as a group)." Consequently, sociologists classify females as a *minority group*. Because females outnumber males, you may find this strange. The term *minority group* applies, however, because it refers to people who are discriminated against on the basis of physical or cultural characteristics, regardless of their numbers (Hacker 1951). For an overview of gender discrimination in a changing society, see the Cultural Diversity box on page 269.

Have females always been a minority group? Some analysts speculate that in hunting and gathering societies, women and men were social equals (Leacock 1981; Hendrix 1994) and that horticultural societies also had less gender discrimination than is common today (Collins et al. 1993). In these societies, women may have contributed about 60 percent of the group's total food. Yet, around the world, gender is the basis for discrimination.

# Work and Gender

## Women at Work in India

traveling through India was both a pleasant and an eye-opening experience. The country is incredibly diverse, the people friendly, and the land culturally rich. For this photo essay, wherever I went—whether city, village, or countryside—I took photos of women at work.

From these photos, you can see that Indian women work in a wide variety of occupations. Some of their jobs match traditional Western expectations, and some diverge sharply from our gender stereotypes. Although women in India remain subservient to men—with the women's movement hardly able to break the cultural surface—women's occupations are hardly limited to the home. I was surprised at some of the hard, heavy labor that Indian women do.

Indian women are highly visible in public places. A storekeeper is as likely to be a woman as a man. This woman is selling glasses of water at a beach on the Bay of Bengal. The structure on which her glasses rest is built of sand.

The villages of India have no indoor plumbing. Instead, each village has a community well with a hand pump, and it is the women's job to fetch the water. This is backbreaking work, for, after pumping the water, the women wrestle the heavy buckets onto their heads and carry them home. This was one of the few occupations I saw that was limited to women.

Women also take care of livestock. It looks as though this woman dressed up and posed for her photo, but this is what she was wearing and doing when I saw her in the field and stopped to talk to her. While the sheep are feeding, her job is primarily to "be" there, to make certain the sheep don't wander off or that no one steals them.

Sweeping the house is traditional work for Western women. So it is in India, but the sweeping has been extended to areas outside the home. These women are sweeping a major intersection in Chennai. When the traffic light changes here, the women will continue sweeping, with the drivers swerving around them. This was one of the few occupations that seems to be limited to women.

As in the West, food preparation in India is traditional women's work. Here, however, food preparation takes an unexpected twist. Having poured rice from the 60-pound sack onto the floor, these women in Chittoor search for pebbles or other foreign objects that might be in the rice.

When I saw this unusual sight, I had to stop and talk to the workers. From historical pictures, I knew that belt-driven machines were common on U.S. farms 100 years ago. This one in Tamil Nadu processes sugar cane. The woman feeds sugar cane into the machine, which disgorges the stalks on one side and sugar cane juice on the other.

This woman belongs to the Dhobi subcaste, whose occupation is washing clothes. She stands waist deep at this same spot doing the same thing day after day. The banks of this canal in Hyderabad are lined with men and women of her caste, who are washing linens for hotels and clothing for more well-to-do families.

I visited quarries in different parts of India, where I found men, women, and children hard at work in the tropical sun. This woman works 8½ hours a day, six days a week. She earns 40 rupees a day (about ninety cents). Men make 60 rupees a day (about $1.35). Like many quarry workers, this woman is a bonded laborer. She must give half of her wages to her master.

A common sight in India is women working on construction crews. As they work on buildings and on highways, they mix cement, unload trucks, carry rubble, and, following Indian culture, carry loads of bricks atop their heads. This photo was taken in Raipur, Chhattisgarh.

## Down-to-Earth Sociology
### The Gender Gap in Math and Science: A National Debate

Overwhelmingly, engineers and scientists are men. Why? A national debate erupted in 2005 when Larry Summers, then the president of Harvard University, suggested that the reason might be innate differences between men and women. In essence, he was suggesting that women's inborn characteristics might make them less qualified to succeed in these endeavors.

Harvard's Arts and Sciences faculty, which was already upset over what they called Summers' authoritarian manner, took his statement as a "last straw." The faculty called an emergency meeting and gave Summers a vote of "no confidence," the equivalent of saying that he should resign. This was the first such repudiation of a president since Harvard was founded in 1636 (Finer 2005). In the face of such opposition, Summers resigned from the presidency of Harvard.

Summers' suggestion that biology *might* be the reason why men dominate science and engineering indicated that he had touched a sore spot in academia. Among the many who weighed in with replies to Summers was the Council of the American Sociological Association ("ASA Council . . ." 2005). The council replied that research gives us clear and compelling evidence that social factors, not genetics, are the reason that women have not done as well as men in science and engineering. To support its position, the council made this compelling argument:

Gender differences in test results in math and science abilities have changed over time. There are now hardly any differences in test scores among male and female U.S. students. In Great Britain, girls now outperform boys on these tests. Biology didn't change—but social factors did: more access to courses in school, changed attitudes of school counselors, and more role models for women.

The council added that women's interests change as opportunities open to them. This, too, is social, not biological. As a result, we can expect many more women to enter the fields of science and engineering. These women, unfortunately, will have to struggle against negative stereotypes about their abilities, as their predecessors have.

### For Your Consideration
Why do you think that Summers' statement made national news—and was the official basis for his rejection as president of Harvard—when such statements used to be routine? Do you think that Summers simply made the mistake of being "politically incorrect," or that the reaction to what he said indicates some fundamental social change?

How, then, did it happen that women became a minority group? Let's consider the primary theory that has been proposed.

## The Origins of Patriarchy

The major theory of the origin of **patriarchy**—men dominating society—points to social consequences of human reproduction (Lerner 1986; Friedl 1990). In early human history, life was short. To balance the high death rate and maintain the population, women had to give birth to many children. And to survive, an infant needed a nursing mother. With a child at her breast or in her uterus, or one carried on her hip or on her back, women were physically encumbered. Consequently, around the world women assumed tasks that were associated with the home and child care, while men took over the hunting of large animals and other tasks that required both greater speed and longer absences from the base camp (Huber 1990).

As a result, men became dominant. It was the men who left camp to hunt animals, who made contact with other

## Cultural Diversity around the World

### "Pssst. You Wanna Buy a Bride?" China in Transition

Nguyen Thi Hoan, age 22, thanked her lucky stars. A Vietnamese country girl, she had just arrived in Hanoi to look for work, and while she was still at the bus station, a woman offered her a job in a candy factory.

It was a trap. After Nguyen had loaded a few sacks of sugar, the woman took her into the country to "get supplies." There some men took her to China, which was only 100 miles away. Nguyen was put up for auction, along with a 16-year-old Vietnamese girl. Each brought $350. Nguyen was traded from one bride dealer to another until she was taken to a Chinese village. There she was introduced to her new husband, who had paid $700 for her (Marshall 1999).

Why are thousands of women kidnapped and sold as brides in China each year (Rosenthal 2001; Yardley 2007)? First, parts of China have a centuries-old tradition of bride selling. Second, China has a shortage of women. The government enforces a "one couple—one child" policy. Since sons are preferred, female infanticide has become common. The result is a huge imbalance: For every 100 girl babies there are about 120 baby boys (Kurlantzick 2007). As you can anticipate, this leaves a shortage of women of marriageable age. Yet all the men are expected to marry and produce heirs.

Actually, Nguyen was lucky. Some kidnapped women are sold as prostitutes.

Bride selling and forced prostitution are ancient practices. But China is also entering a new era, which is bringing with it new pressures for Chinese women. Ideas of beauty are changing, and blonde, blue-eyed women are becoming a fetish. As a consequence, Chinese women feel a pressure to "Westernize" their bodies. Surgeons promise to give them bigger breasts and Western-looking eyes. A Western style of advertising is gaining ground, too: Ads now show scantily clad women perched on top of sports cars (Chen 1995; Johansson 1999; Yat-ming Sin and Hon-ming Yau 2001).

China in transition.  It is continuing the old—bride selling—while moving toward new, Western ideas of beauty and advertising. In both the old and new, women are commodities for the consumption of men.

#### For Your Consideration

What do you think Chinese authorities should do about bride selling? Do you think different penalties are appropriate for those who kidnap the women, those who sell them to the men, and those who buy them? If so, what penalties? Finally, how can the status of women in China be raised?

---

tribes, who traded with these other groups, and who quarreled and waged war with them. It was also the men who made and controlled the instruments of death, the weapons that were used for hunting and warfare. It was they who accumulated possessions in trade and gained prestige by returning to the camp triumphantly, leading captured prisoners or bringing large animals they had killed to feed the tribe. In contrast, little prestige was given to the routine, taken-for-granted activities of women—who were not perceived as risking their lives for the group. Eventually, men took over society. Their sources of power were their weapons, items of trade, and knowledge gained from contact with other groups. Women became second-class citizens, subject to men's decisions.

Is this theory correct? Remember that the answer lies buried in human history, and there is no way of testing it. Male dominance may be the result of some entirely different cause. For example, anthropologist Marvin Harris (1977) proposed that because most men are stronger than most women and hand-to-hand combat was necessary in tribal groups, men became the warriors, and women became the reward that enticed men to risk their lives in battle. Frederick Engels proposed that patriarchy came with the development of private property (Lerner 1986;

Mezentseva 2001). He could not explain why private property should have produced male dominance, however. Gerda Lerner (1986) suggests that patriarchy may even have had different origins in different places.

Whatever its origins, a circular system of thought evolved. Men came to think of themselves as inherently superior—based on the evidence that they dominated society. They shrouded many of their activities with secrecy, and constructed elaborate rules and rituals to avoid "contamination" by females, whom they openly deemed inferior by that time. Even today, patriarchy is always accompanied by cultural supports designed to justify male dominance—such as designating certain activities as "not appropriate" for women.

As tribal societies developed into larger groups, men, who enjoyed their power and privileges, maintained their dominance. Long after hunting and hand-to-hand combat ceased to be routine, and even after large numbers of children were no longer needed to maintain the population, men held on to their power. Male dominance in contemporary societies, then, is a continuation of a millennia-old pattern whose origin is lost in history.

## Global Violence Against Women

A global human rights issue is violence against women. Historical examples are foot binding in China, witch burning in Europe, and *suttee* (burning the living widow with the body of her dead husband) in India. Today we have rape, wife beating, female infanticide, and the bride selling discussed on page 279. There is also forced prostitution, which was probably the case in our opening vignette. Another notorious example is female circumcision, the topic of the Cultural Diversity box on the next page.

A theory of how *patriarchy* originated centers on childbirth. Because only women give birth, they assumed tasks associated with home and child care, while men hunted and performed other survival tasks that required greater strength, speed, and absence from home. This woman farmer in Myanmar (Burma), also takes care of her child—just as her female ancestors have done for centuries.

Another form of violence against women is "honor killings." In some societies, such as Pakistan, Jordan, and Kurdistan, a woman who is thought to have brought disgrace on her family is killed by a male relative—usually a brother or husband, but sometimes her father or uncles. What threat to the family's honor can be so severe that the men kill a daughter, wife, or sister? The usual reason is sex outside of marriage. Even a woman who has been raped is in danger of becoming the victim of an honor killing (Zoepf 2007). Killing the girl or woman removes the "stain" she has brought to the family and restores its honor in the community. Sharing this perspective, the police in these countries generally ignore honor killings, viewing them as private family matters.

**In Sum:** Gender inequality is not some accidental, hitor-miss affair. Rather, each society's institutions work together to maintain the group's particular forms of inequality. Customs, often venerated throughout history, both justify and maintain these arrangements. In some cases, the prejudice and discrimination directed at females are so extreme they result in their enslavement and death.

Foot binding was practiced in China until about 1900. Tiny feet were a status symbol. Making it difficult for a woman to walk, small feet indicated that a woman's husband did not need his wife's labor. To make the feet even smaller, sometimes the baby's feet were broken and wrapped tightly. Some baby's toes were cut off. This photo was taken in Hubei Province, China. The woman getting the pedicure is reportedly 105 years old.

# Cultural Diversity around the World

## Female Circumcision

"Lie down there," the excisor suddenly said to me [when I was 12], pointing to a mat on the ground. No sooner had I laid down than I felt my frail, thin legs grasped by heavy hands and pulled wide apart....Two women on each side of me pinned me to the ground....I underwent the ablation of the labia minor and then of the clitoris. The operation seemed to go on forever. I was in the throes of agony, torn apart both physically and psychologically. It was the rule that girls of my age did not weep in this situation. I broke the rule. I cried and screamed with pain...!

Afterwards they forced me, not only to walk back to join the other girls who had already been excised, but to dance with them. I was doing my best, but then I fainted....It was a month before I was completely healed. When I was better, everyone mocked me, as I hadn't been brave, they said. (Walker and Parmar 1993:107–108)

*This poster is used in Sudan to try to get parents to stop circumcising their daughters.*

Worldwide, between 100 million and 200 million females have been circumcised, mostly in Muslim Africa and in some parts of Malaysia and Indonesia. In Egypt, 97 percent of the women have been circumcised (Boyle et al. 2001; Douglas 2005). In some cultures, the surgery occurs seven to ten days after birth, but in others it is not performed until girls reach adolescence. Among most groups, it takes place between the ages of 4 and 8. Because the surgery is usually done without anesthesia, the pain is so excruciating that adults hold the girl down. In urban areas, physicians sometimes perform the operation; in rural areas, a neighborhood woman usually does it.

In some cultures, only the girl's clitoris is cut off; in others, more is removed. In Sudan, the Nubia cut away most of the girl's genitalia, then sew together the remaining outer edges. They bind the girl's legs from her ankles to her waist for several weeks while scar tissue closes up the vagina. They leave a small opening the diameter of a pencil for the passage of urine and menstrual fluids.

When a woman marries, the opening is cut wider to permit sexual intercourse. Before a woman gives birth, the opening is enlarged further. After birth, the vagina is again sutured shut; this cycle of surgically closing and opening begins anew with each birth.

What are the reasons for this custom? Some groups believe that it reduces female sexual desire, making it more likely that a woman will be a virgin at marriage and, afterward, remain faithful to her husband. Others think that women can't bear children if they aren't circumcised.

The surgery has strong support among many women. Some mothers and grandmothers even insist that the custom continue. Their concern is that their daughters marry well, and in some of these societies uncircumcised women are considered impure and are not allowed to marry.

Feminists respond that female circumcision is a form of ritual torture to control female sexuality. They point out that men dominate the societies that practice it.

## For Your Consideration

Do you think that the United States should try to make other nations stop this custom? Or would this be ethnocentric, the imposition of Western values on other cultures? As one Somali woman said, "The Somali woman doesn't need an alien woman telling her how to treat her private parts." Do you think that it is ever legitimate for members of one culture to interfere with another?

How would you respond to those who oppose male circumcision, also a growing movement? How would you respond to those who point out that female circumcision was a custom of Victorian England (Silverman 2004)?

*Sources:* As cited, and Lightfoot-Klein 1989; Merwine 1993; Chalkley 1997; Collymore 2000; "Ethiopia" 2005; Tuhus-Dubrow 2007.

# Gender Inequality in the United States

Gender inequality used to be a central characteristic of U.S. society, so let's begin by taking a brief look at how change in this vital area of social life came about.

## Fighting Back: The Rise of Feminism

In the nation's early history, the second-class status of U.S. women was taken for granted. A husband and wife were legally one person—him (Chafetz and Dworkin 1986). Women could not vote, buy property in their own name, make legal contracts, or serve on juries. How could things have changed so much in the last hundred years that these examples sound like fiction?

A central lesson of conflict theory is that power yields privilege; like a magnet, power draws society's best resources to the elite. Because men tenaciously held onto their privileges and used social institutions to maintain their position, basic rights for women came only through prolonged and bitter struggle.

**Feminism**—the view that biology is not destiny and that stratification by gender is wrong and should be resisted—met with strong opposition, both by men who had privilege to lose and by women who accepted their status as morally correct. In 1894, for example, Jeannette Gilder said that women should not have the right to vote because "Politics is too public, too wearing, and too unfitted to the nature of women" (Crossen 2003).

Feminists, then known as suffragists, struggled against such views. In 1916, they founded the National Woman's Party, and in 1917 they began to picket the White House. After picketing for six months, the women were arrested. Hundreds were sent to prison, including Lucy Burns, a leader of the National Woman's Party. The extent to which these women had threatened male privilege is demonstrated by how they were treated in prison.

> **Two men brought in Dorothy Day [the editor of a periodical that promoted women's rights], twisting her arms above her head. Suddenly they lifted her and brought her body down twice over the back of an iron bench. . . . They had been there a few minutes when Mrs. Lewis, all doubled over like a sack of flour, was thrown in. Her head struck the iron bed and she fell to the floor senseless. As for Lucy Burns, they handcuffed her wrists and fastened the handcuffs over [her] head to the cell door. (Cowley 1969)**

This *first wave* of the women's movement had a radical branch that wanted to reform all the institutions of society and a conservative branch whose concern was to win the vote for women (Freedman 2001). The conservative branch dominated, and after the right to vote was won in 1920, the movement basically dissolved.

The *second wave* began in the 1960s. Sociologist Janet Chafetz (1990) points out that up to this time most women thought of work as a temporary activity intended to fill the time between completing school and getting married. To see how children's books reinforced such thinking, see Figure 10.1 on the next page. As more women took jobs and began to regard them as careers, however, they began to compare their working conditions with those of men. This shift in their reference group changed the way women viewed their conditions at work. The result was a second wave of protest against gender inequalities. The goals of this second wave (which continues today) are broad, ranging from raising women's pay to changing policies on violence against women.

A *third wave* of feminism has emerged. Three main aspects are apparent. The first is a greater focus on the problems of women in the Least Industrialized Nations (Spivak 2000; Hamid 2006). Some of them are fighting battles against conditions long since overcome by women in the Most Industrialized Nations. The second is a criticism of the

The struggle for equal rights for women has been long and hard. Shown here is a 1919 photo from the first wave of the U.S. women's movement. Only against enormous opposition from men did U.S. women win the right to vote. They first voted in national elections in 1920.

## FIGURE 10.1   Teaching Gender

**Mother and Sally**
25

**Mother can sew.**
**Jane can sew.**
59

**Father**
21

"I will help," said Dick.
"I will help you with the pigs."
120

The "Dick and Jane" readers were the top selling readers in the United States in the 1940s and 1950s. In addition to reading, they taught "gender messages." What gender message do you see here?

Housework is "women's work," and girls should learn this lesson early in life.

What does this page teach students other than how to read "Father"? (Look left to see what Jane and Mother are doing.)

Besides learning words like "pigs" (relevant at that historical period), boys and girls also learned that rough outside work was for men.

*Source:* From *Dick and Jane: Fun with Our Family,* illustrations © copyright 1951, 1979, and *Dick and Jane: We Play Outside,* copyright © 1965, 1979 Pearson Education, Inc., published by Scott, Foresman and Company. Used with permission.

values that dominate work and society. Some feminists argue that competition, toughness, calloused emotions, and independence represent "male" qualities and need to be replaced with cooperation, connection, openness, and interdependence (England 2000). A third aspect is the removal of impediments to women's love and sexual pleasure (Gilligan 2002). As this third wave develops, we can assume that it, too, will have its liberal and conservative branches.

Although U.S. women enjoy fundamental rights today, gender inequality continues to play a central role in social life. Let's look at gender relations in health care, education, the world of work, violence, and politics.

## Gender Inequality in Health Care

**Medical researchers were perplexed. Reports were coming in from all over the country: Women were twice as likely as men to die after coronary bypass surgery. Researchers at Cedars-Sinai Medical Center in Los Angeles checked their own records. They found that of 2,300 coronary bypass patients, 4.6 percent of the women died as a result of the surgery, compared with 2.6 percent of the men.**

These findings presented a sociological puzzle. To solve it, researchers first turned to biology (Bishop 1990).

In coronary bypass surgery, a blood vessel is taken from one part of the body and stitched to an artery on the surface of the heart. Perhaps this operation was more difficult to perform on women because they have smaller arteries. To find out, researchers measured the amount of time that surgeons kept patients on the heart-lung machine while they operated. They were surprised to learn that women spent *less* time on the machine than men. This indicated that the operation was not more difficult to perform on women.

As the researchers probed, a surprising answer unfolded: unintended sexual discrimination. Physicians had not taken the chest pains of their female patients as seriously as they took the complaints of their male patients. The physicians were *ten* times more likely to give men exercise stress tests and radioactive heart scans. They also sent men to surgery on the basis of abnormal stress tests but waited until women showed clear-cut symptoms of heart disease before sending them to surgery. Patients who have surgery after the disease is more advanced are less likely to survive.

As more women become physicians, perhaps such subconscious discrimination will change. Women doctors are more likely to order Pap smears and mammograms (Lurie et al. 1993). There are also indications that they offer more encouragement to their patients and engage them more in making decisions about their care. If this turns out to be true—and the conclusion is tentative—they likely will be more responsive to the health problems of women (Levinson and Lurie 2004).

In contrast to the heart surgery we just discussed, there is a type of surgery that is a blatant form of discrimination against women. This is the focus of the Down-to-Earth Sociology box below.

## Gender Inequality in Education

Gender inequality in U.S. education is not readily apparent. From a minority of students a generation ago, women now attend college in such large numbers that 57 percent

of all college students are women. Women also earn 57 percent of all bachelor's degrees and 59 percent of all master's degrees (*Statistical Abstract* 2007:Table 288). Look at Figure 10.2, which shows how women have increased their share of professional degrees. The greatest change is in dentistry: In 1970, across the entire United States, only 34 women earned degrees in dentistry. Today, 1,900 women become dentists each year. As you can also see, almost as many women as men now graduate from U.S. medical and law schools. With the change so extensive and established, I anticipate that women will soon outnumber men in earning these professional degrees.

So where is there inequality for women? If we probe beneath the surface, we still find *gender tracking*; that is, degrees tend to follow gender, which reinforces male–female

## *Down-to-Earth Sociology*
### Surgical Sexism: Cold-Hearted Surgeons and Their Women Victims

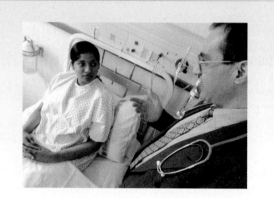

Sociologist Sue Fisher (1986), who did participant observation in a hospital, was surprised to hear surgeons recommend total hysterectomy (removal of both the uterus and the ovaries) *when no cancer was present.* When she asked why, the male doctors explained that the uterus and ovaries are "potentially disease producing." They also said that these organs are unnecessary after the childbearing years, so why not remove them? Doctors who reviewed hysterectomies confirmed this bias: They found that three out of four of these surgeries were, in their term, inappropriate (Broder et al. 2000).

Greed is a powerful motivator in life, and it certainly shows up in surgical sexism. Surgeons perform hysterectomies to make money, but since women, to understate the matter, are reluctant to part with these organs, surgeons have to "sell" this operation. As you read how one resident explained the "hard sell" to sociologist Diana Scully (1994), you might think of a used car salesperson:

> You have to look for your surgical procedures; you have to go after patients. Because no one is crazy enough to come and say, "Hey, here I am. I want you to operate on me." You have to sometimes convince the patient that she is really sick—if she is, of course [laughs], and that she is better off with a surgical procedure.

The surgeon can wield a powerful weapon that used car salespeople would love to have: To "convince" a

woman to have this surgery, the doctor puts on a serious face and tells her that the examination has turned up fibroids in her uterus—and they *might* turn into cancer. This statement is often sufficient, for it frightens women, who picture themselves lying at death's door, their sorrowful family gathered at their death bed. To clinch the sale, the surgeon withholds the rest of the truth—that fibroids are common, that they most likely will *not* turn into cancer, and that the patient has several nonsurgical alternatives.

I wonder how men would feel if surgeons systematically suggested that they be castrated when they get older—since "that organ is no longer necessary, and it might cause disease."

### For Your Consideration

Hysterectomies have become so common that one of three U.S. women eventually has her uterus surgically removed (Elson 2004). Why do you think that surgeons are so quick to operate? How can women find nonsurgical alternatives?

## FIGURE 10.2    Gender Changes in Professional Degrees

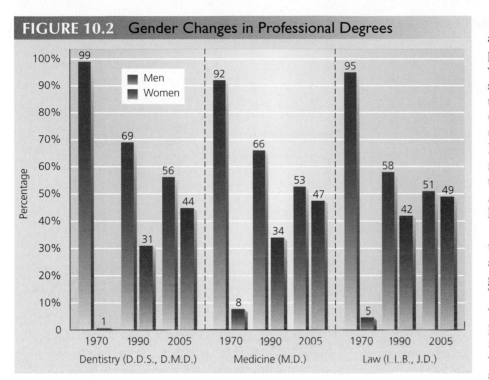

Source: Digest of Education Statistics 2007:Table 262.

If we follow students into graduate school, we see that with each passing year the proportion of women drops. Table 10.1 gives us a snapshot of doctoral programs in the sciences. Note how aspirations (enrollment) and accomplishments (doctorates earned) are sex linked. In five of these doctoral programs, men outnumber women, and in three, women outnumber men. In *all* of them, however, women are less likely to complete the doctorate.

If we follow those who earn doctoral degrees to their teaching careers at colleges and universities, we find gender stratification in rank and pay. Throughout the United States, women are less likely to become full professors, the highest-paying and most prestigious rank. In both private and public colleges, professors average more than twice the salary of instructors (*Statistical Abstract* 2007:Table 284). Even when women do become full professors, their average pay is less than that of men who are full professors (AAUP 2007:Table 5).

distinctions. Here are two extremes: Men earn 94 percent of the associate degrees in the "masculine" field of construction trades, while women are awarded 89 percent of the associate degrees in the "feminine" field of library science (*Statistical Abstract* 2007:Table 290). Because gender socialization gives men and women different orientations to life, they enter college with gender-linked aspirations. It is their socialization—not some presumed innate characteristics—that channels men and women into different educational paths.

## Gender Inequality in the Workplace

To examine the work setting is to make visible basic relations between men and women. I just mentioned the differences in what male and female professors are paid, which takes us to one of the most remarkable areas of gender inequality at work, the pay gap.

## TABLE 10.1    Doctorates in Science, By Sex

| Field | Students Enrolled | | Doctorates Conferred | | Completion Ratio[1] (Higher or Lower Than Expected) | |
|---|---|---|---|---|---|---|
| | Women | Men | Women | Men | Women | Men |
| Mathematics | 36% | 64% | 28% | 72% | −22 | +13 |
| Computer Sciences | 27% | 73% | 21% | 79% | −22 | +8 |
| Social Sciences | 53% | 47% | 44% | 56% | −17 | +19 |
| Biological Sciences | 55% | 45% | 46% | 54% | −16 | +20 |
| Agriculture | 45% | 55% | 38% | 62% | −16 | +13 |
| Physical Sciences | 31% | 69% | 26% | 74% | −16 | +7 |
| Engineering | 21% | 79% | 18% | 82% | −14 | +4 |
| Psychology | 74% | 26% | 67% | 33% | −9 | +27 |

[1]The formula for the completion ratio is X minus Y divided by Y, where X is the doctorates conferred and Y is the proportion enrolled in a program.
Source: By the author. Based on *Statistical Abstract* 2007:Tables 785, 789.

## FIGURE 10.3   Women's and Men's Proportion of the U.S. Labor Force

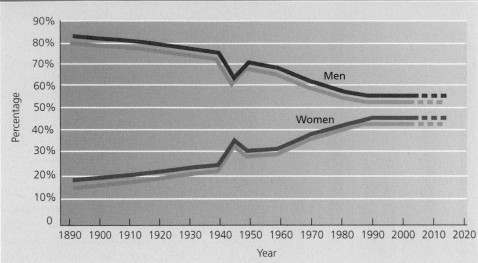

*Note:* Pre-1940 totals include women 14 and over; totals for 1940 and after are for women 16 and over. Broken lines are the author's projections.

*Sources:* By the author. Based on 1969 *Handbook on Women Workers,* 1969:10; *Manpower Report to the President,* 1971:203, 205; Mills and Palumbo, 1980:6, 45; *Statistical Abstract* 2007:Table 574.

**The Pay Gap**   One of the chief characteristics of the U.S. workforce is a steady growth in the numbers of women who work for wages outside the home. Figure 10.3 shows that in 1890 about one of every five paid workers was a woman. By 1940, this ratio had grown to one of four; by 1960 to one of three; and today it is almost one of two. As shown on this figure, the projections are that the ratio will remain 55 percent men and 45 percent women for the next few years.

Women who work for wages are not distributed evenly throughout the United States. From the Social Map below, you can see that where a woman lives makes a difference in how likely she is to work outside the home. Why is there such a clustering among the states? The geographical patterns evident in this map reflect regional-subcultural differences about which we currently have little understanding.

## FIGURE 10.4   Women in the Workforce

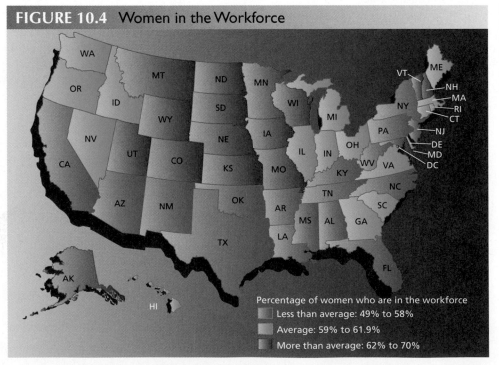

Percentage of women who are in the workforce
- Less than average: 49% to 58%
- Average: 59% to 61.9%
- More than average: 62% to 70%

*Note:* At 49.1%, West Virginia has the lowest rate of women in the workforce, while South Dakota, at 69.4%, has the highest.

*Source:* By the author. Based on *Statistical Abstract* 2007:Table 579.

After college, you might like to take a few years off, travel around Europe, sail the oceans, or maybe sit on a beach in some South American paradise and drink piña coladas. But chances are, you are going to go to work instead. Since you have to work, how would you like to earn an extra $1,300,000 on your job? If this sounds appealing, read on. I'm going to reveal how you can make an extra $2,700 a month between the ages of 25 and 65.

Is this hard to do? Actually, it is simple for some, but impossible for others. As Figure 10.5 shows, all you have to do is be born a male and graduate from college. If we compare full-time workers, based on current differences in earnings, this is how much more money the *average male* college graduate can expect to earn over the course of his career. Hardly any single factor pinpoints gender discrimination better than this total. As you can see, the pay gap shows up at *all* levels of education.

The pay gap is so great that U.S. women who work full time average *only 69 percent* of what men are paid. As you can see from Figure 10.6 on the next page, the pay gap used to be even worse. The gender gap in pay occurs not only in the United States but also in *all* industrialized nations.

If $1,300,000 additional earnings aren't enough, how would you like to make another $166,000 extra at work? If so, just make sure that you are not only a man but also a *tall* man. Over their lifetimes, men who are over 6 feet

tall average $166,000 more than men who are 5 feet 5 inches or less (Judge and Cable 2004). Taller women also make more than shorter women. But even when it comes to height, the gender pay gap persists, and tall men make more than tall women.

What logic can underlie the gender pay gap? As we just saw, college degrees are gender linked, so perhaps this gap is due to career choices. Maybe women are more likely to choose lower-paying jobs, such as teaching grade school, while men are more likely to go into better-paying fields, such as business and engineering. Actually, this is true, and researchers have found that about *half* of the gender pay gap is due to such factors. And the balance? It consists of a combination of gender discrimination (Jacobs 2003; Roth 2003) and what is called the "child penalty"—women missing out on work experience and opportunities while they care for children (Hundley 2001; Chaker and Stout 2004).

For college students, the gender gap in pay begins with the first job after graduation. You might know of a particular woman who was offered a higher salary than most men in her class, but she would be an exception. On average, men enjoy a "testosterone bonus," and employers start them out at higher salaries than women (Fuller and Schoenberger 1991; Harris et al. 2005). Depending on your sex, then, you will either benefit from the pay gap or be victimized by it.

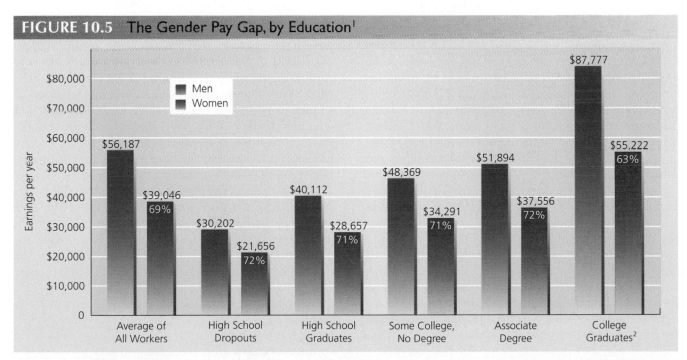

**FIGURE 10.5    The Gender Pay Gap, by Education[1]**

[1]Full-time workers in all fields.
[2]Bachelor's and all higher degrees, including professional degrees.

*Source:* By the author. Based on *Statistical Abstract* 2008:Table 681.

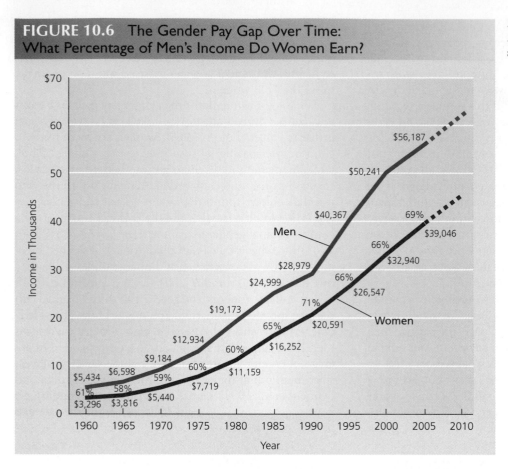

**FIGURE 10.6   The Gender Pay Gap Over Time: What Percentage of Men's Income Do Women Earn?**

*Source:* By the author. Based on *Statistical Abstract* 2008: Table 681, and earlier years.

As a final indication of the extent of the U.S. gender pay gap, consider this. Of the nation's top 500 corporations (the so-called "Fortune 500"), only 10 are headed by women (Fuhrmans and Hymowitz 2007). And 10 is a record-breaking number! I examined the names of the CEOs of the 350 largest U.S. corporations, and I found that your best chance to reach the top is to be named (in this order) John, Robert, James, William, or Charles. Edward, Lawrence, and Richard are also advantageous names. Amber, Katherine, Leticia, and Maria, however, apparently draw a severe penalty. Naming your baby girl John or Robert might seem a little severe, but it could help her reach the top. (I say this only slightly tongue-in-cheek. One of the few women to head a Fortune 500 company—before she was fired and given $21 million severance pay—had a man's first name: Carleton Fiorina of Hewlett-Packard. Carleton's first name was actually Cara, but knowing what she was facing in the highly competitive business world, she dropped this feminine name to go by her masculine middle name.)

**The Cracking Glass Ceiling**   What keeps women from breaking through the **glass ceiling,** the mostly invisible barrier that prevents women from reaching the executive suite? The "pipelines" that lead to the top are the marketing, sales, and production positions that directly affect the corporate bottom line (Hymowitz 2004; DeCrow 2005). Men, who dominate the executive suite, stereotype women as being less capable of leadership but good at "support" (Belkin 2007). They steer women into human resources or public relations. There, successful projects are not appreciated in the same way as those that bring corporate profits—and bonuses for their managers.

Another reason the glass ceiling is so powerful is that women lack mentors—successful executives who take an interest in them and teach them the ropes. Lack of a mentor is no trivial matter, for mentors can provide opportunities to develop leadership skills that open the door to the executive suite (Heilman 2001; Hymowitz 2007).

The glass ceiling is cracking, however (Solomon 2000; Hymowitz 2004). A look at women who have broken through reveals highly motivated individuals with a fierce competitive spirit who are willing to give up sleep and recreation for the sake of career advancement. They also learn to play by "men's rules," developing a style that makes men comfortable. Most of these women also have

**Dilbert**

One of the frustrations felt by many women in the labor force is that no matter what they do, they hit a glass ceiling. Another is that to succeed they feel forced to abandon characteristics they feel are essential to their self.

supportive husbands who share household duties and adapt their careers to accommodate the needs of their executive wives (Lublin 1996). In addition, women who began their careers twenty to thirty years ago are now running many major divisions within the largest companies (Hymowitz 2004). With this background, some of these women have begun to emerge as the new CEOs.

Then there is the *glass escalator*. Sociologist Christine Williams (1995) interviewed men and women who worked in traditionally female jobs—as nurses, elementary school teachers, librarians, and social workers. Instead of bumping their heads against a glass ceiling, the men in these occupations found themselves aboard a **glass escalator.** They were given higher-level positions, more desirable work assignments, and higher salaries. The motor that drives the glass escalator is gender—the stereotype that because someone is male he is more capable.

## Sexual Harassment—and Worse

**Sexual harassment**—unwelcome sexual attention at work or at school, which may affect a person's job or school performance or create a hostile environment—was not recognized as a problem until the 1970s. Before this, women considered unwanted sexual comments, touches, looks, and pressure to have sex to be a personal matter.

With the prodding of feminists, women began to perceive unwanted sexual advances at work and school as part of a *structural* problem. That is, they began to realize that the issue was more than a man here or there doing obnoxious things because he was attracted to a woman; rather, men were using their positions of authority to pressure women to have sex. Now that women have moved into positions of authority, they, too, have become sexual harassers (Wayne et al. 2001). With most authority still vested in men, however, most of the sexual harassers are men.

As symbolic interactionists stress, labels affect our perception. Because we have the term *sexual harassment,* we perceive actions in a different light than did our predecessors. The meaning of sexual harassment is vague and shifting, however, and court cases constantly change what this term does and does not include. Originally, sexual desire was an element of sexual harassment, but it no longer is. This changed when the U.S. Supreme Court considered the lawsuit of a homosexual who had been tormented by his supervisors and fellow workers. The Court ruled that sexual desire is not necessary—that sexual harassment laws also apply to homosexuals who are harassed by heterosexuals while on the job (Felsenthal 1998). By extension, the law applies to heterosexuals who are sexually harassed by homosexuals.

## Gender and Violence

Around the world, one of the consistent characteristics of violence is its gender inequality. That is, females are more likely to be the victims of males, not the other way around. Let's see how this almost-one-way street in gender violence applies to the United States.

**Forcible Rape**    Being raped is a common fear of U.S. women, a fear that is far from groundless. As high as the official rate of rape is, the real rate is even higher. We know this from the National Crime Victimization Survey, an annual survey of 135,000 people. Only 41 percent of rapes are reported to the police. If we eliminate males from this report, since male victims are the exception, each year about 22 of every 10,000 females age 12 and older are raped (Rand and Catalano 2007). Despite these high numbers, women are safer now than they were ten and twenty years ago, as the rape rate has declined.

Women's most common fear seems to be that of strangers—who, appearing as though from nowhere, abduct and beat and rape them. Contrary to the stereotypes that underlie these fears, most victims know their attacker. As you can see from Table 10.2, about one of three rapes is committed by strangers.

An aspect of rape that is usually overlooked is the rape of men in prison. With prison officials reluctant to let the public know about the horrible conditions behind bars, our studies are far from perfect. Those we have, however, indicate that about 15 to 20 percent of men in prison are raped. From court cases, we know that some guards even punish prisoners by placing them in cells with sexual predators (Donaldson 1993; Lewin 2001).

**Date (Acquaintance) Rape** What has shocked so many about date rape (also known as *acquaintance rape*) are studies showing that it does not consist of a few isolated events (Collymore 2000; Goode 2001). Some researchers even report that most women students experience unwanted, forced, or coerced sex (Kalof 2000). Others report much smaller numbers. Researchers who used a representative sample of courses to survey the students at Marietta College, a private school in Ohio, found that 2.5 percent of the women had been physically forced to have sex (Felton et al. 2001). About as many men (23 percent) as women (24 percent) had given in to pressure to have sex when they didn't want to, but—and this is no surprise—none of the men had been physically forced to have sex.

Most date rapes go unreported. A primary reason is that the victim feels partially responsible because she knows the person and was with him voluntarily. However, as a physician who treats victims of date rape said, "Would you feel responsible if someone hit you over the head with a shovel—just because you knew the person?" (Carpenito 1999).

**Murder** All over the world, men are more likely than women to be killers. Figure 10.7 illustrates this gender pattern in U.S. murders. Note that although females make up about 51 percent of the U.S. population, they don't even come close to making up 51 percent of the nation's killers. As you can see from this figure, when women are murdered, about 8 or 9 times out of 10 the killer is a man.

**Violence in the Home** Women are also the typical victims of family violence. Spouse battering, marital rape, and incest are discussed in Chapter 12, pages 354–355. A particular form of violence against women, genital circumcision, is the focus of the Cultural Diversity box on page 271.

**Feminism and Gendered Violence** Feminist sociologists have been especially effective in bringing violence against women to the public's attention. Some use symbolic interactionism, pointing out that to associate strength and

| TABLE 10.2 Relationship of Rapists to Their Victims | |
|---|---|
| Relationship | Percentage |
| Knows her attacker | 56.8% |
|   Knows well | 27.1% |
|   Casual acquaintance | 26.1% |
|   A relative | 3.6% |
| A stranger | 33.5% |
| Not reported | 9.7% |

*Source:* By the author. Based on *Statistical Abstract* 2007:Table 315.

virility with violence—as is done in many cultures—is to promote violence. Others use conflict theory. They argue that men are losing power and that some men turn violently against women as a way to reassert their declining power and status (Reiser 1999; Meltzer 2002).

**Solutions** There is no magic bullet for this problem of gendered violence, but to be effective, any solution must break the connection between violence and masculinity. This would require an educational program that encompasses schools, churches, homes, and the media. Given the gun-slinging heroes of the Wild West and other American icons, as well as the violent messages that are so prevalent in the mass media, it is difficult to be optimistic that a change will come any time soon.

Our next topic, women in politics, however, gives us much more reason for optimism.

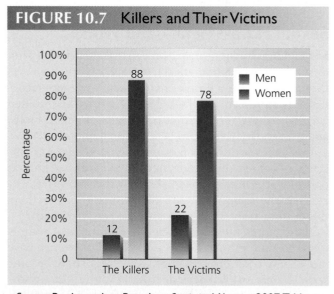

**FIGURE 10.7 Killers and Their Victims**

*Source:* By the author. Based on *Statistical Abstract* 2007:Tables 300, 317.

## The Changing Face of Politics

Women could take over the United States! Think about it. Eight million more women than men are of voting age, and more women than men vote in U.S. national elections. As Table 10.3 shows, however, men greatly outnumber women in political office. Despite the gains women have made in recent elections, since 1789 over 1,800 men have served in the U.S. Senate, but only 35 women have served, including 16 current senators. Not until 1992 was the first African American woman (Carol Moseley-Braun) elected to the U.S. Senate. No Latina or Asian American woman has yet been elected to the Senate (National Women's Political Caucus 1998; *Statistical Abstract* 2007:Table 395).

Why are women underrepresented in U.S. politics? First, women are still underrepresented in law and business, the careers from which most politicians emerge. Most women also find that the irregular hours kept by those who run for office are incompatible with their role as mother. Fathers, in contrast, whose traditional roles are more likely to take them away from home, are less likely to feel this conflict. Women are also not as likely to have a supportive spouse who is willing to play an unassuming background role while providing solace, encouragement, child care, and voter appeal. Finally, preferring to hold on to their positions of power, men have been reluctant to incorporate women into centers of decision making or to present them as viable candidates.

These conditions are changing. Watershed events occurred when Nancy Pelosi was elected by her colleagues in 2002 as the first woman minority leader, and then in 2007 as the first woman Speaker of the House. These posts made her the most powerful woman ever in the House of Representatives. In 2008, Hillary Clinton became the first

| TABLE 10.3 | U.S. Women in Political Office | |
|---|---|---|
| | Percentage of Offices Held by Women | Number of Offices Held by Women |
| **National Office** | | |
| U.S. Senate | 16% | 16 |
| U.S. House of Representatives | 16% | 71 |
| **State Office** | | |
| Governors | 18% | 9 |
| Lt. Governors | 22% | 11 |
| Attorneys General | 8% | 4 |
| Secretaries of State | 24% | 12 |
| Treasurers | 22% | 11 |
| State Auditors | 12% | 6 |
| State Legislators | 24% | 1,734 |

*Source:* Center for American Women and Politics 2007.

woman to win a presidential primary, in New Hampshire. We can also note that more women are becoming corporate executives, and, as indicated in Figure 10.2 (on page 274), more women are also becoming lawyers. In these positions, women are doing more traveling and making statewide and national contacts. Another change is that child care is increasingly seen as a responsibility of both mother and father. This generation, then, is likely to mark a fundamental change in women's political participation, and it is only a matter of time until a woman occupies the Oval Office.

## Glimpsing the Future—with Hope

Women's fuller participation in the decision-making processes of our social institutions has shattered stereotypes that tended to limit females to "feminine" activities and to push males into "masculine" ones. As structural barriers and stereotypes continue to fall, both males and females will have greater freedom to pursue their interests, capacities, and potential. Distinctions between the sexes will not disappear, but there is no reason for biological differences to be translated into social inequalities. If current trends continue, we may see a growing appreciation of sexual differences coupled with greater equality of opportunity—which has the potential of transforming society (Gilman 1911/1971; Offen 1990). If this happens, as sociologist Alison Jaggar (1990) observed, gender equality can become less a goal than a background condition for living in society.

Hillary Clinton broke through the glass ceiling in politics when she was elected senator from New York. She also came within a hair of becoming the Democratic nominee for president.

# INEQUALITIES OF AGING

In 1928, Charles Hart, who was working on his Ph.D. in anthropology, did fieldwork with the Tiwi who live on an island off the northern coast of Australia. Because every Tiwi belongs to a clan, they assigned Hart to the bird (Jabijabui) clan and told him that a particular woman was his mother. Hart described the woman as "toothless, almost blind, withered." He added that she was "physically quite revolting and mentally rather senile." He then recounted this remarkable event:

Toward the end of my time on the islands an incident occurred that surprised me because it suggested that some of them had been taking my presence in the kinship system much more seriously than I had thought. I was approached by a group of about eight or nine senior men. . . . They were the senior members of the Jabijabui clan and they had decided among themselves that the time had come to get rid of the decrepit old woman who had first called me son and whom I now called mother. . . . As I knew, they said, it was Tiwi custom, when an old woman became too feeble to look after herself, to "cover her up." This could only be done by her sons and brothers and all of them had to agree beforehand, since once it was done, they did not want any dissension among the brothers or clansmen, as that might lead to a feud. My "mother" was now completely blind, she was constantly falling over logs or into fires, and they, her senior clansmen, were in agreement that she would be better out of the way. Did I agree?

I already knew about "covering up." The Tiwi, like many other hunting and gathering peoples, sometimes got rid of their ancient and decrepit females. The method was to dig a hole in the ground in some lonely place, put the old woman in the hole and fill it in with earth until only her head was showing. Everybody went away for a day or two and then went back to the hole to discover to their great surprise, that the old woman was dead, having been too feeble to raise her arms from the earth. Nobody had "killed" her; her death in Tiwi eyes was a natural one. She had been alive when her relatives last saw her. I had never seen it done, though I knew it was the custom, so I asked my brothers if it was necessary for me to attend the "covering up."

They said no and that they would do it, but only after they had my agreement. Of course I agreed, and a week or two later we heard in our camp that my "mother" was dead, and we all wailed and put on the trimmings of mourning. (C. W. M. Hart in Hart and Pilling 1979:125–126)

# Aging in Global Perspective

We won't deal with the question of whether it was moral or ethical for Hart to agree that the old woman should be "covered up." What is of interest for our purposes is how the Tiwi treated their frail elderly—or, more specifically, their frail *female* elderly. You probably noticed that the Tiwi "covered up" only old women. As was noted earlier, females are discriminated against throughout the world. As this case makes evident, in some places that discrimination extends even to death.

Every society must deal with the problem of people growing old and of some becoming frail. Although few societies choose to bury old people alive, all societies must decide how to allocate limited resources among their citizens. With the percentage of the population that is old increasing in many nations, these decisions are generating tensions between the generations.

## The Social Construction of Aging

The way the Tiwi treated frail elderly women reflects one extreme of how societies cope with aging. Another extreme, one that reflects an entirely different attitude, is illustrated by the Abkhasians, an agricultural people who live in a mountainous region of Georgia, a republic

The man riding the horse is Temir Tarba, who was 100 years old when the photo was taken. As discussed in the text, the Abkhasians have an extraordinarily large number of elderly, but due to a lack of records, there are questions about their exact age.

of the former Soviet Union. The Abkhasians pay their elderly high respect and look to them for guidance. They would no more dispense with their elderly by "covering them up" than we would "cover up" a sick child in our culture.

The Abkhasians may be the longest-lived people on earth. Many claim to live past 100—some beyond 120 and even 130 (Benet 1971; Robbins 2006). Although it is difficult to document the accuracy of these claims, government records indicate that an extraordinary number of Abkhasians do live to a very old age.

Three main factors appear to account for their long lives. The first is their diet, which consists of little meat, much fresh fruit, vegetables, garlic, goat cheese, cornmeal, buttermilk, and wine. The second is their lifelong physical activity. They do slow down after age 80, but even after the age of 100 they still work about four hours a day. The third factor—a highly developed sense of community—lies at the very heart of the Abkhasian culture. From childhood, each individual is integrated into a primary group and remains so throughout life. There is no such thing as a nursing home, nor do the elderly live alone. Because they continue to work and contribute to the group's welfare, the elderly aren't a burden to anyone.

They don't vegetate, nor do they feel the need to "fill time" with bingo and shuffleboard. In short, the elderly feel no sudden rupture between what they "were" and what they "are."

The examples of the Tiwi and the Abkhasians reveal an important sociological principle: *Like gender, aging is socially constructed.* That is, nothing in the nature of aging summons forth any particular viewpoint. Rather, attitudes toward the aged are rooted in society and, therefore, differ from one social group to another.

## Industrialization and the Graying of the Globe

As noted in previous chapters, industrialization is a worldwide trend. The higher standard of living that industrialization brings includes more food, a purer water supply, and more effective ways of fighting the diseases that kill children. Consequently, when a country industrializes, more of its people live longer and reach older ages. The Social Map below illustrates this principle.

From this global map, you can see that the industrialized countries have the highest percentage of elderly. The range among nations is broad, from just 1 of 48 citizens

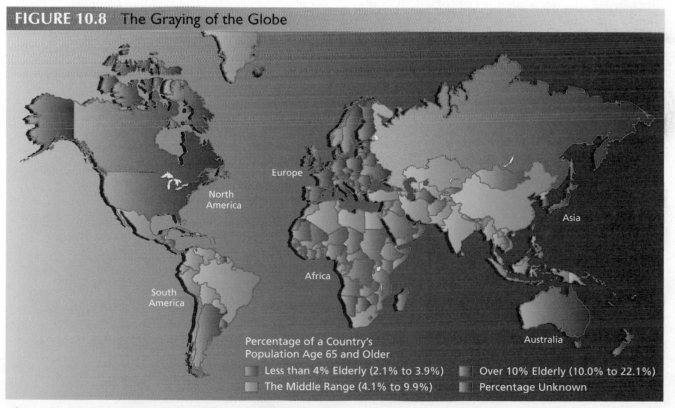

**FIGURE 10.8    The Graying of the Globe**

Percentage of a Country's Population Age 65 and Older

- Less than 4% Elderly (2.1% to 3.9%)
- The Middle Range (4.1% to 9.9%)
- Over 10% Elderly (10.0% to 22.1%)
- Percentage Unknown

*Source:* By the author. Based on *Statistical Abstract* 2007:Table 1309.

in nonindustrialized Uganda to *ten* times higher than this, almost 1 of 4.5, in postindustrial Japan (*Statistical Abstract* 2007:Table 1309). In just two decades, *half* the population of Italy and Japan will be older than 50 (Kinsella and Phillips 2005). The graying of the globe is so new that *two-thirds of all people who have ever passed age 50 in the history of the world are alive today* (Zaslow 2003).

As a nation's elderly population increases, so, too, does the bill its younger citizens pay to provide for their needs. This expense has become a major social issue. Although Americans complain that Social Security taxes are too high, the U.S. rate of 15.3 percent is comparatively low. Polish workers are hit the hardest; they pay 37 percent of their wages into social security. Only a percentage or two less is paid by workers in Austria, France, Greece, Holland, and Hungary (*Statistical Abstract* 2007:Tables 531, 1335). Workers in the Least Industrialized Nations pay no social security taxes. There, families are expected to take care of their own elderly, with no help from the government.

As the numbers of elderly continue to grow, analysts have become alarmed about future liabilities for their care. This issue is especially troubling in western Europe, which has the largest percentage of citizens over the age of 60. The basic issue is, How can nations provide high-quality care for their growing numbers of elderly without burdening future generations with impossible taxes? No one has found a solution yet, and more and more nations around the world are confronting this issue.

## The Graying of America

As Figure 10.9 illustrates, the United States is part of this global trend. This figure shows how U.S. **life expectancy,** the number of years people can expect to live, has increased since 1900. To me, and perhaps to you, it is startling to realize that a hundred years ago the average American could not even expect to see age 50. Since then, we've added about *30* years to our life expectancy, and Americans born today can expect to live into their 70s or 80s.

The term **graying of America** refers to this increasing percentage of older people in the U.S. population. Look at Figure 10.10 on the next page. In 1900 only 4 percent of Americans were age 65 and older. Today about 13 percent are. The average 65-year-old can expect to live another eighteen years (*Statistical Abstract* 2007:Table 100). U.S. society has become so "gray" that, as Figure 10.11 shows, the median age has almost *doubled* since 1850. Today, there are 7 million *more* elderly Americans than there are teenagers (*Statistical Abstract* 2007:Table 11). Despite this vast change, on a global scale Americans rank 10th in life expectancy. With its overall average of 82, Japan holds the record for the longest life expectancy.

As anyone who has ever visited Florida has noticed, the elderly population is not evenly distributed around the country. (As Jerry Seinfeld sardonically noted, "There's a law that when you get old, you've got to move to Florida.") The Social Map on the next page shows how uneven this distribution is.

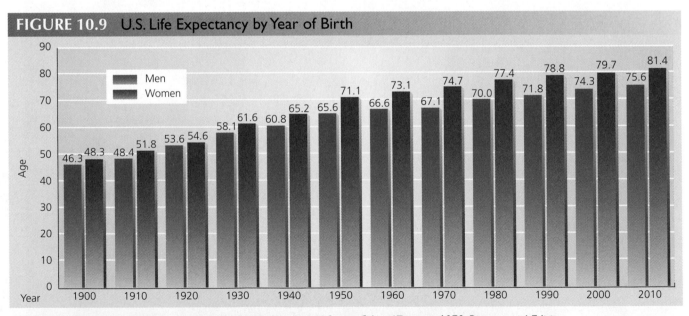

**FIGURE 10.9**   U.S. Life Expectancy by Year of Birth

*Sources:* By the author. Based on *Historical Statistics of the United States, Colonial Times to 1970,* Bicentennial Edition, Part I, Series B, 107–115; *Statistical Abstract* 2007:Table 98.

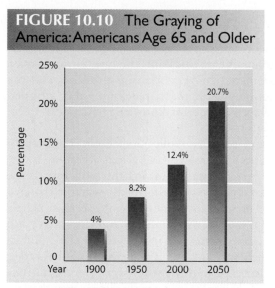

**FIGURE 10.10  The Graying of America: Americans Age 65 and Older**

*Source:* By the author. Based on *Statistical Abstract* 2007: Tables 11 and 12, and earlier years.

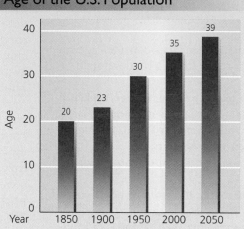

**FIGURE 10.11  The Median Age of the U.S. Population**

*Source:* By the author. Based on *Statistical Abstract* 2007: Tables 11 and 12, and earlier years.

Although more people are living to old age, the maximum length of life possible, the **life span,** has not increased. No one knows, however, just what the maximum is. We do know that it is at least 122, for this was the well-documented age of Jeanne Louise Calment of France at her death in 1997. If the reports on the Abkhasians are correct (a matter of controversy), the human life span may exceed even this number by a comfortable margin. It is also likely that advances in genetics will extend the human life span.

Let's see the different pictures of aging that emerge when we apply the three theoretical perspectives.

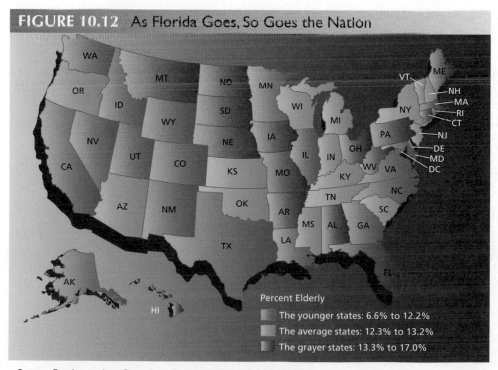

**FIGURE 10.12  As Florida Goes, So Goes the Nation**

*Source:* By the author. Based on *Statistical Abstract* 2007: Table 21.

# The Symbolic Interactionist Perspective

To apply symbolic interactionism, let's consider ageism and how negative stereotypes of the elderly developed.

> At first, the audience sat quietly as the developers explained their plans to build a high-rise apartment building. After a while, people began to shift uncomfortably in their seats. Then they began to show open hostility.
>
> "That's too much money to spend on those people," said one.
>
> "You even want them to have a swimming pool?" asked another incredulously.
>
> Finally, one young woman put their attitudes in a nutshell when she asked, "Who wants all those old people around?"

When physician Robert Butler (1975, 1980) heard these complaints about plans to build apartments for senior citizens, he began to realize how deeply antagonistic feelings toward the elderly can run. He coined the term **ageism** to refer to prejudice, discrimination, and hostility directed against people because of their age. Let's see how ageism developed in U.S. society.

## Shifting Meanings of Growing Old

As we have seen, there is nothing inherent in old age to produce any particular attitude, negative or not. Old age may even have been regarded positively in early U.S. society (Cottin 1979; Kart 1990; Clair et al. 1993). In colonial times, growing old was seen as an accomplishment because so few people made it to old age. With no pensions, the elderly continued to work at jobs that changed little over time. They were viewed as storehouses of knowledge about work skills and sources of wisdom about how to live a long life.

The coming of industrialization eroded these bases of respect. With better sanitation and medical care, more people reached old age. No longer was being elderly an honorable distinction. The new forms of mass production made young workers as productive as the elderly. Coupled with mass education, this stripped away the elderly's superior knowledge (Cowgill 1974; Hunt 2005).

A basic principle of symbolic interactionism is that people perceive both themselves and others according to the symbols of their culture. Following this principle, as the meaning of old age was transformed—when it changed from an asset to a liability—not only did younger people come to view the elderly differently but the elderly also began to perceive themselves in a new light. This shift in meaning is demonstrated in the way people lie about their age: They used to claim that they were older than they were, but now they say that they are younger than they are (Clair et al. 1993).

When does old age begin? And what activities are appropriate for the elderly? From this photo that I took of Munimah, a 65-year-old bonded laborer in Chennai, India, you can see how culturally relative these questions are. No one in Chennai thinks it is extraordinary that this woman makes her living by carrying heavy rocks all day in the burning, tropical sun.

Stereotypes, which play such a profound role in social life, are a basic area of sociological investigation. In contemporary society, the mass media are a major source of stereotypes.

PEANUTS® by Charles M. Schulz

The meaning of old age is shifting once again. Today, most U.S. elderly can take care of themselves financially, and many are well-off. In addition, members of the baby boom generation are now in their late 50s. With their vast numbers, better health, and financial strength, they also are destined to positively affect our images of the elderly. The next step in this symbolic shift, now in process, is to celebrate old age as a time of renewal—not simply as a period that precedes death, but, rather, as a new stage of growth.

Even in scholarly theories, perceptions of the elderly have become more positive. A theory that goes by the mouthful *gerotranscendence* was developed by Swedish sociologist Lars Tornstam. The thrust of this theory is that as people grow old they transcend their more limited views of life. They begin to feel more at one with the universe and come to see things as less black and white. As they develop more subtle ways of viewing right and wrong, they tolerate more ambiguity (Manheimer 2005). This theory is not likely to be universal. I have seen some elderly people grow softer and more spiritual, but I have also seen others grow bitter, close up, and become even more judgmental of life. The theory's limitations should become apparent shortly.

## The Influence of the Mass Media

In Chapter 3 (pages 71–73), we noted that the mass media help to shape our ideas about both gender and relationships between men and women. As a powerful source of symbols, the media also influence our ideas of the elderly, the topic of the Mass Media box on the next page.

## The Functionalist Perspective

Functionalists analyze how the parts of society work together. Among the components of society are **age cohorts**—people who were born at roughly the same time

and who pass through the life course together. Although not visible to us, our age cohort has major effects on our lives. For example, if the age cohort nearing retirement is large (a "baby boom" generation), many jobs open up at roughly the same time. In contrast, if it is a small group (a "baby bust" generation), fewer jobs open up. Let's look at theories that focus on how people adjust to retirement.

## Disengagement Theory

Elaine Cumming and William Henry (1961) analyzed how society prevents disruption when the elderly leave their positions of responsibility. In what is called **disengagement theory,** they explained how it would be disruptive if the elderly left their positions only when they died or became incompetent. To avoid this, pensions are offered to entice the elderly to hand over their positions to younger people. Retirement (or disengagement), then, is a mutually beneficial arrangement between two parts of society. It helps to smooth the transition between the generations.

Cumming (1976) also examined disengagement from the individual's perspective. She pointed out that people start to disengage during middle age, long before retirement. This happens when they sense that the

# MASS MEDIA in SOCIAL LIFE

## Shaping Our Perceptions of the Elderly

The mass media profoundly influence our lives. What we hear and see on television and in the movies, the songs we listen to, the books and magazines we read—all become part of our world view. Without our knowing it, the media shape our images of people. They influence how we view minorities and dominant groups; men, women, and children; people with disabilities; people from other cultures—and the elderly.

The shaping of our images and perception of the elderly is subtle, so much so that it usually occurs without our awareness. The elderly, for example, are underrepresented on television and in most popular magazines. This leaves a covert message—that the elderly are of little consequence and can be safely ignored.

The media also reflect and reinforce stereotypes of *gender age*. Older male news anchors are likely to be retained, while female anchors who turn the same age are more likely to be transferred to less visible positions. Similarly, in movies older men are more likely to play romantic leads—and to play them opposite much younger rising stars.

Although usually subtle, the message is not lost. The more television that people watch, the more they perceive the elderly in negative terms. The elderly, too, internalize these negative images, which, in turn, affects the way they view themselves. These images are so powerful that they affect the elderly's health, even the way they walk (Donlon et al. 2005).

We become fearful of growing old, and we go to great lengths to deny that this is happening to us. Fear and denial play into the hands of advertisers, of course, who exploit our concerns about losing our youth. They help us deny this biological reality by selling us hair dyes, skin creams, and other products that are designed to conceal even the appearance of old age. For these same reasons, Americans visit plastic surgeons to remove telltale signs of aging.

*Age is more than biology. In some cultures, Demi Moore, 46, would be considered elderly. Moore is shown here with her husband, Ashton Kutcher, 30. Almost inevitably, when there is a large age gap between a husband and wife, it is the husband who is the older one. The marriage of Kutcher and Moore is a reversal of the typical pattern.*

The elderly's growing numbers and affluence translate into economic clout and political power. It is inevitable, then, that the media's images of the elderly will change. An indication of that change is shown in the photo above.

### For Your Consideration

What other examples of fear and denial of growing old are you familiar with? What examples of older males playing romantic leads with younger costars can you give? Of older females and younger males? Why do you think we have gender age?

---

end of life is closer than its start. Realizing that their time is limited, they gradually begin to assign priority to goals and tasks. Disengagement begins in earnest when their children leave home and increases with retirement and eventually widowhood.

**Evaluation of the Theory**    Disengagement theory came under attack almost as soon as the ink dried on the theorists' paper. One of the main criticisms is that this theory contains an implicit bias against older people—assumptions that the elderly disengage from productive social roles and then slink into oblivion (Manheimer

2005). Instead of disengaging, say the critics, the elderly *exchange* one set of roles for another (Jerrome 1992). The elderly find new roles, which often center on friendship, no less satisfying than their earlier roles. These new roles are less visible to researchers, however, who tend to have a youthful orientation—and who show their bias by assuming that productivity is the measure of self-worth.

Changing technology is also changing what it means to "disengage." Computers, the Internet, and new types of work have blurred the dividing line between work and retirement. Less and less does retirement mean to abruptly stop working. Many workers just slow down. Some continue at their jobs, but put in fewer hours. Others work as occasional consultants. Some switch careers, even though they are in their 60s or, in some instances, even in their 70s. Many never "retire"—at least not in the sense of sinking into a recliner or being forever on the golf course. If disengagement theory is ever resurrected, it must come to grips with this fundamental change.

## Activity Theory

Are retired people more satisfied with life? Are intimate activities more satisfying than formal ones? Such questions are the focus of **activity theory,** which assumes that the more activities elderly people engage in, the more they find life satisfying. Although we could consider this theory from other perspectives, we are examining it from the functionalist perspective because its focus is how disengagement is functional or dysfunctional.

**Evaluation of the Theory**    The results are mixed. In general, researchers have found that more active people are more satisfied. But not always. A study of retired people in France found that some people are happier when they are more active, but others when they are less involved (Keith 1982). Similarly, most people find informal, intimate activities, such as spending time with friends, to be more satisfying than formal activities. But not everyone does. In one study, 2,000 retired U.S. men reported formal activities to be as important as informal ones. Even solitary activities, such as doing home repairs, had about the same impact as intimate activities on these men's life satisfaction (Beck and Page 1988). It is the same for spending time with adult children. "Often enough" for some parents is "not enough" or even "too much" for others. In short, researchers have discovered the obvious: What makes life satisfying for one person doesn't work for another.

## Continuity Theory

Another theory of how people adjust to growing old is **continuity theory.** As its name implies, the focus of this theory is how people adjust to old age by maintaining ties with their past (Kinsella and Phillips 2005). When they

retire, many people take on new roles that are similar to the ones they gave up. For example, a former CEO might serve as a consultant, a retired electrician might do small electrical repairs, or a pensioned banker might volunteer to direct the finances of her church. Researchers have found that people who are active in multiple roles (wife, author, mother, intimate friend, church member, etc.) are better equipped to handle the changes that growing old entails. They have also found that with their greater resources to meet the challenges of old age, people from higher social classes adjust better to aging.

**Evaluation of the Theory**    The basic criticism of continuity theory is that it is too broad (Hatch 2000). We all have anchor points based on our particular experiences in life, and we all rely on them to make adjustments to the changes we encounter. This applies to people of all ages beyond infancy. This theory is really a collection of loosely connected ideas, with no specific application to the elderly.

**In Sum:** The *broader* perspective of the functionalists is how society's parts work together to keep society running smoothly. Although it is inevitable that younger workers replace the elderly, this transition could be disruptive. To entice the elderly out of their positions so that younger people can take over, the elderly are offered pensions. Functionalists also use a *narrower* perspective, focusing on how individuals adjust to their retirement. The findings of this narrower perspective are too mixed to be of much value—except that people who have better resources and are active in multiple roles adjust better to old age (Crosnoe and Elder 2002).

Because workers do not have to retire by any certain age, a major thrust of theory should be people's decision making. How do people choose to retire or to keep working? Especially important is how people reconstruct their identities and come to terms with the new life they choose. As the United States grows even grayer, this should prove a productive area of sociological theory and research.

As the numbers of U.S. elderly grow, researchers are exploring their mental and social development, as well as the causes of physical and emotional well-being. As research progresses, do you think we will reach the point where the average old person will be in this couple's physical condition?

# The Conflict Perspective

As you know, the conflict perspective's guiding principle of social life is the struggle of social groups for power and resources. How does this apply to society's age groups? Regardless of whether the young and old recognize it, say conflict theorists, they are opponents in a struggle that threatens to throw society into turmoil. The passage of Social Security legislation is an example of this struggle.

## Social Security Legislation

In the 1920s, before Social Security provided an income for the aged, two-thirds of all citizens over 65 had no savings and could not support themselves (Holtzman 1963; Crossen 2004a). The fate of workers sank even deeper during the Great Depression, and in 1930 Francis Townsend, a physician, started a movement to rally older citizens. He soon had one-third of all Americans over age 65 enrolled in his Townsend Clubs. They demanded that the federal government impose a national sales tax of 2 percent to provide $200 a month for every person over 65 ($2,100 a month in today's money). In 1934, the Townsend Plan went before Congress. Because it called for such high payments and many were afraid that it would destroy people's incentive to save for the future, members of Congress looked for a way to reject the plan without appearing to oppose the elderly. When President Roosevelt announced his more modest Social Security plan in 1934, Congress embraced it (Schottland 1963; Amenta 2006).

To provide jobs for younger people, the new Social Security law required that workers retire at age 65. It did not matter how well people did their work or how much they needed the pay. For decades, the elderly protested. Finally, in 1986, Congress eliminated mandatory retirement. Today, almost 90 percent of Americans retire by age 65, but most do so voluntarily. No longer can they be forced out of their jobs simply because of their age.

Conflict theorists point out that Social Security did not come about because the members of Congress had generous hearts. Rather, Social Security emerged from a struggle between competing interest groups. As conflict theorists stress, when competing groups are in equilibrium, it is only a temporary balancing of oppositional forces, one that can be upset at any time. Perhaps more direct conflict may emerge. Let's consider this possibility.

## Intergenerational Conflict

Will the future bring conflict between the elderly and the young? Although violence is not likely, if you listen closely, you can hear ripples of grumbling—complaints that the elderly are getting more than their fair share of society's resources. The huge costs of Social Security and Medicare have become a national concern. These two programs alone account for *one of every three* (31 percent) tax dollars (*Statistical Abstract* 2007:Table 462). As Figure 10.13 shows, Social Security payments were $781 million in 1950; now they run more than *700 times* higher.

As the government transferred resources to the elderly, their condition improved. On Figure 10.14 on the next page, you can trace their declining rate of poverty. As you do so, look at how the poverty rate of U.S. children increased from 1967 until the early 1990s, fell during the 1990s, and is again on the rise. When some analysts suggested that the decline in the elderly's rate of poverty

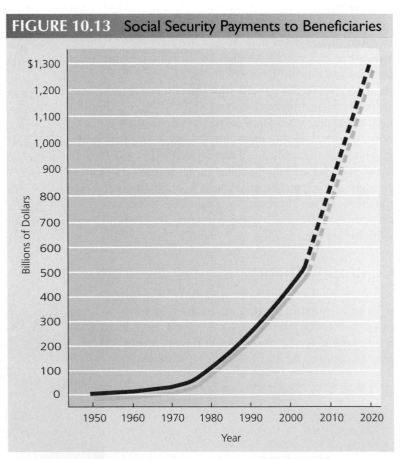

**FIGURE 10.13    Social Security Payments to Beneficiaries**

*Source:* By the author. Based on *Statistical Abstract* 1997:Table 518; 2007:Table 462. Broken line indicates the author's projections.

## FIGURE 10.14  Trends in Poverty

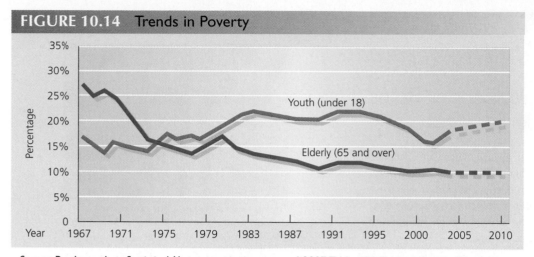

*Source:* By the author. *Statistical Abstract,* various years, and 2007:Table 694. Broken lines indicate the author's projections.

came at the expense of the nation's children, conflict sociologists Meredith Minkler and Ann Robertson (1991) pointed out how misleading this comparison is. Would anyone say that the money the government gives to flood victims comes from the children? Or to build highways? Of course not. Politicians make choices about where to spend taxes, and, if they want to they can increase spending to relieve the poverty of both the elderly and children.

As conflict theorists point out, framing the issue as a case of money going to one group at the expense of another group can divide the working class. To get working-class people to think that they must choose between pathetic children and suffering old folks can splinter them into opposing groups, breaking their power to work together to improve society.

Some form of conflict seems inevitable. The graying of the United States leaves fewer workers to pay for the benefits received by the increasing millions who collect Social Security. The shift in the **dependency ratio**—the number of people who collect Social Security compared with the number of workers who contribute to it—is especially troubling. As Figure 10.15 shows, sixteen workers used to support each person who was collecting Social Security. Now the dependency ratio has dropped to four to one. In another generation, it could hit two to one. If it does, how will younger workers be able to pay the huge sums it will take to support the older generation? How will they be able to pay for the soaring costs of health care shown in Figure 10.16 on the next page?

## FIGURE 10.15  Fewer Workers Supporting a Larger Number of Retirees and Disabled Workers

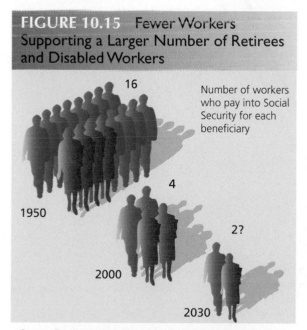

*Source:* By the author. Based on Social Security Administration; *Statistical Abstract* 2007:Tables 531 and 533.

# Gender Roles Among the Elderly

As I stressed at the beginning of this chapter, gender roles are a master status. We learn them early, we refine them during youth, and we play them during the rest of our lives. Even in old age, our gender roles remain a part of us. I think you will enjoy the Down-to-Earth Sociology box with which we close this chapter.

# Down-to-Earth Sociology

## Feisty to the End: Gender Roles Among the Elderly

This image of my father always makes me smile—not because he was arrested as an old man, but, rather, because of the events that led to his arrest. My dad had always been a colorful character, ready with endless, ribald jokes and a hearty laugh. He carried these characteristics into his old age.

*During their elderly years, men and women continue to exhibit aspects of the gender roles that they learned and played in their younger years.*

---

**FIGURE 10.16   Health Care Costs for the Elderly and Disabled**

Medicare is intended for the elderly and disabled, Medicaid for the poor. About 24 percent of Medicaid payments ($55 billion) go to the elderly (*Statistical Abstract* 2007:Table 138).

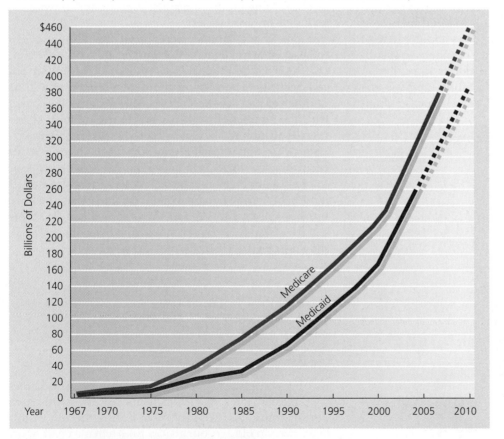

*Note:* Broken lines indicate the author's projections.
*Source:* By the author. Based on *Statistical Abstract,* various years, and 2008:Tables 134, 140.

My dad, in his late 70s, was living in a small apartment in a complex for the elderly in Minnesota. The adjacent building was a nursing home, the next destination for the residents of these apartments. None of them liked to think about this "home," because no one survived it—yet they all knew what was in store for them. Under the watchful eye of these elderly neighbors, care in the nursing home was fairly good. Until they were transferred to this unwelcome last stopping-place, life went on "as usual" in the complex for the elderly.

According to the police report and my dad's account, here is what happened:

Dad was sitting in the downstairs lounge with other residents, waiting for the mail to arrive, a daily ritual that the residents looked forward to. For some reason known only to my dad, he hooked his cane under the dress of an elderly woman, lifted up her skirt, and laughed. Understandably, this upset her, as well as her husband, who was standing next to her. Angry, the man moved toward my father, threatening him.

I say "moved," rather than "lunged," because this man was using a walker. My dad started to run away from this threat. Actually, "run" isn't quite the right word. "Hobbled" would be a better term.

My dad fled as fast as he could using his cane, while this other man pursued him as fast as he could using his walker. Wheezing, puffing, and panting as they went from the lounge into the long adjoining hall, the two paused to catch their breath now and then. Tiring the most, the other man gave up the pursuit. He then called the police.

When the police officer arrived, he said, "Uncle Marv, I'm sorry, but I'm going to have to arrest you." (This event occurred in a small town, and the officer assigned this case turned out to be Dad's nephew.)

Dad went before a judge, who could hardly keep a straight face. He gave Dad a small fine and warned him to behave himself. The apartment manager also gave Dad a warning: One more incident, and he would have to move out of the complex.

Dad's wife wasn't too happy about the situation, either.

This event was brought to mind by a newspaper account of a fight that broke out at the food bar of a retirement home ("Melee Breaks . . ." 2004). It seems that one elderly man criticized the way another man was picking through the salad. When a fight broke out between the two, several elderly people were hurt as they tried either to intervene or to flee.

## For Your Consideration

People carry their personalities, values, and other traits into old age. Among these characteristics are their gender roles. What examples of gender roles do you see in the events related here? Are you familiar with how old people continue to show their femininity or masculinity?

# SUMMARY *and* REVIEW

## Issues of Sex and Gender

### What is gender stratification?

The term **gender stratification** refers to unequal access to property, power, and prestige on the basis of sex. Each society establishes a structure that, on the basis of sex and gender, opens and closes doors to its privileges. P. 262.

### How do sex and gender differ?

**Sex** refers to biological distinctions between males and females. It consists of both primary and secondary sex characteristics. **Gender,** in contrast, is what a society considers proper behaviors and attitudes for its male and female members. *Sex* physically distinguishes males from females; *gender* refers to what people call "masculine" and "feminine." P. 262.

### Why do the behaviors of males and females differ?

The "nature versus nurture" debate refers to whether differences in the behaviors of males and females are caused by inherited (biological) or learned (cultural) characteristics. Almost all sociologists take the side of nurture. In recent years, however, sociologists have begun to cautiously open the door to biology. Pp. 262–265.

## How Females Became a Minority Group

**Patriarchy,** or male dominance, appears to be universal. The origin of discrimination against females is lost in history, but the primary theory of how females became a minority group in their own societies focuses on the physical limitations imposed by childbirth. Pp. 265–270.

*What are some forms of global violence against females?*

The major forms discussed here are honor killing, bride selling, and female circumcision. Pp. 270–272.

## Gender Inequality in the United States

*Is the feminist movement new?*

In what is called the "first wave," feminists made political demands for change in the early 1900s—and were met with hostility, and even violence. The "second wave" began in the 1960s and continues today. A "third wave" has emerged. Pp. 272–273.

*What forms do gender inequality in health care and education take?*

Physicians don't take women's health complaints as seriously as those of men, and they exploit women's fears, performing unnecessary hysterectomies. More women than men attend college, but each tends to select fields that are categorized as "feminine" or "masculine." Women are less likely to complete the doctoral programs in science. Pp. 273–275.

*How does gender inequality show up in the workplace?*

All occupations show a gender gap in pay. For college graduates, the lifetime pay gap runs well over a million dollars in favor of men. **Sexual harassment** also continues to be a reality of the workplace. Pp. 275–279.

*What is the relationship between gender and violence?*

Overwhelmingly, the victims of rape and murder are females. Conflict theorists point out that men use violence to maintain their power and privilege. Pp. 279–280.

*What is the trend in gender inequality in politics?*

A traditional division of gender roles—women as child care providers and homemakers, men as workers outside the home—used to keep women out of politics. Women continue to be underrepresented in politics, but the trend toward greater political equality is firmly in place. Pp. 281–282.

## Aging in Global Perspective

*How are the elderly treated around the world?*

No single set of attitudes, beliefs, or policies regarding the aged characterizes the world's nations. Rather, they vary from exclusion and killing to integration and honor. The global trend is for more people to live longer. Pp. 282–285.

## The Symbolic Interactionist Perspective

*What does the social construction of aging mean?*

Nothing in the nature of aging produces any particular set of attitudes. Rather, attitudes toward the elderly are rooted in society and differ from one social group to another. Pp. 285–287.

## The Functionalist Perspective

*How is retirement functional for society?*

Functionalists focus on how the withdrawal of the elderly from positions of responsibility benefits society. **Disengagement theory** examines retirement as a device for ensuring that a society's positions of responsibility will be passed smoothly from one generation to the next. **Activity theory** examines how people adjust when they disengage from productive roles. **Continuity theory** focuses on how people adjust to growing old by maintaining their roles and coping techniques. Pp. 287–290.

## The Conflict Perspective

*Is there conflict among different age groups?*

Social Security legislation is an example of one generation making demands on another generation for limited resources. As the number of retired people grows, there are relatively fewer workers to support them. Pp. 290–291.

## Gender Roles Among the Elderly

*Do the elderly give up their gender roles?*

Gender roles are master traits, and people don't discard them as they age. As with their values and other orientations to life, people carry their gender roles into old age. Pp. 291–293.

# THINKING CRITICALLY *about* Chapter 10

1. What is your position on the "nature versus nurture" (biology or culture) debate? What materials in this chapter support your position?

2. Why do you think that the gender gap in pay exists all over the world?

3. How does culture influence our ideas about the elderly?

# BY THE NUMBERS: Changes Over Time

- Percentage of medical school graduates who were women in 1970: **8**
- Percentage of medical school graduates today who are women: **44**

- Number of men who have served in the U.S. Senate since 1789: **1,800**
- Number of women who have served in the Senate: **33**

- Percentage of men's salary earned by women in 1970: **59**
- Percentage of men's salary earned by women today: **69**

- Median age in the United States in 1900: **23**
- Median age in the United States today: **35**

- Number of workers for each person who received Social Security in 1950: **16**
- Number of workers for each person who receives Social Security today: **4**

- Amount of Social Security payments in 1950: **$781 million**
- Amount of Social Security payments today: **$550 billion**

- Cost of Medicare in 1975: **$17 billion**
- Cost of Medicare today: **$380 billion**

- Percentage of U.S. children in poverty in 1970: **25%**
- Percentage of U.S. children in poverty today: **17%**

- Percentage of U.S. elderly in poverty in 1970: **25%**
- Percentage of U.S. elderly in poverty today: **10%**

- Percentage of Americans who were elderly in 1900: **4%**
- Percentage of Americans who are elderly today: **13%**

- U.S. life expectancy in 1900: **47 years**
- U.S. life expectancy today: **78 years**

- Women's percentage of the U.S. labor force in 1900: **20%**
- Women's percentage of the U.S. labor force today: **45%**

# ADDITIONAL RESOURCES

## What can you find in MySocLab? mysoclab  www.mysoclab.com

- **Complete Ebook**
- **Practice Tests and Video and Audio activities**
- **Mapping and Data Analysis exercises**

- **Sociology in the News**
- **Classic Readings in Sociology**
- **Research and Writing advice**

## Where Can I Read More on This Topic?

Suggested readings for this chapter are listed at the back of this book.

Chapter

11

# Politics and the Economy

In 1949, George Orwell wrote *1984,* a book about a time in the future in which the government, known as "Big Brother," dominates society, dictating almost every aspect of each individual's life. Even loving someone is considered sinister—a betrayal of the supreme love and total allegiance that all citizens owe Big Brother.

> Even loving someone is considered sinister—a betrayal of the supreme love and total allegiance that all citizens owe Big Brother.

Despite the danger, Winston and Julia fall in love. They delight in each other, but they must meet furtively, always with the threat of discovery hanging over their heads. When informers turn them in, interrogators separate Julia and Winston and try to destroy their affection and restore their loyalty to Big Brother.

Winston's tormentor is O'Brien, who straps Winston into a chair so tightly that he can't even move his head. O'Brien explains that inflicting pain is not always enough to break a person's will, but everyone has a breaking point. There is some worst fear that will push anyone over the edge.

O'Brien tells Winston that he has discovered his worst fear. Then he sets a cage with two starving giant sewer rats on the table next to Winston. O'Brien picks up a hood connected to the door of the cage and places it over Winston's head. He then explains that when he presses the lever, the door of the cage will slide up, and the rats will shoot out like bullets and bore straight into Winston's face. Winston's eyes, the only part of his body that he can move, dart back and forth, revealing his terror. Speaking so quietly that Winston has to strain to hear him, O'Brien adds that the rats sometimes attack the eyes first, but sometimes they burrow through the cheeks and devour the tongue. When O'Brien places his hand on the lever, Winston realizes that the only way out is for someone else to take his place. But who? Then he hears his own voice screaming, "Do it to Julia! . . . Tear her face off. Strip her to the bones. Not me! Julia! Not me!"

Orwell does not describe Julia's interrogation, but when Julia and Winston see each other later, they realize that each has betrayed the other. Their love is gone. Big Brother has won.

Winston's and Julia's misplaced loyalty had made them political heretics, a danger to the state, for every citizen had the duty to place the state above all else in life. To preserve the state's dominance over the individual, their allegiance to one another had to be stripped from them. As you see, it was.

# POLITICS: ESTABLISHING LEADERSHIP

To exist, every society must have a system of leadership. Some people must have power over others.

## Power, Authority, and Violence

As Max Weber (1913/1947) pointed out, we perceive power as either legitimate or illegitimate. *Legitimate* power is called **authority.** This is power that people accept as right. In contrast, *illegitimate* power—called **coercion**—is power that people do not accept as just.

Imagine that you are on your way to buy the hot new cell phone that just came on sale for $250. As you approach the store, a man jumps out of an alley and shoves a gun in your face. He demands your money. Frightened for your life, you hand over your $250. After filing a police report, you head back to college to take a sociology exam. You are running late, so you step on the gas. As you hit 85, you see flashing blue and red lights in your rearview mirror. Your explanation about the robbery doesn't faze the officer—or the judge who hears your case a few weeks later. She first lectures you on safety and then orders you to pay $50 in court costs plus $10 for every mile over 65. You pay the $250.

The mugger, the police officer, and the judge—all have power, and in each case you part with $250. What, then, is the difference? The difference is that the mugger has no authority. His power is *illegitimate*—he has no *right* to do what he did. In contrast, you acknowledge that the officer has the right to stop you and that the judge has the right to fine you. They have authority, or *legitimate* power.

## Authority and Legitimate Violence

As sociologist Peter Berger observed, it makes little difference whether you willingly pay the fine that the judge levies against you or refuse to pay it. The court will get its money one way or another.

> There may be innumerable steps before its application [of violence], in the way of warnings and reprimands. But if all the warnings are disregarded, even in so slight a matter as paying a traffic ticket, the last thing that will happen is that a couple of cops show up at the door with handcuffs and a Black Maria [billy club]. Even the moderately courteous cop who hands out the initial traffic ticket is likely to wear a gun—just in case. (Berger 1963)

The *government,* then, also called the **state,** claims a monopoly on legitimate force or violence. This point, made by Max Weber (1946, 1922/1978)—that the state claims both the exclusive right to use violence and the right to punish everyone else who uses violence—is crucial to our understanding of politics. If someone owes you a debt, you cannot take the money by force, much less imprison that person. The state, however, can. The ultimate proof of the state's authority is that you cannot kill someone because he or she has done something that you consider absolutely horrible—but the state can. As Berger (1963) summarized this matter, *"Violence is the ultimate foundation of any political order."*

Why do people accept power as legitimate? Max Weber (1922/1978) identified three sources of authority: traditional, rational–legal, and charismatic. Let's examine each.

The ultimate foundation of any political order is violence. At no time is this more starkly demonstrated than when government takes a human life. Shown in this 1979 photo are Iranian soldiers executing Kurdish rebels.

## Traditional Authority

Throughout history, the most common basis for authority has been tradition. **Traditional authority,** which is based on custom, is the hallmark of tribal groups. In these societies, custom dictates basic relationships. For example, birth into a particular family makes an individual the chief, king, or queen. As far as members of that society are concerned, this is the right way to determine who shall rule because "We've always done it this way."

Traditional authority declines with industrialization, but it never dies out. Even though we live in a postindustrial society, parents continue to exercise authority over their children *because* parents always have had such authority. From generations past, we inherit the idea that parents should discipline their children, choose their children's doctors and schools, and teach their children religion and morality.

## Rational–Legal Authority

The second type of authority, **rational–legal authority,** is based not on custom but on written rules. *Rational* means reasonable, and *legal* means part of law. Thus *rational–legal* refers to matters that have been agreed to by reasonable people and written into law (or regulations of some sort). The matters that are agreed to may be as broad as a constitution that specifies the rights of all members of a society or as narrow as a contract between two individuals. Because bureaucracies are based on written rules, rational–legal authority is sometimes called *bureaucratic authority.*

Rational–legal authority comes from the *position* that someone holds, not from the person who holds that position. In a democracy, for example, the president's authority comes from the legal power assigned to that office, as specified in a written constitution, not from custom or the individual's personal characteristics. In rational–legal authority, everyone—no matter how high the office held—is subject to the organization's written rules. In governments based on traditional authority, the ruler's word may be law, but in those based on rational–legal authority, the ruler's word is subject to the law.

## Charismatic Authority

A few centuries back, in 1429, the English controlled large parts of France. When they prevented the coronation of a new French king, a farmer's daughter heard a voice telling her that God had a special assignment for her—that she should put on men's clothing, recruit an army, and go to war against the English. Inspired, Joan of Arc raised an army, conquered cities, and defeated the English. Later that year, her visions were fulfilled as she stood next to Charles VII while he was crowned king of France. (Bridgwater 1953)

Joan of Arc is an example of **charismatic authority,** the third type of authority Weber identified. (*Charisma* is a Greek word that means a gift freely and graciously given [Arndt and Gingrich 1957].) People are drawn to a charismatic individual because they believe that individual has been touched by God or has been endowed by nature with exceptional qualities (Lipset 1993). The armies did not follow Joan of Arc because it was the custom to do so, as in traditional authority. Nor did they risk their lives alongside her because she held a position defined by written rules, as in rational–legal authority. Instead, people followed her because they were attracted by her outstanding traits. They saw her as a messenger of God, fighting on the side of justice, and they accepted her leadership because of these appealing qualities.

One of the best examples of *charismatic authority* is Joan of Arc, shown here at the coronation of Charles VII, whom she was instrumental in making king. Uncomfortable at portraying Joan of Arc wearing only a man's coat of armor, the artist has made certain she is wearing plenty of makeup and also has added a ludicrous skirt.

**The Threat Posed by Charismatic Leaders**    Kings and queens owe allegiance to tradition, and presidents to written laws. To what, however, do charismatic leaders owe allegiance? Their authority resides in their ability to attract followers, which is often based on their sense of a special mission or calling. Not tied to tradition or the regulation of law, charismatic leaders pose a threat to the established political order. Following their personal inclination, charismatic leaders can inspire followers to disregard—or even to overthrow—traditional and rational–legal authorities.

This threat does not go unnoticed, and traditional and rational–legal authorities often oppose charismatic leaders. If they are not careful, however, their opposition may arouse even more positive sentiment in favor of the charismatic leader, with him or her viewed as an underdog persecuted by the powerful. Occasionally the Roman Catholic Church faces such a threat, as when a priest claims miraculous powers that appear to be accompanied by amazing healings. As people flock to this individual, they bypass parish priests and the formal ecclesiastical structure. This transfer of allegiance from the organization to an individual threatens the church hierarchy. Consequently, church officials may encourage the priest to withdraw from the public eye, perhaps to a monastery, to rethink matters. This defuses the threat, reasserts rational–legal authority, and maintains the stability of the organization.

## The Transfer of Authority

The orderly transfer of authority from one leader to another is crucial for social stability. Under traditional authority, people know who is next in line. Under rational–legal authority, people might not know who the next leader will be, but they do know how that person will be selected. South Africa provides a remarkable example of the orderly transfer of authority under a rational–legal organization. This country had been ripped apart by decades of racial–ethnic strife, including horrible killings committed by each side. Yet, by maintaining its rational–legal authority, the country was able to transfer power peacefully from the dominant group led by President de Klerk to the minority group led by Nelson Mandela.

*Charismatic authorities* can be of any morality, from the saintly to the most bitterly evil. Like Joan of Arc, Adolf Hitler attracted throngs of people, providing the stuff of dreams and arousing them from disillusionment to hope.

Charismatic authority has no such rules of succession, however. This makes it less stable than either traditional or rational–legal authority. Because charismatic authority is built around a single individual, the death or incapacitation of a charismatic leader can mean a bitter struggle for succession. To avoid this, some charismatic leaders make arrangements for an orderly transition of power by appointing a successor. This step does not guarantee orderly succession, of course, for the followers may not have the same confidence in the designated heir as did the charismatic leader. A second strategy is for the charismatic leader to build an organization. As the organization develops a system of rules or regulations, it transforms itself into a rational–legal organization. Weber used the term the **routinization of charisma** to refer to the transition of authority from a charismatic leader to either traditional or rational–legal authority.

# Types of Government

How do the various types of government—monarchies, democracies, dictatorships, and oligarchies—differ? As we compare them, let's also look at how the state arose and why the concept of citizenship was revolutionary.

## Monarchies: The Rise of the State

Early societies were small and needed no extensive political system. They operated more like an extended family. As surpluses developed and societies grew larger, cities evolved—perhaps around 3500 B.C. (Fischer 1976). **City-states** then came into being, with power radiating

outward from the city like a spider's web. Although the ruler of each city controlled the immediate surrounding area, the land between cities remained in dispute. Each city-state had its own **monarchy,** a king or queen whose right to rule was passed on to the monarch's children. If you drive through Spain, France, or Germany, you can still see evidence of former city-states. In the countryside, you will see only scattered villages. Farther on, your eye will be drawn to the outline of a castle on a faraway hill. As you get closer, you will see that the castle is surrounded by a city. Several miles farther, you will see another city, also dominated by a castle. Each city, with its castle, was once a center of power.

City-states often quarreled, and wars were common. The victors extended their rule, and eventually a single city-state was able to wield power over an entire region. As the size of these regions grew, the people slowly began to identify with the larger region. That is, they began to see distant inhabitants as "we" instead of "they." What we call the **state**—the political entity that claims a monopoly on the use of violence within a territory—came into being.

## Democracies: Citizenship as a Revolutionary Idea

The United States had no city-states. Each colony, however, was small and independent like a city-state. After the American Revolution, the colonies united. With the greater strength and resources that came from political unity, they conquered almost all of North America, bringing it under the power of a central government.

The government formed in this new country was called a **democracy.** (Derived from two Greek words—*demos,* "common people," and *kratos,* "power"—*democracy* literally means "power to the people.") Because of the bitter antagonisms associated with the **revolution** against the British king, the founders of the new country were distrustful of monarchies. They wanted to put political decisions into the hands of the people.

This was not the first democracy the world had seen, but such a system had been tried before only with smaller groups. Athens, a city-state of Greece, practiced democracy 2,500 years ago, with each free male above a certain age having the right to be heard and to vote. Members of some Native American tribes, such as the Iroquois, also elected their chiefs, and in some, women were able to vote and to hold the office of chief. (The Incas and Aztecs of Mexico and Central America had monarchies.)

Because of their small size, tribes and cities were able to practice **direct democracy.** That is, they were small enough for the eligible voters to meet together, express their opin-

ions, and then vote publicly—much like a town hall meeting today. As populous and spread out as the United States was, however, direct democracy was impossible, and the founders invented **representative democracy.** Certain citizens (at first, only white male landowners) voted for men to represent them in Washington. Later, the vote was extended to men who didn't own property, to African American men, and, finally, to women. Our new communications technologies, which make "electronic town meetings" possible, could even allow a new form of direct democracy to develop.

Today we take the concept of citizenship for granted. What is not evident to us is that this idea had to be envisioned in the first place. There is nothing natural about citizenship; it is simply one way in which people choose to define themselves. Throughout most of human history, people were thought to *belong* to a clan, to a tribe, or even to a ruler. The idea of **citizenship**—that by virtue of birth and residence people have basic rights—is quite new to the human scene (Turner 1990; Abowitz and Harnish 2006).

The concept of representative democracy based on citizenship—perhaps the greatest gift the United States has given to the world—was revolutionary. Power was to be vested in the people themselves, and government was to flow from the people. That this concept was revolutionary is generally forgotten, but its implementation meant *the reversal of traditional ideas. It made the government responsive to the people's will, not the people responsive to the government's will.* To keep the government responsive to the needs of its citizens, people were expected to express dissent. In a widely quoted statement, Thomas Jefferson observed that

> A little rebellion now and then is a good thing. . . . It is a medicine necessary for the sound health of government. . . . God forbid that we should ever be twenty years without such a rebellion. . . . The tree of liberty must be refreshed from time to time with the blood of patriots and tyrants. (In Hellinger and Judd 1991)

The idea of **universal citizenship**—of *everyone* having the same basic rights by virtue of being born in a country (or by immigrating and becoming a naturalized citizen)—flowered slowly and came into practice only through fierce struggle. When the United States was founded, for example, this idea was still in its infancy. Today it seems inconceivable to Americans that gender or race–ethnicity should be the basis to deny anyone the right to vote, hold office, make a contract, testify in court, or own property. For earlier generations of property-owning white American men, however, it seemed just as inconceivable that women, racial–ethnic minorities, and the poor should be *allowed* such rights.

## Dictatorships and Oligarchies: The Seizure of Power

If an individual seizes power and then dictates his will to the people, the government is known as a **dictatorship.** If a small group seizes power, the government is called an **oligarchy.** The occasional coups in Central and South America and Africa, in which military leaders seize control of a country, are examples of oligarchies. Although one individual may be named president, often it is military officers, working behind the scenes, who make the decisions. If their designated president becomes uncooperative, they remove him from office and appoint another.

Monarchies, dictatorships, and oligarchies vary in the amount of control they wield over their citizens. **Totalitarianism** is almost *total* control of a people by the government. In Nazi Germany, Hitler organized a ruthless secret police force, the Gestapo, which searched for any sign of dissent. Spies even watched how moviegoers reacted to newsreels, reporting those who did not respond "appropriately" (Hippler 1987). Saddam Hussein acted just as ruthlessly toward Iraqis. The lucky ones who opposed Hussein were shot; the unlucky ones had their eyes gouged out, were bled to death, or were buried alive (Amnesty International 2005). The punishment for telling a joke about Hussein was to have your tongue cut out.

People around the world find great appeal in the freedom that is inherent in citizenship and representative democracy. Those who have no say in their government's decisions, or who face prison or even death for expressing dissent, find in these ideas the hope for a brighter future. With today's electronic communications, people no longer remain ignorant of whether they are more or less politically privileged than others. This knowledge produces pressure for greater citizen participation in government. As electronic communications develop further, this pressure will increase.

# The U.S. Political System

With this global background, let's examine the U.S. political system. We shall consider the two major political parties, compare the U.S. political system with other democratic systems, and examine voting patterns and the role of lobbyists and PACs.

## Political Parties and Elections

After the founding of the United States, numerous political parties emerged. By the time of the Civil War, however, two parties dominated U.S. politics: the Democrats, who in the public mind are associated with the working class, and the Republicans, who are associated with wealthier people (Burnham 1983). In pre-elections, called *primaries,* the voters decide who will represent their party. The candidate chosen by each party then campaigns, trying to appeal to the most voters. The Social Map on the next page shows how Americans align themselves with political parties.

Although the Democrats and Republicans represent somewhat different philosophical principles, each party appeals to a broad membership, and it is difficult to distinguish a conservative Democrat from a liberal Republican. The extremes are easy to discern, however. Deeply committed Democrats support legislation that transfers income from those who are richer to those who are poorer or that controls wages, working conditions, and competition. Deeply committed Republicans, in contrast, oppose such legislation.

Those who are elected to Congress may cross party lines. That is, some Democrats vote for legislation proposed by Republicans, and vice versa. This happens because officeholders support their party's philosophy, but not necessarily its specific proposals. When it comes to a particular bill, such as raising the minimum wage, some conservative Democrats may view the measure as unfair to small employers and vote with the Republicans against the bill. At the same time, liberal Republicans—feeling that the proposal is just, or sensing a dominant sentiment in voters back home—may side with its Democratic backers.

Regardless of their differences and their public quarrels, the Democrats and Republicans represent *different slices of the center.* Although each party may ridicule the opposing party and promote different legislation, they both firmly support such fundamentals of U.S. political philosophy as free public education; a strong military; freedom of religion, speech, and assembly; and, of course, capitalism—especially the private ownership of property.

Third parties also play a role in U.S. politics, but to gain power, they must also support these centrist themes. Any party that advocates radical change is doomed to a short life. Because most Americans consider a vote for a third party a waste, third parties do notoriously poorly at the polls. Two exceptions are the Bull Moose party, whose candidate, Theodore Roosevelt, won more votes in 1912 than Robert Taft, the Republican presidential candidate, and the United We Stand (Reform) party, founded by billionaire Ross Perot, which won 19 percent of the vote in 1992. Amidst internal bickering, the Reform Party declined rapidly, dropping to 8 percent of the presidential vote in 1996, and then fell off the political map (Bridgwater 1953; *Statistical Abstract* 1995:Table 437; 2007:Table 386).

## FIGURE 11.1    Which Political Party Dominates?

Democrat States
Republican States

*Note:* Domination by a political party does *not* refer to votes for president or Congress. This social map is based on the composition of the states' upper and lower houses. When different parties dominate a state's houses, the total number of legislators was used. In case of ties (or, as with Nebraska, which has no party designation), the percentage vote for president was used.
*Source:* By the author. Based on *Statistical Abstract* 2007: Tables 389, 400.

## Voting Patterns

Year after year, Americans show consistent voting patterns. From Table 11.1 on the next page, you can see that the percentage of people who vote increases with age. This table also shows how significant race–ethnicity is. Non-Hispanic whites are more likely to vote than are African Americans, while Latinos and Asian Americans are the least likely to vote. The significance of race–ethnicity is so great that Latinos are only half as likely to vote as are African Americans and non-Hispanic whites.

From Table 11.1, you can see how voting increases with education—that college graduates are almost twice as likely to vote as are high school graduates. You can also see how much more likely the employed are to vote. And look at how powerful income is in determining voting. At each higher income level, people are more likely to vote. Finally, note that women are slightly more likely than men to vote.

**Social Integration**    How can we explain the voting patterns shown in Table 11.1? Look at the extremes. Those who are most likely to vote are whites who are older, more educated, affluent, and employed. Those who are least

likely to vote are Latinos who are younger, less educated, poor, and unemployed. From these extremes, we can draw this principle: *The more that people feel they have a stake in the political system, the more likely they are to vote.* They have more to protect, and they feel that voting can make a difference. In effect, people who have been rewarded more by the political and economic system feel more socially integrated. They vote because they perceive that elections make a difference in their lives, including the type of society in which they and their children live.

**Alienation and Apathy**    In contrast, those who gain less from the system—in terms of education, income, and jobs—are more likely to feel alienated from politics. Perceiving themselves as outsiders, many feel hostile toward the government. Some feel betrayed, believing that politicians have sold out to special-interest groups. They are convinced that all politicians are liars. Minorities who feel that the U.S. political system is a "white" system are less likely to vote.

From Table 11.1, we see that many highly educated people with good incomes also stay away from the polls. Many people do not vote because of **voter apathy,** or indifference. Their view is that "next year will just bring

**TABLE 11.1    Who Votes for President?**

|  | 1980 | 1984 | 1988 | 1992 | 1996 | 2000 | 2004 |
|---|---|---|---|---|---|---|---|
| **Overall** | | | | | | | |
| Americans Who Vote | 59% | 60% | 57% | 61% | 54% | 55% | 58% |
| **Age** | | | | | | | |
| 18–20 | 36% | 37% | 33% | 39% | 31% | 28% | 41% |
| 21–24 | 43% | 44% | 46% | 46% | 33% | 35% | 43% |
| 25–34 | 55% | 58% | 48% | 53% | 43% | 44% | 47% |
| 35–44 | 64% | 64% | 61% | 64% | 55% | 55% | 57% |
| 45–64 | 69% | 70% | 68% | 70% | 64% | 64% | 67% |
| 65 and older | 65% | 68% | 69% | 70% | 67% | 68% | 69% |
| **Sex** | | | | | | | |
| Male | 59% | 59% | 56% | 60% | 53% | 53% | 56% |
| Female | 59% | 61% | 58% | 62% | 56% | 56% | 60% |
| **Race/Ethnicity** | | | | | | | |
| Whites | 61% | 61% | 59% | 64% | 56% | 56% | 60% |
| African Americans | 51% | 56% | 52% | 54% | 51% | 54% | 56% |
| Latinos | 30% | 33% | 29% | 29% | 27% | 28% | 28% |
| Asians | NA | NA | NA | NA | NA | 25% | 30% |
| **Education** | | | | | | | |
| High school dropouts | 46% | 44% | 41% | 41% | 34% | 34% | 40% |
| High school graduates | 59% | 59% | 55% | 58% | 49% | 49% | 56% |
| College dropouts | 67% | 68% | 65% | 69% | 61% | 60% | 69% |
| College graduates | 80% | 79% | 78% | 81% | 73% | 72% | 74% |
| **Marital Status** | | | | | | | |
| Married | NA | NA | NA | NA | 66% | 67% | 71% |
| Divorced | NA | NA | NA | NA | 50% | 53% | 58% |
| **Labor Force** | | | | | | | |
| Employed | 62% | 62% | 58% | 64% | 55% | 56% | 60% |
| Unemployed | 41% | 44% | 39% | 46% | 37% | 35% | 46% |
| **Income**[1] | | | | | | | |
| Under $20,000 | NA | NA | NA | NA | NA | NA | 48% |
| $20,000 to $30,000 | NA | NA | NA | NA | NA | NA | 58% |
| $30,000 to $40,000 | NA | NA | NA | NA | NA | NA | 62% |
| $40,000 to $50,000 | NA | NA | NA | NA | NA | NA | 69% |
| $50,000 to $75,000 | NA | NA | NA | NA | NA | NA | 72% |
| $75,000 to $100,000 | NA | NA | NA | NA | NA | NA | 78% |
| Over $100,000 | NA | NA | NA | NA | NA | NA | 81% |

[1]The primary source used different income categories for 2004, making the data from earlier presidential election years incompatible.

*Sources:* By the author. Data on marital status are from Casper and Bass 1998, Jamieson et al. 2002, and Holder 2006. Data on income are from Holder 2006. The other data are from *Statistical Abstract* 1991:Table 450; 1997:Table 462; 2007:Table 405.

From *The Wall Street Journal*, permission Cartoon Features Syndicate.

pattern. The reason could be a lesser emphasis on individualism in the Asian American subculture.

## Lobbyists and Special-Interest Groups

Suppose that you are president of the United States, and you want to make milk more affordable for the poor. As you check into the matter, you find that part of the reason that prices are high is because the government is paying farmers billions of dollars a year in price supports. You propose to eliminate these subsidies.

Immediately, large numbers of people leap into action. They contact their senators and representatives and hold news conferences. Your office is flooded with calls, faxes, and e-mail. Reuters and the Associated Press distribute pictures of farm families—their Holsteins grazing contentedly in the background—and inform readers that your harsh proposal will destroy these hard-working, healthy, happy, good Americans who are struggling to make a living. President or not, you have little chance of getting your legislation passed.

more of the same, regardless of who is in office." A common attitude of those who are apathetic is "What difference will my one vote make when there are millions of voters?" Many also see little difference between the two major political parties. Alienation and apathy are so widespread that only *half* of the nation's eligible voters cast ballots in presidential elections, and even fewer vote for candidates for Congress (*Statistical Abstract* 2007:Table 408).

**The Gender and Racial–Ethnic Gap in Voting**  Historically, men and women voted the same way, but now we have a *political gender gap*. That is, when they go to the polls, men and women are somewhat more likely to vote for different presidential candidates. As you can see from Table 11.2, men are more likely to favor the Republican candidate, while women are more likely to vote for the Democratic candidate. This table also illustrates the much larger racial–ethnic gap in politics. Note how few African Americans vote for a Republican presidential candidate.

As we saw in Table 11.1, voting patterns reflect life experiences, especially people's economic conditions. On average, women earn less than men, and African Americans earn less than whites. As a result, at this point in history, women and African Americans tend to look more favorably on government programs that redistribute income, and they are more likely to vote for Democrats. As you can see, the Asian American vote is an exception to this

### TABLE 11.2  How the Two-Party Presidential Vote Is Split

| | 1988 | 1992 | 1996 | 2000 | 2004 |
|---|---|---|---|---|---|
| **Women** | | | | | |
| Democrat | 50% | 61% | 65% | 56% | 53% |
| Republican | 50% | 39% | 35% | 44% | 47% |
| **Men** | | | | | |
| Democrat | 44% | 55% | 51% | 47% | 46% |
| Republican | 56% | 45% | 49% | 53% | 54% |
| **African Americans** | | | | | |
| Democrat | 92% | 94% | 99% | 92% | 90% |
| Republican | 8% | 6% | 1% | 8% | 10% |
| **Whites** | | | | | |
| Democrat | 41% | 53% | 54% | 46% | 42% |
| Republican | 59% | 47% | 46% | 54% | 58% |
| **Latinos** | | | | | |
| Democrat | NA | NA | NA | 61% | 58% |
| Republican | NA | NA | NA | 39% | 42% |
| **Asian Americans** | | | | | |
| Democrat | NA | NA | NA | 62% | 77% |
| Republican | NA | NA | NA | 38% | 23% |

Sources: *Statistical Abstract* 1999:Table 464; 2002:Table 372; 2007:Table 387.

What happened? The dairy industry went to work to protect its special interests. A **special-interest group** consists of people who think alike on a particular issue and who can be mobilized for political action. The dairy industry is just one of thousands of such groups that employ **lobbyists,** people who are paid to influence legislation on behalf of their clients. Special-interest groups and lobbyists have become a major force in U.S. politics. Members of Congress who want to be reelected must pay attention to them, for they represent blocs of voters who share a vital interest in the outcome of specific bills. Well financed and able to contribute huge sums, lobbyists can deliver votes to you—or to your opponent.

Some members of Congress who lose an election have a pot of gold waiting for them. So do people who have served in the White House as assistants to the president. With their influence and contacts swinging open the doors of the powerful, they are sought after as lobbyists (Revkin and Wald 2007). Some can demand $2 million a year (Shane 2004). *Half* of the top one hundred White House officials go to work for or advise the very companies that they regulated while they worked for the president (Ismail 2003).

To reduce the influence of special-interest groups on legislation, Congress passed a law that limits the amount of money that any individual, corporation, or special-interest group can donate to a candidate. This law also requires all contributions over $1,000 to be reported. To get around this law, special-interest groups form **political action committees (PACs).** These organizations solicit contributions from many donors—each contribution being within the legal limit—and then use the large total to influence legislation.

PACs are powerful, for they bankroll lobbyists and legislators. To influence politics, about 4,000 PACs shell out hundreds of millions of dollars a year directly to their candidates (*Statistical Abstract* 2007:Tables 409, 410, 414). PACs also contribute millions in indirect ways. Some give "honoraria" (a gift of money) to senators who agree to say a few words at a breakfast. A few PACs represent broad social interests such as environmental protection. Most, however, represent the financial interests of specific groups, such as the banking, dairy, defense, and oil industries.

**Criticism of Lobbyists and PACs**   The major criticism leveled against lobbyists and PACs is that their money, in effect, buys votes. Rather than representing the people who elected them, legislators support the special interests of groups that have the ability to help them stay in power. The PACs that have the most clout in terms of money and votes

gain the ear of Congress. To politicians, the sound of money talking apparently sounds like the voice of the people.

Even if the United States were to outlaw PACs, special-interest groups would not disappear from U.S. politics. Lobbyists walked the corridors of the Senate long before PACs, and since the time of Alexander Graham Bell they have carried the unlisted numbers of members of Congress. For good or for ill, lobbyists play an essential role in the U.S. political system.

# Who Rules the United States?

With lobbyists and PACs wielding such influence, just whom do U.S. senators and representatives really represent? This question has led to a lively debate among sociologists.

## The Functionalist Perspective: Pluralism

Functionalists view the state as having arisen out of the basic needs of the social group. To protect themselves from oppressors, people formed a government and gave it the monopoly on violence. The risk is that the state can turn that force against its own citizens. To return to the example used earlier, states have a tendency to become muggers. Thus, people must find a balance between having no government—which would lead to **anarchy,** a condition of disorder and violence—and having a government that protects them from violence, but also may turn against them. When functioning well, then, the state is a balanced system that protects its citizens both from one another *and* from government.

What keeps the U.S. government from turning against its citizens? Functionalists say that **pluralism,** a diffusion of power among many special-interest groups, prevents any one group from gaining control of the government and using it to oppress the people (Polsby 1959; Dahl 1961, 1982; Newman 2006). To keep the government from coming under the control of any one group, the founders of the United States set up three branches of government: the executive branch (the president), the judiciary branch (the courts), and the legislative branch (the Senate and House of Representatives). Each is sworn to uphold the Constitution, which guarantees rights to citizens, and each can nullify the actions of the other two. This system, known as **checks and balances,** was designed to ensure that no one branch of government dominates the others.

Our pluralist society has many parts—women, men, racial–ethnic groups, farmers, factory and office workers, religious organizations, bankers, bosses, the unemployed, the retired—as well as such broad categories as the rich, middle class, and poor. No group dominates. Rather, as each group pursues its own interests, it is balanced by other groups that are pursuing theirs. To attain their goals, groups must negotiate with one another and make compromises. This minimizes conflict. Because these groups have political muscle to flex at the polls, politicians try to design policies that please as many groups as they can. This, say functionalists, makes the political system responsive to the people, and no one group rules.

## The Conflict Perspective: The Power Elite

If you focus on the lobbyists scurrying around Washington, stress conflict theorists, you get a blurred image of superficial activities. What really counts is the big picture, not its fragments. The important question is, Who holds the power that determines the country's overarching policies? For example, who determines interest rates—and

their impact on the price of our homes? Who sets policies that encourage the transfer of jobs from the United States to countries where labor costs less? And the ultimate question of power: Who is behind the decision to go to war?

Sociologist C. Wright Mills (1956) took the position that the country's most important matters are decided not by lobbyists or even by Congress. Rather, the decisions that have the greatest impact on the lives of Americans—and people across the globe—are made by a **power elite.** As depicted in Figure 11.2, the power elite consists of the top leaders of the largest corporations, the most powerful generals and admirals of the armed forces, and certain elite politicians—the president, the president's cabinet, and senior members of Congress who chair the major committees. It is they who wield power, who make the decisions that direct the country and shake the world.

Are the three groups that make up the power elite—the top business, political, and military leaders—equal in power? Mills said that they were not, but he didn't point to the president and his staff or even to the generals and admirals as the most powerful. The most powerful, he said, are the corporate leaders. Because all three segments of the power elite view capitalism as essential to the welfare of the country, Mills said that business interests take center stage in setting national policy.

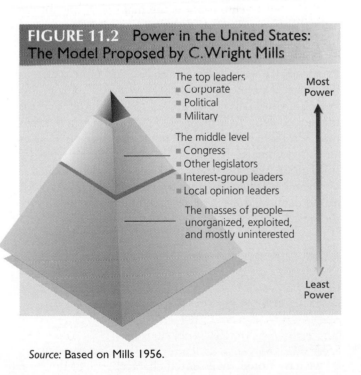

### FIGURE 11.2    Power in the United States: The Model Proposed by C. Wright Mills

The top leaders
- Corporate
- Political
- Military

The middle level
- Congress
- Other legislators
- Interest-group leaders
- Local opinion leaders

The masses of people—unorganized, exploited, and mostly uninterested

Most Power

Least Power

*Source:* Based on Mills 1956.

Sociologist William Domhoff (1990, 2006) uses the term **ruling class** to refer to the power elite. He focuses on the 1 percent of Americans who belong to the super-rich, the powerful capitalist class analyzed in Chapter 8 (pages 207–208). Members of this class control our top corporations and foundations, even the boards that oversee our major universities. It is no accident, says Domhoff, that from this group come most members of the president's cabinet and the ambassadors to the most powerful countries of the world.

Conflict theorists point out that we should not think of the power elite (or ruling class) as some secret group that meets to agree on specific matters. Rather, the group's unity springs from the similarity of its members' backgrounds and orientations to life. All have attended prestigious private schools, belong to exclusive clubs, and are millionaires many times over. Their behavior stems not from some grand conspiracy to control the country but from a mutual interest in solving the problems that face big business (Useem 1984). With political connections extending to the highest centers of power, this elite determines the economic and political conditions under which the rest of the country operates (Domhoff 1990, 1998).

## Which View Is Right?

The functionalist and conflict views of power in U.S. society cannot be reconciled. Either competing interests block any single group from being dominant, as functionalists assert, or a power elite oversees the major decisions of the United States, as conflict theorists maintain. The answer may have to do with the level you look at. Perhaps at the middle level of power depicted in Figure 11.2, the competing groups do keep each other at bay, and none is able to dominate. If so, the functionalist view would apply to this level. But which level holds the key to U.S. power? Perhaps the functionalists have not looked high enough, and activities at the peak remain invisible to them. On that level, does an elite dominate? To protect its mutual interests, does a small group make the major decisions of the United States?

Sociologists passionately argue this issue, but with mixed data, we don't yet know the answer. We await further research.

# War and Terrorism: Implementing Political Objectives

As we have noted, an essential characteristic of the state is that it claims a monopoly on violence. At times, a state may direct that violence against other nations. **War,** armed conflict between nations (or politically distinct groups), is often part of national policy. Let's look at this aspect of politics.

## War

Why do nations choose war as a means to handle disputes? Sociologists answer this question not by focusing on factors *within* humans, such as aggressive impulses, but by looking for *social* causes—conditions in society that encourage or discourage combat between nations.

Sociologist Nicholas Timasheff (1965) identified three essential conditions of war. The first is an antagonistic situation in which two or more states confront incompatible objectives. For example, each may want the same land or resources. The second is a cultural tradition of war. Because their nation has fought wars in the past, the leaders of a group see war as an option for dealing with serious disputes with other nations. The third is a "fuel" that heats the antagonistic situation to a boiling point, so that politicians cross the line from thinking about war to actually waging it.

Timasheff identified seven such "fuels." He found that war is likely if a country's leaders see the antagonistic situation as an opportunity to achieve one or more of these objectives:

1. *Revenge:* settling "old scores" from earlier conflicts
2. *Power:* dominating a weaker nation
3. *Prestige:* defending the nation's "honor"
4. *Unity:* uniting rival groups within their country
5. *Position:* protecting the leaders' positions
6. *Ethnicity:* bringing under their rule "our people" who are living in another country
7. *Beliefs:* forcibly converting others to religious or political beliefs

Timasheff's analysis is excellent, and you can use these three essential conditions and seven fuels to analyze any war. They will help you understand why politicians at that time chose this political action.

### Dehumanization During War

**Proud of his techniques, the U.S. trainer was demonstrating to the South American soldiers how to torture a prisoner. As the victim screamed in anguish, the trainer was interrupted by a phone call from his wife. His students could hear him say, "A dinner and a movie sound nice. I'll see you right after work." Hanging up the phone, he then continued the lesson. (Stockwell 1989)**

War exacts many costs in addition to killing people and destroying property. One of the most remarkable is its effect

The hatred and vengeance of adults becomes the children's heritage. The headband on this 4-year old Palestinian boy reads "Friends of Martyrs."

on morality. Exposure to brutality and killing often causes **dehumanization,** the process of reducing people to objects that do not deserve to be treated as humans. From the quote on the previous page, you can see how people's conscience can become numb, allowing them to participate in acts they would ordinarily condemn. To help understand how this occurs, read the Down-to-Earth Sociology box on the next two pages.

## Terrorism

> Mustafa Jabbar in Najaf, Iraq, is proud of his first born, a baby boy, but he said, "I will put mines in the baby and blow him up." (Sengupta 2004)

How can feelings run so deep that a father would sacrifice his only son? Such hatred is nourished by groups endlessly recounting the atrocities committed by their archenemy. Nurtured in such a cauldron of bitterness, hatred spans generations, sometimes continuing for centuries. Such bitter antagonisms encourage **terrorism,** the use of violence to create fear in an effort to bring about political objectives. Stronger groups use terrorism "just because they can." They delight to see the suffering of their opponents. Terrorism, however, is most often used by weaker groups, for if a weaker group wants to attack a more powerful group, terrorism is one of its few options. It cannot meet its enemy on the battlefield, but it can use terror as a weapon—even if that means blowing up one's only child.

*Suicide terrorism,* a weapon sometimes chosen by the weaker group, captures headlines around the world. Among the groups that have used suicide terrorism effectively are the Palestinians against the Israelis and the Iraqis against the U.S.-led occupation. The most dramatic example of suicide terrorism, of course, was the attack on the World Trade Center and the Pentagon under the direction of Osama bin Laden.

The suicide attacks on New York and Washington were tiny in comparison with the real danger: that of biological, nuclear, and chemical weapons. Unleashed against a civilian population, such weapons could cause millions of deaths. In 2001, Americans caught a glimpse of how easily such weapons can be unleashed when anthrax powder was mailed to a few select victims. When the Soviet empire broke up, its nuclear weapons were no longer secure. The interception of enriched uranium as it was being smuggled out of a former Soviet republic foreshadowed the chilling possibility of terrorism on U.S. soil so great that it could dwarf the 9/11 attacks (Sheets and Broad 2007a, b).

It is sometimes difficult to tell the difference between war and terrorism. This is especially the case in civil wars, when the opposing sides don't wear uniforms, and they often attack civilian populations. Africa is embroiled in such wars. One of the unfortunate developments arising from this situation is that of child soldiers, a topic discussed in the Down-to-Earth Sociology box on page 312.

**In Sum:** Some students wonder why I include war and terrorism as subtopics of politics. The reason is that war and terrorism are tools used to try to accomplish political goals. The Prussian military analyst Carl von Clausewitz, who entered the military at the age of twelve and rose to the rank of Major-General, put it best when he said: "War is merely a continuation of politics by other means."

# THE ECONOMY: WORK IN THE GLOBAL VILLAGE

If you are like most students, you are wondering how changes in the economy are going to affect your chances of getting a good job. Let's see if we can shed some light on this question. We'll begin with this story:

> The sound of her alarm rang in Kim's ears. "Not Monday already," she groaned. "There must be a better way of starting

the week." She pressed the snooze button on the clock (from Germany) to sneak another ten minutes' sleep. In what seemed like just thirty seconds, the alarm shrilly insisted that she get up and face the week.

Still bleary-eyed after her shower, Kim peered into her closet and picked out a silk blouse (from China), a plaid wool skirt (from Scotland), and leather shoes (from Italy). She nodded, satisfied, as she added a pair of simulated pearls (from Taiwan). Running late, she hurriedly ran a brush (from Mexico) through her hair. As Kim wolfed down a bowl of cereal (from the United States) topped with milk (from the United States), bananas (from Costa Rica), and sugar (from the Dominican Republic), she turned on her kitchen television (from Korea) to listen to the weather forecast.

Gulping the last of her coffee (from Brazil), Kim grabbed her briefcase (from India), purse (from Spain), and jacket (from Malaysia), left her house, and quickly climbed into her car (from Japan). As she glanced at her watch (from Switzerland), she hoped that the traffic would be in her favor. She muttered to herself as she pulled up at a stoplight (from Great Britain) and eyed her gas gauge. She muttered again when she pulled into a station and paid for gas (from Saudi Arabia), for the price had risen over the weekend. "My paycheck never keeps up with prices," she moaned.

When Kim arrived at work, she found the office abuzz. Six months ago, New York headquarters had put the company up for sale, but there had been no takers. The big news was that both a German company and a Canadian

## Down-to-Earth Sociology
### How Can "Good" People Torture Others?

When the Nuremberg Trials revealed the crimes of the Nazis to the world, people wondered what kind of abnormal, bizarre humans did those horrific acts. The trials, however, revealed that the officials who authorized the torture and murder of Jews and the soldiers who followed those orders were ordinary, "good" people (Hughes 1962/2005). This revelation came as a shock to the world.

Later, we learned that in Rwanda Hutus hacked their Tutsi neighbors to death. Some Hutu teachers even killed their Tutsi students. Similar revelations of "good" people torturing prisoners have come from all over the world—Iraq, Afghanistan, Mexico. We have also learned that when the torturers finish their "work," they go home to their families, where they are ordinary fathers and husbands.

Let's try to understand how "good, ordinary people" can torture prisoners and still feel good about themselves. Consider the four main characteristics of dehumanization (Bernard et al. 1971):

1. *Increased emotional distance from others.* People stop identifying with others, no longer seeing them as having qualities similar to themselves. They perceive them as "the enemy," or as objects of some sort. Sometimes they think of their opponents as less than human or even not as people at all.

2. *Emphasis on following orders.* The individual clothes acts of brutality in patriotic language: To follow orders is "a soldier's duty." Torture is viewed as a tool that helps soldiers do their duty. People are likely to say, "I don't like doing this, but I have to follow orders—and someone has to do the 'dirty work.'"

3. *Inability to resist pressures.* Ideas of morality take a back seat to fears of losing one's job, losing the respect of peers, or having one's integrity and loyalty questioned.

4. *A diminished sense of personal responsibility.* People come to see themselves as only small cogs in a large machine. The higher-ups who give the orders are thought to have more complete or even secret information that justifies the torture. The thinking becomes, "Those who make the decisions are responsible, for they are in a position to judge what is right and wrong. In my low place in the system, who am I to question these acts?"

Sociologist Martha Huggins (2004) interviewed Brazilian police who used torture to extract confessions. She identified a fifth method that torturers sometimes use: They *blame the victim.* "He was just stupid. If he had confessed in the first place, he wouldn't have been tortured."

This technique removes the blame from the torturer—who is just doing a job—and places it on the victim.

There is a sixth technique of neutralization, a favorite of U.S. government officials who have authorized the torture of terrorists. Their technique of neutralization is to say that what they have authorized is *not* torture. A fair summary of their many statements on this topic would be: "What we have authorized is a harsh, but necessary, method of interrogation, selectively used on designated individuals, to extract information to protect Americans." In one of these approved interrogation methods, called *waterboarding*, the interrogators force a prisoner's head backward and pour water over his or her face. This produces a gag reflex, forcing the prisoner to inhale water. The prisoner experiences the intense sensation of drowning. When the interrogators stop pouring the water, they ask their questions again. If they don't get a satisfactory answer, they continue the procedure.

In several contexts in this book, I have emphasized how important labels are in social life. Notice how powerful they are in this extreme situation. By calling waterboarding "not torture," it becomes "not torture" for those who authorize and practice it. This protects the conscience, allowing the individuals who authorize and practice torture to retain the sense of a "good" self.

One of my students, a Vietnam veteran, who read this section, told me, "You missed the major one we used. We killed kids. Our dehumanizing technique was this saying, 'The little ones are the soldiers of tomorrow.'"

*"Not torture—just a way to get information"—so said U.S. officials. Shown here are human rights activists as they demonstrate waterboarding on a volunteer outside the Senate Office Building in Washington, D.C.*

Such sentiments may be more common than we suppose—and the torturers' uniforms don't have to display swastikas.

## For Your Consideration

Do you think you could torture people? Instead of just saying, "Of course not!" think about this: If "good, ordinary" people can become torturers, why not you? Aren't you a "good, ordinary" person? To answer this question properly, then, let's rephrase it: Based on what you read here, what conditions could get you to cooperate in the torture of prisoners?

---

company had put in bids over the weekend. No one got much work done that day, as the whole office speculated about how things might change.

As Kim walked to the parking lot after work, she saw a tattered "Buy American" bumper sticker on the car next to hers. "That's right," she said to herself. "If people were more like me, this country would be in better shape."

# The Transformation of Economic Systems

Although this vignette may be slightly exaggerated, many of us are like Kim: We use a multitude of products from around the world, and yet we're concerned about our country's ability to compete in global markets. Today's

economy—our system of producing and distributing goods and services—differs radically from past economies. The products that Kim uses make it apparent that today's economy knows no national boundaries. To better understand how global forces affect the U.S. economy—and your life—let's begin by summarizing the sweeping historical changes we reviewed in Chapter 4 (pages 91–96).

## Preindustrial Societies: The Birth of Inequality

The earliest human groups, *hunting and gathering societies*, had a **subsistence economy.** In small groups of about twenty-five to forty, people lived off the land. They gathered plants and hunted animals in one location and then moved to another place as these sources of food ran low.

# Down-to-Earth Sociology
## Child Soldiers

When rebels entered 12-year-old Ishmael Beah's village in Sierra Leone, they lined up the boys (Beah 2007). One of the rebels said, "We are going to initiate you by killing these people. We will show you blood and make you strong."

Before the rebels could do the killing, shots rang out and the rebels took cover. In the confusion, Ishmael escaped into the jungle. When he returned, he found his family dead and his village burned.

With no place to go and rebels attacking the villages, killing, looting, and raping, Ishmael continued to hide in the jungle. As he peered out at a village one day, he saw a rebel carrying the head of a man, which he held by the hair. With blood dripping from where the neck had been, Ishmael said that the head looked as though it were still feeling its hair being pulled.

Months later, government soldiers found Ishmael. The "rescue" meant that he had to become a soldier—on their side, of course.

Ishmael's indoctrination was short but to the point. Hatred is a strong motivator.

"You can revenge the death of your family, and make sure that more children do not lose their parents," the lieutenant said. "The rebels cut people's heads off. They cut open pregnant women's stomachs and take the babies out and kill them. They force sons to have sex with their mothers. Such people do not deserve to live. This is why we must kill every single one of them. Think of it as destroying a great evil. It is the highest service you can perform for your country."

Along with thirty other boys, most of whom were ages 13 to 16, with two just 7 and 11, Ishmael was trained to shoot and clean an AK-47.

Banana trees served for bayonet practice. With thoughts of disemboweling evil rebels, the boys would slash at the leaves.

The things that Ishmael had seen, he did.

Killing was difficult at first, but after a while, as Ishmael says, "killing became as easy as drinking water."

The corporal thought that the boys were sloppy with their bayonets. To improve their performance, he held a contest. He chose five boys. Placing opposite each boy a prisoner with his hands tied, he told the boys to slice the

*Child soldiers in El Salvador.*

men's throats on his command. The boy whose prisoner died the quickest would win the contest.

"I stared at my prisoner," said Ishmael. "He was just another rebel who was responsible for the death of my family. The corporal gave the signal with a pistol shot, and I grabbed the man's head and sliced his throat in one fluid motion. His eyes rolled up, and he looked me straight in the eyes before [his eyes] suddenly stopped in a frightful glance. I dropped him on the ground and wiped my bayonet on him. I reported to the corporal who was holding a timer. I was proclaimed the winner. The other boys clapped at my achievement."

"No longer was I running away from the war," adds Ishmael. "I was in it. I would scout for villages that had food, drugs, ammunition, and the gasoline we needed. I would report my findings to the corporal, and the entire squad would attack the village. We would kill everyone."

Ishmael was one of the lucky ones. Of the approximately 300,000 child soldiers worldwide, Ishmael is one of the few who has been rescued and given counseling at a UNICEF rehabilitation center. Ishmael has also had the remarkable turn of fate of graduating from college in the United States and becoming a permanent U.S. resident.

*Note:* The quotations are summaries.

## For Your Consideration

1. Why are there child soldiers?
2. What can be done to prevent the recruitment of child soldiers? Why don't we just pass a law that requires a minimum age to serve in the military?
3. How can child soldiers be helped? What agencies can take what action?

Because these people had few possessions, they did little trading with one another. With no excess to accumulate, as was mentioned in Chapter 4, everybody owned as much (or, really, as little) as everyone else.

Then people discovered how to breed animals and cultivate plants. The more dependable food supply in what became *pastoral and horticultural societies* allowed humans to settle down in a single place. Human groups grew larger, and for the first time in history, it was no longer necessary for everyone to work at producing food. Some people became leather workers, others weapon makers, and so on. This new division of labor produced a surplus, and groups traded items with one another. The primary sociological significance of surplus and trade is this: They fostered *social inequality,* for some people accumulated more possessions than others. The effects of that change remain with us today.

The plow brought the next major change, ushering in *agricultural societies.* Plowed land was much more productive, allowing even more people to specialize in activities other than producing food. More specialized divisions of labor followed, and trade expanded. Trading centers then developed, which turned into cities. As power passed from the heads of families and clans to a ruling elite, social, political, and economic inequalities grew.

## Industrial Societies: The Birth of the Machine

The steam engine, invented in 1765, ushered in *industrial societies.* Based on machines powered by fuels, these societies created a surplus unlike anything the world had seen. This, too, stimulated trade among nations and brought even greater social inequality. A handful of individuals opened factories and exploited the labor of many.

Then came more efficient machines. As the surpluses grew even greater, the emphasis gradually changed—from producing goods to consuming them. In 1912, sociologist Thorstein Veblen coined the term **conspicuous consumption** to describe this fundamental change in people's orientations. By this term, Veblen meant that the Protestant ethic identified by Weber—an emphasis on hard work, savings, and a concern for salvation (discussed on pages 379 and 382)—was being replaced by an eagerness to show off wealth by the "elaborate consumption of goods."

## Postindustrial Societies: The Birth of the Information Age

In 1973, sociologist Daniel Bell noted that *a new type of society was emerging.* This new society, which he called the *postindustrial society,* has six characteristics: (1) a service sector so large that *most* people work in it; (2) a vast surplus of goods; (3) even more extensive trade among nations; (4) a wider variety and quantity of goods available to the average person; (5) an information explosion; and (6) a *global village*—that is, the world's nations are linked by fast communications, transportation, and trade.

Look at Figure 11.3, which illustrates how work changed as we made our transition to the postindustrial society. In the 1800s, most U.S. workers were farmers. Today, farmers make up only about 2 percent of the workforce. We need so few farmers because of changes in technology. With the farming tools of the 1800s, a typical farmer produced enough food for only five people. With today's machinery and hybrid seeds, a typical farmer now feeds about eighty. In 1940, as you can see, about half of U.S. workers wore a blue collar. As changing technology shrank the market for blue-collar jobs, white-collar work continued its ascent, reaching the dominant position it holds today.

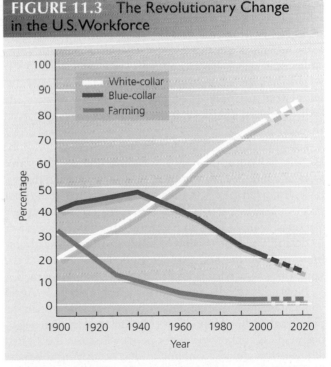

**FIGURE 11.3    The Revolutionary Change in the U.S. Workforce**

*Note:* From 1900 to 1940, "workers" refers to people age 14 and over; from 1970 to people age 16 and over. Broken lines are the author's projections. The totals shown here are broadly accurate only, as there is disagreement on how to classify some jobs. Agriculture, for example, includes forestry, fishing, and hunting. *Source:* By the author. Based on *Statistical Abstract,* various years, and 2007: Tables 602, 1341.

## Biotech Societies: The Merger of Biology and Economics

We may be on the verge of yet another new type of society. This one is being ushered in by advances in biology, especially the deciphering of the human genome system. While the specifics of this new society have yet to unfold, the marriage of biology and economics should yield even greater surpluses and more extensive trade. The global village will continue to expand. The technological advances that will emerge in this new society may also allow us to lead longer and healthier lives. As history is our guide, it also may create even greater inequality between the rich and poor nations.

## Implications for Your Life

The broad changes in societies that I just sketched may seem to be abstract matters, but they are far from irrelevant to your life. Whenever society changes, so do our lives. Consider the information explosion. When you graduate from college, you will most likely do some form of "knowledge work." Instead of working in a factory, you will manage information or design, sell, or service products. The type of work you do has profound implications for your life. It produces social networks, nurtures attitudes, and even affects how you view yourself and the world. To better understand this, consider how vastly different your perspectives on life would be if you were one of the children discussed in the Cultural Diversity box on the next page.

It is the same with the global village. Think of the globe as being divided into three neighborhoods—the three worlds of industrialization and postindustrialization that we reviewed in Chapter 7. Some nations are located in the poor part of the village. Their citizens do menial work and barely eke out a living. Life is so precarious that some even starve to death, while their fellow villagers in the rich neighborhood feast on the best that the globe has to offer. It's the same village, but what a difference the neighborhood makes.

Now visualize any one of the three neighborhoods. Again you will see gross inequalities. Not everyone who lives in the poor neighborhood is poor, and some areas of the rich neighborhood are packed with poor people. Because the United States is the global economic leader, occupying the most luxurious mansion in the best neighborhood, and is spearheading the new biotech society, let's look at U.S. trends.

## Ominous Trends in the United States

Suppose that you own a business manufacturing widgets. You are paying your workers an average of $20 an hour (including their fringe benefits, vacation pay, sick pay, unemployment benefits, Social Security, and so on). Widgets similar to yours are being manufactured in Thailand, where workers are paid $8 a day. Those imported widgets are being sold in the same stores that feature your widgets.

How long do you think you can stay in business? Even if your workers were willing to drop their pay in half—which they aren't willing to do—you would still be undersold.

What do you do? Your choices are simple. You can continue as you are and go broke, try to find some other product to manufacture (which, if successful, will soon be made in Thailand or India or China)—or you can close up your plants here and manufacture your widgets in Thailand.

The globalization of capitalism is bringing many changes, including these stark choices facing many U.S. manufacturers. And for workers? One disruption after another. No matter how productive they are, how can they compete with people who work for peanuts? The transfer of jobs overseas and the closing of U.S. plants have brought a special challenge to small towns, which were already suffering severe losses because of urbanization. We explore this disruption in the photo essay on pages 316–317.

**Stagnant Paychecks**  U.S. workers are some of the most productive in the world (*Statistical Abstract* 2007:Table 1361). One might think, therefore, that their pay would be increasing. This brings us to a disturbing trend.

Look at Figure 11.4 on page 318. The gold bars show current dollars. These are the dollars the average worker finds in his or her paycheck. You can see that since 1970 the average pay of U.S. workers has soared from just over $3 an hour to almost $17 an hour. Workers today are bringing home *five* times as many dollars as workers used to.

But let's strip away the illusion. Look at the green bars, which show the dollars adjusted for inflation, the *buying power* of those paychecks. You can see how inflation has whittled away the value of the dollars that workers earn. Today's workers, with their $17 an hour, can buy only the same amount of goods as workers in 1970 could with their "measly" $3 an hour. The question is not "How could workers live on just $3 an hour back then?" but, rather, *"How can workers get by on a 21-cent-an-hour raise that it took 36 years to get?"* Incredibly, despite higher education and technical training of workers, the use of computers, and increased productivity, this is how much the average worker's purchasing power has increased from 1970 to 2006.

The growing gap between the "haves" and the "have-nots" of our society reveals a related ominous trend. Look

# Cultural Diversity around the World

## The Child Workers

Nine-year-old Alone Banda works in an abandoned quarry in Zambia. Using a bolt, he breaks rocks into powder. In a week, he makes enough powder to fill half a cement bag. Alone gets $3 for the half bag: The amount is pitiful, but without it he and his grandmother would starve to death.

It is still a slow death for Alone. Robbed of his childhood and breathing rock dust continuously, Alone is likely to come down with what the quarry workers call a "heavy chest," an early sign of silicosis.

Some of the children who work at the quarry are only 7 years old. As one mother said, "If I feel pity for them, what are they going to eat?" (Wines 2006a).

In Ghana, 6-year-old Mark Kwadwo, who weighs about 30 pounds, works for a fisherman. For up to fourteen hours a day, seven days a week, he paddles a boat and takes fish out of nets. Exhausted, he falls asleep at night in a mud hut that he shares with five other boys. If Mark doesn't paddle hard enough, or pull in the fish from a net fast enough, Takyi hits him on the head with a paddle.

Mark is too little to dive, but he knows what is coming when he is older. His fear is that he will dive to free a tangled net—and never resurface.

"I prefer to have my boy home with me," says the mother of Kwabena, whom she leased to the fisherman four years ago when Kwabena was 7, "but I need the money to survive." Kwabena's

*Child labor is common in the early stages of industrialization. This photo was taken in the Pennsylvania coal mines in the 1800s.*

*A four-year old quarry worker in West Bengal.*

mother has received $66 for the four years' work (LaFraniere 2006).

Around the world, children are forced to work. Some work in construction (see the photo on page 175). Others work as miners, pesticide sprayers, street vendors, and household servants. Children weave carpets in India, race camels in the Middle East, and, all over the world, work as prostitutes. Their parents, too, say that they don't like it, but they need the money to survive.

The underlying cause of children working is poverty so severe that the few dollars the children bring in can make the difference between life and death. In Ghana, where Mark works on the fishing boat, two out of three people live on less than $1 a day (LaFraniere 2006).

Then, too, there is the cultural factor. In many parts of the world, people view children differently than we do in the West. The idea that children have the right to be educated and to be spared from adult burdens is fairly new. When prosperity comes, so will this perspective.

## For Your Consideration

How do you think the wealthier nations can help alleviate the suffering of child workers? Before industrialization, and for a period afterwards, having children work was also common in the West. Just because our economic system has changed, bringing with it different ideas of childhood and of the rights of children, what right do we have to impose our changed ideas on other nations?

# Small Town USA

## Struggling to Survive

all across the nation, small towns are struggling to survive. Parents and town officials are concerned because so few young adults remain in their home town. There is little to keep them there, and when they graduate from high school, most move to the city. With young people leaving and old ones dying, the small towns are shriveling.

How can small towns contend with cutthroat global competition when workers in some countries are paid a couple of dollars a day? Even if you open a store down the road, Wal-Mart sells the same products for about what you pay for them—and offers much greater variety.

There are exceptions: Some small towns are located close to a city, and they receive the city's spillover. A few possess a rare treasure—some unique historical event or a natural attraction—that draws visitors with money to spend. Most of the others, though, are drying up, left in a time warp as history shifts around them. This photo essay tells the story.

The small towns are filled with places like this—small businesses, locally owned, that have enough clientele for the owner and family to eke out a living. They have to offer low prices because there is a fast-food chain down the road. Fixing the sign? That's one of those "I'll get-to-its."

People do whatever they can to survive. This enterprising proprietor uses the building for an unusual combination of purposes: a "plant world," along with the sale of milk, eggs, bread, and, in a quaint southern touch, cracking pecans.

I was struck by the grandiosity of people's dreams, at least as reflected in the names that some small-towners give their businesses. Donut Palace has a nice ring to it—inspiring thoughts of wealth and royalty (note the crowns). Unfortunately, like so many others, this business didn't make it.

In striking contrast to the grandiosity of some small town business names is the utter simplicity of others. Cafe tells everyone that some type of food and drinks are served here. Everyone in this small town knows the details.

© James M. Henslin, all photos

One of the few buildings consistently in good repair in the small towns is the U.S. Post Office. Although its importance has declined in the face of telecommunications, for "small towners" the post office still provides a vital link with the outside world.

With little work available, it is difficult to afford adequate housing. This house, although cobbled together and in disrepair, is a family's residence.

There is no global competition for this home-grown business. Shirley has located her sign on a main highway just outside Niceville, Florida. By the looks of the building, business could be better.

This is a successful business. The store goes back to the early 1900s, and the proprietors have capitalized on the "old timey" atmosphere.

This general store used to be the main business in the area; it even has a walk-in safe. It has been owned by the same family since the 1920s, but is no longer successful. To get into the building, I had to find out where the owner (shown here) lived, knock on her door, and then wait while she called around to find out who had the keys.

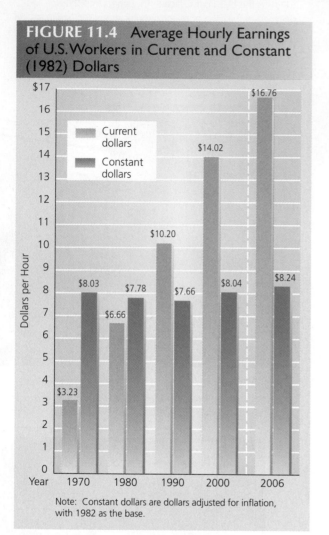

**FIGURE 11.4** Average Hourly Earnings of U.S. Workers in Current and Constant (1982) Dollars

Note: Constant dollars are dollars adjusted for inflation, with 1982 as the base.

*Source:* By the author. Based on *Statistical Abstract* 1992:Table 650; 1999:Table 698; 2008:Table 623.

at Figure 11.5. Each rectangle on the left represents a fifth of the U.S. population, about 60 million people. The rectangles of the inverted pyramid on the right show the percentage of the nation's income that goes to each fifth of the population. You can see that half—*50 percent*—of the entire country's income goes to the richest fifth of Americans; only *3 percent* goes to the poorest fifth. This gap is now greater than it has been in generations. Rather than bringing equality, then, the postindustrial economy has perpetuated and enlarged the income inequalities of the industrial economy. What implications for our future do you see from Figure 11.5?

# World Economic Systems

Now that we have sketched the main historical changes in economic systems, let's compare capitalism and socialism, the two main economic systems in force today. This will help us to understand where the United States stands in the world economic order.

## Capitalism

People who live in a capitalist society may not understand its basic tenets, even though they see them reflected in their local shopping malls and fast-food chains. Table 11.3 distills the many businesses of the United States down to their basic components. As you can see, **capitalism** has three essential features: (1) *private ownership of the means of production* (individuals own the land, machines, and factories); (2) *market competition* (competing with one another, the owners decide what to produce and set the prices for their products); and (3) *the pursuit of profit* (the owners try to sell their products for more than what they cost).

Some people believe that the United States is an example of pure capitalism. Pure capitalism, however, known as **laissez-faire capitalism** (literally "hands off" capitalism), means that the government doesn't interfere in the market. Such is not the case in the United States. The current form of U.S. capitalism is **welfare** or **state capitalism.** Private citizens own the means of production and pursue profits, but they do so within a vast system of laws designed to protect the welfare of the population.

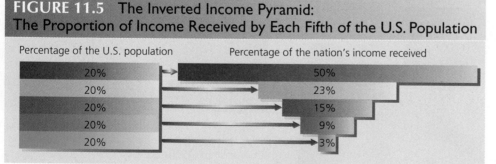

**FIGURE 11.5** The Inverted Income Pyramid:
The Proportion of Income Received by Each Fifth of the U.S. Population

| Percentage of the U.S. population | Percentage of the nation's income received |
|---|---|
| 20% | 50% |
| 20% | 23% |
| 20% | 15% |
| 20% | 9% |
| 20% | 3% |

*Source:* By the author. Based on *Statistical Abstract* 2008:Table 675.

## TABLE 11.3    Comparing Capitalism and Socialism

| Capitalism | Socialism |
|---|---|
| 1. Individuals own the means of production.<br>2. Based on competition, the owners determine production and set prices.<br>3. The pursuit of profit is the reason for distributing goods and services. | 1. The public owns the means of production.<br>2. Central committees plan production and set prices; there is no competition.<br>3. There is no profit motive in the distribution of goods and services. |

Consider this example:

Suppose that you discover what you think is a miracle tonic: It will grow hair, erase wrinkles, and dissolve excess fat. If your product works, you will become an overnight sensation—not only a multimillionaire, but also the toast of television talk shows and the darling of Hollywood.

But don't count on your money or fame yet. You still have to reckon with market restraints, the laws and regulations of welfare capitalism that limit your capacity to produce and sell. First, you must comply with local and state rules. You must obtain a business license and a state tax number that allows you to buy your ingredients without paying sales taxes. Then come the federal regulations. You cannot simply take your product to local stores and ask them to sell it; you first must seek approval from federal agencies that monitor compliance with the Pure Food and Drug Act. This means that you must prove that your product will not cause harm to the public. Your manufacturing process is also subject to federal, state, and local laws concerning fraud, hygiene, and the disposal of hazardous wastes.

Suppose that you overcome these obstacles, and your business prospers. Other federal agencies will monitor your compliance with laws concerning racial, sexual, and disability discrimination; minimum wages; and Social Security taxes. State agencies will examine your records to see whether you have paid unemployment taxes and sales taxes. Finally, the Internal Revenue Service will look over your shoulder and demand a share of your profits (about 35 percent).

In short, the U.S. economic system is highly regulated and is far from an example of laissez-faire capitalism.

## Socialism

As Table 11.3 shows, **socialism** also has three essential components: (1) public ownership of the means of production; (2) central planning; and (3) the distribution of goods without a profit motive.

In socialist economies, the government owns the means of production—not only the factories but also the land, railroads, oil wells, and gold mines. Unlike capitalism, in which **market forces**—supply and demand—determine both what will be produced and the prices that will be charged, a central committee decides that the country needs X number of toothbrushes, Y toilets, and Z shoes. The committee decides how many of each will be produced, which factories will produce them, what price will be charged for the items, and where they will be distributed.

Socialism is designed to eliminate competition, for goods are sold at predetermined prices regardless of the demand for an item or the cost of producing it. The goal is not to make a profit, nor is it to encourage the consumption of goods that are in low demand (by lowering the price) or to limit the consumption of hard-to-get goods (by raising the price). Rather, the goal is to produce goods for the general welfare and to distribute them according to people's needs, not their ability to pay.

In a socialist economy *everyone* in the economic chain works for the government. The members of the central committee who set production goals are government employees, as are the supervisors who implement their plans, the factory workers who produce the merchandise, the truck drivers who move it, and the clerks who sell it. Those who buy the items may work at different jobs—in offices, on farms, or in day care centers—but they, too, are government employees.

Just as capitalism does not exist in a pure form, neither does socialism. Although the ideology of socialism calls for resources to be distributed according to need and not the ability to pay, socialist countries found it necessary to pay higher salaries for some jobs in order to entice people to take on greater responsibilities. For example, in socialist countries factory managers always earned more than factory workers. These differences in pay follow the functionalist argument of social stratification presented in Chapter 7 (page 179). By narrowing the huge pay gaps that characterize capitalist nations, however, socialist nations established considerably greater equality of income.

Dissatisfied with the greed and exploitation of capitalism and the lack of freedom and individuality of socialism, Sweden and Denmark developed **democratic socialism** (also called *welfare socialism*). In this form of socialism, both the state and individuals produce and distribute goods and services. The government owns and runs the

This advertisement from 1885 represents an early stage of capitalism when individuals were free to manufacture and market products with little or no interference from the government. Today, the production and marketing of goods take place under detailed, complicated government laws and regulations.

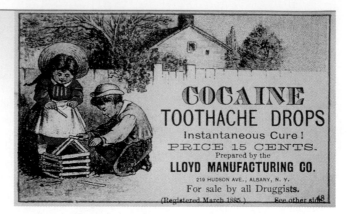

steel, mining, forestry, and energy concerns, as well as the country's telephones, television stations, and airlines. Remaining in private hands are the retail stores, farms, factories, and most service industries.

## Ideologies of Capitalism and Socialism

Not only do capitalism and socialism have different approaches to producing and distributing goods but they also represent opposing belief systems. *Capitalists* believe that market forces should determine both products and prices. They also believe that profits are good for humanity. Striving for profit stimulates people to produce and distribute goods efficiently, as well as to develop new products. This benefits society, bringing a more abundant supply of goods at cheaper prices.

*Socialists,* in contrast, consider profit to be immoral. Karl Marx said that an item's value is based on the work that goes into it. The only way there can be profit, he stressed, is by paying workers less than the value of their labor. Profit, then, is the *excess value* that has been withheld from workers. Socialists believe that the government should protect workers from this exploitation. To do so, the government should own the means of production, using them not to generate profit but to produce items that match people's needs, not their ability to pay.

Adherents to these ideologies paint each other in such stark colors that *each perceives the other system as one of exploitation.* Capitalists believe that socialists violate the basic human rights of freedom of decision and opportunity. Socialists believe that capitalists violate the basic human right of freedom from poverty. With each side claiming moral superiority while viewing the other as a threat to its very existence, the last century witnessed the world split into two main blocs. In what was known as the *Cold War,* the West armed itself to defend and promote capitalism, the East to defend and promote socialism.

## Criticisms of Capitalism and Socialism

The primary criticism leveled against capitalism is that it leads to social inequality. Capitalism, say its critics, produces a tiny top layer of wealthy, powerful people who exploit an immense bottom layer of poorly paid workers.

Another criticism is that the tiny top layer wields vast political power. Those few who own the means of production reap huge profits, accrue power, and get legislation passed that goes against the public good.

The primary criticism leveled against socialism is that it does not respect individual rights (Berger 1991). Others (in the form of some government body) control people's lives. They decide where people will live, work, and go to school. In China, they even decide how many children women may bear (Mosher 1983, 2006). Critics also argue that central planning is grossly inefficient and that socialism is not capable of producing much wealth. They say that its greater equality really amounts to giving almost everyone an equal chance to be poor.

## The Convergence of Capitalism and Socialism

Regardless of the validity of these mutual criticisms, as nations industrialize they come to resemble one another. They urbanize, produce similar divisions of labor (such as professionals and skilled technicians), and encourage higher education. Even similar values emerge (Kerr 1983). By itself, this tendency would make capitalist and socialist nations grow more alike, but another factor also brings them closer to one another (Form 1979): Despite their incompatible ideologies, both capitalist and socialist systems have adopted certain of each other's features.

That capitalism and socialism are growing similar is known as **convergence theory.** This view points to a coming hybrid, or mixed, economy. Fundamental changes in socialist countries give evidence for convergence theory. The people of Russia and China suffered from the production of shoddy goods, they were plagued by shortages, and their standard of living lagged severely behind that of the West. To try to catch up, in the 1980s and 1990s, the governments of Russia and China reinstated

The success of the Barbie doll, bringing in over a billion dollars a year, has spawned numerous competitors. After 40 years as the top seller, Barbie has been outsold—by the brash, "street smart" Flava dolls. What changes do you think this reflects in U.S. culture?

## Capitalism in a Global Economy

**Corporate Capitalism**    Capitalism is driving today's global interdependence. Its triumph as the world's dominant economic force can be traced to a social invention called the corporation. A **corporation** is a business that is treated legally as a person. A corporation can make contracts, incur debts, sue and be sued. Its liabilities and obligations, however, are separate from those of its owners. For example, each shareholder of Ford Motor Company—whether he or she has 1 or 100,000 shares—owns a portion of the company. However, Ford, not its individual owners, is responsible for fulfilling its contracts and paying its debts. To indicate how corporations have come to dominate the economy, sociologists use the term **corporate capitalism.**

**Separation of Ownership and Management**    One of the most surprising aspects of corporations is their *separation of ownership and management.* Unlike most businesses, it is not the owners—those who own the company's stock—who run the day-to-day affairs of the company (Walters 1995; Sklair 2001). Instead, managers run the corporation, and they are able to treat it *as though it were their own.* The result is the "ownership of wealth without appreciable control, and control of wealth without appreciable ownership" (Berle and Means 1932). Sociologist Michael Useem (1984) put it this way:

> When few owners held all or most of a corporation's stock, they readily dominated its board of directors, which in turn selected top management and ran the corporation. Now that a firm's stock [is] dispersed among many unrelated owners, each holding a tiny fraction of the total equity, the resulting power vacuum allow[s] management to select the board of directors; thus management [becomes] self-perpetuating and thereby acquire[s] de facto control over the corporation.

Because of this power vacuum, at their annual meetings the stockholders ordinarily rubber-stamp management's recommendations. It is so unusual for this *not* to happen that these rare cases are called a **stockholders' revolt.** The irony of this term is generally lost, but remember

market forces. They made the private ownership of property legal, and they auctioned off many of their state-owned industries. Making a profit—which had been a crime—was encouraged. In China, capitalists were even invited to join the Communist party (Kahn 2002). Even Vietnam, whose communism the United States was so concerned about, has embraced capitalism (Mydans 2006).

Changes in capitalism also support this theory. The United States has adopted many socialist practices. One of the most obvious is extracting money from some individuals to pay for the benefits it gives to others. Examples include unemployment compensation (taxes paid by workers are distributed to those who no longer produce a profit); subsidized housing (shelter, paid for by the many, is given to the poor and elderly, with no motive of profit); welfare (taxes from the many are distributed to the needy); a minimum wage (the government, not the employer, determines the minimum that workers receive); and Social Security (the retired do not receive what they paid into the system but, rather, receive money that the government collects from current workers). Such an embrace of socialist principles indicates that the United States has produced its own version of a mixed economy.

Perhaps, then, convergence is unfolding before our very eyes. On the one hand, capitalists have assumed, reluctantly, that their system should provide workers with at least minimal support during unemployment, extended illness, and old age. On the other hand, socialist leaders have admitted, reluctantly, that profit and private ownership do motivate people to work harder.

that in such cases it is not the workers who are rebelling at the control of the owners but the owners who are rebelling at the control of the workers!

**Interlocking Directorates and the Concentration of Power**
Conflict theorists stress how the wealthy expand their power through **interlocking directorates;** that is, they serve on the board of directors of several companies. Their fellow members on those boards also sit on the boards of other companies, and so on. Like a spider's web that starts at the center and then fans out in all directions, the top companies are interlocked into a network (Mintz and Schwartz 1985; Davis 2003). The chief executive officer of a firm in England, who sits on the board of directors of half a dozen other companies, said:

> If you serve on, say, six outside boards, each of which has, say, ten directors, and let's say out of the ten directors, five are experts in one or another subject, you have a built-in panel of thirty friends who are experts who you meet regularly, automatically each month, and you really have great access to ideas and information. You're joining a club, a very good club. (Useem 1984)

This concentration of power reduces competition, for a director is not going to approve a plan that will be harmful to another company in which he or she (mostly he) has a stake. The top executives of the top U.S. companies are part of the powerful capitalist class described on pages 207–208. They even get together in recreational settings, where they renew their sense of solidarity, purpose, and destiny (Domhoff 1999b, 2002, 2006).

## Multinational Corporations and Global Investing

> "This Bud is for you!"—Thanks to InBev, a Belgian brewer.
>
> "Fill up at Shell!"—Thanks to a Dutch refinery.
>
> "Tums for your tummy!"—Thanks to Beecham Group, a British corporation.

Corporations have outgrown their national boundaries, as illustrated by the Social Map below and on the next page. Cross-border investments have become so extensive

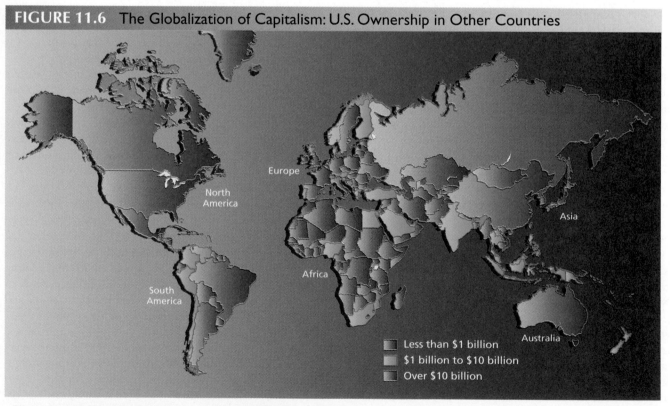

**FIGURE 11.6**    The Globalization of Capitalism: U.S. Ownership in Other Countries

■ Less than $1 billion
■ $1 billion to $10 billion
■ Over $10 billion

*Source:* By the author. Based on *Statistical Abstract* 2007:Table 1288.

## FIGURE 11.7   The Globalization of Capitalism: Foreign Ownership of U.S. Business

Businesses in which at least 10 percent of the voting interest is controlled by a non-U.S. owner.

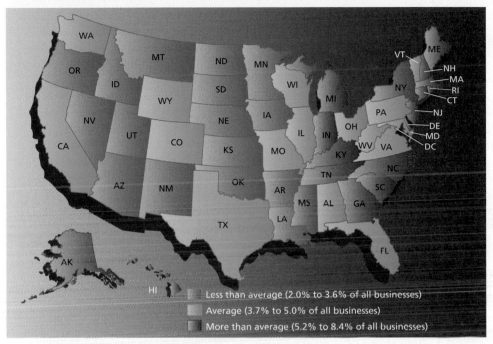

Less than average (2.0% to 3.6% of all businesses)
Average (3.7% to 5.0% of all businesses)
More than average (5.2% to 8.4% of all businesses)

*Source:* By the author. Based on *Statistical Abstract* 2007:Table 1275.

that about 1 of every 20 U.S. businesses—employing over 5 million workers—is now owned by people in other countries (*Statistical Abstract* 2008:Table 1275).

Although we take multinational corporations for granted—as well as their cornucopia of products—their power and presence are new to the world scene. As **multinational corporations**—corporations that operate across national borders—do business, they tend to become detached from the interests and values of their country of origin. A U.S. executive made this revealing statement: "The United States does not have an automatic call on our resources. There is no mindset that puts the country first" (Greider 2001). These global giants move investments and production from one part of the globe to another—with no concern for consequences other than profits. How opening or closing factories affects workers is of no concern to them. With profit as their moral guide, the conscience of multinational corporations is written in dollar signs. As they soar past geographical barriers in the attempt to conquer markets, the road is not without bumps. As discussed in the Cultural Diversity box on the next page, this can lead to humorous situations.

This primary allegiance to profits and market share, rather than to their workers or to any country, accompanied by a web of interconnections around the globe, is of high sociological significance. The shift in orientation and organization is so new, however, that we don't yet know its implications. But we can consider two stark contrasts. The first: Removed from tribal loyalties and needing easy access across national boundaries, the global interconnections of the multinational corporations may be a force for global peace. The second: They could create a New World Order dominated by a handful of corporate leaders. If so, we all may find ourselves at the mercy of a global elite in a system of interconnected societies, directed by the heads of the world's corporate giants.

Let's consider this possibility.

## Global Trade: Inequalities and Conflict

The giant multinational corporations are carving up the world into major trading blocs and pushing for the reduction or elimination of tariffs. As a result, we can expect trade among nations to increase beyond anything the

# Cultural Diversity around the World

## Doing Business in the Global Village

The globalization of capitalism means that business people face cultural hurdles as they sell products in other countries. Some of the cultural mistakes they make as they try to clear these hurdles are downright humorous.

*United States*

In trying to reach Spanish-speaking Americans and Mexico's growing middle class, some companies have stumbled over their Spanish. Parker Pen was using a slogan "It won't leak in your pocket and embarrass you." The translation, however, came out as "It won't leak in your pocket and make you pregnant." Frank Perdue's cute chicken slogan "It takes a strong man to make a tender chicken" didn't fare any better. It came out as "It takes an aroused man to make a chicken affectionate." And

*Japan*

when American Airlines launched a "Fly in Leather" campaign to promote its leather seats in first class, the Mexican campaign stumbled just a bit. "Fly in Leather" (*vuela en cuero*), while literally correct, came out as "Fly Naked." I suppose that slogan did appeal to some (Archbold and Harmon 2001).

The Spanish-speaking market is so huge that it keeps enticing more companies to run marketing campaigns to reach it. The American Dairy Association made a hit in the United States with its humorous campaign, "Got Milk?" In Mexico, though, the Spanish translation read "Are you lactating?" All those mouths with white milk on them suddenly took on new meaning. Coors didn't fare any better. Their slogan, "Turn It Loose," was a hit in the United States, but in Spanish it came out as "Get Diarrhea."

Then there is Hershey's new candy bar, *Cajeta Elegancita,* marketed to Spanish-speaking customers. While *cajeta* can mean nougat, its most common meaning is "little box." The literal translation of *cajeta elegancita* is elegant or fancy little box. Some customers are snickering about this one, too, for *cajeta* is also slang for an intimate part of the female anatomy ("Winner . . ." 2006).

It isn't only Spanish that has given U.S. companies problems. Vicks decided to sell its cough drops in Germany. In German, the "v" is pronounced "f." Unfortunately, this made Vicks sound like the "f" word in English, which is just what ficks means in German.

Cultural mistakes are a two-way street, of course. Electrolux is a vacuum cleaner made in Sweden. Their cute slogan reads just fine in Swedish, but the translation for their U.S. ads came out as "Nothing sucks like an Electrolux."

Some businesspeople have managed to avoid such problems. They have seized profit opportunities in cultural differences. For example, Japanese women are embarrassed by the sounds they make in public toilets. To drown out the offensive sounds, they flush the toilet an average of 2.7 times a visit (Iori 1988). This wastes a lot of water, of course. Seeing this cultural trait as an opportunity, a U.S. entrepreneur developed a battery-powered device that is mounted in the toilet stall. When a woman activates the device, it emits a 25-second flushing sound. A toilet-sound duplicator may be useless in our culture, but the Japanese have bought thousands of them.

To be accepted in another culture, some items have to be changed. In a process called *transcreation*, cartoons designed originally for U.S. audiences are modified to match the tastes of an audience in another culture. The illustration in this box shows this process. At the top is the U.S. version of the Powerpuff Girls; at the bottom is how the Powerpuff Girls appear on Japanese television. It turns out that portraying Blossom, Buttercup, and Bubbles as leggy and dressed in skimpy outfits has broadened their appeal: Not only do little girls look forward to this cartoon on Saturday mornings, but so do many adult Japanese men (Fowler and Chozick 2007).

## For Your Consideration

1. Why do you think that it is often difficult to do business across cultures?
2. How can businesspeople avoid cross-cultural mistakes?
3. If a company offends a culture in which it is trying to do business, what should it do?

world has ever seen. U.S. corporations will continue to support an expansion of global trade, for world markets have become crucial for their success.

Not all nations will benefit equally, of course. The Most Industrialized Nations (even as they transition to their postindustrial phase) will continue to garner the lion's share of the world's wealth.

If economic inequality between the richer and the poorer nations increases, it spells trouble. The growing wealth of the nations that control global trade does not sit easily with the Least Industrialized Nations. Their poverty and powerlessness—illuminated and reinforced by televised images of wealth and privilege beamed from the Most Industrialized Nations—breed discontent. So do growing pressures on their limited resources from their mushrooming populations. All this provides fertile ground for the recruitment of terrorists, who, if able, will vent their frustrations against those nations that they perceive as exploiting them.

## A New World Order?

Today, the world's nations are almost frantically embracing capitalism. With nations forming coalitions of trading partners, national borders are becoming increasingly insignificant. The United States, Canada, and Mexico have formed a North American Free Trade Association (NAFTA). We also have CAFTA, the Central American Free Trade Association. Eventually, all of North and South America may belong to such an organization. Ten Asian countries with a combined population of a half billion people have formed a regional trading partnership called ASEAN (Association of South East Asian Nations). Struggling for dominance is an even more encompassing group called the *World* Trade Organization.

The European Union (EU) may point to this unifying future. Transcending their national boundaries, twenty-seven European countries (with a combined population of 450 million) formed this economic and political unit. These nations have adopted a single, cross-national currency, the Euro, which has replaced their marks, francs, liras, lats, and pesetas. The EU has also established a military staff in Brussels, Belgium (Mardell 2007).

Could this process continue until there is just one state or empire that envelops the earth? The major trend is heading in this direction. The United Nations is striving to become the legislative body of the world, wanting its decisions to supersede those of any individual nation. The UN operates a World Court (formally titled the International Court of Justice). It also has a rudimentary army and has sent "peacekeeping" troops to several nations.

Although we can identify the trend toward a single worldwide government—forged through increasingly encompassing trade organizations—we are unlikely to see its conclusion during our lifetimes. National boundaries, national patriotism, and ethnic loyalties die only hard deaths. The EU is not as united as it appears to be on the surface. In 2005 France and Holland rejected a proposed constitution, and in 2008 Ireland scuttled a proposed treaty that would have given the EU a single foreign minister. The United Nations, too, is divided by power inequality: Any one of the five nations that are the permanent members of its Security Council (Russian Federation, China, France, Great Britain, and the United States) can veto any action decided by the entire United Nations.

Despite occasional obstacles, the broad historical trend is toward increasingly broader, cross-national units. We occasionally catch a glimpse of what is going on behind the scenes. When Russia was struggling to join the capitalist club, its communist background made it an object of suspicion. When Russia was finally acknowledged as "capitalist enough" to be accepted into NATO, its prime minister made this remarkable statement: "We must now together build the New World Order" (Purdum 2002).

It is fascinating to speculate on the type of government that might emerge if global political and economic unity were to come about. Certainly a New World Order holds potential benefits for human welfare. It could bring global peace. And if we had a benevolent government, our lives and participation in politics could be satisfying. But we must be mindful of Hitler. If his conquests had resulted in world domination, we not only would be speaking German but we also would be living under a single dictator in a global totalitarian regime based on racial identification. If the world's resources and people come under the control of a dictatorship or an oligarchy, then the future for humanity could be bleak. We could end up with living under a government like that of Winston and Julia in our opening vignette.

# SUMMARY *and* REVIEW

## Power, Authority, and Violence

*How are authority and coercion related to power?*

**Authority** is **power** that people view as legitimately exercised over them, while **coercion** is power they consider unjust. The **state** is a political entity that claims a monopoly on violence over some territory. If enough people consider a state's power illegitimate, **revolution** is possible. P. 298.

*What kinds of authority are there?*

Max Weber identified three types of authority. In **traditional authority,** power is derived from custom—patterns set down in the past serve as rules for the present. In **rational–legal authority** (also called *bureaucratic authority*), power is based on law and written procedures. In **charismatic authority,** power is derived from loyalty to an individual to whom people are attracted. Charismatic authority, which undermines traditional and rational–legal authority, has built-in problems in transferring authority to a new leader. Pp. 299–300.

## Types of Government

*How are the types of government related to power?*

In a **monarchy,** power is based on hereditary rule; in a **democracy,** power is given to the ruler by citizens; in a **dictatorship,** power is seized by an individual; and in an **oligarchy,** power is seized by a small group. Pp. 300–302.

## The U.S. Political System

*What are the main characteristics of the U.S. political system?*

The U.S. political system is dominated by the Democratic and Republican parties, which represent slightly different centralist positions. The differences are most obvious in those who take extreme positions. P. 302.

Voter turnout is higher among people who are more socially integrated—those who sense a greater stake in the outcome of elections, such as the more educated and well-to-do. **Lobbyists** and **special-interest groups,** such as **political action committees** (PACs), play a significant role in U.S. politics. Pp. 303–306.

## Who Rules the United States?

*Is the United States controlled by a ruling class?*

In a view known as **pluralism,** functionalists say that no one group holds power, that the country's many competing interest groups balance one another. Conflict theorists, who focus on the top level of power, say that the United States is governed by a **power elite,** a **ruling class** made up of the top corporate, political, and military leaders. At this point, the matter is not settled. Pp. 306–308.

## War and Terrorism: Implementing Political Objectives

*How are war and terrorism related to politics?*

**War** and **terrorism** are both means of attempting to accomplish political objectives. Timasheff identified three essential conditions of war and seven fuels that bring about war. His analysis can be applied to terrorism. Nuclear, biological, and chemical terrorism are major threats. One of the chief costs of war and terrorism is **dehumanization.** Pp. 308–309.

## The Transformation of Economic Systems

*How are economic systems linked to types of societies?*

In the earliest societies (hunting and gathering), small groups lived off the land and produced little or no surplus. Economic systems grew more complex as people discovered how to domesticate animals and grow plants (pastoral and horticultural societies), farm (agricultural societies), and manufacture (industrial societies). As people produced a *surplus,* trade developed. Trade, in turn, brought social inequality as some people accumulated more than others. Service industries dominate the postindustrial societies. If a biotech society is emerging, it is too early to know its consequences. Pp. 309–318.

## World Economic Systems

*How do the major economic systems differ?*

The world's two major economic systems are capitalism and socialism. In **capitalism,** private citizens own the means of production and pursue profits. In **socialism,** the state owns the means of production and has no goal of profit. Adherents of each have developed ideologies that defend their own systems and paint the other as harmful or even evil. As expected from **convergence theory,** each system has adopted features of the other. Pp. 318–321.

## Capitalism in a Global Economy

*What is the role of corporations in global capitalism?*

The term **corporate capitalism** indicates that giant corporations dominate capitalism. The profit goal of **multinational corporations** removes their allegiance from any particular nation. Pp. 321–323.

*Is humanity headed toward a world political system?*

The globalization of capitalism and the trend toward regional economic and political unions may indicate that a world political system is developing. If a New World Order develops, the possible consequences for human welfare range from excellent to calamitous. Pp. 323–325.

# THINKING CRITICALLY *about* Chapter 11

1. What are the three sources of authority, and how do they differ from one another?

2. Apply the three essential conditions of war and its seven fuels to a recent war that the United States has been a part of.

3. What global forces are affecting the U.S. economy? What consequences are they having? How might they affect your own life?

# BY THE NUMBERS: Changes Over Time

- Percentage of college graduates who voted in the 1980 presidential election: **80%**
- Percentage of college graduates who voted in the 2004 presidential election: **73%**

- Percentage of U.S. workforce that were farmers in 1900: **30%**
- Percentage of U.S. workforce that are farmers today: **2%**

- Percentage of U.S. workforce that were white-collar workers in 1900: **20%**
- Percentage of U.S. workforce that are white-collar workers today: **78%**

- Percentage of U.S. workforce that were blue-collar workers in 1940: **46%**
- Percentage of U.S. workforce that are blue-collar workers today: **20%**

- The typical U.S. farmer produced enough food to feed this number of people in the 1800s: **5**
- The typical U.S. farmer produces enough food to feed this number of people today: **80**

- Average hourly earnings, in current U.S. dollars, received by workers in 1970: **$3.23**
- Average hourly earnings, in current U.S. dollars, received by workers today: **$16.76**

- Average hourly earnings, in constant (1982) U.S. dollars, received by workers in 1970: **$8.03**
- Average hourly earnings, in constant (1982) U.S. dollars, received by workers today: **$8.24**

# ADDITIONAL RESOURCES

## What can you find in MySocLab? mysoclab　www.mysoclab.com

- **Complete Ebook**
- **Practice Tests and Video and Audio activities**
- **Mapping and Data Analysis exercises**

- **Sociology in the News**
- **Classic Readings in Sociology**
- **Research and Writing advice**

## Where Can I Read More on This Topic?

Suggested readings for this chapter are listed at the back of this book.

Chapter

12

# Marriage and Family

"Hold still. We're going to be late," said Sharon as she tried to put shoes on 2-year-old Michael, who kept squirming away.

Finally succeeding with the shoes, Sharon turned to 4-year-old Brittany, who was trying to pull a brush through her hair. "It's stuck, Mom," Brittany said.

"Well, no wonder. Just how did you get gum in your hair? I don't have time for this, Brittany. We've got to leave."

Getting to the van fifteen minutes behind schedule, Sharon strapped the kids in, and then herself. Just as she was about to pull away, she remembered that she had not checked the fridge for messages.

"Just a minute, kids. I'll be right back."

Running into the house, she frantically searched for a note from Tom. She vaguely remembered him mumbling something about being held over at work. She grabbed the Post-It and ran back to the van.

"He's picking on me," complained Brittany when her mother climbed back in.

"Oh, shut up, Brittany. He's only 2. He can't pick on you."

"Yes, he did," Brittany said, crossing her arms defiantly as she stretched out her foot to kick her brother's seat.

"Oh, no! How did Mikey get that smudge on his face? Did you do that, Brit?"

Brittany crossed her arms again, pushing out her lips in her classic pouting pose.

As Sharon drove to the day care center, she tried to calm herself. "Only two more days of work this week, and then the weekend. Then I can catch up on housework and have a little relaxed time with the kids. And Tom can finally cut the grass and buy the groceries," she thought. "And maybe we'll even have time to make love. Boy, that's been a long time."

At a traffic light, Sharon found time to read Tom's note. "Oh, no. That's what he meant. He has to work Saturday. Well, there go those plans."

What Sharon didn't know was that her boss had also made plans for Sharon's Saturday. And that their emergency Saturday babysitter wouldn't be available. And that Michael was coming down with the flu. And that Brittany would follow next. And that . . .

> "Yes, he did," Brittany said, crossing her arms defiantly as she kicked her brother's seat.

329

# Marriage and Family in Global Perspective

To better understand U.S. patterns of marriage and family, let's first look at how customs differ around the world. This will give us a context for interpreting our own experience with this vital social institution.

## What Is a Family?

The family is so significant to humanity that every human group in the world organizes its members in families. But the world's cultures display so much variety that the term *family* is difficult to define. Although the Western world regards a family as a husband, wife, and children, other groups have family forms in which men have more than one wife (**polygyny**) or women more than one husband (**polyandry**). How about the obvious? Can we define the family as the approved group into which children are born? Then we would be overlooking the Banaro of New Guinea. In this group, a young woman must give birth *before* she can marry—and she *cannot* marry the father of her child (Murdock 1949).

What if we were to define the family as the unit in which parents are responsible for disciplining children and providing for their material needs? This, too, is not universal. Among the Trobriand Islanders, it is not the parents but the wife's eldest brother who is responsible for providing the children's discipline and their food (Malinowski 1927).

Such remarkable variety means that we have to settle for a broad definition. A **family** consists of people who consider themselves related by blood, marriage, or adoption. A **household,** in contrast, consists of people who occupy the same housing unit—a house, apartment, or other living quarters.

We can classify families as **nuclear** (husband, wife, and children) and **extended** (including people such as grandparents, aunts, uncles, and cousins in addition to the nuclear unit). Sociologists also refer to the **family of orientation** (the family in which an individual grows up) and the **family of procreation** (the family that is formed when a couple has its first child).

## What Is Marriage?

We have the same problem here. For just about every element you might regard as essential to marriage, some group has a different custom.

Consider the sex of the bride and groom. In several countries, people of the same sex can marry. Even sexual relationships don't universally characterize marriage. The Nayar of Malabar never allow a bride and groom to have sex. After a three-day celebration of the marriage, they send the groom packing—and never allow him to see his bride again (La Barre 1954). (In case you're wondering, the groom comes from another tribe. Nayar women are allowed to have sex, but only with approved lovers—who can never be the husband. This system keeps family property intact—along matrilineal lines.)

At least we can be certain that those who marry have to be alive—or so you would think. But even here, we find an exception. On the Loess Plateau in China, if a man dies without a wife, his parents look for a dead woman to be his bride. (Some parents sell their dead unmarried daughters.) The dead man and woman are married and then buried together (Fremson 2006).

With such cultural variety, we can conclude that, regardless of its form, **marriage** is a group's approved mating arrangement—usually marked by a ritual of some sort (the wedding) to indicate the couple's new public status.

Often one of the strongest family bonds is that of mother and daughter. The young artist, an eleventh-grader, wrote "This painting expresses the way I feel about my future with my child. I want my child to be happy and I want her to love me the same way I love her. In that way we will have a good relationship so that nobody will be able to take us apart. I wanted this picture to be alive; that is why I used a lot of bright colors."

# Common Cultural Themes

Despite this diversity, several common themes run through marriage and family. As Table 12.1 illustrates, all societies use marriage and family to establish patterns of mate selection, descent, inheritance, and authority. Let's look at these patterns.

**Mate Selection**    Each human group establishes norms to govern who marries whom. If a group has norms of **endogamy,** it specifies that its members must marry *within* their group. For example, some groups prohibit interracial marriage. In some societies, these norms are written into law, but in most cases they are informal. In the United States most whites marry whites and most African Americans marry African Americans—not because of any laws but because of informal norms. In contrast, norms of **exogamy** specify that people must marry *outside* their group. The best example of exogamy is the **incest taboo,** which prohibits sex and marriage among designated relatives.

As you can see from Table 12.1, how people find mates varies around the world, from fathers selecting them, with no input from those who are to marry, to the highly individualistic, personal choices common in Western cultures. Changes in mate selection are the focus of the Sociology and the New Technology box on the next page.

**Descent**    How are you related to your father's father or to your mother's mother? The answer to this question is not the same all over the world. Each society has a **system of descent,** the way people trace kinship over generations. We use a **bilineal system,** for we think of ourselves as related to *both* our mother's and our father's sides of the family. "Doesn't everyone?" you might ask. Ours, however, is only one logical way to reckon descent. Some groups use a **patrilineal system,** tracing descent only on the father's side; they don't think of children as being related to their mother's relatives. Others follow a **matrilineal system,** tracing descent only on the mother's side, and not considering children to be related to their father's relatives. The Naxi of China, for example, don't even have a word for father (Hong 1999).

**Inheritance**    Marriage and family—in whatever forms are customary in a society—are also used to determine rights of inheritance. In a bilineal system, property is passed to both males and females, in a patrilineal system only to males, and in a matrilineal system (the rarest form), only to females. No system is natural. Rather, each matches a group's ideas of justice and logic.

**Authority**    Historically, some form of **patriarchy,** a social system in which men dominate women, has formed a thread that runs through all societies. Contrary to what some think,

| TABLE 12.1 | Common Cultural Themes: Marriage in Traditional and Industrialized Societies | |
|---|---|---|
| **Characteristic** | **Traditional Societies** | **Industrial (and Postindustrial) Societies** |
| What is the structure of marriage? | *Extended* (marriage embeds spouses in a large kinship network of explicit obligations) | *Nuclear* (marriage brings fewer obligations toward the spouse's relatives) |
| What are the functions of marriage? | Encompassing (see the six functions listed on p. 333) | More limited (many functions are fulfilled by other social institutions) |
| Who holds authority? | *Patriarchal* (authority is held by males) | Although some patriarchal features remain, authority is divided more equally |
| How many spouses at one time? | Most have one spouse (*monogamy*), while some have several (*polygamy*) | One spouse |
| Who selects the spouse? | Parents, usually the father, select the spouse | Individuals choose their own spouse |
| Where does the couple live? | Couples usually reside with the groom's family (*patrilocal residence*), less commonly with the bride's family (*matrilocal residence*) | Couples establish a new home (*neolocal residence*) |
| How is descent figured? | Usually figured from male ancestors (*patrilineal kinship*), less commonly from female ancestors (*matrilineal kinship*) | Figured from male and female ancestors equally (*bilineal kinship*) |
| How is inheritance figured? | Rigid system of rules; usually patrilineal, but can be matrilineal | Highly individualistic; usually bilineal |

# SOCIOLOGY and the NEW TECHNOLOGY

## Finding a Mate: Not the Same as It Used to Be

Things haven't changed entirely. Boys and girls still get interested in each other at their neighborhood schools, and men and women still meet at college. Friends still serve as matchmakers and introduce friends, hoping they might click. People still meet at churches and bars, at the mall and at work.

But technology is bringing about some fundamental changes. Americans are turning more and more to the Internet. Numerous sites advertise that they offer thousands of potential companions, lovers, or spouses. For a low monthly fee, you, too, can meet the person of your dreams.

The photos on these sites are fascinating. Some seem to be lovely people, attractive and vivacious, and one wonders why they are posting their photos and personal information online. Do they have some secret flaw that they need to do this? Others seem okay, although perhaps a bit needy. Then there are the pitiful, and one wonders if they will ever find a mate, or even a hookup, for that matter. Some are desperate, begging for someone—anyone—to make contact with them: women who try for sexy poses, exposing too much flesh, suggesting the promise of at least a good time, and men who try their best to look like hulks, their muscular presence promising the same.

The Internet dating sites are not filled with losers, although there are plenty of them. A lot of regular,

ordinary people post their profiles, too. And some do find the person of their dreams—or at least good matches. More and more, Internet posting is losing its stigma, and couples are finding mates via electronic matchmaking.

A frustrating aspect of these sites is that the "thousands of eligible prospects" that they tout are spread over the nation. You might find that a person who piques your interest lives in another part of the country. You can do a search for your area, but there are likely to be few from it.

Not to worry. More technology to the rescue.

The latest is dating on demand. You sit at home, turn on your TV, and search for your partner. Your local cable company does all the hard work for you. They host singles events at bars and malls and help singles make three-to-five minute tapes talking about themselves and what they are looking for in a mate (Grant 2005).

You can view the videos free. And if you get interested in someone, for just a small fee you can contact the individual.

Now all you need is to hire a private detective—also available online for another fee—to see if this engaging person is already married, has a dozen kids, has been sued for paternity or child support, or is a child molester or a rapist.

## For Your Consideration

What is your opinion of electronic dating sites? Have you used one? Would you consider using an electronic dating site (if you were single and unattached)?

there are no historical records of a true **matriarchy,** a social system in which women as a group dominate men as a group. Our marriage and family customs, then, developed within a framework of patriarchy. Although U.S. family patterns are becoming more **egalitarian,** or equal, some of today's customs still reflect their patriarchal origin. One of the most obvious examples is U.S. naming patterns. Despite some changes, the typical bride still takes the groom's last name, and children usually receive the father's last name.

# Marriage and Family in Theoretical Perspective

As we have seen, human groups around the world have many forms of mate selection, ways to trace descent, and ways to view the parent's responsibility. Although these patterns are arbitrary, each group perceives its own forms of marriage and family as natural. Now let's see what picture emerges when we view marriage and family theoretically.

## The Functionalist Perspective: Functions and Dysfunctions

Functionalists stress that to survive, a society must fulfill basic functions (that is, meet its basic needs). When functionalists look at marriage and family, they examine how they are related to other parts of society, especially the ways they contribute to the well-being of society.

**Why the Family Is Universal**    Although the form of marriage and family varies from one group to another, the family is universal. The reason for this, say functionalists, is that the family fulfills six needs that are basic to the survival of every society. These needs, or functions, are (1) economic production, (2) socialization of children, (3) care of the sick and aged, (4) recreation, (5) sexual control, and (6) reproduction. To make certain that these functions are performed, every human group has adopted some form of the family.

**Functions of the Incest Taboo**    Functionalists note that the incest taboo helps families avoid *role confusion.* This, in turn, facilitates the socialization of children. For example, if father–daughter incest were allowed, how should a wife treat her daughter— as a daughter, as a subservient second wife, or even as a rival? Should the daughter consider her mother as a mother, as the first wife, or as a rival? Would her father be a father or a lover? And would

the wife be the husband's main wife, a secondary wife—or even the "mother of the other wife" (whatever role that might be)? And if the daughter had a child by her father, what relationships would everyone have? Maternal incest would also lead to complications every bit as confusing as these.

The incest taboo also forces people to look outside the family for marriage partners. Anthropologists theorize that *exogamy* was especially functional in tribal societies, for it forged alliances between tribes that otherwise might have killed each other off. Today, exogamy still extends both the bride's and the groom's social networks by adding and building relationships with their spouse's family and friends.

**Isolation and Emotional Overload**    As you know, functionalists also analyze dysfunctions. One of those dysfunctions comes from the relative isolation of today's nuclear family. Because extended families are enmeshed in large kinship networks, their members can count on many people for material and emotional support. In nuclear families, in contrast, the stresses that come with crises such as the loss of a job—or even the routine pressures of a harried life, as depicted in our opening vignette—are spread among fewer people. This places greater strain on each family member, creating *emotional overload.* In addition, the relative isolation of the nuclear family makes it vulnerable to a "dark side"—incest and various other forms of abuse, matters that we examine later in this chapter.

This January 1937 photo from Sneedville, Tennesse, shows Eunice Johns, age 9, and her husband, Charlie Johns, age 22. The groom gave his wife a doll as a wedding gift. The new husband and wife planned to build a cabin and, as Charlie Johns phrased it, "go to housekeeping." Is this an example of gender age as symbolic interactionists might say? Or, as conflict theorists would say, of gender exploitation?

## The Conflict Perspective: Struggles Between Husbands and Wives

Anyone who has been married or who has seen a marriage from the inside knows that—regardless of a couple's best intentions—conflict is a part of marriage. It is inevitable that conflict will arise between two people who live intimately and who share most everything in life—from their goals and checkbooks to their bedroom and children. At some point, their desires and approaches to life clash, sometimes mildly and sometimes quite harshly. Conflict among married people is so common that it is the grist of soap operas, movies, songs, and novels.

Throughout the generations, power has been a major source of conflict between wives and husbands: Husbands have had more power, and wives have resented it. Power differences show up throughout marriage, from disagreements over responsibilities for doing housework and taking care of children to quarrels about spending money and the lack of attention, respect, and sex.

As you know well, divorce is one way that couples try to end marital conflict. Divorce can mark the end of hostilities, or it can merely indicate a changed legal relationship within which the hostilities persist as the couple continues to quarrel about finances and children. We will return to the topic of divorce later in this chapter.

## The Symbolic Interactionist Perspective: Gender and Family Responsibilities

**Changes in Traditional Orientations**  Throughout the generations, housework has been regarded as "women's work," and men have resisted getting involved. Child care, too, has traditionally been considered women's work. As more women began to work for wages, however, men came to feel pressure to do housework and to be more involved in the care of their children. But no man wanted to be thought of as a sissy, under the control of a woman. That would conflict with his culturally rooted feelings of manhood and the reputation he wanted to maintain in the community, especially among his friends.

As women put in more hours at paid work, men gradually began to do more housework and to take on more responsibility for the care of their children. When men first began to change diapers—at least openly—it was big news. Comedians even told jokes about Mr. Mom, giving expression to common concerns about what the future would be like if men continued to be feminized.

Ever so slowly, cultural ideas changed, and housework, care of children, and paid labor came to be regarded as the responsibilities of both men and women. Not all segments of the population have accepted these changes to the same degree, and we have not reached equality, but let's examine these changing responsibilities in the family.

**Who Does What?**  Figure 12.1 on the next page illustrates several significant changes that have taken place in U.S. families. The first is likely to surprise you, as it contradicts common ideas. If you look closely at this figure, you will see that not only are husbands spending more time taking care of the children but so are wives. This is fascinating: *Both* husbands and wives are spending more time in child care.

Contrary to popular assumptions, children are getting *more* attention from their parents than they used to. This

In Hindu marriages, the roles of husband and wife are firmly established. Neither this woman, whom I photographed in Chittoor, India, nor her husband question whether she should carry the family wash to the village pump. Women here have done this task for millennia. As India industrializes, as happened in the West, who does the wash will be questioned—and may eventually become a source of strain in marriage.

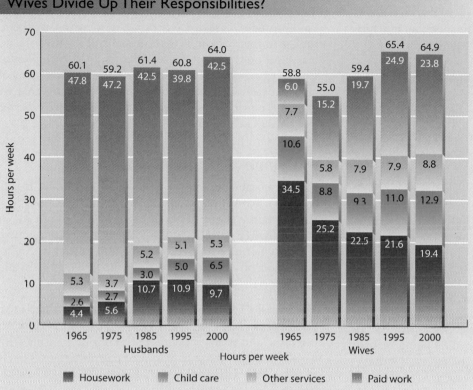

**FIGURE 12.1** In Two Paycheck Marriages, How Do Husbands and Wives Divide Up Their Responsibilities?

*Source:* By the author. Based on Bianchi et al. 2006. Housework hours are from Table 5.1, child care from Table 4.1, and work hours and total hours from Table 3.4. The total for "other services" is derived by subtracting the hours for housework, child care, and paid work from the total hours.

flics in the face of the *Leave It to Beaver* images of families we carry around in our heads, part of our mythical past that colors our perception of the present. But if parents are spending more time with their children, just where is the time coming from?

Today's parents have squeezed out more hours for their children by visiting other couples less and by reducing their participation in organizations. But this accounts for only some of the time. Look again at Figure 12.1, but this time focus on the hours that husbands and wives spend doing housework. Although men are doing more housework than they used to, women are spending so much less time on housework that the total hours that husbands and wives spend on housework have dropped from 38.9 to 29.1 hours a week. This leaves a lot more time to spend with the children.

Does this mean that today's parents aren't as fussy as their parents were, and today's houses are dirtier and

messier? That is one possibility. Or technology could be the explanation. Perhaps microwaves, dishwashers, more efficient washing machines and clothes dryers, and wrinkle-free clothing have saved hours of drudgery, leaving home hygiene about the same as before (Bianchi et al. 2006). The time savings from the "McDonaldization" we discussed in Chapter 5, with people eating more "fast foods," are also substantial. It is likely that this is not an either-or situation and both explanations are true.

Finally, from Figure 12.1, you can see that husbands and wives divide their time differently. In what sociologists call a *gendered division of labor*, husbands take the primary responsibility for earning the income and wives the primary responsibility for taking care of the house and children. The trend, however, is a shift in these responsibilities, with wives spending more time earning the family income and husbands increasing the time they spend on housework and child care. It is also significant that when you add everything up, today's husbands and wives put in about the same total number of hours per week in supporting the family. With shifting responsibilities and changing ideas of what is appropriate for husbands and wives changing, we can anticipate greater marital equality in the future.

# The Family Life Cycle

We have seen how the forms of marriage and family vary widely, looked at marriage and family theoretically, and examined major changes in family relationships. Now let's discuss love, courtship, and the family life cycle.

## Love and Courtship in Global Perspective

Until recently, social scientists thought that romantic love originated in western Europe during the medieval period (Mount 1992). When anthropologists William Jankowiak and Edward Fischer (1992) surveyed the data available on 166 societies around the world, however, they found that this was not so. **Romantic love**—people being sexually attracted to one another and idealizing each other—showed up in 88 percent (147) of these groups. The role of love, however, differs from one society to another. As the Cultural Diversity box on the next page details, for example, Indians don't expect love to occur until *after* marriage.

Because love plays such a significant role in Western life—and often is regarded as the *only* proper basis for marriage—social scientists have probed this concept with the tools of the trade: experiments, questionnaires, interviews, and observations. In a fascinating experiment, psychologists Donald Dutton and Arthur Aron discovered that fear can produce romantic love (Rubin 1985). Here's what they did.

> About 230 feet above the Capilano River in North Vancouver, British Columbia, a rickety footbridge sways in the wind. It makes you feel like you might fall into the rocky gorge below. A more solid footbridge crosses only ten feet above the shallow stream.
>
>   The experimenters had an attractive woman approach men who were crossing these bridges. She told them she was studying "the effects of exposure to scenic attractions on creative expression." She showed them a picture, and they wrote down their associations. The sexual imagery in their stories showed that the men on the unsteady, frightening bridge were more sexually aroused than were the men on the solid bridge. More of these men also called the young woman afterward—supposedly to get information about the study.

You may have noticed that this research was really about sexual attraction, not love. The point, however, is that romantic love usually begins with sexual attraction. Finding ourselves sexually attracted to someone, we spend time with that person. If we discover mutual interests, we may label our feelings "love." Apparently, then, *romantic love has two components.* The first is emotional, a feeling of sexual attraction. The second is cognitive, a label that we attach to our feelings. If we attach this label, we describe ourselves as being "in love."

## Marriage

In the typical case, marriage in the United States is preceded by "love," but, contrary to folklore, whatever love is, it certainly is not blind. That is, love does not hit us willy-nilly, as if Cupid had shot darts blindly into a crowd. If it did, marital patterns would be unpredictable. An examination of who marries whom, however, reveals that love is socially channeled.

**The Social Channels of Love and Marriage**   The most highly predictable social channels are age, education, social class, and race–ethnicity. For example, a Latina with a college degree whose parents are both physicians is likely to fall in love with and marry a Latino slightly older than herself who has graduated from college. Similarly, a girl who drops out of high school and whose parents are on welfare is likely to fall in love with and marry a man who comes from a background similar to hers.

Sociologists use the term **homogamy** to refer to the tendency of people who have similar characteristics to marry one another. Homogamy occurs largely as a result of *propinquity,* or spatial nearness. That is, we tend to "fall in love" with and marry people who live near us or whom we meet at school, church, or work. The people with whom we associate are far from a random sample of the population, for social filters produce neighborhoods, schools, and places of worship that follow racial–ethnic and social class lines.

As with all social patterns, there are exceptions. Although 93 percent of Americans who marry choose someone of their same racial–ethnic background, 7 percent do not. Because there are 60 million married couples in the United States, those 7 percent add up, totaling over 4 million couples (*Statistical Abstract* 2007:Table 58).

One of the more dramatic changes in U.S. marriage patterns is a sharp increase in marriages between African Americans and whites. Today it is difficult to realize how norm shattering such marriages are, but in some states they used to be illegal and carry a jail sentence. In Mississippi, the penalty for interracial marriage was life in prison (Crossen 2004b). The last law of this type (called

# Cultural Diversity around the World

## East Is East and West Is West: Love and Arranged Marriage

After Arun Bharat Ram returned to India with a degree from the University of Michigan, his mother announced that she wanted to find him a wife. Arun would be a good catch anywhere: 27 years old, educated, well mannered, intelligent, handsome—and, not incidentally, heir to a huge fortune.

Arun's mother already had someone in mind. Manju came from a middle-class family and was a college graduate. Arun and Manju met in a coffee shop at a luxury hotel—along with both sets of parents. He found her pretty and quiet. He liked that. She was impressed that he didn't boast about his background.

After four more meetings, including one at which the two young people met by themselves, the parents asked their children whether they were willing to marry. Neither had any major objections.

*This billboard in Chennai, India, caught my attention. Even though India is industrializing, most of its people still follow traditional customs. This billboard is a sign of changing times.*

The Prime Minister of India and fifteen hundred other guests came to the wedding.

"I didn't love him," Manju says. "But when we talked, we had a lot in common." She then adds, "But now I couldn't live without him. I've never thought of another man since I met him."

Although India has undergone extensive social change, Indian sociologists estimate that parents still arrange 90 to 95 percent of marriages. Today, however, as with Arun and Manju, couples have veto power over their parents' selection. Another innovation is that the prospective bride and groom are allowed to talk to each other before the wedding—unheard of just a generation ago.

Why do Indians have arranged marriages? And why does this practice persist today, even among the educated and upper classes? We can also ask why the United States has such an individualistic approach to marriage.

The answers to these questions take us to two sociological principles. First, *a group's marriage practices match its values.* Individual mate selection matches U.S. values of individuality and independence, while arranged marriages match the Indian value of children deferring to parental authority. To Indians, allowing unrestricted dating would mean entrusting important matters to inexperienced young people.

Second, *a group's marriage practices match its patterns of social stratification.* Arranged marriages in India affirm caste lines by channeling marriage within the same caste. Unchaperoned dating would encourage premarital sex, which, in turn, would break down family lines. Virginity at marriage, in contrast, assures the upper castes that they know the fatherhood of the children. In the United States, where family lines are less important and caste is an alien concept, the practice of young people choosing their own dating partners mirrors the relative openness of our social class system.

These different backgrounds have produced contrasting ideas of love. Americans idealize love as being mysterious, a passion that suddenly seizes an individual. Indians view love as a peaceful feeling that develops when a man and a woman are united in intimacy and share common interests and goals in life. For Americans, love just "happens," while Indians think of love as something that can be created between two people by arranging the right conditions. Marriage is one of those right conditions.

The end result is this startling difference: *For Americans, love produces marriage—while for Indians, marriage produces love.*

*Sources:* Based on Gupta 1979; Bumiller 1992; Sprecher and Chandak 1992; Dugger 1998; Derne 2003; Easley 2003; Berger 2007.

## For Your Consideration

What advantages do you see to the Indian approach to love and marriage? Do you think that the Indian system could work in the United States? Why or why not? Do you think that love can be created? Or does love suddenly "seize" people? What do you think love is?

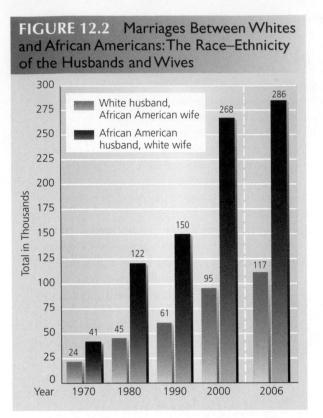

**FIGURE 12.2** Marriages Between Whites and African Americans: The Race–Ethnicity of the Husbands and Wives

Legend:
- White husband, African American wife
- African American husband, white wife

Year / values:
- 1970: 24, 41
- 1980: 45, 122
- 1990: 61, 150
- 2000: 95, 268
- 2006: 117, 286

*Source:* By the author. Based on *Statistical Abstract* 1990: Table 53; 2008: Table 59.

*antimiscegenation* laws) was not repealed until 2000. It had been a part of the Alabama constitution (Lee and Edmonston 2005). There always have been a few couples who crossed the "color line," but the social upheaval of the 1960s broke this barrier permanently.

Figure 12.2 illustrates this increase. Look at the race–ethnicity of the husbands and wives in these marriages. You can see that here, too, Cupid's arrows don't hit random targets. If you look closely, you can see an emerging change. Since 2000, marriages between African American women and white men are increasing faster than those between African American men and white women.

## Child Rearing

As you saw in Figure 12.2, today's parents—both mothers and fathers—are spending more time with their chil-

dren than parents did in the 1970s and 1980s. Despite this trend, with mothers and fathers spending so many hours away from home at work, we must ask, Who's minding the kids while the parents are at work?

**Married Couples and Single Mothers**  Figure 12.3 on the next page compares the child care arrangements of married couples and single mothers. As you can see, their overall arrangements are similar. A main difference is the role of the child's father while the mother is at work. For married couples, about one of five children is cared for by the father, while for single mothers, care by the father drops to one of ten. As you can see, grandparents help fill the gap left by the absent father. Single mothers also rely more on organized day care.

**Day Care**  Figure 12.3 also shows that about one of four or five children is in day care. The broad conclusions of research on day care were reported in Chapter 3 (pages 74–75). Apparently only a minority of U.S. day care centers offer high-quality care as measured by whether they provide stimulating learning activities, safety, and emotional warmth (Bergmann 1995; Blau 2000). A primary reason for this dismal situation is the low salaries paid to day care workers, who average only about $15,000 a year (*Statistical Abstract* 2007:Table 561, adjusted for inflation).

It is difficult for parents to judge the quality of day care, since they don't know what takes place when they are not there. If you ever look for day care, two factors best predict that children will receive quality care: staff who have taken courses in early childhood development and a low ratio of

One of the most demanding, exasperating—and also fulfilling—roles in life is that of parent. To really appreciate this cartoon, however, perhaps one has to have experienced this part of the life course.

*"Your attitude is sucking all the fulfillment out of motherhood."*

## FIGURE 12.3 Who Takes Care of Preschoolers While Their Parents Are at Work?

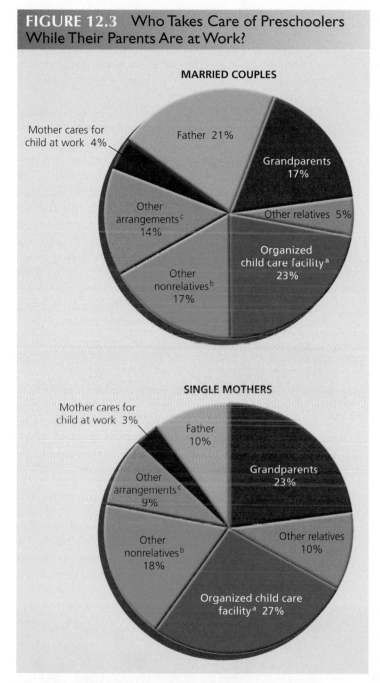

**MARRIED COUPLES**

Mother cares for child at work 4%
Father 21%
Grandparents 17%
Other arrangements[c] 14%
Other relatives 5%
Other nonrelatives[b] 17%
Organized child care facility[a] 23%

**SINGLE MOTHERS**

Mother cares for child at work 3%
Father 10%
Grandparents 23%
Other arrangements[c] 9%
Other relatives 10%
Other nonrelatives[b] 18%
Organized child care facility[a] 27%

[a]Includes in-home babysitters and other nonrelatives providing care in either the child's or the provider's home.
[b]Includes self-care and no regular arrangements.
[c]Includes day care centers, nursery schools, preschools, and Head Start programs.
*Source: America's Children 2005: Table POP8.B.*

children per staff member (Blau 2000; Belsky et al. 2007). If you have nagging fears that your children might be neglected or even abused, choose a center that streams live Webcam images on the Internet. While at work, you can "visit" each room of the day care center via cyberspace and monitor your toddler's activities and care.

**Nannies** For upper-middle-class parents, nannies have become a popular alternative to day care centers. Parents love the one-on-one care. They also like the convenience of in-home care, which eliminates the need to transport the child to an unfamiliar environment, reduces the chances that the child will catch illnesses, and eliminates the hardship of parents having to take time off from work when their child becomes ill. A recurring problem, however, is tension between the parents and the nanny: jealousy that the nanny might see the first step, hear the first word, or—worse yet—be called "mommy." There are also tensions over different discipline styles; disdain on the part of the nanny that the mother isn't staying home with her child; and feelings of guilt or envy as the child cries when the nanny leaves but not when the mother goes to work.

**Social Class** Do you think that social class makes a difference in how people rear their children? If you answered "yes," you are right. But what difference? And why? Sociologists have found that working-class parents tend to think of children as wildflowers that develop naturally. Middle-class parents, in contrast, are more likely to think of children as garden flowers that need a lot of nurturing if they are to bloom (Lareau 2002). These contrasting views make a world of difference. Working-class parents are more likely to set limits on their children and then let them choose their own activities. Middle-class parents, in contrast, are more likely to try to push their children into activities that they think will develop the children's thinking and social skills.

Sociologist Melvin Kohn (1963, 1977; Kohn and Schooler 1969) also found that the type of work that parents do has an impact on how they rear their children. Because members of the working class are closely supervised on their jobs, where they are expected to follow explicit rules, their concern is less with their children's motivation and more with their outward conformity. These parents are more apt to use physical punishment—which brings about outward conformity without regard for internal attitude.

Middle-class workers, in contrast, are expected to take more initiative on the job. Consequently, middle-class parents have more concern that their children develop curiosity and self-expression. They are also more likely to withdraw privileges or affection than to use physical punishment.

## Family Transitions

The later stages of family life bring their own pleasures to be savored and problems to be solved. Let's look at two transitions.

**"Adultolescents" and the Not-So-Empty Nest**    When the last child leaves home, the husband and wife are left, as at the beginning of their marriage, "alone together." This situation, sometimes called the *empty nest,* is not as empty as it used to be. With prolonged education and the high cost of establishing a household, U.S. children are leaving home later. Many stay home during college, and others move back after college. Some (called "boomerang children") strike out on their own, but then find the cost or responsibility too great and return home. Much to their own disappointment, some even leave and return to the parents' home several times. As a result, 42 percent of all U.S. 25- to 29-year-olds are living with their parents (U.S. Census Bureau 2006:Table A2).

Although these "adultolescents" enjoy the protection of home, they have to work out issues of remaining dependent on their parents at the same time that they are grappling with concerns and fears about establishing independent lives. For the parents, "boomerang children" mean not only a disruption of routines but also disagreements about turf, authority, and responsibilities—items they thought were long ago resolved.

**Widowhood**    As you know, women are more likely than men to become widowed. There are two reasons for this: Women usually marry men older than they are—and most outlive their husbands. For either women or men, the death of a spouse tears at the self, clawing at identities that had merged through the years. When the one who had become an essential part of the self is gone, the survivor, as in adolescence, is forced once again to wrestle with the perplexing question "Who am I?"

Most of the widowed adjust well within a year of the death of their spouse. Some even experience a gain in self-esteem, especially those who had been the most dependent on their spouse. They apparently feel better about themselves because they learn to do things on their own (Carr 2004). Deaths that are unexpected are more difficult to adjust to. Spouses who know that death is impending are able to make preparations that smooth the transition—from arranging finances to preparing themselves psychologically for being alone (Hiltz 1989). You can see how saying goodbye and cultivating treasured last memories would help people adjust to the impending death of an intimate companion. Sudden death, in contrast, rips the loved one away, offering no chance at this predeath healing process.

# Diversity in U.S. Families

It is important to note that there is no such thing as *the* American family. Rather, family life varies widely throughout the United States. The significance of social class, noted earlier, will continue to be evident as we examine diversity in U.S. families.

## African American Families

Note that the heading reads African American *families,* not *the* African American family. There is no such thing as *the* African American family any more than there is *the* white family or *the* Latino family. The primary distinction

There is no such thing as *the* African American family, any more than there is *the* Native American, Asian American, Latino, or Irish American family. Rather, each racial–ethnic group has different types of families, with the primary determinant being social class.

is not between African Americans and other groups, but between social classes (Willie and Reddick 2003). Because African Americans who are members of the upper class follow the class interests reviewed in Chapter 8—preservation of privilege and family fortune—they are especially concerned about the family background of those whom their children marry (Gatewood 1990). To them, marriage is viewed as a merger of family lines. Children of this class marry later than children of other classes.

Middle-class African American families focus on achievement and respectability. Both husband and wife are likely to work outside the home. A central concern is that their children go to college, get good jobs, and marry well—that is, marry people like themselves, respectable and hardworking, who want to get ahead in school and pursue a successful career.

African American families in poverty face all the problems that cluster around poverty (Wilson 1987, 1996; Anderson 1990/2006; Venkatesh 2006). Because the men are likely to have few skills and to be unemployed, it is difficult for them to fulfill the cultural roles of husband and father. Consequently, these families are likely to be headed by a woman and to have a high rate of births to single women. Divorce and desertion are also more common than among other classes. Sharing scarce resources and "stretching kinship" are primary survival mechanisms. People who have helped out in hard times are considered brothers, sisters, or cousins to whom one owes obligations as though they were blood relatives; and men who are not the biological fathers of their children are given fatherhood status (Stack 1974; Fischer et al. 2005). Sociologists use the term *fictive kin* to refer to this stretching of kinship.

From Figure 12.4 you can see that, compared with other groups, African American families are the least likely to be headed by married couples and the most likely to be headed by women. Because African American women tend to go farther in school than African American men, they are more likely than women in other racial–ethnic groups to marry men who are less educated than themselves (South 1991; Eshleman 2000).

## Latino Families

As Figure 12.4 shows, the proportion of Latino families headed by married couples and women falls in between that of whites and African Americans. The effects of social class on families, which I just sketched, also apply to Latinos. In addition, families differ by country of origin. Families from Mexico, for example, are more likely to be headed by a married couple than are families from Puerto Rico (*Statistical Abstract* 2007:Table 44). The longer that Latinos have lived in the United States, the more their families resemble those of middle-class Americans (Saenz 2004).

With such a wide variety, experts disagree on what is distinctive about Latino families. Some point to the Spanish language, the Roman Catholic religion, and a strong family orientation coupled with a disapproval of divorce. Others add that Latinos emphasize loyalty to the extended family, with an obligation to support the extended family in times of need (Cauce and Domenech-Rodriguez 2002). Descriptions of Latino families used to include **machismo**—an emphasis on male strength, sexual vigor, and dominance—but current studies show that *machismo* now characterizes

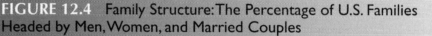

**FIGURE 12.4**    Family Structure: The Percentage of U.S. Families Headed by Men, Women, and Married Couples

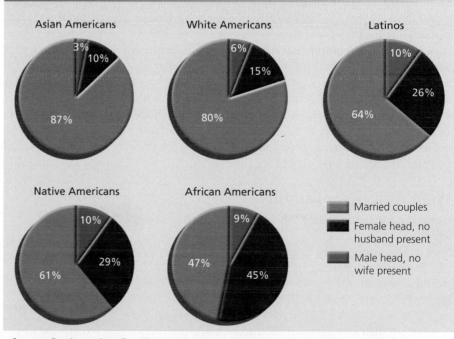

*Sources:* By the author. For Native Americans, "American Community . . ." 2004. For other groups, *Statistical Abstract* 2007:Tables 41, 44, 62. Data for Asian Americans are for families with children under 18, while the other groups don't have this limitation. Totals may not equal 100 percent due to rounding.

As with other groups, there is no such thing as *the* Latino family. Some Latino families have assimilated into U.S. culture to such an extent that they no longer speak Spanish. Others maintain Mexican customs, such as this family, which is celebrating quinceañera, the "coming of age" of girls at age 15 (traditionally, an announcement to the community that a girl is eligible for courtship).

only a small proportion of Latino husband-fathers (Torres et al. 2002). *Machismo* apparently decreases with each generation in the United States (Hurtado et al. 1992; D. B. Wood 2001). Some researchers have found that the husband-father plays a stronger role than in either white or African American families (Vega 1990; Torres et al. 2002). Apparently, the wife-mother is usually more family-centered than her husband, displaying more warmth and affection for her children.

It is difficult to draw generalizations because, as with other racial–ethnic groups, individual Latino families vary considerably (Contreras et al. 2002). Some Latino families, for example, have acculturated to such an extent that they are Protestants who do not speak Spanish.

## Asian American Families

As you can see from Figure 12.4 on the previous page, Asian American children are more likely than children in any other racial–ethnic group to grow up with both parents. As with the other groups, family life also reflects social class. In addition, because Asian Americans emigrated from many different countries, their family life reflects those many cultures (Xie and Goyette 2004). As with Latino families, the more recent their immigration, the more closely their family life reflects the patterns in their country of origin (Kibria 1993; Glenn 1994).

Despite such differences, sociologist Bob Suzuki (1985), who studied Chinese American and Japanese American families, identified several distinctive characteristics of Asian American families. Although Asian Americans have adopted the nuclear family structure, they have retained Confucian values that provide a framework for family life: humanism, collectivity, self-discipline, hierarchy, respect for the elderly, moderation, and obligation. Obligation means that each member of a family owes respect to other family members and has a responsibility never to bring shame on the family. Conversely, a child's success brings honor to the family (Zamiska 2004). To control their children, Asian American parents are more likely to use shame and guilt than physical punishment.

The ideal does not always translate into the real, however, and so it is here. The children born to Asian immigrants confront a bewildering world of incompatible expectations—those of the new culture and those of their parents. As a result, they experience more family conflict and mental problems than do children of Asian Americans who are not immigrants (Meyers 2006).

## Native American Families

Perhaps the single most significant issue that Native American families face is whether to follow traditional values or to assimilate into the dominant culture (Garrett 1999). This

To search for *the* Native American family would be fruitless. There are rural, urban, single-parent, extended, nuclear, rich, poor, traditional, and assimilated Native American families, to name just a few. Shown here is an Onondaga Nation family. The wife is a teacher, the husband a Webmaster.

primary distinction creates vast differences among families. The traditionals speak native languages and emphasize distinctive Native American values and beliefs. Those who have assimilated into the broader culture do not.

Figure 12.4 on page 341 depicts the structure of Native American families. You can see how close it is to that of Latinos. In general, Native American parents are permissive with their children and avoid physical punishment. Elders play a much more active role in their children's families than they do in most U.S. families: Elders, especially grandparents, not only provide child care but also teach and discipline children. Like others, Native American families differ by social class.

**In Sum:** From this brief review, you can see that race–ethnicity signifies little for understanding family life. Rather, social class and culture hold the keys. The more resources a family has, the more it assumes the characteristics of a middle-class nuclear family. Compared with the poor, middle-class families have fewer children and fewer unmarried mothers. They also place greater emphasis on educational achievement and deferred gratification.

## One-Parent Families

Another indication of how extensively U.S. families are changing is the increase in one-parent families. From Figure 12.5, you can see that the percentage of U.S. children who

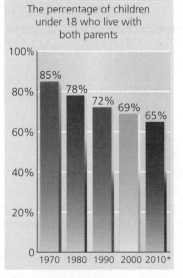

**FIGURE 12.5**
### The Decline of Two-Parent Families

The percentage of children under 18 who live with both parents

*Author's estimate
*Source:* By the author. Based on *Statistical Abstract* 1995: Table 79; 2007: Table 62.

live with two parents (not necessarily their biological parents) has dropped sharply. The concerns that are often expressed about one-parent families may have more to do with their poverty than with children being reared by one parent. Because women head most one-parent families, these families tend to be poor. Most divorced women earn less than their former husbands, yet about 85 percent of children of divorce live with their mothers ("Child Support" 1995; Aulette 2002).

To understand the typical one-parent family, then, we need to view it through the lens of poverty, for that is its primary source of strain. The results are serious, not just for these parents and their children but also for society as a whole. Children from one-parent families are more likely to drop out of school, to get arrested, to have emotional problems, and to get divorced (McLanahan and Sandefur 1994; Menaghan et al. 1997; McLanahan and Schwartz 2002; Amato and Cheadle 2005). If female, they are more likely to become sexually active at a younger age and to bear children while still unmarried teenagers.

## Families Without Children

While most married women give birth, about one of five (19 percent) do not (DeOilos and Kapinus 2003). The number of childless couples has *doubled* from what it was twenty years ago. As you can see from Figure 12.6, this percentage varies by racial–ethnic group, with whites and Latinas representing the extremes. Some couples are infertile, but most childless couples have made a *choice* to not have children. Why do they make this choice? Some women believe they would be stuck at home—bored, lonely, with dwindling career opportunities. Some couples perceive their marriage as too fragile to withstand the strains that a child would bring (Gerson 1985). A common reason is to attain a sense of freedom—to pursue a career, to be able to change jobs, to travel, and to have less stress (Lunneborg 1999; Letherby 2002).

With trends firmly in place—more education and careers for women, advances in contraception, legal abortion, the high cost of rearing children, and an emphasis on possessing more material things—the proportion of women who never bear children is likely to increase. Consider this statement in a newsletter:

> We are DINKS (Dual Incomes, No Kids). We are happily married. I am 43; my wife is 42. We have been married for almost twenty years. . . . Our investment strategy has a lot to do with our personal philosophy: "You can have kids—or you can have everything else!"

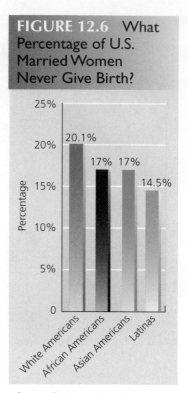

**FIGURE 12.6** What Percentage of U.S. Married Women Never Give Birth?

*Source:* By the author. Based on Bachu and O'Connell 2000: Table A.

## Blended Families

The **blended family,** one whose members were once part of other families, is an increasingly significant type of family in the United States. Two divorced people who marry and each bring their children into a new family unit form a blended family. With divorce common, millions of children spend some of their childhood in blended families. One result is more complicated family relationships. Consider this description written by one of my students:

> I live with my dad. I should say that I live with my dad, my brother (whose mother and father are also my mother and father), my half sister (whose father is my dad, but whose mother is my father's last wife), and two stepbrothers and stepsisters (children of my father's current wife). My father's wife (my current stepmother, not to be confused with his second wife who, I guess, is no longer my stepmother) is pregnant, and soon we all will have a new brother or sister. Or will it be a half brother or half sister?
>
> If you can't figure this out, I don't blame you. I have trouble myself. It gets very complicated around Christmas. Should we all stay together? Split up and go to several other homes? Who do we buy gifts for, anyway?

## Gay and Lesbian Families

In 1989, Denmark became the first country to legalize marriage between people of the same sex. Since then, several European countries, Canada, and the states of Massachusetts, New Hampshire, and California allow people of the same sex to marry. Other states recognize "registered domestic partnerships." Walking a fine conceptual tightrope, they give legal status to same-sex unions but avoid the term *marriage*.

At this point, most gay and lesbian couples lack both legal marriage and the legal protection of registered "partnerships." Although these couples live throughout the United States, about half are concentrated in just twenty cities. The greatest concentrations are in San Francisco, Los Angeles, Atlanta, New York City, and Washington, D.C. About one-fifth of gay and lesbian couples were previously married to heterosexuals. Twenty-two percent of female couples and 5 percent of male couples have children from their earlier heterosexual marriages (Bianchi and Casper 2000).

What are same-sex relationships like? Like everything else in life, these couples cannot be painted with a single brush stroke. As with opposite-sex couples, social class is significant, and orientations to life differ according to education, occupation, and income. Sociologists Philip Blumstein and Pepper Schwartz (1985) interviewed same-sex couples and found their main struggles to be housework, money, careers, problems with relatives, and sexual adjustment—the same problems that face heterosexual couples. Some also confront discrimination at work, which can add stress to their relationship (Todosijevic et al. 2005). Same-sex couples are more likely to break up, and one argument for legalizing gay marriages is that the marriage contract will make these relationships more stable. If they were surrounded by laws, same-sex marriages would be like opposite-sex marriages—to break them would require negotiating around legal obstacles.

# Trends in U.S. Families

As is apparent from this discussion, marriage and family life in the United States is undergoing fundamental shifts. Let's examine other indicators of changes.

## Postponing Marriage and Childbirth

Figure 12.7 on the next page illustrates one of the most significant changes in U.S. marriages. As you can see, the average age of first-time brides and grooms declined from 1890 to about 1950. In 1890, the typical first-time bride was 22, but by 1950, she had just left her teens. For about twenty years, there was little change. Then in 1970, the average age started to increase sharply. *Today's average first-time bride and groom are older than at any other time in U.S. history.*

Since postponing marriage is today's norm, it may come as a surprise to many readers to learn that *most* U.S. women used to be married by the time they reached age 24. To see this remarkable change, look at Figure 12.8 on the next page.

A major issue that has caught the public's attention is whether same-sex couples should have the right of legal marriage. This issue will be decided not by public protest but by legislation and the courts.

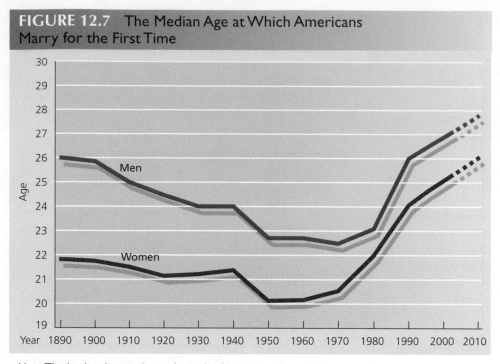

**FIGURE 12.7    The Median Age at Which Americans Marry for the First Time**

Note: The broken lines indicate the author's estimate.

Source: By the author. Based on *Statistical Abstract* 1999: Table 158 (table dropped in later editions); U.S. Bureau of the Census 2003; Fields 2004.

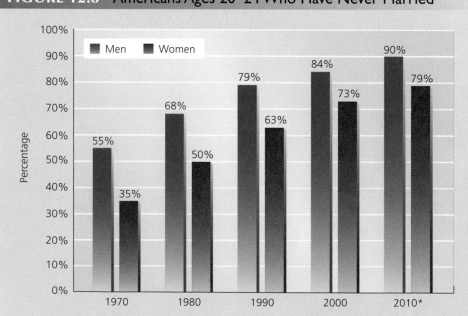

**FIGURE 12.8    Americans Ages 20–24 Who Have Never Married**

*Author's estimate.

Source: By the author. Based on *Statistical Abstract* 1993: Table 60; 2002: Table 48; 2007: Table 55.

Postponing marriage has become so common that the percentage of women of this age who are unmarried is now more than *double* what it was in 1970. Another consequence of postponing marriage is that the average age at which U.S. women have their first child is also the highest in U.S. history (Mathews and Hamilton 2002).

Why have these changes occurred? The primary reason is cohabitation (Michael et al. 2004). Although Americans have postponed the age at which they first marry, they have *not* postponed the age at which they first set up housekeeping with someone of the opposite sex. Let's look at this trend.

## Cohabitation

Figure 12.9 shows the increase in **cohabitation,** adults living together in a sexual relationship without being married. This figure is one of the most remarkable in sociology. Hardly ever do we have totals that rise this steeply and consistently. Cohabitation is *almost ten times* more common today than it was 30 years ago. Today, 60 percent of the couples who marry for the first time have lived together before marriage. A generation ago, it was just 8 percent (Bianchi and Casper 2000; Batalova and Cohen 2002). Cohabitation has become so common that about 40 percent of U.S. children will spend some time in a cohabiting family (Scommegna 2002).

*Commitment* is the essential difference between cohabitation and marriage. In marriage, the assumption is permanence; in cohabitation, couples agree to remain together for "as long as it works out." For marriage, individuals make public vows that legally bind them as a couple; for cohabitation, they simply move in together. Marriage requires a judge to authorize its termination; if a cohabiting relationship sours, the couple separates, telling friends that "it didn't work out." Perhaps the single statement that pinpoints the difference in commitment between marriage and cohabitation is this: Cohabiting couples are less likely than married couples to have a joint bank account (Brines and Joyner 1999). As you know, some cohabiting couples do marry. But do you know how this is related to what cohabitation means to them? This is the subject of our Down-to-Earth Sociology box on the next page.

Are the marriages of couples who cohabited stronger than the marriages of couples who did not live together before they married? It would seem that cohabiting couples might have worked out a lot of problems prior to marriage. To find out, sociologists compared their divorce rates. It turns out that couples who cohabit before marriage are *more* likely to divorce. This presented another

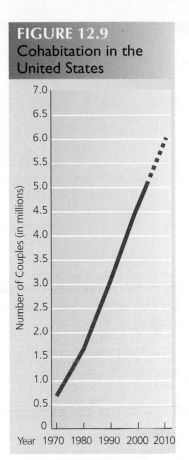

**FIGURE 12.9**
Cohabitation in the United States

*Note:* Broken line indicates author's estimate.
*Source:* By the author. Based on *Statistical Abstract* 1995:Table 60; 2007:Table 61.

sociological puzzle. The key to solving it, suggest some sociologists, is the greater ease of ending a cohabiting relationship than a marriage (Dush et al. 2003). As a result, people are less picky about whom they live with than whom they marry. After they cohabit, however, they experience a push toward marriage. Some of this "push" comes from having common possessions, pets, and children. Other comes from pressure—some subtle and some rather direct—applied by friends and family. Many end up marrying a partner that they would not otherwise have chosen.

## Unmarried Mothers

Births to single women in the United States have increased steadily during the past decades, going from 10 percent in 1970 to 37 percent today (*Statistical Abstract*

# Down-to-Earth Sociology

## "You Want Us to Live Together? What Do You Mean By That?"

What has led to the surge of cohabitation in the United States? Let's consider two fundamental changes in U.S. culture.

The first is changed ideas of sexual morality. It is difficult for today's college students to grasp the sexual morality that prevailed before the 1960s sexual revolution. Almost everyone used to consider sex before marriage to be immoral. Premarital sex existed, to be sure, but it took place furtively and often with guilt. To live together before marriage was called "shacking up," and the couple was said to be "living in sin." A double standard prevailed. It was the woman's responsibility to say no to sex before marriage. Consequently, she was considered to be the especially sinful one in cohabitation.

The second cultural change is the high U.S. divorce rate. Although the rate has declined since 1980, today's young adults have seen more divorce than any prior generation. This makes marriage seem fragile, as if it is something that is not likely to last regardless of how much you devote yourself to it. This is scary. Cohabitation reduces the threat by offering a relationship of intimacy in which divorce is impossible. You can break up, but you can't get divorced.

From the outside, all cohabitation may look the same, but not to the people who are living together. As you can see from Table 12.2, for about 10 percent of couples,

cohabitation is a substitute for marriage. These couples consider themselves married but for some reason don't want a marriage certificate. Some object to marriage on philosophical grounds ("What difference does a piece of paper make?"); others do not yet have a legal divorce from a spouse. Almost half of cohabitants (46 percent) view cohabitation as a step on the path to marriage. For them, cohabitation is more than "going steady" but less than engagement. Another 15 percent of couples are simply "giving it a try." They want to see what marriage to one another might be like. For the least committed, about 29 percent, cohabitation is a form of dating. It provides a dependable source of sex and emotional support.

Do these distinctions make a difference in whether couples marry? Let's look at these couples a half dozen years after they began to live together. As you can see from Table 12.2, couples who view cohabitation as a substitute for marriage are the least likely to marry and the most likely to continue to cohabit. For couples who see cohabitation as a step toward marriage, the outcome is just the opposite: They are the most likely to marry and the least likely to still be cohabiting. Couples who are the most likely to break up are those who "tried" cohabitation and those for whom cohabitation was a form of dating.

## For Your Consideration

Can you explain why the meaning of cohabitation makes a difference in whether couples marry? Can you classify cohabiting couples you know into these four types? Do you think there are other types? If so, what would they be?

| TABLE 12.2 | What Cohabitation Means: Does It Make a Difference? | | | | |
|---|---|---|---|---|---|
| | | | | After 5 to 7 years | |
| | | | | Of those still together | |
| What Cohabitation Means | Percent of Couples | Split Up | Still Together | Married | Cohabitating |
| Substitute for Marriage | 10% | 35% | 65% | 37% | 63% |
| Step toward Marriage | 46% | 31% | 69% | 73% | 27% |
| Trial Marriage | 15% | 51% | 49% | 66% | 34% |
| Coresidential Dating | 29% | 46% | 54% | 61% | 39% |

Source: Recomputed from Bianchi and Casper 2000.

1995:Table 94; 2008:Table 85). Let's place these births in global perspective. As Figure 12.10 shows, the United States is not alone in its increase. Of the twelve nations for which we have data, all except Japan have experienced sharp increases in births to unmarried mothers. As you can see, the U.S. rate falls higher than average but not at the extreme.

From this figure, it would seem fair to conclude that industrialization sets in motion social forces that encourage out-of-wedlock births. There are several problems with this conclusion, however. Why was the rate so much lower in 1960? These nations had all been industrialized for many decades by that time. Why are the rates in Japan and Italy so much lower than those of the other nations? Why does Japan's rate remain low? Why is Sweden's rate so high? Why have the rates of some nations leveled off—and all at about the same time? Industrialization is too simple an answer. A fuller explanation must focus on customs and values embedded within these cultures. For those answers, we will have to await further research.

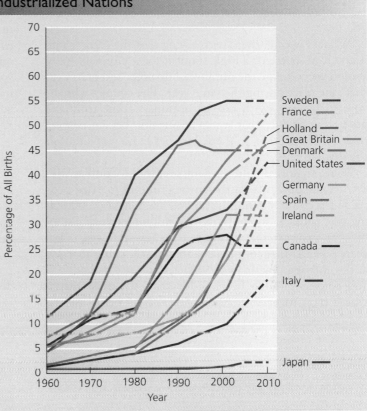

**FIGURE 12.10**   Births to Unmarried Women in Ten Industrialized Nations

*Note:* The broken lines indicate the author's estimates.
*Source:* By the author. Based on *Statistical Abstract* 1993:Table 1380; 2001:Table 1331; 2007:Table 1311.

## The "Sandwich Generation" and Elder Care

The "sandwich generation" refers to people who find themselves sandwiched between and responsible for two other generations, their children and their own aging parents. Typically between the ages of 40 and 55, these people find themselves pulled in two compelling directions. Many feel overwhelmed as these competing responsibilities collide. Some are plagued with guilt and anger because they can be in only one place at a time and have little time to pursue personal interests.

Concerns about elder care have gained the attention of the corporate world, and half of the 1,000 largest U.S. companies offer elder care assistance to their employees (Hewitt Associates 2004). This assistance includes seminars, referral services, and flexible work schedules to help employees meet their responsibilities without missing so much work. Why are companies responding more positively to the issue of elder care than to child care? Most CEOs are older men whose wives stayed home to take care of their children, so they don't understand the stresses of balancing work and child care. In contrast, nearly all have

aging parents, and many have faced the turmoil of trying to cope with both their parents' needs and those of work and their own family.

With people living longer, this issue is likely to become increasingly urgent.

# Divorce and Remarriage

The topic of family life would not be complete without considering divorce. Let's first try to determine how much divorce there really is.

## Problems in Measuring Divorce

You probably have heard that the U.S. divorce rate is 50 percent, a figure that is popular with reporters. The statistic is true in the sense that each year about half as many divorces are granted as there are marriages performed. The totals are 2.2 million marriages and about 1.1 million divorces (*Statistical Abstract* 2007:Tables 17, 76, 119).

What is wrong, then, with saying that the divorce rate is about 50 percent? Think about it for a moment. Why should we compare the number of divorces and marriages that take place during the same year? The couples who divorced do not—with rare exceptions—come from the group that married that year. The one number has *nothing* to do with the other, so these statistics in no way establish the divorce rate.

What figures should we compare, then? Couples who divorce are drawn from the entire group of married people in the country. Since the United States has 60,000,000 married couples, and only about 1 million of them obtain divorces in a year, the divorce rate for any given year is less than 2 percent. A couple's chances of still being married at the end of a year are over 98 percent—not bad odds— and certainly much better odds than the mass media would have us believe. As the Social Map below shows,

the "odds"—if we want to call them that—depend on where you live.

Over time, of course, each year's small percentage adds up. A third way of measuring divorce, then, is to ask, "Of all U.S. adults, what percentage are divorced?" Figure 12.12 on the next page answers this question. You can see how divorce has increased over the years and how race–ethnicity makes a difference for the likelihood that couples will divorce. If you look closely, you can also see that the rate of divorce has slowed down.

Figure 12.12 shows us the percentage of Americans who are currently divorced, but we get yet another answer if we ask the question, "What percentage of Americans have *ever* been divorced?" This percentage increases with each age group, peaking when people reach their 50s. Forty percent of women in their 50s have been divorced at some point in their lives; for men, the total is 43 percent ("Marital History . . ." 2004).

What most of us want to know is what *our* chances of divorce are. It is one thing to know that a certain percentage of Americans are divorced, but have sociologists found

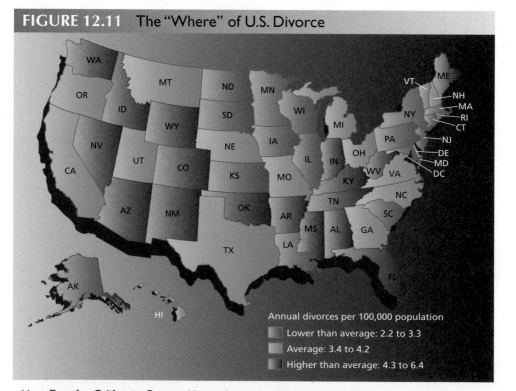

**FIGURE 12.11    The "Where" of U.S. Divorce**

Annual divorces per 100,000 population
- Lower than average: 2.2 to 3.3
- Average: 3.4 to 4.2
- Higher than average: 4.3 to 6.4

*Note:* Data for California, Georgia, Hawaii, Indiana, and Louisiana, based on the earlier editions in the source, have been decreased by the average decrease in U.S. divorce.
*Source:* By the author. Based on *Statistical Abstract* 1995:Table 149; 2002:Table 111; 2007:Table 119.

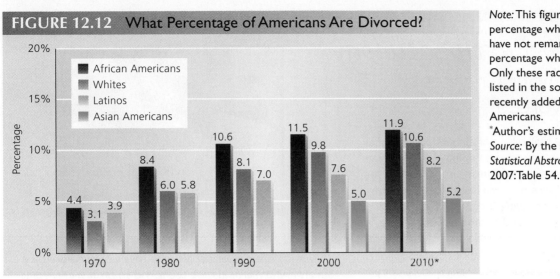

**FIGURE 12.12    What Percentage of Americans Are Divorced?**

- African Americans
- Whites
- Latinos
- Asian Americans

Percentage

1970: 4.4, 3.1, 3.9
1980: 8.4, 6.0, 5.8
1990: 10.6, 8.1, 7.0
2000: 11.5, 9.8, 7.6, 5.0
2010*: 11.9, 10.6, 8.2, 5.2

*Note:* This figure shows the percentage who are divorced and have not remarried, not the percentage who have *ever* divorced. Only these racial–ethnic groups are listed in the source. The source only recently added data on Asian Americans.
*Author's estimate
*Source:* By the author. Based on *Statistical Abstract* 1995:Table 58; 2007:Table 54.

out anything that will tell me about *my* chances of divorce? This is the topic of the Down-to-Earth Sociology box on the next page.

## Children of Divorce

Each year, more than 1 million U.S. children learn that their parents are divorcing. These children are more likely than children reared by both parents to experience emotional problems, both during childhood and after they grow up (Amato and Sobolewski 2001; Weitoft et al. 2003). They are also more likely to become juvenile delinquents (Wallerstein et al. 2001) and less likely to complete high school, to attend college, and to graduate from college (McLanahan and Schwartz 2002). Finally, the children of divorce are themselves more likely to divorce (Wolfinger 2003), perpetuating a marriage–divorce cycle.

Is the greater maladjustment of the children of divorce a serious problem? This question initiated a lively debate between two researchers, both psychologists. Judith Wallerstein claims that divorce scars children, making them depressed and leaving them with insecurities that follow them into adulthood (Wallerstein et al. 2001). Mavis Hetherington replies that 75 to 80 percent of children of divorce function as well as children who are reared by both of their parents (Hetherington and Kelly 2003).

Without meaning to weigh in on either side of this debate, it doesn't seem to be a simple case of the glass being half empty or half full. If 75 to 80 percent of children of divorce don't suffer long-term harm, this leaves one-fourth to one-fifth who do. Any way you look at it, one-fourth or one-fifth of a million children each year is a lot of kids who are having a lot of problems.

What helps children adjust to divorce? Children of divorce who feel close to both parents make the best adjustment, and those who don't feel close to either parent make the worst adjustment (Richardson and McCabe 2001). Other studies show that children adjust well if they experience little conflict, feel loved, live with a parent who is making a good adjustment, and have consistent routines. It also helps if their family has adequate money to meet its needs. Children also adjust better if a second adult can be counted on for support (Hayashi and Strickland 1998). Urie Bronfenbrenner (1992) says this person is like the third leg of a stool, giving stability to the smaller family unit. Any adult can be the third leg, he says—a relative, friend, or even a former mother-in-law—but the most powerful stabilizing third leg is the father, the ex-husband.

As mentioned, when the children of divorce grow up and marry, they are more likely to divorce than are adults who grew up in intact families. Have researchers found any factors that increase the chances that the children of divorce will have successful marriages? Actually, they have. They are more likely to have a lasting marriage if they marry someone whose parents did not divorce. In these marriages, the level of trust is higher and the amount of conflict is less. If both husband and wife come from broken families, however, it is not good news. Those marriages tend to have more distrust and conflict, leading to a higher chance of divorce (Wolfinger 2003).

## Grandchildren of Divorce

Paul Amato and Jacob Cheadle (2005), the first sociologists to study the grandchildren of people who had divorced, found that the effects of divorce continue across generations. Using a national sample, they compared

# Down-to-Earth Sociology
## "What Are Your Chances of Getting Divorced?"

It is probably true that over a lifetime about half of all marriages fail (Whitehead and Popenoe 2004). If you have that 50 percent figure dancing in your head, you might as well make sure that you have an escape door open even while you're saying "I do."

Not every group carries the same risk of divorce. Some have a much higher risk, and some much lower. Let's look at some factors that reduce people's risk.

As Table 12.3 shows, sociologists have worked out percentages that you might find useful (Whitehead and Popenoe 2004). As you can see, people who go to college, participate in a religion, wait to get married before having children, and earn higher incomes have a much better chance that their marriage will last. You can also see that having parents who did not divorce is significant. If you reverse these factors, you will see how the likelihood of

divorce increases for people who have a baby before they marry, who marry in their teens, and so on. It is important to note, however, that these factors reduce the risk of divorce for groups of people, not for any certain individual.

Here are two other factors that increase the risk for divorce (Aberg 2003). For these, sociologists have not computed percentages. Having co-workers who are of the opposite sex (I'm sure you can figure out why) and working with people who are recently divorced increase the risk of divorce. Apparently, divorce is "contagious," following a pattern like measles. Perhaps being around divorced people makes divorce more acceptable. This would increase the likelihood that married people will act on their inevitable dissatisfactions and attractions. Or it could be that divorced people are more likely to "hit" on their fellow workers—and human nature being what it is . . .

## For Your Consideration

Why do you think that people who go to college have a lower risk of divorce? How would you explain the other factors shown in Table 12.3? What other factors discussed in this chapter indicate a greater or lesser risk of divorce?

Why can't you figure your own chances of divorce by starting with some percentage (say 30 percent likelihood of divorce for the first 10 years of marriage) and then reducing it according to this table (subtracting 13 percent of the 30 percent for going to college, and so on)? To better understand this, you might want to read the section on the misuse of statistics on page 355.

| TABLE 12.3   What Reduces the Risk of Divorce? | |
| --- | --- |
| Factors that Reduce People's Chances of Divorce | How Much Does This Decrease the Risk of Divorce? |
| Some college (vs. high school dropout) | −13% |
| Affiliated with a religion (vs. none) | −14% |
| Parents not divorced | −14% |
| Age 25 or over at marriage (vs. under 18) | −24% |
| Having a baby 7 months or longer after marriage (vs. before marriage) | −24% |
| Annual income over $50,000 (vs. under $25,000) | −30% |

Note: These percentages apply to the first ten years of marriage.

grandchildren—those whose grandparents had divorced with those whose grandparents had not divorced. Their findings are astounding. The grandchildren of divorce have weaker ties to their parents, don't go as far in

school, and don't get along as well with their spouses. As these researchers put it, when parents divorce, the consequences ripple through the lives of children who are not yet born.

## The Absent Father and Serial Fatherhood

With divorce common and mothers usually granted custody of the children, a new fathering pattern has emerged. In this pattern, known as **serial fatherhood,** a divorced father maintains high contact with his children during the first year or two after the divorce. As the man develops a relationship with another woman, he begins to play a fathering role with the woman's children and reduces contact with his own children. With another breakup, this pattern may repeat. Only about one-sixth of children who live apart from their fathers see their dad as often as every week. Actually, *most* divorced fathers stop seeing their children altogether (Ahlburg and De Vita 1992; Furstenberg and Harris 1992; Seltzer 1994). Apparently, for many men, fatherhood has become a short-term commitment.

## The Ex-Spouses

Anger, depression, and anxiety are common feelings at divorce. But so is relief. Women are more likely than men to feel that divorce is giving them a "new chance" in life. A few couples manage to remain friends through it all—but they are the exception. The spouse who initiates the divorce usually gets over it sooner (Kelly 1992; Wang and Amato 2000) and also usually remarries sooner (Sweeney 2002).

Divorce does not necessarily mean the end of a couple's relationship. Many divorced couples maintain contact because of their children (Fischer et al. 2005). For others, the "continuities," as sociologists call them, represent lingering attachments (Vaughan 1985; Masheter 1991; author's file 2005). The former husband may help his former wife paint a room or move furniture; she may invite him over for a meal or to watch television. They might even go to dinner or to see a movie together. Some couples even continue to make love after their divorce.

After divorce, the ex-spouses' cost of living increases—two homes, two utility bills, and so forth. But the financial impact hits women the hardest. For them, divorce often spells economic hardship. This is especially true for mothers of small children, whose standard of living drops about a third (Seltzer 1994). Finally, as you would expect, women with more education cope better financially.

## Remarriage

Despite the number of people who emerge from divorce court swearing "Never again!" many do remarry. The rate at which they remarry, however, has slowed, and today only half of women who divorce remarry (Bramlett and Mosher 2002). As Figure 12.13 on the next page shows, most divorced people marry other divorced people. You may be surprised that the women who are most likely to remarry are young mothers and those with less education (Glick and Lin 1986; Schmiege et al. 2001). Apparently women who are more educated and more independent (no children) can afford to be more selective. Men are more likely than women to remarry, perhaps because they have a larger pool of potential mates.

How do remarriages work out? The divorce rate of remarried people *without* children is the same as that of first marriages. Those who bring children into a new marriage,

It is difficult to capture the anguish of the children of divorce, but when I read these lines by the fourth-grader who drew these two pictures, my heart was touched:

Me alone in the park . . .
All alone in the park.
My Dad and Mom are divorced
that's why I'm all alone.

This is me in the picture with my son
We are taking a walk in the park.
I will never be like my father.
I will never divorce my wife and kid.

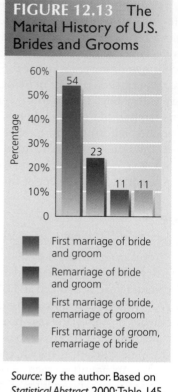

**FIGURE 12.13** The Marital History of U.S. Brides and Grooms

First marriage of bride and groom

Remarriage of bride and groom

First marriage of bride, remarriage of groom

First marriage of groom, remarriage of bride

*Source:* By the author. Based on *Statistical Abstract* 2000: Table 145. Table dropped in later editions.

however, are more likely to divorce again (MacDonald and DeMaris 1995). Certainly these relationships are more complicated and stressful. A lack of clear norms to follow may also play a role (Coleman et al. 2000). As sociologist Andrew Cherlin (1989) noted, we lack satisfactory names for stepmothers, stepfathers, stepbrothers, stepsisters, stepaunts, stepuncles, stepcousins, and stepgrandparents. At the very least, these are awkward terms to use, but they also represent ill-defined relationships.

# Two Sides of Family Life

Let's first look at situations in which marriage and family have gone seriously wrong and then try to answer the question of what makes marriage work.

## The Dark Side of Family Life: Battering, Child Abuse, and Incest

The dark side of family life involves events that people would rather keep in the dark. We shall look at spouse battering, child abuse, and incest.

**Spouse Battering**  To study spouse abuse, some sociologists have studied just a few victims in depth (Goetting 2001), while others have interviewed nationally representative samples of U.S. couples (Straus and Gelles 1988; Straus 1992). Although not all sociologists agree (Dobash et al. 1992, 1993; Pagelow 1992), Murray Straus concludes that husbands and wives are about equally likely to attack one another. If gender equality exists here, however, it certainly vanishes when it comes to the effects of violence— 85 percent of the injured are women (Rennison 2003). A good part of the reason, of course, is that most husbands are bigger and stronger than their wives, putting women at a physical disadvantage in this literal battle of the sexes.

Violence against women is related to the sexist structure of society, which we reviewed in Chapter 10, and to the socialization that we analyzed in Chapter 3. Because they grew up with norms that encourage aggression and the use of violence, some men feel that it is their right to control women. When frustrated in a relationship—or even by events outside it—some men become violent. The basic sociological question is how to socialize males to handle frustration and disagreements without resorting to violence (Rieker et al. 1997). We do not yet have this answer.

### Child Abuse

I answered an ad about a lakeside house in a middle-class neighborhood that was for sale by the owner. As the woman showed me through her immaculate house, I was surprised to see a plywood box in the youngest child's bedroom. About 3 feet high, 3 feet wide, and 6 feet long, the box was perforated with holes and had a little door with a padlock. Curious, I asked what it was. The woman replied matter-of-factly that her son had a behavior problem, and this was where they locked him for "time out." She added that other times they would tie him to a float, attach a line to the dock, and put him in the lake.

I left as soon as I could. With thoughts of a terrorized child filling my head, I called the state child abuse hotline.

As you can tell, what I saw upset me. Most of us are bothered by child abuse—helpless children being victimized by their parents and other adults who are supposed to love, protect, and nurture them. The most gruesome of these cases make the evening news: The 4-year-old girl who was beaten and raped by her mother's boyfriend, passed into a coma, and then three days later passed out of this life; the 6- to 10-year-old children whose stepfather videotaped them engaging in sex acts. Unlike these cases, which made headlines in my area, most child abuse is never brought to our attention: the children who live in filth, who are neglected—left alone for hours or even days at a time—or who are beaten with extension cords—cases like the little boy I learned about when I went house hunting.

Child abuse is extensive. Each year, about 3 million U.S. children are reported to the authorities as victims of abuse or neglect. About 900,000 of these cases are substantiated (*Statistical Abstract* 2007:Table 333). The excuses that parents make are incredible. Of those I have read, one I can only describe as fantastic is this statement, made by a mother to a Manhattan judge: "I slipped in a moment of anger, and my hands accidentally wrapped around my daughter's windpipe" (LeDuff 2003).

**Incest**    Sexual relations between certain relatives (for example, between brothers and sisters or between parents and children) constitute **incest.** Incest is most likely to occur in families that are socially isolated (Smith 1992). Sociologist Diana Russell (n.d.) found that incest victims who experience the greatest trauma are those who were victimized the most often, whose assaults occurred over longer periods of time, and whose incest was "more intrusive"—for example, sexual intercourse as opposed to sexual touching.

Who are the offenders? The most common incest is apparently between brothers and sisters, with the sex initiated by the brother (Canavan et al. 1992; Carlson et al. 2006). With no random samples, however, we do not know how common incest is, and researchers report different results. Russell found that uncles are the most common offenders, followed by first cousins, fathers (stepfathers especially), brothers, and, finally, other relatives ranging from brothers-in-law to stepgrandfathers. From the studies we have, we can conclude that incest between mothers and their children is rare, more so than between fathers and their children.

# The Bright Side of Family Life: Successful Marriages

**Successful Marriages**    After examining divorce and family abuse, one could easily conclude that marriages seldom work out. This would be far from the truth, however, for about three of every five married Americans report that they are "very happy" with their marriages (Whitehead and Popenoe 2004). (Keep in mind that each year divorce removes the most unhappy marriages from this population.) To find out what makes marriage successful, sociologists Jeanette and Robert Lauer (1992) interviewed 351 couples who had been married fifteen years or longer. Fifty-one of these marriages were unhappy, but the couples stayed together for religious reasons, because of family tradition, or "for the sake of the children."

Of the others, the 300 happy couples, all

1. Think of their spouse as their best friend
2. Like their spouse as a person

3. Think of marriage as a long-term commitment
4. Believe that marriage is sacred
5. Agree with their spouse on aims and goals
6. Believe that their spouse has grown more interesting over the years
7. Strongly want the relationship to succeed
8. Laugh together

Sociologist Nicholas Stinnett (1992) used interviews and questionnaires to study 660 families from all regions of the United States and parts of South America. He found that happy families

1. Spend a lot of time together
2. Are quick to express appreciation
3. Are committed to promoting one another's welfare
4. Do a lot of talking and listening to one another
5. Are religious
6. Deal with crises in a positive manner

Sociologists have uncovered two other factors: Marriages are happier when couples get along with their in-laws (Bryant et al. 2001) and when they do leisure activities that they both enjoy (Crawford et al. 2002).

**Symbolic Interactionism and the Misuse of Statistics**
Many students express concerns about their own marital future, a wariness born out of the divorces of their parents, friends, neighbors, relatives—even their pastors and rabbis. They wonder about their chances of having a successful marriage. Because sociology is not just about abstract ideas, but is really about our lives, it is important to stress that you are an individual, not a statistic. That is, if the divorce rate were 33 percent or 50 percent, this would *not* mean that if you marry, your chances of getting divorced are 33 percent or 50 percent. That is a misuse of statistics—and a common one at that. Divorce statistics represent all marriages and have absolutely *nothing* to do with any individual marriage. Our own chances depend on our own situations—especially the way we approach marriage.

To make this point clearer, let's apply symbolic interactionism. From a symbolic interactionist perspective, we create our own worlds. That is, because our experiences don't come with built-in meanings, we interpret our experiences and act accordingly. As we do so, we can create a self-fulfilling prophecy. For example, if we think that our marriage might fail, we are more likely to run when things become difficult. If we think that our marriage is going to work out, we are more likely to stick around and to do things to make the marriage successful. The folk saying "There are no guarantees in life" is certainly true, but it does help to have a vision that a good marriage is possible and that it is worth the effort to achieve.

# The Future of Marriage and Family

What can we expect of marriage and family in the future? Despite its many problems, marriage is in no danger of becoming a relic of the past. Marriage is so functional that it exists in every society. Consequently, the vast majority of Americans will continue to find marriage vital to their welfare.

Certain trends are firmly in place. Cohabitation, births to single women, and age at first marriage will increase. As more married women join the workforce, wives will continue to gain marital power. As the number of elderly increase, more couples will find themselves sandwiched between caring for their parents and rearing their own children.

Our culture will continue to be haunted by distorted images of marriage and family: the bleak ones portrayed in the mass media and the rosy ones perpetuated by cultural myths. Sociological research can help to correct these distortions and allow us to see how our own family experiences fit into the patterns of our culture. Sociological research can also help to answer the big question: How do we formulate social policies that will support and enhance family life?

# SUMMARY *and* REVIEW

## Marriage and Family in Global Perspective

### What is a family—and what themes are universal?

Family is difficult to define. There are exceptions to every element that one might consider essential. Consequently, **family** is defined broadly—as people who consider themselves related by blood, marriage, or adoption. Universally, **marriage** and family are mechanisms for governing mate selection, reckoning descent, and establishing inheritance and authority. Pp. 330–333.

## Marriage and Family in Theoretical Perspective

### What is a functionalist perspective on marriage and family?

Functionalists examine the functions and dysfunctions of family life. Examples include the **incest taboo** and how weakened family functions increase divorce. P. 333.

### What is a conflict perspective on marriage and family?

Conflict theorists focus on inequality in marriage, especially unequal power between husbands and wives. P. 334.

### What is a symbolic interactionist perspective on marriage and family?

Symbolic interactionists examine the contrasting experiences and perspectives of men and women in marriage. They stress that only by grasping the perspectives of wives and husbands can we understand their behavior. Pp. 334–336.

## The Family Life Cycle

### What are the major elements of the family life cycle?

The major elements are love and courtship, marriage, childbirth, child rearing, and the family in later life. Most mate selection follows predictable patterns of age, social class, race–ethnicity, and religion. Child-rearing patterns also vary by social class. Pp. 336–340.

## Diversity in U.S. Families

### How significant is race–ethnicity in family life?

The primary distinction is social class, not race–ethnicity. Families of the same social class are likely to be similar, regardless of their race–ethnicity. Pp. 340–343.

### What other diversity in U.S. families is there?

Also discussed are one-parent, childless, **blended,** and gay and lesbian families. Each has its unique characteristics, but social class is significant in determining their primary characteristics. Poverty is especially significant for single-parent families, most of which are headed by women. Pp. 343–345.

## Trends in U.S. Families

### What major changes characterize U.S. families?

Two changes are postponement of first marriage and an increase in **cohabitation.** With more people living longer, many middle-aged couples find themselves sandwiched between rearing their children and taking care of their aging parents. Pp. 345–349.

## Divorce and Remarriage

### What is the current divorce rate?

Depending on what numbers you choose to compare, you can produce almost any rate you wish, from 50 percent to less than 2 percent. Pp. 349–351.

### How do children and their parents adjust to divorce?

Divorce is difficult for children, whose adjustment problems often continue into adulthood. Most divorced fathers do not maintain ongoing relationships with their children. Financial problems are usually greater for the former wives. The rate at which divorced people remarry has slowed. Pp. 351–354.

### Two Sides of Family Life

*What are the two sides of family life?*

The dark side is abuse—spouse battering, child abuse, and **incest.** All these are acts that revolve around the misuse of family power. The bright side is that most people find marriage and family to be rewarding. Pp. 354–355.

### The Future of Marriage and Family

*What is the likely future of marriage and family?*

We can expect cohabitation, births to unmarried women, and age at first marriage to increase. The growing numbers of women in the workforce are likely to continue to shift the balance of marital power. P. 356.

---

## THINKING CRITICALLY *about* Chapter 12

1. Functionalists stress that the family is universal because it provides basic functions for individuals and society. What functions does your family provide? Hint: In addition to the section "The Functionalist Perspective," also consider the section "Common Cultural Themes."

2. Explain why social class is more important than race–ethnicity in determining a family's characteristics.

3. Apply this chapter's contents to your own experience with marriage and family. What social factors affect your family life? In what ways is your family life different from that of your grandparents when they were your age?

---

## BY THE NUMBERS: Changes Over Time

- Number of marriages between a white woman and an African American man in 1970: **41,000**
- Number of marriages between a white woman and an African American man today: **287,000**

- Age of average first-time bride in 1970: **20**
- Age of average first-time bride today: **25**

- Percentage of children living with both of their parents in 1970: **85**
- Percentage of children living with both of their parents today: **65**

- Number of cohabitating couples in 1970: **500,000**
- Number of cohabitating couples today: **5,000,000**

- Percentage of births to unmarried women in 1970: **10**
- Percentage of births to unmarried women today: **37**

---

## ADDITIONAL RESOURCES

### What can you find in MySocLab? mysoclab  www.mysoclab.com

- **Complete Ebook**
- **Practice Tests and Video and Audio activities**
- **Mapping and Data Analysis exercises**

- **Sociology in the News**
- **Classic Readings in Sociology**
- **Research and Writing advice**

### Where Can I Read More on This Topic?

Suggested readings for this chapter are listed at the back of this book.

# Education and Religion

Kathy Spiegel was upset. Horace Mann, the school principal in her hometown in Oregon, had asked her to come to his office. He explained that Kathy's 11-year-old twins had been acting up in class. They were disturbing other children and the teacher—and what was Kathy going to do about this?

Kathy didn't want to tell Mr. Mann what he could do with the situation. *That* would have gotten her kicked out of the office. Instead, she bit her tongue and said she would talk to her daughters.

> Kathy's 11-year-old twins were disturbing other children and the teacher—and what was Kathy going to do about this?

\* \* \* \* \*

On the other side of the country, Jim and Julia Attaway were pondering their own problem. When they visited their son's school in the Bronx, they didn't like what they saw. The boys looked like they were gang members, and the girls dressed and acted as though they were sexually active. Their own 13-year-old son had started using street language at home, and it was becoming increasingly difficult to communicate with him.

\* \* \* \* \*

In Minneapolis, Denzil and Tamika Jefferson were facing a much quieter crisis. They found life frantic as they hurried from one school activity to another. Their 13-year-old son attended a private school, and the demands were so intense that it felt like the junior year in high school. They no longer seemed to have any relaxed family time together.

\* \* \* \* \*

In Atlanta, Jaime and Maria Morelos were upset at the ideas that their 8-year-old daughter had begun to express at home. As devout first-generation Protestants, Jaime and Maria felt moral issues were a top priority, and they didn't like what they were hearing.

\* \* \* \* \*

Kathy talked the matter over with her husband, Bob. Jim and Julia discussed their problem, as did Denzil and Tamika and Jaime and Maria. They all came to the same conclusion: The problem was not their children. The problem was the school their children attended. All four sets of parents also came to the same solution: home schooling for their children.

Home schooling might seem to be a radical solution to today's education problems, but it is one that the parents of over a million U.S. children have chosen. We'll come back to this topic, but first let's take a broad look at education.

# EDUCATION: TRANSFERRING KNOWLEDGE AND SKILLS

## Education in Global Perspective

Have you ever wondered why people need a high school diploma to sell cars or to join the U.S. Marines? You will learn what you know on the job. Why do employers insist on diplomas and degrees? Why don't they simply use on-the-job training?

In some cases, job skills must be mastered before you are allowed to do the work. On-the-job training was once adequate to become an engineer or an airline pilot, but with changes in information and technology it is no longer sufficient. This is precisely why doctors display their credentials so prominently. Their framed degrees declare that an institution of higher learning has certified them to work on your body.

But testing in algebra or paragraph construction to sell gizmos at Radio Shack? Sociologist Randall Collins (1979) observed that industrialized nations have become **credential societies.** By this, he means that employers use diplomas and degrees as *sorting devices* to determine who is eligible for a job. Because employers don't know potential workers, they depend on schools to weed out the incapable. For example, when you graduate from college, potential employers will presume that you are a responsible person—that you have shown up

for numerous classes, have turned in scores of assignments, and have demonstrated basic writing and thinking skills. They will then graft their particular job skills onto this foundation, which has been certified by your college.

## Education and Industrialization

In the early years of the United States, there was no free public education. Parents with an average income could not afford to send their children to grade school. As the country industrialized during the 1800s, political and civic leaders recognized the need for an educated workforce. They also feared the influx of "foreign" values, for this was a period of high immigration. They looked on public education as a way to reach two major goals: producing more educated workers and "Americanizing" immigrants (Hellinger and Judd 1991).

As industrialization progressed and fewer people made their living from farming, formal education came to be regarded as essential to the well-being of society. With the distance to the nearest college too far and the cost of tuition and lodging too great, many high school graduates were unable to attend college. As is discussed

In hunting and gathering societies, there is no separate social institution called *education*. Instead, children learn from their parents and elders. These boys in the Kalahari desert of Botswana are learning survival skills as they watch their father skin a duiker.

This 1902 photo from Tuskegee, Alabama, provides a glimpse into the past, when free public education, pioneered in the United States, was still in its infancy. In these one-room rural schools, a single teacher had charge of grades 1 to 8. Children were assigned a grade not by age but by mastery of subject matter.

in the Down-to-Earth Sociology box on the next page, this predicament gave birth to community colleges. As you can see from Figure 13.1, receiving a bachelor's degree in the United States is now *twice* as common as completing high school used to be.

To further place our own educational system in perspective, let's look at education in three countries at different levels of industrialization. This will help us see how education is related to a nation's culture and its economy.

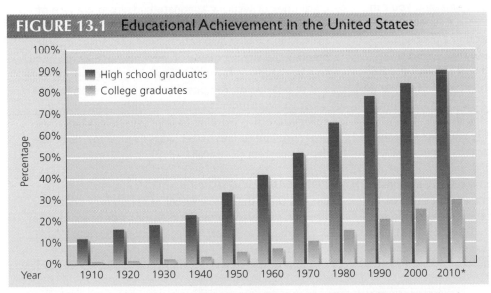

**FIGURE 13.1    Educational Achievement in the United States**

*Note:* Americans 25 years and over. Asterisk indicates author's estimate. Official high school graduation rates should be viewed skeptically. A private study of the high schools of the nation's 50 largest cities found the 2004 graduation rate to be 70 percent (Swanson 2008).
*Sources:* By the author. Based on National Center for Education Statistics 1991:Table 8; *Statistical Abstract* 2007:Table 214.

# Down-to-Earth Sociology
## Community Colleges: Challenges Old and New

*Community colleges have opened higher education to millions of students who would not otherwise have access to college because of cost or distance.*

I attended a junior college in Oakland, California. From there, with fresh diploma in hand, I transferred to a senior college—a college in Fort Wayne, Indiana, that had no freshmen or sophomores.

I didn't realize that my experimental college matched the vision of some of the founders of the community college movement. In the early 1900s, they foresaw a system of local colleges that would be accessible to the average high school graduate—a system so extensive that it would be unnecessary for universities to offer courses at the freshman and sophomore levels (Manzo 2001).

A group with an equally strong opinion questioned whether preparing high school graduates for entry to four-year colleges and universities should be the goal of junior colleges. They insisted that the purpose of junior colleges should be vocational preparation, to equip people for the job market as electricians and other technicians. In some regions, where the proponents of transfer dominated, the admissions requirements for junior colleges were higher than those of Yale (Pedersen 2001). This debate was never won by either side, and you can still hear its echoes today.

The name *junior* college also became a problem. Some felt that the word *junior* made their institution sound as though it weren't quite a real college. A struggle to change the name ensued, and several decades ago *community* college won out.

The name change didn't settle the debate about whether the purpose was preparing students to transfer to universities or training them for jobs, however. Community colleges continue to serve this dual purpose.

Community colleges have become such an essential part of the U.S. educational system that about two of every five of all undergraduates in the United States are enrolled in them (*Statistical Abstract* 2007:Table 268). Most students are *nontraditional* students: Many are age 25 or older, are from the working class, have jobs, and attend college part time (Bryant 2001; Panzarella 2008).

To help their students transfer to four-year colleges and universities, many community colleges work closely with top-tier public and private universities (Chaker 2003). Some provide admissions guidance on how to enter flagship state schools. Others coordinate courses, making sure that they match the university's title and numbering system, as well as its rigor of instruction and grading. More than a third offer honors programs that prepare talented students to transfer with ease into these schools (Padgett 2005).

The challenges that community colleges face are the usual ones of securing adequate budgets in the face of declining resources, meeting changing job markets, and maintaining quality instruction. New challenges include meeting the shifting needs of students, such as the need to teach students for whom English is a second language and to provide on-campus day care for parents. In their quest to help students complete college, community colleges are also working to improve their orientation programs and to find better ways to monitor their students' progress (Panzarella 2008).

## For Your Consideration
Do you think the primary goal of community colleges should be to prepare students for jobs or prepare them to transfer to four-year colleges and universities? Why?

# Education in the Most Industrialized Nations: Japan

*A central sociological principle of education is that a nation's education reflects its culture.* Because a core Japanese value is solidarity with the group, the Japanese discourage competition among individuals. In the workforce, people who are hired together work as a team. They are not expected to compete with one another for promotions; instead, they are promoted as a group (Ouchi 1993). Japanese education reflects this group-centered approach to life. Children in grade school work as a group, all mastering the same skills and materials. On any one day, children all over Japan study the same page from the same textbook ("Less Rote . . ." 2000).

In a fascinating cultural contradiction, college admissions in Japan are highly competitive. The Scholastic Assessment Test (SAT), taken by college-bound high school juniors and seniors in the United States, is voluntary, but Japanese seniors who want to attend college must take a national test. U.S. high school graduates who perform poorly on their tests can usually find some college to attend—as long as their parents can pay the tuition. In Japan, however, only the top scorers—rich and poor alike—are admitted to college. Japanese sociologists have found that even though the tests are open to all, children from the richer families are more likely to be admitted to college. The reason is not favoritism on the part of college officials, but, rather, that the children of richer parents score higher on these tests. One reason is that their parents spend more for tutors and intensive training classes to prepare their children for the college entrance exams (Ono 2001).

# Education in the Industrializing Nations: Russia

After the Russian Revolution of 1917, the Soviet Communist party changed the nation's educational system. At that time, as in most countries, education was limited to children of the elite. The communists expanded the educational system until eventually it encompassed all children. Following the sociological principle that education reflects culture, the new government made certain that socialist values dominated its schools, for it saw education as a means to undergird the new political system. As a result, schoolchildren were taught that capitalism was evil and that communism was the salvation of the world. Every classroom was required to prominently display photographs of Lenin and Stalin.

Education, including college, was free. Just as the economy was directed from central headquarters in Moscow, so was education. Schools stressed mathematics and the natural sciences. Each school followed the same state-prescribed curriculum, and all students in the same grade used the same textbooks. To prevent critical thinking, which might lead to criticisms of communism, few courses in the social sciences were taught, and students memorized course materials, repeating lectures on oral exams (Deaver 2001).

Russia's switch from communism to capitalism brought a change in culture—especially new ideas about profit, private property, and personal freedom. This, in turn, meant that the educational system had to adjust to the country's changing values and views of the world. Not only did the photos of Lenin and Stalin come down, but also, for the first time, private, religious, and even foreign-run schools were allowed. For the first time as well, teachers were able to encourage students to think for themselves.

The problems that Russia confronted in "reinventing" its educational system are mind-boggling. Tens of thousands of teachers who were used to teaching rote political answers had to learn new methods of instruction. As the economy faltered during Russia's early transition to capitalism, school budgets dwindled. Some teachers went unpaid for months; instead of money, at one school teachers were given toilet paper and vodka (Deaver 2001). Teachers are now paid regularly (and in money), but the salaries are low. University professors are paid between $470 and $980 a month. Abysmal salaries have encouraged corruption, and some students pay for good grades and for admission to the better schools ("Russia Sets Out to . . ." 2007).

Because it is true of education everywhere, we can confidently predict that Russia's educational system will continue to reflect its culture. Its educational system will glorify Russia's historical exploits and reinforce its values and world views—no matter how they might change.

# Education in the Least Industrialized Nations: Egypt

Education in the Least Industrialized Nations stands in sharp contrast to that in the industrialized world. Because most of the citizens of these nations work the land or take care of families, there is little emphasis on formal schooling. Even if a Least Industrialized Nation has mandatory attendance laws, they are not enforced. Formal education is expensive, and most of these nations

The poverty of some of the Least Industrialized Nations defies the imagination of most people who have been reared in the industrialized world. Their educational systems are similarly marked by poverty. This photo shows a street school in Bobo Dioulasso, Burkina Faso.

cannot afford it. As we saw in Figure 7.2 (pages 186–187), many people in the Least Industrialized Nations live on less than $1,000 a year. Consequently, in some of these nations few children go to school beyond the first couple of grades. Figure 13.2 on the next page contrasts education in China with that of the United States. As was once common around the globe, it is primarily the wealthy in the Least Industrialized Nations who have the means and the leisure for formal education—especially anything beyond the basics. As an example, let's look at education in Egypt.

Although the Egyptian constitution guarantees five years of free grade school for all children, many poor children receive no education at all. For those who do attend school, qualified teachers are few and classrooms are crowded (Cook 2001). As a result, one-third of Egyptian men and over half of Egyptian women are illiterate (UNESCO 2005). Those who go beyond the five years of grade school attend a preparatory school for three years. High school also lasts for three years. During the first two years, all students take the same courses, but during the third year they specialize in arts, science, or mathematics. The emphasis has been on memorizing facts to pass national tests. Reflecting growing concerns that this approach leaves minds less capable of evaluating life and opens the door to religious extremism, critical thinking is being added to the curriculum (Gauch 2006).

# The Functionalist Perspective: Providing Social Benefits

A central position of functionalism is that when the parts of society are working properly, each contributes to the well-being or stability of that society. The positive things that people intend their actions to accomplish are known as **manifest functions.** The positive consequences they did not intend are called **latent functions.** Let's look at the functions of education.

## Teaching Knowledge and Skills

Education's most obvious manifest function is to teach knowledge and skills—whether the traditional three R's or their more contemporary counterparts, such as computer literacy. Each generation must train the next to fill the group's significant positions. Because our postindustrial society needs highly educated people, the schools supply them.

## Cultural Transmission of Values

Another manifest function of education is the **cultural transmission of values,** a process by which schools pass on a society's core values from one generation to the next. Consequently, schools in a socialist society stress values of

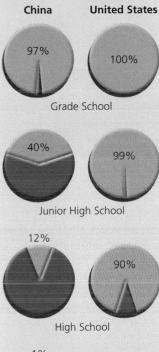

## FIGURE 13.2
### Education in a Most Industrialized (Postindustrial) Nation and a Least Industrialized Nation

**Who Goes to These Schools? Comparing China and the United States**

China          United States

97%            100%

Grade School

40%            99%

Junior High School

12%            90%

High School

1%             40%

College

*Note:* These are initial attendance rates, not completion rates. The U.S. junior high school total is the author's estimate.
*Source:* Brauchli 1994; Kahn 2004; Zeng and Wang 2007; *Statistical Abstract* 2007: Tables 208, 210, 262.

socialism, while schools in a capitalist society teach values that support capitalism. U.S. schools, for example, stress respect for private property, individualism, and competition.

Regardless of a country's economic system, loyalty to the state is a cultural value, and schools around the world teach patriotism. U.S. schools—as well as those of Russia, France, China, and others around the world—extol the society's founders, their struggle for freedom from oppression, and the goodness of the country's basic social institutions. Seldom is this function as explicit as it is in Japan, where the law requires that schools "cultivate a respect for tradition and culture, and love for the nation and homeland that have fostered them" (Nakamura 2006).

To visualize this point of the functionalists, consider how differently a course in current events or U.S. history would be taught in Cuba, Iran, and Muncie, Indiana.

## Social Integration

Schools also bring about *social integration.* They promote a sense of national identity by having students salute the flag and sing the national anthem, as in the photo on the next page. One of the best examples of how schools promote political integration is how they have taught mainstream ideas and values to tens of millions of immigrants. Coming to regard themselves as Americans, the immigrants gave up their earlier national and cultural identities (Rodriguez 1995; Carper 2000).

This integrative function of education goes far beyond making people similar in their appearance, speech, or even ways of thinking. *To forge a national identity is to stabilize the political system.* If people identify with a society's institutions and *perceive them as the basis of their own welfare,* they have no reason to rebel. This function is especially significant when it comes to the lower social classes, from which most social revolutionaries emerge. The wealthy already have a vested interest in maintaining the status quo, but getting the lower classes to identify with a social system *as it is* goes a long way toward preserving the system in its current state.

People with disabilities often have found themselves left out of the mainstream of society. To overcome this, U.S. schools have added a manifest function, **mainstreaming,** or inclusion. This means that educators try to incorporate students with disabilities into regular school activities. As a matter of routine policy, students with disabilities used to be placed in special classes or schools. There, however, they learned to adjust to a specialized situation, leaving them ill prepared to cope with the dominant world. Educational philosophy then shifted to encourage or even to require students with disabilities to attend regular schools. Wheelchair ramps are provided for people who cannot walk; interpreters who use sign language may attend classes with those who

These students are learning that the identity of "American" overrides family, gender, and racial–ethnic identities. They are also learning patriotism and civic duties.

cannot hear. Most students who are blind attend special schools, as do people with severe learning disabilities. Overall, one half of students with disabilities now attend school in regular classrooms (U.S. Department of Education 2007).

## Gatekeeping

**Gatekeeping,** or determining which people will enter what occupations, is another function of education. One type of gatekeeping is *credentialing*— using diplomas and degrees to determine who is eligible for a job—which opens the door of opportunity for some and closes it to others. Gatekeeping is often accomplished by **tracking,** sorting students into different educational programs on the basis of their perceived abilities. Some U.S. high schools funnel students into one of three tracks: general, college prep, or honors. Students on the lowest track are likely to go to work after high school or to take vocational courses. Those on the highest track usually attend prestigious colleges. Those in between usually attend a local college or regional state university. The impact is lifelong, affecting opportunities for jobs, income, and lifestyle. Schools have retreated from formal tracking, but placing students in "ability groups" and "advanced" classes serves the same purpose (Lucas 1999; Tach and Farkas 2003).

Gatekeeping sorts people on the basis of merit, said functionalists Talcott Parsons (1940) and Kingsley Davis and Wilbert Moore (1945). They pioneered a view known as **social placement,** arguing that some jobs require few skills and can be performed by people of lesser intelligence. Other jobs, however, such as that of physician, require high intelligence and advanced education. To motivate capable people to postpone gratification and to put up with years of rigorous education, rewards of high income and prestige are offered. Thus, functionalists look at education as a system that, to benefit society, sorts people according to their abilities and ambitions.

## Replacing Family Functions

Over the years, the functions of U.S. schools have expanded, and they now rival some family functions. Child care is an example. Grade schools do double duty as babysitters for families in which both parents work or for single working mothers. Child care has always been a latent function of formal education, for it was an unintended consequence. Now, however, with two wage earners in most families, child care has become a manifest function, and some schools offer child care both before and after the school day. Some high schools even provide nurseries for the children of their teenaged students (Bosman 2007). Another function is providing sex education and, as in 500 school-based health centers, birth control (Elliott 2007). This has stirred controversy, for some families resent schools taking this function away from them. Disagreement over values has fueled the social movement for home schooling, featured in our opening vignette and in the Down-to-Earth Sociology box on the next page.

# Down-to-Earth Sociology
## Home Schooling: The Search for Quality and Values

"You're doing what? You're going to teach your kids at home?" is the typical, incredulous response to parents who decide to home school their children. The unspoken questions are, "How can you teach? You're not trained. And taking your kids out of the public schools—Do you want your kids to be dumb and social misfits?"

The home-schooling movement was small at first, just a trickle of parents who were dissatisfied with the rigidity of the school bureaucracy, lax discipline, incompetent teachers, low standards, lack of focus on individual needs, and, in some instances, hostility to their religion.

*As the home schooling social movement has grown, it has become increasingly institutionalized. Home schoolers now have their own class rings.*

The trickle has grown. While not yet a raging river, the number of children who are being taught at home is more than twice the size of the public school system of Chicago. More than one million children are being home schooled (Princiotta et al. 2004; *Statistical Abstract* 2007:Table 227).

Home schooling is far from new. In the colonial era, home schooling was the *typical* form of education (Carper 2000). Today's home-schooling movement is restoring this earlier pattern, but it also reflects a fascinating shift in U.S. politics. Political and religious *liberals* began the contemporary home-schooling movement in the 1950s and 1960s. Their objection was that the schools were too conservative. Then the schools changed, and in the 1970s and 1980s, political and religious *conservatives* embraced home schooling (Lines 2000; Stevens 2001). Their objection was that the schools were too liberal. Other parents have no political motivation. They are home schooling their children because of concerns about safety at school and the lack of individual attention (Shellenbarger 2006).

Does home schooling work? Can parents who are not trained as teachers actually teach? The early results of testing home schoolers were promising, but they were limited to small groups or to single states. Then in 1990, a national sample of 2,000 home schoolers showed that these students did better than students who were in public schools. Could this really be true?

To find out, researchers tested 21,000 home schoolers across the nation (Rudner 1999). The results are astounding.

The median scores for every test at every grade were in the 70th to 80th percentiles. The home schoolers outscored students in both public and Catholic schools.

The basic reason for the stunning success of home schooling appears to be the parents' involvement in their children's education. Home schoolers receive an intense, one-on-one education. Their curriculum—although it includes the subjects that are required by the state—is designed around the student's interests and needs. Ninety percent of students are taught by their mothers, ten percent by their fathers (Lines 2000). The parents' income is also above average.

We do not know what these home schoolers' test scores would have been if they had been taught in public schools. With their parents' involvement in their education, they likely would have done very well there, too. Although the Rudner study was large, it was not a random sample, and we cannot say how the *average* home schooler is doing. But, then, we have no random sample of all public school students, either.

What about the children's social skills? Since they don't attend school with dozens and even hundreds of other students, do they become social misfits? The studies show that they do just fine on this level, too. They actually have fewer behavior problems than children who attend conventional schools (Lines 2000). Contrary to stereotypes, home-schooled children are not isolated. As part of their educational experience, their parents take them to libraries, museums, factories, and nursing homes (Medlin 2000). Some home schoolers participate in the physical education and sports programs of the public schools. For social activities, many of the children meet with other home-schooled children and go on field trips together. There are even home-schooling associations, which run conferences for parents and children and hold sporting events. As the photo shows, the same companies that sell class rings to public high schools also sell class rings to home schoolers (McGinn and McLure 2003).

## For Your Consideration

Two of every one hundred students across the country are being taught at home. Why do you think that home schooling has become so popular? Do you think this social movement could eventually become a threat to U.S. public schools? Would you consider home schooling your children? Why or why not?

# The Conflict Perspective: Perpetuating Social Inequality

Unlike functionalists, who look at the benefits of education, conflict theorists examine how *the educational system reproduces the social class structure.* By this, they mean that schools perpetuate the social divisions of society and help members of the elite to maintain their dominance. Let's look at how this happens.

## The Hidden Curriculum

The term **hidden curriculum** refers to the attitudes and the unwritten rules of behavior that schools teach in addition to the formal curriculum. Examples are obedience to authority and conformity to mainstream norms. Conflict theorists stress that the hidden curriculum helps to perpetuate social inequalities.

To understand this central point, consider the way English is taught. Middle-class schools—whose teachers know where their students are headed—stress "proper" English and "good" manners. In contrast, the teachers in inner-city schools—who also know where *their* students are headed—allow ethnic and street language in the classroom. Each type of school is helping to reproduce the social class structure. That is, each is preparing students to work in positions similar to those of their parents. The social class of some children destines them for higher positions. For these jobs, they need "refined" speech and manners. The social destiny of others is low-status jobs. For this type of work, they need only to obey rules (Bowles and Gintis 1976; 2002). Teaching these students

"refined" speech and manners would be a wasted effort. In other words, even the teaching of English and manners helps keep the social classes intact across generations.

## Tilting the Tests: Discrimination by IQ

Even intelligence tests help to keep the social class system intact. Let's look at an example. How would you answer this question?

**A symphony is to a composer as a book is to a(n)**
_____ paper        _____ sculptor       _____ musician
_____ author       _____ man

You probably had no difficulty coming up with "author" as your choice. Wouldn't any intelligent person have done so?

In point of fact, this question raises a central issue in intelligence testing. Not all intelligent people would know the answer. This question contains *cultural biases.* Children from some backgrounds are more familiar with the concepts of symphonies, composers, and sculptors than are other children. Consequently, the test is tilted in their favor.

To make the bias clearer, try to answer this question:

**If you throw two dice and "7" is showing on the top, what is facing down?**
_____ seven        _____ snake eyes     _____ box cars
_____ little Joes  _____ eleven

Adrian Dove (n.d.), a social worker in Watts, a poor area of Los Angeles, suggested this question. Its cultural bias should be obvious—that it allows children from certain social backgrounds to perform better than others. Unlike the first question, this one is not tilted to the middle-class

Conflict theorists stress that education reproduces a country's social class system. As part of the evidence to support this position, they point out that the U.S. social classes attend separate schools, where they learn perspectives of the world that match their place in it. Shown here is a student at The Andrews School in Willoughby, Ohio. What do you think the *hidden curriculum* is at this school?

experience. In other words, IQ (intelligence quotient) tests measure not only intelligence but also acquired knowledge.

You should now be able to perceive the bias of IQ tests that use such words as *composer* and *symphony*. A lower-class child may have heard about rap, rock, hip hop, or jazz, but not about symphonies. One consequence of this bias to the middle and upper social classes is that the children of the poor score lower on IQ tests. Then, to match their supposedly inferior intelligence, they are assigned to less demanding courses. Their inferior education helps them reach their social destiny, their lower-paying jobs in adult life. As conflict theorists view them, then, IQ tests are another weapon in an arsenal designed to maintain the social class structure across the generations.

## Stacking the Deck: Unequal Funding

Conflict theorists stress that the way schools are funded stacks the deck against the poor. Because public schools are supported largely by local property taxes, the richer communities (where income and property values are higher) have more to spend on their children, and the poorer communities have less to spend on theirs. Consequently, the richer communities can offer higher salaries and take their pick of the most highly qualified and motivated teachers. They can also afford to buy the latest textbooks, computers, and software, as well as offer courses in foreign languages, music, and the arts.

## The Bottom Line: Family Background

Conflict theorists end their analysis of education with a flourish, taking us back to their main point, that education reproduces the social class structure. The end result of the hidden curriculum, IQ tests, and school funding is this: Family background is more important than test scores in predicting who attends college. In a classic study, sociologist Samuel Bowles (1977) compared the college attendance of the brightest 25 percent of high school students with that of the intellectually weakest 25 percent. Figure 13.3 shows the results. Of the *brightest* 25 percent of high school students, 90 percent of those from affluent homes went to college, while only half of those from low-income homes did. Of the *intellectually weakest* students, 26 percent from affluent homes went to college, while only 6 percent from poorer homes did so.

Other sociologists have confirmed this classic research. Anthony Carnevale and Stephen Rose (2003) compared students' college attendance with their intellectual abilities and their parents' social class. Regardless of personal abilities, children from more well-to-do families are more likely not only to go to college but also to attend the nation's most elite schools. This, in turn, piles advantage upon advantage,

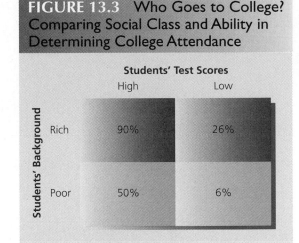

**FIGURE 13.3  Who Goes to College? Comparing Social Class and Ability in Determining College Attendance**

|  | Students' Test Scores | |
|---|---|---|
|  | High | Low |
| Rich | 90% | 26% |
| Poor | 50% | 6% |

Students' Background

*Source:* Bowles 1977.

because they get higher paying and more prestigious jobs when they graduate. The elite colleges are the icing on the cake of these students' more privileged birth.

Conflict theorists point out that the educational system reproduces not only the U.S. social class structure but also its racial–ethnic divisions. From Figure 13.4 on the next page, you can see that, compared with whites, African Americans and Latinos are less likely to complete high school and less likely to go to college. Because adults without college degrees usually end up with low-paying, dead-end jobs, you can see how this supports the conflict view—that education is helping to reproduce the racial–ethnic structure for the next generation.

# The Symbolic Interactionist Perspective: Teacher Expectations

Functionalists look at how education benefits society, and conflict theorists examine how education perpetuates social inequality. Symbolic interactionists, in contrast, study face-to-face interaction in the classroom. They have found that the expectations of teachers have profound consequences for their students.

## The Rist Research

Why do some people get tracked into college prep courses and others into vocational ones? There is no single answer, but in what has become a classic study, sociologist Ray

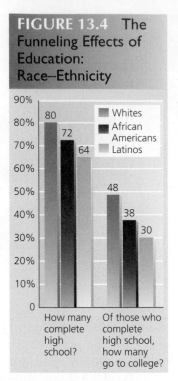

**FIGURE 13.4  The Funneling Effects of Education: Race–Ethnicity**

Legend:
- Whites
- African Americans
- Latinos

How many complete high school?
- 80 (Whites)
- 72 (African Americans)
- 64 (Latinos)

Of those who complete high school, how many go to college?
- 48 (Whites)
- 38 (African Americans)
- 30 (Latinos)

*Note:* The source gives totals only for these three groups.
*Source:* By the author. Based on *Statistical Abstract* 2007:Table 262.

Rist came up with some intriguing findings. Rist (1970, 2000) did participant observation in an African American grade school with an African American faculty. He found that after only eight days in the classroom, the kindergarten teacher felt that she knew the children's abilities well enough to assign them to three separate work-tables. To Table 1, Mrs. Caplow assigned those she considered to be "fast learners." They sat at the front of the room, closest to her. Those whom she saw as "slow learners," she assigned to Table 3, located at the back of the classroom. She placed "average" students at Table 2, in between the other tables.

This seemed strange to Rist. He knew that the children had not been tested for ability, yet their teacher was certain that she could identify the bright and slow children. Investigating further, Rist found that social class was the underlying basis for assigning the children to the different tables. Middle-class students were separated out for Table 1, and children from poorer homes were assigned to Tables 2 and 3. The teacher paid the most attention to the children at Table 1, who were closest to her, less to Table 2, and the least to Table 3. As the year went on, children from Table 1 perceived that they were treated better and came to see themselves as smarter. They became the leaders in class activities and even ridiculed children at the other tables, calling them "dumb." Eventually, the children at Table 3 disengaged themselves from many classroom activities. At the end of the year, only the children at Table 1 had completed the lessons that prepared them for reading.

This early tracking stuck. Their first-grade teacher looked at the work these students had done, and she placed students from Table 1 at her Table 1. She treated her tables much as the kindergarten teacher had, and the children at Table 1 again led the class.

The children's reputations continued to follow them. The second-grade teacher reviewed their scores and also divided her class into three groups. The first she named the "Tigers" and, befitting their name, gave them challenging readers. Not surprisingly, the Tigers came from the original Table 1 in kindergarten. The second group she called the "Cardinals." They came from the original Tables 2 and 3. Her third group consisted of children she had failed the previous year, whom she called the "Clowns." The Cardinals and Clowns were given less advanced readers.

Rist concluded that *each child's journey through school was determined by the eighth day of kindergarten!* As happened with the Saints and Roughnecks reported in Chapter 4, labels can be so powerful that they can set people on courses of action that affect the rest of their lives.

What occurred was a **self-fulfilling prophecy.** This term, coined by sociologist Robert Merton (1949/1968), refers to a false assumption of something that is going to happen but which then comes true simply because it was predicted. For example, if people believe an unfounded rumor that a credit union is going to fail because its officers have embezzled their money, they all rush to the credit union to demand their money. The prediction—although originally false—is now likely to come true.

## How Do Teacher Expectations Work?

Sociologist George Farkas (1990a, 1990b, 1996) became interested in how teacher expectations affect grades. Using a stratified sample of students in a large school district in Texas, he found that teacher expectations produced gender and racial–ethnic biases. *On the gender level:* Even though boys and girls had the same test scores, girls on average were given higher course grades. *On the racial–ethnic level:* Asian Americans who had the same test scores as the other groups averaged higher grades than did African Americans, Latinos, and whites.

At first, this may sound like more of the same old news—another case of discrimination. But this explanation doesn't fit, which is what makes the finding fascinating. Look at who the victims are. It is most unlikely that the teachers would be prejudiced against boys and whites. To interpret these unexpected results, Farkas used symbolic interactionism. He observed that some students "signal" to their teachers that they are "good students." They show an eagerness to cooperate, and they quickly agree with what the teacher says. They also show that they are "trying hard." The teachers pick up these signals and reward these "good students" with better grades. Girls and Asian Americans, the researcher concluded, are better at displaying these characteristics so coveted by teachers.

We do not have enough information on how teachers communicate their expectations to students. Nor do we know much about how students "signal" messages to teachers. Perhaps you will become the educational sociologist who will shed more light on this significant area of human behavior.

# Problems in U.S. Education—and Their Solutions

To conclude this section, let's examine two problems facing U.S. education—and consider their potential solutions.

## Problems: Mediocrity and Violence

**The Rising Tide of Mediocrity**   Since I know you love taking tests, let's see how you do on these three questions:

1. How many goals are on a basketball court?
   a. 1  b. 2  c. 3  d. 4
2. How many halves are in a college basketball game?
   a. 1  b. 2  c. 3  d. 4
3. How many points does a three-point field goal account for in a basketball game? a. 1  b. 2  c. 3  d. 4

I know that this sounds like a joke, but it isn't. Sociologist Robert Benford (2007) got his hands on a copy of a 20-question final examination given to basketball players who took a credit course on coaching principles at the University of Georgia. It is usually difficult to refer to athletes, sports, and academics in the same breath, but this is about as mediocre as mediocrity can get.

Here are broader examples of how mediocrity plagues our educational system:

- All Arizona high school sophomores took a math test. It covered the math that sophomores should know. *One of ten passed.*
- Tennessee state officials were so pleased at their test results that they called a news conference. They

boasted that 87 percent of their students were proficient at math—and they had the test results to prove it. When the federal government retested the students, the results dropped just a bit—to 21 percent (Dillon 2005b).

We haven't done too well on our SAT tests, either. In Figure 13.5, you can see how the scores dropped from the 1960s to 1980. At that point, educators—and even Congress—expressed concern. Schools raised their standards, and the scores started to climb. The recovery in math has been encouraging. Today's high school seniors now score the same in math as seniors did in the 1960s. Administrators are requiring more of teachers, and teachers are requiring more of students. Each is performing according to these higher expectations. This looks good, right? But going back to past levels isn't enough. Compared with students from 40 other nations, U.S. students rank 25th in math (Chaddock 2004).

As you can see from Figure 13.5, the verbal scores have not returned to earlier levels. Today's students perform so poorly that the makers of the SAT eliminated the analogy part of the verbal test. Analogies demand penetrating thinking, and, unfortunately, today's students just couldn't handle it. No one knows exactly why the verbal scores are so low, but the culprits are often identified as "dummied down" textbooks, less rigorous teaching, and less reading because of watching television and playing video and computer games.

**How to Cheat on the SATs**   If you receive poor grades this semester, wouldn't you like to use a magic marker—

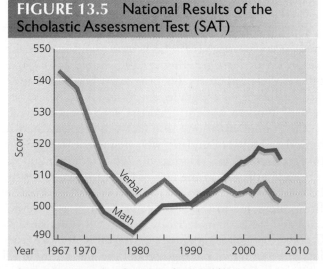

**FIGURE 13.5   National Results of the Scholastic Assessment Test (SAT)**

*Source:* By the author. Based on *Statistical Abstract* 2008:Table 258.

to—presto!—change them into higher grades? I suppose every student would. Now imagine that you had that power. Would you use it?

Some people in authority apparently have found such a magic marker, and they have used it to raise our low national SAT scores. Table 274 of the 1996 edition of the *Statistical Abstract of the United States* reports that in 1995 only 8.3 percent of students earned 600 or more on the verbal portion of the SAT test. The very next edition, in 1997, however, holds a pleasant surprise. Table 276 tells us that it was really 21.9 percent of students who scored 600 or higher in 1995. Later editions of this source retain the higher figure. What a magic marker!

In the twinkle of an eye, we get another bonus. Somehow, between 1996 and 1997 the scores of *everyone* who took the test in previous years improved. Now that's the kind of power we all would like to have. Students, grab your report cards. Workers, change those numbers on your paycheck.

It certainly is easier to give simpler tests than to teach more effectively. And this is what has happened to the SAT. The results were so embarrassing to U.S. educators that the SAT was made easier. Not only was testing on antonyms and analogies dropped, but the test was also shortened and students were given more time to answer the fewer questions. The test makers then "rescored" the totals of previous years to match the easier test. This "dummying down" of the SAT is yet another form of grade inflation, the topic to which we shall now turn.

### Grade Inflation, Social Promotion, and Functional Illiteracy

High school teachers used to give about twice as many *C*'s as *A*'s, but now they give more *A*'s than *C*'s. Grades are so inflated that some of today's *A*'s are the *C*'s of years past. **Grade inflation** is so pervasive that *47 percent* of all college freshmen have an overall high school grade point average of *A*. This is more than *twice* what it was in 1970 (*Statistical Abstract* 2007:Table 274). Grade inflation has also hit the Ivy League. At Harvard University, *half* of the course grades are *A*'s and *A*–'s. *Ninety* percent of Harvard students graduate with honors. To rein in the "honor inflation," the Harvard faculty voted to limit the number of students who graduate with honors to 60 percent of a class (Hartocollis 2002; Douthat 2005).

Grade inflation in the face of declining standards has been accompanied by **social promotion,** passing students from one grade to the next even though they have not mastered the basic materials. One result is **functional illiteracy,** high school graduates having difficulty with reading and writing. Some high school graduates cannot fill out job applications; others can't even figure out whether they get the right change at the grocery store.

**The Influence of Peer Groups**   What do you think is the most important factor in how teenagers do in school? Two psychologists and a sociologist, who studied 20,000 high school students in California and Wisconsin, found that it is the student's peer group (Steinberg et al. 1996). Simply put: Teens who hang out with good students tend to do well, and those who hang out with friends who do poorly in school do poorly. Student subcultures include informal norms about grades. Some groups have norms of classroom excellence, while others sneer at good grades. The applied question that arises from this research, of course, is how to build educational achievement into student culture.

**Violence in Schools**   Some U.S. schools have deteriorated to the point that safety is an issue. In these schools, uniformed guards and metal detectors have become permanent fixtures. Some grade schools even supplement their traditional fire drills with "drive-by shooting drills." Because they might be targeted by terrorists, other schools hold "Code Blue" drills: The classrooms—each equipped with a phone—are locked, the windows are locked, and the shades are drawn. Whether these measures create feelings of security or produce fear is yet to be studied by sociolgists.

School shootings are another concern. For a surprising analysis of deaths at school, read the Mass Media box on the next page.

## Solutions: Safety and Standards

It is one thing to identify problems, quite another to find solutions for them. Let's consider solutions to the problems we just reviewed.

**A Secure Learning Environment**   The first step in offering a good education is to keep students safe and free from fear. With the high rate of violence in U.S. society, we can expect some violence to spill over into the schools. To minimize this spillover, school administrators can expel all students who threaten the welfare of others. They also can refuse to tolerate threats, violence, and weapons. The zero tolerance policy for guns and other weapons on school property that school boards and administrators have adopted helps to make schools safer.

**Higher Standards for Teachers and Students**   To offer a quality education, we need quality teachers. Don't we already have them? Most teachers are qualified and, if motivated, can do an excellent job. But a large number of teachers are not qualified. Consider just a couple of items. California requires that its teachers pass an educational skills test. California's teachers did so poorly that to get enough teachers to fill their classrooms, officials had to drop the passing grade to the tenth-grade level. These are college graduates who are teachers—and they are expected

# MASS MEDIA in SOCIAL LIFE

## School Shootings: Exploring a Myth

The media sprinkle their reports of school shootings with such dramatic phrases as "alarming proportions," "outbreak of violence," and "out of control." They give us the impression that wackos walk our hallways, ready to spray our schools with gunfire. Parents used to consider schools safe havens, but no longer. Those naïve thoughts have been shattered by the bullets that have ripped through schools—or at least by the media's portrayal of growing danger and violence in our schools.

Have our schools really become war zones, as the mass media would have us believe? Certainly events such as those at Columbine High School and Virginia Tech are disturbing, but we need to probe deeper than newspaper headlines and televised images.

When we do, we find that the media's sensationalist reporting has created a myth. Contrary to "what everyone knows," there is

*This frame from a home video shows Eric Harris (on the left) and Dylan Klebold (on the right) as they pretend that they are searching for victims. They put their desires into practice in the infamous Columbine High School shootings.*

| TABLE 13.1 | Exploding a Myth: Deaths at U.S. Schools[1] | | | | |
|---|---|---|---|---|---|
| | | | VICTIMS | | |
| School Year | Shooting Deaths | Other Deaths[2] | Boys | Girls | Total |
| 1992–1993 | 45 | 11 | 49 | 7 | 56 |
| 1993–1994 | 41 | 12 | 41 | 12 | 53 |
| 1994–1995 | 16 | 5 | 18 | 3 | 21 |
| 1995–1996 | 29 | 7 | 26 | 10 | 36 |
| 1996–1997 | 15 | 11 | 18 | 8 | 26 |
| 1997–1998 | 36 | 8 | 27 | 17 | 44 |
| 1998–1999 | 25 | 6 | 24 | 7 | 31 |
| 1999–2000 | 16 | 16 | 26 | 6 | 32 |
| 2000–2001 | 19 | 5 | 20 | 4 | 24 |
| 2001–2002 | 4 | 1 | 5 | 0 | 5 |
| 2002–2003 | 14 | 8 | 16 | 6 | 22 |
| 2003–2004 | 29 | 13 | 37 | 5 | 42 |
| 2004–2005 | 20 | 8 | 20 | 8 | 28 |
| 2005–2006 | 5 | 0 | 4 | 1 | 5 |
| 2006–2007 | 16 | 3 | 12 | 7 | 19 |
| Total 1992–2007 | 330 | 114 | 343 | 101 | 444 |
| Mean 1992–2007 | 22.0 | 7.6 | 22.9 | 6.7 | 29.6 |

[1] Includes all school-related homicides, even those that occurred on the way to or from school. Includes suicides, school personnel killed at school by other adults, and even adults who had nothing to do with the school but who were found dead on school property. Source does not report on deaths at colleges, only K–12 (kindergarten through high school).
[2] Beating, hanging, jumping, stabbing, slashing, strangling, or heart attack.
*Source:* By the author. Based on National School Safety Center 2007.

no trend toward greater school violence. In fact, the situation is just the opposite—*the trend is toward greater safety.* Despite the dramatic school shootings that make headlines, as Table 13.1 shows, shooting deaths at schools are decreasing.

This is not to say that school shootings are not a serious problem. Even one student being wounded or killed is too many. But, contrary to the impression fostered by the media, we are not seeing an increase of school shooting deaths.

This is one reason that we need sociology: to quietly, dispassionately search for facts so we can better understand the events that shape our lives. The first requirement for solving any problem is accurate data, for how can we create rational solutions that are based on hysteria? The information presented in this box may not make for sensational headlines, but it does serve to explode one of the myths that the media have created.

### For Your Consideration

How do you think we can reduce school shootings? How about school violence of any sort?

to perform at the tenth-grade level! It gets even worse. For fifteen of our states, teachers need to be able to read only at the lowest quarter of the national average (Schemo 2002). I don't know about you, but I think this situation is a national disgrace. If we want to improve teaching, we need to insist that teachers meet high standards.

What else can we do to improve the quality of education? An older study by sociologists James Coleman and Thomas Hoffer (1987) provides helpful guidelines. They wanted to see why the test scores of students in Roman Catholic schools average 15 to 20 percent higher than those of students in public schools. Is it because Catholic schools attract better students, while public schools have to put up with everyone? To find out, they tested 15,000 students in public and Catholic high schools.

Their findings? From the sophomore through the senior years, students at Catholic schools pull ahead of public school students by a full grade in verbal and math skills. The superior test performance of students in Catholic schools, they concluded, is due not to better students, but to higher standards. Catholic schools have not watered down their curricula as have public schools. The researchers also underscored the importance of parental involvement. Parents and teachers in Catholic schools reinforce each other's commitment to learning.

**A Warning About Higher Standards**   If we raise standards, we can expect protest. It is less upsetting to use low standards and to tell students that they are doing well than it is to do rigorous teaching and use high standards to measure student performance. When Florida decided that its high school seniors needed to pass an assessment test in order to receive a diploma, 13,000 students failed the test. Parents of failed students banded together—not to demand better teaching but to pressure the state to drop the new test. They asked people to boycott Disney World and to not buy Florida orange juice (Canedy 2003). Those actions would certainly improve their children's learning!

# RELIGION: ESTABLISHING MEANING

Let's look at the main characteristics of a second significant social institution.

## What Is Religion?

Sociologists who do research on religion analyze the relationship between society and religion and study the role that religion plays in people's lives. They do not try to prove that one religion is better than another. Nor is it their goal to verify or disprove anyone's faith. As was mentioned in Chapter 1, sociologists have no tools for deciding that one course of action is more moral than another, much less for determining that one religion is "the" correct one. Religion is a matter of faith—and sociologists deal with empirical matters, things they can observe or measure. When it comes to religion, then, sociologists study the effects of religious beliefs and practices on people's lives. They also analyze how religion is related to stratification systems. Unlike theologians, however, sociologists do not try to evaluate the truth of a religion's teachings.

In 1912 Emile Durkheim published an influential book, *The Elementary Forms of the Religious Life,* in which he tried to identify the elements that are common to all religions. After surveying religions around the world, Durkheim could find no specific belief or practice that all religions share. He did find, however, that all religions develop a community around their practices and beliefs. All religions also separate the sacred from the profane. By **sacred,** Durkheim referred to aspects of life having to do with the supernatural that inspire awe, reverence, deep respect, even fear. By **profane,** he meant aspects of life that are not concerned with religion or religious purposes but, instead, are part of ordinary, everyday life.

Durkheim (1912/1965) summarized his conclusions by saying:

> A religion is a unified system of beliefs and practices relative to sacred things, that is to say, things set apart and forbidden—beliefs and practices which unite into one single moral community called a Church, all those who adhere to them.

When I visited a Hindu temple in Chattisgargh, India, I was impressed by the colorful and expressive figures on its roof. Each figure represents one of the millions of gods that Hindus worship, each deity considered part of the same divine energy or Supreme Being..

**Religion,** then, has three elements:

1. *Beliefs* that some things are sacred (forbidden, set apart from the profane)
2. *Practices* (rituals) centering on the things considered sacred
3. *A moral community* (a church) resulting from a group's beliefs and practices

Durkheim used the word **church** in an unusual sense, to refer to any "moral community" centered on beliefs and practices regarding the sacred. In Durkheim's sense, *church* refers to Buddhists bowing before a shrine, Hindus dipping in the Ganges River, and Confucians offering food to their ancestors. Similarly, the term *moral community* does not imply morality in the sense familiar to most of us—of ethical conduct. Rather, a moral community is simply a group of people who are united by their religious practices—and that would include sixteenth-century Aztec priests who each day gathered around an altar to pluck out the beating heart of a virgin.

To better understand the sociological approach to religion, let's see what pictures emerge when we apply the three theoretical perspectives.

# The Functionalist Perspective

Functionalists stress that religion is universal because it meets basic human needs. Let's look at some of the functions—and dysfunctions—of religion.

## Functions of Religion

**Questions about Ultimate Meaning**    Around the world, religions provide answers to perplexing questions about ultimate meaning—such as the purpose of life, why people suffer, and the existence of an afterlife. Those answers give followers a sense of purpose, a framework in which to live. Instead of seeing themselves buffeted by random events in an aimless existence, believers see their lives as fitting into a divine plan.

**Emotional Comfort**    The answers that religion provides about ultimate meaning also comfort people by assuring them that there is a purpose to life, even to suffering. Similarly, religious rituals that enshroud crucial events such as illness and death provide emotional comfort at times of crisis. The individual knows that others care and can find consolation in following familiar rituals.

**Social Solidarity**    Religious teachings and practices unite believers into a community that shares values and perspectives ("we Jews," "we Christians," "we Muslims"). The religious rituals that surround marriage, for example, link the bride and groom with a broader community that wishes them well. So do other religious rituals, such as those that celebrate birth and mourn death.

**Guidelines for Everyday Life**    The teachings of religion are not all abstractions. They also provide practical instructions. For example, four of the ten commandments delivered by Moses to the Israelites concern God, but the other six contain instructions on how to live everyday life, from how to get along with parents and neighbors to warnings about lying, stealing, and having affairs.

Religion can promote social change, as was evident in the U.S. civil rights movement. Dr. Martin Luther King, Jr., a Baptist minister, shown here in his famous "I have a dream" speech, was the foremost leader of this movement.

The consequences for people who follow these guidelines can be measured. People who attend church are less likely to abuse alcohol, nicotine, and illegal drugs than are people who don't go to church (Gillum 2005; Wallace et al. 2007). In general, churchgoers follow a healthier lifestyle, and they live longer than those who don't go to church.

**Social Control**    Religion not only provides guidelines for everyday life but also sets limits on people's behaviors. Most norms of a religious group apply only to its members, but nonmembers also feel a spillover. Religious teachings, for example, are incorporated into criminal law. In the United States, blasphemy and adultery were once crimes for which people could be arrested, tried, and sentenced. Some states still have laws that prohibit the sale of alcohol before noon on Sunday, laws whose purpose was to get people out of the saloons and into the churches.

**Social Change**    Although religion is often so bound up with the prevailing social order that it resists social change, religion occasionally spearheads change. In the 1960s, for example, the civil rights movement, whose goal was to desegregate public facilities and abolish racial discrimination at southern polls, was led by religious leaders, especially leaders of African American churches such as Martin Luther King, Jr. Churches also served as centers at which demonstrators were trained and rallies were organized.

## Dysfunctions of Religion

Functionalists also examine ways in which religion is *dysfunctional*— that is, how it can bring harmful results. Two dysfunctions are religious persecution and war and terrorism.

**Religion as Justification for Persecution**    Beginning in the 1200s and continuing into the 1800s, in what has become known as the Inquisition, special commissions of the Roman Catholic Church tortured women to make them confess that they were witches and then burned them at the stake. In 1692, Protestant leaders in Salem, Massachusetts, executed twenty-one women and men who were accused of being witches. In 2001, in the Democratic Republic of the Congo, about 1,000 alleged witches were hacked to death (Jenkins 2002). Similarly, it seems fair to say that the Aztec religion had its dysfunctions— at least for the virgins who were offered to appease angry gods. In short, religion has been used to justify oppression and any number of brutal acts.

**War and Terrorism**    History is filled with wars based on religion—commingled with politics. Between the eleventh and fourteenth centuries, for example, Christian monarchs conducted nine bloody Crusades in an attempt to wrest control of the region they called the Holy Land from the Muslims. Terrorist acts, too, are sometimes committed in the name of religion, as discussed in the Down-to-Earth Sociology box on the next page.

## The Symbolic Interactionist Perspective

Symbolic interactionists focus on the meanings that people give their experiences, especially how they use symbols. Let's apply this perspective to religious symbols, rituals, and beliefs to see how they help to forge a community of like-minded people.

### Religious Symbols

Suppose that it is about two thousand years ago, and you have just joined a new religion. You have come to believe that a recently crucified Jew named Jesus is the Messiah, the Lamb of God offered for your sins. The Roman leaders are persecuting the followers of Jesus. They hate your religion because you and your fellow believers will not acknowledge Caesar as God.

Christians are few in number, and you are eager to have fellowship with other believers. But how can you tell who is a believer? Spies are everywhere. The government has sworn to destroy this new religion, and you do not relish the thought of being fed to lions in the Colosseum.

You use a simple technique. While talking with a stranger, as though doodling absentmindedly in the sand or dust, you casually trace the outline of a fish. Only fellow believers know the meaning—that, taken together, the first letter of each word in the Greek sentence "Jesus (is) Christ the Son of God" spell the Greek word for fish. If the other person gives no response, you rub out the outline and continue the interaction as usual. If there is a response, you eagerly talk about your new faith.

All religions use symbols to provide identity and social solidarity for their members. For Muslims, the primary symbol is the crescent moon and star; for Jews, the Star of David; for Christians, the cross. For members, these are not ordinary symbols, but sacred emblems that evoke feelings of awe and reverence. In Durkheim's terms, religions use symbols to represent what the group considers sacred and to separate the sacred from the profane.

A symbol is a condensed way of communicating. Worn by a fundamentalist Christian, for example, the cross says, "I am a follower of Jesus Christ. I believe that He is the Messiah, the promised Son of God, that He loves me, that

# Down-to-Earth Sociology
## Terrorism and the Mind of God

WARNING: The "equal time" contents of this box are likely to offend just about everyone.

After September 11, 2001, the question on many people's minds was some form of "How can people do such evil in the name of God?"

To answer this question, we need to broaden the context. The question is fine, but it cannot be directed solely at Islamic terrorists. If it is, it misses the point.

We need to consider other religions, too. For Christians, we don't have to go back centuries to the Inquisition or to the Children's Crusades. We only have to look at Ireland and the bombings in Belfast. There, Protestants and Catholics slaughtered each other in the name of God.

In the United States, we can consider the killing of abortion doctors. Paul Hill, a minister who was executed for killing a doctor in Florida, was convinced that his act was good, that he had saved the lives of unborn babies. Before his execution, he said that he was looking forward to heaven.

Since I want to give equal time to the major religions, we can't forget the Jews. Dr. Baruch Goldstein was convinced that Yahweh wanted him to take an assault rifle, go to the Tomb of the Patriarchs, and shoot into a crowd of praying Palestinian men and boys. His admirers built a monument on his grave (Juergensmeyer 2000).

Finally, for the sake of equality, let's not let the Hindus, Buddhists, and Sikhs off the hook. In India, they continue to slaughter one another. In the name of their gods, they attack the houses of worship of the others and blow one another up. (The Hindus are actually equal opportunists—they kill Christians, too. I visited a state in India where Hindus had doused a jeep with gasoline and burned alive an Australian missionary and his two sons.)

None of these terrorists—Islamic, Christian, Jew, Sikh, Buddhist, or Hindu—represent the mainstream of their religion, but they do commit violence for religious reasons. How can they do so? Here are five elements that religious terrorists seem to have in common.

First, the individuals believe that they are under attack. Evil forces are bent on destroying the good of their world—whether that be their religion, their way of life, or unborn babies.

*Woodcuts (prints made from engraved blocks of wood coated with ink to leave an impression on paper) were used to illustrate books shortly after the printing press was invented. This woodcut commemorates a dysfunction of religion, the burning of witches at the stake. This particular event occurred at Derneburg, Germany, in 1555.*

Second, they become convinced that God wants the evil destroyed.

Third, they conclude that only violence will resolve the situation.

Fourth, they become convinced that God has chosen them for this task.

Fifth, these perspectives are nurtured by a community, a group in which the individuals find identity. This group may realize that most members of their faith do not support their views, but those others are mistaken. The smaller community holds the truth.

Under these conditions, morality is turned upside down. Killing becomes a moral act, a good done for a greater cause.

There is just enough truth in these points of view to keep the delusion alive. After all, wouldn't it have been better for the millions of victims of Hitler, Stalin, or Pol Pot if someone had had the nerve and foresight to kill them? Wouldn't their deaths and one's own self-sacrifice have been a greater good? Today, there are those bad Protestants, those bad Catholics, those bad Jews, those bad Palestinians, those bad abortionists, those bad Americans—an endless list. And the violence is for the Greater Good: what God wants.

Once people buy into this closed system of thought, they become convinced that they have access to the mind of God.

## For Your Consideration

How do you think this type of thinking can be broken?

One of the functions of religion is to create community—a sense of being connected with one another and, in this case, also a sense of being connected with God. To help accomplish this, religions often use rituals. Shown here are Javanese Muslim women in Surinam as they celebrate Id al Fatr at the end of Ramadan.

He died to take away my sins, that He rose from the dead and is going to return to earth, and that through Him I will receive eternal life."

That is a lot to pack into one symbol—and it is only part of what the symbol means to a fundamentalist believer. To people in other traditions of Christianity, the cross conveys somewhat different meanings—but to all Christians, the cross is a shorthand way of expressing many meanings. So it is with the Star of David, the crescent moon and star, the cow (expressing to Hindus the unity of all living things), and the various symbols of the world's many other religions.

## Rituals

**Rituals,** ceremonies or repetitive practices, are also symbols that help to unite people into a moral community. Some rituals, such as the bar mitzvah of Jewish boys and the holy communion of Christians, are designed to create in devout believers a feeling of closeness with God and unity with one another. Rituals include kneeling and praying at set times; bowing; crossing oneself; singing; lighting candles and incense; reading scripture; and following prescribed traditions at processions, baptisms, weddings, and funerals. The photo essay on pages 380–381 features annual rituals held in Spain during Holy Week.

## Beliefs

Symbols, including rituals, develop from beliefs. The belief may be vague ("God is") or highly specific ("God wants us to prostrate ourselves and face Mecca five times each day"). Religious beliefs include not only *values* (what is considered good and desirable in life—how we ought to live) but also a **cosmology,** a unified picture of the world. For example, the Jewish, Christian, and Muslim belief that there is only one God, the creator of the universe, who is concerned about the actions of humans and who will hold us accountable for what we do, is a cosmology. It presents a unifying picture of the universe.

## Religious Experience

The term **religious experience** refers to a sudden awareness of the supernatural or a feeling of coming into contact with God. Some people

Symbolic interactionists stress that a basic characteristic of humans is that they attach meaning to objects and events and then use representations of those objects or events to communicate with one another. Some religious symbols are used to communicate feelings of awe and reverence. Michaelangelo's *Pietà*, depicting Mary tenderly holding her son, Jesus, after his crucifixion, is one of the most acclaimed symbols in the Western world. It is admired for its beauty by believers and nonbelievers alike.

undergo a mild version, such as feeling closer to God when they look at a mountain, watch a sunset, or listen to a certain piece of music. Others report a life-transforming experience. St. Francis of Assisi, for example, said that he became aware of God's presence in every living thing.

Some Protestants use the term **born again** to describe people who have undergone a life-transforming religious experience. These people say that they came to the realization that they had sinned, that Jesus had died for their sins, and that God wants them to live a new life. Their worlds become transformed. They look forward to the Resurrection and to a new life in heaven, and they see relationships with spouses, parents, children, and even bosses in a new light. They also report a need to make changes in how they interact with others so that their lives reflect their new, personal commitment to Jesus as their "Savior and Lord." They describe a feeling of beginning life anew; hence the term *born again.*

# The Conflict Perspective

In general, conflict theorists are highly critical of religion. They stress that religion supports the status quo and helps to maintain social inequalities. Let's look at some of their analyses.

## Opium of the People

Karl Marx, an avowed atheist who believed that the existence of God was impossible, set the tone for conflict theorists with his most famous statement on this subject: "Religion is the sigh of the oppressed creature, the sentiment of a heartless world. . . . It is the opium of the people" (Marx 1844/1964). By this statement, Marx meant that oppressed workers find escape in religion. For them, religion is like a drug that helps them to forget their misery. By diverting their thoughts toward future happiness in an afterlife, religion takes their eyes off their suffering in this world, reducing the possibility that they will rebel against their oppressors.

## A Legitimation of Social Inequalities

Conflict theorists say that religion legitimates the social inequalities of the larger society. By this, they mean that religion teaches that the existing social arrangements of a society represent what God desires. For example, during the Middle Ages, Christian theologians decreed the *divine right of kings.* This doctrine meant that God determined who would become king and set him on the throne. The king ruled in God's place, and it was the duty of a king's

subjects to be loyal to him (and to pay their taxes). To disobey the king was to disobey God.

In what was perhaps the supreme technique of legitimating the social order (and one that went even a step farther than the *divine right of kings*), the religion of ancient Egypt held that the pharaoh himself was a god. The emperor of Japan was similarly declared divine. If this were so, who could ever question his decisions? Today's politicians would give their right arm for such a religious teaching.

Conflict theorists point to many other examples of how religion legitimates the social order. In India, Hinduism supports the caste system by teaching that an individual who tries to change caste will come back in the next life as a member of a lower caste—or even as an animal. In the decades before the American Civil War, Southern ministers used scripture to defend slavery, saying that it was God's will—while Northern ministers legitimated *their* region's social structure by using scripture to denounce slavery as evil (Ernst 1988; Nauta 1993; White 1995).

# Religion and the Spirit of Capitalism

Sociologist Max Weber disagreed with Marx that religion merely reflects and legitimates the social order. Weber had become intrigued with the origin of *capitalism.* Why, he wondered, did some societies embrace capitalism while others clung to their traditional ways? As Weber explored this puzzle, he found the answer in an unexpected place, in religion's focus on the afterlife.

To explain his conclusions, Weber wrote *The Protestant Ethic and the Spirit of Capitalism* (1904–1905/1958). He said that

1. Capitalism is not just a superficial change. Rather, capitalism represents a fundamentally different way of thinking about work and money. *Traditionally, people worked just enough to meet their basic needs, not so that they could have a surplus to invest.* To accumulate money (capital) as an end in itself, not just to spend it, was a radical departure from traditional thinking. People even came to consider it a duty to invest money so they could make profits. They reinvested these profits to make even more profits. Weber called this new approach to work and money the **spirit of capitalism.**

2. Why did the spirit of capitalism develop in Europe and not, for example, in China or India, where the people had similar material resources and education? According to Weber, *religion was the key.* The religions of China and India, and indeed Roman Catholicism

# Holy Week in Spain

**r**eligious groups develop rituals designed to evoke memories, create awe, inspire reverence, and stimulate social solidarity. One of the primary means by which groups, religious and secular, accomplish these goals is through the display of symbols.

I took these photos during Holy Week in Spain—in Malaga and Almuñecar. Throughout Spain, elaborate processions feature *tronos* that depict the biblical account of Jesus' suffering, death, and resurrection. During the processions in Malaga, the participants walk slowly for one or two minutes, then because of the weight of the *tronos*, they rest for one or two minutes. This process repeats for about six hours.

One group of participants exiting the Church of the Incarnation for Malaga's Easter procession.

Parents gave a lot of attention to their children both during the preparations and during the processions. This photo was taken during one of the recurring short breaks.

The procession in the village was more informal. This Roman soldier has an interesting way of participating—and keeping tabs—on his little daughter. The girl is distributing candy.

Bands, sometimes several of them, are part of the processions.

For the Good Friday procession, I was fortunate to be able to photograph the behind-the-scenes preparations, which are seldom seen by visitors. Shown here are finishing touches being given to the Mary figure.

During the short breaks at the night processions, children from the audience would rush to collect dripping wax to make wax balls. This was one way that the audience made themselves participants in the drama.

Beneath the costumes are townspeople and church members who know one another well. They enjoy themselves prior to the procession. This man is about ready to put on his hood.

The town square was packed with people awaiting the procession. From one corner of the square, the *trono* of Jesus was brought in. Then from another, that of Mary ("reuniting" them, as I was told). During this climactic scene the priest on the balcony on the left read a message.

These parents are giving last-minute instructions to their children, who are dressed alike. Although the processions were made up primarily of men and boys, girls and women also participated.

Some *tronos* were so heavy that they required many men to carry them. (Some required over 100 men.) This photo was taken in Malaga, on Monday of Holy Week.

in Europe, encouraged a traditional approach to life, not thrift and investment. Capitalism appeared when Protestantism came on the scene.

3. What was different about Protestantism, especially Calvinism? John Calvin taught that God had predestined some people to go to heaven and others to hell. Neither church membership nor feelings about your relationship with God could assure you that you were saved. You wouldn't know your fate until after you died.

4. This doctrine created intense anxiety among Calvin's followers: "Am I predestined to hell or to heaven?" they wondered. As Calvinists wrestled with this question, they concluded that church members have a duty to prove that they are one of God's elect and to live as though they are predestined to heaven—for good works are a demonstration of salvation.

5. This conclusion motivated Calvinists to lead moral lives *and* to work hard, to use their time productively, and to be frugal—for idleness and needless spending were signs of worldliness. Weber called this self-denying approach to life the **Protestant ethic.**

6. As people worked hard and spent money only on necessities (a pair of earrings or a second pair of dress shoes would have been defined as sinful luxuries), they had money left over. Because it couldn't be spent, this capital was invested, which led to a surge in production.

7. Weber's analysis can be summed up this way: The change in religion (from Catholicism to Protestantism, especially Calvinism) led to a fundamental change in thought and behavior (the *Protestant ethic*). The result was the *spirit of capitalism.* For this reason, capitalism originated in Europe and not in places where religion did not encourage capitalism's essential elements: the accumulation of capital and its investment and reinvestment.

At this point in history, the Protestant ethic and the spirit of capitalism are not confined to any specific religion or even to any one part of the world. Rather, they have become cultural traits that have spread to societies around the globe (Greeley 1964;

Yinger 1970). U.S. Catholics have about the same approach to life as do U.S. Protestants. In addition, Hong Kong, Japan, Malaysia, Singapore, South Korea, and Taiwan—not exactly Protestant countries—have embraced capitalism (Levy 1992). China is in the midst of doing so.

# Types of Religious Groups

Sociologists have identified four types of religious groups: cult, sect, church, and ecclesia. Why do some of these groups meet with hostility, while others are more accepted? For an explanation, look at Figure 13.6.

Let's explore what sociologists have found about these four types of religious groups. The summary that follows is a modification of analyses by sociologists Ernst Troeltsch (1931), Liston Pope (1942), and Benton Johnson (1963).

## Cult

The word *cult* conjures up bizarre images—shaven heads, weird music, brainwashing—even ritual suicide may come to mind. Cults, however, are not necessarily weird, and few practice "brainwashing" or bizarre rituals. In fact, *all religions began as cults* (Stark 1989). A **cult** is simply a new or different religion whose teachings and practices put it at odds with the dominant culture and religion. Because the term *cult* arouses such negative meanings in the public mind, however, some scholars prefer to use the term *new religion* instead.

*"We're thinking maybe it's time you started getting some religious instruction. There's Catholic, Protestant, and Jewish—any of those sound good to you?"*

For some Americans, religion is an "easy-going, makes-little-difference" matter, as expressed in this cartoon. For others, religious matters are firmly held, and followers find even slight differences of faith to be significant.

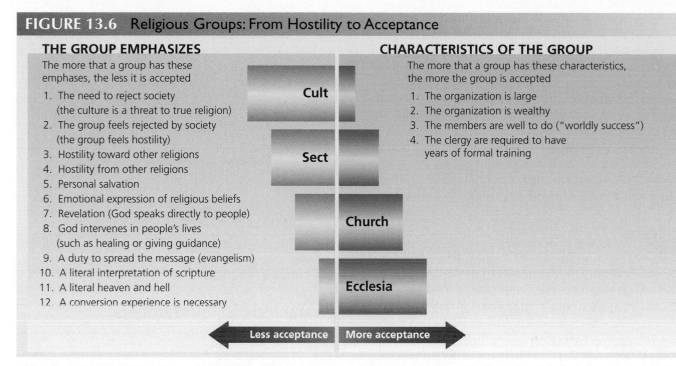

**FIGURE 13.6  Religious Groups: From Hostility to Acceptance**

**THE GROUP EMPHASIZES**

The more that a group has these emphases, the less it is accepted

1. The need to reject society (the culture is a threat to true religion)
2. The group feels rejected by society (the group feels hostility)
3. Hostility toward other religions
4. Hostility from other religions
5. Personal salvation
6. Emotional expression of religious beliefs
7. Revelation (God speaks directly to people)
8. God intervenes in people's lives (such as healing or giving guidance)
9. A duty to spread the message (evangelism)
10. A literal interpretation of scripture
11. A literal heaven and hell
12. A conversion experience is necessary

**CHARACTERISTICS OF THE GROUP**

The more that a group has these characteristics, the more the group is accepted

1. The organization is large
2. The organization is wealthy
3. The members are well to do ("worldly success")
4. The clergy are required to have years of formal training

Cult

Sect

Church

Ecclesia

← Less acceptance | More acceptance →

*Note:* Any religious organization can be placed somewhere on this continuum, based on its having "more" or "less" of these characteristics and emphases. The varying proportions of the rectangles are intended to represent the group's relative characteristics and emphases. *Source:* By the author. Based on Troeltsch 1931; Pope 1942; and Johnson 1963.

Cults often originate with a **charismatic leader,** an individual who inspires people because he or she seems to have extraordinary qualities. **Charisma** refers to an outstanding gift or to some exceptional quality. People feel drawn to both the person and the message because they find something highly appealing about the individual—in some instances, almost a magnetic charm.

The most popular religion in the world began as a cult. Its handful of followers believed that an unschooled carpenter who preached in remote villages in a backwater country was the Son of God, that he was killed and came back to life. Those beliefs made the early Christians a cult, setting them apart from the rest of their society. Persecuted by both religious and political authorities, these early believers clung to one another for support. Many cut off associations with friends who didn't accept the new message. To others, the early Christians must have seemed deluded and brainwashed.

Most cults fail. Not many people believe the new message, and the cult fades into obscurity. Some, however, succeed and make history. Over time, large numbers of people may come to accept the message and become followers of the religion. If this happens, the new religion changes from a cult to a sect.

## Sect

A **sect** is larger than a cult, but its members still feel tension between their views and the prevailing beliefs and values of the broader society. A sect may even be hostile to the society in which it is located. At the very least, its members remain uncomfortable with many of the emphases of the dominant culture; in turn, nonmembers tend to be uncomfortable with members of the sect.

If a sect grows, its members tend to gradually make peace with the rest of society. To appeal to a broader base, the sect shifts some of its doctrines, redefining matters to remove some of the rough edges that create tension between it and the rest of society. As the members become more respectable in the eyes of the society, they feel less hostility and little, if any, isolation. If a sect follows this course, as it grows and becomes more integrated into society, it changes into a church.

## Church

At this point, the religious group is highly bureaucratized—probably with national and international headquarters that give direction to the local congregations, enforce rules about who can be ordained, and control finances.

The relationship with God has grown less intense. The group is likely to have less emphasis on personal salvation and emotional expression. Worship services are likely to be more sedate, with sermons more formal and written prayers read before the congregation. Rather than being recruited from the outside by fervent, personal evangelism, most new members now come from within, from children born to existing members. Rather than joining through conversion—seeing the new truth—children may be baptized, circumcised, or dedicated in some other way. At some designated age, children may be asked to affirm the group's beliefs in a confirmation or bar mitzvah ceremony.

## Ecclesia

Finally, some groups become so well integrated into a culture, and so strongly allied with their government, that it is difficult to tell where one leaves off and the other takes over. In these *state religions,* also called **ecclesia,** the government and religion work together to try to shape society. There is no recruitment of members, for citizenship makes everyone a member. For most people in the society, the religion provides little meaning: The religion is part of a cultural identity, not an eye-opening experience. Sweden provides a good example of how extensively religion and government intertwine in an ecclesia. In the 1860s, all citizens had to memorize Luther's *Small Catechism* and be tested on it yearly (Anderson 1995). Today, Lutheranism is still associated with the state, but most Swedes come to church only for baptisms, marriages, and funerals.

## Variations in Patterns

Obviously, not all religious groups go through all these stages—from cult to sect to church to ecclesia. Some die out because they fail to attract enough members. Others, such as the Amish, remain sects. And, as is evident from the few countries that have state religions, very few religions ever become ecclesias.

In addition, these classifications are not perfectly matched in the real world. For example, although the Amish are a sect, they place little or no emphasis on recruiting others. The early Quakers, another sect, shied away from emotional expressions of their beliefs. They would quietly meditate in church, with no one speaking, until God gave someone a message to share with others. Finally, some groups that become churches may retain a few characteristics of sects, such as an emphasis on evangelism (recruiting members) or a personal relationship with God.

Although all religions began as cults, not all varieties of a particular religion begin that way. For example, some **denominations**—"brand names" within a major religion, such as Methodism or Reform Judaism—begin as splinter groups. Some members of a church disagree with *particular* aspects of the church's teachings (not its major message), and they break away to form their own organization. An example is the Southern Baptist Convention, which was formed in 1845 to defend the right to own slaves (Ernst 1988; Nauta 1993; White 1995).

# Religion in the United States

To better understand religion in U.S. society, let's first find out who belongs to religious groups and then look at the groups they belong to.

## Characteristics of Members

As you can see from Table 13.2, about 62 percent of Americans belong to a church, synagogue, or mosque. What are the characteristics of people who hold formal membership in a religion?

**Social Class**    Religion in the United States is stratified by social class. As you can see from Figure 13.7 on the next page, some religious groups are "top-heavy," and others are "bottom-heavy." The most top-heavy are Jews and Episcopalians; the most bottom-heavy are Assembly of God, Southern Baptists, and Jehovah's Witnesses. This figure provides further confirmation that churchlike groups tend to appeal to people who are more economically successful, while the more sectlike groups attract the less successful.

| TABLE 13.2 | Growth in Religious Membership |
|---|---|
| **The Percentage of Americans Who Belong to a Church or Synagogue** | |
| Year | Percentage Who Claim Membership |
| 1776 | 17% |
| 1860 | 37% |
| 1890 | 45% |
| 1926 | 58% |
| 1975 | 71% |
| 2000 | 68% |
| 2007 | 62% |

*Note:* The sources do not contain data on mosque membership.
*Sources:* Finke and Starke 1992; *Statistical Abstract* 2002: Table 64. Gallup Poll 2007.

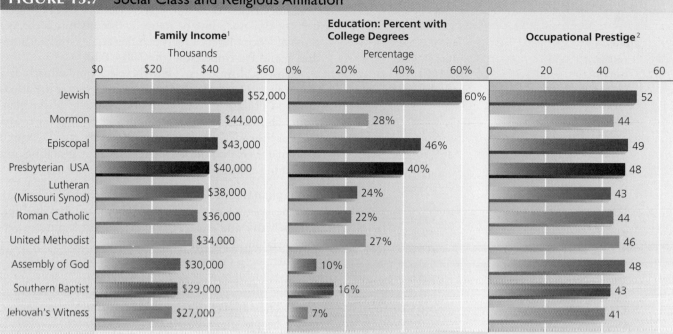

**FIGURE 13.7   Social Class and Religious Affiliation**

| | Family Income[1] (Thousands) | Education: Percent with College Degrees (Percentage) | Occupational Prestige[2] |
|---|---|---|---|
| Jewish | $52,000 | 60% | 52 |
| Mormon | $44,000 | 28% | 44 |
| Episcopal | $43,000 | 46% | 49 |
| Presbyterian USA | $40,000 | 40% | 48 |
| Lutheran (Missouri Synod) | $38,000 | 24% | 43 |
| Roman Catholic | $36,000 | 22% | 44 |
| United Methodist | $34,000 | 27% | 46 |
| Assembly of God | $30,000 | 10% | 48 |
| Southern Baptist | $29,000 | 16% | 43 |
| Jehovah's Witness | $27,000 | 7% | 41 |

[1] Since the income data were reported, inflation has run approximately 24 percent.

[2] Higher numbers mean that more of the group's members work at occupations that have higher prestige, generally those that require more education and pay more. For more information on occupational prestige, see Table 8.2 on page 203.

*Source:* By the author. Based on Smith and Faris 2005.

From this figure, you can see how *status consistency* (a concept we reviewed in Chapter 4) applies to religious groups. If a group ranks high (or low) on education, it is also likely to rank high (or low) on income and occupational prestige. Jews, for example, rank the highest on education, income, and occupational prestige, while Jehovah's Witnesses rank the lowest on these three measures of social class. As you can see, the Mormons are status inconsistent. They rank second in income, fourth in education, and tie for sixth in occupational prestige. Even more status inconsistent is the Assembly of God. Their members tie for third in occupational prestige but rank only eighth in income and ninth in education. This inconsistency is so jarring that there could be a problem with the sample.

**Race–Ethnicity**   All major religious groups draw from the nation's many racial–ethnic groups. Like social class, however, race–ethnicity tends to cluster. People of Irish descent are likely to be Roman Catholics; those with Greek ancestors are likely to belong to the Greek Orthodox Church. African Americans are likely to be Protestants—more specifically, Baptists—or to belong to fundamentalist sects.

Although many churches are integrated, it is with good reason that Sunday morning between 10 and 11 A.M. has been called "the most segregated hour in the United States." African Americans tend to belong to African American churches, while most whites see only whites in theirs. The segregation of churches is based on custom, not on law.

## Characteristics of Religious Groups

Let's examine features of the religious groups in the United States.

**Diversity**   With its 300,000 congregations and hundreds of denominations, no religious group even comes close to being a dominant religion in the United States (*Statistical Abstract* 2007:Tables 73, 74). Table 13.3 on the next page illustrates some of this remarkable diversity.

**Competition and Recruitment**   The many religious groups of the United States compete for clients. They even

## TABLE 13.3    How U.S. Adults Identify with Religion[1]

| | |
|---|---|
| **Christian** | 160,000,000 |
| Protestant | 108,000,000 |
| Baptist | 34,000,000 |
| No denomination | 21,300,000 |
| Methodist | 14,000,000 |
| Lutheran | 9,600,000 |
| Pentecostal | 7,600,000 |
| Presbyterian | 5,600,000 |
| Churches of Christ | 4,000,000 |
| Episcopalian/Anglican | 3,500,000 |
| Mormon | 2,800,000 |
| United Church of Christ | 1,400,000 |
| Jehovah's Witness | 1,300,000 |
| Evangelical Church | 1,000,000 |
| Seventh Day Adventist | 700,000 |
| Church of the Nazarene | 550,000 |
| Disciples of Christ | 500,000 |
| Reformed Churches | 500,000 |
| Church of the Brethren | 360,000 |
| Mennonite | 350,000 |
| Quakers | 200,000 |
| Other | 350,000 |
| Roman Catholic | 51,000,000 |
| Eastern Orthodox | 650,000 |
| **Other Religions** | 8,000,000 |
| Jewish | 2,800,000 |
| Islamic | 2,300,000 |
| Buddhist | 1,100,000 |
| Hindu | 800,000 |
| Unitarian/Universalist | 600,000 |
| Pagan | 150,000 |
| Wican | 150,000 |
| Native American | 100,000 |
| Spiritualist | 100,000 |
| Other and unclassified | 850,000 |
| **No Religion** | 30,000,000 |
| **Refused to answer** | 11,000,000 |

[1]All totals must be taken as approximate. Some groups ignore reporting forms. Totals are rounded to the nearest 100,000.
*Sources: Muslim Americans* 2007 (for Muslim total); *Statistical Abstract* 2000: Table 74; 2007: Table 73.

advertise in the Yellow Pages of the telephone directory and insert appealing advertising—under the guise of news—in the religion section of the Saturday or Sunday edition of the local newspapers.

**The Electronic Church**    What began as a ministry to shut-ins and those who do not belong to a church blos-

somed into its own type of church. Its preachers, called "televangelists," reach millions of viewers and raise millions of dollars. Some of its most famous ministries are those of Joyce Meyer, Robert Schuller (the "Crystal Cathedral"), and Pat Robertson (the 700 Club).

Many local ministers view the electronic church as a competitor. They complain that it competes for the attention and dollars of their members. Leaders of the electronic church reply that the money goes to good causes and that through its conversions, the electronic church feeds members into the local churches, strengthening, not weakening them.

**Fundamentalist Revival**    The fundamentalist Christian churches are undergoing a revival. They teach that the Bible is literally true and that salvation comes only through a personal relationship with Jesus Christ. They also denounce what they see as the degeneration of U.S. culture: flagrant sex on television, in movies, and in videos; abortion; corruption in public office; premarital sex and cohabitation; and drug abuse. Their answer to these problems is firm, simple, and direct: People whose hearts are changed through religious conversion will change their lives. The mainstream churches, which offer a more remote God and less emotional involvement, fail to meet the basic religious needs of large numbers of Americans. For an example, see the Cultural Diversity in the United States box on the next page.

## Secularization and the Splintering of U.S. Churches

As the model, fashionably slender, paused before the head table of African American community leaders, her gold necklace glimmering above the low-cut bodice of her emerald-green dress, the hostess, a member of the Church of God in Christ, said, "It's now OK to wear more revealing clothes—as long as it's done in good taste." Then she added, "You couldn't do this when I was a girl, but now it's OK—and you can still worship God." (Author's files)

When I heard these words, I grabbed a napkin and quickly jotted them down, my sociological imagination stirred by their deep implication. As strange as it may seem, this simple event pinpoints the essence of why the Christian churches in the United States have splintered. Let's see how this could possibly be.

The simplest explanation for why Christians don't have just one church, or at most several, instead of the hundreds of sects and denominations that dot the U.S. landscape, is disagreements about doctrine (church teaching).

# Cultural Diversity in the United States

## The New Face of Religion: Pentecostals and the Spanish-Speaking Immigrants

That millions of immigrants from Spanish-speaking countries have become part of the U.S. social scene is not news. That most of them are poor isn't news, either. Almost all the immigrants who came before them were poor, too.

What is news is that many of these Latinos are abandoning the Roman Catholic religion and are embracing a form of Protestantism called Pentecostalism. Pentecostals, often referred to by the derisive term *holy rollers*, take the Bible literally. They believe there is a real heaven and hell. They lay hands on each other and pray for healings. They expect God to act in their lives in a personal way. They speak in tongues.

And they are noisily joyful about their faith.

Go into one of their storefront churches, such as those on Amsterdam Avenue in New York City—or in any of the thousands of little churches that have sprung up around the country. You'll hear music and clapping. The preachers talk about a God who is concerned about the troubles people are going through. They warn the congregation, too, about the dangers of sin—the adultery that seductively beckons; the downfall of drugs and alcohol; the dead end of laziness and extravagance. They also extol the values of thrift and hard work. As the preacher preaches, the congregation breaks out into "Amens." "Amen, brother! Bring it on!" will shout one person, while another says, "Amen, sister. Tell it like it is!"

The preachers know what they are talking about. They work at factory jobs during the day. They know what it is to sweat for a living and that J-O-B is really spelled B-R-O-K-E. Cantankerous bosses, unpaid bills, and paychecks that run out before the month does are part of their own lives.

*Religion often helps immigrants adapt to their new culture. What indications of this do you see in this photo?*

As people clap and sway to the sounds of the drums and guitars—like salsa music with religious lyrics—some pray silently in tongues. Others shout out the strange sounds. Some tongues, they believe, are messages straight from God. But no one can understand them unless someone else is given the interpretation. When this happens, people listen intently for what God has to say to them personally.

The worshippers don't come just for an hour on Sunday mornings. They come night after night, finding comfort in community and encouragement In the message and music. They can also give expression to their emotions among a like-minded people.

Pentecostalism is the fastest-growing religion in the United States, and there are perhaps 400 million Pentecostals worldwide. This religion is also being welcomed by some among the middle class and the educated, but the middle-class arms aren't open as wide. The appeal is mainly to the poor. When the poor make the transition to the middle class—as their religion, with its emphasis on work and thrift will help them do—they are likely to seek new forms of religious expression.

When this happens, we can expect that Pentecostalism will also adapt, that the form will remain recognizable, but the fervor will be lost. For now, though, it is the fervor—the intensity that connects the individuals to God and to one another—that is the driving force of this religion. The Pentecostals would phrase this a little differently. They would say that the fervor is merely the expression of the driving force of their religion, which is the Holy Spirit.

Either way you put it, these people are on fire. And that fire is burning a new imprint on the face of religion.

## For Your Consideration

Why do you think the Pentecostals are growing so fast? What effect do you think they might have on mainstream Christianity?

As theologian and sociologist Richard Niebuhr pointed out, however, there are many ways of settling doctrinal disputes besides splintering off and forming other religious organizations. Niebuhr (1929) suggested that the answer lies more in *social* change than it does in *religious* conflict.

The explanation goes like this. As was noted earlier, when a sect becomes more churchlike, tension lessens between it and the mainstream culture. Quite likely, when a sect is first established, its founders and first members are poor, or at least not very successful in worldly pursuits. Feeling like strangers in the dominant culture, they derive a good part of their identity from their religion. In their church services and lifestyle, they stress how different their values are from those of the dominant culture. They are also likely to emphasize the joys of the coming afterlife, when they will be able to escape from their present pain.

As time passes, the group's values—such as frugality and the avoidance of gambling, alcohol, and drugs—help the members become successful. As their children attain more education and become more middle class, members of this group grow more respectable in the eyes of society. They no longer experience the alienation that was felt by the founders of their group. Life's burdens don't seem as heavy, and the need for relief through an afterlife becomes less pressing. Similarly, the pleasures of the world no longer appear as threatening to the "truth." As is illustrated by the woman at the fashion show, people then attempt to harmonize their religious beliefs with their changing ideas about the culture.

This process is called the **secularization of religion**—shifting the focus from spiritual matters to the affairs of this world. Anyone familiar with today's mainstream Methodists would be surprised to know that they once were a sect. Methodists used to ban playing cards, dancing, and going to movies. They even considered circuses to be sinful. As Methodists grew more middle class, however, they began to change their views on sin. They started to dismantle the barriers that they had constructed between themselves and the outside world (Finke and Stark 1992).

Secularization leads to a splintering of the group. Adjusting to the secular culture displeases some of the group's members, especially those who have had less worldly success. These people still feel a gulf between themselves and the broader culture. For them, tension and hostility continue to be real. They see secularization as deserting the group's fundamental truths, a "selling out" to the secular world.

After futile attempts to bring the group back to its senses, the group splinters. Those who protested the secularization of Methodism, for example, were kicked out— even though *they* represented the values around which the group had organized in the first place. The dissatisfied— who have come to be viewed as complainers—then form a sect that once again stresses its differences from the world; the need for more personal, emotional religious experiences; and salvation from the pain of living in this world. As time passes, the cycle repeats: adjustment to the dominant culture by some, continued dissatisfaction by others, and further splintering.

This process is not limited to sects, but also occurs in churches. When U.S. Episcopalians elected an openly gay bishop in 2003, some pastors and congregations splintered from the U.S. church and affiliated with the more conservative African archbishops. In an ironic twist, this made them mission congregations from Africa. Sociologists have not yet compared the income or wealth of those who stayed with the group that elected the gay bishop and those who joined the splinter groups. If such a study is done and it turns out that there is no difference, we will have to modify the secularization thesis.

# The Future of Religion

Religion thrives in the most advanced scientific nations— and, as officials of Soviet Russia were disheartened to learn—in even the most ideologically hostile climate. Humans are inquiring creatures. As they reflect on life, they ask: What is the purpose of it all? Why are we born? Is there an afterlife? If so, where are we going? Out of these concerns arises this question: If there is a God, what does God want of us in this life? Does God have a preference about how we should live?

Science, including sociology, cannot answer such questions. By its very nature, science cannot tell us about four main concerns that many people have:

1. *The existence of God.* About this, science has nothing to say. No test tube has either isolated God or refuted God's existence.
2. *The purpose of life.* Although science can provide a definition of life and describe the characteristics of

living organisms, it has nothing to say about ultimate purpose.

3. *An afterlife.* Science can offer no information on this at all, for it has no tests to prove or disprove a "hereafter."

4. *Morality.* Science can demonstrate the consequences of behavior, but not the moral superiority of one action compared with another. This means that science cannot even prove that loving your family and neighbor is superior to hurting and killing them. Science can describe death and measure consequences, but it cannot determine the moral superiority of any action, even in such an extreme example.

There is no doubt that religion will last as long as humanity lasts, for what could replace it? And if something did, and answered such questions, would it not be religion under a different name?

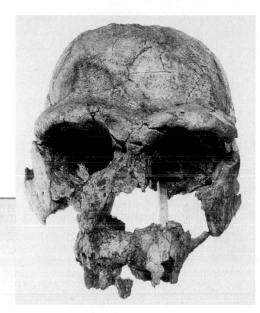

A basic principle of symbolic interactionism is that meaning is not inherent in an object or event, but is determined by people as they interpret the object or event. Old bones and fossils are an excellent illustration of this principle. Does this skull of *Homo erectus* "prove" evolution? Does it "disprove" creation? Such "proof" and "disproof" lie in the eye of the beholder, based on the background assumptions by which it is interpreted.

# SUMMARY *and* REVIEW

## Education in Global Perspective

*What is a credential society, and how did it develop?*

A **credential society** is one in which employers use diplomas and degrees to determine who is eligible for a job. One reason that credentialism developed is that large, anonymous societies lack the personal knowledge common to smaller groups. Educational certification is taken as evidence of a person's ability. P. 360.

*How does education compare among the Most Industrialized, Industrializing, and Least Industrialized Nations?*

In general, formal education reflects a nation's economy. Consequently, education is extensive in the Most Industrialized Nations, undergoing vast change in the Industrializing Nations, and spotty in the Least Industrialized Nations.

Japan, Russia, and Egypt provide examples of education in countries at three levels of industrialization. Pp. 363–364.

## The Functionalist Perspective: Providing Social Benefits

*What is the functionalist perspective on education?*

Among the functions of education are the teaching of knowledge and skills, **cultural transmission of values,** social integration, **gatekeeping,** and **mainstreaming.** Functionalists also note that education has replaced some traditional family functions. Pp. 364–367.

## The Conflict Perspective: Perpetuating Social Inequality

*What is the conflict perspective on education?*

The basic view of conflict theorists is that *education reproduces the social class structure;* that is, through such mechanisms as the **hidden curriculum** and the unequal funding of schools, education perpetuates a society's basic social inequalities from one generation to the next. Pp. 368–369.

## The Symbolic Interactionist Perspective: Teacher Expectations

*What is the symbolic interactionist perspective on education?*

Symbolic interactionists focus on face-to-face interaction. In examining what occurs in the classroom, they have found that student performance tends to conform to teacher and peer expectations, whether they are high or low. Pp. 369–371.

## Problems in U.S. Education— and Their Solutions

*What are the chief problems that face U.S. education?*

In addition to violence, the major problems are low achievement as shown by SAT scores and international comparisons, **grade inflation, social promotion,** and **functional illiteracy.** Pp. 371–372.

*What are the potential solutions to these problems?*

The primary solution is to restore high educational standards, which can be done only after providing basic security for students. Any solution for improving quality must be based on expecting more of *both* students and teachers. Pp. 372–374.

## What Is Religion?

Durkheim identified three essential characteristics of religion: beliefs that set the **sacred** apart from the **profane, rituals,** and a moral community (a **church**). Pp. 374–375.

## The Functionalist Perspective

*What are the functions and dysfunctions of religion?*

Among the functions of religion are answering questions about ultimate meaning, providing emotional comfort, social solidarity, guidelines for everyday life, social control, and fostering social change. Among the dysfunctions of religion are religious persecution and war and terrorism. Pp. 375–376.

## The Symbolic Interactionist Perspective

*What aspects of religion do symbolic interactionists study?*

Symbolic interactionists focus on the meanings of religion for its followers. They examine religious symbols, **rituals,** beliefs, and **religious experiences.** Pp. 376–379.

## The Conflict Perspective

*What aspects of religion do conflict theorists study?*

Conflict theorists examine the relationship of religion to social inequalities, especially how religion reinforces a society's stratification system. P. 379.

## Religion and the Spirit of Capitalism

*What does the spirit of capitalism have to do with religion?*

Max Weber saw religion as a primary source of social change. He analyzed how Protestantism gave rise to the **Protestant ethic,** which stimulated what he called the **spirit of capitalism.** The result was capitalism, which transformed society. Pp. 379–382.

## Types of Religious Groups

*What types of religious groups are there?*

Sociologists divide religious groups into cults, sects, churches, and ecclesias. All religions began as **cults.** Those that survive tend to develop into **sects** and eventually into **churches. Ecclesias,** or state religions, are rare. Pp. 382–384.

## Religion in the United States

*What are the main characteristics of religion in the United States?*

Membership varies by social class and race–ethnicity. Major characteristics of religious groups are diversity, competition, the electronic church, and a fundamentalist revival. Pp. 384–386.

*What is the connection between secularization of religion and the splintering of churches?*

**Secularization of religion,** a change in a religion's focus from spiritual matters to concerns of "this world," is the key to understanding why churches divide. Basically, as a cult or sect changes to accommodate its members' upward social class mobility, it changes into a church. Left dissatisfied are members who are not upwardly mobile. They tend to splinter off and form a new cult or sect, and the cycle repeats itself. Pp. 386–388.

## The Future of Religion

*What is the future of religion?*

Because science cannot answer questions about ultimate meaning, the existence of God, or an afterlife—nor provide guidelines for morality—the need for religion will remain. In any foreseeable future, religion will prosper. Pp. 388–389.

# THINKING CRITICALLY *about* Chapter 13

1. How have your experiences in education (including teachers and assignments) influenced your goals, attitudes, and values? How have your classmates influenced you? Be specific.

2. How do you think that U.S. schools can be improved?

3. Since 9/11, many people have wondered how anyone can use religion to defend or promote terrorism. How does the Down-to-Earth Sociology box on terrorism and the mind of God on page 377 help to answer this question? How do the analyses of group-think in Chapter 5 (pages 136–137) and dehumanization in Chapter 11 (pages 308–311) fit into your analysis?

# BY THE NUMBERS: Changes Over Time

- Percentage of U.S. population that were college graduates in 1960: 8%
- Percentage of U.S. population that are college graduates today: 30%

- National average verbal scores on SATs in 1967: 543
- National average verbal scores on SATs today: 503

- National average math scores on SATs in 1967: 516
- National average math scores on SATs today: 518

- Percentage of Americans claiming membership in a church or synagogue in 1890: 45%
- Percentage of Americans claiming membership in a church or synagogue today: 65%

- Number of violent deaths of students at school, K–12, in 1992: 56
- Number of violent deaths of students at school, K–12, today: 19

# ADDITIONAL RESOURCES

## What can you find in MySocLab?  mysoclab  www.mysoclab.com

- **Complete Ebook**
- **Practice Tests and Video and Audio activities**
- **Mapping and Data Analysis exercises**
- **Sociology in the News**
- **Classic Readings in Sociology**
- **Research and Writing advice**

## Where Can I Read More on This Topic?

Suggested readings for this chapter are listed at the back of this book.

# Population
# and Urbanization

The image still haunts me. There stood Celia, age 30, her distended stomach visible proof that her thirteenth child was on its way. Her oldest was only 14 years old! A mere boy by our standards, he had already gone as far in school as he ever would. Each morning, he joined the men to work in the fields. Each evening around twilight, I saw him return home, exhausted from hard labor in the subtropical sun.

**There stood Celia, age 30, her distended stomach visible proof that her thirteenth child was on its way.**

I was living in Colima, Mexico, and Celia and Angel had invited me for dinner. Their home clearly reflected the family's poverty. A thatched hut consisting of only a single room served as home for all fourteen members of the family. At night, the parents and younger children crowded into a double bed, while the eldest boy slept in a hammock. As in many homes in the village, the other children slept on mats spread on the dirt floor—despite the crawling scorpions.

The home was meagerly furnished. It had only a gas stove, a table, and a cabinet where Celia stored her few cooking utensils and clay dishes. There were no closets; clothes hung on pegs in the walls. There also were no chairs, not even one. I was used to the poverty in the village, but this really startled me. The family was too poor to afford even a single chair.

Celia beamed as she told me how much she looked forward to the birth of her next child. Could she really mean it? It was hard to imagine that any woman would want to be in her situation.

Yet Celia meant every word. She was as full of delighted anticipation as she had been with her first child—and with all the others in between.

How could Celia have wanted so many children—especially when she lived in such poverty? That question bothered me. I couldn't let it go until I understood why.

This chapter helps to provide an answer.

# POPULATION IN GLOBAL PERSPECTIVE

Celia's story takes us into the heart of **demography,** the study of the size, composition, growth, and distribution of human populations. It brings us face to face with the question of whether we are doomed to live in a world so filled with people that there will be very little space for anybody. Will our planet be able to support its growing population? Or are chronic famine and mass starvation the sorry fate of most earthlings?

Let's look at how concern about population growth began.

## A Planet with No Space for Enjoying Life?

The story begins with the lowly potato. When the Spanish *conquistadores* found that people in the Andes Mountains ate this vegetable, which was unknown in Europe, they brought some home to cultivate. At first, Europeans viewed the potato with suspicion, but gradually it became the main food of the lower classes. With a greater abundance of food, fertility increased, and the death rate dropped. Europe's population soared, almost doubling during the 1700s (McKeown 1977; McNeill 1999).

Thomas Malthus (1766–1834), an English economist, saw this surging growth as a sign of doom. In 1798, he wrote a book that became world famous, *An Essay on the Principle of Population* (1798). In it, Malthus proposed what became known as the **Malthus theorem.** He argued that although population grows geometrically (from 2 to 4 to 8 to 16 and so forth), the food supply increases only arithmetically (from 1 to 2 to 3 to 4 and so on). This meant, he claimed, that if births go unchecked, the population of a country, or even of the world, will outstrip its food supply.

### The New Malthusians

Was Malthus right? This question has become a matter of heated debate among demographers. One group, which can be called the *New Malthusians,* is convinced that today's situation is at least as grim as—if not grimmer than—Malthus ever imagined. For example, *the world's population is growing so fast that in just the time it takes you to read this chapter, another 20,000 to 40,000 babies will be born!* By this time tomorrow, the earth will have over 200,000 more people to feed. This increase goes on hour after hour, day after day, without letup. For an illustration of this growth, see Figure 14.1.

The New Malthusians point out that the world's population is following an **exponential growth curve.** This means

In earlier generations, large farm families were common. Having many children was functional—there were many hands to help with crops, food production, and food preparation. As the country industrialized and urbanized, this changed to a dysfunction—children became expensive and nonproducing. Consequently, the size of families shrank as we entered Stage 3 of the demographic transition. In 1939, when this photo was taken in McIntosh County, Oklahoma, many farm families had more children than the number shown here.

## FIGURE 14.1    How Fast Is the World's Population Growing?

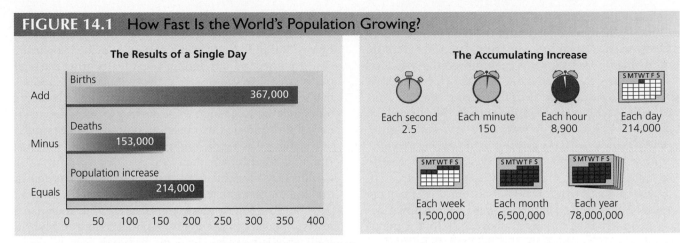

### The Results of a Single Day

Add — Births — 367,000

Minus — Deaths — 153,000

Equals — Population increase — 214,000

(scale: 0  50  100  150  200  250  300  350  400)

### The Accumulating Increase

Each second — 2.5

Each minute — 150

Each hour — 8,900

Each day — 214,000

Each week — 1,500,000

Each month — 6,500,000

Each year — 78,000,000

*Source:* By the author. Based on Haub 2002, 2005, 2006; McFalls 2007.

that if growth doubles during approximately equal intervals of time, it suddenly accelerates. To illustrate the far-reaching implications of exponential growth, sociologist William Faunce (1981) retold an old parable about a poor man who saved a rich man's life. The rich man was grateful and said that he wanted to reward the man for his heroic deed.

The man replied that he would like his reward to be spread out over a four-week period, with each day's amount being twice what he received on the preceding day. He also said he would be happy to receive only one penny on the first day. The rich man immediately handed over the penny and congratulated himself on how cheaply he had gotten by.

At the end of the first week, the rich man checked to see how much he owed and was pleased to find that the total was only $1.27. By the end of the second week he owed only $163.83. On the twenty-first day, however, the rich man was surprised to find that the total had grown to $20,971.51. When the twenty-eighth day arrived the rich man was shocked to discover that he owed $1,342,177.28 for that day alone and that the total reward had jumped to $2,684,354.56!

This is precisely what alarms the New Malthusians. They claim that humanity has just entered the "fourth week" of an exponential growth curve. Figure 14.2 shows why they think the day of reckoning is just around the corner. It took from the beginning of time until 1800 for the world's population to reach its first billion. It then took only 130 years (1930) to add the second billion. Just 30 years later (1960), the world population hit 3 billion. The time it took to reach the fourth billion was cut in half, to only 15 years (1975).

## FIGURE 14.2    World Population Growth over 2,000 Years

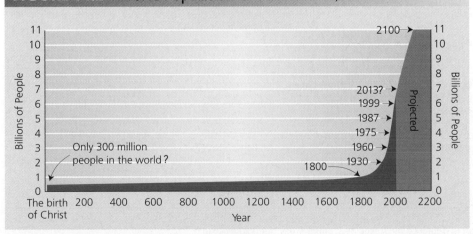

Only 300 million people in the world?

2100
2013?
1999 →
1987 →
1975 →
1960 →
1930 →
1800

Projected

(y-axis: Billions of People, 0–11; x-axis: The birth of Christ, 200, 400, 600, 800, 1000, 1200, 1400, 1600, 1800, 2000, 2200; Year)

*Source:* Modified from Piotrow 1973; McFalls 2007.

Then just 12 years later (in 1987), the total reached 5 billion, and in another 12 years it hit 6 billion (in 1999).

On average, every minute of every day, 150 babies are born. As Figure 14.1 shows, at each sunset, the world has 214,000 more people than it did the day before. In a year, this comes to 78 million people. During the next four years, this increase will total more than the entire U.S. population. Think of it this way: *In just the next 12 years, the world will add as many people as it did during the entire time from when the first humans began to walk the earth until the year 1800.*

These totals terrify the New Malthusians. They are convinced that we are headed toward a showdown between population and food. In the year 2025, the population of just India, Pakistan, and Bangladesh is expected to be more than the entire world's population was 100 years ago (Haub 2006). It is obvious that we will run out of food if we don't curtail population growth. Soon we are going to see more pitiful, starving Pakistani and Bangladeshi children on television.

## The Anti-Malthusians

All of this seems obvious, and no one wants to live shoulder-to-shoulder and fight for scraps. How, then, can anyone argue with the New Malthusians?

An optimistic group of demographers, whom we can call the *Anti-Malthusians,* paint a far different picture. They believe that Europe's **demographic transition** provides a more accurate glimpse into the future. This transition is diagrammed in Figure 14.3. During most of its history, Europe was in Stage 1. Its population remained about the same from year to year, for high death rates offset the high birth rates. Then came Stage 2, the "population explosion" that so upset Malthus. Europe's population surged because birth rates remained high while death rates went down. Finally, Europe made the transition to Stage 3: The population stabilized as people brought their birth rates into line with their lower death rates.

This, say the Anti-Malthusians, will also happen in the Least Industrialized Nations. Their current surge in population growth simply indicates that they have reached Stage 2 of the demographic transition. Hybrid seeds, medicine from the Most Industrialized Nations, and purer public drinking water have cut their death rates, but their birth rates remain high. When they move into Stage 3, as surely they will, we will wonder what all the fuss was about. In fact, their growth is already slowing.

## Who Is Correct?

As you can see, both the New Malthusians and the Anti-Malthusians have looked at historical trends and projected them onto the future. The New Malthusians project continued world growth and are alarmed. The Anti-Malthusians project Stage 3 of the demographic transition onto the Least Industrialized Nations and are reassured.

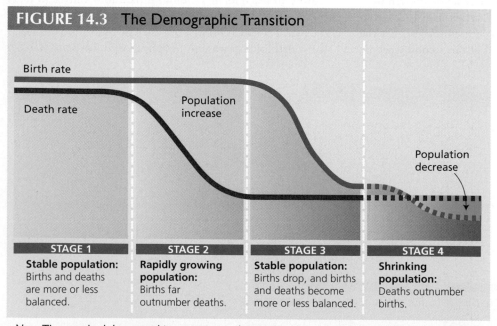

**FIGURE 14.3** The Demographic Transition

| STAGE 1 | STAGE 2 | STAGE 3 | STAGE 4 |
|---|---|---|---|
| **Stable population:** Births and deaths are more or less balanced. | **Rapidly growing population:** Births far outnumber deaths. | **Stable population:** Births drop, and births and deaths become more or less balanced. | **Shrinking population:** Deaths outnumber births. |

*Note:* The standard demographic transition is depicted by Stages 1–3. Stage 4 has been suggested by some Anti-Malthusians.

There is no question that the Least Industrialized Nations are in Stage 2 of the demographic transition. The question is, Will these nations enter Stage 3? After World War II, the West exported its hybrid seeds, herbicides, and techniques of public hygiene around the globe. Death rates plummeted in the Least Industrialized Nations as their food supply increased and health improved. Because their birth rates stayed high, their populations mushroomed. Just as Malthus had done 200 years earlier, demographers predicted worldwide catastrophe if something were not done immediately to halt the population explosion (Ehrlich and Ehrlich 1972, 1978).

We can use the conflict perspective to understand what happened when this message reached the leaders of the industrialized world. They saw the mushrooming populations of the Least Industrialized Nations as a threat to the global balance of power they had so carefully worked out. With swollen populations, the poorer countries might demand a larger share of the earth's resources. The leaders found the United Nations to be a willing tool, and they used it to spearhead efforts to reduce world population growth. The results have been remarkable. The annual growth of the Least Industrialized Nations has dropped 29 percent, from an average of 2.1 percent a year in the 1960s to 1.5 percent today (Haub and Yinger 1994; Haub 2006).

The New Malthusians and Anti-Malthusians have greeted this news with significantly different interpretations. For the Anti-Malthusians, this slowing of growth is the signal they had been waiting for: Stage 3 of the demographic transition has begun. First, the death rate in the Least Industrialized Nations fell—now, just as they predicted, birth rates are also falling. Did you notice, they would say, if they looked at Figure 14.2, that it took 12 years to add the fifth billion to the world's population—and also 12 years to add

the sixth billion? Population momentum is slowing. The New Malthusians reply that a slower growth rate still spells catastrophe—it just will take longer for it to hit.

The Anti-Malthusians also argue that our future will be the opposite of what the New Malthusians worry about: There are going to be too few children in the world, not too many. The world's problem will not be a population explosion, but **population shrinkage**—populations getting smaller. They point out that births in sixty-five countries have already dropped so low that those countries no longer produce enough children to maintain their populations. *All* of the forty-two countries in Europe fill more coffins than cradles (Haub 2006).

Some Anti-Malthusians even predict a "demographic free fall" (Mosher 1997). As more nations enter Stage 4 of the demographic transition, the world's population will peak at about 8 or 9 billion, then begin to grow smaller. Two hundred years from now, they say, we will have a lot fewer people on earth.

Who is right? It simply is too early to tell. Like the proverbial pessimists who see the glass of water half empty, the New Malthusians interpret changes in world population growth negatively. And like the eternal optimists who see the same glass half full, the Anti-Malthusians view the figures positively. Sometime during our lifetime we should know the answer.

## Why Are People Starving?

Pictures of starving children gnaw at our conscience. We live in such abundance, while these children and their parents starve before our very eyes. Why don't they have enough food? Is it because there are too many of them or simply because the abundant food produced around the world does not reach them?

Photos of starving people, such as this mother and her child, haunt Americans and other members of the Most Industrialized Nations. Many of us wonder why, when some are starving, we should live in the midst of such abundance, often overeating and even casually scraping excess food into the garbage. We even have eating contests to see who can eat the most food in the least time. The text discusses reasons for such disparities.

The Anti-Malthusians make a point that seems irrefutable. As Figure 14.4 below shows, *there is now more food for each person in the world than there was in 1950.* Although the world's population has more than doubled since 1950, improved seeds and fertilizers have made more food available for *each* person on earth. Even more food may be on the way, for bioengineers are making breakthroughs in agriculture. The United Nations estimates that even without agricultural gains through bioengineering, there will be ample food to keep up with the world's growing population for at least the next thirty years (United Nations 2000).

Then why do people die of hunger? From Figure 14.4, we can conclude that starvation occurs not because the earth produces too little food, but because particular places lack food. Droughts and wars are the main reasons. Just as droughts slow or stop food production, so does war. In nations ravaged by civil war, opposing sides either confiscate or burn crops, and farmers flee to the cities (Thurow 2005). While some countries have their food supply disrupted, others are producing more food than their people can consume. At the same time that countries of Africa are hit by drought and civil wars—and people are starving—the U.S. government pays farmers to *reduce* their output of crops. The United States' problem is too much food; West Africa's is too little.

The New Malthusians counter with the argument that the world's population is still growing and that we do not know how long the earth will continue to produce enough food. They add that the recent policy of turning food (such as corn and sugar cane) into biofuels (such as gasoline and diesel fuel) presents another serious threat to the world's food supply. They also remind us of the penny doubling each day. It is only a matter of time, they insist, until the earth no longer produces enough food—not "if," but "when."

Both the New Malthusians and the Anti-Malthusians have contributed significant ideas, but theories will not eliminate famines. Starving children are going to continue to peer out at us from our televisions and magazines, their tiny, shriveled bodies and bloated stomachs nagging at our conscience and imploring us to do something. Regardless of the underlying causes of this human misery, it has a simple solution: Food can be transferred from nations that have a surplus.

These pictures of starving Africans leave the impression that Africa is overpopulated. Why else would all those people be starving? The truth, however, is far different. Africa has 23 percent of the earth's land, but only 14 percent of the earth's population (Haub 2006). Africa even has vast areas of fertile land that have not yet been farmed. The reason for famines in Africa, then, *cannot* be too many people living on too little land.

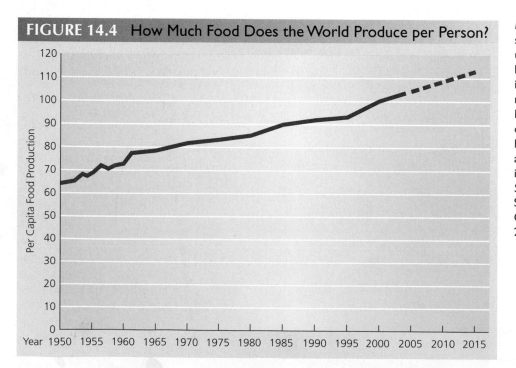

**FIGURE 14.4    How Much Food Does the World Produce per Person?**

*Note:* Julian Simon provided the stimulus for producing this figure. I used to reproduce a figure that he had developed, but since his death in 1998 inconsistencies in data have made it difficult to update his work. Based on UN data, this figure overcomes that limitation. Production per person is the amount produced for each individual in the entire world.
*Source:* By the author. Based on Simon 1981; Food and Agriculture Organization of the United Nations 2006.

# Population Growth

Even if starvation is the result of a maldistribution of food rather than overpopulation, the fact remains that the Least Industrialized Nations are growing *fifteen times faster* than the Most Industrialized Nations—1.5 percent a year compared with 0.1 percent (Haub 2006). At these rates, it will take 1,000 years for the average Most Industrialized Nation to double its population, but just 48 years for the average Least Industrialized Nation to do so. Figure 14.5 puts the matter in stark perspective. So does the Down-to-Earth Sociology box on the next page. Why do the nations that can least afford it have so many children?

## Why the Least Industrialized Nations Have So Many Children

Why do people in the countries that can least afford it have so many children? To understand this, let's figure out why Celia is so happy about having her thirteenth child. Here, we need to apply the symbolic interactionist perspective. We must take the role of the other so that we can understand the world of Celia and Angel as *they* see it. As our culture does for us, their culture provides a perspective on life that guides their choices. Celia and Angel's culture tells them that twelve children are *not* enough, that they ought to have a thirteenth—as well as a fourteenth and fifteenth. How can this be? Let's consider three reasons why bearing many children plays a central role in their lives—and in the lives of millions upon millions of poor people around the world.

First is the status of parenthood. In the Least Industrialized Nations, motherhood is the most prized status a woman can achieve. The more children a woman bears, the more she is thought to have achieved the purpose for which she was born. Similarly, a man proves his manhood by fathering children. The more children he fathers, especially sons, the better—for through them his name lives on.

Second, the community supports this view. Celia and those like her live in *Gemeinschaft* communities, where people identify closely with one another and share similar views of life. To them, children are a sign of God's blessing. By producing children, people reflect the values of their community, achieve status, and are assured that they are blessed by God. It is the barren woman, not the woman with a dozen children, who is to be pitied.

These factors certainly provide strong motivations for bearing many children. Yet there is a third powerful

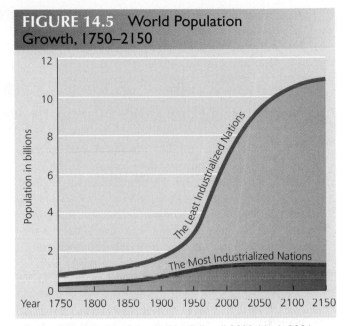

**FIGURE 14.5** World Population Growth, 1750–2150

*Source:* "The World of the Child 6 Billion," 2000; Haub 2006.

incentive: For poor people in the Least Industrialized Nations, children are economic assets. Like Celia and Angel's eldest son, children begin contributing to the family income at a young age. (See Figure 14.6 on page 401.) But even more important: Children are also the equivalent of our Social Security. In the Least Industrialized Nations, the government does not provide social security or medical and unemployment insurance. This motivates people to bear *more* children, for when parents become too old to work, or when no work is to be found, their children take care of them. The more children they have, the broader their base of support will be.

To those of us who live in the Most Industrialized Nations, it seems irrational to have many children. And *for us it would be.* Understanding life from the framework of people who are living it, however—the essence of the symbolic interactionist perspective—reveals how it makes perfect sense to have many children. Consider this report by a government worker in India:

> **Thaman Singh (a very poor man, a water carrier) . . . welcomed me inside his home, gave me a cup of tea (with milk and "market" sugar, as he proudly pointed out later), and said: "You were trying to convince me that I shouldn't have any more sons. Now, you see, I have six sons and two daughters and I sit at home in leisure. They are grown up and they bring me money. One even works outside the**

# Down-to-Earth Sociology

## How the Tsunami Can Help Us to Understand Population Growth

*This photo was snapped at Koh Raya in Thailand, just as the tsunami wave of December 26, 2004, landed.*

On December 26, 2004, the world witnessed the worst tsunami in modern history. As the giant waves rolled over the shores of unsuspecting countries, they swept away people from all walks of life—from lowly sellers of fish to wealthy tourists visiting the fleshpots of Sri Lanka. Over the next several days, as the government reports came in, the media kept increasing the death toll. When those reports were tallied two months later, the total stood at 286,000 people.

In terms of lives lost, this was not the worst single disaster the world had seen. Several hundred thousand people had been killed in China's Tangshan earthquake in 1976. In terms of geography, however, this was the broadest. It involved more countries than any other disaster in modern history. And, unlike its predecessors, this tsunami occurred during a period of instantaneous, global reporting of events.

As news of the tsunami was transmitted around the globe, the response was almost immediate. Aid poured in—in unprecedented amounts. Governments gave over $3 billion. Citizens pitched in, too, from Little Leaguers and religious groups to the "regulars" at the local bars.

I want to use the tsunami disaster to illustrate the incredible population growth that is taking place in the Least Industrialized Nations. My intention is not to dismiss the tragedy of these deaths, for they were horrible—as were the maiming of so many, the sufferings of families, and the lost livelihoods.

Let's consider Indonesia first. With 233,000 deaths, this country was hit the hardest. Indonesia had an annual growth rate of 1.6 percent (its "rate of natural increase," as demographers call it). With a population of 220 million, Indonesia is growing by 3,300,000 people each year (Haub 2004). This increase, coming to 9,041 people each day, means that it took Indonesia less than four weeks (twenty-six days) to replace the huge number of people it lost to the tsunami.

The next greatest loss of lives took place in Sri Lanka. With its lower rate of natural increase of 1.3 and its smaller population of 19 million, it took Sri Lanka a little longer to replace the 31,000 people it lost: forty-six days.

India was the third hardest hit. With India's 1 billion people and its 1.7 rate of natural increase, India is adding 17 million people to its population each year. This comes to 46,575 people each day. At an increase of 1,940 people per hour, India took just eight or nine hours to replace the 16,000 people it lost to the tsunami.

The next hardest hit was Thailand. It took Thailand four or five days to replace the 5,000 people that it lost.

For the other countries, the losses were smaller: 298 for Somalia, 82 for the Maldives; 68 for Malaysia; 61 for Myanmar, 10 for Tanzania, 2 for Bangladesh, and 1 for Kenya ("Tsunami deaths . . ." 2005).

Again, I don't want to detract from the horrifying tragedy of the 2004 tsunami. But by using this event as a comparative backdrop, we can gain a better grasp of the unprecedented population growth that is taking place in the Least Industrialized Nations.

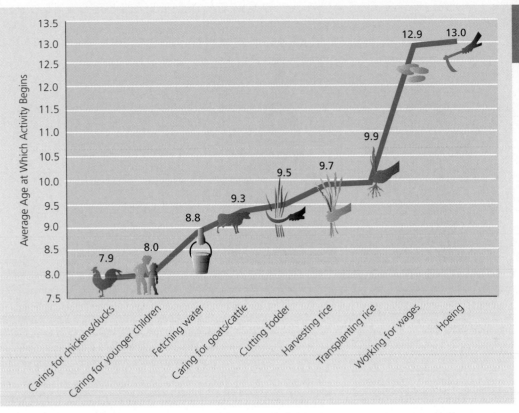

**FIGURE 14.6**
Why the Poor
Need Children

Children are an economic asset
in the Least Industrialized
Nations. Based on a survey in
Indonesia, this figure shows that
boys and girls can be net
income earners for their
families by the age of 9 or 10.

*Source:* U.N. Fund for
Population Activities.

village as a laborer. You told me I was a poor man and couldn't support a large family. Now, you see, because of my large family I am a rich man." (Mamdani 1973)

Conflict theorists offer a different view of why women in the Least Industrialized Nations bear so many children. Feminists argue that women like Celia have internalized values that support male dominance. In Latin America, *machismo*—an emphasis on male virility and dominance—is common. To father many children, especially sons, shows that a man is sexually potent, giving him higher status in the community. From a conflict perspective, then, the reason poor people have so many children is that men control women's reproductive choices.

## Implications of Different Rates of Growth

The result of Celia and Angel's desire for many children—and of the millions of Celias and Angels like them—is that Mexico's population will double in thirty-five years. In contrast, women in the United States are having so few children that if it weren't for immigration, the U.S. population would begin to shrink. To illustrate population

dynamics, demographers use **population pyramids.** These depict a country's population by age and sex. Look at Figure 14.7 on the next page, which shows the population pyramids of the United States, Mexico, and the world.

To see why population pyramids are important, I would like you to imagine a miracle. Imagine that, overnight, Mexico is transformed into a nation as industrialized as the United States. Imagine also that overnight the average number of children per woman drops to 2.0, the same as in the United States. If this happened, it would seem that Mexico's population would grow at the same rate as that of the United States, right?

But this isn't at all what would happen. Instead, the population of Mexico would continue to grow much faster. As you can see from these population pyramids, a much higher percentage of Mexican women are in their childbearing years. Even if Mexico and the United States had the same birth rate (2.0 children per woman), a larger percentage of women in Mexico would be giving birth, and Mexico's population would grow faster. As demographers like to phrase this, Mexico's *age structure* gives it greater *population momentum.*

Mexico's population momentum is so strong that, as we saw earlier, its population will double in thirty-five years.

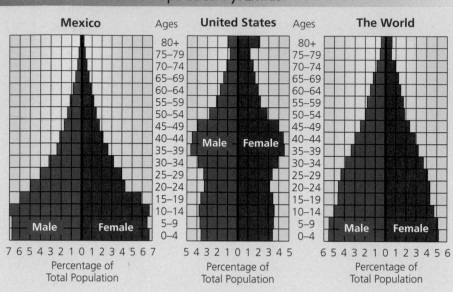

**FIGURE 14.7**    Three Population Pyramids

Source: *Population Today, 26, 9, September 1998:4, 5.*

The implications of a doubling population are mind-boggling. *Just to stay even,* within thirty-five years Mexico must double the number of available jobs and housing facilities; its food production; its transportation and communication facilities; its water, gas, sewer, and electrical systems; and its schools, hospitals, churches, civic buildings, theaters, stores, and parks. If Mexico fails to double them, its already meager standard of living will drop even further.

Conflict theorists point out that a declining standard of living poses the threat of political instability—protests, riots, even revolution—and, in response, repression by the government. Political instability in one country can spill into others, threatening an entire region's balance of power. Fearing such disruptions, leaders of the Most Industrialized Nations are using the United Nations to direct a campaign of worldwide birth control. With one hand they give agricultural aid, IUDs, and condoms to the masses in the Least Industrialized Nations—while, with the other, they sell weapons to the elites in these countries. Both actions, say conflict theorists, serve the same purpose: that of promoting political stability in order to maintain the dominance of the Most Industrialized Nations in global stratification.

## The Three Demographic Variables

How many people will live in the United States fifty years from now? What will the world's population be then? These are important questions. Educators want to know

how many schools to build. Manufacturers want to anticipate changes in the market for their products. The government needs to know how many doctors, engineers, and executives to train. Politicians want to know how many people will be paying taxes—and how many young people will be available to fight a war.

To project the future of populations, demographers use three **demographic variables:** fertility, mortality, and migration. Let's look at each.

**Fertility**    The number of children that the average woman bears is called the **fertility rate.** The world's overall fertility rate is 2.7, which means that during her lifetime the average woman in the world bears 2.7 children. At 2.0, the fertility rate of U.S. women is considerably less (Haub 2006). A term that is sometimes confused with fertility is **fecundity,** the number of children that women are *capable* of bearing. This number is rather high, as some women have given birth to 30 children (McFalls 2007).

The region of the world that has the highest fertility rate is Middle Africa, where the average woman gives birth to 6.3 children; the lowest is Eastern Europe, where the average woman bears 1.3 children (Haub 2006). As you can see from Table 14.1, Macao has the world's lowest fertility rate. There, the average woman gives birth to only 0.9 children. Four of the lowest-birth countries are in Asia. The rest are located in Europe. The countries with the highest birth rate are also clustered. With the exception of Afghanistan, all of them are in Africa. Niger in West Africa holds the

| TABLE 14.1 | Extremes in Childbirth | | |
|---|---|---|---|
| Where Do Women Give Birth to the Fewest Children? | | Where Do Women Give Birth to the Most Children? | |
| Country | Number of Children | Country | Number of Children |
| Macao | 0.9 | Niger | 7.9 |
| Hong Kong | 1.0 | Guinea-Bissau | 7.1 |
| South Korea | 1.1 | Mali | 7.1 |
| Taiwan | 1.1 | Somalia | 6.9 |
| Poland | 1.2 | Uganda | 6.9 |
| Slovenia | 1.2 | Afghanistan | 6.8 |
| Ukraine | 1.2 | Angola | 6.8 |
| Germany | 1.3 | Burundi | 6.8 |
| Italy | 1.3 | Liberia | 6.8 |
| Russia | 1.3 | Chad | 6.7 |

Note: Other countries with 1.2 children per woman are Belarus, Bosnia-Herzegovina, and Moldova; others that average 1.3 children are Bulgaria, Greece, Hungary, and Spain.

record for the world's highest birth rate. There, the average woman gives birth to 7.9 children, *nine* times as many children as the average woman in Macao.

To compute the fertility rate of a country, demographers analyze the government's records of births. From these, they figure the country's **crude birth rate,** the annual number of live births per 1,000 population. There may be considerable inaccuracies here, of course. The birth records in many of the Least Industrialized Nations are haphazard, at best.

**Mortality**    The second demographic variable is measured by the **crude death rate,** the annual number of deaths per 1,000 population. It, too, varies widely around the world. The highest death rate is 28, a record held by Botswana and Lesotho in southern Africa. At 1, the oil-rich country of Kuwait holds the world's record for the lowest death rate (Haub 2006).

**Migration**    The third demographic variable is the **net migration rate,** the difference between the number of *immigrants* (people moving into a country) and *emigrants* (people moving out of a country) per 1,000 population. Unlike fertility and mortality, migration does not affect the global population, for people are simply shifting their residence from one country or region to another.

As you know, immigrants are seeking a better life. They are willing to give up the security of their family and friends to move to a country with a strange language and unfamiliar customs. What motivates people to embark on such a venture? To understand migration, we need to look at both push and pull factors. The *push* factors are what

people want to escape: poverty or persecution for their religious and political ideas. The *pull* factors are the magnets that draw people to a new land, such as opportunities for education, higher wages, better jobs, the freedom to worship or to discuss political ideas, and a more promising future for their children.

Around the world, the flow of migration is from the Least Industrialized Nations to the industrialized countries. After "migrant paths" are established, immigration often accelerates as networks of kin and friends become additional magnets that attract more people from the same nation—and even from the same villages.

By far, the United States is the world's number one choice of immigrants. The United States admits more immigrants each year than all the other nations of the world combined. Thirty-six million residents—one of every eight Americans—were born in other countries (*Statistical Abstract* 2008:Table 44). Table 14.2 on the next page shows where recent U.S. immigrants were born. To escape grinding poverty, such as that which surrounds Celia and Angel, millions of people also enter the United States illegally. As surprising as it may seem, as Figure 14.8 on the next page shows, U.S. officials have sufficient information on these approximately 11 million people to estimate their country of origin.

Experts cannot agree about whether immigrants are a net contributor to the U.S. economy or a drain on it. Some economists claim that immigrants benefit the economy. After subtracting what immigrants collect in welfare, what they cost the medical and school systems, and then adding what they produce in jobs and taxes, they conclude that immigrants produce more than they cost (Simon 1986, 1993). Looking at the same data, other economists conclude that immigrants drain taxpayers of billions of dollars a year (Huddle 1993; Davis and Weinstein 2002). Evidence seems strong that immigrants lower the income of the native-born Americans with whom they compete (Borjas 2004, 2005, 2006). The fairest conclusion seems to be that the more educated immigrants produce more than they cost, while the less educated cost more than they produce.

## Problems in Forecasting Population Growth

The total of the three demographic variables—fertility, mortality, and net migration—gives us a country's **growth rate,** the net change after people have been added to and subtracted from a population. What demographers call the **basic demographic equation** is quite simple:

$$\text{Growth rate} = \text{births} - \text{deaths} + \text{net migration}$$

If population increase depended only on biology, the demographer's job would be easy. But social factors—wars,

**TABLE 14.2**   Country of Birth of U.S. Immigrants

| North America | 2,161,000 | Vietnam | 186,000 | Brazil | 70,000 |
|---|---|---|---|---|---|
| Mexico | 1,051,000 | Pakistan | 84,000 | Peru | 82,000 |
| Cuba | 167,000 | Iran | 68,000 | Ecuador | 65,000 |
| Dominican Republic | 166,000 | | | Venezuela | 45,000 |
| Canada | 108,000 | **Europe** | **922,000** | Guyana | 50,000 |
| El Salvador | 173,000 | Ukraine | 108,000 | Argentina | 29,000 |
| Haiti | 111,000 | United Kingdom | 96,000 | | |
| Jamaica | 101,000 | Russia | 104,000 | **Africa** | **431,000** |
| Guatemala | 104,000 | Poland | 82,000 | Ethiopia | 54,000 |
| | | Bosnia and Herzegovina | 83,000 | Nigeria | 58,000 |
| **Asia** | **2,089,000** | Germany | 49,000 | Egypt | 37,000 |
| India | 407,000 | Romania | 34,000 | Ghana | 34,000 |
| China | 371,000 | | | Somalia | 29,000 |
| Philippines | 342,000 | **South America** | **511,000** | | |
| Korea | 124,000 | Colombia | 138,000 | | |

*Note:* Totals are for the top countries of origin for 2000–2006, the latest year available.
*Source:* By the author. Based on *Statistical Abstract* 2008: Table 49.

economic booms and busts, plagues, and famines—push rates of birth and death and migration up or down. As is shown in the Cultural Diversity box on the next page, even infanticide can affect population growth. Politicians also complicate projections. Sometimes governments try to persuade women to bear fewer—or more—children. When

Hitler decided that Germany needed more "Aryans," the German government outlawed abortion and offered cash bonuses to women who gave birth. The population increased. Today, European leaders are alarmed that their birth rates have dropped so low that their populations will shrink. With its population dropping, Russia's leaders are offering incentives to women to have children: cash grants for each child and subsidies for day care (Chivers 2006).

In China, we find the opposite situation. Many people know that China tries to limit population growth with its "One couple, one child" policy, but few know how ruthlessly officials enforce this policy. Steven Mosher (2006), an anthropologist who did fieldwork in China, revealed that—whether she wants it or not—after the birth of her first child, each woman is fitted with an IUD (intrauterine device). If a woman has a second child, she is sterilized. If a woman gets pregnant without government permission (yes, you read that right), the fetus is aborted. If she does not consent to an abortion, one is performed on her anyway—even if she is nine months pregnant. No unmarried women are allowed to give birth; any unmarried woman who gets pregnant is arrested and forced to have an abortion.

In the face of Western disapproval and in an effort to present a better image to accompany its new role on the world political stage, Chinese leaders have relented somewhat. They have kept their "One couple, one child" policy, but they have begun to make exceptions to it. In rural areas, authorities allow a woman to bear a second child—if the first child is a girl. This improves the couple's chances of getting a son (Baochang et al. 2007).

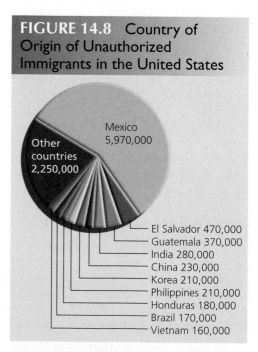

**FIGURE 14.8   Country of Origin of Unauthorized Immigrants in the United States**

Mexico 5,970,000
Other countries 2,250,000
El Salvador 470,000
Guatemala 370,000
India 280,000
China 230,000
Korea 210,000
Philippines 210,000
Honduras 180,000
Brazil 170,000
Vietnam 160,000

*Source:* By the author. Based on *Statistical Abstract* 2008: Table 46.

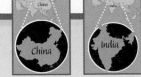

# *Cultural Diversity around the World*

## Killing Little Girls: An Ancient and Thriving Practice

"The Mysterious Case of the Missing Girls" could have been the title of this box. Around the globe, for every 100 girls born, about 105 boys are born. In China, however, for every 100 baby girls, there are 120 baby boys. Given China's huge population, this means that China has several million fewer baby girls than it should have. Why?

The answer is *female infanticide,* the killing of baby girls. When a Chinese woman goes into labor, the village midwife sometimes grabs a bucket of water. If the newborn is a girl, she is plunged into the water before she can draw her first breath.

At the root of China's sexist infanticide is economics. The people are poor, and they have no pensions. When parents can no longer work, sons support them. In contrast, a daughter must be married off, at great expense, and at that point, her obligations transfer to her husband and his family.

In the past few years, the percentage of boy babies has grown. The reason, again, is economics, but this time it has a new twist. As China opened the door to capitalism, travel and trade opened up—but primarily to men, for it is not thought appropriate for women to travel alone. With men finding themselves in a better position to bring profits home to the family, parents have one more reason to want male children.

*These women in New Delhi, India, are protesting sex-selection abortion.*

The gender ratio is so lopsided that for people in their 20s there are six bachelors for every five potential brides. Concerned about this gender imbalance, officials have begun a campaign to stop the drowning of girl babies. They are also trying to crack down on the abortions of girl fetuses.

It is likely that the preference for boys, and the resulting female infanticide, will not disappear until the social structures that perpetuate sexism are dismantled. This is unlikely to take place until women hold as much power as men, a development that, should it ever occur, apparently lies far in the future.

In the meantime, politicians have become concerned about a primary sociological implication of female infanticide—that large numbers of young men who cannot marry pose a political threat. These "bare branches," as they are referred to in China, disgruntled and lacking the stabilizing influences of marriage and children, could become a breeding ground for political dissent. This threat could motivate the national elites to take steps against female infanticide.

### For Your Consideration
What do you think can be done to reduce female infanticide? Why do you think this issue receives so little publicity?

*Sources:* Jordan 2000; Dugger 2001; Eckholm 2002; French 2004; Hudson and den Boer 2004; Riley 2004; Wonacott 2007; Yardley 2007.

Government actions can change a country's growth rate, yet the main factor is not the government, but industrialization. *In every country that industrializes, the birth rate declines.* Not only does industrialization open up economic opportunities but it also makes rearing children more expensive. Children require more education and remain dependent longer. Significantly, the basis for conferring status also changes—from having many children to attaining education and displaying material wealth. People like Celia and Angel begin to see life differently, and their motivation to have many children drops sharply. Not knowing how rapidly industrialization will progress or how quickly changes in values and reproductive behavior will follow adds to the difficulty of making accurate projections.

Because of these many complications, demographers play it safe by making several projections of population

The Chinese government uses billboards to remind people of its "one couple, one child" policy. The fat on the child's face on this billboard in Chengdu carries an additional message—that curtailing childbirth brings prosperity, abundant food for all. The portrayal of a girl baby is part of the government's attempt to reduce infanticide.

growth. For example, what will the U.S. population be in the year 2050? Between now and then, will we have **zero population growth,** with every 1,000 women giving birth to 2,100 children? (The extra 100 children make up for those who do not survive or reproduce.) Will a larger proportion of women go to college? (The more education women have, the fewer children they bear [Sutton and Matthews 2004].) How will immigration change? Will some devastating disease appear? With such huge variables, it is easy to see why demographers make the three projections of the U.S. population shown in Figure 14.9.

Let's look at a different aspect of population, where people live. Because more and more people around the world are living in cities, we shall concentrate on urban trends and urban life.

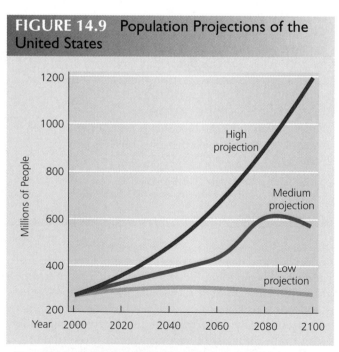

**FIGURE 14.9    Population Projections of the United States**

High projection

Medium projection

Low projection

Millions of People

1200
1000
800
600
400
200

Year    2000    2020    2040    2060    2080    2100

*Note:* The projections are based on different assumptions of fertility, mortality, and, especially, immigration.
*Source:* By the author. Based on *Statistical Abstract* 2002:Table 3.

# URBANIZATION

As I was climbing a steep hill in Medellin, Colombia, in a district called El Tiro, my informant, Jaro, said, "This used to be a garbage heap." I stopped to peer through the vegetation alongside the path we were on, and sure enough, I could see bits of refuse still sticking out of the dirt. The "town" had been built on top of garbage.

This was just the first of my many revelations that day. The second was that El Tiro was so dangerous that the Medellin police refused to enter it. I shuddered for a moment, but I had good reason to trust Jaro. He had been a pastor in El Tiro for several years, and he knew the people well. I knew that if I stayed close to him I would be safe.

Actually, El Tiro was safer now than it had been. A group of young men had banded together to make it so, Jaro told me. A sort of frontier justice prevailed. The vigilantes told the prostitutes and drug dealers that there would be no prostitution or drug dealing in El Tiro and to "take it elsewhere."

They killed anyone who robbed or killed someone. And they even made families safer—they would beat up any man who got drunk and beat "his" woman. With the threat of instant justice, the area had become much safer.

Jaro then added that each household had to pay the group a monthly fee, which turned out to be less than a dollar in U.S. money. Each business had to pay a little more. For this, they received security.

As we wandered the streets of El Tiro, it did look safe—but I still stayed close to Jaro. And I wondered about this group of men who had made the area safe. What kept them from turning on the residents? Jaro had no answer. When Jaro pointed to two young men, whom he said were part of the ruling group, I asked if I could take their picture. They refused. I did not try to snap one on the sly.

My final revelation was El Tiro itself. On the next two pages, you can see some of the things I saw that day.

In this second part of the chapter, I will try to lay the context for understanding urban life    and El Tiro. Let's begin by first finding out how the city itself came about.

# The Development of Cities

Cities are not new to the world scene. Perhaps as early as 7,000 years ago, people built small cities with massive defensive walls, such as biblically famous Jericho (Homblin 1973). Cities on a larger scale appeared about 3500 B.C., around the time that writing was invented (Chandler and Fox 1974; Hawley 1981). At that time, cities emerged in several parts of the world—first in Mesopotamia (Iraq and Iran) and later in the Nile, Indus, and Yellow River valleys, in West Africa, along the shores of the Mediterranean, in Central America, and in the Andes (Fischer 1976; Flanagan 1990). In the Americas, the first city was Caral, in what is now Peru (Fountain 2001).

The key to the origin of cities is the development of more efficient agriculture (Lenski and Lenski 1987). Only when farming produces a surplus can some people stop producing food and gather in cities to spend time in other economic pursuits. A **city,** in fact, can be defined as a place in which a large number of people are permanently based and do not produce their own food. The invention of the plow about 5,000 years ago created widespread agricultural surpluses, stimulating the development of towns and cities.

Most early cities were tiny, merely a collection of a few thousand people in agricultural centers or on major trade routes. The most notable exceptions are two cities that reached 1 million residents for a brief period of time before they declined—Changan (now Xi'an) in China about A.D. 800 and Baghdad in Persia (Iraq) about A.D. 900 (Chandler and Fox 1974). Even Athens at the peak of its power in the fifth century B.C. had about 250,000 inhabitants. Rome, at

Early cities were small economic centers surrounded by walls to keep out enemies. These cities had to be fortresses, for they were constantly threatened by armed, roving tribesmen and by leaders of nearby city states who raised armies to enlarge their domain and enrich their coffers by sacking neighboring cities. Pictured here is Cologne, Germany, as depicted in a 1545 manuscript.

# A Walk Through El Tiro in Medellin, Colombia

This is the "richer" area below El Tiro. As you can see, some of the residents own cars.

Kids are kids the world over. These children don't know they are poor. They are having a great time playing on a pile of dirt in the street.

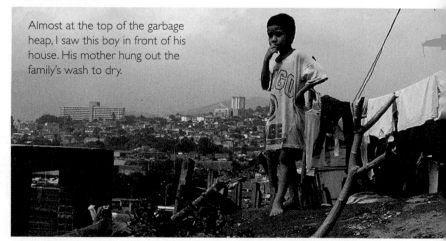

Almost at the top of the garbage heap, I saw this boy in front of his house. His mother hung out the family's wash to dry.

This is one of my favorite photos. The woman is happy that she has a home—and proud of what she has done with it. What I find remarkable is the flower garden she so carefully tends, and has taken great effort to protect from children and dogs. I can see the care she would take of a little suburban home.

It doesn't take much skill to build your own house in El Tiro. A hammer and saw, some nails, and used lumber will provide most of what you need. This man is building his house on top of another house.

The road to El Tiro. On the left, going up the hill, is a boardwalk. To the right is a meat market (*carnicería*). Note the structure above the meat market, where the family that runs the store lives.

El Tiro has home delivery.

An infrastructure has developed to serve El Tiro. This woman is waiting in line to use the only public telephone.

"What does an El Tiro home look like inside?," I kept wondering. Then Jaro, my guide at the left, took me inside the home of one of his parishioners. Amelia keeps a neat house with everything highly organized.

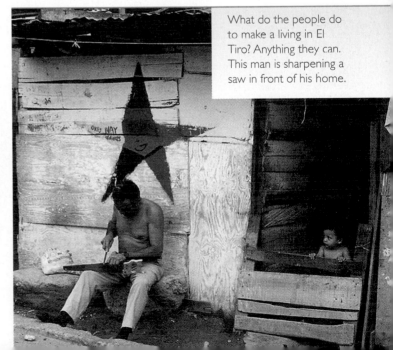

What do the people do to make a living in El Tiro? Anything they can. This man is sharpening a saw in front of his home.

its peak, may have had a million people or more, but as it declined, its population fell to just 35,000 (Palen 2005).

Even 200 years ago, the only city in the world that had a population of more than a million was Peking (now Beijing), China (Chandler and Fox 1974). Then in just 100 years, by 1900, the number of such cities jumped to sixteen. The reason was the Industrial Revolution, which drew people to cities by providing work. The Industrial Revolution also stimulated rapid transportation and communication and allowed people, resources, and products to be moved efficiently—all essential factors (called *infrastructure*) on which large cities depend. Figure 14.10 shows the global growth in the number of cities that have a million or more people.

## The Process of Urbanization

Although cities are not new to the world scene, urbanization is. **Urbanization** refers to masses of people moving to cities and these cities having a growing influence on society. Urbanization is taking place all over the world. In 1800, only 3 percent of the world's population lived in cities (Hauser and Schnore 1965). Then in 2007, for the first time in history, more people lived in cities than in rural areas. Urbanization is uneven across the globe. For the in-

dustrialized world, it is 77 percent, and for the Least Industrialized Nations, it is 41 percent (Haub 2006; Robb 2007). Without the Industrial Revolution this remarkable growth could not have taken place, for an extensive infrastructure is needed to support hundreds of thousands and even millions of people in a relatively small area.

To understand the city's attraction, we need to consider the "pulls" of urban life. Because of its exquisite division of labor, the city offers incredible variety—music ranging from rap and salsa to death metal and classical, shops that feature imported delicacies from around the world and those that sell special foods for vegetarians and diabetics. Cities also offer anonymity, which so many find refreshing in light of the tighter controls of village and small-town life. And, of course, the city offers work.

Some cities have grown so large and have so much influence over a region that the term *city* is no longer adequate to describe them. The term **metropolis** is used instead. This term refers to a central city surrounded by smaller cities and their suburbs. They are linked by transportation and communication and connected economically, and sometimes politically, through county boards and regional governing bodies. St. Louis is an example.

> Although this name, St. Louis, properly refers to a city of 350,000 people in Missouri, it also refers to another 3 million people who live in more than a hundred separate towns in both Missouri and Illinois. Altogether, the region is known as the "St. Louis or Bi-State Area." Although these towns are independent politically, they form an economic unit. They are linked by work (many people in the smaller towns work in St. Louis or are served by industries from St. Louis), by communications (they share the same area newspaper and radio and television stations), and by transportation (they use the same interstate highways, the Bi-State Bus system, and international airport). As symbolic interactionists would note, shared symbols (the Arch, the Mississippi River, Busch Brewery, the Cardinals, the Rams, the Blues—both the hockey team and the music) provide the residents a common identity.
>
> Most of the towns run into one another, and if you were to drive through this metropolis, you would not know that you were leaving one town and entering another—unless you had lived there for some time and were aware of the fierce small-town identifications and rivalries that coexist within this overarching identity.

Some metropolises have grown so large and influential that the term **megalopolis** is used to describe them. This term refers to an overlapping area consisting of at least two metropolises and their many suburbs. Of the twenty

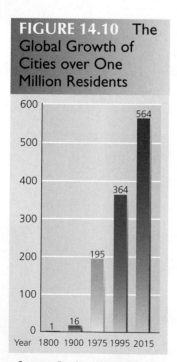

**FIGURE 14.10  The Global Growth of Cities over One Million Residents**

| Year | 1800 | 1900 | 1975 | 1995 | 2015 |
|------|------|------|------|------|------|
| | 1 | 16 | 195 | 364 | 564 |

*Sources:* By the author. Based on Chandler and Fox 1974; Brockerhoff 2000.

or so megalopolises in the United States, the three largest are the Eastern seaboard running from Maine to Virginia, the area in Florida between Miami, Orlando, and Tampa, and California's coastal area between San Francisco and San Diego. The California megalopolis extends into Mexico and includes Tijuana and its suburbs.

This process of urban areas turning into a metropolis, and a metropolis developing into a megalopolis, occurs worldwide. When a city's population hits 10 million, it is called a **megacity.** In 1950, New York City was the only megacity in the world. Today there are nineteen. Figure 14.11 shows the world's ten largest megacities. Note that most megacities are located in the Least Industrialized Nations.

## U.S. Urban Patterns

**From Country to City**    In its early years, the United States was almost exclusively rural. In 1790, only about 5 percent of Americans lived in cities. By 1920, this figure had jumped to 50 percent. Urbanization has continued without letup, and today 79 percent of Americans live in cities.

The U.S. Census Bureau divides the country into 274 **metropolitan statistical areas (MSAs).** Each MSA consists of a central city of at least 50,000 people and the urbanized areas linked to it. About three of five Ameri-

cans live in just fifty or so MSAs. As you can see from the Social Map on the next page, like our other social patterns, urbanization is uneven across the United States.

**From City to City**    As Americans migrate in search of work and better lifestyles, some cities increase in population while others shrink. Table 14.3 on the next page compares the fastest-growing U.S. cities with those that are losing people. This table reflects a major shift of people, resources, and power that is occurring between regions of the United States. As you can see, six of the ten fastest-growing cities are in the West, and four are in the South. Of the ten declining cities, eight are in the Northeast and two are in a state that borders the Northeast and the South.

**Between Cities**    As Americans migrate, **edge cities** have developed to meet their needs. This term refers to clusters of buildings and services near the intersection of major highways. These areas of shopping malls, hotels, office parks, and apartment complexes are not cities in the traditional sense. Rather than being political units with their own mayor or city manager, they overlap political boundaries and include parts of several cities or towns. Yet, edge cities—such as Tysons Corner in Washington and those clustering along the LBJ Freeway in Dallas, Texas—provide a sense of place to those who live or work there.

**FIGURE 14.11    How Many Millions of People Live in the World's Largest Megacities?**

| Tokyo | |
|---|---|
| 2015 | 26 |
| 2000 | 26 |
| 1975 | 19 |

| New York | |
|---|---|
| 2015 | 17 |
| 2000 | 17 |
| 1975 | 16 |

| Lagos | |
|---|---|
| 2015 | 23 |
| 2000 | 13 |
| 1975 | 3 |

| Shanghai | |
|---|---|
| 2015 | 15 |
| 2000 | 13 |
| 1975 | 11 |

| Los Angeles | |
|---|---|
| 2015 | 14 |
| 2000 | 13 |
| 1975 | 9 |

| Bombay | |
|---|---|
| 2015 | 26 |
| 2000 | 18 |
| 1975 | 7 |

| Mexico City | |
|---|---|
| 2015 | 19 |
| 2000 | 18 |
| 1975 | 11 |

| Sao Paulo | |
|---|---|
| 2015 | 20 |
| 2000 | 18 |
| 1975 | 10 |

| Buenos Aires | |
|---|---|
| 2015 | 14 |
| 2000 | 13 |
| 1975 | 9 |

| Calcutta | |
|---|---|
| 2015 | 17 |
| 2000 | 13 |
| 1975 | 8 |

*Source:* United Nations 2000.

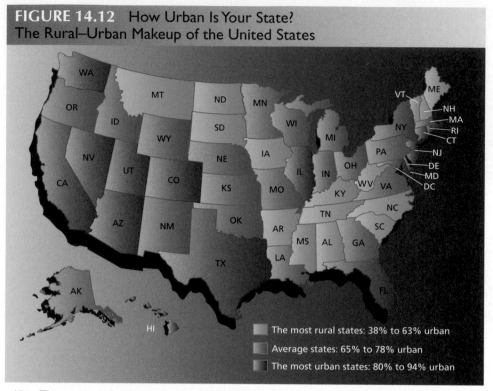

**FIGURE 14.12    How Urban Is Your State?
The Rural–Urban Makeup of the United States**

The most rural states: 38% to 63% urban

Average states: 65% to 78% urban

The most urban states: 80% to 94% urban

*Note:* The most rural state is Vermont (38% urban). The most urban states are California and New Jersey (94% urban).
*Source:* By the author. Based on *Statistical Abstract* 2007: Table 33.

**Within the City**    Another U.S. urban pattern is **gentrification,** the movement of middle-class people into rundown areas of a city. They are attracted by the low prices for large houses that, although deteriorated, can be restored. A positive consequence is an improvement in the appearance of some urban neighborhoods—freshly painted buildings, well-groomed lawns, and the absence of boarded-up windows. A negative

## TABLE 14.3    The Shrinking and the Fastest-Growing Cities

| The Shrinking Cities | | The Fastest-Growing Cities | |
|---|---|---|---|
| 1.  −1.9% | Buffalo–Niagara Falls, NY | 1.  +24.3% | Las Vegas, NV |
| 2.  −1.9% | Pittsburgh, PA | 2.  +23.6% | Cape Coral–Ft. Myers, FL |
| 3.  −1.8% | Scranton, PA | 3.  +22.2% | Naples, FL. |
| 4.  −1.6% | Youngstown, OH | 4.  +20.2% | Provo, UT |
| 5.  −1.0% | Cleveland, OH | 5.  +20.1% | Riverside, CA |
| 6.  −1.0% | Charleston, WV | 6.  +19.3% | Port St. Lucie, FL |
| 7.  −0.9% | Huntington, WV | 7.  +19.2% | Raleigh, NC |
| 8.  −0.7% | Utica–Rome, NY | 8.  +19.1% | McAllen, TX |
| 9.  −0.5% | Dayton, OH | 9.  +18.9% | Phoenix, AZ |
| 10.  −0.4% | Toledo, OH | 10.  +17.8% | Stockton, CA |

*Note:* Population change from 2000 to 2005.
*Source:* By the author. Based on *Statistical Abstract* 2007: Table 25.

consequence is that the poor residents are displaced by the more well-to-do newcomers. Tension between the gentrifiers and those being displaced is common (Anderson 1990, 2006).

The usual pattern is for the gentrifiers to be whites and the displaced to be minorities. As is discussed in the Down-to-Earth Sociology box on the next page, in the Harlem neighborhood of New York City, both the gentrifiers and the displaced are African Americans. As middle-class and professional African Americans reclaim this area, an infrastructure—which includes everything from Starbucks coffee shops to dentists—follows. So do soaring real estate prices.

**From City to Suburb** The term **suburbanization** refers to people moving from cities to **suburbs,** the communities located just outside a city. Suburbanization is not new. Archaeologists recently found that the Mayan city of Caracol (in what is now Belize) had suburbs, perhaps even with specialized subcenters, the equivalent of today's strip malls (Wilford 2000). The extent to which people have left U.S. cities in search of their dreams is remarkable. Fifty years ago, about 20 percent of Americans lived in the suburbs (Karp et al. 1991). Today, over half of all Americans live in them (Palen 2005).

The automobile was a major impetus for suburbanization. Beginning about one hundred years ago, whites began to move to small towns near the cities where they worked. After the racial integration of U.S. schools in the 1950s and 1960s, suburbanization picked up pace as whites fled the cities. Minorities began to move to the suburbs about 1970. In some of today's suburbs, minorities are the majority.

**Smaller Centers** The most recent urban trend is the development of *micropolitan areas.* A *micropolis* is a city of 10,000 to 50,000 residents that is not a suburb (McCarthy 2004), such as Gallup, New Mexico, or Carbondale, Illinois. Most micropolises are located "next to nowhere." They are fairly self-contained in terms of providing work, housing, and entertainment, and few of their residents commute to urban centers for work. Micropolises are growing, as residents of both rural and urban areas find their cultural attractions and conveniences appealing, especially in the absence of the city's crime and pollution.

## The Rural Rebound

The desire to retreat to a safe haven has led to a migration to rural areas that is without precedent in the history of the United States. Some small farming towns are making a comeback, their boarded-up stores and schools once again open for business and learning.

The "push" factors for this fundamental shift are fears of urban crime and violence. The "pull" factors are safety, lower cost of living, and more living space. Interstate highways have made airports—and the city itself—accessible from longer distances. With satellite communications, cell phones, fax machines, and the Internet, people can be "plugged in"—connected with others around the world—even though they live in what just a short time ago were remote areas.

Listen to the wife of one of my former students as she explains why she and her husband moved to a rural area, three hours from the international airport that they fly out of each week:

I work for a Canadian company. Paul works for a French company, with headquarters in Paris. He flies around the country doing computer consulting. I give motivational seminars to businesses. When we can, we drive to the airport together, but we often leave on different days. I try to go with my husband to Paris once a year.

We almost always are home together on the weekends. We often arrange three- and four-day weekends, because I can plan seminars at home, and Paul does some of his consulting from here.

Sometimes shopping is inconvenient, but we don't have to lock our car doors when we drive, and the new Wal-Mart superstore has most of what we need. E-commerce is a big part of it. I just type in www—whatever, and they ship it right to my door. I get make-up and books online. I even bought a part for my stove.

Why do we live here? Look at the lake. It's beautiful. We enjoy boating and swimming. We love to walk in this park-like setting. We see deer and wild turkeys. We love the sunsets over the lake. (author's files)

## Models of Urban Growth

In the 1920s, Chicago was a vivid mosaic of immigrants, gangsters, prostitutes, the homeless, the rich, and the poor—much as it is today. Sociologists at the University of Chicago studied these contrasting ways of life. One of these sociologists, Robert Park, coined the term **human ecology** to describe how people adapt to their environment (Park and Burgess 1921; Park 1936). (This concept is also known as *urban ecology.*) The process of urban growth is of special interest to sociologists. Let's look at four models they developed.

**The Concentric Zone Model** To explain how cities expand, sociologist Ernest Burgess (1925) proposed a

# Down-to-Earth Sociology
## Reclaiming Harlem: "It Feeds My Soul"

*West 125th Street in Harlem*

The story is well known. The inner city is filled with crack, crime, and corruption. It stinks from foul, festering filth strewn on the streets and piled up around burned-out buildings. Only those who have no choice live in this desolate, despairing environment where danger lurks around every corner.

What is not so well known is that affluent African Americans are reclaiming some of these areas.

Howard Sanders was living the American Dream. After earning a degree from Harvard Business School, he took a position with a Manhattan investment firm. He lived in an exclusive apartment on Central Park West, but he missed Harlem, where he had grown up. He moved back, along with his wife and daughter.

African American lawyers, doctors, professors, and bankers are doing the same.

What's the attraction? The first is nostalgia, a cultural identification with the Harlem of legend and folklore. It was here that black writers and artists lived in the 1920s, here that the blues and jazz attracted young and accomplished musicians.

The second reason is a more practical one. Harlem offers housing value. Five-bedroom homes with 6,000 square feet are available. Some feature Honduran mahogany. Some brownstones are only shells and have to be renovated; others are in perfect condition.

What is happening is the rebuilding of a community. Some people who "made" it want to be role models. They want children in the community to see them going to and returning from work.

When the middle class moved out of Harlem, so did its amenities. Now that young professionals are moving back in, the amenities are returning, too. There were no coffee shops, restaurants, jazz clubs, florists, copy centers, dentist and optometrist offices, or art galleries—the types of things urbanites take for granted. Now there are.

The police have also returned, changing the character of Harlem. Their more visible presence and enforcement of laws have shut down the open-air drug markets. With residents running a high risk of arrest if they carry guns, the shootouts that used to plague this area have become a thing of the past. With the enforcement of laws against public urination and vagrancy, the area has become much safer, further attracting the middle class.

The same thing is happening on Chicago's West Side and in other U.S. cities.

The drive to find community—to connect with others and with one's roots—is strong. As an investment banker who migrated to Harlem said, "It feeds my soul."

"But at what cost?" ask others. This change might be fine for investment bankers and professionals who want to move back and try to rediscover their roots, but what about the people who are displaced? Gentrification always has a cost: residents of an area being pushed out as the area becomes middle class and more expensive. Tenant associations have sprung up to protest the increase in rents and the displacement of residents. And homeowners' associations have emerged to fight to keep renters out of their rehabilitated areas. All are African Americans. The issue is not race, but social class antagonisms.

The "invasion–succession cycle," as sociologists call it, is continuing, but this time with a twist—a flight back in.

## For Your Consideration

One of the costs of gentrification is the displacement of the poor as people with higher incomes move into the area. What can be done to prevent this? Would you be willing to move into an area of high crime in order to get a good housing bargain?

*Sources:* Based on Cose 1999; McCormick 1999a; Scott 2001; Taylor 2002; Leland 2003; Hampson 2005; Hyra 2006.

*concentric-zone model.* As shown in part A of Figure 14.13 below, Burgess noted that a city expands outward from its center. Zone 1 is the central business district. Zone 2, which encircles the downtown area, is in transition. It contains rooming houses and deteriorating housing, which, Burgess said, breed poverty, disease, and vice. Zone 3 is the area to which thrifty workers have moved in order to escape the zone in transition and yet maintain easy access to their work. Zone 4 contains more expensive apartments, residential hotels, single-family homes, and exclusive areas where the wealthy live. Commuters live in Zone 5, which consists of suburbs or satellite cities that have grown up around transportation routes.

Burgess intended this model to represent "the tendencies of any town or city to expand radially from its central business district." He noted, however, that no "city fits

perfectly this ideal scheme." Some cities have physical obstacles such as a lake, river, or railroad that cause their expansion to depart from the model. Burgess also noted that businesses had begun to deviate from the model by locating in outlying zones (see Zone 10). That was in 1925. Burgess didn't know it, but he was seeing the beginning of a major shift that led businesses away from downtown areas to suburban shopping malls. Today, these malls account for most of the country's retail sales.

**The Sector Model** Sociologist Homer Hoyt (1939, 1971) noted that a city's concentric zones do not form a complete circle, and he modified Burgess' model of urban growth. As shown in part B of Figure 14.13, a concentric zone can contain several sectors—one of working-class housing, another of expensive homes, a

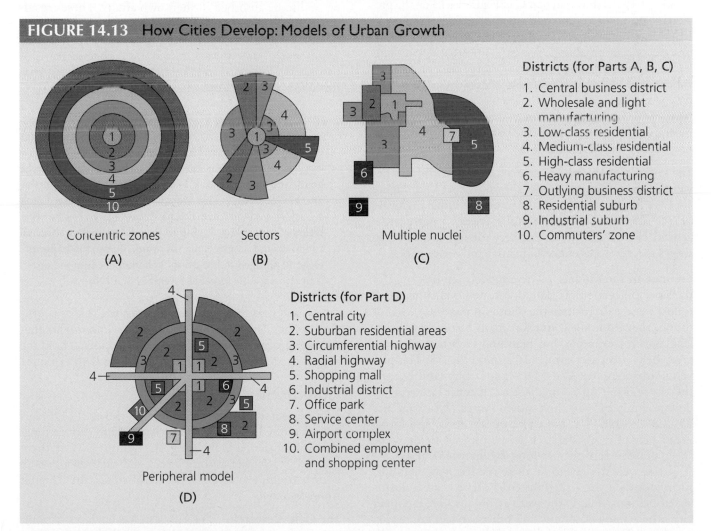

**FIGURE 14.13   How Cities Develop: Models of Urban Growth**

Concentric zones (A)   Sectors (B)   Multiple nuclei (C)

Districts (for Parts A, B, C)
1. Central business district
2. Wholesale and light manufacturing
3. Low-class residential
4. Medium-class residential
5. High-class residential
6. Heavy manufacturing
7. Outlying business district
8. Residential suburb
9. Industrial suburb
10. Commuters' zone

Peripheral model (D)

Districts (for Part D)
1. Central city
2. Suburban residential areas
3. Circumferential highway
4. Radial highway
5. Shopping mall
6. Industrial district
7. Office park
8. Service center
9. Airport complex
10. Combined employment and shopping center

*Source:* Cousins and Nagpaul 1970; Harris 1997.

third of businesses, and so on—all competing for the same land.

An example of this dynamic competition is what sociologists call an **invasion–succession cycle.** Poor immigrants and rural migrants settle in low-rent areas. As their numbers swell, they spill over into adjacent areas. Upset by their presence, the middle class moves out, which expands the sector of low-cost housing. The invasion–succession cycle is never complete, for later another group will replace this earlier one. As discussed in the Down-to-Earth Sociology box on page 414, in Harlem there has been a switch in the sequence: the "invaders" are the middle class.

**The Multiple-Nuclei Model**    Geographers Chauncey Harris and Edward Ullman noted that some cities have several centers, or nuclei (Harris and Ullman 1945; Ullman and Harris 1970). As shown in part C of Figure 14.13 on the previous page, each nucleus contains some specialized activity. A familiar example is the clustering of fast-food restaurants in one area and automobile dealers in another. Sometimes similar activities are grouped together because they profit from cohesion; retail districts, for example, draw more customers if there are more stores. Other clustering occurs because some types of land use, such as factories and expensive homes, are incompatible with one another. One result is that services are not spread evenly throughout the city.

**The Peripheral Model**    Chauncey Harris (1997) also developed the peripheral model shown in part D of Figure 14.13. This model portrays the impact of radial highways on the movement of people and services away from the central city to the city's periphery, or outskirts. It also shows the development of industrial and office parks.

**Critique of the Models**    These models tell only part of the story. They are time bound, for medieval cities didn't follow these patterns (see the photo on page 407). In addition, they do not account for urban planning policies. England, for example, has planning laws that preserve green belts (trees and farmlands) around the city. This prevents urban sprawl: Wal-Mart cannot buy land outside the city and put up a store; instead, it must locate in the downtown area with the other stores. Norwich has 250,000 people—yet the city ends abruptly, and on its green belt pheasants skitter across plowed fields while sheep graze in verdant meadows (Milbank 1995).

If you were to depend on these models, you would be surprised when you visited the cities of the Least Industrialized Nations. There, the wealthy often claim the inner city, where fine restaurants and other services are readily accessible. Tucked behind walls and protected from public scrutiny, they enjoy luxurious homes and gardens. The poor, in contrast, especially rural migrants, settle in areas outside the city—or, as in the case of El Tiro, featured in the photo essay on pages 408–409, on top of piles of garbage in what used to be the outskirts of a city.

# City Life

Life in cities is filled with contrasts. Let's look at two of those contrasts, alienation and community.

## Alienation in the City

**Impersonality and Self-Interest**    If you know urban life, you know that impersonality and self-interest are ordinary characteristics of the city. As you traverse city streets, you can expect people to avoid needless interaction with others and to be absorbed in their own affairs. These are adjustments that people have made to deal with the crowds of strangers with whom they temporarily share the same urban space. Sometimes, however, these characteristics of urban life are carried to extremes. Here is an event that made national headlines when it occurred:

> In crowded traffic on a bridge going into Detroit, Deletha Word bumped the car ahead of her. The damage was minor, but the driver, Martell Welch, jumped out. Cursing, he pulled Deletha from her car, pushed her onto the hood, and began beating her. Martell's friends got out to watch. One of them held Deletha down while Martell took a car jack and smashed Deletha's car. Scared for her life, Deletha broke away, fleeing to the bridge's railing. Martell and his friends taunted her, shouting, "Jump, bitch, jump!" Deletha plunged to her death. Whether she jumped or fell is unknown. (*Newsweek,* September 4, 1995)

Anyone who lives in a large city knows that it is prudent to be alert to danger. You never know who that stranger near you really is. Even traffic accidents hold the danger of angry people whose wrath is ready to explode.

## Community in the City

The city is not inevitably alienating, however. The drivers who witnessed the attack on Deletha Word did nothing. But after Deletha went over the railing, two of them jumped in after her, risking injury and their own lives in a futile attempt to save her. Some urbanites, then, are far from alienated.

**The Gans Research**    The city also has enclaves of community. Sociologist Herbert Gans, a symbolic interactionist, did participant observation in the West End of Boston.

He was so impressed with the sense of community that he titled his book *The Urban Villagers* (1962). In this book, which has become a classic in sociology, Gans said:

> After a few weeks of living in the West End, my observations—and my perceptions of the area—changed drastically. The search for an apartment quickly indicated that the individual units were usually in much better condition than the outside or the hallways of the buildings. Subsequently, in wandering through the West End, and in using it as a resident, I developed a kind of selective perception, in which my eye focused only on those parts of the area that were actually being used by people. Vacant buildings and boarded-up stores were no longer so visible, and the totally deserted alleys or streets were outside the set of paths normally traversed, either by myself or by the West Enders. The dirt and spilled-over garbage remained, but, since they were concentrated in street gutters and empty lots, they were not really harmful to anyone and thus were not as noticeable as during my initial observations.
>
> Since much of the area's life took place on the street, faces became familiar very quickly. I met my neighbors on the stairs and in front of my building. And, once a shopping pattern developed, I saw the same storekeepers frequently, as well as the area's "characters" who wandered through the streets every day on a fairly regular route and schedule. In short, the exotic quality of the stores and the residents also wore off as I became used to seeing them.

In short, Gans found a *community,* people who identified with the area and with one another. Its residents enjoyed networks of friends and acquaintances. Despite the area's substandard buildings, most West Enders had chosen to live here. *To them, this was a low-rent district, not a slum.*

Most West Enders had low-paying, insecure jobs. Other residents were elderly, living on small pensions. Unlike the middle class, these people didn't care about their "address." The area's inconveniences were something they put up with in exchange for cheap housing. In general, they were content with their neighborhood.

## Who Lives in the City?

Whether people find alienation or community in the city, then, depends on whom you are talking about. Here are five types of urban dwellers that Gans (1962, 1968, 1991) identified. They certainly have vastly different experiences in the city. The first three live in the city by choice and are not alienated; the latter two are outcasts of industrial society who live in the city despairingly, without choice or hope.

**The Cosmopolites**  These are the intellectuals, professionals, artists, and entertainers who have been attracted to the city. They value its conveniences and cultural benefits.

**The Singles**  Usually in their early 20s to early 30s, the singles have settled in the city temporarily. For them, urban life is a stage in their life course. Businesses and services, such as singles bars and apartment complexes, cater to their needs and desires. After they marry, many move to the suburbs.

**The Ethnic Villagers**  Feeling a sense of identity, working-class members of the same ethnic group band together. They form tightly knit neighborhoods that resemble villages and small towns. Family- and peer-oriented, they try to isolate themselves from the dangers and problems of urban life.

**The Deprived**  Destitute, emotionally disturbed, and having little income, education, or work skills, the deprived live in neighborhoods that are more like urban jungles than urban villages. Some of them stalk those jungles in search of prey. Neither predator nor prey has much hope for anything better in life—for themselves or for their children.

The city dwellers whom Gans identified as ethnic villagers find community in the city. Living in tightly knit neighborhoods, they know many other residents. Some first-generation immigrants have even come from the same village in the "old country." This photo was taken in New York City.

**The Trapped**   These people don't live in the area by choice, either. Some were trapped when an ethnic group "invaded" their neighborhood and they could not afford to move. Others found themselves trapped in a downward spiral. They started life in a higher social class, but because of personal problems—mental or physical illness or addiction to alcohol or other drugs—they drifted downward. There also are the elderly who are trapped by poverty and not wanted elsewhere. Like the deprived, the trapped suffer from high rates of assault, mugging, and rape.

**In Sum:** Gans' typology illustrates the complexity of urban life. With the city a mosaic of social diversity, not all urban dwellers experience the city in the same way. Each group has its own lifestyle, and each has distinct experiences. Some people welcome the city's cultural diversity and mix with several groups. Others find community by retreating into the security of ethnic enclaves. Still others feel trapped and deprived. To them, the city is an urban jungle. It poses threats to their health and safety, and their lives are full of despair.

## The Norm of Noninvolvement and the Diffusion of Responsibility

Urban dwellers try to avoid intrusions from strangers. As they go about their everyday lives in the city, they follow a *norm of noninvolvement.*

> To do this, we sometimes use props such as newspapers to shield ourselves from others and to indicate our inaccessibility for interaction. In effect, we learn to "tune others out." In this regard, we might see the Walkman [or iPod] as the quintessential urban prop in that it allows us to be tuned in and tuned out at the same time. It is a device that allows us to enter our own private world and thereby effectively to close off encounters with others. The use of such devices protects our "personal space," along with our body demeanor and facial expression (the passive "mask" or even scowl that persons adopt on subways). (Karp et al. 1991)

Social psychologists John Darley and Bibb Latané (1968) ran the series of experiments featured in Chapter 5, page 132. In their experiments, Darley and Latané uncovered the *diffusion of responsibility*—the more bystanders there are, the less likely people are to help. As a group grows, people's sense of responsibility becomes diffused, with each person assuming that *another* will do the responsible thing. "With these other people here, it is not *my* responsibility," they reason.

The diffusion of responsibility, along with the norm of noninvolvement, helps to explain why people can ignore the plight of others. Those who did nothing to intervene in the attack on Deletha Ward were *not* uncaring people. With the diffusion of responsibility, each felt that others might do something. Then, too, there was the norm of noninvolvement—helpful for getting people through everyday city life but, unfortunately, dysfunctional in some crucial situations.

To this dispassionate analysis of diffusion of responsibility and norm of noninvolvement, we can add this: These people were scared. They didn't want to get hurt. The fears nurtured by events like the sudden attack on a motorist, as well as the city's many rapes and muggings, make many people want to retreat to a safe haven. This topic is discussed in the Down-to-Earth Sociology box on the next page.

# Urban Problems and Social Policy

To close this chapter, let's look at the primary reasons that U.S. cities have declined and then consider the potential of urban revitalization.

## Suburbanization

The U.S. city has been the loser in the transition to the suburbs. As people moved out of the city, businesses and jobs followed. White-collar corporations, such as insurance companies, were the first to move their offices to the suburbs. They were soon followed by manufacturers. This process has continued so relentlessly that today twice as many manufacturing jobs are located in the suburbs as in the city (Palen 2005). As the city's tax base shrank, it left a budget squeeze that affected not only parks, zoos, libraries, and museums, but also the city's basic services—its schools, streets, sewer and water systems, and police and fire departments.

This shift in population and resources left behind people who had no choice but to stay in the city. As we reviewed in Chapter 9, sociologist William Julius Wilson (1987) says that this exodus transformed the inner city into a ghetto. Left behind were families and individuals who, lacking training and skills, were trapped by poverty, unemployment, and welfare dependency. Also left behind were those who prey on others through street crime. The term *ghetto*, says Wilson, "suggests that a fundamental social transformation has taken place . . . that groups represented by this term are collectively different from and much more socially isolated from those that lived in these communities in earlier years" (quoted in Karp et al. 1991).

**City Versus Suburb**   Having made the move out of the city—or having been born in a suburb and preferring to stay

# Down-to-Earth Sociology
## Urban Fear and the Gated Fortress

Gated neighborhoods—where gates open and close to allow or prevent access to a neighborhood—are not new. They always have been available to the rich. What is new is the rush of the upper middle class to towns where they pay high taxes to keep all of the town's facilities private. Even the city's streets are private.

Towns cannot discriminate on the basis of religion or race–ethnicity, but they can—and do—discriminate on the basis of social class. Klahanie, Washington, is an excellent example. Begun in 1985, it was supposed to take twenty years to develop. With its winding streets, pavilions, gardens, swimming pools, parks, private libraries, infant–toddler playcourt, and 25 miles of hiking-bicycling-running trails on 300 acres of open space, demand for the $300,000 to $500,000 homes nestled by a lake in this private community exceeded supply (Egan 1995; Klahanie Association Web site 2007).

As the upper middle class flees urban areas and tries to build a bucolic dream, we will see many more private towns. A strong sign of the future is Celebration, a town of 20,000 people planned and built by the Walt Disney Company just five minutes from Disney World. Celebration boasts the usual school, hospital, and restaurants. In addition, Celebration offers a Robert Trent Jones golf course, walking and bicycling paths, a hotel with a lighthouse tower and bird sanctuary, a health and fitness center with a rock-climbing wall, and its own cable TV channel. With fiber-optic technology, the residents of private communities can remain locked

*The U.S. economic system has proven highly beneficial to most citizens, but it also has left many in poverty. To protect themselves, primarily from the poor, the upper middle class increasingly seeks sanctuary behind gated communities. Some seek even more safety and privacy by living behind gates within a gated community, as shown here in Miami Beach, Florida.*

within their sanctuaries and still be connected to the outside world.

## For Your Consideration

Community involves a sense of togetherness, a sense of identity with one another. Can you explain how this concept also contains the idea of separateness from others (not just in the example of gated communities)? What will our future be if we become a nation of gated communities, where middle-class homeowners withdraw into private domains, separating themselves from the rest of the nation?

---

there—suburbanites want the city to keep its problems to itself. They reject proposals to share suburbia's revenues with the city and oppose measures that would allow urban and suburban governments joint control over what has become a contiguous mass of people and businesses. Suburban leaders generally believe that it is in their best interests to remain politically, economically, and socially separate from their nearby city. They do not mind going to the city to work or venturing there on weekends for the diversions it offers, but they do not want to help pay the city's expenses.

It is likely that the mounting bill ultimately will come due, however, and that suburbanites will have to pay for their uncaring attitude toward the urban disadvantaged. Karp et al. (1991) put it this way:

**It may be that suburbs can insulate themselves from the problems of central cities, at least for the time being. In the long run, though, there will be a steep price to pay for the failure of those better off to care compassionately for those at the bottom of society.**

Our occasional urban riots may be part of that bill—perhaps just the down payment.

**Suburban Flight**    In some places, the bill is coming due quickly. As they age, some suburbs are becoming mirror images of the city that their residents so despise. Suburban crime, the flight of the middle class, a shrinking tax base, and eroding services create a spiraling sense of insecurity, stimulating more middle-class flight (Herrick 2007). Figure 14.14 on the next page illustrates this process, which is new to the urban-suburban scene.

## Disinvestment and Deindustrialization

As the cities' tax base shrank and their services declined, neighborhoods deteriorated, and banks began **redlining:** Afraid of loans going bad, bankers would draw a line around a problem area on a map and refuse to make loans for housing or businesses there. This **disinvestment** (withdrawal of investment) pushed these areas into further decline. Youth gangs, muggings, and murders are common in these areas, but good jobs are not. All are woven into this process of disinvestment.

The globalization of capitalism has also left a heavy mark on U.S. cities. As we reviewed in Chapter 11, to compete in the global market, many U.S. industries abandoned local communities and moved their factories to countries where labor costs are lower. This process, called **deindustrialization,** made U.S. industries more competitive, but it eliminated millions of U.S. manufacturing jobs. Lacking training in the new information technologies,

many poor people are locked out of the benefits of the postindustrial economy that is engulfing the United States. Left behind in the inner cities, many live in despair.

## The Potential of Urban Revitalization

Social policy usually takes one of two forms. The first is to tear down and rebuild—something that is fancifully termed **urban renewal.** The result is the renewal of an area—but *not* for the benefit of its inhabitants. Stadiums, high-rise condos, luxury hotels, and boutiques replace run-down, cheap housing. Outpriced, the area's inhabitants are displaced into adjacent areas.

The second is some sort of **enterprise zone,** a designated area of the city that offers economic incentives, such as reduced taxes, to businesses that move into it. Although the intention is good, the usual result is failure. Most businesses refuse to locate in high-crime areas. Those that do relocate pay a high price for security and losses from crime, which can eat up the tax savings. If workers are hired from within the problem area and the jobs pay a decent wage, which most do not, the workers move to better neighborhoods—which doesn't help the area (Lemann 1994). After all, who chooses to live with the fear of violence?

A form of the enterprise zone, called *Federal Empowerment Zones,* has brought some success. In addition to tax breaks, this program offers low-interest loans targeted for redeveloping an area. It is, in effect, the opposite of disinvestment, which devastates areas. The Down-to-Earth Sociology box on page 414 featured the renaissance of

As cities evolve, so does architecture. This is the design of the headquarters for China's flagship television network to be built in Beijing. As a sign of changing times and of China's evolving partnership with the West, the architect is a Westerner, Rem Koolhaas of Holland.

## FIGURE 14.14 Urban Growth and Urban Flight

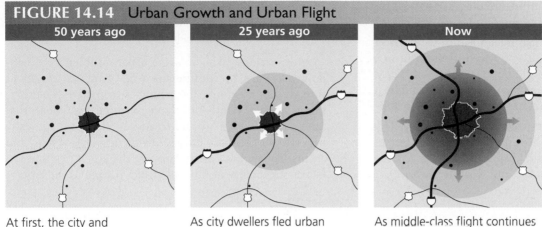

| 50 years ago | 25 years ago | Now |
|---|---|---|
| At first, the city and surrounding villages grew independently. | As city dwellers fled urban decay, they created a ring of suburbs. | As middle-class flight continues outward, urban problems are arriving in the outer rings. |

Harlem. Stimulating this change was the designation of Harlem as a Federal Empowerment Zone. The economic incentives lured grocery stores, dry cleaners, and video stores, attracting urbanites who expect such services. As middle-class people moved back in, the demand for more specialty shops followed. A self-feeding cycle of investment and hope began, replacing the self-feeding cycle of despair, crime, and drug use that accompanies disinvestment.

U.S. cities can be revitalized and made into safe and decent places to live. There is nothing in the nature of cities that turns them into dangerous slums. Most European cities, for example, are both safe and pleasant. If U.S. cities are to change, they need to become top agenda items of the U.S. government. Adequate resources in terms of money and human talents must be focused on overcoming urban woes. That we are beginning to see success in Harlem, Chicago's North Town, and even in formerly riot-torn East Los Angeles indicates that the transformation can be brought about.

Replacing old buildings with new ones, however, is not the answer. Instead, sociological principles of building community need to be followed. Here are three guiding principles suggested by sociologist William Flanagan (1990):

***Scale.*** Regional and national planning is necessary. Local jurisdictions, with their many rivalries,

U.S. suburbs were once unplanned, rambling affairs that took irregular shapes as people moved away from the city. Today's suburbs tend to be planned to precise details even before the first resident moves in. This photo is of a suburb outside of Venice, California.

competing goals, and limited resources, end up with a hodgepodge of mostly unworkable solutions.

***Livability.*** Cities must be appealing and meet human needs, especially the need of community. This will attract the middle classes into the city, which will increase its tax base. In turn, this will help finance the services that make the city more livable.

***Social justice.*** In the final analysis, social policy must be evaluated by how it affects people. "Urban renewal" programs that displace the poor for the benefit of the middle class and wealthy do not pass

this standard. The same would apply to solutions that create "livability" for select groups but neglect the poor and the homeless.

Most actions taken to solve urban problems are window dressings for politicians who want to *appear* as though they are doing something constructive. The solution is to avoid Band-Aids that cover up the problems that hurt our quality of life and to address their *root* causes—poverty, poor schools, crimes of violence, lack of jobs, and an inadequate tax base to provide the amenities that enhance our quality of life and attract people to the city.

# SUMMARY *and* REVIEW

## A Planet with No Space for Enjoying Life?

### What debate did Thomas Malthus initiate?

In 1798, Thomas Malthus analyzed the surge in Europe's population. He concluded that the world's population will outstrip its food supply. The debate between today's New Malthusians and those who disagree, the Anti-Malthusians, continues. Pp. 394–397.

### Why are people starving?

Starvation is not due to a lack of food in the world, for there is now *more* food for each person in the entire world than there was fifty years ago. Rather, starvation is the result of a maldistribution of food, which is primarily due to drought and civil war. Pp. 397–399.

## Population Growth

### Why do people in the poor nations have so many children?

In the Least Industrialized Nations, children are often viewed as gifts from God. In addition, they cost little to rear, contribute to the family income at an early age, and provide the parents' social security. These are powerful motivations to have large families. Pp. 399–402.

### What are the three demographic variables?

To compute population growth, demographers use *fertility, mortality,* and *migration.* The **basic demographic equation** is births minus deaths plus net migration equals the growth rate. Pp. 402–403.

### Why is forecasting population difficult?

A nation's growth rate is affected by unanticipated variables—from economic cycles, wars, and famines to industrialization and government policies. Pp. 403–406.

## The Development of Cities

### How are cities to related to the Industrial Revolution?

**Cities** can develop only if there is a large agricultural surplus, which frees people from food production. The primary impetus to the development of cities was the invention of the plow. After the Industrial Revolution stimulated rapid transportation and communication, cities grew quickly and became much larger. Today **urbanization** is so extensive that some cities have become **metropolises,** dominating the area adjacent to them. The areas of influence of some metropolises have merged, forming a **megalopolis.** Pp. 406–413.

### What models of urban growth have been proposed?

The primary models are concentric zone, sector, multiple-nuclei, and peripheral. These models fail to account for ancient and medieval cities, many European cities, cities in the Least Industrialized Nations, and urban planning. Pp. 413–416.

## City Life

### Who lives in the city?

Some people experience **alienation** in the city; others find **community** in it. What people find depends largely on their background and urban networks. Five types of people who live in cities are cosmopolites, singles, ethnic villagers, the deprived, and the trapped. Pp. 414–416.

## Urban Problems and Social Policy

*Why have U.S. cities declined?*

Three primary reasons for the decline of U.S. cities are **suburbanization** (as people moved to the suburbs, the tax base of cities eroded and services deteriorated), **disinvestment** (banks withdrawing their financing), and **deindustrialization** (which caused a loss of jobs). Pp. 418–420.

*What social policy can salvage U.S. cities?*

Three guiding principles for developing urban social policy are scale, livability, and social justice. Pp. 420–422.

# THINKING CRITICALLY *about* Chapter 14

1. Do you think that the world is threatened by a population explosion? Use data from this chapter to support your position.

2. Why do people find alienation or community in the city?

3. What are the causes of urban problems, and what can we do to solve those problems?

# BY THE NUMBERS: Changes Over Time

- World population at the birth of Christ: **About 300 million**
- World population today: **Closing in on 7 billion**

- Per capita food production in 1970: **80**
- Per capita food production today: **105**

- Number of years it will take for the Most Industrialized Nations to double in population: **1,000**
- Number of years it will take for the Least Industrialized Nations to double in population: **48**

- Annual population increase of the Least Industrialized Nations in the 1960s: **2.1%**
- Annual population increase of the Least Industrialized Nations today: **1.5%**

- Number of cities in the world with over 1 million residents in 1975: **195**
- Projected number of cities in the world with over 1 million residents in 2015: **564**

- Number of cities in the world with over 10 million residents in 1950: **1**
- Number of cities in the world with over 10 million residents today: **19**

# ADDITIONAL RESOURCES

## What can you find in MySocLab? mysoclab www.mysoclab.com

- **Complete Ebook**
- **Practice Tests and Video and Audio activities**
- **Mapping and Data Analysis exercises**

- **Sociology in the News**
- **Classic Readings in Sociology**
- **Research and Writing advice**

## Where Can I Read More on This Topic?

Suggested readings for this chapter are listed at the back of this book.

# 15

# Social Change and the Environment

A mong technology's amazing feats is the capacity to transplant human organs from one person to another. Some organs come from living donors, but the dead provide most of them. Bizarrely, this technological advance makes some people more valuable dead than alive.

> This technological advance makes some people more valuable dead than alive.

Because body organs deteriorate quickly, they must be harvested immediately after someone's death. This requires highly trained medical specialists, such as Hootan Roozrokh. As a toddler, Roozrokh emigrated with his family from Iran to the United States. After graduating from medical school, he won a coveted fellowship in transplant medicine at Stanford University. As Roozrokh's skills grew, so did his reputation. Eventually, Dr. Roozrokh was hired as a transplant surgeon—to harvest organs from patients who have agreed to be organ donors.

To be ready to remove the organs, a transplant team is called before a patient dies. To be sure the team doesn't get impatient and do something rash, the team is not allowed in the patient's room. The team has to wait for another doctor—one not on the team—to declare the patient dead. Only then can the team rush in to begin surgery. That wait is a terrible waste of time.

In February 2006, Ruben Navarro, a disabled, brain-damaged 25-year-old, was admitted to Sierra Vista Regional Medical Center in San Luis Obispo, California. This time, the transplant team didn't wait. They entered Navarro's room, ready to go to work. Most people die within a few minutes after their breathing tubes are removed. Not Navarro. He kept on breathing, while the transplant team grew increasingly impatient.

What do you do in a case like this? Go sit in the hallway? These medical specialists are highly paid and hard to come by. They have better things to do than to wait for someone to die.

Dr. Roozrokh came up with a solution. He ordered that Navarro be given morphine and Ativan—10 to 20 times the normal dosages. When that didn't hasten his death, he ordered that Navarro be given Betadine, "a substance that may cause death if ingested."

Navarro still hung in there. Roozrokh then suggested that Navarro really was dead, that the electronic monitors were only showing "pulseless electronic activity."

425

Dr. Laura Lubarsky, assigned by the hospital to determine exactly when Navarro was dead—so that those waiting surgical knives weren't put to use prematurely—disagreed. Using a stethoscope, she said she could hear Navarro's heart beating.

A slow, agonizing eight hours later, Navarro's heart finally gave up.

Finally! But it was too late. You can imagine the disappointment Roozrokh felt. Navarro's death had been so slow that his organs had deteriorated and were worthless as transplants.

What a wasted day for Roozrokh (for Navarro, too, of course). But the worst was yet to come for Roozrokh.

Some of the witnesses to this incident didn't like what they had seen. After thinking about it for a couple of days, a nurse broke the medical norm against squealing on doctors. The sheriff investigated, and the district attorney ordered Dr. Roozrokh arrested. Roozrokh was charged with the felonies of abusing a dependent adult, administering a harmful substance (Betadine), and prescribing a controlled substance (morphine) without a legitimate medical purpose.

Many people don't want to sign consent forms to have their organs removed after their death. Some feel a repugnance at the thought of having someone cut up their bodies after they die. Others have a nagging feeling that maybe they won't really be dead when the surgeons start to harvest their organs.

That's ridiculous. Of course, you'll be dead. The surgeons will make sure of that.

*Sources:* Based on Committee on Non-Heart-Beating Transplantation II; Associated Press 2008; Chawkins 2008; Elsworth 2008; McKinley 2008.

If any characteristic describes social life today, it is rapid social change. As we shall see in this chapter, technology, such as that which allows livers, kidneys, hearts, and other essential organs to be replaced, is a driving force behind this change. If we want a better understanding of society— and our own lives—we need to understand how technology underlies social change.

# How Social Change Transforms Social Life

**Social change,** a shift in the characteristics of culture and society, is such a vital part of social life that it has been a recurring theme throughout this book. To make this theme more explicit, let's review the main points about social change that were made in the preceding chapters.

## The Four Social Revolutions

The rapid social change that the world is currently experiencing did not "just happen." Rather, today's social change is the result of forces that were set in motion thousands of years ago, beginning with the domestication of plants and animals. This first social revolution allowed hunting and gathering societies to develop into horticultural and pastoral societies (see pages 91–94). The plow brought about the second social revolution, from which agricultural societies emerged. The third social revolution, prompted by the invention of the steam engine, ushered in the Industrial Revolution. Now we are in the midst of the fourth social revolution, stimulated by the invention of the microchip. The process of change has accelerated so greatly that the mapping of the human genome system could be pushing us into yet another new type of society, one based on biotechnology.

*Social change* comes in many forms. Shown here are students in a Fort Myer, Virginia, elementary school on the first day of desegregation in 1954. The school, operated by the military for the children of military personnel, was desegregated by order of the Defense Department.

## From *Gemeinschaft* to *Gesellschaft*

Although so many aspects of our lives have already changed, we have seen only the tip of the iceberg. By the time this fourth—and perhaps fifth—social revolution is full-blown, little of our current way of life will remain. We can assume this because that is how it was with the earlier social revolutions. For example, the change from agricultural to industrial society meant not only that people moved from villages to cities but also that many intimate, lifelong relationships were replaced by impersonal, short-term associations. Paid work, contracts, and money replaced the reciprocal obligations (such as exchanging favors) that were essential to relationships based on kinship, social status, and friendship. As reviewed on page 98, sociologists use the terms *Gemeinschaft* and *Gesellschaft* to indicate this fundamental shift in society.

## Capitalism, Modernization, and Industrialization

Just why did societies change from *Gemeinschaft* to *Gesellschaft*? Karl Marx pointed to a social invention called *capitalism*. He analyzed how the breakup of feudal society threw people off the land, creating a surplus of labor. These masses moved to cities, where they were exploited by the owners of the means of production (factories, machinery, tools). This set in motion antagonistic relationships between capitalists and workers that remain today.

Max Weber, in contrast, traced capitalism to the Protestant Reformation (see page 8). He noted that the Reformation stripped Protestants of the assurance that church membership saved them. As they agonized over heaven and hell, they concluded that God did not want the elect to live in uncertainty. Surely God would give a sign to assure them that they were predestined to heaven. That sign, they decided, was prosperity. An unexpected consequence of the Reformation, then, was to make Protestants work hard and be thrifty. This created an economic surplus, which stimulated capitalism. In this way, Protestantism laid the groundwork for the Industrial Revolution that transformed the world.

The sweeping changes ushered in by the Industrial Revolution are called **modernization.** Table 15.1 on the next page summarizes these changes. The traits listed on this table are *ideal types* in Weber's sense of the term, for no society exemplifies all of them to the maximum degree. Our new technology has also brought about a remarkable unevenness in the characteristics of nations. For example, in Uganda, a traditional society, the elite have computers. Thus the characteristics shown in Table 15.1 should be interpreted as "more" or "less" rather than "either-or."

When technology changes, societies change. Consider how technology from the industrialized world is transforming traditional societies. When the West exported medicine to the Least Industrialized Nations, for example, death rates dropped while birth rates remained high. As a result, the population exploded. This second stage of the demographic transition upset traditional balances of family and property. It brought hunger and caused mass migration to cities—but these cities have little industrialization to support the throngs of people moving into them. The photo essay on pages 408–409 illustrates some of these problems.

The Protestant Reformation ushered in not only religious change but also, as Max Weber analyzed, fundamental social–economic change. This painting by Hans Holbein, the Younger, shows the new prosperity of the merchant class. Previously, only the nobility and higher clergy could afford such possessions.

**TABLE 15.1    Comparing Traditional and Industrialized (and Information) Societies**

| Characteristics | Traditional Societies | Industrialized (and Information) Societies |
|---|---|---|
| **General Characteristics** | | |
| Social change | Slow | Rapid |
| Size of group | Small | Large |
| Religious orientation | More | Less |
| Formal education | No | Yes |
| Place of residence | Rural | Urban |
| Family size | Larger | Smaller |
| Infant mortality | High | Low |
| Life expectancy | Short | Long |
| Health care | Home | Hospital |
| Temporal orientation | Past | Future |
| Demographic transition | First stage | Third stage (or Fourth) |
| **Material Relations** | | |
| Industrialized | No | Yes |
| Technology | Simple | Complex |
| Division of labor | Simple | Complex |
| Income | Low | High |
| Material possessions | Few | Many |
| **Social Relationships** | | |
| Basic organization | *Gemeinschaft* | *Gesellschaft* |
| Families | Extended | Nuclear |
| Respect for elders | More | Less |
| Social stratification | Rigid | More open |
| Statuses | More ascribed | More achieved |
| Gender equality | Less | More |
| **Norms** | | |
| View of life and morals | Absolute | Relativistic |
| Social control | Informal | Formal |
| Tolerance of differences | Less | More |

*Source:* By the author.

## Conflict, Power, and Global Politics

In our fast-paced world, we pay most attention to changes that directly affect our own lives. Mostly out of sight is one of the most significant changes of all, the shifting arrangement of power among nations. By the sixteenth century, global divisions had begun to emerge. Nations with the most advanced technology (at that time, the swiftest ships and the most powerful cannons) became wealthy by conquering other nations and taking control of their resources. Then, as capitalism emerged, some nations industrialized. The newly industrialized nations exploited the resources of those countries that had not yet industrialized. According to *world system theory,* this made the nonindustrialized nations dependent and unable to develop their own resources (see page 190).

**G-7 Plus**    Since World War II, a realignment of the world's powers (called *geopolitics*) has resulted in a triadic division of the globe: a Japan-centered East (soon to be dominated by China), a Germany-centered Europe, and a United States–centered western hemisphere. These three powers, along with four lesser ones—Canada, France, Great Britain, and Italy—dominate the globe. They called themselves G-7, meaning the "Group of 7." Fear of Russia's nuclear arsenal and an attempt to gain Russia's cooperation in global affairs prompted G-7 to let Russia join their elite club. The fragility of Russia's membership, which depends on its continued cooperation, became apparent with the armed conflict in Georgia in 2008.

No longer can this group ignore the growing wealth and power of China. Wanting to recapture the glory of centuries past, China is expanding its domain of influence. Bowing to the inevitable and attempting to reduce the likelihood of conflict as China steps on turf claimed by others, G-7 has allowed China to become an observer at its annual summits. As mentioned in Chapter 11, if China cooperates adequately, the next step will be to incorporate China into this exclusive club.

**Dividing Up the World**    At their annual meetings, these world powers set policies to guide global economic matters. Their goal is to perpetuate their global dominance, which includes trying to maintain low prices on the raw materials they buy from the Least Industrialized Nations. Access to abundant oil, essential to this goal, requires that they dominate the Middle East, not letting it become an independent power. To the degree that these nations fail to control prices, policies, and international relations that implement their own interests, they undermine the New World Order they are trying to orchestrate.

**Two Threats to This Coalition of Powers**    There are two major threats to the global divisions that this group is trying to work out. The first is dissension within. Currently, Russia and the United States are at the center of the intrafamilial feuding that threatens this coalition of powers. Because Russia is still stinging after losing its empire and wants a more powerful presence on the world stage, Russia is quick to see insult and threat—and to retaliate. In the dead of winter of 2006, amidst a dispute with Ukraine over the price of gas, Russia turned off the oil supply that runs from it through Ukraine to western Europe, endangering lives in several countries (Crossland 2006). In 2007, after fuming for months about a U.S. plan to put missiles in Poland as part of a missile-defense shield, Russia threatened to aim its missiles at cities in Europe if the United States didn't back down (Blomfield 2007). In 2008, when the United States went ahead and signed the missile agreement with Poland, Russia threatened a nuclear attack on Poland (McElroy 2008). Despite snarling back and forth, it is likely that these nations will realign their structure of power successfully, working out their New World Order.

I was in Riga, Latvia, as this feud began to unfold. While there, I took the photos below, a foreshadowing of the armed conflict in Georgia.

The second threat is the resurgence of ethnic rivalries and conflicts. In Europe, ethnic violence in the former Yugoslavia split the country into seven nations. Ossetians and Georgians recently killed one another, the Flemish say they are not Belgian, and Turks in Germany live in fear of the young Germans who threaten their lives. In Africa, violence erupts between Kenya's Kalenjin and Kikuyu, and in Nigeria the Igbo won't let the government count them because, as they say, "We are not Nigerians." Ethnic conflicts threaten the peace in many parts of the world—from the United States and Mexico in North America to China and Vietnam in Asia. We do not know how long the lid can be kept on these seemingly bottomless ethnic antagonisms or whether they will ever play themselves out.

For global control, the Most Industrialized Nations require political and economic stability, both in their own backyards and in those countries that provide the raw materials essential for their industrial machine. This explains why they care little when African nations self-destruct in ethnic slaughter but refuse to tolerate interethnic warfare in their own neighborhoods. To let interethnic warfare in Bosnia, Kosovo, or Georgia go unchecked would be to tolerate conflict that could spread and engulf Europe. In contrast, the deaths of hundreds of thousands of Tutsis in Rwanda had little or no political significance for these powerful countries.

# Theories and Processes of Social Change

Social change has always fascinated theorists. Of the many attempts to explain why societies change, we shall consider just four: cultural evolution, natural cycles, conflict and power, and the pioneering views of sociologist William Ogburn.

## Cultural Evolution

Evolutionary theories of how societies change are of two types, unilinear and multilinear. *Unilinear* theories assume that all societies follow the same path: Each evolves from

Armored vehicles blocked streets when NATO held a summit in Riga, Latvia, in 2006. Disregarding broadcast warnings to stay off the streets, I wandered around the city, taking photos. I expected to be stopped, perhaps arrested, but I wasn't.

Angry that NATO was meeting in Latvia, a country Russia still claims as its own, Vladimir Putin, then the president of Russia, boycotted the meetings. I took this photo from an apartment window overlooking the ship on which NATO held secret meetings on November 29.

Despite the globe's vast social change, people all over the world continue to make race a fundamental distinction. Shown here is a Ukrainian being measured to see if he is really "full lipped" enough to be called a Tartar.

simpler to more complex forms. This journey takes each society through uniform sequences (Barnes 1935). Of the many versions of this theory, the one proposed by Lewis Morgan (1877) once dominated Western thought. Morgan said that all societies go through three stages: savagery, barbarism, and civilization. In Morgan's eyes, England, his own society, was the epitome of civilization. All other societies were destined to follow the same path.

*Multilinear* views of evolution replaced unilinear theories. Instead of assuming that all societies follow the same sequence, multilinear theorists proposed that different routes lead to the same stage of development. Although the paths all lead to industrialization, societies need not pass through the same sequence of stages on their journey (Sahlins and Service 1960; Lenski and Lenski 1987).

Central to all evolutionary theories, whether unilinear or multilinear, is the assumption of *cultural progress*. Tribal societies are assumed to have a primitive form of human culture. As these societies evolve, they will reach a higher state—the supposedly advanced and superior form that characterizes the Western world. Growing appreciation of the rich diversity—and complexity—of tribal cultures discredited this idea. In addition, Western culture is now in crisis (poverty, racism, war, terrorism, sexual assaults, unsafe streets) and is no longer regarded as the apex of human civilization. Consequently, the idea of cultural progress has been cast aside, and evolutionary theories have been rejected (Eder 1990; Smart 1990).

## Natural Cycles

Cyclical theories attempt to account for the rise of entire civilizations. Why, for example, did Egypt, Greece, and Rome wield such power and influence, only to crest and fall into a decline? Cyclical theories assume that civilizations are like organisms: They are born, see an exuberant youth, come to maturity, then decline as they reach old age, and finally die (Hughes 1962).

Why do civilizations go through this cycle? Historian Arnold Toynbee (1946) said that each civilization faces challenges to its existence. Solutions to these challenges are worked out, but they are not satisfactory to all, and oppositional forces remain. The ruling elite manages to keep these forces under control, but at a civilization's peak, when it has become an empire, the ruling elite loses its

capacity to keep the masses in line "by charm rather than by force." The fabric of society eventually rips apart. Force may hold the empire together for hundreds of years, but the civilization is doomed.

In a book that provoked widespread controversy, *The Decline of the West* (1926–1928), Oswald Spengler, a high school teacher in Germany, proposed that Western civilization had passed its peak and was in decline. Although the West succeeded in overcoming the crises provoked by Hitler and Mussolini, as Toynbee noted, civilizations don't end in sudden collapse. Because the decline can last hundreds of years, perhaps the crisis in Western civilization mentioned earlier (poverty, rape, murder, and so on) indicates that Spengler was right, and we are now in decline. If so, it appears that China is waiting on the horizon to be the next global power and to forge a new civilization.

## Conflict over Power

Long before Toynbee, Karl Marx identified a recurring process of social change. He said that each *thesis* (a current arrangement of power) contains its own *antithesis* (contradiction or opposition). A struggle develops between the thesis and its antithesis, leading to a *synthesis* (a new arrangement of power). This new social order, in turn, becomes a thesis that will be challenged by its own antithesis, and so on. Figure 15.1 gives a visual summary of this process.

According to Marx's view (called a **dialectical process** of history), each ruling group sows the seeds of its own destruction. Consider capitalism. Marx said that capitalism (the thesis) is built on the exploitation of workers (an antithesis, or built-in opposition). With workers and owners on a collision course, the dialectical process will not stop until workers establish a classless state (the synthesis).

The analysis of the world's most powerful nations in the previous section follows conflict theory. Their current division of the globe's resources and markets is a thesis. Resentment on the part of have-not nations is an antithesis. If one of the Least Industrialized Nations gains in military power, that nation will press for a redistribution of resources. China, India, Pakistan, and, soon, North Korea and Iran, with their nuclear weapons, fit this scenario. So do the efforts of al-Qaeda to change the balance of power between the Middle East and the industrialized West. Any new arrangement, a new synthesis, will contain its own antitheses. These may be ethnic hostilities or leaders feeling that their country has been denied its fair share of resources. These antitheses will haunt the arrangement of power and must at some point be resolved into a synthesis. The process repeats itself.

## Ogburn's Theory

Sociologist William Ogburn (1922/1938, 1961, 1964) proposed a theory of social change that is based largely on technology. As you can see from Table 15.2, technology, he said, changes society by three processes: invention, discovery, and diffusion. Let's consider each.

**Invention**    Ogburn defined **invention** as a combining of existing elements and materials to form new ones. We usually think of inventions as being only material items, such

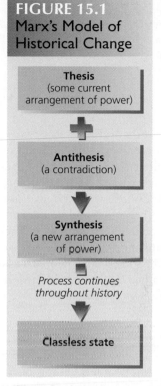

**FIGURE 15.1**
**Marx's Model of Historical Change**

**Thesis**
(some current arrangement of power)

**+**

**Antithesis**
(a contradiction)

**Synthesis**
(a new arrangement of power)

*Process continues throughout history*

**Classless state**

*Source:* By the author.

---

| TABLE 15.2 | Ogburn's Processes of Social Change | | |
| --- | --- | --- | --- |
| Process of Change | What It Is | Examples | Social Changes |
| Invention | Combination of existing elements to form new ones | 1. Cars | 1. Urban sprawl and long commutes to work |
| | | 2. Computers | 2. Telework, downloading music, watching movies at home |
| | | 3. Plastics | 3. Building new types of furniture and construction |
| Discovery | New way of seeing some aspect of the world | 1. Columbus and N. America | 1. Realignment of global power |
| | | 2. Gold in California | 2. Westward expansion of United States |
| | | 3. DNA | 3. Identification of criminals |
| Diffusion | Spread of an invention or discovery | 1. Airplanes | 1. Global tourism |
| | | 2. Money | 2. Global trade |
| | | 3. Condom | 3. Smaller families |

*Note:* For each example, there are many social changes. For social changes ushered in by the computer, see pages 433–435. Any particular change, such as global trade, depends not just on one item, but on several preceding changes.

*Source:* By the author.

*Culture contact* is the source of *diffusion,* the spread of an *invention* or *discovery* from one area to another. Shown here are members of the Samburu tribe in Kenya. How do you think cell phones will affect their lives if their use becomes common among this group?

as computers, but there also are *social inventions.* We have considered many social inventions in this text including democracy and citizenship (301), capitalism (pages 318–319), socialism (pages 319–320), bureaucracy (pages 124–128), the corporation (pages 321–323), and in Chapter 10, gender equality. As we saw in these instances, social inventions can have far-reaching consequences on society and people's relationships to one another. So can material inventions, and in this chapter we will examine how the computer has transformed society.

**Discovery**    Ogburn identified **discovery,** a new way of seeing reality, as a second process of change. The reality is already present, but people see it for the first time. An example is Columbus' "discovery" of North America, which had consequences so huge that they altered the course of human history. This example also illustrates another principle: A discovery brings extensive change only when it comes at the right time. Other groups, such as the Vikings, had already "discovered" North America in the sense of learning that a new land existed—obviously no discovery to the Native Americans already living in it. Viking settlements disappeared into history, however, and Norse culture was untouched by the discovery.

**Diffusion**    Ogburn stressed how **diffusion,** the spread of an invention or discovery from one area to another, can have extensive effects on people's lives. Consider an object as simple as the axe. When missionaries introduced steel axes to the Aborigines of Australia, it upset their whole society. Before this, the men controlled axe-making. They used a special stone that was available only in a remote region, and fathers passed axe-making skills on to their sons. Women had to request permission to use the axe. When steel axes became common, women also possessed them, and the men lost both status and power (Sharp 1995).

Diffusion also includes the spread of ideas. As we saw in Chapter 11, the idea of citizenship changed political structure around the world. It removed monarchs as an unquestioned source of authority. The concept of gender equality is now circling the globe. Although taken for granted in a few parts of the world, the idea that it is

wrong to withhold rights on the basis of someone's sex is revolutionary. Like citizenship, this idea is destined to transform basic human relationships and entire societies.

**Cultural Lag**    Ogburn coined the term **cultural lag** to refer to how some elements of a culture lag behind the changes that come from invention, discovery, and diffusion. Technology, he suggested, usually changes first, with culture lagging behind. In other words, we play catch-up with changing technology, adapting our customs and ways of life to meet its needs.

As with the organ transplants featured in the chapter's opening vignette, technology underlies the rapid change that is engulfing us today. As we consider technology, let's focus on the computer, which, for good or ill, is transforming society and, with it, our way of life.

# How Technology Changes Society

## The Sociological Significance of Technology

As you may recall from Chapter 2, *technology* has a double meaning. It refers to both the *tools,* the items used to accomplish tasks, and the skills or procedures needed to make and use those tools. Technology refers to tools as simple as a comb and as complicated as a computer. Technology's second meaning—the skills or procedures needed to make and use tools—refers in this case not only to the procedures used to manufacture combs and computers but also to those that are required to "produce" an acceptable hairdo or to go

In the photo on the left, Henry Ford proudly displays his 1905 car, the latest in automobile technology. As is apparent, especially from the spokes on the car's wheels, new technology builds on existing technology. At the time this photo was taken, who could have imagined that this vehicle would transform society? Mazda's Nagare, a concept car, is said to embody the word "flow."

online. Apart from its particulars, technology always refers to *artificial means of extending human abilities.*

All human groups make and use technology, but the chief characteristic of technology in postindustrial societies (also called **postmodern societies**) is that it greatly extends our abilities to communicate, to travel, and to analyze information. These *new technologies,* as they are called, allow us to do what had never been done before: to transplant organs; to communicate almost instantaneously anywhere on the globe; to probe space; to travel greater distances faster; and to store, retrieve, and analyze vast amounts of information. In our coming biotech society, we may even "wear" computers, storing data on holograms located in our own proteins (bacteriorhodopsin) (Guessous et al. 2004).

*The sociological significance of technology is not the apparatus but how technology changes our way of life.* It is obvious, for example, that without automobiles, telephones, and televisions, our entire way of life would be strikingly different. Although our journey to the future is going to have many twists and turns, it is intriguing to try to peer over the edge of the present to catch a glimpse of that future. Let's examine some of the computer's effect on education, business, and the waging of war. We'll then consider its impact on social control and social inequality.

## Computers in Education

Computers are having a major impact on education. Students can take courses in Russian, German, and Spanish—even when their schools have no teachers who speak these languages. Even though they have no sociology instructors, they can take courses in the sociology of gender, race, social class, or even sex, and sports. (The comma is important. It isn't sex and sports. That course isn't offered—yet.)

We've barely begun to harness the power of computers, but I imagine that the day will come when you will be able to key in the terms *social interaction* and *gender,* select your preference of historical period, geographical area, age, and ethnic group—and the computer will spew out text, maps, moving images, and sounds. You will be able to compare sexual discrimination in the military in 1985 and today or compare the prices of marijuana and cocaine in Los Angeles and New Orleans. If you wish, the computer will give you a test—geared to the level of difficulty you choose—so that you can check your mastery of the material.

*Distance learning,* courses taught to students who are not physically present with their instructor, will become such a part of mainstream education that most students will take at least some of their high school, college, and graduate courses through this arrangement. Cameras in laptops allow everyone in the class to see everyone else simultaneously, even though the students live in different countries. Imagine this—and likely it soon will be a reality: Your fellow students in a course on diversity in human culture will be living in Thailand, Latvia, South Africa, Egypt, China, and Australia. With zero-cost conference calls and e-mail and file exchanges, you will be able to compare your countries' customs on eating, dating, marriage, family, or burial—whatever is of interest to you. You can then write a team paper in which you compare your experiences with one another, applying the theories taught in the text, and then e-mail your paper to your mutual instructor.

## Computers in Business and Finance

Not long ago, the advanced technology of businesses consisted of cash registers and adding machines. Connection to the outside world was managed by telephone. Today, those same businesses are electronically "wired" to suppliers, salespeople, and clients around the country—and around the world. Computers track sales of items, tabulate inventory, and set in motion the process of reordering and restocking. Their detailed reports of sales alert managers to changes in their customers' tastes or preferences.

National borders have become meaningless as computers instantaneously transfer billions of dollars from one country to another. No "cash" changes hands in these transactions. The money consists of digits in computer memory banks. In the same day, this digitized money can be transferred from the United States to Switzerland, from there to the Grand Cayman Islands, and then to the Isle of Man. Its zigzag, instantaneous path around the globe leaves few traces for sleuths to follow. "Where's my share?" governments around the world are grumbling, as they consider how to control—and tax—this new technology.

## Computers in Warfare

Computers are also having a major impact on the way war is fought. Let's review their impact on warfare in the following Thinking Critically section.

# ThinkingCRITICALLY

## The Coming Star Wars

Star Wars is on its way.

We already have the Predator, an unmanned plane that flies thousands of feet above enemy lines and beams streaming video back to the base. Sensors from the Global Positioning System report the Predator's precise location. When operators at the base identify a target, they press a button; the Predator beams a laser onto the target, and the

operators launch guided bombs (Barry and Thomas 2001).

The enemy doesn't know what hit them. They see neither the Predator nor the laser. Perhaps, however, just before they are blown to bits, they do hear the sound of an incoming bomb (Barry 2001).

On its way is Warfighter I, a camera that uses hyperspectral imaging, a way of identifying objects by detecting their "light signatures." This camera is so precise that it can report from space whether a field of grain contains natural or genetically altered grain—and whether the grain has adequate nitrogen. The military use of this camera? It can also locate tanks that are camouflaged or even hiding under trees (Hitt 2001).

Robot soldiers are on their way, too. In a project called Future Combat Systems, the Pentagon is developing robots that will see and react like humans. They might not look like humans. In fact, they might look like hummingbirds—or tractors or cockroaches. They will gather intelligence, search buildings, and fire weapons (Weiner 2005).

The first robots are already being used in Iraq. These are primitive versions, however, simply remote-controlled devices that dispose of bombs. The next ones are likely to have the capacity to drive vehicles.

The Pentagon is also building its own Internet called the Global Information Grid (GIG). The goal of GIG, encircling the globe, is grandiose: to give the Pentagon a "God's eye view" of every enemy everywhere (Weiner 2004).

All this is but a prelude. The U.S. Defense Department is planning to "weaponize" space. Concerned that other nations will also launch intelligence-gathering devices and space weapons, the United States is set to launch microsatellites the size of a suitcase. These satellites will be able to pull alongside an enemy satellite and, using a microwave gun, fry its electronic system.

Coming also is a laser whose beam will bounce off a mirror in space, making the night battlefield visible to ground soldiers who are wearing special goggles. Also on its way is a series of Star Wars weapons: space-based lasers, pyrotechnic electromagnetic pulsers, holographic decoys, suppression clouds, oxygen suckers, robo-bugs—and whatever else the feverish imaginations of military planners can devise.

The Air Force has nicknamed one of its space programs "Rods from God." Tungsten cylinders would be hurled from space at targets on the ground. Striking at speeds of 7,000 miles an hour, the rods would have the force of a small nuclear weapon. In another program, radio waves would be directed to targets on the earth. As the Air Force explains it, the power of the radio waves could be "just a tap on the shoulder—or they could turn you into toast" (Weiner 2005).

We are on the edge of a surrealistic world. Politicians and the military assume that it is normal both to dominate the world and to weaponize space. The chilling reality is reflected in a report by a congressional commission: "Every medium—air, land and sea—has seen conflict. Reality indicates that space will be no different" (Hitt 2001).

### For Your Consideration

Do you think we should militarize space? What if other countries do the same? In 2006, China launched a missile to shoot down one of its own orbiting satellites, which could indicate that it is ready to play this deadly space game. What do you think of this comment, made to Congress by the head of the U.S. Air Force Space Command? "We must establish and maintain space superiority. It's the American way of fighting" (Weiner 2005).

## Reservations About the Computer

**Big Brother** Some people have deep reservations about our computerized society. They worry that errors will creep into computerized records, that their identity will be stolen and their privacy invaded. Then there is the matter of political control. The Federal Drug Administration has approved an identity chip the size of a grain of rice

that can be injected under the skin (Stein 2004). The chip is designed to store a patient's medical records, including blood type. Besides name, address, age, weight, height, hair and skin color, and race–ethnicity, the chip can also store our school grades, our work history, the names and addresses of our friends and associates—even any suspected acts of disloyalty. The chip can be activated by a scanner, so none of us would even know that we are under surveillance. It isn't difficult to jump from the capacities of this chip to Orwell's Big Brother society.

**Social Inequality** This new technology carries severe implications for national and global stratification. On the national level, computer technology could perpetuate present inequalities: We could end up with information have-nots, primarily inner-city residents cut off from the flow of information on which prosperity depends. Or this technology could provide an opportunity to break out of the inner city and the rural centers of poverty. On the global level, the question is similar, but on a grander scale, taking us to one of the more profound issues of this century: Will unequal access to advanced technology destine the Least Industrialized Nations to a perpetual pauper status? Or will access to this new technology be their passport to affluence?

**In Sum:** Technology wraps itself around us, changing our society, our culture, and our everyday lives. Apart from the disruptions that technology brings, there are two primary issues: What type of future will technology lead us into? Will the new technology perpetuate or alleviate social inequalities on both national and global levels?

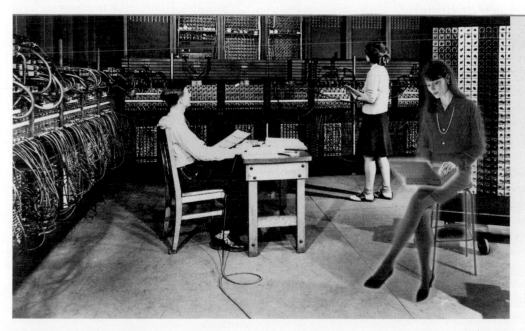

Most of us take computers for granted, but they are new to the world scene—as are their effects on our lives. This photo captures a significant change in the evolution of computers. The laptop held by the superimposed model has more power than the room-size ENIAC of 1946.

# Social Movements as a Source of Social Change

The contradictions of social inequality that are built into arrangements of power, summarized in Figure 15.1, create discontent. One result is **social movements,** large numbers of people who organize either to promote or to resist social change. Members of social movements hold strong ideas about what is wrong with the world—or some part of it—and how to make things right. Examples include the civil rights movement, the white supremacist movement, the women's movement, the animal rights movement, and the environmental movement.

At the heart of social movements lies a sense of injustice (Klandermans 1997). Some find a particular condition of society intolerable, and their goal is to promote social change. Theirs is called a **proactive social movement.** Others, in contrast, feel threatened because some condition of society is changing, and they *react* to resist that change. Theirs is a **reactive social movement.**

To further their goals, people develop **social movement organizations.** Those who want to promote social change establish organizations such as the National Association for the Advancement of Colored People (NAACP). In contrast, those who are trying to resist these particular changes form organizations such as the Ku Klux Klan or Aryan Nations. To recruit followers and publicize their grievances, leaders of social movements use attention-getting devices, from marches and protest rallies to sit-ins and boycotts. Some stage "media events," sometimes quite effectively.

Social movements are like a rolling sea, observed sociologist Mayer Zald (1992). During one period, few social movements may appear, but shortly afterward, a wave of them rolls in, each competing for the public's attention. Zald suggests that a *cultural crisis* can give birth to a wave of social movements. By this, he means that there are times when a society's institutions fail to keep up with social change. During these times many people's needs go unfulfilled, massive unrest follows, and social movements spring into action to bridge this gap.

Let's see what types of social movements there are, how they use propaganda, and the stages they go through.

## Types of Social Movements

Since social change is their goal, we can classify social movements according to their *target* and the *amount of change* they seek. Look at Figure 15.2. If you read across, you will see that the target of the first two types of social movements is *individuals*. **Alterative social movements** seek only to *alter* some specific behavior. An example is the Woman's Christian Temperance Union, a powerful social movement of the early 1900s. Its goal was to get people to stop drinking alcohol. Its members were convinced that if they could shut down the saloons, such problems as poverty and wife abuse would go away. **Redemptive social movements** also target individuals, but their goal is *total* change. An example is a religious social movement that stresses conversion. In fundamentalist Christianity, for example, when someone converts to Christ, the entire person is supposed to change, not just some specific behavior. Self-centered acts are to be replaced by loving behaviors toward others as the convert becomes, in fundamentalist terms, a "new creation."

The target of the next two types of social movements is *society*. **Reformative social movements** seek to *reform* some specific aspect of society. The animal rights movement, for example, seeks to reform the ways in which society views and treats animals. **Transformative social movements,** in contrast, seek to *transform* the social order itself. Its members want to replace the current social order with their vision of the good society. Revolutions, such as those in the American colonies, France, Russia, and Cuba, are examples.

As Figure 15.2 indicates, some social movements have a global orientation. As with many aspects of life in our new global economy, numerous issues that concern people transcend national boundaries. Participants in **transnational social movements** (also called *new social movements*) want to change some specific condition that cuts across societies. (See Cell 5 of Figure 15.2.) These social movements often center on improving the quality of life (Melucci 1989). Examples are the women's movement, labor movements, and the environmental movement (McAdam et al. 1988; Smith et al. 1997; Walter 2001; Tilly 2004).

*Social movements* involve large numbers of people who, upset about some condition in society, organize to do something about it. Shown here is Carrie Nation, a temperance leader who in 1900 began to break up saloons with a hatchet. Her social movement eventually became so popular and powerful that it resulted in Prohibition.

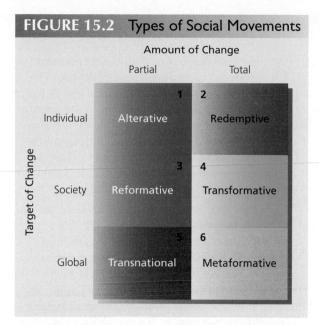

**FIGURE 15.2    Types of Social Movements**

Amount of Change

|  | Partial | Total |
|---|---|---|
| Individual | 1 Alterative | 2 Redemptive |
| Society | 3 Reformative | 4 Transformative |
| Global | 5 Transnational | 6 Metaformative |

*Target of Change* (vertical axis)

*Sources:* The first four types are from Aberle 1966; the last two are by the author.

Cell 6 in Figure 15.2 represents a rare type of social movement. The goal of **metaformative social movements** is to change the social order itself—not just of a specific country, but of an entire civilization or even the whole world. Their objective is to change concepts and practices of race–ethnicity, class, gender, family, religion, government, and the global stratification of nations. These were the aims of the communist social movement of the early to middle twentieth century and the fascist social movement of the 1920s to 1940s. (The fascists consisted of the Nazis in Germany, the Black Shirts of Italy, and other groups throughout Europe and the United States.)

Today, we are witnessing another metaformative social movement, that of Islamic fundamentalism. Like other social movements before it, this movement is not united, but consists of many separate groups with differing goals and tactics. Al-Qaeda, for example, would not only cleanse Islamic societies of Western influences—which they contend are demonic and degrading to men, women, and morality—but also replace Western civilization with an extremist form of Islam. This frightens both Muslims and non-Muslims, who hold sharply differing views of what constitutes quality of life. If the Islamic fundamentalists—like the communists or fascists before them—have their way, they will usher in a New World Order fashioned after their particular views of the good life.

## Propaganda and the Mass Media

The leaders of social movements try to manipulate the mass media to influence **public opinion,** how people think about some issue. The right kind of publicity enables the leaders to arouse sympathy and to lay the groundwork for recruiting more members. Pictures of bloodied, dead baby seals, for example, go a long way toward getting a group's message across.

A key to understanding social movements, then, is **propaganda.** Although this word often evokes negative images, it actually is a neutral term. Propaganda is simply the presentation of information in an attempt to influence people. Its original meaning was positive. *Propaganda* referred to a committee of cardinals of the Roman Catholic Church whose assignment was the care of foreign missions. (They were to *propagate*—multiply or spread—the faith.) The term has traveled a long way since then, however, and today it usually refers to a presentation of information so one-sided that it distorts reality.

Propaganda, in the sense of organized attempts to influence public opinion, is a part of everyday life. Our news is filled with propaganda, as various interest groups—from retailers to the government—try to manipulate our perceptions of the world. Our movies, too, although seemingly intended as simply entertainment devices, are actually propaganda vehicles. The basic techniques that underlie propaganda are discussed in the Down-to-Earth Sociology box on the next page.

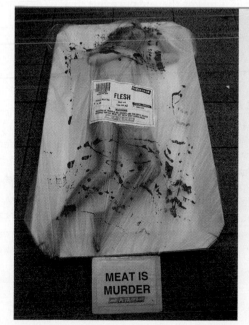

FLESH

MEAT IS MURDER

The use of *propaganda* is popular among those committed to the goals of a social movement. They can see only one side to the social issue about which they are so upset. What attention-getting devices is this demonstrator using? Are they effective? Why is this an example of propaganda?

# Down-to-Earth Sociology
## "Tricks of the Trade"— Deception and Persuasion in Propaganda

Sociologists Alfred and Elizabeth Lee (1939) found that propaganda relies on seven basic techniques, which they termed "tricks of the trade." To be effective, the techniques should be subtle, with the audience unaware that their minds and emotions are being manipulated. If propaganda is effective, people will not know why they support something, but they'll fervently defend it. Becoming familiar with these techniques can help you keep your mind and emotions from being manipulated.

- *Name calling.* This technique aims to arouse opposition to the competing product, candidate, or policy by associating it with a negative image. By comparison, one's own product, candidate, or policy is attractive. Republicans who call Democrats "soft on crime" and Democrats who call Republicans "insensitive to the poor" are using this technique.

- *Glittering generality.* Essentially the opposite of the first technique, this one surrounds the product, candidate, or policy with images that arouse positive feelings. "She's a real Democrat" has little meaning, but it makes the audience feel that something substantive has been said. "This Republican stands for individual rights" is so general that it is meaningless; yet the audience thinks that it has heard a specific message about the candidate.

- *Transfer.* In its positive form, this technique associates the product, candidate, or policy with something the public approves of or respects. You might not be able to get by with saying "Coors is patriotic," but surround a beer with images of the country's flag, and beer drinkers will get the idea that it is more patriotic to drink this brand of beer than some other kind. In its negative form, this technique associates the product, candidate, or policy with something generally disapproved of by the public.

- *Testimonials.* Famous individuals endorse a product, candidate, or policy. Michelle Wie lends her name to Nike products, and Tiger Woods tells you that Buicks make fine SUVs. In the negative form of this technique, a despised person is associated with the competing product. If propagandists (called "spin doctors" in politics) could get away with it, they would show Osama bin Laden announcing support for an opposing candidate.

- *Plain folks.* Sometimes it pays to associate the product, candidate, or policy with "just plain folks." "If Mary or John Q. Public likes it, you will, too." A political candidate who kisses babies, puts on a hard hat, and has lunch at McDonald's while photographers "catch him (or her) in the act" is using the "plain folks" strategy. "I'm just a regular person" is the message of the presidential candidate who poses for photographers in jeans and work shirt—while making certain that the chauffeur-driven Mercedes does not show up in the background.

- *Card stacking.* The aim of this technique is to present only positive information about what you support, and only negative information about what you oppose. The intent is to make it sound as though there is only one conclusion a rational person can draw. Falsehoods, distortions, and illogical statements are often used.

- *Bandwagon.* "Everyone is doing it" is the idea behind this technique. Emphasizing how many other people buy the product or support the candidate or policy conveys the message that anyone who doesn't join in is on the wrong track.

The Lees (1939) added, "Once we know that a speaker or writer is using one of these propaganda devices in an attempt to convince us of an idea, we can separate the device from the idea and see what the idea amounts to on its own merits."

## For Your Consideration

What propaganda techniques have you seen or heard recently? Recall TV ads, political ads, movies, and newspaper articles. Explain why they were propaganda, not simply a source of information or entertainment.

The mass media play such a crucial role that we can say they are the gatekeepers to social movements. If those who control and work in the mass media—from owners to reporters—are sympathetic to some particular "cause," you can be sure that it will receive sympathetic treatment. If the social movement goes against their views, however, it likely will be ignored or receive unfavorable treatment. If you ever get the impression that the media are trying to manipulate your opinions and attitudes—even your feelings—on some particular issue or social movement, you probably are right. Far from providing unbiased reporting, the media are under the control and influence of people who have an agenda to get across. To the materials in the Down-to-Earth Sociology box on propaganda, then, we need to add the biases of the media establishment—the topics it chooses to publicize, those it chooses to ignore, and its favorable and unfavorable treatment of issues and movements.

Sociology can be a liberating discipline (Berger 1963/2007). Sociology sensitizes us to *multiple realities;* that is, for any single point of view on some topic, there are competing points of view. Each represents reality as people see it, their distinct experiences having led them to different perceptions. Consequently, different people find each point of view equally compelling. Although the committed members of a social movement are sincere—and perhaps even make sacrifices for "the cause"—theirs is but one view of the world. If other sides were presented, the issue would look quite different.

## The Stages of Social Movements

Sociologists have identified five stages in the growth and maturity of social movements (Lang and Lang 1961; Mauss 1975; Spector and Kitsuse 1977; Jasper 1991; Tilly 2004):

1. *Initial unrest and agitation.* During this first stage, people are upset about some condition in society and want to change it. Leaders emerge who verbalize people's feelings and crystallize issues. Most social movements fail at this stage. Unable to gain enough support, after a brief flurry of activity, they fade away.

2. *Resource mobilization.* A crucial factor that enables social movements to make it past the first stage is **resource mobilization.** By this term, sociologists mean the gathering and organizing of resources such as time, money, information, people's skills, and the ability to get the attention of the mass media. Those resources may also include access to churches to organize protests (Mirola 2003). A key resource is communications technology such as cell phones, Internet sites, and blogs. Also important is access to mailing lists for direct mailing, faxing, and e-mailing.

In some cases, an indigenous leadership arises to mobilize resources. Other groups, lacking capable leadership, turn to "guns for hire," outside specialists who sell their services. As sociologists John McCarthy and Mayer Zald (1977; Zald and McCarthy 1987) point out, even though large numbers of people may be upset over some condition of society, without resource mobilization they are only upset people, perhaps even agitators, but they do not constitute a social movement.

3. *Organization.* A division of labor is set up. The leadership makes policy decisions, and the rank and file carry out the daily tasks necessary to keep the movement going. There is still much collective excitement about the issue, the movement's focal point of concern.

4. *Institutionalization.* At this stage, the movement has developed a bureaucracy, the type of formal hierarchy that was described in Chapter 5. Control lies in the hands of career officers, who may care more about their own position in the organization than the movement for which the organization's initial leaders made sacrifices. The collective excitement diminishes.

5. *Organizational decline and possible resurgence.* During this phase, managing the day-to-day affairs of the organization dominates the leadership. A change in public sentiment may even have occurred, and there may no longer be a group of committed people who share a common cause. The movement is likely to wither away.

Decline is not inevitable, however. More idealistic and committed leaders can emerge who reinvigorate the movement. Or, as in the case of abortion, the topic of the following Thinking Critically section, conflict between groups on opposing sides of the issue can invigorate both sides and prevent the movement's decline.

# ThinkingCRITICALLY

## Which Side of the Barricades? Prochoice and Prolife as a Social Movement

No issue so divides Americans as abortion. Although most Americans take a more moderate view, on one side are some who believe that abortion should be permitted under any circumstance, even during the last month of pregnancy. They are matched by individuals on the other side who are convinced that abortion should never be allowed under any circumstances, not even in the case of rape or incest or during the first month of pregnancy. This polarization constantly breathes new life into the movement.

When the U.S. Supreme Court made its 1973 decision, *Roe v. Wade,* that states could not prohibit abortion, the prochoice side relaxed. Victory was theirs, and they thought their opponents would quietly disappear. Instead, large numbers of Americans were disturbed by what they saw as the legal right to murder unborn children.

The views of the two sides could not be more incompatible. Those who favor choice view the 1.3 million abortions that are performed annually in the United States as examples of women exercising their basic reproductive rights. Those who gather under the prolife banner see these abortions as legalized murder. To the prochoice side, those who oppose abortion are blocking women's rights— they would force women to continue pregnancies they want to terminate. To the prolife side, those who advocate choice are perceived as condoning murder—they would sacrifice their unborn children for the sake of school, career, or convenience.

There is no way to reconcile these contrary views. Each sees the other as unreasonable and extremist. And each uses propaganda by focusing on worst-case scenarios: prochoice images of young women raped at gunpoint, forced to bear the children of rapists; prolife images of women who are eight months pregnant killing their babies instead of nurturing them.

With no middle ground, these views remain in perpetual conflict. As each side fights for what it considers to be basic rights, it reinvigorates the other. When in 1989 the

*With sincere people on both sides of the issue—equally committed and equally convinced that their side is right—abortion is destined to remain a controversial force in U.S. life.*

U.S. Supreme Court decided in *Webster v. Reproductive Services* that states could restrict abortion, one side mourned it as a defeat and the other hailed it as a victory. Seeing the political battle going against them, the prochoice side regrouped for a determined struggle. The prolife side, sensing judicial victory within its grasp, gathered forces for a push to complete the overthrow of *Roe v. Wade.*

In 1992, this goal of the prolife side almost became reality in *Casey v. Planned Parenthood.* In a 6–3 decision, the Supreme Court upheld the right of states to require women to wait 24 hours between the confirmation of pregnancy and getting an abortion; to require girls under 18 to obtain the consent of one parent; and to require that women be informed about alternatives to abortion and that they be given materials which describe the fetus. In the same case, however, in a 5–4 decision, the Court ruled that a wife does not have to inform her husband if she intends to have an abortion. In 2007, in another 5–4 decision, the Court ruled a certain type of abortion procedure illegal. The names given this late-term procedure represent the ongoing struggle: One side calls it an "intact dilation and evacuation," while the other side terms it a "partial-birth abortion."

The battle is brought to our attention each time the Senate is asked to confirm the president's nominee to the U.S. Supreme Court. To watch these hearings is to view a skirmish between the opposing sides of this issue.

Because the two sides do not share the same reality, this social movement cannot end unless an overwhelming majority of Americans commit to one side or the other. Every legislative and judicial outcome—including the extremes of a constitutional amendment that declares abortion to be either murder or a woman's right—is a victory to one and a defeat to the other. To committed activists, then, no battle is ever complete. Rather, each action is only one small part of a long, hard-fought moral struggle.

## For Your Consideration

Typically, the last stage of a social movement is decline. Why hasn't this social movement declined? Under what conditions will it decline?

The longer the duration of the pregnancy, the fewer the number of Americans who approve of abortion. How do you feel about abortion during the second month versus the eighth month? What do you think about abortion in cases of rape and incest? Can you identify some of the social reasons that underlie your opinions?

*Sources:* Neikirk and Elsasser 1992; McKenna 1995; Williams 1995; *Statistical Abstract* 2007: Table 96; Henslin 2008.

# The Growth Machine Versus the Earth

Of all the changes swirling around us, those that affect the natural environment seem to hold the most serious implications for human life.

Underlying today's environmental decay is the *globalization* of capitalism, which I have stressed throughout this text. To maintain their dominance and increase their wealth, the Most Industrialized Nations, spurred by multinational corporations, continue to push for economic growth. At the same time, the Industrializing Nations, playing catch-up, are striving to develop their economies. Meanwhile, the Least Industrialized Nations are anxious to enter the race: Because they start from even farther behind, they have to strive for even faster growth.

Many people are convinced that the earth cannot withstand such an onslaught. Global economic production creates extensive pollution, and faster-paced production means faster-paced destruction of our environment. In this relentless pursuit of economic development, many animal species are endangered or on the verge of extinction. If the goal is a **sustainable environment,** a world system in which we use our physical environment to meet our needs without destroying humanity's future, we cannot continue to trash the earth. In short, the ecological message is incompatible with an economic message that implies it is OK to rape the earth for the sake of profits.

Before looking at the social movement that has emerged about this issue, let's examine major environmental problems. We'll begin with pollution in the Most Industrialized Nations.

## Environmental Problems in the Most Industrialized Nations

Although even tribal groups produced pollution, the frontal assault on the natural environment did not begin in earnest until nations industrialized. Industrialization was equated with progress and prosperity. For the Most Industrialized Nations, the slogan has been "Growth at any cost."

Industrial growth did come, but at a high cost to the natural environment. Today, for example, formerly pristine streams are polluted sewers, and the water supply of some cities is unfit to drink. Nuclear wastes, which will remain lethal for thousands of years, have been stored in rusting containers (Madslien 2006). We simply don't know what to do with this deadly garbage. Despite the danger to people and the environment, much toxic waste has simply been dumped. The Social Map on the next page shows the locations of the worst hazardous waste sites in the United States. These sites represent corporate garbage, some of it subsidized by corporate welfare, the topic of the Down-to-Earth Sociology box on page 443.

The major polluters are the Most Industrialized Nations. Our follies include harming the ozone layer in order to have the convenience of aerosol spray bottles, refrigerators, and air conditioners. With limited space to address this issue, I would like to focus on an overarching aspect of the pollution of our environment, the burning of fossil fuels.

**Fossil Fuels and the Environment**   Burning fossil fuels to run factories, motorized vehicles, and power plants has been especially harmful. Fish can no longer survive in some lakes in Canada and the northeastern United States because of **acid rain.** As Figure 15.4 on the next page illustrates, the burning of fossil fuels releases sulfur dioxide and nitrogen oxide, which react with moisture in the air to become sulfuric and nitric acids.

An invisible but infinitely more serious consequence is the **greenhouse effect.** Burning fossil fuels releases gases that, like the glass of a greenhouse, allow sunlight to enter the earth's atmosphere freely but inhibit the release of heat. It is as though the gases have smudged the windows of our earth's greenhouse, and our planet can no longer breathe the way it should. The buildup of heat is causing **global warming:** Glaciers are melting and the seas are rising, threatening to flood the world's shorelines. Some island nations will disappear, washed away into the ocean (Kanter and Revkin 2007). As the climate boundaries move north several hundred miles, many animal and plant species will become extinct.

For decades, scientists argued about global warming. Many said that it was part of a natural cycle that the earth goes through. Some even said that it did not exist. As evidence accumulated, more and more scientists concluded that global warming did exist and that human activity—primarily the burning of coal and oil—was its cause. Today, the world's leading climate scientists, forming the United Nations' Intergovernmental Panel on Climate Change, have concluded that global warming is "unequivocal" and that human activity is its main driver (Rosenthal and Revkin 2007). The consequences, they predict, are likely to be catastrophic, and we should immediately reduce the burning of fossil fuels.

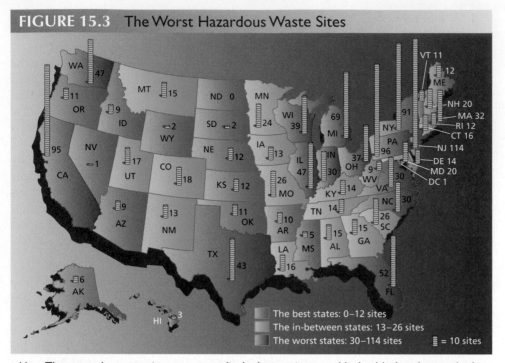

**FIGURE 15.3    The Worst Hazardous Waste Sites**

The best states: 0–12 sites
The in-between states: 13–26 sites
The worst states: 30–114 sites          = 10 sites

*Note:* These are the waste sites so outstandingly threatening to public health that they made the national priority list. New Jersey is in a class by itself. This small state has 18 more hazardous waste sites than its nearest competition Pennsylvania, with 96.
*Source:* By the author. Based on *Statistical Abstract of the United States* 2007:Table 368.

**The Energy Shortage and Multinational Corporations**    If you ever read about an energy shortage, you can be sure that what you read is false. There is no energy shortage, nor can there ever be. We can produce unlimited low-cost power, which can help to raise the living standards of humans across the globe. The sun, for example, produces more energy than humanity could ever use. Boundless energy is also available from the tides and the winds. In some cases, we need better technology to harness these sources of energy; in others, we need only to apply the technology we already have.

Burning fossil fuels in internal combustion engines is the main source of pollution in the Most Industrialized Nations. Of the technologies being developed to use alternative sources of energy in vehicles, the most prominent is the gas-electric hybrid. Some of these cars are expected to eventually get several hundred miles per gallon of gasoline. The hybrid, however, is simply a bridge until vehicles powered by fuel cells become practical. Fuel cells convert hydrogen into electricity; water, instead of carbon monoxide, will come out of a car's exhaust pipe.

**Environmental Injustice**    Unequal power has led to **environmental injustice**—minorities and the poor being the ones who suffer the most from the effects of pollution (Mohal and Saha 2007). Industries locate where land is cheaper, which is *not* where the wealthy live.

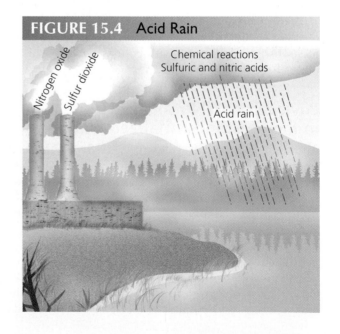

**FIGURE 15.4    Acid Rain**

Nitrogen oxide

Sulfur dioxide

Chemical reactions
Sulfuric and nitric acids

Acid rain

Nor will the rich allow factories to spew pollution near their homes. As a result, low-income communities, which are often inhabited by minorities, are more likely to be exposed to pollution. Sociologists have studied, formed, and joined *environmental justice* groups that fight to close polluting plants and block construction of polluting industries.

## Environmental Problems in the Industrializing and Least Industrialized Nations

Pollution and the destruction of the environment cannot be laid solely at the feet of the Most Industrialized Nations. With their rush to industrialize, along with

## *Down-to-Earth Sociology*
### Corporations and Big Welfare Bucks: How to Get Paid to Pollute

Welfare is one of the most controversial topics in the United States. It arouses the ire of many wealthy and middle-class Americans, who view the poor who collect welfare as parasites. But have you heard about *corporate welfare*?

**Corporate welfare** refers to handouts that are given to corporations. Some states will reduce a company's taxes if it locates within the state or if it remains after threatening to leave. Some states provide land and buildings at bargain prices. The reason: jobs.

Corporate welfare even goes to companies that foul the land, water, and air. Borden Chemicals in Louisiana has buried hazardous wastes without a permit and released clouds of hazardous chemicals so thick that to protect drivers, the police have sometimes had to shut down the highway that runs near the plant. Borden even contaminated the groundwater beneath its plant, threatening the aquifer that provides drinking water for residents of Louisiana and Texas.

Borden's pollution has cost the company dearly: $3.6 million in fines, $3 million to clean up the groundwater, and $400,000 for local emergency response units. That's a hefty $7 million. But if we add corporate welfare, the company didn't make out so badly. With $15 million in reduced and canceled property taxes, Borden has enjoyed a net gain of $8 million (Bartlett and Steele 1998). And that's not counting the savings the company racked up by not having to properly dispose of its toxic wastes in the first place.

Louisiana has added a novel twist to corporate welfare. It offers an incentive to help start-up companies.

*Some companies that pollute are rewarded with reduced taxes.*

This itself isn't novel; the owners of that little "mom and pop" grocery store on your corner may have received some benefits when they first opened. Louisiana's twist is what it counts as a start-up company. One of these little start-ups is called Exxon Mobil Corp. Although Exxon Mobil opened for business in 1870 and is one of the world's richest corporations, it had $213 million in property taxes canceled under this start-up program. Another little company that the state figured could use a nudge to help it get started was Shell Oil Co., which had $140 million slashed from its taxes (Bartlett and Steele 1998). Then there were International Paper, Dow Chemical, Union Carbide, Boise Cascade, Georgia Pacific, and another tiny one called Procter & Gamble.

### For Your Consideration
Apply the functionalist, symbolic interactionist, and conflict perspectives to corporate welfare. Which do you think provides the best explanation of corporate welfare? Why?

nonexistent or unenforced environmental laws, the Industrializing Nations have become major polluters (Bradsher 2007a). Pollution in China is taking a huge environmental toll, as rivers and lakes become depositories for industrial waste and smoke consumes China's cities. The attempts to reduce pollution have been feeble. As China secures its place in the industrialized world, its leaders will take the need to control pollution seriously.

The lack of environmental protection laws in some of the Least Industrialized Nations has not gone unnoticed by opportunists in the industrialized ones. Some dump poisonous wastes in these countries (Polgreen and Simons 2006). Others produce chemicals there that have been outlawed in their own countries (Smith 1995; Mol 2001). Alarmed at the growing environmental destruction, the World Bank, the monetary arm of the world's most powerful nations, has pressured the Least Industrialized Nations to reduce pollution. When New Delhi officials tried to comply, workers blocked traffic and set fires, closing down the city for several days (Freund 2001). Understandably, the basic concern of workers is to provide food for their families first and to worry about the environment later.

A special concern is the rain forests. Although they cover just 7 percent of the earth's land area, the rain forests are home to *one-third to one-half* of all the earth's plant and animal species. Despite our knowledge that the rain forests are essential for humanity's welfare, we seem bent on destroying them for the sake of timber and farms. In the process, we extinguish plant and animal species, perhaps thousands a year (Wolfensohn and Fuller 1998). As biologists remind us, once a species is lost, it is gone forever.

As the rain forests disappear, so do the Indian tribes who live in them. With their extinction goes their knowledge of the environment, the topic of the Cultural Diversity box on page 446. Like Esau who traded his birthright for a bowl of porridge, we are exchanging our future for some lumber, farms, and pastures.

## The Environmental Movement

Concern about environmental problems has produced a worldwide social movement. One result is *green parties,* political parties whose central issue is the environment. In some European countries, these parties have made a political impact. In Germany, for example, the Green Party has won seats in the national legislature. Green parties have had little success in the United States, but in the 2000 election, a green party headed by Ralph Nader arguably

tipped the balance and gave the presidential election to George W. Bush.

Activists in the environmental movement generally seek solutions in politics, education, and legislation. Despairing that pollution continues, that the rain forests are still being cleared, and that species continue to become extinct, some activists are convinced that the planet is doomed unless we act immediately. Choosing a more radical course, they use extreme tactics to try to arouse indignation among the public and to force the government to act. Convinced that they stand for true morality, many are willing to break the law and go to jail for their actions. Such activists are featured in the following Thinking Critically section.

# ThinkingCRITICALLY
## Ecosabotage

Chaining oneself to a giant Douglas fir that is slated for cutting, tearing down power lines and ripping up survey stakes, driving spikes into redwood trees, sinking whaling vessels, and torching SUVs and Hummers—are these the acts of dangerous punks who have little understanding of the needs of modern society? Or are they the acts of brave men and women who are willing to put their freedom, and even their lives, on the line on behalf of the earth itself?

To understand why **ecosabotage**—actions taken to sabotage the efforts of people who are thought to be legally harming the environment—is taking place, consider the Medicine Tree, a 3,000-year-old redwood in the Sally Bell Grove near the northern California coast. Georgia Pacific, a lumber company, was determined to cut down the Medicine Tree, the oldest and largest of the region's redwoods, which rests on a sacred site of the Sinkyone Indians. Members of Earth First! chained themselves to the tree. After they were arrested, the sawing began. Other protesters jumped over the police-lined barricade and stood defiantly in the path of men wielding axes and chain saws. A logger swung an axe and barely missed a demonstrator. At that moment, the sheriff radioed a restraining order, and the cutting stopped.

Twenty-four-year-old David Chain's dedication cost him his life. The federal government and the state of California were trying to purchase 10,000 acres of pristine redwoods for half a billion dollars. As last-minute negotiations dragged on, loggers from the Pacific Lumber Company kept felling trees, and Earth First! activists kept trying to stop them. David Chain died of a crushed skull when a felled tree struck him.

How many 3,000-year-old trees remain on this planet? Does our desire for fences and picnic tables for backyard barbecues justify cutting them down? Issues like these—as well as the slaughter of seals, the destruction of the rain forests, and the drowning of dolphins in mile-long drift nets—spawned Earth First! and other organizations devoted to preserving the environment, such as Greenpeace, Rainforest Action Network, the Ruckus Society, and the Sea Shepherds.

"We feel like there are insane people who are consciously destroying our environment, and we are compelled to fight back," explains a member of one of the militant groups. "No compromise in defense of Mother Earth!" says another. "With famine and death approaching, we're in the early stages of World War III," adds another.

Radical environmentalists represent a broad range of activities and purposes. They are united neither on tactics nor on goals. Most propose a simpler lifestyle that will consume less energy and reduce pressure on the earth's resources. Some want to stop a specific action, such as the killing of whales. Others want to destroy all nuclear weapons and dismantle nuclear power plants. Some want everyone to become a vegetarian. Still others want the earth's population to drop to one billion, roughly what it was in 1800. Some even want humans to return to hunting and gathering societies. These groups are so splintered that Dave Foreman, the founder of Earth First!, quit his own organization when it became too confrontational for his taste.

Radical groups have had some successes. They have brought a halt to the killing of dolphins off Japan's Iki Island, achieved a ban on whaling, established trash recycling programs, and saved hundreds of thousands of acres of trees, including, of course, the Medicine Tree.

## For Your Consideration

Should we applaud ecosaboteurs or jail them? As symbolic interactionists stress, it all depends on how you view their actions. And as conflict theorists emphasize, your view likely depends on your location in the economy. That is, if you own a lumber company, you will see ecosaboteurs differently from the way a camping enthusiast will. How does your own view of ecosaboteurs depend on your life situation? What effective alternatives to ecosabotage are there for people who are convinced that we are destroying the very life support system of our planet?

*Sources:* Carpenter 1990; Eder 1990; Foote 1990; Parfit 1990; Reed and Benet 1990; Knickerbocker 2003; Gunther 2004; Fattig 2007.

Julia "Butterfly" Hill lived for two years in this 1,000-year-old redwood tree, which she named Luna. The Pacific Lumber Company finally agreed to save the tree and a 200-foot buffer zone.

## Environmental Sociology

About 1970, **environmental sociology** emerged. The focus of this subdiscipline of sociology is the relationship between human societies and the environment (Dunlap and Catton 1979, 1983; Casper 2003). Its main assumptions are

1. The physical environment should be a significant variable in sociological investigation.
2. Human beings are but one species among many that depend on the natural environment.

# *Cultural Diversity around the World*

## The Rain Forests: Lost Tribes, Lost Knowledge

Since 1900, 90 of Brazil's 270 Indian tribes have disappeared. Other tribes have moved to villages as settlers have taken over their lands. Tribal knowledge is lost as group members adapt to village life.

Tribal groups are not just "wild" people who barely survive despite their ignorance. On the contrary, they have intricate forms of social organization and possess knowledge that has accumulated over thousands of years. The 2,500 Kayapo Indians, for example, belong to one of the Amazon's endangered tribes. The Kayapo use 250 types of wild fruit and hundreds of nut and tuber species. They cultivate thirteen types of bananas, eleven kinds of manioc (cassava), sixteen strains of sweet potato, and seventeen kinds of yams. Many of these varieties are unknown to non-Indians. The Kayapo also use thousands of medicinal plants, one of which contains a drug that is effective against intestinal parasites.

Until recently, Western scientists dismissed tribal knowledge as superstitious and worthless. Now, however, some have come to realize that to lose tribes is to lose valuable knowledge. In the Central African Republic, a man whose chest was being eaten away by an amoeboid infection lay dying because his infection did not respond to drugs. Out of desperation, the Roman Catholic nuns who were treating him sought the advice of a native doctor. He applied crushed termites to the open wounds. To the amazement of the nuns, the man made a remarkable recovery.

*A Tari Huli dancer in the New Guinea highlands. The way of life of the world's few remaining rain forest tribes is threatened.*

The disappearance of the rain forests means the destruction of plant species that may have healing properties. Some of the discoveries from the rain forests have been astounding. The needles from a Himalayan tree in India contain taxol, a drug that is effective against ovarian and breast cancer. A flower from Madagascar is used in the treatment of leukemia; a frog in Peru produces a painkiller that is more powerful, but less addictive, than morphine (Wolfensohn and Fuller 1998).

On average, one tribe of Amazonian Indians has been lost each year for the past century—because of violence, greed for their lands, and exposure to infectious diseases against which they have little resistance. Ethnocentrism underlies much of this assault. Perhaps the extreme is represented by the cattle ranchers in Colombia who killed eighteen Cueva Indians. The cattle ranchers were perplexed when they were put on trial for murder. They asked why they should be charged with a crime, since everyone knew that the Cuevas were animals, not people. They pointed out that there was even a verb in Colombian Spanish, *cuevar,* which means "to hunt Cueva Indians." So what was their crime, they asked? The jury found them not guilty because of "cultural ignorance."

### For Your Consideration
What do you think we can do to stop the destruction of the rain forests?

*Sources:* Durning 1990; Gorman 1991; Linden 1991; Stipp 1992; Nabhan 1998; Simons 2006.

The social movement that centers on the environment has become global. In all nations, people are concerned about the destruction of the earth's resources. This photo is a sign of changing times. Instead of jumping on this beached whale and carving it into pieces, these Brazilians are doing their best to save its life.

3. Because of feedback to nature, human actions have many unintended consequences.
4. The world is finite, so there are physical limits to economic growth.
5. Economic expansion requires increased extraction of resources from the environment.
6. Increased extraction of resources leads to ecological problems.
7. These ecological problems place limits on economic expansion.
8. Governments create environmental problems by encouraging the accumulation of capital.

The goal of environmental sociology is not to stop pollution or nuclear power but, rather, to study how humans (their cultures, values, and behavior) affect the physical environment and how the physical environment affects human activities. Environmental sociologists, however, generally are also environmental activists, and the Section on Environment and Technology of the American Sociological Association tries to influence governmental policies (American Sociological Association n.d.).

**Technology and the Environment: The Goal of Harmony**
It is inevitable that humans will continue to develop new technologies. But the abuse of our environment by those technologies is not inevitable. To understate the matter, the destruction of our planet is an unwise choice.

If we are to live in a world that is worth passing on to coming generations, we must seek harmony between technology and the natural environment. This will not be easy. At one extreme are people who claim that to protect the environment we must eliminate industrialization and go back to a tribal way of life. At the other extreme are people who are blind to the harm being done to the natural environment, who want the entire world to industrialize at full speed. Somewhere, there must be a middle ground, one that recognizes not only that industrialization is here to stay but also that we *can* control it, for it is our creation. Controlled, industrialization can enhance our quality of life; uncontrolled, it will destroy us.

It is essential, then, that we develop ways to reduce or eliminate the harm that technology does to the environment. This includes mechanisms to monitor the production, use, and disposal of technology. The question, of course, is whether we have the resolve to take the steps necessary to preserve the environment for future generations. What is at stake is nothing less than the welfare of planet Earth. Surely that is enough to motivate us to make wise choices.

# SUMMARY *and* REVIEW

## How Social Change Transforms Social Life

*What major trends have transformed the course of human history?*

The primary changes in human history are the four social revolutions (domestication, agriculture, industrialization, and information); the change from *Gemeinschaft* to *Gesellschaft* societies; capitalism and industrialization; modernization; and global stratification. Social movements indicate cutting edges of social change. Ethnic conflicts and power rivalries threaten the global divisions that the most powerful nations are working out. We may also be on the cutting edge of a new biotech society. Pp. 426–430.

## Theories and Processes of Social Change

*Besides technology, capitalism, modernization, and so on, what other theories of social change are there?*

*Evolutionary* theories presuppose that societies move from the same starting point to some similar ending point. *Unilinear* theories, which assume the same evolutionary path for every society, were replaced by *multilinear* theories, which assume that different paths lead to the same stage of development. *Cyclical* theories view civilizations as going through a process of birth, youth, maturity, decline, and death. Conflict theorists view social change as inevitable, for each *thesis* (basically an arrangement of power) contains *antithesis* (contradictions). A new *synthesis* develops to resolve these contradictions, but it, too, contains contradictions that must be resolved, and so on. This is called a **dialectical** process. Pp. 430–431.

*What is Ogburn's theory of social change?*

William Ogburn identified technology as the basic cause of social change, which comes through three processes: **invention, discovery,** and **diffusion.** The term **cultural lag** refers to symbolic culture lagging behind changes in technology. Pp. 431–432.

## How Technology Changes Society

*How does new technology affect society?*

Because **technology** is an organizing force of social life, changes in technology can have profound effects. The computer is changing the way we learn, do business, and fight wars. The implications for social control are serious, and we don't yet know whether information technologies

will help to perpetuate or to reduce social inequalities on both a national and a global level. Pp. 432–435.

## Social Movements as a Source of Social Change

*What types of social movements are there?*

**Social movements** consist of large numbers of people who organize to promote or resist social change. Depending on their target (individuals or society) and the amount of social change that is desired (partial or complete), social movements can be classified as **alterative, redemptive, reformative, transformative, transnational,** and **metaformative.** Pp. 436–437.

*How are the mass media related to social movements?*

The mass media are gatekeepers for social movements. Leaders use **propaganda** to influence **public opinion.** Pp. 437–439.

*What stages do social movements go through?*

Sociologists have identified five stages of social movements: initial unrest and agitation, mobilization, organization, institutionalization, and, finally, decline. Resurgence is also possible, if, as in the case of abortion, opposing sides revitalize one another. Pp. 439–440.

## The Growth Machine Versus the Earth

*What are the environmental problems of the Most Industrialized Nations?*

The environmental problems of the Most Industrialized Nations range from smog and acid rain to the **greenhouse effect. Global warming** is likely to have severe consequences for the world. Burning fossil fuels in internal combustion engines lies at the root of many environmental problems. The location of factories and hazardous waste sites creates **environmental injustice,** environmental problems having a greater impact on minorities and the poor. Pp. 441–444.

*Do the Industrializing and Least Industrialized Nations have environmental problems?*

The worst environmental problems are found in the nations that are rushing into industrialization, especially China. The world is facing a basic conflict between the lust for profits through the exploitation of the earth's resources and the need to establish a **sustainable environment.** P. 444.

*What is the environmental movement?*

The environmental movement is an attempt to restore a healthy environment for the world's people. This global social movement takes many forms, from peaceful attempts to influence the political process to **ecosabotage.** Pp. 444–446.

*What is environmental sociology?*

**Environmental sociology** is not an attempt to change the environment, but, rather, is a study of the relationship between humans and the environment. Environmental sociologists are generally also environmental activists. P. 447.

# THINKING CRITICALLY *about* Chapter 15

1. Pick a social movement and analyze it according to the sociological principles and findings reviewed in this chapter.

2. In what ways does technology change society? How has social change affected your life? Be specific—what changes, how? Does Ogburn's theory help to explain your experiences? Why or why not?

3. Do you think that a sustainable environment should be a goal of the world's societies? Why or why not? If so, what practical steps do you think we can take to produce a sustainable environment?

# ADDITIONAL RESOURCES

## What can you find in MySocLab?  mysoclab  www.mysoclab.com

- Complete Ebook
- Practice Tests and Video and Audio activities
- Mapping and Data Analysis exercises

- Sociology in the News
- Classic Readings in Sociology
- Research and Writing advice

## Where Can I Read More on This Topic?

Suggested readings for this chapter are listed at the back of this book.

# EPILOGUE: WHY MAJOR IN SOCIOLOGY?

As you explored social life in this textbook, I hope that you found yourself thinking along with me. If so, you should have gained a greater understanding of why people think, feel, and act as they do—as well as insights into why *you* view life the way you do. Developing your sociological imagination was my intention in writing this book. I have sincerely wanted to make sociology come alive for you.

## Majoring in Sociology

If you feel a passion for peering beneath the surface—for seeking out the social influences in people's lives, and for seeing these influences in your own life—this is the best reason to major in sociology. As you take more courses in sociology, you will continue this enlightening process of social discovery. Your sociological perspective will grow, and you will become increasingly aware of how social factors underlie human behavior.

In addition to people who have a strong desire to continue this fascinating process of social discovery, there is a second type of person whom I also urge to major in sociology. Let's suppose that you have a strong, almost unbridled sense of wanting to explore many aspects of life. Let's also assume that because you have so many interests, you can't make up your mind about what you want to do with your life. You can think of so many things you'd like to try, but for each one there are other possibilities that you find equally as compelling. Let me share what one student who read this text wrote me:

> I'd love to say what my current major is—if only I truly knew. I know that the major you choose to study in college isn't necessarily the field of work you'll be going into. I've heard enough stories of grads who get jobs in fields that are not even related to their majors to believe it to a certain extent. My only problem is that I'm not even sure what it is I want to study, or what I truly want to be in the future for that matter.
>
> The variety of choices I have left open for myself are very wide, which creates a big problem, because I know I have to narrow it down to just one, which isn't something easy at all for me. It's like I want to be the best and do the best (medical doctor), yet I also wanna do other things (such as being a paramedic, or a cop, or firefighter, or a pilot), but I also realize I've only got one life to live. So the big question is: What's it gonna be?

This note reminded me of myself. In my reply, I said:

> You sound so much like myself when I was in college. In my senior year, I was plagued with uncertainty about what would be the right course for my life. I went to a counselor and took a vocational aptitude test. I still remember the day when I went in for the test results. I expected my future to be laid out for me, and I hung on every word. But then I heard the counselor say, "Your tests show that mortician should be one of your vocational choices."
>
> Mortician! I almost fell off my chair. That choice was so far removed from anything that I wanted that I immediately gave up on such tests.
>
> I like your list of possibilities: physician, cop, firefighter, and paramedic. In addition to these, mine included cowboy, hobo, and beach bum. One day, I was at the dry cleaners (end of my sophomore year in college), and the guy standing next to me was a cop. We talked about his job, and when I left the dry cleaners, I immediately went to the police station to get an application. I found out that I had to be 21, and I was just 20. I went back to college.
>
> I'm very happy with my choice. As a sociologist, I am able to follow my interests. I was able to become a hobo (or at least a traveler and able to experience different cultural settings). As far as being a cop, I developed and taught a course in the sociology of law.
>
> One of the many things I always wanted to be was an author. I almost skipped graduate school to move to Greenwich Village and become a novelist. The problem was that I was too timid, too scared of the unknown—and I had no support at all—to give it a try. My ultimate choice of sociologist has allowed me to fulfill this early dream.

It is sociology's breadth that is so satisfying to those of us who can't seem to find the limit to our interests, who can't pin ourselves down to just one thing in life. Sociology covers *all* of social life. Anything and everything that people do is part of sociology. For those of us who feel such broad, and perhaps changing interests, sociology is a perfect major.

But what if you already have a major picked out, yet you really like thinking sociologically? You can *minor* in sociology. Take sociology courses that continue to pique your sociological imagination. Then after college, continue to stimulate your sociological interests through your reading, including novels. This ongoing development of your sociological imagination will serve you well as you go through life.

# But What Can You Do With a Sociology Major?

I can just hear someone say: "That's fine for you, since you became a sociologist. I don't want to go to graduate school, though. I just want to get my bachelor's degree and get out of college and get on with life. So, how can a bachelor's in sociology help me?"

This is a fair question. Just what can you do with a bachelor's degree in sociology?

A few years ago, in my sociology department we began to develop a concentration in applied sociology. At that time, since this would be a bachelor's degree, I explored this very question. I was surprised at the answer: *Almost anything!*

It turns out that most employers don't care what you major in. (Exceptions are some highly specialized fields such as nursing, computers, and engineering.) *Most* employers just want to make certain that you have completed college, and for most of them one degree is the same as another. *College provides the base on which the employer builds.*

Because you have your bachelor's degree—no matter what it is in—employers assume that you are a responsible person. This credential implies that you have proven yourself: You were able to stick with a four-year course, you showed up for classes, listened to lectures, took notes,

passed tests, and carried out whatever assignments you were given. On top of this base of presumed responsibility, employers add the specifics necessary for you to perform their particular work, whether that be in sales or service, in insurance, banking, retailing, marketing, product development, or whatever.

If you major in sociology, you don't have to look for a job as a sociologist. If you ever decide to go on for an advanced degree, that's fine. But such plans are not necessary. The bachelor's in sociology can be your passport to most types of work in society.

# Final Note

I want to conclude by stressing the reason to major in sociology that goes far beyond how you are going to make a living. It is the sociological perspective itself, the way of thinking and understanding that sociology provides. Wherever your path in life may lead, the sociological perspective will accompany you.

You are going to live in a fast-paced, rapidly changing society that, with all its conflicting crosscurrents, is going to be in turmoil. The sociological perspective will cast a different light on life's events, allowing you to perceive them in more insightful ways. As you watch television, attend a concert, converse with a friend, listen to a boss or co-worker—you will be more aware of the social contexts that underlie such behavior. The sociological perspective that you develop as you major in sociology will equip you to view what happens in life differently from someone who does not have your sociological background. Even events in the news will look different to you.

The final question that I want to leave you with, then, is, "If you enjoy sociology, why not major in it?"

With my best wishes for your success in life,

*Jim Henslin*

# GLOSSARY

**achieved statuses** positions that are earned, accomplished, or involve at least some effort or activity on the individual's part

**acid rain** rain containing sulfuric and nitric acids (burning fossil fuels release sulfur dioxide and nitrogen oxide that become sulfuric and nitric acids when they react with moisture in the air)

**activity theory** the view that satisfaction during old age is related to a person's amount and quality of activity

**age cohort** people born at roughly the same time who pass through the life course together

**ageism** prejudice, discrimination, and hostility directed against people because of their age; can be directed against any age group, including youth

**agents of socialization** people or groups that affect our self-concept, attitudes, behaviors, or other orientations toward life

**aggregate** individuals who temporarily share the same physical space but who do not see themselves as belonging together

**agricultural society** a society based on large-scale agriculture

**alienation** Marx's term for workers' lack of connection to the product of their labor; caused by their being assigned repetitive tasks on a small part of a product—which leads to a sense of powerlessness and normlessness; others use the term in the general sense of not feeling a part of something

**alterative social movement** a social movement that seeks to alter some specific aspect of people and institutions

**anarchy** a condition of lawlessness or political disorder caused by the absence or collapse of governmental authority

**anomie** Durkheim's term for a condition of society in which people become detached from the norms that usually guide their behavior

**anticipatory socialization** the process of learning in advance a role or status one anticipates having

**applied sociology** the use of sociology to solve problems—from the micro level of classroom interaction and family relationships to the macro level of crime and pollution

**ascribed status** a position an individual either inherits at birth or receives involuntarily later in life

**assimilation** the process of being absorbed into the mainstream culture

**authoritarian leader** an individual who leads by giving orders

**authoritarian personality** Theodor Adorno's term for people who are highly prejudiced and also rank high on scales of conformity, intolerance, insecurity, respect for authority, and submissiveness to superiors

**authority** power that people consider legitimate, as rightly exercised over them; also called *legitimate power*

**background assumption** a deeply embedded common understanding of how the world operates and of how people ought to act

**basic demographic equation** growth rate equals births minus deaths plus net migration

**basic sociology** sociological research for the purpose of making discoveries about life in human groups, not for making changes in those groups; also called *pure sociology*

**bilineal** (system of descent) a system of reckoning descent that counts both the mother's and the father's side

**biotech society** a society whose economy increasingly centers on the application of genetics—human genetics for medicine, and plant and animal genetics for the production of food and materials

**blended family** a family whose members were once part of other families

**body language** the ways in which people use their bodies to give messages to others

**bonded labor** (indentured service) a contractual system in which someone sells his or her body (services) for a specified period of time in an arrangement very close to slavery, except that it is entered into voluntarily

**born again** a term describing Christians who have undergone a religious experience so life-transforming that they feel they have become new persons

**bourgeoisie** Marx's term for capitalists, those who own the means of production

**bureaucracy** a formal organization with a hierarchy of authority and a clear division of labor; emphasis on impersonality of positions and written rules, communications, and records

**capital punishment** the death penalty

**capitalism** an economic system characterized by the private ownership of the means of production, the pursuit of profit, and market competition

**capitalist class** the wealthy who own the means of production and buy the labor of the working class

**caste system** a form of social stratification in which people's statuses are determined by birth and are lifelong

**category** people who have similar characteristics

**charisma** literally, an extraordinary gift from God; more commonly, an outstanding, "magnetic" personality

**charismatic authority** authority based on an individual's outstanding traits, which attract followers

**charismatic leader** literally, someone to whom God has given a gift; more commonly, someone who exerts extraordinary appeal to a group of followers

**checks and balances** the separation of powers among the three branches of U.S. government—legislative, executive, and judicial—so that each is able to nullify the actions of the other two, thus preventing any single branch from dominating the government

**church** according to Durkheim, one of the three essential elements of religion—a moral community of believers; also refers to a large, highly organized religious group that has formal, sedate worship services and little emphasis on evangelism, intense religious experience, or personal conversion

**citizenship** the concept that birth (and residence or naturalization) in a country imparts basic rights

**city** a place in which a large number of people are permanently based and do not produce their own food

*G*

**city-state**  an independent city whose power radiates outward, bringing the adjacent area under its rule

**class conflict**  Marx's term for the struggle between capitalists and workers

**class consciousness**  Marx's term for awareness of a common identity based on one's position in the means of production

**class system**  a form of social stratification based primarily on the possession of money or material possessions

**clique**  a cluster of people within a larger group who choose to interact with one another

**closed-ended questions**  questions that are followed by a list of possible answers to be selected by the respondent

**coalition**  the alignment of some members of a group against others

**coercion**  power that people do not accept as rightly exercised over them; also called *illegitimate power*

**cohabitation**  unmarried couples living together in a sexual relationship

**colonialism**  the process by which one nation takes over another nation, usually for the purpose of exploiting its labor and natural resources

**common sense**  those things that "everyone knows" are true

**community**  a place people identify with, where they sense that they belong and that others care about what happens to them

**compartmentalize**  to separate acts from feelings or attitudes

**conflict theory**  a theoretical framework in which society is viewed as composed of groups that are competing for scarce resources

**conspicuous consumption**  Thorstein Veblen's term for a change from the Protestant ethic to an eagerness to show off wealth by the consumption of goods

**continuity theory**  the focus of this theory is how people adjust to retirement by continuing aspects of their earlier lives

**contradictory class locations**  Erik Wright's term for a position in the class structure that generates contradictory interests

**control group**  the subjects in an experiment who are not exposed to the independent variable

**control theory**  the idea that two control systems—inner controls and outer controls—work against our tendencies to deviate

**convergence theory**  the view that as capitalist and socialist economic systems each adopt features of the other, a hybrid (or mixed) economic system will emerge

**corporate capitalism**  the domination of an economic system by giant corporations

**corporate crime**  crimes committed by executives in order to benefit their corporation

**corporate culture**  the values, norms, and other orientations that characterize corporate work settings

**corporate welfare**  the financial incentives (tax breaks, subsidies, and even land and stadiums) given to corporations in order to attract them to an area or induce them to remain

**corporation**  a business enterprise whose assets, liabilities, and obligations are separate from those of its owners; as a legal entity, it can enter into contracts, assume debt, and sue and be sued

**cosmology**  teachings or ideas that provide a unified picture of the world

**counterculture**  a group whose values, beliefs, norms, and related behaviors place its members in opposition to the broader culture

**credential society**  the use of diplomas and degrees to determine who is eligible for jobs, even though the diploma or degree may be irrelevant to the actual work

**crime**  the violation of norms written into law

**criminal justice system**  the system of police, courts, and prisons set up to deal with people who are accused of having committed a crime

**crude birth rate**  the annual number of live births per 1,000 population

**crude death rate**  the annual number of deaths per 1,000 population

**cult**  a new religion with few followers, whose teachings and practices put it at odds with the dominant culture and religion

**cultural diffusion**  the spread of cultural traits from one group to another; includes both material and nonmaterial cultural traits

**cultural goals**  the objectives held out as legitimate or desirable for the members of a society

**cultural lag**  Ogburn's term for human behavior lagging behind technological innovations

**cultural leveling**  the process by which cultures become similar to one another; refers especially to the process by which Western culture is being exported and diffused into other nations

**cultural relativism**  not judging a culture but trying to understand it on its own terms

**cultural transmission of values**  the process of transmitting values from one group to another; often used in reference to how cultural traits are transmitted across generations and, in education, the ways in which schools transmit a society's values

**culture**  the language, beliefs, values, norms, behaviors, and even material objects that characterize a group and are passed from one generation to the next

**culture of poverty**  the assumption that the values and behaviors of the poor make them fundamentally different from other people, that these factors are largely responsible for their poverty, and that parents perpetuate poverty across generations by passing these characteristics to their children

**culture shock**  the disorientation that people experience when they come in contact with a fundamentally different culture and can no longer depend on their taken-for-granted assumptions about life

**degradation ceremony**  a term coined by Harold Garfinkel to refer to a ritual whose goal is to remake someone's self by stripping away that individual's self-identity and stamping a new identity in its place

**dehumanization**  the act or process of reducing people to objects that do not deserve the treatment accorded humans

**deindustrialization**  the process of industries moving out of a country or region

**democracy**  a government whose authority comes from the people; the term, based on two Greek words, translates literally as "power to the people"

**democratic leader**  an individual who leads by trying to reach a consensus

**democratic socialism**   a hybrid economic system in which the individual ownership of businesses is mixed with the state ownership of industries thought essential to the public welfare, such as the postal service and the delivery of medicine and utilities

**demographic transition**   a three-stage historical process of population growth: first, high birth rates and high death rates; second, high birth rates and low death rates; and third, low birth rates and low death rates; a fourth stage in which deaths outnumber births has made its appearance in the Most Industrialized Nations

**demographic variables**   the three factors that influence population growth: fertility, mortality, and net migration

**demography**   the study of the size, composition, growth, and distribution of human populations

**denomination**   a "brand name" within a major religion; for example, Methodist or Baptist

**dependency ratio**   the number of workers who are required to support each dependent person—those 65 and older and those 15 and under

**dependent variable**   a factor in an experiment that is changed by an independent variable

**deviance**   the violation of norms (or rules or expectations)

**deviants**   those who violate norms

**dialectical process** (of history)   each arrangement of power (a thesis) contains contradictions (antitheses) which make the arrangement unstable and which must be resolved; the new arrangement of power (a synthesis) contains its own contradictions; this process of balancing and unbalancing continues throughout history as groups struggle for power and other resources

**dictatorship**   a form of government in which an individual has seized power

**differential association**   Edwin Sutherland's term to indicate that people who associate with some groups learn an "excess of definitions" of deviance, increasing the likelihood that they will become deviant

**diffusion**   the spread of an invention or a discovery from one area to another; identified by William Ogburn as one of three processes of social change

**direct democracy**   a form of democracy in which the eligible voters meet together to discuss issues and make their decisions

**discovery**   a new way of seeing reality; identified by William Ogburn as one of three processes of social change

**discrimination**   an act of unfair treatment directed against an individual or a group

**disengagement theory**   the view that society is stabilized by having the elderly retire (disengage from) their positions of responsibility so the younger generation can step into their shoes

**disinvestment**   the withdrawal of investments by financial institutions, which seals the fate of an urban area

**divine right of kings**   the idea that the king's authority comes directly from God; in an interesting gender bender, also applies to queens

**division of labor**   the splitting of a group's or a society's tasks into specialties

**documents**   in its narrow sense, written sources that provide data; in its extended sense, archival material of any sort, including photographs, movies, CDs, DVDs, and so on

**dominant group**   the group with the most power, greatest privileges, and highest social status

**downward social mobility**   movement down the social class ladder

**dramaturgy**   an approach, pioneered by Erving Goffman, in which social life is analyzed in terms of drama or the stage; also called *dramaturgical analysis*

**dyad**   the smallest possible group, consisting of two persons

**ecclesia**   a religious group so integrated into the dominant culture that it is difficult to tell where the one begins and the other leaves off; also called a *state religion*

**economy**   a system of producing and distributing goods and services

**ecosabotage**   actions taken to sabotage the efforts of people who are thought to be legally harming the environment

**edge city**   a large clustering of service facilities and residential areas near highway intersections that provides a sense of place to people who live, shop, and work there

**education**   a formal system of teaching knowledge, values, and skills

**egalitarian**   authority more or less equally divided between people or groups (in marriage, for example, between husband and wife)

**ego**   Freud's term for a balancing force between the id and the demands of society

**electronic community**   individuals who regularly interact with one another on the Internet and who think of themselves as belonging together

**endogamy**   the practice of marrying within one's own group

**enterprise zone**   the use of economic incentives in a designated area to encourage investment

**environmental injustice**   refers to how minorities and the poor are harmed the most by environmental pollution

**environmental sociology**   a specialty within sociology whose focus is how humans affect the environment and how the environment affects humans

**ethnic cleansing**   a policy of eliminating a population; includes forcible expulsion and genocide

**ethnic work**   activities designed to discover, enhance, or maintain ethnic and racial identity

**ethnicity** (and **ethnic**)   having distinctive cultural characteristics

**ethnocentrism**   the use of one's own culture as a yardstick for judging the ways of other individuals or societies, generally leading to a negative evaluation of their values, norms, and behaviors

**ethnomethodology**   the study of how people use background assumptions to make sense out of life

**exchange mobility**   about the same numbers of people moving up and down the social class ladder, such that, on balance, the social class system shows little change

**exogamy**   the practice of marrying outside one's group

**experiment**   the use of control and experimental groups and dependent and independent variables to test causation

**experimental group**   the group of subjects in an experiment who are exposed to the independent variable

**exponential growth curve**   a pattern of growth in which numbers double during approximately equal intervals, showing a steep acceleration in the later stages

**expressive leader**   an individual who increases harmony and minimizes conflict in a group; also known as a *socioemotional leader*

**extended family**  a nuclear family plus other relatives, such as grandparents, uncles, and aunts

**face-saving behavior**  techniques used to salvage a performance (interaction) that is going sour

**false class consciousness**  Marx's term to refer to workers identifying with the interests of capitalists

**family**  two or more people who consider themselves related by blood, marriage, or adoption

**family of orientation**  the family in which a person grows up

**family of procreation**  the family formed when a couple's first child is born

**fecundity**  the number of children that women are capable of bearing

**feminism**  the philosophy that men and women should be politically, economically, and socially equal; organized activities on behalf of this principle

**[the] feminization of poverty**  refers to most U.S. poor families being headed by women

**feral children**  children assumed to have been raised by animals, in the wilderness, isolated from humans

**fertility rate**  the number of children that the average woman bears

**folkways**  norms that are not strictly enforced

**functional analysis**  a theoretical framework in which society is viewed as composed of various parts, each with a function that, when fulfilled, contributes to society's equilibrium; also known as *functionalism* and *structural functionalism*

**functional illiterate**  a high school graduate who has difficulty with basic reading and math

**fundamentalism**  the belief that social change, especially in values, is threatening true religion and that the religion needs to go back to its fundamentals (roots, early beliefs, and practices)

**gatekeeping**  the process by which education opens and closes doors of opportunity; another term for the *social placement* function of education

**Gemeinschaft**  a type of society in which life is intimate; a community in which everyone knows everyone else and people share a sense of togetherness

**gender**  the behaviors and attitudes that a group considers proper for its males and females; masculinity or femininity

**gender age**  the relative value placed on men's and women's ages

**gender role**  the behaviors and attitudes expected of people because they are female or a male

**gender stratification**  males' and females' unequal access to property, power, and prestige

**generalized other**  the norms, values, attitudes, and expectations of people "in general"; the child's ability to take the role of the generalized other is a significant step in the development of a self

**genetic predisposition**  inborn tendencies (for example, a tendency to commit deviant acts)

**genocide**  the systematic annihilation or attempted annihilation of a people because of their presumed race or ethnicity

**gentrification**  middle-class people moving into a rundown area of a city, displacing the poor as they buy and restore homes

**Gesellschaft**  a type of society that is dominated by impersonal relationships, individual accomplishments, and self-interest

**gestures**  the ways in which people use their bodies to communicate with one another

**glass ceiling**  the mostly invisible barrier that keeps women from advancing to the top levels at work

**glass escalator**  the mostly invisible accelerators that push men into higher-level positions, more desirable work assignments, and higher salaries

**global warming**  an increase in the earth's temperature due to the greenhouse effect

**globalization**  the extensive interconnections among nations due to the expansion of capitalism

**globalization of capitalism**  capitalism (investing to make profits within a rational system) becoming the globe's dominant economic system

**goal displacement**  an organization replacing old goals with new ones; also known as *goal replacement*

**grade inflation**  higher grades given for the same work; a general rise in student grades without a corresponding increase in learning

**graying of America**  the growing percentage of older people in the U.S. population

**greenhouse effect**  the buildup of carbon dioxide in the earth's atmosphere that allows light to enter but inhibits the release of heat; believed to cause global warming

**group**  people who have something in common and who believe that what they have in common is significant; also called a *social group*

**group dynamics**  the ways in which individuals affect groups and the ways in which groups influence individuals

**groupthink**  a narrowing of thought by a group of people, leading to the perception that there is only one correct course of action, in which to even suggest alternatives becomes a sign of disloyalty

**growth rate**  the net change in a population after adding births, subtracting deaths, and either adding or subtracting net migration

**hate crime**  a crime that is punished more severely because it is motivated by hatred (dislike, animosity) of someone's race–ethnicity, religion, sexual orientation, disability, or national origin

**hidden curriculum**  the unwritten goals of schools, such as teaching obedience to authority and conformity to cultural norms

**homogamy**  the tendency of people with similar characteristics to marry one another

**Horatio Alger myth**  the belief that due to limitless possibilities anyone can get ahead if he or she tries hard enough

**horticultural society**  a society based on cultivating plants by the use of hand tools

**household**  people who occupy the same housing unit

**human ecology**  Robert Park's term for the relationship between people and their environment (such as land and structures); also known as *urban ecology*

**hunting and gathering society**  a human group that depends on hunting and gathering for its survival

**hypothesis**  a statement of how variables are expected to be related to one another, often according to predictions from a theory

**id**  Freud's term for our inborn basic drives

**ideal culture**  a people's ideal values and norms; the goals held out for them

**ideology**  beliefs about the way things ought to be that justify social arrangements

**illegitimate opportunity structure**  opportunities for crimes that are woven into the texture of life

**impression management**  people's efforts to control the impressions that others receive of them

**incest**  sexual relations between specified relatives, such as brothers and sisters or parents and children

**incest taboo**  the rule that prohibits sex and marriage among designated relatives

**income**  money received, usually from a job, business, or assets

**independent variable**  a factor that causes a change in another variable, called the dependent variable

**individual discrimination**  the negative treatment of one person by another on the basis of that person's perceived characteristics

**Industrial Revolution**  the third social revolution, occurring when machines powered by fuels replaced most animal and human power

**industrial society**  a society based on the harnessing of machines powered by fuels

**inflation**  an increase in prices

**in-groups**  groups toward which one feels loyalty

**institutional discrimination**  negative treatment of a minority group that is built into a society's institutions; also called *systemic discrimination*

**institutionalized means**  approved ways of reaching cultural goals

**instrumental leader**  an individual who tries to keep the group moving toward its goals; also known as a *task-oriented leader*

**intergenerational mobility**  the change that family members make in social class from one generation to the next

**interlocking directorates**  the same people serving on the board of directors of several companies

**internal colonialism**  the policy of economically exploiting minority groups

**invasion–succession cycle**  the process of one group of people displacing a group whose racial–ethnic or social class characteristics differ from their own

**invention**  the combination of existing elements and materials to form new ones; identified by William Ogburn as one of three processes of social change

[the] **iron law of oligarchy**  Robert Michels' term for the tendency of formal organizations to be dominated by a small, self-perpetuating elite

**labeling theory**  the view that the labels people are given affect their own and others' perceptions of them, thus channeling their behavior into either deviance or conformity

**laissez-faire capitalism**  unrestrained manufacture and trade (literally, "hands off" capitalism)

**laissez-faire leader**  an individual who leads by being highly permissive

**language**  a system of symbols that can be combined in an infinite number of ways and can represent not only objects but also abstract thought

**latent functions**  unintended beneficial consequences of people's actions

**leader**  someone who influences other people

**leadership styles**  ways in which people express their leadership

**life course**  the stages of our life as we go from birth to death

**life expectancy**  the number of years that an average person at any age, including newborns, can expect to live

**life span**  the maximum length of life of a species; for humans, the longest that a human has lived

**lobbyists**  people who influence legislation on behalf of their clients

**looking-glass self**  a term coined by Charles Horton Cooley to refer to the process by which our self develops through internalizing others' reactions to us

**machismo**  an emphasis on male strength and dominance

**macro-level analysis**  an examination of large-scale patterns of society

**macrosociology**  analysis of social life that focuses on broad features of society, such as social class and the relationships of groups to one another; usually used by functionalists and conflict theorists

**mainstreaming**  becoming part of the mainstream of society; often refers to people with disabilities

**Malthus theorem**  an observation by Thomas Malthus that although the food supply increases arithmetically (from 1 to 2 to 3 to 4 and so on), population grows geometrically (from 2 to 4 to 8 to 16 and so forth)

**manifest functions**  the intended beneficial consequences of people's actions

**marginal working class**  the most desperate members of the working class, who have little money, few skills, little job security, and are often unemployed

**market forces**  the law of supply and demand

**marriage**  a group's approved mating arrangements, usually marked by a ritual of some sort

**mass media**  forms of communication, such as radio, newspapers, and television that are directed to mass audiences

**master status**  a status that cuts across the other statuses that an individual occupies

**material culture**  the material objects that distinguish a group of people, such as their art, buildings, weapons, utensils, machines, hairstyles, clothing, and jewelry

**matriarchy**  a society in which women as a group dominate men as a group; authority is vested in females

**matrilineal**  (system of descent) a system of reckoning descent that counts only the mother's side

[the] **McDonaldization of society**  the process by which ordinary aspects of life are rationalized and efficiency comes to rule them, including such things as food preparation

**means of production**  the tools, factories, land, and investment capital used to produce wealth

**mechanical solidarity**  Durkheim's term for the unity (a shared consciousness) that people feel as a result of performing the same or similar tasks

**medicalization of deviance** to make deviance a medical matter, a symptom of some underlying illness that needs to be treated by physicians

**megacity** a city of 10 million or more residents

**megalopolis** an urban area consisting of at least two metropolises and their many suburbs

**melting pot** the view that Americans of various backgrounds would blend into a sort of ethnic stew

**meritocracy** a form of social stratification in which all positions are awarded on the basis of merit

**metaformative social movement** a social movement that has the goal to change the social order not just of a country or two, but of a civilization, or even of the entire world

**metropolis** a central city surrounded by smaller cities and their suburbs

**metropolitan statistical area (MSA)** a central city and the urbanized counties adjacent to it

**micro-level analysis** an examination of small-scale patterns of society

**microsociology** analysis of social life that focuses on social interaction; typically used by symbolic interactionists

**minority group** people who are singled out for unequal treatment and who regard themselves as objects of collective discrimination

**modernization** the transformation of traditional societies into industrial societies

**monarchy** a form of government headed by a king or queen

**money** any item (from sea shells to gold) that serves as a medium of exchange; today, currency is the most common form

**mores** norms that are strictly enforced because they are thought essential to core values or the well-being of the group

**multiculturalism** a philosophy or social policy that permits or encourages ethnic difference; also called *pluralism*

**multinational corporations** companies that operate across national boundaries; also called *transnational corporations*

**negative sanction** an expression of disapproval for breaking a norm, ranging from a mild, informal reaction such as a frown to a formal reaction such as a prison sentence or an execution

**neocolonialism** the economic and political dominance of the Least Industrialized Nations by the Most Industrialized Nations

**net migration rate** the difference between the number of immigrants and emigrants per 1,000 population

**networking** using one's social networks for some gain

**new technology** the emerging technologies of an era that have a significant impact on social life

**nonmaterial culture** a group's ways of thinking (including its beliefs, values, and other assumptions about the world) and doing (its common patterns of behavior, including language and other forms of interaction); also called *symbolic culture*

**nonverbal interaction** communication without words through gestures, use of space, silence, and so on

**norms** what is expected of people; the expectations (or rules) intended to guide people's behavior

**nuclear family** a family consisting of a husband, wife, and child(ren)

**objectivity** value neutrality in research

**oligarchy** a form of government in which a small group of individuals holds power; the rule of the many by the few

**open-ended questions** questions that respondents answer in their own words

**operational definition** the way in which a researcher measures a variable

**organic solidarity** Durkheim's term for the interdependence that results from the division of labor; people depending on others to fulfill their jobs

**out-groups** groups toward which one feels antagonism

**pan-Indianism** a movement that focuses on common elements in the cultures of Native Americans in order to develop a cross-tribal group identity and to work toward the welfare of all Native Americans

**participant observation** participating in a research setting in order to observe what is happening in that setting; also called *fieldwork*

**pastoral society** a society based on the pasturing of animals

**patriarchy** a group in which men as a group dominate women as a group; authority is vested in males

**patrilineal** (system of descent) a system of reckoning descent that counts only the father's side

**peer group** a group of individuals of roughly the same age who are linked by common interests

**personality disorders** the view that a personality disturbance of some sort causes an individual to violate social norms

**Peter principle** a tongue-in-cheek observation that the members of an organization are promoted for their accomplishments until they reach their level of incompetence; there they cease to be promoted, remaining at the level at which they can no longer do good work

**pluralism** the diffusion of power among many interest groups that prevents any single group from gaining control of the government

**pluralistic society** a society made up of many different groups

**political action committee (PAC)** a group whose purpose is to solicit and spend funds for the purpose of influencing legislation

**politics** the exercise of power and attempts to maintain or to change power relations

**polyandry** a form of marriage in which women have more than one husband

**polygyny** a form of marriage in which men have more than one wife

**population** a target group to be studied

**population pyramid** a chart or graph intended to represent the age and sex of a population

**population shrinkage** the process by which a country's population becomes smaller because its birth rate and immigration are too low to replace those who die and emigrate

**population transfer** the forced relocation of a minority group

**positive sanction** a reward or positive reaction for following norms, ranging from a smile to a material reward

**positivism** the application of the scientific method to the social world

**postindustrial (information) society** a society based on information, services, and high technology, rather than on raw materials and manufacturing

**postmodern society** another term for postindustrial society; a chief characteristic is the use of tools that extend human abilities to gather and analyze information, to communicate, and to travel

**poverty line** the official measure of poverty; calculated to include incomes that are less than three times a low-cost food budget

**power** the ability to carry out your will, even over the resistance of others

**power elite** C. Wright Mills' term for the top people in U.S. corporations, military, and politics who make the nation's major decisions

**prejudice** an attitude or prejudging, usually in a negative way

**prestige** respect or regard

**primary group** a group characterized by intimate, long-term, face-to-face association and cooperation

**proactive social movement** a social movement that promotes some social change

**profane** Durkheim's term for common elements of everyday life

**proletariat** Marx's term for the exploited class, the mass of workers who do not own the means of production

**propaganda** in its broad sense, information used to try to influence people; in its narrow sense, one-sided information used to try to influence people

**property** material possessions: animals, bank accounts, bonds, buildings, businesses, cars, furniture, land, and stocks

**Protestant ethic** Weber's term to describe the ideal of a self-denying, highly moral life accompanied by hard work and frugality

**public opinion** how people think about some issue

**race** a group whose inherited physical characteristics distinguish it from other groups

**racism** prejudice and discrimination on the basis of race

**random sample** a sample in which everyone in the target population has the same chance of being included in the study

**rapport** (ruh-POUR) a feeling of trust between researchers and the people they are studying

**rational–legal authority** authority based on law or written rules and regulations; also called *bureaucratic authority*

**[the] rationalization of society** a widespread acceptance of rationality and social organizations that are built largely around this idea

**reactive social movement** a social movement that resists some social change

**real culture** the norms and values that people actually follow (as opposed to ideal culture)

**recidivism rate** the proportion of released convicts who are rearrested

**redemptive social movement** a social movement that seeks to change people and institutions totally, to redeem them

**redlining** a decision by the officers of a financial institution not to make loans in a particular area

**reference group** a group whose standards we refer to as we evaluate ourselves

**reformative social movement** a social movement that seeks to reform some specific aspect of society

**reliability** the extent to which research produces consistent or dependable results

**religion** according to Durkheim, beliefs and practices that separate the profane from the sacred and unite its adherents into a moral community

**religious experience** a sudden awareness of the supernatural or a feeling of coming in contact with God

**replication** duplicating some research in order to test its findings

**representative democracy** a form of democracy in which voters elect representatives to meet together to discuss issues and make decisions on their behalf

**research method** one of six procedures that sociologists use to collect data: surveys, participant observation, secondary analysis, documents, experiments, and unobtrusive measures; also called a *research design*

**reserve labor force** the unemployed; unemployed workers are thought of as being "in reserve"—capitalists take them "out of reserve" (put them back to work) during times of high production and then lay them off (put them back in reserve) when they are no longer needed

**resocialization** the process of learning new norms, values, attitudes, and behaviors

**resource mobilization** a theory that social movements succeed or fail based on their ability to mobilize resources such as time, money, and people's skills

**respondents** people who respond to a survey, either in interviews or by self-administered questionnaires

**revolution** armed resistance designed to overthrow and replace a government

**rising expectations** the sense that better conditions are soon to follow, which, if unfulfilled, increases frustration

**rituals** ceremonies or repetitive practices; in religion, often intended to evoke a sense of awe of the sacred

**role** the behaviors, obligations, and privileges attached to a status

**role conflict** conflicts that someone feels *between* roles because the expectations attached to one role are incompatible with the expectations of another role

**role performance** the ways in which someone performs a role; showing a particular "style" or "personality"

**role strain** conflicts that someone feels within a role

**romantic love** feelings of erotic attraction accompanied by an idealization of the other

**routinization of charisma** the transfer of authority from a charismatic figure to either a traditional or a rational–legal form of authority

**ruling class** another term for the power elite

**sacred** Durkheim's term for things set apart or forbidden, that inspire fear, awe, reverence, or deep respect

**sample** the individuals intended to represent the population to be studied

**sanctions** either expressions of approval given to people for upholding norms or expressions of disapproval for violating them

**Sapir-Whorf hypothesis** Edward Sapir's and Benjamin Whorf's hypothesis that language creates ways of thinking and perceiving

**scapegoat** an individual or group unfairly blamed for someone else's troubles

**science** the application of systematic methods to obtain knowledge and the knowledge obtained by those methods

[the] **scientific method**   the use of objective, systematic observations to test theories

**secondary analysis**   the analysis of data that have been collected by other researchers

**secondary group**   compared with a primary group, a larger, relatively temporary, more anonymous, formal, and impersonal group based on some interest or activity

**sect**   a religious group larger than a cult that still feels substantial hostility from and toward society

**secularization of religion**   the replacement of a religion's spiritual or "other worldly" concerns with concerns about "this world"

**segregation**   the policy of keeping racial–ethnic groups apart

**selective perception**   seeing certain features of an object or situation, but remaining blind to others

**self**   the unique human capacity of being able to see ourselves "from the outside"; the views we internalize of how others see us

**self-fulfilling prophecy**   Robert Merton's term for an originally false assertion that becomes true simply because it was predicted

**self-fulfilling stereotype**   preconceived ideas of what someone is like that lead to the person behaving in ways that match the stereotype

**serial fatherhood**   a pattern of parenting in which a father, after a divorce, reduces contact with his own children, serves as a father to the children of the woman he marries or lives with, then ignores these children, too, after moving in with or marrying another woman

**serial murder**   the killing of several victims in three or more separate events

**sex**   biological characteristics that distinguish females and males, consisting of primary and secondary sex characteristics

**sexual harassment**   the abuse of one's position of authority to make unwanted sexual demands on someone

**significant other**   an individual who significantly influences someone else's life

**slavery**   a form of social stratification in which some people own other people

**small group**   a group small enough for everyone to interact directly with all the other members

**social change**   the alteration of culture and societies over time

**social class**   according to Weber, a large group of people who rank close to one another in wealth, prestige, and power; according to Marx, one of two groups: capitalists who own the means of production or workers who sell their labor

**social construction of reality**   the use of background assumptions and life experiences to define what is real

**social control**   a group's formal and informal means of enforcing its norms

**social environment**   the entire human environment, including direct contact with others

**social inequality**   a social condition in which privileges and obligations are given to some but denied to others

**social institution**   the organized, usual, or standard ways by which society meets its basic needs

**social integration**   the degree to which members of a group or a society are united by shared norms, values, behaviors, and other social bonds; also known as *social cohesion*

**social interaction**   what people do when they are in one another's presence

**social location**   the group memberships that people have because of their location in history and society

**social mobility**   movement up or down the social class ladder

**social movement**   a large group of people who are organized to promote or resist some social change

**social movement organization**   an organization founded to promote the goals of a social movement

**social network**   the social ties radiating outward from the self that link people together

**social order**   a group's usual and customary social arrangements, on which its members depend and on which they base their lives

**social placement**   a function of education—funneling people into a society's various positions

**social promotion**   passing students on to the next level even though they have not mastered basic materials

**social stratification**   the division of large numbers of people into layers according to their relative property, power, and prestige; applies to both nations and to people within a nation, society, or other group

**social structure**   the framework that surrounds us, consisting of the relationships of people and groups to one another, which gives direction to and sets limits on behavior

**socialism**   an economic system characterized by the public ownership of the means of production, central planning, and the distribution of goods without a profit motive

**socialization**   the process by which people learn the characteristics of their group—the knowledge, skills, attitudes, values, norms, and actions thought appropriate for them

**socialization of gender**   the ways in which society sets children on different paths in life *because* they are male or female

**society**   people who share a culture and a territory

**sociobiology**   a framework of thought that views human behavior as the result of natural selection and considers biological factors to be the fundamental cause of human behavior

**sociological perspective**   understanding human behavior by placing it within its broader social context

**sociology**   the scientific study of society and human behavior

**special-interest group**   a group of people who support a particular issue and who can be mobilized for political action

**spirit of capitalism**   Weber's term for the desire to accumulate capital—not to spend it, but as an end in itself—and to constantly reinvest it

**split labor market**   workers split along racial, ethnic, gender, age, or any other lines; this split is exploited by owners to weaken the bargaining power of workers

**state**   a political entity that claims monopoly on the use of violence in some particular territory; commonly known as a country

**state religion**   a government-sponsored religion; also called *ecclesia*

**status**   the position that someone occupies in a social group

**status consistency**   ranking high or low on all three dimensions of social class

**status inconsistency**   ranking high on some dimensions of social class and low on others; also called *status discrepancy*

**status set**   all the statuses or positions that an individual occupies

**status symbols**   items used to identify a status

**stereotype**   assumptions of what people are like, whether true or false

**stigma**   "blemishes" that discredit a person's claim to a "normal" identity

**stockholders' revolt**   the refusal of a corporation's stockholders to rubber-stamp decisions made by its managers

**strain theory**   Robert Merton's term for the strain engendered when a society socializes large numbers of people to desire a cultural goal (such as success), but withholds from some the approved means of reaching that goal; one adaptation to the strain is crime, the choice of an innovative means (one outside the approved system) to attain the cultural goal

**stratified random sample**   a sample from selected subgroups of the target population in which everyone in those subgroups has an equal chance of being included in the research

**street crime**   crimes such as mugging, rape, and burglary

**structural mobility**   movement up or down the social class ladder that is due to changes in the structure of society, not to individual efforts

**subculture**   the values and related behaviors of a group that distinguish its members from the larger culture; a world within a world

**subsistence economy**   a type of economy in which human groups live off the land and have little or no surplus

**suburb**   a community adjacent to a city

**suburbanization**   the movement from the city to the suburbs

**superego**   Freud's term for the conscience; the internalized norms and values of our social groups

**survey**   the collection of data by having people answer a series of questions

**sustainable environment**   a world system that takes into account the limits of the environment, produces enough material goods for everyone's needs, and leaves a sound environment for the next generation

**symbol**   something to which people attach meanings and then use to communicate with others

**symbolic culture**   another term for nonmaterial culture

**symbolic interactionism**   a theoretical perspective in which society is viewed as composed of symbols that people use to establish meaning, develop their views of the world, and communicate with one another

**system of descent**   how kinship is traced over the generations

**taboo**   a norm so strong that it often brings revulsion if violated

**taking the role of the other**   putting oneself in someone else's shoes; understanding how someone else feels and thinks and thus anticipating how that person will act

**teamwork**   the collaboration of two or more people to manage impressions jointly

**techniques of neutralization**   ways of thinking or rationalizing that help people deflect (or neutralize) society's norms

**technology**   in its narrow sense, tools; its broader sense includes the skills or procedures necessary to make and use those tools

**terrorism**   the use of violence or the threat of violence to produce fear in order to attain political objectives

**theory**   a general statement about how some parts of the world fit together and how they work; an explanation of how two or more facts are related to one another

**Thomas theorem**   William I. and Dorothy S. Thomas' classic formulation of the definition of the situation: "If people define situations as real, they are real in their consequences."

**total institution**   a place that is almost totally controlled by those who run it, in which people are cut off from the rest of society and the society is mostly cut off from them

**totalitarianism**   a form of government that exerts almost total control over people

**tracking**   in education, the sorting of students into different programs on the basis of real or perceived abilities

**traditional authority**   authority based on custom

**transformative social movement**   a social movement that seeks to change society totally, to transform it

**transitional adulthood**   a term that refers to a period following high school (and often college), when young adults have not yet taken on the responsibilities ordinarily associated with adulthood; also called *adultolescence*

**transnational social movement**   a social movement whose emphasis is on some condition around the world, instead of on a condition in a specific country; also known as a *new social movement*

**triad**   a group of three people

**underclass**   a group of people for whom poverty persists year after year and across generations

**universal citizenship**   the idea that everyone has the same basic rights by virtue of being born in a country (or by immigrating and becoming a naturalized citizen)

**unobtrusive measures**   ways of observing people so they do not know they are being studied

**upward social mobility**   movement up the social class ladder

**urban renewal**   the rehabilitation of a rundown area, which usually results in the displacement of the poor who are living in that area

**urbanization**   the process by which an increasing proportion of a population lives in cities and those cities attain a growing influence on the culture

**validity**   the extent to which an operational definition measures what it is intended to measure

**value cluster**   values that together form a larger whole

**value contradiction**   values that contradict one another; to follow the one means to come into conflict with the other

**value free**   the view that a sociologist's personal values or biases should not influence social research

**values**   the standards by which people define what is desirable or undesirable, good or bad, beautiful or ugly

**variable**   a factor thought to be significant for human behavior, which can *vary* (or change) from one case to another

**voluntary association**   a group made up of people who voluntarily organize on the basis of some mutual interest; also known as *voluntary memberships* and *voluntary organizations*

**voter apathy**   indifference and inaction on the part of individuals or groups with respect to the political process

**war**   armed conflict between nations or politically distinct groups

**WASP**   White Anglo-Saxon Protestant; narrowly, an American of English descent; broadly, an American of western European ancestry

**wealth**   the total value of everything someone owns, minus the debts

**welfare capitalism**   an economic system in which individuals own the means of production but the state regulates many economic activities for the welfare of the population; also called *state capitalism*

**white ethnics**   white immigrants to the United States whose cultures differ from that of WASPs

**white-collar crime**   Edwin Sutherland's term for crimes committed by people of respectable and high social status in the course of their occupations; for example, bribery of public officials, securities violations, embezzlement, false advertising, and price fixing

**working class**   those people who sell their labor to the capitalist class

**world system theory**   economic and political connections that tie the world's countries together

**zero population growth**   women bearing only enough children to reproduce the population

# Chapter 1: The Sociological Perspective

Allan, Kenneth D. *Explorations in Classical Sociological Theory: Seeing the Social World.* Thousand Oaks, Calif.: Pine Forge Press, 2006. The author explains how sociological theory can be a guide for selecting research projects and for interpreting the results.

Berger, Peter L. *Invitation to Sociology: A Humanistic Perspective.* New York: Doubleday, 1972. This analysis of how sociology applies to everyday life has become a classic in sociology.

Brooks, Arthur C. *Gross National Happiness: Why Happiness Matters for America and How We Can Get More of It.* New York: Basic Books, 2008. To see how happiness, ordinarily considered to be an intensely personal matter, can be explained by the sociological perspective, read this book.

Charon, Joel M. *Symbolic Interactionism: An Introduction, an Interpretation, an Integration,* 9th ed. Upper Saddle River, N.J.: Prentice-Hall, 2008. The author lays out the main points of symbolic interactionism, providing an understanding of why this perspective is important in sociology.

Hedstrom, Peter. *Dissecting the Social: On the Principles of Analytical Sociology.* New York: Cambridge University Press, 2005. By examining the personal perspectives of theorists, the author shows how theoretical and historical perspectives underlie our understanding of the world.

Henslin, James M., ed. *Down to Earth Sociology: Introductory Readings,* 14th ed. New York: Free Press, 2007. This collection of readings about everyday life and social structure is designed to broaden the reader's understanding of society and of the individual's place within it.

Lengermann, Patricia Madoo, and Gillian Niebrugge. *The Women Founders: Sociology and Social Theory, 1830–1930.* Long Grove, Ill.: Waveland Press, 1998. Through their analyses and the writings they reprint, the authors/editors illuminate the struggles of female sociologists during the early period of sociology.

Mills, C. Wright. *The Sociological Imagination.* New York: Oxford University Press, 2000. First published in 1960, this classic analysis provides an overview of sociology from the framework of the conflict perspective.

Ritzer, George. *Classic Sociological Theory,* 5th ed. New York: McGraw-Hill, 2008. To help readers understand the personal and historical context of how theory develops, the author includes biographical sketches of the theorists.

## How Sociologists Do Research

Bryman, Alan. *Social Research Methods,* 3rd ed. Oxford: Oxford University Press, 2008. The author provides an overview of the research methods used by sociologists, with an emphasis on the logic that underlies these methods.

Creswell, John W. *Research Design: Qualitative, Quantitative, and Mixed Methods Approaches,* 3rd ed. Beverly Hills, Calif.: Sage, 2008.

This introduction to research methods walks you through the research experience and helps you to understand when to use a particular method.

Drew, Paul, Geoffrey Raymond, and Darin Weinberg. *Talk and Interaction in Social Research Methods.* Thousand Oaks, Calif.: Sage, 2006. The authors stress the importance of talk in a variety of social research methods.

Lee, Raymond M. *Unobtrusive Methods in Social Research.* Philadelphia: Open University Press, 2000. This overview of unobtrusive ways of doing social research summarizes many interesting studies.

Lomand, Turner C. *Social Science Research: A Cross Section of Journal Articles for Discussion and Evaluation,* 5th ed. Los Angeles: Pyrczak, 2007. This overview of the methods of research used by sociologists includes articles on current topics.

Neuman, W. Lawrence. *Social Research Methods: Qualitative and Quantitative Approaches,* 6th ed. Boston: Allyn & Bacon, 2006. A "how-to" book of sociological research that describes how sociologists gather data and the logic that underlies each method.

Whyte, William Foote. *Creative Problem Solving in the Field: Reflections on a Career.* Lanham, Md.: AltaMira Press, 1997. Focusing on his extensive field experiences, the author provides insight into the researcher's role in participant observation.

Wysocki, Diane Kholos, ed. *Readings in Social Research Methods,* 3rd ed. Belmont, Calif.: Wadsworth, 2008. The authors of these articles provide an overview of research methods.

## Journals

*Applied Behavioral Science Review; Clinical Sociology Review; International Clinical Sociology; Journal of Applied Sociology; The Practicing Sociologist; Sociological Practice: A Journal of Clinical and Applied Sociology;* and *Sociological Practice Review* report the experiences of sociologists who work in applied settings, from peer group counseling and suicide prevention to recommending changes to school boards.

*Contexts,* published by the American Sociological Association, uses a magazine format to present sociological research in a down-to-earth fashion.

*Humanity & Society,* the official journal of the Association for Humanist Sociology, publishes articles intended "to advance the quality of life of the world's people."

*Qualitative Sociology, Symbolic Interaction,* and *Urban Life* feature articles on symbolic interactionism and analyses of everyday life.

## Electronic Journals

*Electronic Journal of Sociology* (http://www.sociology.org) and *Sociological Research Online* (http://www. socresonline.org.uk) publish articles on various sociological topics. Access is free.

## About Majoring in Sociology

You like sociology and perhaps are thinking about majoring in it, but what can you do with a sociology major? Be sure to check the epilogue of this book (pages 450–451). Also check out the resources that are available from the American Sociological Association. Go to www.asanet.org. This will bring you to the ASA's home page. Here, you can click around and get familiar with what our professional association offers students.

On the menu at the top of ASA's home page, click *Students.* This will bring you to a page that has links to resources for students. You may be interested in *The Student Sociologist,* a newsletter for students. The link *Careers* will take you to several free online publications, including those that feature information on careers in both basic and applied sociology. You will also see such links as the student forum, student involvement, and funding.

If you want to contact the ASA by snail mail or by telephone or fax, here is the contact information: American Sociological Association, 1430 K Street NW, Suite 600, Washington, D.C. 20005. Tel. (202) 383-9005. Fax (202) 638-0882. E-mail: Executive.Office@asanet.org

You might also be interested in this book. If your library doesn't have it, I'm sure they'll order it if you request it.

Stephens, W. Richard, Jr. *Careers in Sociology,* 4th ed. Boston: Pearson Education, 2004. How can you make a living with a major in sociology? The author explores careers in sociology, from business and government to health care and the law.

# Chapter 2: Culture

Borofsky, Robert, and Bruce Albert. *Yanomami: The Fierce Controversy and What We Can Learn from It.* Berkeley: University of California Press, 2006. The authors criticize the research on the Yanomamö, including that by Chagnon in the next book, with an emphasis on anthropologists' lack of consideration of human rights.

Chagnon, Napoleon A. *Yanomamö: The Fierce People,* 5th ed. New York: Harcourt, Brace, Jovanovich, 1997. This account of a tribal people whose customs are extraordinarily different from ours will help you to see how arbitrary the choices are that underlie human culture.

Fulbeck, Kip. *Permanence: Tattoo Portraits.* New York: Chronicle Books, 2008. Through photographs of tattoos and the accounts of those who have those tattoos, you can gain insight and understanding of the tattoo subcultures, which are being adopted and modified by mainstreamers.

Griswold, Wendy. *Cultures and Societies in a Changing World,* 3rd ed. Thousand Oaks, Calif.: Pine Forge Press, 2008. Analyzes how culture shapes people's individual identity, including their norms, values, beliefs, and behavior; also indicates how globalization is changing cultures.

Inglis, David. *Culture and Everyday Life.* Oxford: Routledge, 2006. An overview of how culture shapes, influences, and structures our everyday lives.

Jacobs, Mark D., and Nancy Weiss Hanrahan, eds. *The Blackwell Companion to the Sociology of Culture.* Malden, Mass.: Blackwell, 2005. The authors of these articles explore cultural systems, everyday life, identity, collective memory, and citizenship in a globalizing world.

Lenski, Gerhard, and Patrick Nolan. *Human Societies,* 10th ed. New York: Paradigm, 2006. A wide-ranging examination of the fundamentals of human societies; also analyzes contemporary social change, including globalization, outsourcing, the end of cheap oil, Islamic fundamentalism, and the rise of China.

Zellner, William W., and Richard T. Schaefer. *Extraordinary Groups: An Examination of Unconventional People,* 8th ed. New York: Worth, 2007. The authors describe the lifestyles of nine unconventional U.S. groups: Amish, Oneida, Gypsies, Unitarian Universalists, Christian Scientists, Hasidim, followers of Father Divine, Mormons, and Jehovah's Witnesses.

# Chapter 3: Socialization

Ariès, Philippe. *Centuries of Childhood: A Social History of Family Life.* New York: Vintage, 1972. The author analyzes how childhood in Europe during the Middle Ages differs from childhood today.

Blumer, Herbert. *George Herbert Mead and Human Conduct.* Lanham, Md.: AltaMira Press, 2004. An overview of symbolic interactionism by a sociologist who studied and lectured on Mead's teachings all of his life.

Corsaro, William A. *The Sociology of Childhood,* 2nd ed. Thousand Oaks, Calif.: Pine Forge Press, 2005. This sociological analysis of childhood includes social indicators of children in the United States and the world.

Grusec, Joan E., and Paul D. Hastings, eds. *Handbook of Socialization: Theory and Research.* New York: Guilford Press, 2007. Extensive overview of socialization from earliest childhood into adulthood.

Handel, Gerald, Spencer Cahill, and Frederick Elkin. *Children and Society: The Sociology of Children and Childhood Socialization.* New York: Oxford University Press, 2007. A symbolic interactionist perspective on childhood from birth to adolescence, with an emphasis on the development of the self.

Hunt, Stephen J. *The Life Course: A Sociological Introduction.* New York: Palgrave Macmillan, 2006. This book gives an overview of the life course while considering what is distinctive about a sociological approach to this topic.

Lareau, Annette. *Unequal Childhoods: Class, Race, and Family Life.* Berkeley: University of California Press, 2003. The author compares childrearing in poor, working-class, and middle-class U.S. families.

Settersten, Richard A., Jr., and Timothy J. Owens, eds. *New Frontiers in Socialization.* Greenwich, Conn.: JAI Press, 2003. The authors of these articles focus on the adult years in the life course, examining the influence of families, neighborhoods, communities, friendship, education, work, volunteer associations, medical institutions, and the media.

*Sociological Studies of Child Development: A Research Annual.* Greenwich, Conn.: JAI Press, published annually. Along with theoretical articles, this publication reports on sociological research on the socialization of children.

# Chapter 4: Social Structure and Social Interaction

Berry, Bonnie. *Beauty Bias: Discrimination and Social Power.* Westport, Conn.: Praeger, 2007. The subject is *looksism*: the many areas of discrimination, negative and positive, that are based on appearance.

Bogle, Kathleen A. *Hooking Up: Sex, Dating, and Relationships on Campus.* New York: New York University Press, 2008. An analysis of the sexual-social interaction of college students.

Cregan, Kate. *The Sociology of the Body: Mapping the Abstraction of Embodiment.* Beverly Hills, Calif.: Sage, 2006. Examines social influences on the body, the smallest unit of sociological analysis.

Day, Graham. *Community and Everyday Life.* New York: Routledge, 2006. The author reviews changing ideas and patterns of community, from urban and rural to communes and electronic or virtual communities.

Goffman, Erving. *The Presentation of Self in Everyday Life.* New York: Peter Smith, 1999. First published in 1959, this classic statement of dramaturgical analysis provides a different way of looking at everyday life. This was one of the best books I read as a student.

Seidman, Steven, Nancy Fischer, and Chet Meeks, eds. *Introducing the New Sexuality Studies: Original Essays and Interviews.* New York: Routledge, 2006. The authors of these articles explore how society influences our sexual choices, our beliefs about sexuality, and our sexual standards.

Tönnies, Ferdinand. *Community and Society (Gemeinschaft und Gesellschaft).* New York: Dover, 2003. Originally published in 1887, this classic work, focusing on social change, provides insight into how society influences personality. It is rather challenging reading.

Waskul, Dennis, and Phillip Vannini, eds. *Body/embodiment: Symbolic Interaction and the Sociology of the Body.* London: Ashgate, 2007. Using a symbolic interactionist perspective, the authors of these articles explore the interrelationship of the body, the self, and social interaction.

Whyte, William Foote. *Street Corner Society: The Social Structure of an Italian Slum,* 4th ed. Chicago: University of Chicago Press, 1993. Originally published in 1943. This sociological classic focuses on interaction in a U.S. Italian slum, demonstrating how social structure affects personal relationships.

# Chapter 5: Social Groups and Formal Organizations

Ackoff, Russell L., and Sheldon Rovin. *Beating the System: Using Creativity to Outsmart Bureaucracies.* San Francisco: Berrett-Koehler, 2005. This analysis can be applied to everyday situations, such as avoiding getting lost in an interminable maze as you try to solve a problem with the phone company or some other bureaucracy.

Fineman, Stephen, Gabriel Yiannis, and David P. Sims. *Organizing and Organizations,* 3rd ed. Beverly Hills, Calif.: Sage, 2006. The authors draw on many firsthand accounts to help enliven the study of formal organizations.

Hall, Richard H., and Pamela S. Tolbert. *Organizations: Structures, Processes, and Outcomes,* 9th ed. Upper Saddle River, N.J.: Prentice-Hall,

2005. The focus of this review of the literature on social organizations is on the impacts that organizations have upon individuals and society.

Homans, George C. *The Human Group.* New Brunswick, N.J.: Transaction, 2001. First published in 1950. In this classic work, the author develops the idea that all human groups share common activities, interactions, and sentiments.

Hughes, Richard L., Robert C. Ginnett, and Gordon J. Curphy. *Leadership: Enhancing the Lessons of Experience,* 5th ed. New York: McGraw-Hill, 2006. Supplementing empirical studies with illustrative anecdotes, the authors focus on what makes effective leaders.

Newman, Mark, Albert-Laszlo Barabasi, and Duncan J. Watts, eds. *The Structure and Dynamics of Networks,* 6th ed. Princeton, N.J.: Princeton University Press, 2007. The authors of these papers analyze the significance of social networks for individuals and the functioning of society.

Parkinson, C. Northcote. *Parkinson's Law.* Boston: Buccaneer Books, 1997. Although this exposé of the inner workings of bureaucracies is delightfully satirical, if what Parkinson analyzes were generally true, bureaucracies would always fail.

Purcell, Patrick, ed. *Networked Neighborhoods: The Connected Community in Context.* New York: Springer, 2007. The authors of these papers analyze the impact of the Internet on our social relationships, community, work patterns, and lifestyles.

Ritzer, George. *The McDonaldization of Society: An Investigation into the Changing Character of Contemporary Life,* 5th ed. Thousand Oaks, Calif.: Pine Forge Press, 2007. The author examines how Durkheim's predictions about the rationalization of society are coming true in everyday life.

Venkatesh, Sudhir. *Gang Leader for a Day: A Rogue Sociologist Takes to the Streets.* New York: Penguin Press, 2008. The adventures of a graduate student in sociology as he explores a drug-dealing gang in a Chicago public housing project.

Want, Jerome. *Corporate Culture: Illuminating the Black Hole.* New York: St. Martin's Press, 2007. The author uses real-life examples to show how culture determines the success of an organization.

Wilson, Gerald L. *Groups in Context: Leadership and Participation in Small Groups,* 7th ed. New York: McGraw-Hill, 2005. The book provides an overview of principles and processes of interaction in small groups, with an emphasis on how to exercise leadership.

# Chapter 6: Deviance and Social Control

Deflin, Mathieu. *Surveillance and Governance: Crime Control and Beyond.* Greenwich, Conn.: JAI Press, 2008. The use of increasingly powerful surveillance techniques to monitor terrorists and other violent criminals is usually taken for granted—but what is to keep those same methods from being turned against ordinary citizens?

Fox, James Alan, and Jack Levin. *Extreme Killing: Understanding Serial and Mass Murder.* Thousand Oaks, Calif.: Sage, 2005. As the authors analyze the various types of serial and mass murders, they examine the characteristics of both killers and their victims.

Goffman, Erving. *Stigma: Notes on the Management of Spoiled Identity.* New York: Simon & Schuster, 1986. First published in 1968. The author outlines the social and personal reactions to "spoiled identity," appearances that—due to disability, weight, ethnicity, birth marks, and so on—do not match dominant expectations.

Goode, Erich, and D. Angus Vail, eds. *Extreme Deviance.* Thousand Oaks, Calif: Pine Forge Press, 2007. As the authors of these article examine behaviors that bring extreme negative reactions, they analyze vocabularies of motive, deviance neutralization, the acquisition of a deviant identity, and the formation of deviant subcultures.

Gu, George Zhibin, and Andre Gunder Frank. *China's Global Reach: Markets, Multinationals, and Globalization*, rev. ed. Palo Alto, Calif.: Fultus Corp., 2006. The author tries to identify the causes and consequences of global development, with a comparison of corporations in China and other nations.

Heiner, Robert, ed. *Deviance Across Cultures.* Oxford: Oxford University Press, 2007. Cross-cultural norms and behavior are the focus of this collection of classic and contemporary articles on deviance.

Lombroso, Cesare, Guglielmo Ferrero, Nicole Hahn Rafter, and Mary Gibson. *Criminal Woman, the Prostitute, and the Normal Woman.* Durham, N.C.: Duke University Press, 2005. This translation of a classic work from the 1800s on women and crime is put into current social context by two researchers on female criminals.

Parmentier, Stephen, and Elmar Weitekamp. *Crime and Human Rights.* Greenwich, Conn.: JAI Press, 2008. The authors analyze how the emphasis on human rights is changing the ways crime and criminal justice are viewed and how this is impacting the U.S. and European justice systems.

Paul, Pamela. *Pornified: How Pornography Is Transforming Our Lives, Our Relationships, and Our Families.* New York: Holt, 2005. Based on interviews, the author's thesis is that for many people pornography is replacing intimacy and creating emotional isolation.

Rathbone, Cristina. *A World Apart: Women, Prison, and Life Behind Bars.* New York: Random House, 2006. A journalist's account of the four years she spent investigating MCI Framingham, the oldest women's prison in the United States.

Reiman, Jeffrey. *The Rich Get Richer and the Poor Get Prison: Ideology, Class, and Criminal Justice*, 8th ed. Boston: Allyn & Bacon, 2007. An analysis of how social class works to produce different types of criminals and different types of justice.

Simon, David R. *Elite Deviance*, 9th ed. Boston: Allyn & Bacon, 2008. A broad overview of deviance, from scandals to organized crime syndicates.

## Journals

*Criminal Justice Review: Issues in Criminal, Social, and Restorative Justice* and *Journal of Law and Society* examine the social forces that shape law and justice.

# Chapter 7: Global Stratification

Grusky, David B., ed. *Social Stratification: Class, Race, and Gender in Sociological Perspective.* Boulder, Colo.: Westview Press, 2008. This reader of over 100 articles and 1,000 pages examines almost every aspect of social stratification, from causes and consequences to likely futures.

Holzner, Burkart, and Leslie Holzner. *Transparency in Global Change: The Vanguard of the Open Society.* Pittsburgh: University of Pittsburgh Press, 2006. The tension between transparency and secrecy as information flows within and across international boundaries.

Lechner, Frank J., and John Boli, eds. *The Globalization Reader*, 3rd ed. Malden, Mass.: Wiley-Blackwell, 2008. A thorough introduction to globalization, including a link with environmentalism.

Ritzer, George. *The Globalization of Nothing*, 2nd ed. Thousand Oaks, Calif: Pine Forge Press, 2007. The author expresses concerns about the short- and long-term effects of globalization.

Rothkopf, David. *Superclass: The Global Power Elite and the World They Are Making.* New York: Farrar, Straus and Giroux, 2008. The author of this overview of the world's wealthiest families has many personal connections with these elite, powerful people.

Sachs, Jeffrey D. *The End of Poverty: Economic Possibilities for Our Time.* East Rutherford, N.J.: Penguin, 2005. After visiting 100 countries, representing 90 percent of the world's population, the author suggests ways that we can end global poverty.

Sernau, Scott. *Worlds Apart: Social Inequalities in a Global Economy*, 2nd ed. Thousand Oaks, Calif.: Pine Forge Press, 2005. The author's thesis is that the market-driven global economy contributes to rather than reduces social inequality.

Wan, Ming. *The Political Economy of East Asia: Striving for Wealth and Power.* Washington, D.C.: CQ Press, 2008. The author analyzes the politics and policies that are increasing the power and wealth of east Asia.

Zakaria, Fareed. *The Post-American World.* New York: W.W. Norton, 2008. Analyzes political and economic megatrends that are making fundamental changes in the distribution of world power.

# Chapter 8: Social Class in the United States

Beeghley, Leonard. *The Structure of Social Stratification in the United States*, 5th ed. Boston: Pearson, 2008. In this brief book, the author presents an overview of the U.S. social classes.

Eitzen, D. Stanley, and Janis E. Johnston, eds. *Inequality: Social Class and Its Consequences.* Boulder, Colo.: Paradigm, 2007. Written from the conflict perspective (class struggle), these selections examine class formation, cultures, and politics.

Engels, Friedrich. *Condition of the Working Class in England.* Sydney, Australia: Read How You Want, 2007. First published as *Die Lage der arbeitenden Klasse in England*, in 1844. One of the significant books in world history, this analysis of people who lived in poverty (the working class of the time) is based on the author's research and parliamentary reports.

Fraser, Steve, and Gary Gerstle, eds. *Ruling America: A History of Wealth and Power in a Democracy.* Cambridge, Mass.: Harvard University Press, 2005. Analyses of the controlling elites in the United States, from its founding to the present.

Gilbert, Dennis. *The American Class Structure in an Age of Growing Inequality*, 7th ed. Thousand Oaks, Calif.: Pine Forge Press, 2008. This basic text on the U.S. social class structure; filled with facts about class, grapples with the question of why social mobility in the United States is decreasing.

Hartmann, Heidi I., ed. *Women, Work, and Poverty: Women Centered Research for Policy Change*. Binghamton, N.Y.: Haworth Press, 2006. The authors present research on women living at or below the poverty line. Major themes are work, marriage, motherhood, and welfare reform.

Iceland, John. *Poverty in America, A Handbook,* 2nd ed. Berkeley, Calif.: University of California Press, 2006. Details how both U.S. poverty and its related public policies have changed over time.

Newman, Katherine S., and Victor Tan Chen. *The Missing Class: Portraits of the Near Poor in America*. Boston: Beacon Press, 2007. The story of nine families who live on the edge of poverty: their experiences in education, leisure, child rearing, romance, work, the police, courts, welfare, shopping, and debt.

Perucci, Robert, and Earl Wyson. *The New Class Society,* 3rd ed. Lanham, Md.: Rowman and Littlefield, 2007. An overview of the U.S. social class structure, with the suggestion that there no longer is a middle class.

Sherman, Rachel. *Class Acts: Service and Inequality in Luxury Hotels*. Berkeley, Calif.: University of California Press, 2007. Based on participant observation, the author explores the relationship between workers and guests at a luxury hotel.

Sumner, William Graham. *What the Social Classes Owe to Each Other*. Charleston, South Carolina: BiblioBazaar, 2008. First published in 1883. Written when sociology had a largely conservative orientation, the author explains why the government should not redistribute wealth.

Van Galen, Jane A., and George W. Noblit, eds. *Late to Class: Social Class and Schooling in the New Economy*. Albany: State University of New York Press, 2007. The authors of these articles compare the educational experiences of poor, working-class, and middle-class students, illustrating how education reproduces social class and suggesting ways to open educational opportunity.

## Journals

*Journal of Children and Poverty* and *Journal of Poverty* analyze issues that affect the quality of life of people who live in poverty.

*Race, Gender, and Class* publishes interdisciplinary articles on the topics listed in its title.

# Chapter 9: Race and Ethnicity

Acosta, Teresa Palomo, and Ruthe Winegarten. *Los Tejanas: 300 Years of History*. Austin: University of Texas Press, 2003. This account traces how Tejanas in the colonial period and from the Republic of Texas up to 1900 overcame obstacles to their success.

Blackmon, Douglas A. *A Different Kind of Slavery. The Re-Enslavement of Black Americans from the Civil War to World War II*. New York, Doubleday, 2008. The author documents the horrible conditions African Americans suffered in Georgia during "post-slavery," especially in its criminal "justice" system.

Castile, George Pierre. *Taking Charge: Native American Self-determination and Federal Indian Policy, 1975–1993*. Tucson: University of Arizona Press, 2006. Examines the background, implications, and implementation of the Indian Self-Determination Act of 1975.

Du Bois, W. E. B. *Black Reconstruction in America: An Essay Toward a History of the Part Which Black Folk Played in the Attempt to Reconstruct Democracy in America, 1860–1880*. New York: Harcourt, Brace 1935; New York: Free Press, 2000. This analysis of the role of African Americans in the Civil War and during the years immediately following provides a glimpse into a neglected part of U.S. history.

Gracia, Jorge J. E. *Race or Ethnicity? On Black and Latino Identity*. Ithaca, N.Y.: Cornell University Press, 2007. In this exploration of history and identity, the reader will come to understand "ethnicized blackness" and "racialized Latinity."

Higginbotham, Elizabeth, and Margaret L. Andersen, eds. *Race and Ethnicity in Society: The Changing Landscape,* 2nd ed. Belmont, Calif.: Wadsworth, 2008. From race–ethnicity as a social issue to its relationship to beliefs, ideology, and personal identity, the authors provide a thorough overview of this topic.

Idler, Jose Enrique. *Officially Hispanic: Classification Policy and Identity*. Lanham, Md.: Lexington Books, 2007. How official categories are inadequate for representing lived racial–ethnic experience.

Parrillo, Vincent, N. *Strangers to These Shores: Race and Ethnic Relations in the United States,* 9th ed. Boston: Allyn & Bacon, 2009. This text reviews the experiences of more than 50 racial–ethnic groups.

Ross, Jeffrey Ian, and Larry Gould, eds. *Native Americans and the Criminal Justice System*. Boulder, Colo.: Paradigm, 2006. The authors of these articles address crime by Native Americans within historical, cultural, and legal contexts and the issue of criminal justice and tribal sovereignty.

Schaefer, Richard T. *Race and Ethnicity in the United States,* 4th ed. Upper Saddle River, New Jersey: Prentice-Hall, 2007. The data and analyses of this basic text can help cut through some of the emotional blinders that often accompany this topic.

Walker, Samuel, Cassia Spohn, and Miriam Delone. *The Color of Justice: Race, Ethnicity, and Crime in America,* 4th ed. Belmont, Calif.: Wadsworth, 2007. The authors analyze racial, ethnic, and gender discrimination in the criminal justice system.

Wilson, George, ed. *Race, Ethnicity, and Inequality in the U.S. Labor Market: Critical Issues in the New Millennium*. Thousand Oaks, Calif.: Sage, 2007. The authors of these articles make evident that the labor market is neither race-neutral nor color blind, that race–ethnicity continues to be a major factor in determining life-chances.

Wilson, William Julius, and Richard P. Taub. *There Goes the Neighborhood: Racial, Ethnic, and Class Tensions in Four Chicago Neighborhoods and Their Meaning for America*. New York: Vintage, 2008. Through their analysis of four working- and lower-middle-class neighborhoods in Chicago, the authors conclude that the "tipping point" of rapid ethnic change depends on the strength of neighborhood social organizations.

Zeitz, Joshua M. *White Ethnic New York: Jews, Catholics, and the Shaping of Postwar Politics*. Chapel Hill: University of North Carolina Press, 2007. Examines the sometimes contentious, fractious, and fragile coalition that became politically and culturally significant in this area of the United States.

# Chapter 10: Gender and Age

## INEQUALITIES OF GENDER

Andersen, Margaret L. *Thinking About Women: Sociological Perspectives on Sex and Gender,* 8th ed. Boston: Allyn & Bacon, 2009. An overview of the main issues of sex and gender in contemporary society, ranging from sexism and socialization to work and health.

Brettell, Caroline B., and Carolyn F. Sargent, eds. *Gender in Cross-Cultural Perspective,* 5th ed. Upper Saddle River, N.J.: Prentice-Hall, 2009. The net is spread wide as the authors examine gender and biology, in prehistory, at home, and the division of labor, and the body, property, kinship, religion, politics, and the global economy.

Casey, Emma, and Lydia Martens, eds. *Gender and Consumption: Domestic Cultures and the Commercialisation of Everyday Life.* Burlington, Vermont: Ashgate, 2007. The articles in this short book focus on how gender is constructed and communicated through the purchase and use of objects.

Colapinto, John. *As Nature Made Him: The Boy Who Was Raised as a Girl.* New York: HarperCollins, 2001. This is a detailed account of the story summarized in this chapter of the boy whose penis was accidentally burned off.

DeFrancisco, Victoria Pruin, and Catherine Helen Palczewski. *Communicating Gender Diversity: A Critical Approach.* Los Angeles: Sage, 2007. Probably the polar opposite of the Colapinto book; gender is viewed not as something that people are but as something that people do; an emphasis on how gender is constructed through communication.

Fuller, Linda K., ed. *Sport, Rhetoric, and Gender: Historical Perspectives and Media Representations.* New York: Palgrave Macmillan, 2006. The articles in this short book focus on how gender is communicated in sports; includes both historical materials and contemporary case studies.

Gilbert, Paula Ruth, and Kimberly K. Eby, eds. *Violence and Gender: An Interdisciplinary Reader.* Upper Saddle River:, N.J.: Prentice-Hall, 2004. The authors of these articles examine violence and youth, the human body, war, intimacy, sports, the media, and how to prevent violence.

Gilman, Charlotte Perkins. *The Man-Made World or, Our Androcentric Culture.* New York: Charlton, 1911. Reprinted in 1971 by Johnson Reprint. This early book on women's liberation provides an excellent view of female–male relations at the beginning of the last century.

Gonas, Lena, and Jan Ch Karlsson, eds. *Gender Segregation: Divisions of Work in Post-Industrial Welfare States.* Burlington, Vermont: Ashgate, 2006. This short book of ten articles focuses on the gendered division of labor.

Johnson, Allan G. *Privilege, Power, and Difference,* 2nd ed. New York: McGraw-Hill, 2006. The author helps us see the nature and consequences of privilege and our connection to it.

Kimmel, Michael S., ed. *The Gendered Society Reader,* 3rd ed. New York: Oxford University Press, 2007. The authors of these articles examine the relationship of gender and violence in the contexts of culture, family, classroom, workplace, and intimacy.

Kimmel, Michael S., and Michael A. Messner, eds. *Men's Lives,* 7th ed. Boston: Allyn & Bacon, 2007. The authors of these articles examine issues of sex and gender as they affect men. The articles often provide different views from those presented in the Andersen book.

McDonagh, Eileen, and Laura Pappano. *Playing with the Boys: Why Separate Is Not Equal in Sports.* New York: Oxford University Press, 2008. A detailed history of how women have challenged men's sports; filled with anecdotes and contains fascinating historical photos.

## Journals

These journals focus on the role of gender in social life: *Feminist Studies; Gender and Behavior; Gender and Society; Forum in Women's and Gender Studies; Gender and History; Gender, Place and Culture: A Journal of Feminist Geography; Journal of Gender, Culture, and Health; Journal of Interdisciplinary Gender Studies; Journal of Men's Health and Gender; Sex Roles;* and *Signs: Journal of Women in Culture and Society.*

## INEQUALITIES OF AGING

Gubrium, Jaber F., and James A. Holstein, eds. *Ways of Aging.* Malden, Mass.: Blackwell, 2003. The authors of these articles examine how people construct their self-definitions as they adjust to the realities of aging bodies.

Harris, Diana K., and Michael L. Benson. *Maltreatment of Patients in Nursing Homes: There Is No Safe Place.* New York: Routledge, 2006. An examination of the physical, financial, and psychological abuse of patients—restraints, verbal abuse, sexual abuse, the theft of belongings, childlike treatment, and learned helplessness.

Hooyman, Nancy, and H. Asuman Kiyak. *Social Gerontology: A Multidisciplinary Perspective,* 8th ed. Boston: Allyn & Bacon, 2008. As the authors consider factors that influence how people experience old age, they cover differences by age and cohort, gender, race–ethnicity, sexual orientation, and socioeconomic status.

Nilan, Pam, and Carles Feixa, eds. *Global Youth? Hybrid Identities, Plural Worlds.* New York: Routledge, 2006. The authors of these articles report research on Eastern youth cultures.

Quadagno, Jill S. *Aging and the Life Course: An Introduction to Social Gerontology,* 4th ed. New York: McGraw-Hill, 2008. In this review of major issues in gerontology, the author examines how the quality of life that people experience in old age is the result of earlier choices, opportunities, and constraints.

Rubin, Lillian B. *Tangled Lives: Daughters, Mothers, and the Crucible of Aging.* Boston: Beacon Press, 2002. The author reflects on her own experiences with illness and death to try to come to grips with the meaning of growing old—and of life.

Schaie, K. Warner, and Laura Carsgtensen. *Social Structures, Aging, and Self-Regulation in the Elderly.* New York: Springer, 2006. The focus is on how social location, especially social class, influences the lives, even the brains, of the elderly; recommended for advanced students.

Vincent, John A., Chris R. Phillipson, and Murna Downs. *The Futures of Old Age.* Thousand Oaks, Calif.: Sage, 2006. Considers how families, services, and economies might adapt to a growing older population.

Xi, Jieying, Yunxiao Sun, and Jin Jian Xiao, eds. *Chinese Youth in Transition.* Burlington, Vermont: Ashgate, 2006. The authors of these articles analyze the changing youth culture of China.

## Journals

*Elderly Latinos; The Gerontologist; Journal of Aging and Identity; Journal of Aging and Social Policy; Journal of Aging Studies; Journal of Cross-Cultural Gerontology; Journal of Elder Abuse and Neglect; Journal of Gerontology;* and *Journal of Women and Aging* focus on issues of aging, while *Journal of Youth Studies* and *Youth and Society* examine adolescent culture.

# Chapter 11: Politics and the Economy

## POLITICS

Amnesty International. *Amnesty International Report.* London: Amnesty International Publications. This annual report summarizes human rights violations around the world, listing specific instances, including names, country by country.

Andreas, Peter, and Ethan Nadelmenn. *Policing the Globe: Crime Control in International Relations.* New York: Oxford University Press, 2006. The authors' thesis in this bridge between criminal justice and international relations is that Western countries gain political benefits by exporting their definitions of crime.

Beah, Ishmael. *A Long Way Gone: Memoirs of a Boy Soldier.* New York: Farrar, Straus, and Giroux, 2007. This first-person account of a boy who was forced into becoming a soldier in Sierra Leone provides an understanding of the social dynamics that transform young teenagers into rapists, torturers, and killers.

Domhoff, G. William. *Who Rules America? Power and Politics,* 5th ed. New York: McGraw-Hill, 2006. An analysis of how the multinational corporations dominate the U.S. government.

Du Bois, William, and R. Dean Wright. Lanham, Md.: Lexington Books, 2007. *Politics in the Human Interest: Applying Sociology in the Real World.* The authors explain how we can use sociology to change politics so it serves the interest of the people.

Liang, Bin. *The Changing Chinese Legal System, 1978–Present: Centralization of Power and Rationalization of the Legal System.* New York: Routledge, 2007. The author places his analysis of changes in the Chinese legal and political system within a global context.

Mills, C. Wright. *The Power Elite,* new ed. New York: Oxford University Press, 2000. First published in 1956. This classic analysis elaborates the conflict thesis summarized in this chapter—that U.S. society is ruled by the nation's top corporate leaders, together with an elite from the military and political institutions.

Nash, Kate. *Contemporary Political Sociology: Globalization, Politics, and Power.* Malden, Mass.: Blackwell, 2008. This overview of the sociology of politics makes the point that globalization is ushering in a major transition, from the nation-state to the internationalized state.

Paxton, Pamela, and Melanie M. Hughes. *Women, Politics, and Power: A Global Perspective.* Thousand Oaks, Calif.: Pine Forge Press, 2007. The authors survey women's political participation in many countries and regions of the world.

*Research in Political Sociology: A Research Annual.* Greenwich, Conn.: JAI Press. This annual publication is not recommended for beginners, as the findings and theories are often difficult and abstract. It does, however, analyze political topics of vital concern to our well-being.

## Journals

Many sociology journals publish articles on politics. Six that focus on this area of social life are *American Political Science Review, Journal of Conflict Resolution, Journal of Peace Research, Journal of Political and Military Sociology, Social Policy,* and *Social Politics.*

## THE ECONOMY

Bales, Kevin. *Disposable People: New Slavery in the Global Economy,* rev. ed. Berkeley: University of California Press, 2005. The author documents the relationship between the globalization of capitalism and current slavery in Brazil, India, Mauritania, Pakistan, and Thailand.

Bergsten, C. Fred. *The United States and the World Economy.* Washington, D.C.: Institute for International Economics, 2005. This analysis of the globalization of capitalism focuses on how the prosperity of the United States is related to the world economy.

Eitzen, D. Stanley, and Maxine Baca Zinn, eds. *Globalization: The Transformation of Social Worlds.* Belmont, Calif.: Wadsworth, 2008. The authors of these articles examine the process of globalization and analyze how globalization is reshaping societies and groups within it.

Kenway, Jane, Elizabeth Bullen, Johannah Fahey, and Simon Robb. *Haunting the Knowledge Economy.* New York: Routledge, 2007. The authors' thesis is that alongside the dominant knowledge economy lie alternative marginalized risk, libidinal, gift, and survival economies.

Lenin, Vladimir Ilyich. *The Development of Capitalism in Russia.* Honolulu: University Press of the Pacific, 2004. This is an English translation of Lenin's 1899 book.

Lucarelli, Bill. *Monopoly Capitalism in Crisis.* New York: Palgrave Macmillan, 2005. Is U.S. prosperity about to end? The author argues that the global economy is about to deflate owing to excess global production capacity.

Noland, Marcus, and Howard Pack. *The Arab Economies in a Changing World.* Washington, D.C.: Institute for International Economics, 2007. Places the economies of the Middle East in global context, comparing them with other economies in transition.

Sweet, Stephen A., and Peter F. Meiksins. *Changing Contours of Work: Jobs and Opportunities in the New Economy.* Thousand Oaks, Calif.: Pine Forge Press, 2008. The authors examine historical changes in work, explain how U.S. workers have become part of an integrated global work force, and make recommendations for how the new economy can help overcome inequality and serve human dignity.

Volti, Rudi. *An Introduction to the Sociology of Work and Occupations.* Thousand Oaks, Calif.: Pine Forge Press, 2008. Reviewing work from hunting and gathering societies to the information age, this basic introduction to the sociology of work stresses the impact of globalization on work today.

# Chapter 12: Marriage and Family

Agger, Ben, and Beth Anne Shelton. *Fast Families, Virtual Children: A Critical Sociology of Families and Schooling.* Boulder, Colo.: Paradigm, 2007. The authors analyze how technology has changed the way families lead their lives, rear their children, and try to maintain a boundary between work and home.

Amato, Paul R., Alan Booth, David R. Johnson, and Stacy J. Rogers. *Alone Together: How Marriage in America Is Changing.* Cambridge, Mass.: Harvard University Press, 2007. The authors' controversial thesis is that the significance of marriage is declining, that marriage is becoming one lifestyle choice among many.

Bianchi, Suzanne M., John P. Robinson, and Melissa A. Milkie. *Changing Rhythms of American Family Life.* New York: Russell Sage, 2006. Based on time-diaries, the authors conclude that despite their greater participation in the paid labor force, U.S. mothers spend just as much time with their children as the previous generation of women did.

Coontz, Stephanie. *Marriage, a History: From Obedience to Intimacy or How Love Conquered Marriage.* New York: Viking, 2005. This analysis of how the fundamental orientations to marriage have changed contains enlightening excerpts from the past.

Epstein, Cynthia Fuchs, and Arne L Kalleberg, eds. *Fighting for Time: Shifting Boundaries of Work and Social Life.* New York: Russell Sage, 2005. The authors explore changes in the time people spend at work and the consequences of those changes for individuals and families.

Gosselin, Denise Kindschi. *Heavy Hands: An Introduction to the Crimes of Family Violence,* 3rd ed. Upper Saddle River, N.J.: Prentice-Hall, 2005. This book explores causes, consequences, and prevalence of domestic violence; it also has an emphasis on law enforcement.

Johnson, Leonor Boulin, and Robert Staples. *Black Families at the Crossroads: Challenges and Prospects.* New York: Jossey-Bass, 2005. After placing today's black families in historical context, the authors analyze the impact of economic policies and social change.

Marquardt, Elizabeth. *Between Two Worlds: The Inner Lives of Children of Divorce.* New York: Crown, 2005. The author weaves her own experiences as a child of divorce into her summary of interviews with children who have had this experience.

Stone, Pamela. *Opting Out? Why Women Really Quit Careers and Head Home.* Berkeley: University of California Press, 2007. A study of high-achieving, highly educated, privileged women who quit their fast-paced professional work in order to become stay-at-home mothers—their decision, the transition, and the consequences.

Wallace, Harvey. *Family Violence,* 5th ed. Boston: Allyn & Bacon, 2008. An overview of family violence through three perspectives: legal, medical, and social.

## Journals

*Family Relations; The History of the Family; International Journal of Sociology of the Family; Journal of Comparative Family Studies; Journal of Divorce; Journal of Divorce and Remarriage; Journal of Family and Economic Issues; Journal of Family Issues; Journal of Family Violence; Journal of Marriage and the Family;* and *Marriage and Family Review* publish articles on almost every aspect of marriage and family life.

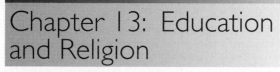

# Chapter 13: Education and Religion

## EDUCATION

Attewell, Paul, David Lavin, Thurston Domina, and Tana Levey. *Passing the Torch: Does Higher Education for the Disadvantaged Pay Off Across the Generations?* New York: Russell Sage, 2007. This study of women from poor families who attended college under open admission programs shows that their children are more likely to succeed in school and to earn college degrees themselves.

Ballantine, Jeanne H., and Floyd Hammock. *The Sociology of Education: A Systematic Analysis,* 6th ed. Upper Saddle River, New Jersey: Prentice-Hall, 2008. A basic reader that covers current issues in education and the social processes that underlie education.

Cotterill, Pamela, Sue Jackson, and Gayle Letherby, ed. *Challenges and Negotiations for Women in Higher Education.* Dordrecht, Netherlands: Springer, 2007. A short book of just twelve articles; addresses issues women face in higher education, from feeling unwelcome to juggling families and schooling.

Hess, Frederick M. *Common Sense School Reform.* New York: Palgrave Macmillan, 2005. Critical of current efforts to reform U.S. education, the author makes the case that reform needs to be based on accountability, competition, and leadership.

Kozol, Jonathan. *The Shame of the Nation: The Restoration of Apartheid Schooling in America.* New York: Crown, 2006. After visiting sixty schools in eleven states, the author concludes that we are offering inferior education for black and Latino children.

Lopez, Nancy. *Hopeful Girls, Troubled Boys: Race and Gender Disparity in Urban Education.* New York: Rutledge, 2003. Building on her thesis that education is failing boys of color, the author suggests ways to improve education.

Rothstein, Richard. *Class and Schools: Using Social, Economic, and Educational Reform to Close the Black-White Achievement Gap.* Washington, D.C.: Economic Policy Institute, 2004. The author's thesis is that because social class influences learning in school, public policy must address the social and economic conditions of children's lives.

Spring, Joel H. *Deculturalization and the Struggle for Equality: A Brief History of the Education of Dominated Cultures in the United States,* 4th ed. New York: McGraw-Hill 2004. The author examines how Anglos have used their control of schools to strip away the cultures of minorities and replace them with Anglo culture.

Stevens, Michael L. *Kingdom of Children: Culture and Controversy in the Homeschooling Movement.* Princeton: Princeton University Press, 2003. This analysis of the home schooling movement, based on interviews and participant observation, contains numerous quotations that provide insight into why parents home school their children.

## Journals

These journals contain articles that examine almost every aspect of education: *Education and Urban Society, Harvard Educational Review, Sociology and Education,* and *Sociology of Education.*

## RELIGION

Ault, James M. *Spirit and Flesh: Life in a Fundamentalist Baptist Church.* New York: Alfred A. Knopf, 2004. This participant observation study of an independent Baptist congregation provides insight into the initiation and maintenance of faith and relationships.

Cateura, Linda Brandi, and Omid Safi. *Voices of American Muslims.* New York: Hippocrene Books, 2006. U.S. Muslims describe their religion, experiences with suspicion and misunderstandings, and, in this heated period of terrorist attacks by Muslims, their devotion to the United States.

Christiano, Kevin, William H. Swatos, Jr., and Peter Kivisto. *Sociology of Religion: Contemporary Developments,* 2nd ed. Lanham, Md.: Rowman and Littlefield, 2008. Examines the foundations of the sociology of religion and charts changes in this field.

Crawford, Suzanne, *Native American Religious Traditions.* Upper Saddle River, New Jersey: Prentice-Hall, 2006. An introduction to the religious traditions of the Lakota, Diné (Navajo), and Coast Salish tribes, placing them within their historical, social, and political contexts.

Gilman, Sander. *Jewish Frontiers: Essays on Bodies, Histories, and Identities.* New York: Macmillan, 2003. The author analyzes Jewish identity from the framework of living on a frontier, and the representation of this identity in the mass media.

Juergensmeyer, Mark. *Terror in the Mind of God: The Global Rise of Religious Violence,* 3rd ed. Berkeley: University of California Press, 2003. The author's summaries of religious violence provide a rich background for understanding this behavior.

McRoberts, Omar M. *Streets of Glory: Church and Community in a Black Urban Neighborhood.* Chicago: University of Chicago Press, 2003. Four Corners, one of the toughest areas of Boston, contains twenty-nine mostly storefront churches. The author finds most of them are attended and run by people who do not live in the neighborhood and who have little or no attachment to the surrounding area.

Smith, Christian, and Melinda Denton. *Soul Searching: The Religious and Spiritual Life of American Teenagers.* Oxford: Oxford University Press, 2006. The authors survey the spiritual life of U.S. teenagers.

## Journals

These journals publish articles that focus on the sociology of religion: *Journal for the Scientific Study of Religion, Review of Religious Research,* and *Sociological Analysis: A Journal in the Sociology of Religion.*

# Chapter 14: Population and Urbanization

Bull, Michael. *Sound Moves: Ipod Culture and Urban Experience.* New York: Routledge, 2008. Using the example of the Apple iPod, the author analyzes how urbanites use sound to construct key areas of their daily lives.

Department of Agriculture. *Yearbook of Agriculture.* Washington, D.C.: Department of Agriculture. This yearbook focuses on specific aspects of U.S. agribusiness, especially international economies and trade.

Lang, Robert E., and Jennifer LeFurgy. *Boomburgs: The Rise of America's Accidental Cities.* Washington, D.C.: Brookings Institution Press, 2007. Contending that many fast-growing "cities" are really overgrown suburbs ("boomburgs"), the authors look at what attracts people to them and how they are governed.

Lin, Jan, and Christopher Mele, eds. *The Urban Sociology Reader.* New York: Routledge, 2006. The authors of these articles review the major issues in urban change and development.

Low, Setha. *Behind the Gates: Life, Security, and the Pursuit of Happiness in Fortress America.* New York: Routledge, 2004. An account of what life is like inside gated communities.

Palen, John J. *The Urban World,* 8th ed. New York: McGraw-Hill, 2008. A short, basic text that summarizes major issues in urban sociology.

Rodriguez, Gregory. *Mongrels, Bastards, Orphans, and Vagabonds: Mexican Immigration and the Future of Race in America.* New York: Random House, 2007. A thorough overview not just of the immigration of Mexicans to the United States but also of the tense and changing relationships between Anglos and Mexican immigrants.

Wacquant, Loic. *Urban Outcasts: A Comparative Sociology of Advanced Marginality.* Malden, Mass.: Polity, 2008. This analysis of U.S. ghettos and French *banlieue* explores polarization, lived realities, and "reserved urban spaces."

Yaukey, David, and Douglas L. Anderton. *Demography: The Study of Human Population,* 3rd ed. Bellevue, Wash.: Waveland Press, 2007. Focusing on both the United States and countries around the world, the authors analyze major issues in population.

Zhao, Zhongwei, and Fei Guo. *Transition and Challenge: China's Population at the Beginning of the 21st Century.* New York: Oxford University Press, 2007. The authors analyze implications of China's family planning policy, changes in marital patterns, high rural-urban migration, and falling birth rates coupled with a rising life expectancy.

## Journals

*City and Community, Journal of Rural Studies, Journal of Urban Affairs, Review of Regional and Urban Development Studies, Rural Sociology,* and *Urban Studies* publish articles whose focus is the city, community, immigration, migration, rural life, and suburbs. *Social Movement Studies* examines the origins, development, organization, context, and impact of social movements.

# Chapter 15: Social Change and the Environment

Bauchspies, Wenda K., Jennifer Croissant, and Sal Restivo. *Science, Technology, and Society: A Sociological Approach.* Malden, Mass.: Wiley-Blackwell, 2005. Analyzes major issues in STS (Science, Technology, and Society) studies: power, culture, race–ethnicity, gender, colonialism, cyberspace, and biotechnology.

Best, Joel. *Flavor of the Month: Why Smart People Fall for Fads.* Berkeley, Calif.: University of California Press, 2006. If you want to smile, perhaps even laugh, as you read a sociological account, this little book is for you.

Brown, Lester R., ed. *State of the World.* New York: Norton. This annual publication uses a New Malthusian perspective to analyze environmental problems throughout the world.

Council on Environmental Quality. *Environmental Quality.* Washington, D.C.: U.S. Government Printing Office. This annual publication evaluates the condition of some aspect of the environment.

DuPuis, E. Melanie, ed. *Smoke and Mirrors: The Politics and Culture of Air Pollution.* New York: New York University Press, 2004. The fifteen articles in this book review the emergence of air pollution as a social problem and the status of air pollution today.

Fox, Nicols. *Against the Machine: The Hidden Luddite Tradition in Literature, Art, and Individual Lives.* Washington, D.C.: Island Press, 2004. The author covers broad historical ground as he analyzes reactions against modernization in the West.

Hannigan, John. *Environmental Sociology: A Social Constructionist Perspective,* 2nd ed. New York: Routledge, 2006. This basic text on environmental sociology links major disasters to environmental change and reviews the escalating global conflict over freshwater resources.

Howard, Russell D., Reid L. Sawyer, and Natasha E. Bajema, eds. *Terrorism and Counterterrorism: Understanding the New Security Environment, Readings and Interpretations,* 3rd ed. New York: McGraw-Hill, 2008. These analyses stress causes of terrorism and suggest steps to take to combat terrorism; includes genomic terrorism; a militaristic emphasis runs through the articles.

Kleinman, Daniel, and Daniel Lee Kleinman. *Science and Technology in Society: From Biotechnology to the Internet.* Malden, Mass.: Blackwell, 2005. Analyzes how power shapes the development of technoscience and how the impact of technology depends on class, race, gender, and location.

McKibben, Bill. *Deep Economy: The Wealth of Communities and the Durable Future.* New York: Holt, 2008. The author's thesis is that we are on the brink of environmental disaster and that we need to take corrective steps now.

Naco, Brigitte Lebens. *Terrorism and Counterterrorism: Understanding Threats and Responses in the Post 9/11 World.* New York: Longman, 2006. This overview of terrorism includes both new terror in the post–Cold War world and historical acts of terror.

Stahler-Sholk, Richard. *Latin American Social Movements in the Twenty-first Century: Resistance, Power, and Democracy.* Lanham, Md.: Rowman and Littlefield, 2008. Focuses on the involvement of socially marginalized Latin Americans in social movements, examining the origins, strategies, and outcomes of their organizing.

Stewart, Charles J., Craig Allen Smith, and Robert E. Denton, Jr. *Persuasion and Social Movements,* 5th ed. Long Grove, Ill.: Waveland Press, 2007. The authors analyze social movements and countermovements in the light of identity, values, and culture, showing how people have shaped society collectively.

## Journals

*Earth First! Journal* and *Sierra,* magazines published by Earth First! and the Sierra Club respectively, are excellent sources for keeping informed of major developments in the environmental movement.

# REFERENCES

**The references new to this edition are printed in blue.**

AAUP (American Association of University Professors). "2006–07 Report on the Economic Status of the Profession," April 2007.

Aberg, Yvonne. *Social Interactions: Studies of Contextual Effects and Endogenous Processes.* Doctoral Dissertation, Department of Sociology, Stockholm University, 2003.

Aberle, David. *The Peyote Religion Among the Navaho.* Chicago: Aldine, 1966.

Abowitz, Kathleen Knight, and Jason Harnish. "Contemporary Discourses of Citizenship." *Review of Educational Research, 76,* 4, Winter 2006:653–690.

Adams, Noah. "All Things Considered." *New England Journal of Medicine* report. NPR. January 12, 2000.

Addams, Jane. *Twenty Years at Hull-House.* New York: Signet, 1981. First published 1910.

Adler, Patricia A., and Peter Adler. *Peer Power: Preadolescent Culture and Identity.* New Brunswick, N.J.: Rutgers University Press, 1998.

Adorno, Theodor W., Else Frenkel-Brunswick, D. J. Levinson, and R. N. Sanford. *The Authoritarian Personality.* New York: Harper & Row, 1950.

Aeppel, Timothy. "More Amish Women Are Tending to Business." *Wall Street Journal,* February 8, 1996:B1, B2.

Ahlburg, Dennis A., and Carol J. De Vita. "New Realities of the American Family." *Population Bulletin, 47,* 2, August 1992:1–44.

Akol, Jacob. "Slavery in Sudan." *New African,* September 1998.

Alba, Richard, and Victor Nee. *Remaking the American Mainstream: Assimilation and Contemporary Immigration.* Cambridge, Mass.: Harvard University Press, 2003.

Albanese, Jennifer. Personal research for the author. March 2007.

Aldrich, Nelson W., Jr. *Old Money: The Mythology of America's Upper Class.* New York: Vintage Books, 1989.

Alexander, Gerianne M., and Melissa Hines. "Sex Differences in Response to Children's Toys in Nonhuman Primates." *Evolution and Human Behavior, 23,* 2002:467–479.

Allport, Floyd. *Social Psychology.* Boston: Houghton Mifflin, 1954.

Amato, Paul R., and Jacob Cheadle. "The Long Reach of Divorce: Divorce and Child Well-Being Across Three Generations." *Journal of Marriage and Family, 67,* February 2005:191–206.

Amato, Paul R., and Juliana M. Sobolewski. "The Effects of Divorce and Marital Discord on Adult Children's Psychological Well-Being." *American Sociological Review, 66,* 6, December 2001:900–921.

Amenta, Edwin. "The Social Security Debate, Now, and Then." *Contexts, 5,* 3, Summer 2006.

"American Community Survey 2003." Washington, D.C.: U.S. Census Bureau, 2004.

American Sociological Association, "Section on Environment and Technology." Pamphlet, no date.

American Sociological Association. "Code of Ethics and Policies and Procedures of the ASA Committee on Professional Ethics." Washington, D.C.: American Sociological Association, 1999.

*America's Children: Key National Indicators of Well-Being 2005.* Washington, D.C.: Federal Interagency Forum on Child and Family Statistics, 2005.

Amnesty International. "Decades of Human Rights Abuse in Iraq." Online, 2005.

Anderson, Chris. "NORC Study Describes Homeless." *Chronicle,* 1986:5, 9.

Anderson, Elijah. *A Place on the Corner.* Chicago: University of Chicago Press, 1978.

Anderson, Elijah. *Streetwise: Race, Class, and Change in an Urban Community.* Chicago: University of Chicago Press, 1990.

Anderson, Elijah. "Streetwise." In *Exploring Social Life: Readings to Accompany Essentials of Sociology, Sixth Edition,* 2nd ed., James M. Henslin, ed. Boston: Allyn & Bacon, 2006:147–156.

Anderson, Nels. *Desert Saints: The Mormon Frontier in Utah.* Chicago: University of Chicago Press, 1966. First published 1942.

Anderson, Philip. "God and the Swedish Immigrants." *Sweden and America,* Autumn 1995:17–20.

Andersson, Hilary. "Born to Be a Slave in Niger." BBC News, World Edition, February 11, 2005.

Angier, Natalie. "Do Races Differ? Not Really, DNA Shows." *New York Times,* August 22, 2000.

Annin, Peter, and Kendall Hamilton. "Marriage or Rape?" *Newsweek,* December 16, 1996:78.

Ansberry, Clare. "Despite Federal Law, Hospitals Still Reject Sick Who Can't Pay." *Wall Street Journal,* November 29, 1988:A1, A4.

Aptheker, Herbert. "W. E. B. Du Bois: Struggle Not Despair." *Clinical Sociology Review, 8,* 1990:58–68.

Archbold, Ronna, and Mary Harmon. "International Success: Acceptance." Online: The Five O'clock Club, 2001.

Ariès, Philippe. *Centuries of Childhood.* R. Baldick, trans. New York: Vintage Books, 1965.

Arlacchi, P. *Peasants and Great Estates: Society in Traditional Calabria.* Cambridge, England: Cambridge University Press, 1980.

Armstrong, David. "Hard Case: When Academics Double as Expert Witnesses." *Wall Street Journal,* June 22, 2007.

Arndt, William F., and F. Wilbur Gingrich. *A Greek-English Lexicon of the New Testament and Other Early Christian Literature.* Chicago: University of Chicago Press, 1957.

Arsneault, Shelly. "Implementing Welfare Reform in Rural and Urban Communities: Why Place Matters." *American Review of Public Administration, 36,* 2, June 2006:173–188.

*R*

"ASA Council Statement on the Causes of Gender Differences in Science and Math Career Achievement." *Footnotes,* March 2005:10.

Asch, Solomon. "Effects of Group Pressure Upon the Modification and Distortion of Judgments." In *Readings in Social Psychology,* Guy Swanson, Theodore M. Newcomb, and Eugene L. Hartley, eds. New York: Holt, Rinehart & Winston, 1952.

Associated Press. "Report: California Surgeon Ordered Huge Drug Doses for Organ Donor." *North County Times,* March 2, 2008.

Aulette, Judy Root. *Changing American Families.* Boston: Allyn & Bacon, 2002.

Ayittey, George B. N. "Black Africans Are Enraged at Arabs." *Wall Street Journal,* interactive edition, September 4, 1998.

Bachu, Amara, and Martin O'Connell. "Fertility of American Women: Population Characteristics." *Current Population Reports.* Washington, D.C.: U.S. Bureau of the Census, September 2000.

Bales, Robert F. *Interaction Process Analysis.* Reading, Mass.: Addison-Wesley, 1950.

Bales, Robert F. "The Equilibrium Problem in Small Groups." In *Working Papers in the Theory of Action,* Talcott Parsons et al., eds. New York: Free Press, 1953:111–115.

Baltzell, E. Digby. *Puritan Boston and Quaker Philadelphia.* New York: Free Press, 1979.

Baltzell, E. Digby, and Howard G. Schneiderman. "Social Class in the Oval Office." *Society, 25,* Sept/Oct, 1988:42–49.

Baochang, Gu, Wang Feng, Guo Zhigang, and Zhang Erli. "China's Local and National Fertility Policies at the End of the Twentieth Century." *Population and Development Review, 33,* 1, March 2007:129–147.

Barlett, Donald L., and James B. Steele. "Wheel of Misfortune." *Time,* December 16, 2002:44–58.

Barnes, Fred. "How to Rig a Poll." *Wall Street Journal,* June 14, 1995:A14.

Barnes, Helen. "A Comment on Stroud and Pritchard: Child Homicide, Psychiatric Disorder and Dangerousness." *British Journal of Social Work, 31,* 3, June 2001.

Barry, John, and Evan Thomas. "Dropping the Bomb." *Newsweek,* June 25, 2001.

Barstow, David, and Lowell Bergman. "Death on the Job, Slaps on the Wrist." *Wall Street Journal,* January 10, 2003.

Barstow, David, and Robin Stein. "Between News and P. R., More Blurred Lines Found." *New York Times,* March 13, 2005.

Bartlett, Donald L., and James B. Steele. "Paying a Price for Polluters." *Time,* November 23, 1998:72–80.

Bartos, Otomar J., and Paul Wehr. *Using Conflict Theory.* New York: Cambridge University Press, 2002.

Batalova, Jeanne A., and Philip N. Cohen. "Premarital Cohabitation and Housework: Couples in Cross-National Perspectives." *Journal of Marriage and the Family, 64,* 3, August 2002:743–755.

Bates, Marston. *Gluttons and Libertines: Human Problems of Being Natural.* New York: Vintage Books, 1967. Quoted in Crapo, Richley H. *Cultural Anthropology: Understanding Ourselves and Others,* 5th ed. Boston: McGraw-Hill, 2002.

Beah, Ishmael. *A Long Way Gone: Memoirs of a Boy Soldier.* New York: Farrar, Straus and Giroux, 2007.

Bean, Frank D., Jennifer Lee, Jeanne Batalova, and Mark Leach. "Immigration and Fading Color Lines in America." Washington, D.C.: Population Reference Bureau, 2004.

Beck, Scott H., and Joe W. Page. "Involvement in Activities and the Psychological Well-Being of Retired Men." *Activities, Adaptation, & Aging, 11,* 1, 1988:31–47.

Becker, Howard S. *Outsiders: Studies in the Sociology of Deviance.* New York: Free Press, 1966.

Beckett, Paul. "Caste Away." *Wall Street Journal,* June 23, 2007.

Beeghley, Leonard. *The Structure of Social Stratification in the United States,* 5th ed. Boston: Allyn & Bacon, 2008.

Begley, Sharon. "Twins: Nazi and Jew." *Newsweek, 94,* December 3, 1979:139.

Belkin, Lisa. "The Feminine Critique." *New York Times,* November 1, 2007.

Bell, Daniel. *The Coming of Post-Industrial Society: A Venture in Social Forecasting.* New York: Basic Books, 1973.

Bell, David A. "An American Success Story: The Triumph of Asian-Americans." In *Sociological Footprints: Introductory Readings in Sociology,* 5th ed., Leonard Cargan and Jeanne H. Ballantine, eds. Belmont, Calif.: Wadsworth, 1991:308–316.

Belsky, Jay. "Early Child Care and Early Child Development: Major Findings of the NICHD Study of Early Child Care." *European Journal of Developmental Psychology, 3,* 1, 2006:95–110.

Belsky, Jay, Deborah Lowe Vandell, Margaret Burchinall, K. Alison Clarke-Stewart, Kathleen McCartney, and Margaret Tresch Owen. "Are There Long-Term Effects of Early Child Care?" *Child Development, 78,* 2, March/April 2007:681–701.

Benet, Sula. "Why They Live to Be 100, or Even Older, in Abkhasia." *New York Times Magazine, 26,* December 1971.

Benford, Robert D. "The College Sports Reform Movement: Reframing the 'Educational' Industry." *The Sociological Quarterly, 48,* 2007:1–28.

Berger, Arthur Asa. *Video Games: A Popular Culture Phenomenon.* New Brunswick, N.J.: Transaction, 2002.

Berger, Joseph. "Family Ties and the Entanglements of Caste." *New York Times,* October 24, 2004.

Berger, Peter L. *Invitation to Sociology: A Humanistic Perspective.* New York: Doubleday, 1963.

Berger, Peter L. *The Capitalist Revolution: Fifty Propositions About Prosperity, Equality, and Liberty.* New York: Basic Books, 1991.

Berger, Peter L. "Invitation to Sociology." In *Down to Earth Sociology: Introductory Readings,* 14th ed., James M. Henslin, ed. New York: Free Press, 2007:3–7. First published 1963.

Bergmann, Barbara R. "The Future of Child Care." Paper presented at the 1995 meetings of the American Sociological Association.

Berle, Adolf A., and Gardiner C. Means. *The Modern Corporation and Private Property.* New York: Harcourt, Brace & World, 1932.

Bernard, Jessie. "The Good-Provider Role." In *Marriage and Family in a Changing Society,* 4th ed., James M. Henslin, ed. New York: Free Press, 1992:275–285.

Bernard, Viola W., Perry Ottenberg, and Fritz Redl. "Dehumanization: A Composite Psychological Defense in Relation to Modern War." In *The Triple Revolution Emerging: Social Problems in Depth,* Robert Perucci and Marc Pilisuk, eds. Boston: Little, Brown, 1971:17–34.

Bernstein, Robert, and Mike Bergman. "Hispanic Population Reaches All-Time High of 38.8 Million, New Census Bureau Estimates Show." *U.S. Department of Commerce News,* June 18, 2003.

Bertrand, Marianne, and Sendhil Mullainathan. "Are Emily and Brendan More Employable than Lakish and Jamal? A Field Experiment on Labor Market Discrimination." Unpublished paper, November 18, 2002.

Bianchi, Suzanne M., and Lynne M. Casper. "American Families." *Population Bulletin, 55,* 4, December 2000:1–42.

Bianchi, Suzanne M., John P. Robinson, and Melissa A. Milkie. *Changing Rhythms of American Family Life.* New York: Russell Sage, 2006.

Bishop, Jerry E. "Study Finds Doctors Tend to Postpone Heart Surgery for Women, Raising Risk." *Wall Street Journal,* April 16, 1990:B4.

Bjerklie, David, Andrea Dorfman, Wendy Cole, Jeanne DeQuine, Helen Gibson, David S. Jackson, Leora Moldofsky, Timothy Roche, Chris Taylor, Cathy Booth Thomas, and Dick Thompson. "Baby, It's You: And You, and You . . . " *Time,* February 19, 2001:47–57.

Blau, David M. "The Production of Quality in Child-Care Centers: Another Look." *Applied Developmental Science, 4,* 3, 2000:136–148.

Blau, Peter M., and Otis Dudley Duncan. *The American Occupational Structure.* New York: John Wiley, 1967.

Blee, Kathleen M. "Inside Organized Racism." In *Life in Society: Readings to Accompany Sociology A Down-to-Earth Approach, Seventh Edition,* James M. Henslin, ed. Boston: Allyn & Bacon, 2005:46–57.

Blomfield, Adrian. "Putin Vows to Aim Nukes at Europe." *London Daily Telegraph,* June 4, 2007.

Blumstein, Alfred, and Joel Wallman. "The Crime Drop and Beyond." *Annual Review of Law and Social Science, 2,* December 2006:125–146.

Blumstein, Philip, and Pepper Schwartz. *American Couples: Money, Work, Sex.* New York: Pocket Books, 1985.

Bond, Rod. "Group Size and Conformity." *Group Processes and Intergroup Relations, 8,* 4, 2005:331–354.

Booth, Alan, and James M. Dabbs, Jr. "Testosterone and Men's Marriages." *Social Forces, 72,* 2, December 1993:463–477.

Booth, Alan, David R. Johnson, and Douglas A. Granger. "Testosterone, Marital Quality, and Role Overload." Paper presented at the 2004 meetings of the American Sociological Association.

Borjas, George J. "Increasing the Supply of Labor Through Immigration: Measuring the Impact on Native-born Workers." *Backgrounder,* May 2004:1–11.

Borjas, George J. "The Labor Market Impact of High-Skill Immigration." *National Bureau of Economic Research Working Paper* 11217, March 2005.

Borjas, George J. "Making It in America: Social Mobility in the Immigrant Population." *National Bureau of Economic Research Working Paper* 12088, March 2006.

Bosman, Ciska M., et al. "Business Success and Businesses' Beauty Capital." National Bureau of Economic Research Working Paper: 6083, July 1997.

Bosman, Julie. "New York Schools for Pregnant Girls Will Close." *New York Times,* May 24, 2007.

"The Boss's Pay." *Wall Street Journal,* April 7, 2007.

Bowles, Samuel, and Herbert Gintis. "*Schooling in Capitalist America* Revisited." *Sociology of Education, 75,* 2002:1–18.

Boxer, Sarah. "When Emotion Worms Its Way Into Law." *New York Times,* April 7, 2001.

Boyle, Elizabeth Heger, Fortunata Songora, and Gail Foss. "International Discourse and Local Politics: Anti-Female-Genital-Cutting Laws in Egypt, Tanzania, and the United States." *Social Problems, 48,* 4, November 2001:524–544.

Bradford, Phillips Verner, and Harvey Blume. *Ota Benga: The Pygmy in the Zoo.* New York: Delta, 1992.

Bradsher, Keith. "As Asia Keeps Cool, Scientists Worry About the Ozone Layer." *New York Times,* February 23, 2007a.

Bradsher, Keith. "China Enacting a High-Tech Plan to Track People." *New York Times,* August 12, 2007b.

Brajuha, Mario, and Lyle Hallowell. "Legal Intrusion and the Politics of Fieldwork: The Impact of the Brajuha Case." *Urban Life, 14,* 4, January 1986:454–478.

Bramlett, M. D., and W. D. Mosher. "Cohabitation, Marriage, Divorce, and Remarriage in the United States." Hyattsville, Md.: National Center for Health Statistics, Vital Health Statistics, Series 23, Number 22, July 2002.

Brauchli, Marcus W. "Wary of Education But Needing Brains, China Faces a Dilemma." *Wall Street Journal,* November 15, 1994:A1, A10.

Bray, Rosemary L. "Rosa Parks: A Legendary Moment, a Lifetime of Activism. *Ms., 6,* 3, November–December 1995:45–47.

"Brazil Arrests U.S. Pilot Over Obscene Gesture." Associated Press, January 15, 2004.

Bretos, Miguel A. "Hispanics Face Institutional Exclusion." *Miami Herald,* May 22, 1994.

Bridgwater, William, ed. *The Columbia Viking Desk Encyclopedia.* New York: Viking Press, 1953.

Brines, Julie. "Economic Dependency, Gender, and the Division of Labor at Home." *American Journal of Sociology, 100,* 3, November 1994:652–688.

Brines, Julie, and Kara Joyner. "The Ties That Bind. Principles of Cohesion in Cohabitation and Marriage." *American Sociological Review, 64,* June 1999:333–355.

Brinkley, Joel. "U.S. Faults 4 Allies Over Forced Labor." *New York Times,* June 4, 2005.

Broad, William J. "The Shuttle Explodes." *New York Times,* January 29, 1986, A1, A5.

Brockerhoff, Martin P. "An Urbanizing World." *Population Bulletin, 55,* 3, September 2000:1–44.

Broder, Michael S., David E. Kanouse, Brian S. Mittman, and Steven J. Bernstein. "The Appropriateness of Recommendations for Hysterectomy." *Obstetrics and Gynecology, 95,* 2, February 2000: 199–205.

Bronfenbrenner, Urie, as quoted in Diane Fassel. "Divorce May Not Harm Children." In *Family in America: Opposing Viewpoints,* Viqi Wagner, ed. San Diego, Calif.: Greenhaven Press, 1992:115–119.

Brooks-Gunn, Jeanne, Greg. J. Duncan, and Lawrence Aber, eds. *Neighborhood Poverty, Volume 1: Context and Consequences for Children.* New York: Russell Sage, 1997.

Browning, Christopher R. *Ordinary Men: Reserve Police Battalion 101 and the Final Solution in Poland.* New York: HarperPerennial, 1993.

Brunello, Giorgio, and Beatrice D'Hombres. "Does Body Weight Affect Wages? Evidence From Europe." *Economics and Human Biology, 5,* 2007:1–19.

Bryant, Alyssa N. "Community College Students: Recent Findings and Trends." *Community College Review, 29,* 3, 2001:77–93.

Bryant, Chalandra M., Rand D. Conger, and Jennifer M. Meehan. "The Influence of In-Laws on Chances in Marital Success." *Journal of Marriage and the Family, 63, 3,* August 2001:614–626.

Budrys, Grace. *Unequal Health: How Inequality Contributes to Health or Illness.* Lanham, Md.: Rowman and Littlefield, 2003.

Bumiller, Elisabeth. "First Comes Marriage—Then, Maybe, Love." In *Marriage and Family in a Changing Society,* 4th ed., James M. Henslin, ed. New York: Free Press, 1992:120–125.

Burawoy, Michael. "The Field of Sociology: Its Power and Its Promise." In *Public Sociology: Fifteen Eminent Sociologists Debate Politics and the Profession in the Twenty-first Century.* Berkeley: University of California Press, 2007:241–258.

Burgess, Ernest W., and Harvey J. Locke. *The Family: From Institution to Companionship.* New York: American Book, 1945.

Burnham, Walter Dean. *Democracy in the Making: American Government and Politics.* Englewood Cliffs, N.J.: Prentice Hall, 1983.

Burris, Val. "Interlocking Directorates and Political Cohesion Among Corporate Elites." *American Journal of Sociology, 111,* 1, 2005:249–283.

Bush, Diane Mitsch, and Robert G. Simmons. "Socialization Processes Over the Life Course." In *Social Psychology: Sociological Perspectives,* eds. Morris Rosenberger and Ralph H. Turner. New Brunswick, N.J.: Transaction, 1990:133–164.

Butler, Robert N. *Why Survive? Being Old in America.* New York: Harper & Row, 1975.

Butler, Robert N. "Ageism: Another Form of Bigotry." *Gerontologist, 9,* Winter 1980:243–246.

Butterfield, Fox. "With Cash Tight, States Reassess Long Jail Terms." *New York Times,* November 10, 2003.

Canavan, Margaret M., Walter J. Meyer, III, and Deborah C. Higgs. "The Female Experience of Sibling Incest." *Journal of Marital and Family Therapy, 18,* 2, 1992:129–142.

Canedy, Dana. "Critics of Graduation Exam Threaten Boycott in Florida." *New York Times,* May 13, 2003.

Carlson, Bonnie E., Katherine Maciol, and Joanne Schneider. "Sibling Incest: Reports from Forty-One Survivors." *Journal of Child Sexual Abuse, 15,* 4, 2006:19–34.

Carlson, Lewis H., and George A. Colburn. *In Their Place: White America Defines Her Minorities, 1850–1950.* New York: Wiley, 1972.

Carnevale, Anthony P., and Stephen J. Rose. "Socioeconomic Status, Race/Ethnicity, and Selective College Admissions." New York: The Century Foundation, March 2003.

Carpenito, Lynda Juall. "The Myths of Acquaintance Rape." *Nursing Forum, 34,* 4, October–December 1999:3.

Carpenter, Betsy. "Redwood Radicals." *U.S. News & World Report, 109,* 11, September 17, 1990:50–51.

Carper, James C. "Pluralism to Establishment to Dissent: The Religious and Educational Context of Home Schooling." *Peabody Journal of Education, 75,* 1–2, 2000:8–19.

Carr, Deborah. "Gender, Preloss Marital Dependence, and Older Adults' Adjustment to Widowhood." *Journal of Marriage and Family, 66,* February 2004:220–235.

Carr, Deborah, Carol D. Ryff, Burton Singer, and William J. Magee. "Bringing the 'Life' Back into Life Course Research: A 'Person-Centered' Approach to Studying the Life Course." Paper presented at the 1995 meetings of the American Sociological Association.

Carrington, Tim. "Developed Nations Want Poor Countries to Succeed on Trade, But Not Too Much." *Wall Street Journal,* September 20, 1993:A10.

Cartwright, Dorwin, and Alvin Zander, eds. *Group Dynamics,* 3rd ed. Evanston, Ill.: Peterson, 1968.

Case, Anne, and Christina Paxson. "Stature and Status: Height, Ability, and Labor Market Outcomes." Working Paper, August 2006.

Casper, Lynne M., and Loretta E. Bass. "Voting and Registration in the Election of November 1996." *Current Population Reports,* July 1998.

Casper, Monica J., ed. *Synthetic Planet: Chemical Politics and the Hazards of Modern Life.* New York: Taylor & Francis, 2003.

Cassel, Russell N. "Examining the Basic Principles for Effective Leadership." *College Student Journal, 33,* 2, June 1999:288–301.

Cauce, Ana Mari, and Melanie Domenech-Rodriguez. "Latino Families: Myths and Realities." In *Latino Children and Families in the United States: Current Research and Future Directions,* Josefina M. Contreras, Kathryn A. Kerns, and Angela M. Neal-Barnett, eds. Westport, Conn.: Praeger, 2002:3–25.

Center for American Women and Politics. "Women in Elective Office 2007." April 2007.

Centers for Disease Control and Prevention. "WISQARS Injury Mortality Reports, 1999–2004." Atlanta, GA: National Center for Injury Prevention and Control, 2006.

Centers for Disease Control and Prevention. "A Glance at the HIV/AIDS Epidemic." January 2007a.

Centers for Disease Control and Prevention. "Native American Suicides per 100,000, Ages 0–19, IHS Areas, 1989–1998." June 13, 2007b.

Chaddock, Gail Russell. "Math + Test = Trouble for U.S. Economy." *Christian Science Monitor,* December 7, 2004.

Chafetz, Janet Saltzman. *Gender Equity: An Integrated Theory of Stability and Change.* Newbury Park, Calif.: Sage, 1990.

Chafetz, Janet Saltzman, and Anthony Gary Dworkin. *Female Revolt: Women's Movements in World and Historical Perspective.* Totowa, N.J.: Rowman & Allanheld, 1986.

Chagnon, Napoleon A. *Yanomamo: The Fierce People,* 2nd ed. New York: Holt, Rinehart & Winston, 1977.

Chaker, Anne Marie. "A Backdoor Route to a College Dream." *Wall Street Journal,* June 26, 2003.

Chaker, Anne Marie, and Hilary Stout. "After Years off, Women Struggle to Revive Careers." *Wall Street Journal,* May 6, 2004.

Chalkley, Kate. "Female Genital Mutilation: New Laws, Programs Try to End Practice." *Population Today, 25,* 10, October 1997:4–5.

Chambliss, William J. *Power, Politics, and Crime.* Boulder: Westview Press, 2000.

Chambliss, William J. "The Saints and the Roughnecks." In *Down to Earth Sociology: Introductory Readings,* 14th ed., James M. Henslin, ed. New York: Free Press, 2007:299–314. First published 1973.

Chandler, Tertius, and Gerald Fox. *3000 Years of Urban Growth.* New York: Academic Press, 1974.

Chandra, Vibha P. "Fragmented Identities: The Social Construction of Ethnicity, 1885–1947." Unpublished paper, 1993a.

Chandra, Vibha P. "The Present Moment of the Past: The Metamorphosis." Unpublished paper, 1993b.

Chawkins, Steve. "Medical Community Eyes Case." *Los Angeles Times,* February 28, 2008.

Chazman, Guy. "Murdered Regulator in Russia Made Plenty of Enemies." *Wall Street Journal,* September 22, 2006.

Chen, Edwin. "Twins Reared Apart: A Living Lab." *New York Times Magazine.* December 9, 1979:112.

Chen, Kathy. "China's Growth Places Strains on a Family's Ties." *Wall Street Journal,* April 13, 2005.

Cherlin, Andrew J. "Remarriage as an Incomplete Institution." In *Marriage and Family in a Changing Society,* 3rd ed., James M. Henslin, ed. New York: Free Press, 1989:492–501.

"Child Support for Custodial Mothers and Fathers." *Current Population Reports,* Series P60–187. Washington, D.C.: U.S. Bureau of the Census, 1995.

Chin, Nancy P., Alicia Monroe, and Kevin Fiscella. "Social Determinants of (Un)Healthy Behaviors." *Education for Health: Change in Learning and Practice, 13,* 3, November 2000:317–328.

Chivers, C. J. "Officer Resigns Before Hearing in D.W.I. Case." *New York Times,* August 29, 2001.

Chivers, C. J. "Putin Urges Plan to Reverse Slide in the Birth Rate." *New York Times,* May 10, 2006.

Chodorow, Nancy J. "What Is the Relation Between Psychoanalytic Feminism and the Psychoanalytic Psychology of Women?" In *Theoretical Perspectives on Sexual Difference,* Deborah L. Rhode, ed. New Haven, Conn.: Yale University Press, 1990:114–130.

Chung, He Len, and Laurence Steinberg. "Relations Between Neighborhood Factors, Parenting Behaviors, Peer Deviance, and Delinquency Among Serious Juvenile Offenders." *Developmental Psychology, 42,* 2, 2006:319–331.

Churchill, Ward. *A Little Matter of Genocide: Holocaust and Denial in the Americas, 1492 to the Present.* San Francisco: City Lights Books, 1997.

Clair, Jeffrey Michael, David A. Karp, and William C. Yoels. *Experiencing the Life Cycle: A Social Psychology of Aging,* 2nd ed. Springfield, Ill.: Thomas, 1993.

Clark, Candace. *Misery and Company: Sympathy in Everyday Life.* Chicago: University of Chicago Press, 1997.

Cloud, John. "For Better or Worse." *Time,* October 26, 1998: 43–44.

Cloward, Richard A., and Lloyd E. Ohlin. *Delinquency and Opportunity: A Theory of Delinquent Gangs.* New York: Free Press, 1960.

Cohen, Patricia. "Forget Lonely. Life Is Healthy at the Top." *New York Times,* May 15, 2004.

Colapinto, John. *As Nature Made Him: The Boy Who Was Raised as a Girl.* New York: HarperCollins, 2001.

Cole, Elizabeth R., and Safiya R. Omari. "Race, Class and the Dilemmas of Upward Mobility for African Americans." *Journal of Social Issues, 59,* 4, 2003:785–802.

Coleman, James S., and Thomas Hoffer. *Public and Private Schools: The Impact of Communities.* New York: Basic Books, 1987.

Coleman, Marilyn, Lawrence Ganong, and Mark Fine. "Reinvestigating Remarriage: Another Decade of Progress." *Journal of Marriage and the Family, 62,* 4, November 2000:1288–1307.

Collins, Randall. *The Credential Society: An Historical Sociology of Education.* New York: Academic Press, 1979.

Collins, Randall. "Socially Unrecognized Cumulation." *American Sociologist, 30,* 2, Summer 1999:41–61.

Collins, Randall, Janet Saltzman Chafetz, Rae Lesser Blumberg, Scott Coltrane, and Jonathan H. Turner. "Toward an Integrated Theory of Gender Stratification." *Sociological Perspectives, 36,* 3, 1993:185–216.

Collymore, Yvette. "Conveying Concerns: Women Report on Gender-Based Violence." Washington, D.C.: Population Reference Bureau, 2000.

Committee on Non-Heart-Beating Transplantation II. *Non-Heart-Beating Organ Transplantation: Practice and Protocols.* Washington, DC: The National Academies Press, 2000.

Conklin, John E. *Why Crime Rates Fell.* Boston: Allyn & Bacon, 2003.

Connors, L. "Gender of Infant Differences in Attachment: Associations with Temperament and Caregiving Experiences." Paper presented at the Annual Conference of the British Psychological Society, Oxford, England, 1996.

Contreras, Josefina M., Kathryn A. Kerns, and Angela M. Neal-Barnett, eds. *Latino Children and Families in the United States: Current Research and Future Directions.* Westport, Conn.: Praeger, 2002.

Cook, Bradley J. "Islam and Egyptian Higher Education: Student Attitudes." *Comparative Education Review, 45,* 3, August 2001:379–403.

Cookson, Peter W., Jr., and Caroline Hodges Persell. "Preparing for Power: Cultural Capital and Elite Boarding Schools." In *Life in Society: Readings to Accompany Sociology: A Down-to-Earth Approach, Seventh Edition,* James M. Henslin, ed. Boston: Allyn & Bacon, 2005:175–185.

Cooley, Charles Horton. *Human Nature and the Social Order.* New York: Scribner's, 1902.

Cooley, Charles Horton. *Social Organization.* New York: Schocken Books, 1962. First published by Scribner's, 1909.

Corcoran, Mary. "Mobility, Persistence, and Consequences of Poverty for Children: Child and Adult Outcomes." In *Understanding Poverty,* Sheldon H. Danziger and Robert H. Haveman, eds. New York: Russell Sage, 2001:127–161.

Cose, Ellis. "The Good News About Black America." *Newsweek,* June 7, 1999:29–40.

Cose, Ellis. "What's White Anyway?" *Newsweek,* September 18, 2000:64–65.

Cose, Ellis. "Black Versus Brown." *Newsweek,* July 3, 2006:44–45.

Coser, Lewis A. *Masters of Sociological Thought: Ideas in Historical and Social Context,* 2nd ed. New York: Harcourt Brace Jovanovich, 1977.

Cottin, Lou. *Elders in Rebellion: A Guide to Senior Activism.* Garden City, N.Y.: Anchor Doubleday, 1979.

Cousins, Albert N., and Hans Nagpaul. *Urban Man and Society: A Reader in Urban Sociology.* New York: McGraw-Hill, 1970.

Cowen, Emory L., Judah Landes, and Donald E. Schaet. "The Effects of Mild Frustration on the Expression of Prejudiced Attitudes." *Journal of Abnormal and Social Psychology.* January 1959:33–38.

Cowgill, Donald. "The Aging of Populations and Societies." *Annals of the American Academy of Political and Social Science, 415,* 1974:1–18.

Cowley, Geoffrey. "Attention: Aging Men." *Newsweek,* November 16, 1996:66–75.

Cowley, Joyce. *Pioneers of Women's Liberation.* New York: Merit, 1969.

Crawford, Duane W., Renate M. Houts, Ted L. Huston, and Laura J. George. "Compatibility, Leisure, and Satisfaction in Marital Relationships." *Journal of Marriage and Family, 64,* May 2002:433–449.

*Crime in the United States.* Washington, D.C.: Department of Justice, Federal Bureau of Investigation, published annually.

Crosnoe, Robert, and Glen H. Elder, Jr. "Successful Adaptation in the Later Years: A Life Course Approach to Aging. " *Social Psychology Quarterly, 65,* 4, 2002:309–328.

Crossen, Cynthia. "Margin of Error: Studies Galore Support Products and Positions, But Are They Reliable?" *Wall Street Journal,* November 14, 1991:A1.

Crossen, Cynthia. "Deja Vu." *Wall Street Journal,* March 5, 2003.

Crossen, Cynthia. "How Pygmy Ota Benga Ended Up in Bronx Zoo as Darwinism Dawned." *Wall Street Journal,* February 6, 2006.

Crossette, Barbara. "Caste May Be India's Moral Achilles' Heel." *New York Times,* October 20, 1996.

Crossland, David. "Gas Dispute Has Europe Trembling." *Spiegel Online,* January 2, 2006.

Cumming, Elaine. "Further Thoughts on the Theory of Disengagement." In *Aging in America: Readings in Social Gerontology,* Cary S. Kart and Barbara B. Manard, eds. Sherman Oaks, Calif.: Alfred, 1976:19–41.

Cumming, Elaine, and William E. Henry. *Growing Old: The Process of Disengagement.* New York: Basic Books, 1961.

Dabbs, James M., Jr., Timothy S. Carr, Robert L. Frady, and Jasmin K. Riad. "Testosterone, Crime, and Misbehavior Among 692 Male Prison Inmates." *Personality and Individual Differences, 18,* 1995:627–633.

Dabbs, James M., Jr., Marian F. Hargrove, and Colleen Heusel. "Testosterone Differences Among College Fraternities: Well-Behaved vs. Rambunctious." *Personality and Individual Differences, 20,* 1996: 157–161.

Dabbs, James M., Jr., and Robin Morris. "Testosterone, Social Class, and Antisocial Behavior in a Sample of 4,462 Men." *Psychological Science, 1,* 3, May 1990:209–211.

Dahl, Robert A. *Who Governs?* New Haven, Conn.: Yale University Press, 1961.

Dahl, Robert A. *Dilemmas of Pluralist Democracy: Autonomy vs. Control.* New Haven, Conn.: Yale University Press, 1982.

Dao, James. "Instant Millions Can't Halt Winners' Grim Side." *New York Times,* December 5, 2005.

Darley, John M., and Bibb Latané. "Bystander Intervention in Emergencies: Diffusion of Responsibility." *Journal of Personality and Social Psychology, 8,* 4, 1968:377–383.

Dasgupta, Nilanjana, Debbie E. McGhee, Anthony G. Greenwald, and Mahzarin R. Banaji. "Automatic Preference for White Americans: Eliminating the Familiarity Explanation." *Journal of Experimental Social Psychology, 36,* 3, May 2000:316–328.

Davies, W. Martin. "Cognitive Contours: Recent Work on Cross-Cultural Psychology and Its Relevance for Education." *Studies in the Philosophy of Education, 26,* 2007:13–42.

Davis, Ann, Joseph Pereira, and William M. Bulkeley. "Security Concerns Bring Focus on Translating Body Language." *Wall Street Journal,* August 15, 2002.

Davis, Donald R., and David E. Weinstein. "Technological Superiority and the Losses From Migration." Working Paper. National Bureau of Economic Research. June 2002.

Davis, Gerald F. "American Cronyism: How Executive Networks Inflated the Corporate Bubble." *Contexts, 2,* 3, Summer 2003:34–40.

Davis, Kingsley. "Extreme Social Isolation of a Child." *American Journal of Sociology, 45,* 4 Jan. 1940:554–565.

Davis, Kingsley. "Extreme Isolation." In *Down to Earth Sociology: Introductory Readings,* 14th ed., James M. Henslin, ed. New York: Free Press, 2007:151–160.

Davis, Kingsley, and Wilbert E. Moore. "Some Principles of Stratification." *American Sociological Review, 10,* 1945:242–249.

Davis, Kingsley, and Wilbert E. Moore. "Reply to Tumin." *American Sociological Review, 18,* 1953:394–396.

Davis, Nancy J., and Robert V. Robinson. "Class Identification of Men and Women in the 1970s and 1980s." *American Sociological Review, 53,* February 1988:103–112.

Davis, Stan. *Lessons From the Future: Making Sense of a Blurred World.* New York: Capstone, 2001.

Dawley, Richard Lee. *Amish in Wisconsin.* New Berlin, Wis.: Amish Insight, 2003.

Deaver, Michael V. "Democratizing Russian Higher Education." *Demokratizatsiya, 9,* 3, Summer 2001:350–366.

Deck, Leland P. "Buying Brains by the Inch." *Journal of the College and University Personnel Association, 19,* 1968:33–37.

DeCrow, Karen. Foreword to *Why Men Earn More* by Warren Farrell. New York: AMACOM, 2005:xi–xii.

Deegan, Mary Jo. "W. E. B. Du Bois and the Women of Hull-House, 1895–1899." *American Sociologist,* Winter 1988:301–311.

Deflem, Mathieu, ed. *Sociological Theory and Criminological Research: Views from Europe and the United States.* San Diego: JAI Press, 2006.

Deliege, Robert. *The Untouchables of India.* New York: Berg, 2001.

DeMartini, Joseph R. "Basic and Applied Sociological Work: Divergence, Convergence, or Peaceful Co-existence?" *The Journal of Applied Behavioral Science, 18,* 2, 1982:203–215.

DeMause, Lloyd. "Our Forebears Made Childhood a Nightmare." *Psychology Today 8,* 11, April 1975:85–88.

Denney, Nancy W., and David Quadagno. *Human Sexuality,* 2nd ed. St. Louis: Mosby, 1992.

Denzin, Norman K. "The Suicide Machine." *Society,* July–August, 1992:7–10.

Denzin, Norman K. *Symbolic Interactionism and Cultural Studies: The Politics of Interpretation.* Cambridge, Mass.: Blackwell 2007.

DeOilos, Ione Y., and Carolyn A. Kapinus. "Aging Childless Individuals and Couples: Suggestions for New Directions in Research." *Sociological Inquiry, 72,* 1, Winter 2002:72–80.

Derne, Steve. "Arnold Schwarzenegger, Ally McBeal and Arranged Marriages: Globalization on the Ground in India." *Contexts,* Summer 2003:12–18.

Deutscher, Irwin. *Accommodating Diversity: National Policies that Prevent Ethnic Conflict.* Lanham, Md.: Lexington Books, 2002.

Diamond, Milton, and Keith Sigmundson. "Sex Reassignment at Birth: Long-term Review and Clinical Implications." *Archives of Pediatric and Adolescent Medicine, 151,* March 1997:298–304.

Dickey, Christopher, and John Barry. "Iran: A Rummy Guide." *Newsweek,* May 8, 2006.

Dietz, Tracy L. "An Examination of Violence and Gender Role Portrayals in Video Games." *Women and Language, 23,* 2, Fall 2000:64–77.

Dillon, Sam. "Public Schools Begin to Offer Classes Online." *New York Times,* August 2, 2005a.

Dillon, Sam. "Students Ace State Tests, But Earn D's From U.S." *New York Times,* November 25, 2005b.

DiSilvestro, Roger L. *In the Shadow of Wounded Knee: The Untold Final Chapter of the Indian Wars.* New York: Walker, 2006.

Doane, Ashley W., Jr. "Dominant Group Ethnic Identity in the United States: The Role of 'Hidden' Ethnicity in Intergroup Relations." *The Sociological Quarterly, 38,* 3, Summer 1997:375–397.

Dobash, Russell P., R. Emerson Dobash, Margo Wilson, and Martin Daly. "The Myth of Sexual Symmetry in Marital Violence." *Social Problems, 39,* 1, February 1992:71–91.

Dobash, Russell P., R. Emerson Dobash, Margo Wilson, and Martin Daly. "Marital Violence Is Not Symmetrical: A Response to Campbell." *SSSP Newsletter, 24,* 3, Fall 1993:26–30.

Dobriner, William M. "The Football Team as Social Structure and Social System." In *Social Structures and Systems: A Sociological Overview.* Pacific Palisades, Calif.: Goodyear, 1969a:116–120.

Dobriner, William M. *Social Structures and Systems.* Pacific Palisades, California: Goodyear, 1969b.

Dobyns, Henry F. *Their Numbers Became Thinned: Native American Population Dynamics in Eastern North America.* Knoxville: University of Tennessee Press, 1983.

Dodds, Peter Sheridan, Roby Muhamad, and Duncan J. Watts. "An Experimental Study of Search in Global Social Networks." *Science, 301,* August 8, 2003:827–830.

Dollard, John, et al. *Frustration and Aggression.* New Haven, Conn.: Yale University Press, 1939.

Domhoff, G. William. *The Power Elite and the State: How Policy Is Made in America.* Hawthorne, N. Y.: Aldine de Gruyter, 1990.

Domhoff, G. William. *Who Rules America? Power and Politics in the Year 2000,* 3rd ed. Mountain View, Calif: Mayfield, 1998.

Domhoff, G. William. "The Bohemian Grove and Other Retreats." In *Down to Earth Sociology: Introductory Readings,* 10th ed., James M. Henslin, ed. New York: Free Press, 1999a:391–403.

Domhoff, G. William. "State and Ruling Class in Corporate America (1974): Reflections, Corrections, and New Directions." *Critical Sociology, 25,* 2–3, July 1999b:260–265.

Domhoff, G. William. *Who Rules America? Power, Politics, and Social Change,* 5th ed. New York: McGraw-Hill, 2006.

Donaldson, Stephen. "A Million Jockers, Punks, and Queens: Sex Among American Male Prisoners and Its Implications for Concepts of Sexual Orientation." February 4, 1993. Online.

Donlon, Margie M., Ori Ash, and Becca R. Levy. "Re-Vision of Older Television Characters: A Stereotype-Awareness Intervention." *Journal of Social Issues, 61,* 2, June 2005.

Douglas, Carol Anne, et al. "Kenya: FGM Increasingly Occurring in Hospitals." *Off Our Backs, 35,* January–February 2005:5.

Douthat, Ross. "The Truth About Harvard." *Atlantic Monthly,* March 2005.

Dove, Adrian. "Soul Folk 'Chitling' Test or the Dove Counterbalance Intelligence Test." no date. (Mimeo)

Dowd, Maureen. "The Knife Under the Tree." *New York Times,* December 5, 2002.

Drivonikou, G. V., P. Kay, T. Regler, R. B. Ivry, A. L. Gilbert, A. Franklin, and I. R. L. Davies. "Further Evidence That Whorfian Effects Are Stronger in the Right Visual Field Than in the Left." *PNAS, 104,* 3, January 16, 2007:1097–1102.

Du Bois, W. E. B. *The Souls of Black Folk: Essays and Sketches.* Chicago: McClurg, 1903.

Du Bois, W. E. B. *Black Reconstruction in America: An Essay Toward a History of the Part Which Black Folk Played in the Attempt to Reconstruct Democracy in America, 1860–1880.* New York: Atheneum, 1992. First published 1935.

Du Bois, W. E. B. *The Philadelphia Negro: A Social Study.* New York: Schocken Books, 1967. First published 1899.

Du Bois, W. E. B. *The Autobiography of W. E. B. Du Bois: A Soliloquy on Viewing My Life from the Last Decade of Its First Century.* New York: International, 1968.

Duff, Christina. "Superrich's Share of After-Tax Income Stopped Rising in Early '90s, Data Show." *Wall Street Journal,* November 22, 1995:A2.

Dugger, Celia W. "Wedding Vows Bind Old World and New." *New York Times,* July 20, 1998.

Dugger, Celia W. "Abortion in India Is Tipping Scales Sharply Against Girls." *New York Times,* April 22, 2001.

Duneier, Mitchell. *Sidewalk.* New York: Farrar, Straus & Giroux, 1999.

Dunlap, Riley E., and William R. Catton, Jr. "Environmental Sociology." *Annual Review of Sociology, 5,* 1979:243–273.

Dunlap, Riley E., and William R. Catton, Jr. "What Environmental Sociologists Have in Common Whether Concerned with 'Built' or 'Natural' Environments." *Sociological Inquiry, 53,* 2–3, 1983:113–135.

Durkheim, Emile. *The Division of Labor in Society.* George Simpson, trans. New York: Free Press, 1933. First published 1893.

Durkheim, Emile. *The Rules of Sociological Method.* Sarah A. Solovay and John H. Mueller, trans. New York: Free Press, 1938, 1958, 1964. First published 1895.

Durkheim, Emile. *The Elementary Forms of the Religious Life.* New York: Free Press, 1965. First published 1912.

Durkheim, Emile. *Suicide: A Study in Sociology.* John A. Spaulding and George Simpson, trans. New York: Free Press, 1966. First published 1897.

Durning, Alan. "Cradles of Life." In *Social Problems 90/91,* LeRoy W. Barnes, ed. Guilford, Conn.: Dushkin, 1990:231–241.

Dush, Claire M. Kamp, Catherine L. Cohan, and Paul R. Amato. "The Relationship Between Cohabitation and Marital Quality and Stability: Change Across Cohorts?" *Journal of Marriage and Family,* 65, 3, August 2003:539–549.

Dye, Jane Lawler. "Fertility of American Women, June 2004." U.S. Bureau of the Census. *Current Population Reports,* December 2005.

Dyer, Gwynne. "Anybody's Son Will Do." In *Down to Earth Sociology: Introductory Readings,* 14th ed., James M. Henslin, ed. New York: Free Press, 2007:481–492.

Easley, Hema. "Indian Families Continue to Have Arranged Marriages." *The Journal News,* June 9, 2003.

Ebner, Johanna. "Fighting International Terrorism with Social Science Knowledge." *Footnotes,* February 2005.

Eckholm, Erik. "Desire for Sons Drives Use of Prenatal Scans in China." *New York Times,* June 21, 2002.

Eder, Donna. *School Talk: Gender and Adolescent Culture.* New Brunswick, N.J.: Rutgers University Press, 1995.

Eder, Donna. "On Becoming Female: Lessons Learned in School." In *Down to Earth Sociology: Introductory Readings,* 14th ed., James M. Henslin, ed. New York: Free Press, 2007:173–179.

Eder, Klaus. "The Rise of Counter-Culture Movements Against Modernity: Nature as a New Field of Class Struggle." *Theory, Culture & Society,* 7, 1990:21–47.

Edgerton, Robert B. *Deviance: A Cross-Cultural Perspective.* Menlo Park, Calif.: Benjamin/Cummings, 1976.

Egan, Timothy. "Many Seek Security in Private Communities." *New York Times,* September 3, 1995:1, 22.

Ehrlich, Paul R., and Anne H. Ehrlich. *Population, Resources, and Environment: Issues in Human Ecology,* 2nd ed. San Francisco: Freeman, 1972.

Ehrlich, Paul R., and Anne H. Ehrlich. "Humanity at the Crossroads." *Stanford Magazine,* Spring–Summer 1978:20–23.

Ekman, Paul. *Faces of Man: Universal Expression in a New Guinea Village.* New York: Garland Press, 1980.

Ekman, Paul, Wallace V. Friesen, and John Bear. "The International Language of Gestures." *Psychology Today,* May 1984:64.

Elder, Glen H., Jr. "Age Differentiation and Life Course." *Annual Review of Sociology,* 1, 1975:165–190.

Elder, Glen H., Jr. *Children of the Great Depression: Social Change in Life Experience.* Boulder: Westview Press, 1999.

Elias, Paul. "'Molecular Pharmers' Hope to Raise Human Proteins in Crop Plants." *St. Louis Post-Dispatch,* October 28, 2001:F7.

Elliott, Joel. "Birth Control Allowed at Maine Middle School." *New York Times,* October 18, 2007.

Elson, Jean. *Am I Still a Woman? Hysterectomy and Gender Identity.* Philadelphia: Temple University Press, 2004.

Elsworth, Catherine. "Doctor 'Hastened Death of Patient for Organs.'" *London Telegraph,* February 29, 2008.

England, Paula. "The Impact of Feminist Thought on Sociology." *Contemporary Sociology: A Journal of Reviews,* 2000:263–267.

Epstein, Cynthia Fuchs. "Great Divides: The Cultural, Cognitive, and Social Bases of the Global Subordination of Women." *American Sociological Review,* 72, February 2007:1–22.

Ernst, Eldon G. "The Baptists." In *Encyclopedia of the American Religious Experience: Studies of Traditions and Movements,* Vol. 1, Charles H. Lippy and Peter W. Williams, eds. New York: Scribner's, 1988:555–577.

Eshleman, J. Ross. *The Family,* 9th ed. Boston: Allyn & Bacon, 2000.

"Ethiopia: Fighting Female Circumcision at Local Level." African News Service, February 16, 2005.

Evans, Peter, and James E. Rauch. "Bureaucracy and Growth: A Cross-National Analysis of the Effects of 'Weberian' State Structures on Economic Growth." *American Sociological Review,* 64, October 1999: 748–765.

Fabrikant, Geraldine. "Old Nantucket Warily Meets the New." *New York Times,* June 5, 2005.

Fadiman, Anne. *The Spirit Catches You and You Fall Down.* Farrar, Straus and Giroux, 1997.

Fagot, Beverly I., Richard Hagan, Mary Driver Leinbach, and Sandra Kronsberg. "Differential Reactions to Assertive and Communicative Acts of Toddler Boys and Girls." *Child Development,* 56, 1985: 1499–1505.

Faris, Robert E. L., and Warren Dunham. *Mental Disorders in Urban Areas.* Chicago: University of Chicago Press, 1939.

Farkas, George. *Human Capital or Cultural Capital?: Ethnicity and Poverty Groups in an Urban School District.* New York: Walter DeGruyter, 1996.

Farkas, George, Robert P. Grobe, Daniel Sheehan, and Yuan Shuan. "Cultural Resources and School Success: Gender, Ethnicity, and Poverty Groups Within an Urban School District." *American Sociological Review,* 55, February 1990a:127–142.

Farkas, George, Daniel Sheehan, and Robert P. Grobe. "Coursework Mastery and School Success: Gender, Ethnicity, and Poverty Groups Within an Urban School District." *American Educational Research Journal,* 27, 4, Winter 1990b:807–827.

Fattah, Hassan M. "After First Steps, Saudi Reformers See Efforts Stall." *New York Times,* April 26, 2007.

Fattig, Paul. "Good Intentions Gone Bad." *Mail Tribune,* June 6, 2007.

Faunce, William A. *Problems of an Industrial Society,* 2nd ed. New York: McGraw-Hill, 1981.

*FBI Uniform Crime Reports.* Washington, D.C.: U.S. Government Printing Office, published annually.

Feagin, Joe R. "The Continuing Significance of Race: Antiblack Discrimination in Public Places." In *Majority and Minority: The Dynamics of Race and Ethnicity in American Life,* 6th ed., Norman R. Yetman, ed. Boston: Allyn & Bacon, 1999:384–399.

Featherman, David L. "Opportunities Are Expanding." *Society,* 13, 1979:4–11.

Featherman, David L., and Robert M. Hauser. *Opportunity and Change.* New York: Academic Press, 1978.

Feder, Barnaby. "Billboards That Know You by Name." *New York Times,* January 29, 2007.

Feldman, Saul D. "The Presentation of Shortness in Everyday Life—Height and Heightism in American Society: Toward a Sociology of Stature." Paper presented at the 1972 meetings of the American Sociological Association.

Felsenthal, Edward. "Maine Limits Liability for Doctors Who Meet Treatment Guidelines." *Wall Street Journal,* May 3, 1993:A1, A9.

Felton, Lee Ann, Andrea Gumm, and David J. Pittenger. "The Recipients of Unwanted Sexual Encounters Among College Students." *College Student Journal, 35,* 1, March 2001:135–143.

Fernandez, Manny. "Study Finds Disparities in Mortgages by Race." *New York Times,* October 15, 2007.

Fessenden, Ford. "Subprime Mortgages Concentrated in City's Minority Neighborhoods." *New York Times,* October 15, 2007.

Finer, Jonathan. "Faculty Group Rebukes Harvard President With Vote." *Washington Post,* March 16, 2005.

Finke, Roger, and Roger Stark. *The Churching of America, 1776–1990: Winners and Losers in Our Religious Economy.* New Brunswick, N.J.: Rutgers University Press, 1992.

Fischer, Claude S. *The Urban Experience.* New York: Harcourt, 1976.

Fischer, Tamar F. C., Paul M. De Graaf, and Matthijs Kalmijn. "Friendly and Antagonistic Contact Between Former Spouses After Divorce." *Journal of Family Issues, 26,* 8, November 2005:1131–1163.

Fish, Jefferson M. "Mixed Blood." *Psychology Today, 28,* 6, November–December 1995:55–58, 60, 61, 76, 80.

Fisher, Sue. *In the Patient's Best Interest: Women and the Politics of Medical Decisions.* New Brunswick, N.J.: Rutgers University Press, 1986.

Flanagan, William G. *Urban Sociology: Images and Structure.* Boston: Allyn & Bacon, 1990.

Flavel, John H., et al. *The Development of Role-Taking and Communication Skills in Children.* New York: Wiley, 1968.

Flavel, John, Patricia H. Miller, and Scott A. Miller. *Cognitive Development,* 4th ed. Upper Saddle River, N.J.: Prentice Hall, 2002.

Flippen, Annette R. "Understanding Groupthink From a Self-Regulatory Perspective." *Small Group Research, 30,* 2, April 1999:139–165.

Food and Agriculture Organization of the United Nations. "World and Regional Review: Facts and Figures." 2006.

Foote, Jennifer. "Trying to Take Back the Planet." *Newsweek, 115,* 6, February 5, 1990:24–25.

Form, William. "Comparative Industrial Sociology and the Convergence Hypothesis." In *Annual Review of Sociology, 5,* 1, 1979, Alex Inkeles, James Coleman, and Ralph H. Turner, eds.

Fountain, Henry. "Archaeological Site in Peru Is Called Oldest City in Americas." *New York Times,* April 27, 2001.

Fowler, Geoffrey A., and Amy Chozick. "Cartoon Characters Get Big Makeover for Overseas Fans." *Wall Street Journal,* October 16, 2007.

Fox, Elaine, and George E. Arquitt. "The VFW and the 'Iron Law of Oligarchy.'" In *Down to Earth Sociology,* 4th ed., James M. Henslin, ed. New York: Free Press, 1985:147–155.

Fraser, Graham. "Fox Denies Free Trade Exploiting the Poor in Mexico." *Toronto Star,* April 20, 2001.

Freedman, Jane. *Feminism.* Philadelphia: Open University Press, 2001.

Freidson, Eliot. *Professionalism: The Third Logic.* Chicago: University of Chicago Press, 2001.

Fremson, Ruth. "Dead Bachelors in Remote China Still Find Wives." *New York Times,* October 5, 2006.

French, Howard W. "As Girls 'Vanish,' Chinese City Battles Tide of Abortions." *New York Times,* April 14, 2004.

French, Howard W. "Chinese Censors and Web Users Match Wits." *New York Times,* March 4, 2005.

Freund, Charles Paul. "A Riot of Our Own." *Reason, 32,* 10, March 2001:10.

Friedl, Ernestine. "Society and Sex Roles." In *Conformity and Conflict: Readings in Cultural Anthropology,* James P. Spradley and David W. McCurdy, eds. Glenview, Ill.: Scott, Foresman, 1990: 229–238.

Fuhrmans, Vanessa, and Carol Hymowitz. "WellPoint's CEO Takes the Reins, Facing Challenges." *Wall Street Journal,* June 6, 2007.

Fuller, Rex, and Richard Schoenberger. "The Gender Salary Gap: Do Academic Achievement, Internship Experience, and College Major Make a Difference?" *Social Science Quarterly, 72,* 4, December 1991:715–726.

Furstenberg, Frank F., Jr., and Kathleen Mullan Harris. "The Disappearing American Father? Divorce and the Waning Significance of Biological Fatherhood." In *The Changing American Family: Sociological and Demographic Perspectives,* Scott J. South and Stewart E. Tolnay, eds. Boulder, Colo.: Westview Press, 1992: 197–223.

Furstenberg, Frank F., Jr., Sheela Kennedy, Vonnie C. McLoyd, Ruben G. Rumbaut, and Richard A. Settersten, Jr. "Growing Up Is Harder to Do." *Contexts, 3,* 3, Summer 2004:33–41.

Galbraith, John Kenneth. *The Nature of Mass Poverty.* Cambridge Mass.: Harvard University Press, 1979.

Gallup Poll. "Americans More Likely to Believe in God Than the Devil, Heaven More Than Hell." June 13, 2007.

Gallup Poll. "Questions and Answers about Americans' Religion." December 24, 2007.

Gans, Herbert J. *The Urban Villagers.* New York: Free Press, 1962.

Gans, Herbert J. *People and Plans: Essays on Urban Problems and Solutions.* New York: Basic Books, 1968.

Gans, Herbert J. *People, Plans, and Policies: Essays on Poverty, Racism, and Other National Urban Problems.* New York: Columbia University Press, 1991.

Garfinkel, Harold. "Conditions of Successful Degradation Ceremonies." *American Journal of Sociology, 61,* 2, March 1956:420–424.

Garfinkel, Harold. *Studies in Ethnomethodology.* Englewood Cliffs, N.J.: Prentice Hall, 1967.

Garfinkel, Harold. *Ethnomethodology's Program: Working Out Durkheim's Aphorism.* Lanham, MD: Rowman & Littlefield, 2002.

Garrett, Michael Tlanusta. "Understanding the 'Medicine' of Native American Traditional Values: An Integrative Review." *Counseling and Values, 43,* 2, January 1999:84–98.

Gatewood, Willard B. *Aristocrats of Color: The Black Elite, 1880–1920.* Bloomington, Ind.: Indiana University Press, 1990.

Gauch, Sarah. "In Egyptian Schools, a Push for Critical Thinking." *Christian Science Monitor,* February 9, 2006.

Gautham S. "Coming Next: The Monsoon Divorce." *New Statesman, 131,* 4574, February 18, 2002:32–33.

Gerhard, Jane. "Revisiting 'The Myth of the Vaginal Orgasm': The Female Orgasm in American Sexual Thought and Second Wave Feminism." *Feminist Studies, 26,* 2, Fall 2000:449–477.

Gerson, Kathleen. *Hard Choices: How Women Decide about Work, Career, and Motherhood.* Berkeley: University of California Press, 1985.

Gerth, H. H., and C. Wright Mills. *From Max Weber: Essays in Sociology.* New York: Galaxy, 1958.

Gerth, Jeff. "Two Companies Pay Penalties for Improving China Rockets." *New York Times,* March 3, 2003.

Gilbert, Dennis L. *The American Class Structure in an Age of Growing Inequality,* 6th ed. Belmont, Calif.: Wadsworth, 2003.

Gilbert, Dennis, and Joseph A. Kahl. *The American Class Structure: A New Synthesis,* 4th ed. Belmont, Calif.: Wadsworth, 1998.

Gilligan, Carol. *The Birth of Pleasure.* New York: Knopf, 2002.

Gillum, R. F. "Frequency of Attendance at Religious Services and Smoking: The Third National Health and Nutrition Examination Survey." *Preventive Medicine, 41,* 2005:607–613.

Gilman, Charlotte Perkins. *The Man-Made World or, Our Androcentric Culture.* New York: 1971. First published 1911.

Gitlin, Todd. *The Twilight of Common Dreams: Why America Is Wracked by Culture Wars.* New York: Metropolitan Books, 1997.

Glascock, Jack. "Gender Roles on Prime-Time Network Television: Demographics and Behaviors." *Journal of Broadcasting and Electronic Media, 45,* Fall 2001:656–669.

Glenn, Evelyn Nakano. "Chinese American Families." In *Minority Families in the United States: A Multicultural Perspective,* Ronald L. Taylor, ed. Englewood Cliffs, N.J.: Prentice Hall, 1994:115–145.

Glick, Paul C., and S. Lin. "More Young Adults Are Living with Their Parents: Who Are They?" *Journal of Marriage and Family, 48,* 1986: 107–112.

Goetting, Ann. *Getting Out: Life Stories of Women Who Left Abusive Men.* New York: Columbia University Press, 2001.

Gofen, Anat. "Family Capital: How First-Generation Higher-Education Students Break the Intergenerational Cycle." Institute for Research on Poverty, Discussion Paper 1322–07, 2007.

Goffman, Erving. *Asylums: Essays on the Social Situation of Mental Patients and Other Inmates.* Chicago: Aldine, 1961.

Goffman, Erving. *Stigma: Notes on the Management of Spoiled Identity.* Englewood Cliffs, N.J.: Prentice Hall, 1963.

Gold, Ray. "Janitors Versus Tenants: A Status-Income Dilemma." *American Journal of Sociology, 58,* 1952:486–493.

Goldberg, Susan, and Michael Lewis. "Play Behavior in the Year-Old Infant: Early Sex Differences." *Child Development, 40,* March 1969:21–31.

Goleman, Daniel. "Pollsters Enlist Psychologists in Quest for Unbiased Results." *New York Times,* September 7, 1993:C1, C11.

Gonzales, Alberto R. "Memorandum for Albert R. Gonzales, Counsel to the President: Re: Standards of Conduct for Interrogation Under *18 U.S.C. 2340–2340A.*" August 2, 2002.

Goode, Erica. "Study Says 20% of Girls Reported Abuse by a Date." *New York Times,* August 1, 2001.

Goozen, Stephanie H. M. van, Graeme Fairchild, Heddeke Snoek, and Gordon T. Harold. "The Evidence for a Neurobiological Model of Childhood Antisocial Behavior." *Psychological Bulletin, 133,* 1, 2007: 149–182.

Gorman, Peter. "A People at Risk: Vanishing Tribes of South America." *The World & I.* December 1991:678–689.

Gottfredson, Michael R., and Travis Hirschi. *A General Theory of Crime.* Stanford, Calif.: Stanford University Press, 1990.

Gottschalk, Peter, Sara McLanahan, and Gary Sandefur, "The Dynamics and Intergenerational Transmission of Poverty and Welfare Participation." In *Confronting Poverty: Prescriptions for Change,* Sheldon H. Danziger, Gary D. Sandefur, and Daniel H. Weinberg, eds. Cambridge, Mass.: Harvard University Press, 1994.

Grant, Peter. "Looking for Love (Or a Date) on Cable TV." *Wall Street Journal,* December 15, 2005.

Gray Panthers. "Age and Youth in Action." No date.

Gray, William S. *Dick and Jane: We Play Outside.* New York: Scott, Foresman, 1951.

Greeley, Andrew M. "The Protestant Ethic: Time for a Moratorium." *Sociological Analysis, 25,* Spring 1964:20–33.

Greenhouse, Linda. "Justices Decline Case on 200-Year Sentence for Man Who Possessed Child Pornography." *New York Times,* February 27, 2007.

Greenwald, Anthony G., and Linda Hamilton Krieger. "Implicit Bias: Scientific Foundations." *California Law Review,* July 2006.

Greider, William. "Pro Patria, Pro Mundus." *Nation, 273,* 15, November 12, 2001:22–24.

Gross, Jan T. *Neighbors.* New Haven: Yale University Press, 2001.

Gross, Jane. "In the Quest for the Perfect Look, More Girls Choose the Scalpel." *New York Times,* November 29, 1998.

Guensburg, Carol. "Bully Factories." *American Journalism Review, 23,* 6, 2001:51–59.

Guessous, Fouad, Thorsten Juchem, and Norbert A. Hampp. In *Optical Security and Counterfeit Deterrence Techniques,* Rudolf L. van Renesse, ed. *Proceedings of the SPIE, 5310,* 2004.

Guice, Jon. "Sociologists Go to Work in High Technology." *Footnotes,* November 1999:8.

Gunther, Marc. "The Mosquito in the Tent." *Fortune, 149,* 11, May 31, 2004:158.

Gupta, Giri Raj. "Love, Arranged Marriage, and the Indian Social Structure." In *Cross-Cultural Perspectives of Mate Selection and Marriage,* George Kurian, ed. Westport, Conn.: Greenwood Press, 1979.

Hacker, Helen Mayer. "Women as a Minority Group." *Social Forces, 30,* October 1951:60–69.

Hage, Dave. *Reforming Welfare by Rewarding Work.* Minneapolis: University of Minnesota Press, 2004.

Hall, Edward T. *The Hidden Dimension.* Garden City, N.Y.: Anchor Books, 1969.

Hall, Edward T., and Mildred R. Hall. "The Sounds of Silence." In *Down to Earth Sociology: Introductory Readings,* 14th ed., James M. Henslin, ed. New York: Free Press, 2007:109–117.

Hall, G. Stanley. *Adolescence: Its Psychology and Its Relations to Physiology, Anthropology, Sociology, Sex, Crime, Religion, and Education.* New York: Appleton, 1904.

Hall, Ronald E. "The Tiger Woods Phenomenon: A Note on Biracial Identity." *The Social Science Journal, 38,* 2, April 2001:333–337.

Hamermesh, Daniel S., and Jeff E. Biddle. "Beauty and the Labor Market." *American Economic Review, 84,* 5, December 1994: 1174–1195.

Hamid, Shadi. "Between Orientalism and Postmodernism: The Changing Nature of Western Feminist Thought Towards the Middle East." *HAWWA, 4,* 1, 2006:76–92.

Hampson, Rick. "Studies: Gentrification a Boost for Everyone." *USA Today,* April 19, 2005.

*Handbook on Women Workers.* Washington, D.C.: Women's Bureau of the U.S. Department of Labor, 1969.

Harlow, Harry F., and Margaret K. Harlow. "Social Deprivation in Monkeys." *Scientific American, 207,* 1962:137–147.

Harlow, Harry F., and Margaret K. Harlow. "The Affectional Systems." In *Behavior of Nonhuman Primates: Modern Research Trends,* Vol. 2, Allan M. Schrier, Harry F. Harlow, and Fred Stollnitz, eds. New York: Academic Press, 1965:287–334.

Harrington, Michael. *The Vast Majority: A Journey to the World's Poor.* New York: Simon & Schuster, 1977.

Harris, Chauncey D. "The Nature of Cities and Urban Geography in the Last Half Century." *Urban Geography, 18,* 1997.

Harris, Chauncey D., and Edward Ullman. "The Nature of Cities." *Annals of the American Academy of Political and Social Science, 242,* 1945:7–17.

Harris, Kim, Dwight R. Sanders, Shaun Gress, and Nick Kuhns. "Starting Salaries for Agribusiness Graduates From an AASCARR Institution: The Case of Southern Illinois University." *Agribusiness, 21,* 1, 2005:65–80.

Harris, Marvin. "Why Men Dominate Women." *New York Times Magazine,* November 13, 1977:46, 115, 117–123.

Harrison, Paul. *Inside the Third World: The Anatomy of Poverty,* 3rd ed. London: Penguin, 1993.

Hart, Charles W. M., and Arnold R. Pilling. *The Tiwi of North Australia,* Fieldwork Edition. New York: Holt, Rinehart & Winston, 1979.

Hart, Paul. "Groupthink, Risk-Taking and Recklessness: Quality of Process and Outcome in Policy Decision Making." *Politics and the Individual, 1,* 1, 1991:67–90.

Hartley, Eugene. *Problems in Prejudice.* New York: King's Crown Press, 1946.

Hartocollis, Anemona. "Harvard Faculty Votes to Put the Excellence Back in the A." *New York Times,* May 22, 2002.

Hatch, Laurie Russell. *Beyond Gender Differences: Adaptation to Aging in Life Course Perspective.* Amityville, N.Y.: Baywood, 2000.

Haub, Carl. "Has Global Growth Reached Its Peak?" *Population Today, 30,* 6, August–September 2002:6.

Haub, Carl. "World Population Data Sheet." Washington, D.C.: Population Reference Bureau, 2004, 2005, 2006.

Haub, Carl, and Nancy Yinger. "The U.N. Long-Range Population Projections: What They Tell Us." Washington, D.C.: Population Reference Bureau, 1994.

Hauser, Philip, and Leo Schnore, eds. *The Study of Urbanization.* New York: Wiley, 1965.

Hawley, Amos H. *Urban Society: An Ecological Approach.* New York: Wiley, 1981.

Hayashi, Gina M., and Bonnie R. Strickland. "Long-Term Effects of Parental Divorce on Love Relationships: Divorce as Attachment Disruption." *Journal of Social and Personal Relationships, 15,* 1, February 1998, 23–38.

Heames, Joyce Thompson, Michael G. Harvey, and Darren Treadway. "Status Inconsistency: An Antecedent to Bullying Behavior in Groups." *International Journal of Human Resource Management, 17,* 2, February 2006:348–361.

Heilman, Madeline E. "Description and Prescription: How Gender Stereotypes Prevent Women's Ascent Up the Organizational Ladder." *Journal of Social Issues, 57,* 4, Winter 2001:657–674.

Hellinger, Daniel, and Dennis R. Judd. *The Democratic Facade.* Pacific Grove, Calif.: Brooks/Cole, 1991.

Hendrix, Lewellyn. "What Is Sexual Inequality? On the Definition and Range of Variation." *Gender and Society, 28,* 3, August 1994: 287–307.

Henley, Nancy, Mykol Hamilton, and Barrie Thorne. "Womanspeak and Manspeak." In *Beyond Sex Roles,* Alice G. Sargent, ed. St Paul, Minn.: West, 1985.

Henslin, James M. "On Becoming Male: Reflections of a Sociologist on Childhood and Early Socialization." In *Down to Earth Sociology: Introductory Readings,* 14th ed., James M. Henslin, ed. New York: Free Press, 2007:161–172.

Henslin, James M. *Social Problems: A Down-to-Earth Approach,* 8th ed. Boston: Allyn & Bacon, 2008.

Henslin, James M., and Mae A. Biggs. "Behavior in Pubic Places: The Sociology of the Vaginal Examination." In *Down to Earth Sociology: Introductory Readings,* 14th ed., James M. Henslin, ed. New York: Free Press, 2007:229–241.

Herrick, Thaddeus. "Aging Areas Around Cities Push Suburban Renewal." *New York Times,* January 31, 2007.

Herring, Cedric. "Is Job Discrimination Dead?" *Contexts,* Summer 2002:13–18.

Hetherington, Mavis, and John Kelly. *For Better or For Worse: Divorce Reconsidered.* New York: W.W. Norton, 2003.

Hewitt Associates. *Worklife Benefits Provided by Major U.S. Employers, 2003–2004.* Lincolnshire, Ill.: Hewitt Associates, 2004.

Higginbotham, Elizabeth, and Lynn Weber. "Moving with Kin and Community: Upward Social Mobility for Black and White Women." *Gender and Society, 6,* 3, September 1992:416–440.

Hill, Andrew J. "Motivation for Eating Behaviour in Adolescent Girls: The Body Beautiful." *Proceedings of the Nutrition Society, 65,* 2006: 376–384.

Hill, Mark E. "Skin Color and the Perception of Attractiveness Among African Americans: Does Gender Make a Difference?" *Social Psychology Quarterly, 65,* 1, 2002:77–91.

Hiltz, Starr Roxanne. "Widowhood." In *Marriage and Family in a Changing Society,* 3rd ed., James M. Henslin, ed. New York: Free Press, 1989:521–531.

Hipler, Fritz. Interview with Bill Moyers in television documentary "*Propaganda,*" part of the series *Walk Through the 20th Century,* 1987.

Hirschi, Travis. *Causes of Delinquency.* Berkeley: University of California Press, 1969.

*Historical Statistics of the United States: From Colonial Times to the Present.* New York: Basic Books, 1976.

Hitt, Jack. "The Next Battlefield May Be in Outer Space." *New York Times,* August 5, 2001.

Hochschild, Arlie Russell. "The Sociology of Feeling and Emotion: Selected Possibilities." In *Another Voice: Feminist Perspectives on Social Life and Social Science,* Marcia Millman and Rosabeth Moss Kanter, eds. Garden City, N.Y.: Anchor Books, 1975.

Hochschild, Arlie Russell. *The Managed Heart: Commercialization of Human Feeling.* Chicago: University of Chicago Press, 1983.

Hochschild, Arlie Russell. *The Second Shift: Working Parents and the Revolution at Home.* New York: Viking, 1989.

Hofferth, Sandra. "Did Welfare Reform Work? Implications for 2002 and Beyond." *Contexts,* Spring 2002:45–51.

Holder, Kelly. "Voting and Registration in the Election of November 2004." *Current Population Reports,* March 2006.

Holmwood, John. "Sociology as Public Discourse and Professional Practice: A Critique of Michael Burawoy." *Sociological Theory, 25,* 1, March 2007:46–66.

Holtzman, Abraham. *The Townsend Movement: A Political Study.* New York: Bookman, 1963.

Homblin, Dora Jane. *The First Cities.* Boston: Little, Brown, Time-Life Books, 1973.

Honeycutt, Karen. "Disgusting, Pathetic, Bizarrely Beautiful: Representations of Weight in Popular Culture." Paper presented at the 1995 meetings of the American Sociological Association.

Hong, Lawrence. "Marriage in China." In *Til Death Do Us Part: A Multicultural Anthology on Marriage,* Sandra Lee Browning and R. Robin Miller, eds. Stamford, Conn.: JAI Press, 1999.

hooks, bell. *Where We Stand: Class Matters.* New York: Routledge, 2000.

Horn, James P. *Land As God Made It: Jamestown and the Birth of America.* New York: Basic Books, 2006.

Horowitz, Ruth. *Honor and the American Dream: Culture and Identity in a Chicano Community.* New Brunswick, N.J.: Rutgers University Press, 1983.

Horowitz, Ruth. "Community Tolerance of Gang Violence." *Social Problems, 34,* 5, December 1987:437–450.

Horowitz, Ruth. "Studying Violence Among the 'Lions.'" In James M. Henslin, *Social Problems.* Upper Saddle River, New Jersey: Prentice-Hall, 2005:135.

Hostetler, John A. *Amish Society,* 3rd ed. Baltimore: Johns Hopkins University Press, 1980.

Hotz, Robert Lee. "Most Science Studies Appear to Be Tainted by Sloppy Analysis." *Wall Street Journal,* September 14, 2007.

"House Divided." *People Weekly,* May 24, 1999:126.

Houtman, Dick. "What Exactly Is a 'Social Class'? On the Economic Liberalism and Cultural Conservatism of the 'Working Class.'" Paper presented at the 1995 meetings of the American Sociological Association.

Howells, Lloyd T., and Selwyn W. Becker. "Seating Arrangement and Leadership Emergence." *Journal of Abnormal and Social Psychology, 64,* February 1962:148–150.

Hoyt, Homer. "Recent Distortions of the Classical Models of Urban Structure." In *Internal Structure of the City: Readings on Space and Environment,* Larry S. Bourne, ed. New York: Oxford University Press, 1971:84–96.

Hoyt, Homer. *The Structure and Growth of Residential Neighborhoods in American Cities.* Washington, D.C.: Federal Housing Administration, 1939.

Hsu, Francis L. K. *The Challenge of the American Dream: The Chinese in the United States.* Belmont, Calif.: Wadsworth, 1971.

Huber, Joan. "Micro-Macro Links in Gender Stratification." *American Sociological Review, 55,* February 1990:1–10.

Huddle, Donald. "The Net National Cost of Immigration." Washington, D.C.: Carrying Capacity Network, 1993.

Hudson, Valerie M., and Andrea M. den Boer. *Bare Branches: The Security Implications of Asia's Surplus Male Population.* Cambridge, Mass.: MIT Press, 2004.

Huggins, Martha K., and Sandra Rodrigues. "Kids Working on Paulista Avenue." *Childhood, 11,* 2004:495–514.

Huggins, Martha K., Mika Haritos-Fatouros, and Philip G. Zimbardo. *Violence Workers: Police Torturers and Murderers Reconstruct Brazilian Atrocities.* Berkeley: University of California Press, 2002.

Hughes, Everett C. "Good People and Dirty Work." In *Life in Society: Readings to Accompany Sociology: A Down-to-Earth Approach, Seventh Edition,* James M. Henslin, ed. Boston: Allyn & Bacon, 2005:125–134. Article originally published in 1962.

Hughes, H. Stuart. *Oswald Spengler: A Critical Estimate.* Revised edition. New York: Scribner's, 1962.

Hughes, Kathleen A. "Even Tiki Torches Don't Guarantee a Perfect Wedding." *Wall Street Journal,* February 20, 1990:A1, A16.

Humphreys, Laud. "Impersonal Sex and Perceived Satisfaction." In *Studies in the Sociology of Sex,* James M. Henslin, ed. New York: Appleton-Century-Crofts, 1971:351–374.

Humphreys, Laud. *Tearoom Trade: Impersonal Sex in Public Places,* enlarged ed. Chicago: Aldine, 1970, 1975.

Hundley, Greg. "Why Women Earn Less Than Men in Self-Employment." *Journal of Labor Research, 22,* 4, Fall 2001:817–827.

Hunt, Stephen. *The Life Course: A Sociological Introduction.* London: Palgrave Macmillan, 2005.

Hurtado, Aída, David E. Hayes-Bautista, R. Burciaga Valdez, and Anthony C. R. Hernández. *Redefining California: Latino Social Engagement in a Multicultural Society.* Los Angeles: UCLA Chicano Studies Research Center, 1992.

Huttenbach, Henry R. "The Roman *Porajmos:* The Nazi Genocide of Europe's Gypsies." *Nationalities Papers, 19,* 3, Winter 1991: 373–394.

Hutton, Will. *The Writing on the Wall: Why We Must Embrace China as a Partner or Face It as an Enemy.* New York: Free Press, 2007.

Hymowitz, Carol. "Through the Glass Ceiling." *Wall Street Journal,* November 8, 2004.

Hymowitz, Carol. "Raising Women to Be Leaders." *Wall Street Journal,* February 12, 2007.

Hyra, Derek S. "Racial Uplift? Intra-Racial Class Conflict and the Economic Revitalization of Harlem and Bronzeville." *City and Community,* 5, 1, March 2006:71–92.

Iori, Ron. "The Good, the Bad and the Useless." *Wall Street Journal,* June 10, 1988:18R.

Ismail, M. Asif. "The Clinton Top 100: Where Are They Now?" Washington, D.C.: The Center for Public Integrity, 2003.

Itard, Jean Marc Gospard. *The Wild Boy of Aveyron.* Translated by George and Muriel Humphrey. New York: Appleton-Century-Crofts, 1962.

Jacobs, Jerry A. "Detours on the Road to Equality: Women, Work and Higher Education." *Contexts,* Winter 2003:32–41.

Jacobs, Margaret A. "'New Girl' Network Is Boon for Women Lawyers." *Wall Street Journal,* March 4, 1997:B1, B7.

Jaffrelot, Christophe. "The Impact of Affirmative Action in India: More Political than Socioeconomic." *India Review,* 5, 2, April 2006:173–189.

Jaggar, Alison M. "Sexual Difference and Sexual Equality." In *Theoretical Perspectives on Sexual Difference,* Deborah L. Rhode, ed. New Haven, Conn.: Yale University Press, 1990:239–254.

Jamieson, Amie, Hyon B. Shin, and Jennifer Day. "Voting and Registration in the Election of November 2000." *Current Population Reports,* February 2002.

Janis, Irving L. *Victims of Groupthink.* Boston, Mass.: Houghton Mifflin, 1972.

Janis, Irving. L. *Groupthink: Psychological Studies of Policy Decisions and Fiascoes.* Boston: Houghton Mifflin, 1982.

Jankowiak, William R., and Edward F. Fischer. "A Cross-Cultural Perspective on Romantic Love." *Journal of Ethnology, 31,* 2, April 1992:149–155.

Jasper, James M. "Moral Dimensions of Social Movements." Paper presented at the annual meetings of the American Sociological Association, 1991.

Jenkins, Philip. "The Next Christianity." *Atlantic Monthly,* October 2002:53–68.

Jerrome, Dorothy. *Good Company: An Anthropological Study of Old People in Groups.* Edinburgh: Edinburgh University Press, 1992.

Johansson, Perry. "Consuming the Other: The Fetish of the Western Woman in Chinese Advertising and Popular Culture." *Postcolonial Studies, 2,* 3, November 1999.

Johnson, Benton, "On Church and Sect." *American Sociological Review, 28,* 1963:539–549.

Johnson, Johna Till. "The Costs and Benefits of Remote Workers." *Network World,* December 20, 2004:24.

Johnson-Weiner, Karen. *Train Up a Child: Old Order Amish and Mennonite Schools.* Baltimore: Johns Hopkins University Press, 2007.

Jones, James H. *Bad Blood: The Tuskegee Syphilis Experiment,* 2nd ed. New York: Free Press, 1993.

Jordan, Miriam. "Among Poor Villagers, Female Infanticide Still Flourishes in India." *Wall Street Journal,* May 9, 2000:A1, A12.

Judge, Timothy A., and Daniel M. Cable. "The Effect of Physical Height on Workplace Success and Income: Preliminary Test of a Theoretical Model." *Journal of Applied Psychology, 89,* 3, 2004:428–441.

Juergensmeyer, Mark. *Terror in the Mind of God: The Global Rise of Religious Violence.* Berkeley: University of California Press, 2000.

Jung, Jaehee, and Gordon B. Forbes. *Psychology of Women Quarterly, 31,* 4, December 2007:381–393.

Kaebnick, Gregory E. "On the Sanctity of Nature." *Hastings Center Report, 30,* 5, September–October 2000:16–23.

Kagan, Jerome. "The Idea of Emotions in Human Development." In *Emotions, Cognition, and Behavior,* Carroll E. Izard, Jerome Kagan, and Robert B. Zajonc, eds. New York: Cambridge University Press, 1984:38–72.

Kahn, Joseph. "Some Chinese See the Future, and It's Capitalist." *New York Times,* May 4, 2002.

Kalof, Linda. "Vulnerability to Sexual Coercion Among College Women: A Longitudinal Study." *Gender Issues, 18,* 4, Fall 2000:47–58.

Kanazawa, Satoshi, and Jody L. Kovar. "Why Beautiful People Are More Intelligent." *Intelligence, 32,* 2004:227–243.

Kanter, James, and Andrew C. Revkin. "Scientists Detail Climate Changes, Poles to Tropics." *New York Times,* April 7, 2007.

Kanter, Rosabeth Moss. *Men and Women of the Corporation.* New York: Basic Books, 1977.

Kanter, Rosabeth Moss. *The Change Masters: Innovation and Entrepreneurship in the American Corporation.* New York: Simon & Schuster, 1983.

Karp, David A., Gregory P. Stone, and William C. Yoels. *Being Urban: A Sociology of City Life,* 2nd ed. New York: Praeger, 1991.

Katz, Sidney. "The Importance of Being Beautiful." In *Down to Earth Sociology: Introductory Readings,* 14th ed., James M. Henslin, ed. New York: Free Press, 2007:341–348.

Kaufman, Joanne. "Married Maidens and Dilatory Domiciles." *Wall Street Journal,* May 7, 1996:A16.

Kefalas, Maria. "Looking for the Lower Middle Class." *City and Community, 6,* 1, March 2007:63–68.

Keith, Jennie. *Old People, New Lives: Community Creation in a Retirement Residence,* 2nd ed. Chicago: University of Chicago Press, 1982.

Kelly, Joan B. "How Adults React to Divorce." In *Marriage and Family in a Changing Society,* 4th ed., James M. Henslin, ed. New York: Free Press, 1992:410–423.

Keniston, Kenneth. *Youth and Dissent: The Rise of a New Opposition.* New York: Harcourt, Brace, Jovanovich, 1971.

Kent, Mary, and Robert Lalasz. "In the News: Speaking English in the United States." Population Reference Bureau, January 18, 2007.

Kephart, William M., and William W. Zellner. *Extraordinary Groups: An Examination of Unconventional Life-Styles,* 7th ed. New York: Worth, 2001.

Kerr, Clark. *The Future of Industrialized Societies.* Cambridge, Mass.: Harvard University Press, 1983.

Khattak, Mizuko Ito. "Anime's 'Transnational Geekdom.'" UCLA's Asia Institute, January 23, 2007.

Kibria, Nazli. *Family Tightrope: The Changing Lives of Vietnamese Americans.* Princeton, N.J.: Princeton University Press, 1993.

Kifner, John. "Building Modernity on Desert Mirages." *New York Times,* February 7, 1999.

Kingston, Maxine Hong. *The Woman Warrior.* New York: Vintage Books, 1975:108. Quoted in Frank J. Zulke and Jacqueline P. Kirley, *Through the Eyes of Social Science,* 6th ed. Prospect Heights, Ill.: Waveland Press, 2002.

Kinsella, Kevin, and David R. Phillips. "Global Aging: The Challenge of Success." Washington, D.C.: Population Reference Bureau, 2005.

Klahanie Association Web site. http://www. klahanie.com/

Klandermans, Bert. *The Social Psychology of Protest.* Cambridge, Mass.: Blackwell, 1997.

Kleinfeld, Judith S. "Gender and Myth: Data about Student Performance." In *Through the Eyes of Social Science,* 6th ed., Frank J. Zulke and Jacqueline P. Kirley, eds. Prospect Heights, Ill.: Waveland Press, 2002a:380–393.

Kleinfeld, Judith S. "The Small World Problem." *Society,* January–February, 2002b:61–66.

Kluegel, James R., and Eliot R. Smith. *Beliefs About Inequality: America's Views of What Is and What Ought to Be.* Hawthorne, N.Y.: Aldine de Gruyter, 1986.

Knapp, Daniel. "What Happened When I Took My Sociological Imagination to the Dump." *Footnotes,* May–June, 2005:4.

Knickerbocker, Brad. "Firebrands of 'Ecoterrorism' Set Sights on Urban Sprawl." *Christian Science Monitor,* August 6, 2003.

Kohlberg, Lawrence, and Carol Gilligan. "The Adolescent as a Philosopher: The Discovery of the Self in a Postconventional World." *Daedalus, 100,* 1971:1051–1086.

Kohn, Melvin L. "Social Class and Parental Values." *American Journal of Sociology, 64,* 1959:337–351.

Kohn, Melvin L. "Social Class and Parent-Child Relationships: An Interpretation." *American Journal of Sociology, 68,* 1963: 471–480.

Kohn, Melvin L. "Occupational Structure and Alienation." *American Journal of Sociology, 82,* 1976:111–130.

Kohn, Melvin L. *Class and Conformity: A Study in Values,* 2nd ed. Homewood, Ill.: Dorsey Press, 1977.

Kohn, Melvin L., and Carmi Schooler. "Class, Occupation, and Orientation." *American Sociological Review, 34,* 1969:659–678.

Krane, Vikki, Julie A. Stiles-Shipley, Jennifer Waldron, and Jennifer Michalenok. "Relationships Among Body Satisfaction, Social Physique Anxiety, and Eating Behaviors in Female Athletes and Exercisers." *Journal of Sport Behavior, 24,* 3, September 2001:247–264.

Kraybill, Donald B. *The Riddle of Amish Culture.* Revised edition. Baltimore, Md.: Johns Hopkins University Press, 2002.

Kristoff, Nicholas D. "Interview With a Humanoid." *New York Times,* July 23, 2002.

Kroeger, Brooke. "When a Dissertation Makes a Difference." *New York Times,* March 20, 2004.

Krugman, Paul. "White Man's Burden." *New York Times,* September 24, 2002.

Kubrin, Charis E., and Ronald Weitzer. "Retaliatory Homicide: Concentrated Disadvantage and Neighborhood Culture." *Social Problems, 50,* 2, May 2003:157–180.

Kurian, George Thomas. *Encyclopedia of the First World,* Vols. 1, 2. New York: Facts on File, 1990.

Kurian, George Thomas. *Encyclopedia of the Second World.* New York: Facts on File, 1991.

Kurian, George Thomas. *Encyclopedia of the Third World,* Vols. 1, 2, 3. New York: Facts on File, 1992.

Kurlantzick, Josh. "China's Future: A Nation of Single Men?" *Los Angeles Times,* October 21, 2007.

La Barre, Weston. *The Human Animal.* Chicago: University of Chicago Press, 1954.

Lacayo, Richard. "The 'Cultural' Defense." *Time,* Fall 1993:61.

Lacey, Marc. "Tijuana Journal: Cities Mesh Across Blurry Border, Despite Physical Barrier. *New York Times,* March 5, 2007.

LaFraniere, Sharon. "Africa's World of Forced Labor, in a 6-Year-Old's Eyes." *New York Times,* October 29, 2006.

Lambert, Bruce. "Manufacturer in $2 Million Accord With U.S. on Deficient Kevlar in Military Helmets." *Wall Street Journal,* February 6, 2008.

Landtman, Gunnar. *The Origin of the Inequality of the Social Classes.* New York: Greenwood Press, 1968. First published 1938.

Lang, Kurt, and Gladys E. Lang. *Collective Dynamics.* New York: Crowell, 1961.

Lauer, Jeanette, and Robert Lauer. "Marriages Made to Last." In *Marriage and Family in a Changing Society,* 4th ed., James M. Henslin, ed. New York: Free Press, 1992:481–486.

Leacock, Eleanor. *Myths of Male Dominance.* New York: Monthly Review Press, 1981.

LeDuff, Charlie. "Handling the Meltdowns of the Nuclear Family." *New York Times,* May 28, 2003.

Lee, Alfred McClung, and Elizabeth Briant Lee. *The Fine Art of Propaganda: A Study of Father Coughlin's Speeches.* New York: Harcourt Brace, 1939.

Lee, Raymond M. *Unobtrusive Methods in Social Research.* Philadelphia: Open University Press, 2000.

Lee, Sharon M. "Asian Americans: Diverse and Growing." *Population Bulletin, 53,* 2, June 1998:1–39.

Lee, Sharon M., and Barry Edmonston. "New Marriages, New Families: U.S. Racial and Hispanic Intermarriage." *Population Bulletin, 60,* 2, June 2005:1–36.

Leland, John. "A New Harlem Gentry in Search of Its Latte." *New York Times,* August 7, 2003.

Leland, John, and Gregory Beals. "In Living Colors." *Newsweek,* May 5, 1997:58–60.

Lemann, Nicholas. "The Myth of Community Development." *New York Times Magazine,* January 9, 1994, p. 27.

Lenski, Gerhard. "Status Crystallization: A Nonvertical Dimension of Social Status." *American Sociological Review, 19,* 1954: 405–413.

Lenski, Gerhard. *Power and Privilege: A Theory of Social Stratification.* New York: McGraw-Hill, 1966.

Lenski, Gerhard, and Jean Lenski. *Human Societies: An Introduction to Macrosociology,* 5th ed. New York: McGraw-Hill, 1987.

Lerner, Gerda. *Black Women in White America: A Documentary History.* New York: Pantheon Books, 1972.

Lerner, Gerda. *The Creation of Patriarchy.* New York: Oxford, 1986.

"Less Rote, More Variety: Reforming Japan's Schools." *The Economist,* December 16, 2000:8.

Lester, David. "Adolescent Suicide from an International Perspective." *American Behavioral Scientist, 46,* 9, May 2003:1157–1170.

Letherby, Gayle. "Childless and Bereft? Stereotypes and Realities in Relation to 'Voluntary' and 'Involuntary' Childlessness and Womanhood." *Sociological Inquiry, 72,* 1, Winter 2002:7–20.

Levinson, D. J. *The Seasons of a Man's Life.* New York: Knopf, 1978.

Levinson, Wendy, and Nicole Lurie. "When Most Doctors Are Women: What Lies Ahead." *Annals of Internal Medicine, 141,* 2004:471–474.

Levy, Marion J., Jr. "Confucianism and Modernization." *Society, 24,* 4, May-June 1992:15–18.

Lewin, Tamar. "Little Sympathy or Remedy for Inmates Who Are Raped." *New York Times,* April 15, 2001.

Lewin, Tamar. "Colleges Regroup After Voters Ban Race Preferences." *New York Times,* January 26, 2007.

Lewis, Neil A. "Justice Dept. Toughens Rules on Torture." *New York Times,* January 1, 2005.

Lewis, Oscar. "The Culture of Poverty." *Scientific American, 115,* October 1966a:19–25.

Lewis, Oscar. *La Vida.* New York: Random House, 1966b.

Lewis, Richard S. *Challenger: The Final Voyage.* New York: Columbia University Press, 1988.

Lichter, Daniel T., and Martha L. Crowley. "Poverty in America: Beyond Welfare Reform." *Population Bulletin, 57,* 2, June 2002:1–36.

Liebow, Elliott. *Tally's Corner: A Study of Negro Streetcorner Men.* Boston: Little, Brown, 1999. Originally published in 1967.

Lightfoot-Klein, A. "Rites of Purification and Their Effects: Some Psychological Aspects of Female Genital Circumcision and Infibulation (Pharaonic Circumcision) in an Afro-Arab Society (Sudan)." *Journal of Psychological Human Sexuality, 2,* 1989:61–78.

Lind, Michael. *The Next American Nation: The New Nationalism and the Fourth American Revolution.* New York: Free Press, 1995.

Linden, Eugene. "Lost Tribes, Lost Knowledge." *Time,* September 23, 1991:46, 48, 50, 52, 54, 56.

Lines, Patricia M. "Homeschooling Comes of Age." *Public Interest,* Summer 2000:74–85.

Linton, Ralph. *The Study of Man.* New York: Appleton-Century-Crofts, 1936.

Linz, Daniel, Paul Bryant, et al. "An Examination of the Assumption that Adult Businesses Are Associated with Crime in Surrounding Areas: A Secondary Effects Study in Charlotte, North Carolina." *Law & Society, 38,* 1, March 2004:69–104.

Lippitt, Ronald, and Ralph K. White. "An Experimental Study of Leadership and Group Life." In *Readings in Social Psychology,* 3rd ed., Eleanor E. Maccoby, Theodore M. Newcomb, and Eugene L. Hartley, eds. New York: Holt, Rinehart & Winston, 1958: 340–365. (As summarized in Olmsted and Hare 1978:28–31.)

Lipset, Seymour Martin. "Democracy and Working-Class Authoritarianism." *American Sociological Review, 24,* 1959:482–502.

Lipset, Seymour Martin. "The Social Requisites of Democracy Revisited." Presidential address to the American Sociological Association, Boston, Massachusetts, 1993.

Liu, Haiyong. "Growing Up Poor and Childhood Weight Problems." Institute for Research on Poverty, Discussion Paper. DP 1324-07, April 2007.

Lombroso, Cesare. *Crime: Its Causes and Remedies,* H. P. Horton, trans. Boston: Little, Brown, 1911.

Lublin, Joann S. "Women at Top Still Are Distant from CEO Jobs." *Wall Street Journal,* February 28, 1996:B1.

Lublin, Joann S. "Living Well." *Wall Street Journal,* April 8, 1999.

Lucas, Samuel Roundfield. *Tracking Inequality: Stratification and Mobility in American High Schools.* New York: Teachers College Press, 1999.

Luhnow, David. "As Jobs Move East, Plants in Mexico Retool to Compete." *Wall Street Journal,* March 5, 2004.

Lunneborg, Patricia. *Chosen Lives of Childfree Men.* Westport, Conn.: Bergin & Garvey, 1999.

Lurie, Nicole, Jonathan Slater, Paul McGovern, Jacqueline Ekstrum, Lois Quam, and Karen Margolis. "Preventive Care for Women: Does the Sex of the Physician Matter?" *New England Journal of Medicine, 329,* August 12, 1993:478–482.

Mabry, Marcus. "The Price Tag on Freedom." *Newsweek,* May 3, 1999: 50–51.

MacDonald, William L., and Alfred DeMaris. "Remarriage, Stepchildren, and Marital Conflict: Challenges to the Incomplete Institutionalization Hypothesis." *Journal of Marriage and the Family, 57,* May 1995:387–398.

Madigan, Nick. "Judge Questions Long Sentence in Drug Case." *New York Times,* November 17, 2004.

Madslien, Jorn. "Nuclear Waste Poses Arctic Threat." *BBC News,* October 19, 2006.

Mahoney, John S., Jr., and Paul G. Kooistra. "Policing the Races: Structural Factors Enforcing Racial Purity in Virginia (1630–1930)." Paper presented at the 1995 meetings of the American Sociological Association.

Maier, Mark. "Teaching from Tragedy: An Interdisciplinary Module on the Space Shuttle *Challenger.*" *T. H. E. Journal,* September 1993:91–94.

Malinowski, Bronislaw. *Sex and Repression in Savage Society.* Cleveland, Ohio: World, 1927.

Malthus, Thomas Robert. *First Essay on Population 1798.* London: Macmillan, 1926. Originally published in 1798.

Mamdani, Mahmood. "The Myth of Population Control: Family, Caste, and Class in an Urban Village." New York: Monthly Review Press, 1973.

Manheimer, Ronald J. "The Older Learner's Journey to an Ageless Society." *Journal of Transformative Education, 3,* 3, 2005.

*Manpower Report to the President.* Washington, D.C.: U.S. Department of Labor, Manpower Administration, April 1971.

Manzo, Kathleen Kennedy. "History in the Making." *Community College Week, 13,* 15, March 5, 2001:6–8.

Mardell, Mark. "Europe in Khaki." *BBC News,* June 14, 2007.

"Marital History for People 15 Years Old and Over by Age, Sex, Race and Ethnicity: 2001." Annual Demographic Survey, Bureau of Labor Statistics and the Bureau of the Census. 2004.

Marshall, Samantha. "It's So Simple: Just Lather Up, Watch the Fat Go Down the Drain." *Wall Street Journal,* November 2, 1995:B1.

Marshall, Samantha. "Vietnamese Women Are Kidnapped and Later Sold in China as Brides." *Wall Street Journal,* August 3, 1999.

Martineau, Harriet. *Society in America.* Garden City, N. Y.: Doubleday 1962. First published 1837.

Marx, Gary T. "The Road to the Future." In *Triumph of Discovery: A Chronicle of Great Adventures in Science.* New York: Holt, 1995:63–65.

Marx, Karl. "Contribution to the Critique of Hegel's Philosophy of Right." In *Karl Marx: Early Writings,* T. B. Bottomore, ed. New York: McGraw-Hill, 1964:45. First published 1844.

Marx, Karl, and Friedrich Engels. *Communist Manifesto.* New York: Pantheon, 1967. First published 1848.

Masheter, Carol. "Postdivorce Relationships Between Ex-spouses: The Role of Attachment and Interpersonal Conflict." *Journal of Marriage and the Family, 53,* February 1991:103–110.

Mathews, T. J., and Brady E. Hamilton. "Mean Age of Mother, 1970–2000." *National Vital Statistics Report, 51,* 1, December 11, 2002.

Mauss, Armand. *Social Problems as Social Movements.* Philadelphia: Lippincott, 1975.

Mayer, John D. *Personality: A Systems Approach.* Boston: Allyn & Bacon, 2007.

McAdam, Doug, John D. McCarthy, and Mayer N. Zald. "Social Movements." In *Handbook of Sociology,* Neil J. Smelser, ed. Newbury Park, Calif.: Sage, 1988:695–737.

McCarthy, John D., and Mark Wolfson. "Consensus Movements, Conflict Movements, and the Cooperation of Civic and State Infrastructures." In *Frontiers in Social Movement Theory,* Aldon D. Morris and Carol McClurg Mueller, eds. New Haven, Conn.: Yale University Press, 1992:273–297.

McCarthy, Michael J. "Granbury, Texas, Isn't a Rural Town: It's a 'Micropolis.'" *Wall Street Journal,* June 3, 2004.

McCormick, John. "Change Has Taken Place." *Newsweek,* June 7, 1999a:34.

McCormick, John. "The Sorry Side of Sears." *Newsweek,* February 22, 1999b:36–39.

McDowell, Bart. "Mexico City: An Alarming Giant." *National Geographic, 166,* 1984:139–174.

McFalls, Joseph A., Jr. "Population: A Lively Introduction, 5th ed." *Population Bulletin, 62,* 1, March 2007:1–30.

McGee, Glenn. "Cloning, Sex, and New Kinds of Families." *Journal of Sex Research, 37,* 3, August 2000:266–272.

McGinn, Daniel, and Jason McLure. "Home School: The Ring." *Newsweek,* November 10, 2003:12.

McIntosh, Peggy. "White Privilege and Male Privilege: A Personal Account of Coming to See Correspondences through Work in Women's Studies." Working Paper #189. Wellesley College Center for Research on Women, 1988.

McKenna, George. "On Abortion: A Lincolnian Position." *Atlantic Monthly,* September 1995:51–67.

McKeown, Thomas. *The Modern Rise of Population.* New York: Academic Press, 1977.

McKinley, Jesse. "Surgeon Accused of Speeding a Death to Get Organs." *New York Times,* February 27, 2008.

McLanahan, Sara, and Gary Sandefur. *Growing Up with a Single Parent: What Hurts, What Helps.* Cambridge, Mass.: Harvard University Press, 1994.

McLanahan, Sara, and Dona Schwartz. "Life Without Father: What Happens to the Children?" *Contexts, 1,* 1, Spring 2002:35–44.

McLemore, S. Dale. *Racial and Ethnic Relations in America.* Boston: Allyn & Bacon, 1994.

McNeill, William H. "How the Potato Changed the World's History." *Social Research, 66,* 1, Spring 1999:67–83.

McShane, Marilyn, and Frank P. Williams, III., eds. *Criminological Theory.* Upper Saddle River, N.J.: Prentice-Hall, 2007.

Mead, George Herbert. *Mind, Self and Society.* Chicago: University of Chicago Press, 1934.

Medlin, Richard G. "Home Schooling and the Question of Socialization." *Peabody Journal of Education, 75,* 1–2, 2000:107–123.

Meese, Ruth Lyn. "A Few New Children: Postinstitutionalized Children of Intercountry Adoption." *Journal of Special Education, 39,* 3, 2005:157–167.

"Melee Breaks Out at Retirement Home." *The Daily News,* March 5, 2004.

Meltzer, Scott A. "Gender, Work, and Intimate Violence: Men's Occupational Spillover and Compensatory Violence." *Journal of Marriage and the Family, 64,* 2, November 2002:820–832.

Melucci, Alberto. *Nomads of the Present: Social Movements and Individual Needs in Contemporary Society.* Philadelphia: Temple University Press, 1989.

Menaghan, Elizabeth G., Lori Kowaleski-Jones, and Frank L. Mott. "The Intergenerational Costs of Parental Social Stressors: Academic and Social Difficulties in Early Adolescence for Children of Young Mothers." *Journal of Health and Social Behavior, 38,* March 1997:72–86.

Mende, Nazer, and Damien Lewis. *Slave: My True Story.* New York: Public Affairs, 2005.

Menzel, Peter. *Material World: A Global Family Portrait.* San Francisco: Sierra Club, 1994.

Merton, Robert K. "The Social-Cultural Environment and *Anomie.*" In *New Perspectives for Research on Juvenile Delinquency,* Helen L. Witmer and Ruth Kotinsky, eds. Washington, D.C.: U.S. Department of Health, Education, and Welfare, 1956:24–50.

Merton, Robert K. *Social Theory and Social Structure.* Glencoe, Ill.: Free Press, 1949. Enlarged edition 1968.

Merwine, Maynard H. "How Africa Understands Female Circumcision." *New York Times,* November 24, 1993.

Messner, Michael. "Boyhood, Organized Sports, and the Construction of Masculinities." *Journal of Contemporary Ethnography, 18,* 4, January 1990:416–444.

Meyers, Laurie. "Asian-American Mental Health." *APA Online,* February 2006.

Mezentseva, E. *Russian Social Science Review, 42,* 4, July–August 2001:4–21.

Michael, Robert T., John H. Gagnon, Edward O. Laumann, and Gina Kolata. "How Many Sexual Partners Do Americans Have?" In *Exploring Social Life: Readings to Accompany Essentials of Sociology: A Down-to-Earth Approach,* 5th ed., James M. Henslin, ed. Boston: Allyn & Bacon, 2004:166–174.

Michels, Robert. *Political Parties.* Glencoe, Ill.: Free Press, 1949. First published 1911.

Milbank, Dana. "Guarded by Greenbelts, Europe's Town Centers Thrive." *Wall Street Journal,* May 3, 1995:B1, B4.

Milgram, Stanley. "Behavioral Study of Obedience." *Journal of Abnormal and Social Psychology, 67,* 4, 1963:371–378.

Milgram, Stanley. "Some Conditions of Obedience and Disobedience to Authority." *Human Relations, 18,* February 1965:57–76.

Milgram, Stanley. "The Small World Problem." *Psychology Today, 1,* 1967:61–67.

Milkie, Melissa A. "Social World Approach to Cultural Studies." *Journal of Contemporary Ethnography, 23,* 3, October 1994:354–380.

Miller, Walter B. "Lower Class Culture as a Generating Milieu of Gang Delinquency." *Journal of Social Issues, 14,* 3, 1958:5–19.

Mills, C. Wright. *The Power Elite.* New York: Oxford University Press, 1956.

Mills, C. Wright. *The Sociological Imagination.* New York: Oxford University Press, 1959.

Mills, Karen M., and Thomas J. Palumbo. *A Statistical Portrait of Women in the United States: 1978.* U.S. Bureau of the Census, *Current Population Reports,* Series P-23, no. 100, 1980.

Minkler, Meredith, and Ann Robertson. "The Ideology of 'Age/Race Wars': Deconstructing a Social Problem." *Ageing and Society, 11,* 1, March 1991:1–22.

Mintz, Beth A., and Michael Schwartz. *The Power Structure of American Business.* Chicago: University of Chicago Press, 1985.

Mirola, William A. "Asking for Bread, Receiving a Stone: The Rise and Fall of Religious Ideologies in Chicago's Eight-Hour Movement." *Social Problems, 50,* 2, May 2003:273–293.

Mohal, Paul, and Robin Saha. "Racial Inequalities in the Distribution of Hazardous Waste: A National-Level Reassessment." *Social Problems, 54,* 3, 2007:343–370.

Mohawk, John C. "Indian Economic Development: An Evolving Concept of Sovereignty." *Buffalo Law Review, 39,* 2, Spring 1991:495–503.

Mol, Arthur P. *Globalization and Environmental Reform: The Ecological Modernization of the Global Economy.* Cambridge, Mass.: MIT Press, 2001.

Money, John, and Anke A. Ehrhardt. *Man and Woman, Boy and Girl.* Baltimore: Johns Hopkins University Press, 1972.

Montagu, M. F. Ashley. *Introduction to Physical Anthropology,* 3rd ed. Springfield, Ill.: Thomas, 1960.

Montagu, M. F. Ashley. *The Concept of Race.* New York: Free Press, 1964.

Montagu, M. F. Ashley, ed. *Race and IQ: Expanded Edition.* New York: Oxford University Press, 1999.

Morgan, Lewis Henry. *Ancient Society.* New York: Holt, 1877.

Morris, Joan M., and Michael D. Grimes. "Moving Up from the Working Class." In *Down to Earth Sociology: Introductory Readings,* 13th ed., James M. Henslin, ed. New York: Free Press, 2005:365–376.

Mosca, Gaetano. *The Ruling Class.* New York: McGraw-Hill, 1939. First published 1896.

Mosher, Steven W. "Why Are Baby Girls Being Killed in China?" *Wall Street Journal,* July 25, 1983:9.

Mosher, Steven W. "Too Many People? Not by a Long Shot." *Wall Street Journal,* February 10, 1997:A18.

Mosher, Steven W. "China's One-Child Policy: Twenty-Five Years Later." *Human Life Review,* Winter 2006:76–101.

Mouawad, Jad. "Saudi Officials Seek to Temper the Price of Oil." *Bloomberg News,* January 27, 2007.

Mount, Ferdinand. *The Subversive Family: An Alternative History of Love and Marriage.* New York: Free Press, 1992.

Moynihan, Daniel Patrick. "Social Justice in the *Next* Century." *America,* September 14, 1991:132–137.

"Mujer 'resucita' en España." BBC Mundo, February 17, 2006.

Murdock, George Peter. *Social Structure.* New York: Macmillan, 1949.

Murray, Christopher J. L., Sandeep C. Kulkarni, Catherine Michard, Niels Tomijima, Maria T. Bulzacchelli, Terrell J. Landiorio, and Majid Ezzati. "Eight Americas: Investigating Mortality Disparities across Races, Counties, and Race-Counties in the United States." *PLoS Medicine, 3,* 9, September 2006:1513–1524.

*Muslim Americans: Middle Class and Mostly Mainstream.* Washington, D.C.: Pew Research Center, May 22, 2007.

Mydans, Seth. "A Fervor of Capitalism Sweeps Vietnam." *International Herald Tribune,* April 26, 2006.

Nabhan, Gary Paul. *Cultures in Habitat: On Nature, Culture, and Story.* New York: Counterpoint, 1998.

Naik, Gautam. "Doing Hard Time in Greenland Isn't Really That Hard." *Wall Street Journal,* January 13, 2004.

Nakamura, Akemi. "Abe to Play Hardball with Soft Education System." *The Japan Times,* October 27, 2006.

Nakao, Keiko, and Judith Treas. "Occupational Prestige in the United States Revisited: Twenty-Five Years of Stability and Change." Paper presented at the annual meetings of the American Sociological Association, 1990. (As referenced in Kerbo, Harold R. *Social Stratification and Inequality: Class Conflict in Historical and Comparative Perspective,* 2nd ed. New York: McGraw-Hill, 1991:181.)

Nash, Gary B. *Red, White, and Black.* Englewood Cliffs, N.J.: Prentice-Hall, 1974.

National Center for Education Statistics. *Digest of Education Statistics.* Washington, D.C.: U.S. Government Printing Office, 1991.

National Institute of Child Health and Human Development. "Child Care and Mother-Child Interaction in the First 3 Years of Life." *Developmental Psychology, 35,* 6, November 1999: 1399–1413.

National School Safety Center. "School Associated Violent Deaths." Westlake Village, California, 2007.

Nauta, André. "That They All May Be One: Can Denominationalism Die?" Paper presented at the annual meetings of the American Sociological Association, 1993.

Navarro, Mireya. "For New York's Black Latinos, a Growing Racial Awareness." *New York Times,* April 28, 2003.

Navarro, Vicente, ed. *The Political Economy of Social Inequalities: Consequences for Health and Quality of Life.* Amityville, N.Y.: Baywood, 2002.

Needham, Sarah E. "Grooming Women for the Top: Tips from Executive Coaches." *Wall Street Journal,* October 31, 2006.

Neikirk, William, and Glen Elsasser. "Ruling Weakens Abortion Right." *Chicago Tribune,* June 30, 1992:1, 8.

Neil, Martha. "New 'Big Brother' Software Will Monitor Workers' Facial Expressions." *ABA Journal,* January 16, 2008.

Nestar, Russell, and Robert Gregory. "Making the Undoable Doable: Milgram, the Holocaust, and Modern Government." *The American Review of Public Administration, 35,* December 1, 2005:327–349.

Neugarten, Bernice L. "Middle Age and Aging." In *Growing Old in America,* Beth B. Hess, ed. New Brunswick, N.J.: Transaction, 1976: 180–197.

Neugarten, Bernice L. "Personality and Aging." In *Handbook of the Psychology of Aging,* James E. Birren and K. Warren Schaie, eds. New York: Van Nostrand Reinhold, 1977:626–649.

Newman, Michael. "Class, State and Democracy: Laski, Miliband and the Search for a Synthesis." *Political Studies, 54,* 2006:328–348.

Niebuhr, Gustav. "Studies Suggest Lower Count for Number of U.S. Muslims." *New York Times,* October 25, 2001.

Niebuhr, H. Richard. *The Social Sources of Denominationalism.* New York: Holt, 1929.

Nisbett, Richard E. *The Geography of Thought: How Asians and Westerners Think Differently . . . and Why.* New York: Free Press, 2003.

Nordland, Rod. "That Joke Is a Killer." *Newsweek,* May 19, 2003:10.

Nusbaum, Marci Alboher. "New Kind of Snooping Arrives at the Office." *New York Times,* July 13, 2003.

Nussenbaum, Evelyn. "Video Game Makers Go Hollywood. Uh-Oh." *New York Times,* August 22, 2004.

O'Brien, John E. "Violence in Divorce-Prone Families." In *Violence in the Family,* Suzanne K. Steinmetz and Murray A. Straus, eds. New York: Dodd, Mead, 1975:65–75.

O'Hare, William P. "A New Look at Poverty in America." *Population Bulletin, 51,* 2, September 1996a:1–47.

O'Hare, William P. "U.S. Poverty Myths Explored: Many Poor Work Year-Round, Few Still Poor After Five Years." *Population Today: News, Numbers, and Analysis, 24,* 10, October 1996b:1–2.

Offen, Karen. "Feminism and Sexual Difference in Historical Perspective." In *Theoretical Perspectives on Sexual Difference,* Deborah L. Rhode, ed. New Haven, Conn.: Yale University Press, 1990:13–20.

Ogburn, William F. *Social Change with Respect to Culture and Human Nature.* New York: W. B. Huebsch, 1922. (Other editions by Viking in 1927, 1938, and 1950.)

Ogburn, William F. "The Family and Its Functions." In *Recent Social Trends in the United States: Report of the President's Research Committee on Social Trends.* New York: McGraw-Hill, 1933:661–708.

Ogburn, William F. "The Hypothesis of Cultural Lag." In *Theories of Society: Foundations of Modern Sociological Theory,* Vol. 2, Talcott Parsons, Edward Shils, Kaspar D. Naegele, and Jesse R. Pitts, eds. New York: Free Press, 1961:1270–1273.

Ogburn, William F. *On Culture and Social Change: Selected Papers,* Otis Dudley Duncan, ed. Chicago: University of Chicago Press, 1964.

Olmsted, Michael S., and A. Paul Hare. *The Small Group,* 2nd ed. New York: Random House, 1978.

"On History and Heritage: John K. Castle." *Penn Law Journal,* Fall 1999.

Ono, Yumiko. "By Dint of Promotion Japanese Entrepreneur Ignites a Soccer Frenzy." *Wall Street Journal,* September 17, 1993:A1, A6.

Orme, Nicholas. *Medieval Children.* New Haven: Yale University Press, 2002.

Orwell, George. *1984.* New York: Harcourt Brace, 1949.

Osborne, Lawrence. "Got Silk." *New York Times Magazine,* June 15, 2002.

Ouchi, William. "Decision-Making in Japanese Organizations." In *Down to Earth Sociology: Introductory Readings,* 7th ed., James M. Henslin, ed. New York: Free Press, 1993:503–507.

Padgett, Tim. "An Ivy Stepladder." *Time,* April 4, 2005.

Pagelow, Mildred Daley. "Adult Victims of Domestic Violence: Battered Women." *Journal of Interpersonal Violence, 7,* 1, March 1992:87–120.

Pager, Devah. "Blacks and Ex-Cons Need Not Apply." *Context, 2,* 3, Fall 2003:58–59.

Pager, Devah. "The Mark of a Criminal Record." *American Journal of Sociology, 108,* 5, March 2003:937–975.

Palen, John J. *The Urban World,* 7th ed. Boston: McGraw-Hill, 2005.

Panzarella, Jamie. "Achieving the Dream: Helping Community Colleges Focus on Student Success." *Footnotes, 36,* 1, January 2008:6.

Parfit, Michael, "Earth First!ers Wield a Mean Monkey Wrench." *Smithsonian, 21,* 1, April 1990:184–204.

Park, Robert Ezra. "Human Ecology." *American Journal of Sociology, 42,* 1, July 1936:1–15.

Park, Robert Ezra, and Ernest W. Burgess. *Human Ecology.* Chicago: University of Chicago Press, 1921.

Parsons, Talcott. "An Analytic Approach to the Theory of Social Stratification." *American Journal of Sociology, 45,* 1940:841–862.

Partington, Donald H. "The Incidence of the Death Penalty for Rape in Virginia." *Washington and Lee Law Review, 22,* 1965: 43–75.

Pascoe, C. J. "Multiple Masculinities? Teenage Boys Talk About Jocks and Gender." *American Behavioral Scientist, 46,* 10, June 2003:1423–1438.

Passell, Peter. "Race, Mortgages and Statistics." *New York Times,* May 10, 1996:D1, D4. Washington, D.C.: Pew Hispanic Center.

Patterson, Orlando. "The Root of the Problem." *Time,* April 26, 2007.

Pearlin, L. I., and Melvin L. Kohn. "Social Class, Occupation, and Parental Values: A Cross-National Study." *American Sociological Review, 31,* 1966:466–479.

Pedersen, R. P. "How We Got Here: It's Not How You Think." *Community College Week, 13,* 15, March 15, 2001:4–5.

Peña, Maria. "Patrullaje de voluntarios destaca urgencia de aprobar reforma." *EFE.* April 3, 2005.

Perry, Barbara. "Nobody Trusts Them! Under- and Over-Policing Native American Communities." *Critical Criminology, 14,* 2006:411–444.

Peter, Laurence J., and Raymond Hull. *The Peter Principle: Why Things Always Go Wrong.* New York: Morrow, 1969.

Peters, Jeremy W., and Danny Hakim. "Ford's Lending Practices Challenged in a Lawsuit." *New York Times,* March 1, 2005.

Peterson, Iver. "1993 Deal for Indian Casino Is Called a Model to Avoid." *New York Times,* June 30, 2003.

Peterson, Janice. "Welfare Reform and Inequality: The TANF and UI Programs." *Journal of Economic Issues, 34,* 2, June 2000:517–526.

Pfann, Gerard A., et al. "Business Success and Businesses' Beauty Capital." *Economics Letters, 67,* 2, May 2000:201–207.

Piaget, Jean. *The Psychology of Intelligence.* London: Routledge & Kegan Paul, 1950.

Piaget, Jean. *The Construction of Reality in the Child.* New York: Basic Books, 1954.

Pines, Maya. "The Civilizing of Genie." *Psychology Today, 15,* September 1981:28–34.

Piotrow, Phylis Tilson. *World Population Crisis: The United States' Response.* New York: Praeger, 1973.

Polgreen, Lydia, and Marlise Simons. "Global Sludge Ends in Tragedy for Ivory Coast." *New York Times,* October 2, 2006.

Polsby, Nelson W. "Three Problems in the Analysis of Community Power." *American Sociological Review, 24,* 6, December 1959:796–803.

Pope, Liston. *Millhands and Preachers: A Study of Gastonia.* New Haven, Conn.: Yale University Press, 1942.

Portés, Alejandro, and Ruben G. Rumbaut. *Immigrant America.* Berkeley: University of California Press, 1990.

Pratt, Laura A., Achintya N. Dey, and Alan J. Cohen. "Characteristics of Adults with Serious Psychological Distress as Measured by the K6 Scale: United States, 2001–04." *Vital and Health Statistics, 382,* March 30 2007:1–18.

Princiotta, Daniel, Stacey Bielick, and Chris Chapman. "1.1 Million Homeschooled Students in the United States in 2003." *Education Statistics Quarterly, 6,* 3, 2004:23–25.

Prystay, Cris, and Geoffrey A. Fowler. "They Shun Hard-Body Look, Preferring Pills, Teas and Gels." *Wall Street Journal,* October 9, 2003.

Purdum, Todd S. "NATO Strikes Deal to Accept Russia in a Partnership." *New York Times,* May 15, 2002.

Quadagno, Jill. *Aging and the Life Course: An Introduction to Gerontology,* 4th ed. New York: McGraw-Hill, 2007.

Rainwater, Lee, and Timothy M. Smeeding. *Poor Kids in a Rich Country: America's Children in Comparative Perspective.* New York: Russell Sage, 2003.

Raisfeld, Robin, and Rob Patronite. "Shirako Season." *New York Magazine,* December 25, 2006.

Ramos, Jorge. "Project Minuteman Is Meaningless." *Oakland Tribune.* April 10, 2005.

Rand, Michael, and Shannan Catalano. "Criminal Victimization, 2006." *Bureau of Justice Statistics Bulletin,* December 2007.

Ray, J. J. "Authoritarianism Is a Dodo: Comment on Scheepers, Felling and Peters." *European Sociological Review, 7,* 1, May 1991:73–75.

Reckless, Walter C. *The Crime Problem,* 5th ed. New York: Appleton, 1973.

Reed, Susan, and Lorenzo Benet. "Ecowarrior Dave Foreman Will Do Whatever It Takes in His Fight to Save Mother Earth." *People Weekly, 33,* 15, April 16, 1990:113–116.

Regalado, Antonio. "Seoul Team Creates Custom Stem Cells from Cloned Embryos." *Wall Street Journal,* May 20, 2005.

Reibstein, Larry. "Managing Diversity." *Newsweek,* January 25, 1996:50.

Reiman, Jeffrey. *The Rich Get Richer and the Poor Get Prison: Ideology, Class, and Criminal Justice,* 7th ed. Boston: Allyn & Bacon, 2004.

Reiser, Christa. *Reflections on Anger: Women and Men in a Changing Society.* Westport, Conn.: Praeger, 1999.

Rennison, Callie Marie. "Intimate Partner Violence, 1993–2001." Washington, D.C.: Bureau of Justice Statistics, February 2003.

Reskin, Barbara F. *The Realities of Affirmative Action in Employment.* Washington, D.C.: American Sociological Association, 1998.

Resnik, David B. "Financial Interests and Research Bias." *Perspectives on Science, 8,* 3, Fall 2000:255–283.

Reuters. "Fake Tiger Woods Gets 200-Years-To-Life in Prison." April 28, 2001.

Revkin, Andrew C., and Matthew L. Wald. "Material Shows Weakening of Climate Reports." *New York Times,* March 20, 2007.

Richardson, Stacey, and Marita P. McCabe. "Parental Divorce During Adolescence and Adjustment in Early Adulthood." *Adolescence, 36,* Fall 2001:467–489.

Richman, Joe. "From the Belgian Congo to the Bronx Zoo." National Public Radio, September 8, 2006.

Richtel, Matt. "For Liars and Loafers, Cellphones Offer an Alibi." *New York Times,* June 26, 2004.

Ricks, Thomas E. "'New' Marines Illustrate Growing Gap Between Military and Society." *Wall Street Journal,* July 27, 1995:A1, A4.

Rideout, Victoria J., and Elizabeth A. Vandewater. "Zero to Six: Electronic Media in the Lives of Infants, Toddlers and Preschoolers." Kaiser Family Foundation, Fall 2003.

Rieker, Patricia P., Chloe E. Bird, Susan Bell, Jenny Ruducha, Rima E. Rudd, and S. M. Miller, "Violence and Women's Health: Toward a Society and Health Perspective." Unpublished paper, 1997.

Riley, Nancy E. "China's Population: New Trends and Challenges." *Population Bulletin, 59,* 2, June 2004:3–36.

Risen, James, David Johnston, and Neil A. Lewis. "Harsh C. I. A. Methods Cited in Top Qaeda Interrogations." *New York Times,* May 13, 2004.

Rist, Ray C. "Student Social Class and Teacher Expectations: The Self-Fulfilling Prophecy in Ghetto Education." *Harvard Educational Review, 40,* 3, August 1970:411–451.

Ritzer, George. "The McDonaldization of Society." In *Down to Earth Sociology: Introductory Readings,* 11th ed., James M. Henslin, ed. New York: Free Press, 2001:459–471.

Ritzer, George. *The McDonaldization of Society: An Investigation into the Changing Character of Contemporary Life.* Thousand Oaks, Calif.: Pine Forge Press, 1993.

Ritzer, George. *The McDonaldization Thesis: Explorations and Extensions.* Thousand Oaks, Calif.: Sage, 1998.

Rivlin, Gary. "Beyond the Reservation." *New York Times,* September 22, 2007.

Robb, John. "The Coming Urban Terror." *City Journal,* Summer 2007. Online.

Robbins, John. *Healthy at 100.* New York: Random House, 2006.

Robertson, Ian. *Sociology,* 3rd ed. New York: Worth, 1987.

"Rodney King." *Time,* April 25, 2007.

Rodriguez, Richard. "The Education of Richard Rodriguez." *Saturday Review,* February 8, 1975:147–149.

Rodriguez, Richard. *Hunger of Memory: The Education of Richard Rodriguez.* Boston: Godine, 1982.

Rodriguez, Richard. "The Late Victorians: San Francisco, AIDS, and the Homosexual Stereotype." *Harper's Magazine,* October 1990:57–66.

Rodriguez, Richard. "Mixed Blood." *Harper's Magazine, 283,* November 1991:47–56.

Rodriguez, Richard. "Searching for Roots in a Changing Society." In *Down to Earth Sociology: Introductory Readings,* 8th ed., James M. Henslin, ed. New York: Free Press, 1995:486–491.

Roediger, David R. *Colored White: Transcending the Racial Past.* Berkeley: University of California Press, 2002.

Rogers, Joseph W. *Why Are You Not a Criminal?* Englewood Cliffs, N.J.: Prentice-Hall, 1977.

Rohwedder, Cecilie. "London Parents Scramble for Edge in Preschool Wars." *Wall Street Journal,* February 12, 2007.

Rosenfeld, Richard. "Crime Decline in Context." *Contexts, 1,* 1, Spring 2002:25–34.

Rosenthal, Elisabeth. "Harsh Chinese Reality Feeds a Black Market in Women." *New York Times,* June 25, 2001.

Rosenthal, Elisabeth. "Cat Lovers Lining Up for No-Sneeze Kitties." *New York Times,* October 6, 2006.

Rosenthal, Elisabeth, and Andrew C. Revkin. "Science Panel Calls Global Warming 'Unequivocal.'" *New York Times,* February 2, 2007.

Ross, Casey. "Jackpot Grandma Busy Eluding Moochers." *Boston Herald,* July 14, 2004:2.

Ross, Emma. "Social Life Helps Prevent Dementia." Associated Press, April 23, 2000.

Rossi, Alice S. "A Biosocial Perspective on Parenting." *Daedalus, 106,* 1977:1–31.

Rossi, Alice S. "Gender and Parenthood." *American Sociological Review, 49,* 1984:1–18.

Roth, Louise Marie. "Selling Women Short: A Research Note on Gender Differences in Compensation on Wall Street." *Social Forces, 82,* 2, December 2003:783–802.

Rotstein, Arthur H. "Minuteman Volunteers May Have Played Prank." Associated Press, April 7, 2005.

Rubin, Zick. "The Love Research." In *Marriage and Family in a Changing Society,* 2nd ed., James M. Henslin, ed. New York: Free Press, 1985.

Rudner, Lawrence M. "The Scholastic Achievement of Home School Students." *ERIC/AE Digest,* September 1, 1999.

Ruggles, Patricia. "Short and Long Term Poverty in the United States: Measuring the American 'Underclass.'" Washington, D.C.: Urban Institute, June 1989.

Russell, Diana E. H. "Preliminary Report on Some Findings Relating to the Trauma and Long-Term Effects of Intrafamily Childhood Sexual Abuse." Unpublished paper.

"Russia Sets Out to Fight Corruption in Education With a New Standardized Test." Associated Press, February 2, 2007.

Saenz, Rogelio. "Latinos and the Changing Face of America." Washington, D.C.: Population Reference Bureau, 2004:1–28.

Sahlins, Marshall D., and Elman R. Service. *Evolution and Culture.* Ann Arbor: University of Michigan Press, 1960.

Salopek, Paul. "Shattered Sudan: Drilling for Oil, Hoping for Peace." *National Geographic, 203,* 2, February 2003:30–66.

Sampson, Robert J., Jeffrey D. Morenoff, and Felton Earls. "Beyond Social Capital: Spatial Dynamics of Collective Efficacy for Children." *American Sociological Review, 64,* October 1999:633–660.

Sampson, Robert J., Gregory D. Squires, and Min Zhou. *How Neighborhoods Matter: The Value of Investing at the Local Level.* Washington, D.C.: American Sociological Association, 2001.

Samuelson, Paul Anthony, and William D. Nordhaus. *Economics,* 18th ed. New York: McGraw-Hill, 2005.

Sanchez, Juan I., and Nohora Medkik. "The Effects of Diversity Awareness Training on Differential Treatment." *Group and Organization Management, 29,* 4, August 2004:517–536.

Sanchez-Jankowski, Martin. "Gangs and Social Change." *Theoretical Criminology, 7,* 2, 2003:191–216.

Sanders, Peter. "Casinos Bet on Radio-ID Gambling Chips." *Wall Street Journal,* May 13, 2005.

Sapir, Edward. *Selected Writings of Edward Sapir in Language, Culture, and Personality.* David G. Mandelbaum, ed. Berkeley, Calif.: University of California Press, 1949.

Saranow, Jennifer. "The Snoop Next Door." *Wall Street Journal,* January 12, 2007.

Schaefer, Richard T. *Sociology,* 3rd ed. New York: McGraw-Hill, 1989.

Schaefer, Richard T. *Racial and Ethnic Groups,* 9th ed. Upper Saddle River, N.J.: Prentice-Hall, 2004.

Schellenberg, James A. *Conflict Resolution: Theory, Research, and Practice.* Albany: New York University Press, 1996.

Schemo, Diana Jean. "When Students' Gains Help Teachers' Bottom Line." *New York Times,* May 9, 2004.

Schmiege, Cynthia J., Leslie N. Richards, and Anisa M. Zvonkovic. "Remarriage: For Love or Money?" *Journal of Divorce and Remarriage,* May-June 2001:123–141.

Schottland, Charles I. *The Social Security Plan in the U.S.* New York: Appleton, 1963.

Schulz, William F. "The Torturer's Apprentice: Civil Liberties in a Turbulent Age." *The Nation,* May 13, 2002.

Scommegna, Paola. "Increased Cohabitation Changing Children's Family Settings." *Population Today, 30,* 7, October 2002:3, 6.

Scott, Janny. "White Flight, This Time Toward Harlem." *New York Times,* February 25, 2001.

Scott, Monster Cody. *Monster: The Autobiography of an L. A. Gang Member.* New York: Penguin, 1994.

Scully, Diana. "Negotiating to Do Surgery." In *Dominant Issues in Medical Sociology,* 3rd ed., Howard D. Schwartz, ed. New York: McGraw-Hill, 1994:146–152.

Scully, Diana, and Joseph Marolla. "Convicted Rapists Vocabulary of Motive: Excuses and Justifications." *Social Problems, 31,* 5, June 1984:530–544.

Scully, Diana, and Joseph Marolla. "'Riding the Bull at Gilley's': Convicted Rapists Describe the Rewards of Rape." In *Down-to-Earth Sociology: Introductory Readings,* 14th ed., James M. Henslin, ed. New York: The Free Press, 2007:48–62.

Segal, Nancy L., and Scott L. Hershberger. "Virtual Twins and Intelligence." *Personality and Individual Differences, 39,* 6, 2005:1061–1073.

Seltzer, Judith A. "Consequences of Marital Dissolution for Children." *Annual Review of Sociology, 20,* 1994:235–266.

Sengupta, Somini. "In the Ancient Streets of Najaf, Pledges of Martyrdom for Cleric." *New York Times,* July 10, 2004.

Shane, Scott. "Through the Revolving Door, a Pot of Gold Still Awaits." *New York Times,* December 28, 2004.

Sharp, Deborah. "Miami's Language Gap Widens." *USA Today,* April 3, 1992:A1, A3.

Sharp, Lauriston. "Steel Axes for Stone-Age Australians." In *Down to Earth Sociology: Introductory Readings,* 8th ed., James M. Henslin, ed. New York: Free Press, 1995:453–462.

Sheets, Lawrence Scott, and William J. Broad. "Georgia Says It Blocked Smuggling of Arms-Grade Uranium." *New York Times,* January 25, 2007a.

Sheets, Lawrence Scott, and William J. Broad. "Smuggler's Plot Highlights Fear Over Uranium." *New York Times,* January 25, 2007b.

Shellenbarger, Sue. "Extreme Juggling: Parents Home-School the Kids While Holding Full-time Jobs." *Wall Street Journal,* September 14, 2006.

Sherif, Muzafer, and Carolyn Sherif. *Groups in Harmony and Tension.* New York: Harper & Row, 1953.

Sherman, Spencer. "The Hmong in America." *National Geographic,* October 1988:586–610.

Shields, Stephanie A. *Speaking from the Heart: Gender and the Social Meaning of Emotion.* New York: Cambridge University Press, 2002.

Shively, JoEllen. "Cultural Compensation: The Popularity of Westerns Among American Indians." Paper presented at the annual meetings of the American Sociological Association, 1991.

Shively, JoEllen. "Cowboys and Indians: Perceptions of Western Films Among American Indians and Anglos." *American Sociological Review, 57,* December 1992:725–734.

Sills, David L. *The Volunteers.* Glencoe, Ill.: Free Press, 1957.

Silverman, Eric K. "Anthropology and Circumcision." *Annual Review of Anthropology, 33,* 2004:419–445.

Simmel, Georg. *The Sociology of Georg Simmel,* Kurt H. Wolff, ed. and trans. Glencoe, Ill.: Free Press, 1950. First published between 1902 and 1917.

Simon, Julian L. *The Ultimate Resource.* Princeton, N.J.: Princeton University Press, 1981.

Simon, Julian L. *Theory of Population and Economic Growth.* New York: Blackwell, 1986.

Simon, Julian L. "The Nativists Are Wrong." *Wall Street Journal,* August 4, 1993:A10.

Simons, Marlise. "Social Change and Amazon Indians." In *Exploring Social Life: Readings to Accompany Essentials of Sociology: A Down-to-Earth Approach, Sixth Edition,* 2nd ed., James M. Henslin, ed. Boston: Allyn & Bacon, 2006:157–165.

Simpson, George Eaton, and J. Milton Yinger. *Racial and Cultural Minorities: An Analysis of Prejudice and Discrimination,* 4th ed. New York: Harper & Row, 1972.

Skeels, H. M. *Adult Status of Children with Contrasting Early Life Experiences: A Follow-up Study.* Monograph of the Society for Research in Child Development, *31,* 3, 1966.

Skeels, H. M., and H. B. Dye. "A Study of the Effects of Differential Stimulation on Mentally Retarded Children." *Proceedings and Addresses of the American Association on Mental Deficiency, 44,* 1939:114–136.

Skinner, Jonathan, James N. Weinstein, Scott M. Sporer, and John E. Wennberg. "Racial, Ethnic, and Geographic Disparities in Rates of Knee Arthroplasty Among Medicare Patients." *New England Journal of Medicine, 349,* 14, October 2, 2003:1350–1359.

Sklair, Leslie. *Globalization: Capitalism and Its Alternatives,* 3rd ed. New York: Oxford: University Press, 2001.

Smart, Barry. "On the Disorder of Things: Sociology, Postmodernity and the 'End of the Social.'" *Sociology, 24,* 3, August 1990:397–416.

Smedley, Brian D., Adrienne Y. Stith, and Alan R. Nelson, eds. *Unequal Treatment: Confronting Racial and Ethnic Disparities in Health Care.* Washington, D.C.: The National Academies Press, 2003.

Smith, Beverly A. "An Incest Case in an Early 20th-Century Rural Community." *Deviant Behavior, 13,* 1992:127–153.

Smith, Christian, and Robert Faris. "Socioeconomic Inequality in the American Religious System: An Update and Assessment." *Journal for the Scientific Study of Religion, 44,* 1, 2005:95–104.

Smith, Craig S. "Abduction, Often Violent, a Kyrgyz Wedding Rite." *New York Times,* April 30, 2005.

Smith, Jackie, Charles Chatfield, and Ron Pagnucco. *Transnational Social Movements and Global Policy: Solidarity Beyond the State.* Syracuse, N.Y.: Syracuse University Press, 1997.

Smith, Simon C. "The Making of a Neo-Colony? Anglo-Kuwaiti Relations in the Era of Decolonization." *Middle Eastern Studies, 37,* 1, January 2001:159–173.

Snyder, Mark. "Self-Fulfilling Stereotypes." In *Down to Earth Sociology: Introductory Readings,* 7th ed., James M. Henslin, ed. New York: Free Press, 1993:153–160.

Solomon, Charlene Marmer. "Cracks in the Glass Ceiling." *Workforce, 79,* 9, September 2000:87–91.

Soss, Joe. "Lessons of Welfare: Policy Design, Political Learning, and Political Action." *American Political Science Review, 93,* 1999:363–380.

*Sourcebook of Criminal Justice Statistics.* Washington, D.C.: U.S. Government Printing Office, published annually.

South, Scott J. "Sociodemographic Differentials in Mate Selection Preferences." *Journal of Marriage and the Family, 53,* November 1991:928–940.

Spector, Malcolm, and John Kitsuse. *Constructing Social Problems.* Menlo Park, Calif.: Cummings, 1977.

Spector, Tim. "Ageing Linked to Social Status." *BBC News,* March 29, 2007.

Spencer, Jane. "Shirk Ethic: How to Face a Hard Day at the Office." *Wall Street Journal,* May 15, 2003:D1, D3.

Spengler, Oswald. *The Decline of the West,* 2 vols. Charles F. Atkinson, trans. New York: Knopf, 1926–1928. First published 1919–1922.

Spickard, P. R. S. *Mixed Blood: Intermarriage and Ethnic Identity in Twentieth Century America.* Madison: University of Wisconsin Press, 1989.

Spitzer, Steven. "Toward a Marxian Theory of Deviance." *Social Problems, 22,* June 1975:608–619.

Spivak, Gayatri Chakravorty. "Feminism 2000: One Step Beyond." *Feminist Review, 64,* Spring 2000:113.

Sprecher, Susan, and Rachita Chandak. "Attitudes About Arranged Marriages and Dating Among Men and Women from India." *Free Inquiry in Creative Sociology, 20,* 1, May 1992:59–69.

Srole, Leo, et al. *Mental Health in the Metropolis: The Midtown Manhattan Study.* Albany, N.Y.: New York University Press, 1978.

Stack, Carol B. *All Our Kin: Strategies for Survival in a Black Community.* New York: Harper, 1974.

Stampp, Kenneth M. *The Peculiar Institution: Slavery in the Ante-Bellum South.* New York: Vintage Books, 1956.

Stark, Rodney. *Sociology,* 3rd ed. Belmont, Calif.: Wadsworth, 1989.

Starr, Paul. *The Social Transformation of American Medicine.* New York: Basic Books, 1982.

"State of the World's Children 2001." *Reading Today, 18,* 4, February–March 2001:24.

*Statistical Abstract of the United States.* See U.S. Bureau of the Census.

Stein, Rob. "FDA Approves Implantable Identity Chip." *Washington Post,* October 14, 2004.

Steinberg, Laurence, Stanford Dornbusch, and Bradford Brown. *Beyond the Classroom.* New York: Simon & Schuster, 1996.

Stenner, Karen. *The Authoritarian Dynamic.* New York: Cambridge University Press, 2005.

Stephens, Bret. "The Foreign Brides." *Wall Street Journal,* May 2, 2006.

Stevens, Mitchell L. *Kingdom of Children: Culture and Controversy in the Homeschooling Movement.* Princeton: Princeton University Press, 2001.

"Sticky Ticket: A New Jersey Mother Sues Her Son Over a Lottery Jackpot She Claims Belongs to Them Both." *People Weekly,* February 9, 1998:68.

Stinnett, Nicholas. "Strong Families." In *Marriage and Family in a Changing Society,* 4th ed., James M. Henslin, ed. New York: Free Press, 1992:496–507.

Stipp, David. "Himalayan Tree Could Serve as Source of Anti-cancer Drug Taxol, Team Says." *Wall Street Journal,* April 20, 1992:B4.

Stockwell, John. "The Dark Side of U.S. Foreign Policy." *Zeta Magazine,* February 1989:36–48.

Stodgill, Ralph M. *Handbook of Leadership: A Survey of Theory and Research.* New York: Free Press, 1974.

Stolberg, Sheryl Gay. "Blacks Found on Short End of Heart Attack Procedure." *New York Times,* May 10, 2001.

*Strategic Energy Policy: Challenges for the 21st Century.* New York: Council on Foreign Relations, 2001.

Straus, Roger A. "The Sociologist as a Marketing Research Consultant." *Journal of Applied Sociology, 8,* 1991:65–75.

Stryker, Sheldon. "Symbolic Interactionism: Themes and Variations." In *Social Psychology: Sociological Perspectives,* Morris Rosenberg and Ralph H. Turner, eds. New Brunswick, N.J.: Transaction, 1990.

Suizzo, Marie-Anne. "The Social-Emotional and Cultural Contexts of Cognitive Development: Neo-Piagetian Perspectives." *Child Development, 71,* 4, August 2000:846–849.

Sullivan, Andrew. "What's So Bad About Hate?" *New York Times Magazine,* September 26, 1999.

Sumner, William Graham. *Folkways: A Study in the Sociological Importance of Usages, Manners, Customs, Mores, and Morals.* New York: Ginn, 1906.

Sutherland, Edwin H. *Criminology.* Philadelphia: Lippincott, 1924.

Sutherland, Edwin H. *Principles of Criminology,* 4th ed. Philadelphia: Lippincott, 1947.

Sutherland, Edwin H. *White Collar Crime.* New York: Dryden Press, 1949.

Sutton, Paul D., and T. J. Matthews. "Trends in Characteristics of Births by State: United States, 1990, 1995, and 2000–2002." *National Vital Statistics Reports, 52,* 19, May 10, 2004:1–150.

Suzuki, Bob H. "Asian-American Families." In *Marriage and Family in a Changing Society,* 2nd ed., James M. Henslin, ed. New York: Free Press, 1985:104–119.

Swanson, Christopher B. *Cities in Crisis: A Special Analytic Report on High School Graduation.* Bethesda, Md.: Editorial Projects in Education, 2008.

Sweeney, Megan M. "Remarriage and the Nature of Divorce: Does It Matter Which Spouse Chose to Leave?" *Journal of Family Issues, 23,* 3, April 2002:410–440.

Sykes, Gresham M., and David Matza. "Techniques of Neutralization." In *Down to Earth Sociology: Introductory Readings,* 5th ed., James M. Henslin, ed. New York: Free Press, 1988: 225–231. First published 1957.

Szasz, Thomas S. *Cruel Compassion: Psychiatric Control of Society's Unwanted.* Syracuse: Syracuse University Press, 1998.

Szasz, Thomas S. "Mental Illness Is Still a Myth." In *Deviant Behavior 96/97,* Lawrence M. Salinger, ed. Guilford, Conn.: Dushkin, 1996:200–205.

Szasz, Thomas S. *The Myth of Mental Illness.* Revised edition. New York: Harper & Row, 1986.

Tach, Laura, and George Farkas. "Ability Grouping and Educational Stratification in the Early School Years." Unpublished paper, 2003.

Tafoya, Sonya M., Hans Johnson, and Laura E. Hill. "Who Chooses to Choose Two?" Washington, D.C.: Population Reference Bureau, 2005.

Taneja, V., S. Sriram, R. S. Beri, V. Sreenivas, R. Aggarwal, R. Kaur, and J. M. Puliyel. "'Not by Bread Alone': Impact of a Structured 90-Minute Play Session on Development of Children in an Orphanage." *Child Care, Health & Development, 28,* 1, 2002:95–100.

Taylor, Chris. "The Man Behind Lara Croft." *Time,* December 6, 1999:78.

Taylor, Howard F. "The Structure of a National Black Leadership Network: Preliminary Findings." Unpublished manuscript, 1992. As cited in Margaret L. Andersen and Howard F. Taylor, *Sociology: Understanding a Diverse Society.* Belmont, Calif.: Wadsworth, 2000.

Taylor, Monique M. *Harlem: Between Heaven and Hell.* Minneapolis: University of Minnesota Press, 2002.

Terhune, Chad. "Pepsi, Vowing Diversity Isn't Just Image Polish, Seeks Inclusive Culture." *Wall Street Journal,* April 19, 2005.

Thomas, Paulette. "U.S. Examiners Will Scrutinize Banks with Poor Minority-Lending Histories." *Wall Street Journal,* October 22, 1991:A2.

Thomas, W. I., and Dorothy Swaine Thomas. *The Child in America: Behavior Problems and Programs.* New York: Knopf, 1928.

Thompson, Ginger. "Chasing Mexico's Dream into Squalor." *New York Times,* February 11, 2001.

Thornton, Russell. *American Indian Holocaust and Survival: A Population History Since 1492*. Norman: University of Oklahoma Press, 1987.

Thurow, Roger. "Farms Destroyed, Stricken Sudan Faces Food Crisis." *Wall Street Journal,* February 7, 2005.

Tilly, Charles. *Social Movements, 1768–2004*. Boulder, Colo.: Paradigm, 2004.

Timasheff, Nicholas S. *War and Revolution*. Joseph F. Scheuer, ed. New York: Sheed & Ward, 1965.

Todosijevic, Jelica, Esther D. Rothblum, and Sondra E. Solomon. "Relationship Satisfaction, Affectivity, and Specific Stressors in Same-Sex Couples Joined in Civil Unions." *Psychology of Women Quarterly, 29,* 2005:158–166.

Tönnies, Ferdinand. *Community and Society (Gemeinschaft und Gesellschaft),* with a new introduction by John Samples. New Brunswick, N.J.: Transaction, 1988. First published 1887.

Torres, Jose B., V. Scott H. Solberg, and Aaron H. Carlstrom. "The Myth of Sameness Among Latino Men and Their Machismo." *American Journal of Orthopsychiatry, 72,* 2, 2002:163–181.

Toynbee, Arnold. *A Study of History,* D. C. Somervell, abridger and ed. New York: Oxford University Press, 1946.

Treiman, Donald J. *Occupational Prestige in Comparative Perspective*. New York: Academic Press, 1977.

Tresniowski, Alex. "Payday Or Mayday?" *People Weekly,* May 17, 1999: 128–131.

Trice, Harrison M., and Janice M. Beyer. "Cultural Leadership in Organization." *Organization Science, 2,* 2, May 1991:149–169.

Troeltsch, Ernst. *The Social Teachings of the Christian Churches*. New York: Macmillan, 1931.

"Tsunami Deaths Over 283,000." *News 24.com,* January 27, 2005.

Tuhus-Dubrow, Rebecca. "Rites and Wrongs." *Boston Globe,* February 11, 2007.

Tumin, Melvin M. "Some Principles of Social Stratification: A Critical Analysis." *American Sociological Review 18,* August 1953:394.

Turner, Bryan S. "Outline of a Theory of Citizenship." *Sociology, 24,* 2, May 1990:189–217.

Turner, Jonathan H. *The Structure of Sociological Theory*. Homewood, Ill.: Dorsey, 1978.

Tyler, Patrick E. "A New Life for NATO? But It's Sidelined for Now." *New York Times,* November 20, 2002.

U.S. Bureau of the Census. "Annual Social and Economic Supplement to Current Population Survey." Washington, D.C.: U.S. Government Printing Office, 2006.

U.S. Bureau of the Census. *Statistical Abstract of the United States: The National Data Book*. Washington, D.C.: U.S. Government Printing Office. Published annually.

U.S. Department of Education, Institute of Education Sciences, National Center for Education Statistics. *The Condition of Education, 2007.*

U.S. Department of Education, National Center for Education Statistics. *Digest of Education Statistics: 2006*. Washington, D.C. U.S. Department of Education, July 2007.

Uchitelle, Louis. "How to Define Poverty? Let Us Count the Ways." *New York Times,* May 28, 2001.

Udry, J. Richard. "Biological Limits of Gender Construction." *American Sociological Review, 65,* June 2000:443–457.

Ullman, Edward, and Chauncey Harris. "The Nature of Cities." In *Urban Man and Society: A Reader in Urban Ecology,* Albert N. Cousins and Hans Nagpaul, eds. New York: Knopf, 1970:91–100.

UNESCO Institute for Statistics. "World Illiteracy Rates." 2005.

UNESCO. *Education for All Global Monitoring Report, 2006.*

United Nations. "World Urbanization Prospects: The 1999 Revision." New York: United Nations, 2000.

Urban Institute. "A Decade of Welfare Reform: Facts and Figures." June 2006.

Usdansky, Margaret L. "English a Problem for Half of Miami." *USA Today,* April 3, 1992:A1, A3, A30.

Useem, Michael. *The Inner Circle: Large Corporations and the Rise of Business Political Activity in the U.S. and U. K.* New York: Oxford University Press, 1984.

Varese, Federico. *The Russian Mafia: Private Protection in a New Market Economy*. Oxford: Oxford University Press, 2005.

Vartabedian, Ralph, and Scott Gold. "New Questions on Shuttle Tile Safety Raised." *Los Angeles Times,* February 27, 2003.

Vaughan, Diane. "Uncoupling: The Social Construction of Divorce." In *Marriage and Family in a Changing Society,* 2nd ed., James M. Henslin, ed. New York: Free Press, 1985:429–439.

Vega, William A. "Hispanic Families in the 1980s: A Decade of Research." *Journal of Marriage and the Family, 52,* November 1990:1015–1024.

Venkatesh, Sudhir. *Gang Leader for a Day: A Rogue Sociologist Takes to the Streets*. New York: Penguin, 2008.

Vincent, John A. "Ageing Contested: Anti-ageing Science and the Cultural Construction of Old Age" *Sociology, 40,* 2006.

Von Hoffman, Nicholas. "Sociological Snoopers." *Transaction 7,* May 1970:4, 6.

Wade, Nicholas. "In Dusty Archives, a Theory of Affluence." *New York Times,* August 7, 2007.

Wagley, Charles, and Marvin Harris. *Minorities in the New World*. New York: Columbia University Press, 1958.

Wald, Matthew L., and John Schwartz. "Alerts Were Lacking, NASA Shuttle Manager Says." *New York Times,* July 23, 2003.

Walker, Alice, and Pratibha Parmar. *Warrior Marks: Female Genital Mutilation and the Sexual Blinding of Women*. New York: Harcourt Brace, 1993.

Wallace, John M., Ryoko Yamaguchi, Jerald G. Bachman, Patrick M. O'Malley, John E. Schulenberg, and Lloyd D. Johnston. "Religiosity and Adolescent Substance Use: The Role of Individual and Contextual Influences." *Social Problems, 54,* 2, 2007:308–327.

Wallerstein, Immanuel. *The Modern World System: Capitalist Agriculture and the Origins of the European World-Economy in the Sixteenth Century*. New York: Academic Press, 1974.

Wallerstein, Immanuel. *The Capitalist World-Economy*. New York: Cambridge University Press, 1979.

Wallerstein, Immanuel. "Culture as the Ideological Battleground of the Modern World-System." In *Global Culture: Nationalism, Globalization, and Modernity,* Mike Featherstone, ed. London: Sage, 1990:31–55.

Wallerstein, Judith S., Sandra Blakeslee, and Julia M. Lewis. *The Unexpected Legacy of Divorce: A 25-Year Landmark Study.* Concord, N.H.: Hyperion Press, 2001.

Walsh, Catherine. "The Life and Legacy of Lawrence Kohlberg." *Society, 37,* 2, January–February 2000:38–44.

Walter, Lynn. *Women's Rights: A Global View.* Westport, Conn.: Greenwood Press, 2001.

Walters, Alan. "Let More Earnings Go to Shareholders." *Wall Street Journal,* October 31, 1995:A23.

Wang, Hongyu, and Paul R. Amato. "Predictors of Divorce Adjustment: Stressors, Resources, and Definitions." *Journal of Marriage and the Family, 62,* 3, August 2000:655–668.

Wang, Yong, and Carl W. Roberts. "*Schadenfreude:* A Case Study of Emotion as Situated Discursive Display." *Comparative Sociology, 5,* 1, 2006:45–63.

Watson, J. Mark. "Outlaw Motorcyclists." In *Society: Readings to Accompany Sociology: A Down-to-Earth Approach, Core Concepts,* James M. Henslin ed. Boston: Allyn & Bacon, 2006:105–114. First published 1980 in *Deviant Behavior, 2,* 1.

Wayne, Julie Holliday, Christine M. Riordan, and Kecia M. Thomas. "Is All Sexual Harassment Viewed the Same? Mock Juror Decisions in Same- and Cross-Gender Cases." *Journal of Applied Psychology, 86,* 2, April 2001:179–187.

Weber, Max. *From Max Weber: Essays in Sociology.* Hans Gerth and C. Wright Mills, trans. and ed. New York: Oxford University Press, 1946.

Weber, Max. *The Theory of Social and Economic Organization,* A. M. Henderson and Talcott Parsons, trans., Talcott Parsons, ed. Glencoe, Ill.: Free Press, 1947. First published 1913.

Weber, Max. *The Protestant Ethic and the Spirit of Capitalism.* New York: Scribner's, 1958. First published 1904–1905.

Weber, Max. *Economy and Society,* G. Roth and C. Wittich, eds. Berkeley: University of California Press, 1978. First published 1922.

Weiner, Tim. "Pentagon Envisioning a Costly Internet for War." *New York Times,* November 13, 2004.

Weiss, Rick. "Mature Human Embryos Cloned." *Washington Post,* February 12, 2004:A1.

Weitoft, Gunilla Ringback, Anders Hjern, Bengt Haglund, and Mans Rosen. "Mortality, Severe Morbidity, and Injury in Children Living with Single Parents in Sweden: A Population-Based Study." *Lancet, 361,* January 25, 2003:289–295.

Werner, Erica. "Indian Casinos Gross $25 Billion in 2006." Associated Press, June 5, 2007.

Wheaton, Blair, and Philippa Clarke. "Space Meets Time: Integrating Temporal and Contextual Influences on Mental Health in Early Adulthood." *American Sociological Review, 68,* 2003:680–706.

White, Jack E. "Forgive Us Our Sins." *Time,* July 3, 1995:29.

White, Joseph B., Stephen Power, and Timothy Aeppel. "Death Count Linked to Failures of Firestone Tires Rises to 203." *Wall Street Journal,* June 19, 2001:A4.

Whitehead, Barbara Dafoe, and David Popenoe. "The Marrying Kind: Which Men Marry and Why." Rutgers University: The State of Our Unions: The Social Health of Marriage in America, 2004.

Whorf, Benjamin. *Language, Thought, and Reality,* J. B. Carroll, ed. Cambridge, Mass.: MIT Press, 1956.

Wilford, John Noble. "In Maya Ruins, Scholars See Evidence of Urban Sprawl." *New York Times,* December 19, 2000.

Williams, Christine L. *Still a Man's World: Men Who Do Women's Work.* Berkeley: University of California Press, 1995.

Williams, Rhys H. "Constructing the Public Good: Social Movements and Cultural Resources." *Social Problems, 42,* 1, February 1995:124–144.

Williams, Robin M., Jr. *American Society: A Sociological Interpretation,* 2nd ed. New York: Knopf, 1965.

Willie, Charles Vert. "Caste, Class, and Family Life Experiences." *Research in Race and Ethnic Relations, 6,* 1991:65–84.

Willie, Charles Vert, and Richard J. Reddick. *A New Look at Black Families,* 5th ed. Walnut Creek, Calif.: AltaMira Press, 2003.

Wilson, James Q., and Richard J. Herrnstein. *Crime and Human Nature.* New York: Simon & Schuster, 1985.

Wilson, William Julius. *The Declining Significance of Race: Blacks and Changing American Institutions.* Chicago: University of Chicago Press, 1978.

Wilson, William Julius. *The Truly Disadvantaged: The Inner City, the Underclass, and Public Policy.* Chicago: University of Chicago Press, 1987.

Wilson, William Julius. *When Work Disappears: The World of the New Urban Poor.* Chicago: University of Chicago Press, 1996.

Wilson, William Julius. *The Bridge over the Racial Divide: Rising Inequality and Coalition Politics.* Berkeley: University of California Press, 2000.

Wines, Michael. "Africa Adds to Miserable Ranks of Child Workers." *New York Times,* August 24, 2006a.

Wines, Michael. "How Bad Is Inflation in Zimbabwe?" *Wall Street Journal,* May 2, 2006b.

"Winner, Dumbest Moment, Marketing." CNN, February 1, 2006.

Wirth, Louis. "The Problem of Minority Groups." In *The Science of Man in the World Crisis,* Ralph Linton, ed. New York: Columbia University Press, 1945.

Wise, Raul Delgado, and James M. Cypher. "The Strategic Role of Mexican Labor Under NAFTA: Critical Perspectives on Current Economic Integration." *Annals of the American Academy of Political and Social Science, 610,* March 2007:120–142.

Wolfensohn, James D., and Kathryn S. Fuller. "Making Common Cause: Seeing the Forest for the Trees." *International Herald Tribune,* May 27, 1998:11.

Wolfinger, Nicholas H. "Family Structure Homogamy: The Effects of Parental Divorce on Partner Selection and Marital Stability." *Social Science Research, 32,* 2003:80–97.

Wonacott, Peter. "India's Skewed Sex Ratio Puts GE Sales in Spotlight." *Wall Street Journal,* April 18, 2007.

Wood, Daniel B., "Latinos Redefine What It Means to Be Manly." *Christian Science Monitor, 93,* 161, July 16, 2001.

"The World of the Child 6 Billion." Population Reference Bureau, 2000.

Wright, Erik Olin. *Class.* London: Verso, 1985.

Wright, Lawrence. "One Drop of Blood." *New Yorker,* July 25, 1994: 46–50, 52–55.

Wright, Lawrence. "Double Mystery." *New Yorker,* August 7, 1995:45–62.

Xie, Yu, and Kimberly A. Goyette. "A Demographic Portrait of Asian Americans." Washington, D.C.: Population Reference Bureau, 2004:1–32.

Yardley, Jim. "Married for the Afterlife in China." *International Herald Tribune,* October 4, 2006.

Yardley, Jim. "Faces of Abortion in China: A Young, Single Woman." *New York Times,* May 13, 2007.

Yat-ming Sin, Leo, and Hon-ming Yau, Oliver. "Female Role Orientation and Consumption Values: Some Evidence from Mainland China." *Journal of International Consumer Marketing, 13,* 2, 2001:49–75.

Yinger, J. Milton. *Toward a Field Theory of Behavior: Personality and Social Structure.* New York: McGraw-Hill, 1965.

Yonas, Michael A., Patricia O'Campo, Jessica G. Burke, and Andrea C. Gielen. "Neighborhood-Level Factors and Youth Violence: Giving Voice to the Perception of Prominent Neighborhood Individuals." *Health, Education, and Behavior OnlineFirst,* July 21, 2006.

Young, Laurie E. "The Overlooked Contributions of Women to the Development of American Sociology: An Examination of AJS Articles from 1895–1926." Paper presented at the 1995 meetings of the American Sociological Association.

Zachary, G. Pascal. "Behind Stocks' Surge Is an Economy in Which Big U.S. Firms Thrive." *Wall Street Journal,* November 22, 1995: A1, A5.

Zald, Mayer N. "Looking Backward to Look Forward: Reflections on the Past and the Future of the Resource Mobilization Research Program." In *Frontiers in Social Movement Theory,* Aldon D. Morris and Carol McClurg Mueller, eds. New Haven, Conn.: Yale University Press, 1992:326–348.

Zald, Mayer N., and John D. McCarthy, eds. *Social Movements in an Organizational Society.* New Brunswick, N.J.: Transaction, 1987.

Zamiska, Nicholas. "Pressed to Do Well on Admissions Tests, Students Take Drugs." *Wall Street Journal,* November 8, 2004.

Zaslow, Jeffrey. "Will You Still Need Me When I'm . . . 84? More Couples Divorce After Decades." *Wall Street Journal,* June 17, 2003:D1.

Zellner, William W. *Countercultures: A Sociological Analysis.* New York: St. Martin's, 1995.

Zeng, Douglas Zhihua, and Shuilin Wang. "China and the Knowledge Economy: Challenges and Opportunity." World Bank Policy Research Working Paper 4223, May 2007.

Zerubavel, Eviatar. *The Fine Line: Making Distinctions in Everyday Life.* New York: Free Press, 1991.

Zielbauer, Paul. "Study Finds Pequot Businesses Lift Economy." *New York Times,* November 29, 2000.

Zoepf, Katherine. "A Dishonorable Affair." *New York Times,* September 23, 2007.

# NAME INDEX